JAVA™ 2
Network Security

ISBN 0-13-015592-6

90000

9 780130 155924

The ITSO Networking Series

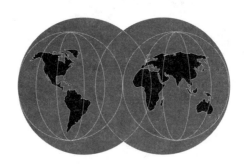

JAVA™ 2 Network Security, Second Edition
    by Pistoia, Reller, Gupta, Nagnur, and Ramani

A Guide to Virtual Private Networks
    by Murhammer, Bourne, Gaidosch, Kunzinger, Rademacher, and Weinfurter

TCP/IP Tutorial and Technical Overview, Sixth Edition
    by Murhammer, Atakan, Bretz, Pugh, Suzuki, and Wood

Understanding Optical Communications
    by Dutton

Asynchronous Transfer Mode (ATM)
    by Dutton and Lenhard

High-Speed Networking Technology
    by Dutton and Lenhard

www.security: How to Build a Secure World Wide Web Connection
    by Macgregor, Aresi, and Siegert

Internetworking over ATM: An Introduction
    by Dorling, Freedman, Metz, and Burger

Inside APPN and HPR
    by Dorling, Lenhard, Lennon, and Uskokovic

JAVA™ 2
Network Security

MARCO PISTOIA ■ **DUANE F. RELLER** ■
DEEPAK GUPTA ■ **MILIND NAGNUR** ■
ASHOK K. RAMANI

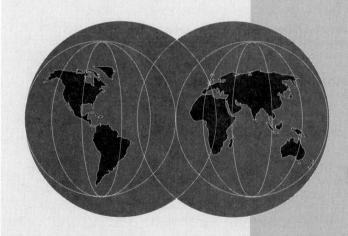

IBM

PRENTICE HALL PTR, UPPER SADDLE RIVER, NEW JERSEY 07458
http://www.phptr.com

For information about redbooks:
`http://www.redbooks.ibm.com`

Send comments to:
`redbooks@us.ibm.com`

Published by Prentice Hall PTR
Prentice-Hall, Inc.
Upper Saddle River, NJ 07458

Prentice Hall books are widely used by corporations and government agencies for training, marketing, and resale. The publisher offers discounts on this book when ordered in bulk quantities. For more information, contact

Corporate Sales Department,
Phone 800-382-3419; FAX: 201-236-7141
E-mail (Internet): corpsales@prenhall.com

Or Write: Prentice Hall PTR
Corporate Sales Department
One Lake Street
Upper Saddle River, NJ 07458

Take Note! Before using this information and the product it supports, be sure to read the general information under Appendix F, "Special Notices" on page 693.

Printed in the United States of America
10 9 8 7 6 5 4 3 2 1

ISBN 0-13-015592-6

Prentice-Hall International (UK) Limited, *London*
Prentice-Hall of Australia Pty. Limited, *Sydney*
Prentice-Hall Canada Inc., *Toronto*
Prentice-Hall Hispanoamericana, S.A., *Mexico*
Prentice-Hall of India Private Limited, *New Delhi*
Prentice-Hall of Japan, Inc., *Tokyo*
Prentice-Hall (Singapore) Pte. Ltd., *Singapore*
Editora Prentice-Hall do Brasil, Ltda., *Rio de Janeiro*

Foreword

As the person who led the JavaSoft team that developed the Java security technology discussed in this book, it is extremely gratifying to see people spend their precious time writing about our technology and products. Every engineer's dream is to have his or her technology deployed and used by thousands of others, and this book is a great help to Java developers who write security-aware applications.

Security is a difficult subject to write about. On the one hand, security is in people's daily consciousness so that it appears easy to get across (to the reader) some of the basic concepts. On the other hand, security applied to computer and networking is often subtle and unexpected. Security also is pervasive in that it touches all aspects of the computing technology, including hardware, software, operating system, software libraries, communication software, networking infrastructure, application software, user interface, and management software. In order to understand security in any situation, one has to understand the entire system under consideration as well as each individual component so that one can identity their strengths and weaknesses and design the appropriate solutions.

Java security is one of the more recent additions to the family of security technologies. Ever since Sun Microsystems announced Java technology in the spring of 1995, there has been strong and growing interest (in industry, research laboratories, and academia) around the security of the Java platform as well as new security issues raised by the deployment of Java technology.

Such close attention being paid to security is almost unprecedented in that new computing technologies normally ignore security considerations when they emerge initially. Most of them remain unsecured forever. In the few cases where efforts are made to secure them later, the efforts are typically not very successful because retrofitting security is usually very difficult, if possible at all, and often causes backward compatibility problems.

Therefore, it is extremely fortunate that the Java technology had security as a primary design goal from the very beginning. (Hats off to the original Java development team. I joined JavaSoft only in 1996.) Although the initial security model was very simplistic, it enabled later improvements in the security architecture.

The Java language is a general-purpose object-oriented programming language and is specifically designed to be platform independent so that application developers can write a program once and then run it securely everywhere on the Internet. To achieve this platform independence, a Java program is compiled to a bytecode instruction set and binary format defined in the Java Virtual Machine Specification. The Java platform consists of the Java language and its associated tools (such as compilers), together with the Java Virtual Machine (JVM) and its associated libraries that define a rich set of application programming interfaces (APIs).

Security for the Java platform has multiple layers. First of all, the Java language is strongly typed and does not include any unsafe constructs, such as array accesses without index checking, because such unsafe constructs may result in unspecified and unpredictable program behavior that can lead to security compromises. Type safety is checked both at the time a piece of bytecode is loaded into the JVM and throughout the lifetime of the bytecode (that is, during run time) until it is no longer used and garbage collected. Second, mechanisms (for example, class loaders) are in place to ensure a sufficient degree of separation between multiple Java programs so that they do not interfere with each other in undesirable ways.

Third, access to crucial system resources is mediated by the JVM. A security manager is installed to deny all requests for unauthorized access. The access control model, in the initial release of the Java Development Kit (JDK 1.0), was to grant full access to local code (that is, trust such code and let it do anything it wants) and to grant very restricted access to code loaded over the network because such code (often referred to as applets) may not be trusted. JDK 1.1 introduced a notion of trusted applets and granted full access to these applets. The latest release, JDK 1.2 (also called Java 2), incorporates a new security architecture that supports policy-driven, fine-grained, flexible, and extensible access control. (For design rationales of this architecture, as well as difficulties and subtleties we encountered during JDK 1.2 development, please refer to my book Inside Java 2 Platform Security.)

On top of type safety and access control, there are the Java Cryptography Architecture (implemented in JDK 1.2 and in the Java Cryptography Extension 1.2), support for secure communication (the Java Secure Socket Extension), and a framework for user-based authentication and access control (the Java Authentication and Authorization Service). These technologies are at various stages in the development and release cycle. Finally, applications can provide their own specific security features and can customize security features that are built into the Java platform.

Our colleagues at IBM, among other industrial partners, have been closely involved with the recent development of Java security technology. They have supported our efforts in many ways, and have provided excellent technical suggestions. This latest book from IBM is a comprehensive guidebook that provides the programmer/reader with well-organized details of the Java security APIs and their usage. The book is also broad in its coverage of the wider security context and related issues.

I am very excited to see such a good book being published on Java security. It will contribute greatly toward making the Java platform the most popular deployment environment for secure computing.

Li Gong
Distinguished Engineer and Chief Java Security Architect
Sun Microsystems
Cupertino, California

May 1999

Contents

Preface

Java is fashionable, but is it reliable? Java is entertaining, but is it secure? Java is useful, but is it safe?

The purpose of this book is to answer those questions, from the point of view of people who want to use Java, but want to do so reliably, securely and safely. That makes this book different from much recent writing on Java, which focuses, perfectly legitimately, on how a Java system can be broken into and how to avoid those dangers. On the contrary, this book focuses on how Java can be made secure and how to exploit its strengths. The goal is to provide practical help to the various groups involved in making a Java-based application or Web site into an industrial-strength commercial proposition.

Various groups have different needs and different skills, which this book meets in its different parts.

- The first part is aimed at the intelligent non-specialist who oversees system management or application development, or incorporates Java into the security policy. Only a basic understanding of computers and a limited exposure to Java is assumed, but all the themes of Java security are introduced in a context that stresses over and over again how Java security must be seen as an integral part of system security.
- The second part goes into more detail on how Java security works, and is aimed more at system and network administrators and programmers, who need to know more of what is going on.
- The third part looks at the broader context in which Java operates, including some extensions to Java security and some aspects of its future.

This book explains the evolution of the Java security model, and then focuses on the Java 2 security architecture and its revolutionary domains of protection. It offers a very large number of examples to give you a better understanding of the technology involved.

The Team That Wrote This Redbook

This redbook was produced by a team of specialists from around the world working at the International Technical Support Organization Raleigh Center.

The leader of this project was Marco Pistoia.

Marco Pistoia is a Network Security Specialist, working as a project leader at the International Technical Support Organization, Raleigh Center. He writes extensively and teaches IBM classes worldwide on all areas of the e-business Application Framework, WebSphere, Java and Internet security. Marco holds a degree with honors in Pure Mathematics from the University of Rome and a masters degree in Computer Science. Before joining the ITSO, he was a System Engineer in IBM Italy. He received an Outstanding Technical Achievement Award in 1996.

Duane F. Reller is a Senior Software Engineer in the System/390 Programming Laboratory in Endicott, New York, USA. He has 25 years of experience in System/390 Hardware and Software development. He has served in technical and management positions. He holds a Bachelor's degree in Electrical Technology and a Master of Science degree in Computer Science from the State University of New York at Binghamton. His areas of expertise include Hardware and Software System's Architecture and Management.

Deepak Gupta is a Senior Software Engineer in IBM, India. He has two and a half years of experience in Internet technologies. He holds a degree in Electronics and Communications from the University of Roorkee, India. His areas of expertise include Internet security and Electronic Commerce. Deepak was involved in IBM India's largest e-Commerce project and in India's first secured e-Commerce site allowing Rupee-based transactions, for which he was conferred the Employee of the Month Award. He has also given several talks on Internet security and e-Commerce.

Milind Nagnur is a Senior Associate in the Operations and Systems Risk Management (OSRM) group of Price Waterhouse Coopers in Mumbai, India. He has a couple of years of exposure in Internet technologies, with emphasis on security and control issues in real business applications. He holds a degree in Mechanical Engineering from the Indian Institute of Technology in Bombay, India, and an MBA from the Indian Institute of Management in Calcutta, India.

Ashok K. Ramani is a Senior Software Engineer in IBM India. He has two and a half years of experience in Internet technologies. He holds a degree in MSc.(Tech.) Information Systems from the Birla Institute of Technology and Science, Pilani, India. His areas of expertise include Internet security and Electronic Commerce. Ashok was involved in IBM India's largest e-Commerce project and in India's first secure e-Commerce site allowing Rupee-based transactions for which he was conferred the Employee of the Month Award. He has won special recognition awards at IBM India for his contribution to e-Commerce projects. He has also presented several talks on Internet security and e-Commerce.

Thanks to the following people for their invaluable contributions to this project:

Anthony J. Nadalin, Julianne Yarsa, Shirley Fox, Donna Smith Skibbie, Bruce Rich
IBM Enterprise Security, Austin Center

Larry Koved
IBM, Thomas J. Watson Research, Hawthorne

Li Gong, Jan Luehe, Roland Schemers
Sun Microsystems, Inc.

Pat Donleycott, Jorge Ferrari, Martin Murhammer, Gail Christensen, Margaret Ticknor, Shawn Walsh, Linda Robinson, Tate Renner
IBM, International Technical Support Organization, Raleigh Center

Rob Macgregor, Dave Durbin, John Owlett, Andrew Yeomans
Authors of the first edition

Pete Lawther, Simon Phipps
Contributors to the first edition

Comments Welcome

Your comments are important to us!

We want our redbooks to be as helpful as possible. Please send us your comments about this or other redbooks in one of the following ways:

- Fax the evaluation form found in "ITSO Redbook Evaluation" on page 713 to the fax number shown on the form.
- Use the online evaluation form found at http://www.redbooks.ibm.com/
- Send your comments in an internet note to redbook@us.ibm.com

Part 1. Introduction to Java and Security

Chapter 1. An Overview of Java and Security

The purpose of this chapter is not only to introduce the themes of the book to those who will later read the more detailed chapters that follow, but also to act as a brief overview for the intelligent non-specialist who does not need all the details. This is because the focus of the book is on helping people to deploy Java in a secure way. There are many people involved in that – managers, administrators, developers, systems programmers, users – all of whom play a part.

1.1 Java Is Not Just a Language

Most of the books on the subject deal with Java as a programming language. As a programming language it has much to recommend it. Its syntax is very like C, but with many of the features that hurt your brain removed. It is strongly object-oriented, but it avoids the more obscure corners of the O-O world.

For most programming languages the question of *how secure is it?* does not arise. It's the application that needs to implement security, not the language it is written in. However, Java is many other things in addition to being a programming language:

- A set of object-oriented frameworks, primarily for graphical user interface (GUI) building and networking
- An operating system
- A client/server management mechanism
- A unifying force that cuts across operating system and network boundaries

1.2 What Java Does

What Java does is to solve the problem of executable content. What's that? Well, the early sites on the World Wide Web were static: pictures and text. That was revolutionary enough. The richness of the pages was a revelation to anyone used to the traditional staid appearance of information downloaded from a server; the hypertext links, which made cross-referencing easy, made it a more useful information source than an encyclopedia; and the amount of information available was staggering. But if you wanted a program to run, you had to send a data file to the server where that program was – you filled in a form on the screen, clicked the send button, and waited for the result.

Some programs are better run on the client than on a server. So why couldn't part of the content of the Web pages be executable? Why couldn't a page comprise some text, some pictures, and some programs that run on the client? There were two reasons:

1. It would be dangerous from a security point of view. There are enough viruses on the Web anyway. With executable content, you might not even realize that you were downloading potentially dangerous code.

2. The programs might not run on a particular operating system. One of the joys of the Web was that you could choose whatever client system was right for you and download pages running on a completely different system.

But executable content, while potentially dangerous, is also extremely valuable:

- Executable content can make a Web page much more exciting. This is what Java became well known for in its early days: dancing cartoon characters, bouncing heads, ticker tapes, etc. You can't do these if all the programs must run on the server. Some of the early examples were indeed just cute – they showed what the technology could do, not why it was important – but appearance, excitement, and even cuteness are important in attracting customers to a business site.

- Many dialogues with a customer are unbearably slow if you have to communicate with a Web server at each interaction. With executable content, the dialogue – an insurance proposal, a request for a credit card, a browse through a catalogue, or whatever – can be completed on the client machine, and the resulting transaction sent across the Web.

Java makes executable content possible while solving the problems noted above by having three components:

1. A *Java Virtual Machine* (JVM) designed to prevent any code from tampering with the client system. The code runs in a *protected space*, and has only limited and always strictly controlled access to the surrounding system. This is to meet Requirement 1 above. The arena of activity for any specific code is defined by the client by way of a security policy. Java 2 provides an implementation for such protected spaces by the use of protected domains, security policy files and security managers which we shall see in greater detail in the later parts of this book.

2. A set of *bytecodes* – JVM instructions – which are interpreted by the JVM. You have to have these to prevent any code from jumping outside the pre-determined area of operation, but they have a benefit of their own. Since they are machine-independent, if you have a JVM for your

workstation, then you can run any applet from any server, satisfying Requirement 2 above.

3. A high-level object-oriented language in which to write the classes that make up the code. This is a language similar in many ways to C++ with some functions (such as pointers) omitted because they could be used by malicious code to escape from its area of operation pre-determined by the client.

There is now a Java Development Kit (JDK) – comprising the JVM, compiler, and basic classes – for most operating systems, and most Web browsers contain a JVM, so executable content is now real.

A Java program that is loaded from the Web and is run on a Web browser system is called an *applet*. A Java program that is loaded locally, rather than from the Web, is called an *application*. In JDK 1.1, an application was not constrained by the sandbox and could access the local machine, just like a program written in any other language.

However, in Java 2, any piece of code, local or remote, is recognized by two characteristics: the location of its origin (URL address) and the identities of the entities signing the code. The user can define in his or her security policy, exactly how much of which resource can be accessed by a code having a particular URL source and signers. This is what is called *fine-grained access control*.

Due to these security features, all you have to do is to write an application once in Java. Then that application can be run anywhere that has a JVM in compliance with the Java Compatibility Kit (JCK)[1]. This makes Java very useful for people writing applications which will be used by a wide variety of users – quite independently of whether they will ever be downloaded from the Web.

1.3 Java Is Not an Island: Java as a Part of Security

Java security must be *holistic*, *adequate* and *perpetual*.

1. First, Java security must be holistic. An attacker who wishes you harm (rather than one who wants to prove his own cleverness) will focus on the weak links in the security, so the security of a system that uses Java must be reviewed as a whole, following the flows of data and applications, and considering the potential for attack or accident at each point. Specifically,

---

[1] Sun Microsystems requires that code obtained by third parties by modifying the original source code of the JVM pass the JCK. This is done to maintain compatibility among the Java platforms implemented by different vendors.

if Java is being used to pass applets over a shared network like the Internet, then you have to consider:

- Private network protection, using a firewall and allied security policies
- Private data protection, using encryption to shield data as it flows over the public network
- User authentication, using digital signatures, or protected passwords

2. Secondly, Java security must be adequate. It has to be strong enough for the purpose in hand: Java must not be the weak link. But there is no need to spend extra money to make it far and away the strongest link, unless one of the two following circumstances occur:

- Your potential attackers don't just want to crack your system, they want to crack your *Java* system.
- Your users have a particular fear of Java, and you need to reassure them (security has to match levels of threat and worry, as well as, levels of potential loss).

3. Thirdly, Java security must be perpetual. This book will help you build a secure Java system to face today's perils of accident and attack. But those perils will change. So you must review your Java security – as a part of your overall security of course – regularly, to stay one jump ahead of potential attackers.

How well does Java meet those needs? Three points:

1. **Java architecture permits secure design**

   The Java 2 security architecture allows a user to predetermine the area of activity for any code local or remote, and enforce strict control over access of any code to system resources. This has been made possible by the use of the concepts of protection domains, user defined security policies and security managers (which are described in great detail in Chapter 3, "The New Java Security Model" on page 69).

2. **Java implementations respond to error reports**

   The attack applets we describe later were all reported by applet hunters. They come not from incidents of loss on the Internet, but from laboratory studies of how Java can be used and abused. The applet hunters have been as responsible as they are clever, and have alerted the Java implementors to the problems before telling the public. So normally you will hear of an implementation loophole at the same time as hearing of the fix. Thus any risk of using Java gets gradually less as loopholes are closed.

3. Nothing in Java should permit complacency

Installers and users of Java must be as willing to respond as the implementors. That is, users must recognize that loopholes will be found and must be closed without delay.

In summary, provided that you have an implementation that is free of known errors, and that you install, maintain and review Java carefully, you can reach levels of security which are appropriate for any business purpose.

1.3.1 Safety and Security

To enthusiastic object-oriented programmers, it is the *Java language* that is important. It contains a number of important differences from C++ which reduce the chance of writing a rogue program by accident, as well as making it more difficult to write a rogue program by design.

But, from a security point of view, it is the *Java Virtual Machine* that matters. The business benefits of Java are the security and portability of the JVM, and these come from the bytecodes, not from the Java source language.

So, we shall be more concerned with bytecode programs, which are different from Java source programs. All valid Java source programs can be compiled to bytecode programs, but there are bytecode programs that have no corresponding Java source. And, of course, it is possible to generate Java bytecode programs from other high-level languages. The first other language was NetREXX, a variant of the REXX language, and others have followed.

This difference between high-level and bytecode is both bad and good:

- It is bad because people can circumvent the design features of the Java language. This was designed to produce well-behaved bytecode programs, a design that has limited security strength if an attacker can write directly in bytecode.

- It is good because you can foil the decompilers. These take bytecode and generate Java source code – source code which is very readable because of the large amount of information a Java class file contains. To prevent people from decompiling your valuable copyright code, you can modify the compiled class file so that there is no decompiled version. We discuss this in detail in 5.4.1, "Beating the Decompilation Threat" on page 134. So the good features of the high-level Java language should be seen as *safety* features, not as *security* features.

1.3.2 Java as an Aid to Security

Sometimes, discussions of Java and security focus only on the perils of Java, as though there was only a downside to using it, from a security point of view anyway. But this is not the whole story. Java can be a great help to the security of a system, and can strengthen weak links, primarily because *code distribution is a risky process*.

Many applications need code running on the client in cooperation with code running on the server – for example, graphical front ends, or dialers to connect to the telephone network – and this code has to be installed there somehow. The distribution of this code is often a weak link in an online system, and it is usually *much* easier to attack this than to waste time trying to decrypt messages flowing over the Internet. What is the danger? If this code can be tampered with, then, for example, a dialer number can be changed so that the client dials the attacker's site rather than the proper server. The client will never realize this because the attacker, acting as a man-in-the-middle (MIM)[2], forwards all traffic between client and server, reading it as it goes. Or a virus can be introduced, or a host of other horrible possibilities.

The options for code distribution are:

- To send a physical diskette or CD-ROM to the client
- To have the client download the code over an existing network
- To use Java

The safest of the three is Java. It isn't always suitable – the client must already have a network connection that is fast enough for the purpose – but it is by far the easiest to update with a new release, it is less easily intercepted than a physical distribution and, unlike a normal download, it is checked on arrival. Moreover, it can be signed and verified for appropriate signatures.

The checking and signing of Java code is central to Java security and very much more will be said about them in Part 2, "Under the Hood" on page 107. In this introductory chapter, it is enough to describe briefly the three components of applet checking:

1. The *class loader* is responsible for bringing together all of the different parts of the program so that it can be executed.

---

[2] A network entity that intercepts data flowing between two machines is commonly known as a *sniffer*. A sniffer could have a more active role than just copying frames off the wire. In fact a more dangerous attack could be accomplished if the sniffer is able to acts as a *man-in-the-middle*, a machine that actively inserts itself in the data flows between two legitimate systems in order to compromise the data flowing between them. To the client, the MIM masquerades as the server and to the server the MIM masquerades as the client.

2. The *class file verifier* (which includes the *bytecode verifier*) checks that the program obeys the rules of the Java Virtual Machine (but note that this does not necessarily mean that it obeys the rules of the Java language).

3. The *security manager* imposes local restrictions on the things that the program is allowed to do. It is perfectly possible to customize this to allow code limited access to carefully controlled resources. This could mean allowing no access to the local file system, and network access only to the location from which the code, or its Web page, came.

You may wish, for example, to print something from an applet. You are unlikely to want your security manager to allow anyone to do that, but you might allow access to especially trustworthy people. So you download the applet; discover that it is located at a trustworthy URL address and encrypted with someone's private key; check the accompanying public key certificate to make sure it is valid, and identify someone especially trustworthy; decrypt the applet with that public key, and then allow it the necessary access.

One important thing that distinguishes Java from other forms of executable content is that it has *both* the web of trust that signatures bring *and* the three security components to validate the downloaded code. These precautions are taken, not because Java users are less trustful than others, but because even the most trusted of code suppliers sometimes make mistakes, or can have their systems compromised. Without the validation, a web of trust can become a web of corruption if any one trusted site is successfully cracked.

1.3.3 Java as a Threat to Security

So, in the absence of implementation errors, either on the part of the browser vendors *or on the part of computer operators, administrators and systems programmers*, Java should be safe. The browser vendors have a good reputation for responding to reports of flaws in their implementations, and one of the key purposes of this book is to help you avoid any slips in your installation.

If something does go wrong, then the most severe threat you face is *system modification*, the result of what are sometimes called *attack applets*. This is worse than someone's being able to read data from your system, because you have no idea what has been left behind. There could be a virus on your computer, or on any computer to which you are connected. Alternatively, some of your business data could have been modified so that it is no longer valid.

This is exactly the sort of thing that Java is intended to prevent, and its defenses against attack applets are strong. They are equally strong against the next, still severe, threat of *privacy invasion*, in which read access rather than update access is gained. This does not leave you having to reinstall all your software and reassemble all your business data, but the loss can be serious enough. In addition to the exposure of business data, if your private key is compromised, then it can be used to sign electronic payments in your name.

Because Java has the strongest security for executable content, it has been seen as a challenge by security specialists, who find both the intellectual challenge exciting and want to help close any loopholes in Java implementations. Up to the date of writing, all the reported attack applets were developed by such specialists, not by malicious or criminal attackers.

There are another couple of, much less severe, threats against which Java does not have strong defenses. The very essence of Java is that a program from a server will come down and run on your client with little, if any, intervention from you. What if the program is not one you want to run... If it is stealing your cycles?

The most extreme form of cycle stealing is a *denial of service* attack. The applet can use so much of the client's machine time that it cannot perform its normal function. This is the Java equivalent of flooding a company with mail or with telephone calls; like those nuisances it cannot readily be prevented – all you can do is find out who is responsible and take action after the event.

Less extreme examples of cycle stealing are the irksome, *nuisance*, applets. These run unhelpful programs intended to show how clever the author is and embarrass the owner of the client machine. They can even pretend to be you (psyche stealing?), for example by sending e-mail that appears to come from you.

1.3.4 Writing Secure Java

Valuable Java code is likely to need to communicate with the server it came from, and to do so securely. All sensitive communication over the Internet needs proper cryptographic protection. From JDK 1.1 onwards, Java provides general purpose APIs for cryptographic functions, collectively known as the Java Cryptography Architecture (JCA) and Java Cryptography Extension (JCE). Java 2 significantly extends the Java Cryptography Architecture. The set of the Java core classes (which are the Java classes shipped with the Java platform[3]) can be divided into two subsets:

- Security related core classes

- Other core classes

[3] In this book, the Java 2 Platform, Standard Edition, V1.2 (J2SE) is often referred to as *Java platform* or *Java 2 platform*.

The Security related core classes in Java 2 can be further subdivided as:

- Access control and permissions related core classes
- Cryptography related core classes

Of these, only the cryptography related core classes form a part of the JCA. In addition to these, all classes in JCE 1.2 form part of the JCA.

Some cryptographic functions are seen as being dangerous in the wrong hands. No government wants to provide organized crime, or terrorist groups, with a cheap effective way of communicating that the police cannot decrypt. Exactly how to prevent this is not so clear, so there are many different export and import rules for cryptographic products. The cryptographic interfaces are divided into two parts, JCA and JCE, which reflect the divide between exportable and unexportable cryptography. We discuss this in more detail in Chapter 13, "Cryptography in Java 2" on page 475.

1.3.5 Staying One Jump Ahead

To get ahead, the owners of a client or a Web site need to develop an overall security policy of which Java is a part, and implement it with care. They need to use the latest information on what is known about Java security. This is bound to change; realistically, Java is so young that it cannot be otherwise.

So how do they find the very latest information? Two key sources are the CERT Coordination Center, which is on the Web at http://www.cert.org/ and Sun Microsystems's list of frequently asked questions about applet security at http://java.javasoft.com/sfaq. This gets you ahead. Staying ahead means that the security policy should include regular checks of these sites, and regular reviews of which are the right sites to check.[4]

Another part of staying ahead involves balancing security with stability. If an implementation error is discovered in the browser you use, and you see on the Web sites a description of the problem together with news of a new beta version of the browser to fix the problem, do you change to the new beta at once? Systems managers are traditionally very cautious about beta code: they want to see a lot of testing before they put it live on their production systems. This caution is one of the most important causes of the very high availability levels of modern systems, so systems managers are not about to change.

Traditionally, a change to include new function is forced to wait until it passes thorough testing, while a security change may be allowed through with less

[4] See also the list of the Java security Web sites in Appendix D, "Sources of Information about Java Security" on page 685.

testing. It's a business decision, and it's worth including guidance in the security policy. The only way in which Java is different from all other areas of security, where similar business decisions must be made, is that news of a loophole can be spread worldwide extremely quickly, so the presumption should be that security fixes must go on quickly.

1.3.6 The Vigilant Web Site

The cure for abuse is proper use, not non-use. Executable content has such a great value to computer systems and to computer business that we need to do it properly, not to ban it.

Proper use of Java involves vigilance on everybody's part, including:

- Vigilance on the part of the systems administrators who need to be sure that they can trust their sources

- Vigilance on the part of the network administrators who need to protect against network attacks such as the MIM attack

- Vigilance on the part of applet developers who need to be sure that the tools they are using do not corrupt their class files: their workstations may not be production machines, but they must be properly protected

There is something of an irony in remarks one sometimes hears about how Java should be turned off, made by people who are happy to download a code patch or a driver from a Web site. It is similar to those who are deeply concerned about sending their credit card information over the Web, but would willingly hand a credit card to a waiter in a restaurant.

If Java is used with vigilance, then its unique combination of web of trust and code validation makes it more secure than forms of executable content which depend on the web of trust alone. And, of course, dramatically more secure than downloading natively executable code from the Web.

1.4 Understanding Java 2 Security

As we already said in 1.1, "Java Is Not Just a Language" on page 3, in most programming languages it is the application that needs to implement security, not the language itself. This is not true in Java. Since its inception, Java has demonstrated that it was built for the net. For this reason, although Java is not just for applets any more, it looks immediately clear that, unlike other programming languages and systems, security mechanisms must be an integral part of Java.

The history of Java security has been parallel to the main releases of Java: JDK 1.0, JDK 1.1 and Java 2 SDK, Standard Edition, V1.2[5]:

1. The JDK 1.0 security model was very strict. Local code was granted access to all the system resources, while a remote applet was always considered untrusted, and could be used almost only for cosmetic functions, like the decoration of a Web page.

2. JDK 1.1 still considered local code as completely trusted, with full access to all of the system resources. However, JDK 1.1 also offered Java developers the possibility to apply a digital signature to the code they wrote. By looking at the digital signature, the user on a client machine could decide whether a particular remote code was to be considered trusted or not. If untrusted, that remote code would run in a restricted environment. If trusted, that code would be considered as a local code, with full access to all of the system resources. The JDK 1.1 security model was more attractive, but still presented several limitations. For example, remote code with a trusted signature was granted full access to all the system resources, as well as local code. So, even when you wanted to grant a signed remote code, say, only read access to a particular file in a particular directory of your system, you had to grant it full read access to all your files and all your directories. Moreover, that code was automatically granted the permission to write on your system, install other code, open a socket, and a lot of other things. This happened without your intervention or your awareness.

3. The Java 2 security model implements fine-grained access control. You can now classify the Java code that is to run on your system basing your judgement on the URL location where that code resides and/or the owners of the code itself. The owners of the code are identified through their digital signatures. Multiple signatures for a single piece of code are allowed in Java 2. Possibilities are now endless. You can say that a piece of code coming from a particular location and/or signed by particular signers can only read that file and write in that directory. Other code coming from another location and/or signed by other entities can open only a specific socket, while still other code can be classified to have full access. Moreover, in Java 2, even local code can be subjected to security restrictions.

In this section we will demonstrate to you that Java is not a threat to security, provided that your Java system is configured in the correct way. On the contrary, the security features that are part of the Java programming language itself can really improve the overall security of your system.

---

[5] In this book, Java 2 SDK, Standard Edition, V1.2 (J2SDK) is sometimes referred to as *Java 2 SDK*.

We will show you two simple examples, and we will explain to you the main concepts that are involved. However, we will not go through all the details, because this will be done in other sections of the book.

1.4.1 An Example of Applet Security in Java 2

In 1.3.2, "Java as an Aid to Security" on page 8, we introduced an interesting scenario, where the user on the client machine may wish to print something from an applet, but does not want the security manager to allow anyone to do that. On the contrary, the user might grant this right only to especially trustworthy entities. So this is the sequence of the operations:

1. An applet packaged in a signed Java Archive (JAR) file is downloaded.

2. The Java Runtime Environment (JRE)[6] detects that it has come from a trustworthy URL location and is signed with the private key of a particular entity[7].

3. The JRE then verifies that the entity that signed the JAR file is the entity that owns the accompanying public key certificate and that the contents of the JAR file have not been tampered with.

4. Finally, the JRE verifies that the entity that signed the JAR file has a matching certificate in the keystore database. This ensures that the entity is trustworthy.

1.4.1.1 The Java Code

Let's consider the following piece of code:

```
import java.awt.*;
import java.awt.event.*;
import java.applet.*;

public class GetPrintJob extends Applet implements ActionListener
{
   boolean p = true;

   public GetPrintJob()
   {
   super();
      Button b = new Button("getPrintJob");
```

Figure 1. (Part 1 of 2). GetPrintJob.java Applet Source Code

[6] In this book, Java 2 Runtime Environment, Standard Edition, V1.2 (J2RE) is often referred to as Java Runtime Environment (JRE) 1.2.

[7] In Java 2, signatures by multiple entities can be applied on the same JAR file.

```
      add(b, BorderLayout.CENTER);
      b.addActionListener(this);
   }

   public void actionPerformed(ActionEvent evt)
   {
      try
      {
         Toolkit.getDefaultToolkit().getPrintJob(null, "PrintJob", null);
      }

      catch(Exception e)
      {
         System.out.println("There was an exception, "+ e.toString());
         p=false;
      }
      if (p)
         System.out.println("No exception. Test is successful.");
   }

   public void paint(Graphics g)
   {
      new GetPrintJob();
   }
}
```

Figure 2. (Part 2 of 2). GetPrintJob.java Applet Source Code

This is the code of an applet that, once downloaded on your system, does nothing but displays a button. If you push the button, the applet attempts to get a PrintJob object, which results in initiating a print operation on the toolkit's platform.

In JDK 1.0, this operation would not have been allowed to a remote applet, by default considered untrusted. In JDK 1.1, the remote applet should have been signed and the signature considered as trusted. However, once granted the permission to access your system resources, that applet could do everything a local code would be allowed to do, not only print to a printer. The fine-grained access control implemented by the Java 2 security model gives you the possibility to grant only the permission to print (since this is the only permission this applet requires) and only to the code you trust.

The applet above can be invoked by a very simple HTML page, such as the following one:

```
<HTML>

   <HEAD>
      <TITLE>GetPrintJob Applet</TITLE>
   </HEAD>

   <BODY>

      <H3>GetPrintJob Applet</H3>

      <APPLET Code="GetPrintJob" Width=250 Height=50>
      </APPLET>

   </BODY>
</HTML>
```

Figure 3. GetPrintJob.html File Invoking the GetPrintJob Applet

The applet source code shown in Figure 1 on page 14 and Figure 2 on page 15 can be compiled by issuing the command:

`javac GetPrintJob.java`

which translates Java source code into Java bytecode. The resulting file produced by the Java compiler `javac` is GetPrintJob.class.

1.4.1.2 Running the Applet without the Necessary Permission

After saving GetPrintJob.class and GetPrintJob.html in the public directory of a Web server, having host name wtr05218.itso.ral.ibm.com, we try to access the HTML file from a client machine using the Java 2 Applet Viewer. The Applet Viewer is a development tool shipped with the SDK. The applet can be invoked from a remote machine running Java 2 by entering the following command:

`appletviewer http://wtr05218.itso.ral.ibm.com/GetPrintJob.html`

The Applet Viewer window with a getPrintJob button is immediately displayed:

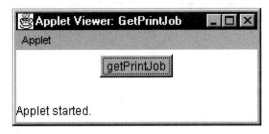

Figure 4. GetPrintJob Applet Running

However, upon clicking on the **getPrintJob** button, no print operation on the toolkit's platform will be initiated and you will see a security exception being displayed on the Command Prompt window from which you launched the Applet Viewer:

```
There was an exception, java.security.AccessControlException: access denied
(java.lang.RuntimePermission queuePrintJob )
```

The same exception will be displayed every time the button is clicked.

The reason for this exception is that the applet has not been granted any permissions before being downloaded, so it has to run in a restricted environment. When its button is pressed and the applet attempts to initiate a print operation on the toolkit's platform, a security exception is thrown because the applet is attempting to run out of its restricted environment.

In a JDK 1.1 environment, we would solve this problem by signing the applet code on the Web server, and recognizing the signer as trusted on the client. However, this would grant the applet all permissions, not only the specific permission that the applet needs to print. In a Java 2 environment the situation is different, since you can limit the permissions the code gets to only what the code claims it needs. In this case the only security-related operation the applet needs to perform is to initiate a print operation on the toolkit's platform. Since the applet resides in the public HTML directory of the Web server wtr05218.itso.ral.ibm.com, we will grant this permission to all the code coming from that location. To further limit the security exposure of our system, we want the remote applet to be signed by a trusted entity, and we will limit the permission by also looking at the digital signature, so that another applet coming from the same location will not be granted the same permission unless signed by the same trusted entity. The sequence of operations to get this is explained in the following sections.

1.4.1.3 Packing the Applet Class in a JAR File

First of all, we sign the code of the GetPrintJob applet on the server machine. To do this, the applet file must be packed in the JAR format, through the command:

```
jar cvf GetPrintJob.jar GetPrintJob.class
```

The command above must be launched on the same directory where the file GetPrintJob.class resides and it automatically creates the JAR file GetPrintJob.jar, which includes a compressed version of the original class file. If you examine the contents of GetPrintJob.jar (on Windows systems this can be done even with the WinZip utility), you will see that it contains also a file called MANIFEST.MF. This is a text file containing general information about the files that have been packed in the JAR file. The file MANIFEST.MF is often called the *manifest* file.

1.4.1.4 Creating a Keystore and a Signer's Key Pair

We also need to generate a *key pair* (a public key and associated private key). With Java 2, this can be done using the Java 2 keytool command line utility with the option –genkey, which generates a key pair and wraps the public key into an X.509 V1 self-signed certificate. The details are shown in the following session screen:

```
C:\>keytool -genkey
Enter keystore password:  Paolina
What is your first and last name?
  [Unknown]:  Marco Pistoia
What is the name of your organizational unit?
  [Unknown]:  ITSO
What is the name of your organization?
  [Unknown]:  IBM Corporation
What is the name of your City or Locality?
  [Unknown]:  Cary
What is the name of your State or Province?
  [Unknown]:  North Carolina
What is the two-letter country code for this unit?
  [Unknown]:  US
Is <CN=Marco Pistoia, OU=ITSO, O=IBM Corporation, L=Cary, ST=North Carolina, C=US> correct?
  [no]:  yes

Enter key password for <mykey>
        (RETURN if same as keystore password):  Centonze
```

The process we have just described creates a public and private key pair and associates the public key with the certificate of the signer, whose alias by default is mykey. The private key and the certificate are stored in a flat keystore file called .keystore, located in the user home directory. A *keystore* is a database of private keys and their associate X.509 certificate chains authenticating the corresponding public keys. The public information in the default implementation of a keystore file is stored unencrypted; however, a keystore password is necessary for the user to verify in the future that the keystore file has not been tampered with. The private key is password-protected.

1.4.1.5 Signing the Code

Once the keystore has been generated, and a certificate has been created for the signer, the JAR file can be signed using the private key of the signer. This is done by launching the Java 2 command line tool `jarsigner` against the JAR file, as shown in the following session:

```
D:\WWW\HTML>jarsigner GetPrintJob.jar mykey
Enter Passphrase for keystore: Paolina
Enter key password for mykey: Centonze

D:\WWW\HTML>
```

The `jarsigner` utility temporarily opens the JAR file, adds the information related to the signature, and packs the JAR file again. At the end of this process, you will see in the D:\WWW\HTML directory that the GetPrintJob.jar file has changed and its size has become larger. Notice that a signed JAR file in Java 2 still has the .jar extension. The `jarsigner` utility does not add a .sig extension to the .jar extension of the JAR file, as it happened with the JDK 1.1 `javakey` command line tool.

At this point, the HTML file invoking the applet must be modified to point to the JAR file GetPrintJob.jar. We open the file GetPrintJob.html, shown in Figure 3 on page 16, and we modify the <APPLET> tag in the following way:

```
<APPLET Archive="GetPrintJob.jar" Code="GetPrintJob" Width=250 Height=50>
```

Then we save the resulting file as GetPrintJobJAR.html.

1.4.1.6 Exporting the Signer's Certificate on the Server

Notice that, on the client machine, the signer of the code must be considered a trusted entity. For this reason, on the server machine, we export the signer's certificate into a file, called marcoCer.cer. This is done using again the `keytool` command with the `-export` option, as shown in the following session:

```
C:\WINNT\Profiles\pistoia.000>keytool -export -alias mykey -file marcoCer.cer
Enter keystore password:  Paolina
Certificate stored in file <marcoCer.cer>

C:\WINNT\Profiles\pistoia.000>
```

1.4.1.7 Importing the Signer's Certificate on the Client

The file marcoCer.cer must be copied on the client machine and then
imported into the local keystore as a trusted certificate. Of course, a local
keystore must have been previously created. The -import option of the
keytool command is used to import a certificate. The following session shows
that we import the certificate giving to the owner of the certificate the alias
marcokey.

```
C:\WINNT\Profiles\pistoia.000>keytool -import -alias marcokey -file marcoCer.cer

Enter keystore password:  np3101r
Owner: CN=Marco Pistoia, OU=ITSO, O=IBM Corporation, L=Cary, ST=North Carolina,
C=US
Issuer: CN=Marco Pistoia, OU=ITSO, O=IBM Corporation, L=Cary, ST=North Carolina,
 C=US
Serial number: 36f3206e
Valid from: Fri Mar 19 23:13:34 EST 1999 until: Fri Jun 18 00:13:34 EDT 1999
Certificate fingerprints:
        MD5:  60:CA:F2:D1:4E:C1:D1:AD:B7:37:68:2B:A5:9C:33:64
        SHA1: FC:CB:F5:30:75:0A:21:6E:F6:21:9C:17:C3:FD:A3:53:A4:E3:45:5C
Trust this certificate? [no]:  yes
Certificate was added to keystore

C:\WINNT\Profiles\pistoia.000>
```

The keytool option in this case asks only for the password of the local
keystore. Since the private key was never exported out of the server machine,
it is not even imported in the client machine, and no password is required to
protect the private key. As you can see from the screen above, the keytool
command shows the particulars of the certificate to be imported, and then,
before actually importing it, it asks for further confirmation that the certificate
is to be considered trusted.

1.4.1.8 Modifying the Security Policy on the Client System

Now the Java security system needs to be informed that code signed by the
signer marcokey and residing in the HTML public directory of the Web server
wtr05218.itso.ral.ibm.com must be granted permission to initiate a print
operation on the toolkit's platform. The security policy of the Java system is
configured in a text file called a *policy file*. By default, after a typical

installation of the Java 2 SDK, Standard Edition, V1.2.*x*, the policy file that affects the Applet Viewer security comes in the directory *drive*:\jdk1.2.*x*\jre\lib\security (in our system, *drive* is D) and is called java.policy. Rather than manually editing this file, with the risks of generating security exposures by doing syntax mistakes, it is convenient to use a new utility available with the Java 2 platform, the *Policy Tool*, that is launched from the command line by entering the command `policytool`.

When the Policy Tool window is brought up, you have to select the policy file you want to configure (this can be done by clicking on **Open** from the File menu) and the keystore where the signer's certificates reside (click on **Change KeyStore** from the Edit menu). The following figure shows the Policy Tool window we used on the client machine:

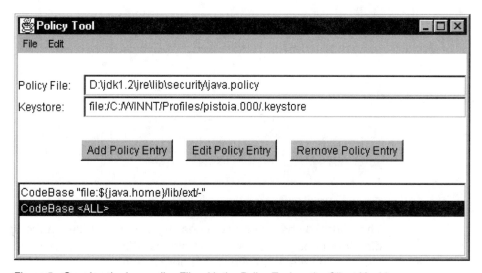

Figure 5. Opening the java.policy File with the Policy Tool on the Client Machine

What we need to do now is to grant permission to initiate a print operation on the toolkit's platform to all the code signed by marcokey and residing in the URL http://wtr05218.itso.ral.ibm.com/. To do this, we click on **Add Policy Entry** and the Policy Entry panel is displayed. Here we type `http://wtr05218.itso.ral.ibm.com/*` in the CodeBase field and `marcokey` in the SignedBy field, as shown next:

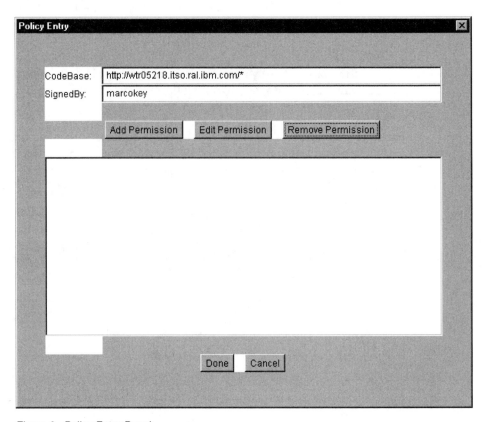

Figure 6. Policy Entry Panel

The wildcard character * is necessary when JAR files in the specified directory need to receive the privileges. Without that character, only class files would receive the specified permissions.

This way we are granting particular security privileges to all the JAR files stored in the public HTML directory of the Web server wtr05218.itso.ral.ibm.com and signed by marcokey.

Then we click on **Add Permission**, and the permission dialog appears:

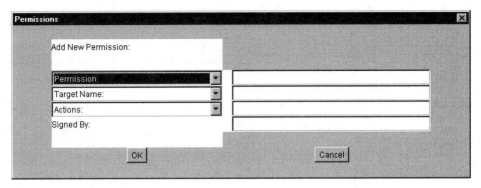

Figure 7. Permission Dialog

The specific permission we need in this case is a RuntimePermission, and the target is queuePrintJob. After selecting these items from the Permission and Target Name menus, the Permission dialog appears as follows:

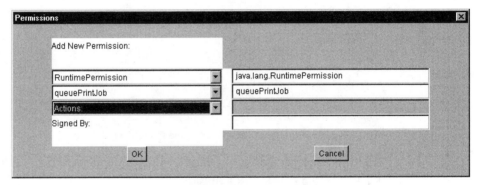

Figure 8. Selecting the Appropriate Values in the Permission Dialog Panel Fields

After pressing **OK**, we see that the Policy Entry panel has registered the new permission:

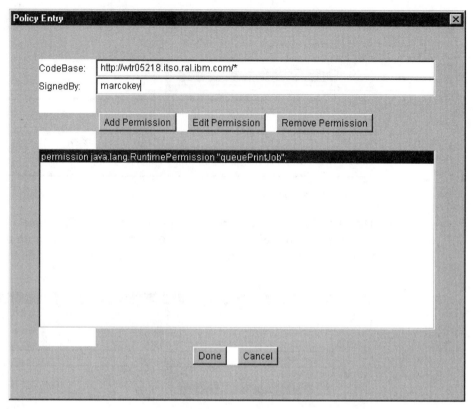

Figure 9. New Permission Registered in the Policy Entry Dialog

Then we click on **Done**, and in the Policy Tool window we see that the new policy entry has been registered:

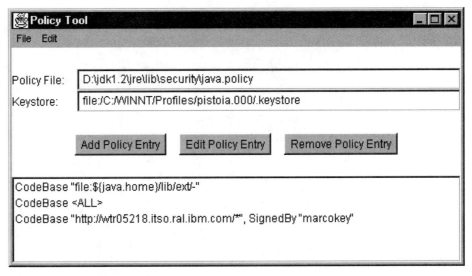

Figure 10. New Policy Entry Registered in the Policy Tool Window

Before closing the Policy Tool, it is necessary to save this configuration, by selecting the **Save** item from the File menu. Upon opening with a text editor the java.policy file in the directory D:\jdk1.2.x\jre\lib\security, we would see that the following entry has been generated:

```
grant signedBy "marcokey",  codeBase "http://wtr05218.itso.ral.ibm.com/*" {
  permission java.lang.RuntimePermission "queuePrintJob";
};
```

1.4.1.9 Running the Applet with the Necessary Permission
At this point, we can run the GetPrintJob signed applet by entering the following command on the command line:

```
appletviewer http://wtr05218.itso.ral.ibm.com/GetPrintJobJAR.html
```

An Applet Viewer window very similar to the one shown in Figure 4 on page 17 is brought up. However, this time the applet is signed and the combination of the signer and the URL where the applet resides have been granted the permission to initiate a print operation on the toolkit's platform. For this reason, when the **getPrintJob** button is pressed, the following Print window will be displayed:

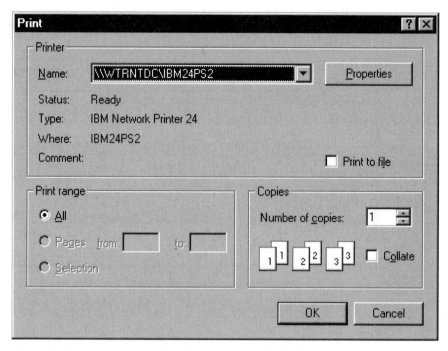

Figure 11. Print Window Opened by the GetPrintJob Applet

No security exceptions are thrown this time. According to the Java code shown in Figure 1 on page 14 and Figure 2 on page 15, the Command Prompt window registers the following message:

```
No exception. Test is successful.
```

However, if the same applet had attempted to read or write a file from the local file system, or open a socket connection, a security exception would have been thrown, because such permissions were not granted to this code.

1.4.2 An Example of Application Security in Java 2

The example of remote code downloading described in 1.4.1, "An Example of Applet Security in Java 2" on page 14 can give you an idea of the reason why the new Java security model adds a security layer to the basic security of your system. Moreover, as you can see, no particular programming efforts are required to use it, since security is part of Java.

Another example that we want to show you in this chapter relates to Java application security. As we have discussed in Point 1 and Point 2 on page 13, in previous versions of Java, the security model granted full permissions to all the local code. In other words, a Java application launched from the command line was not subjected to any security restrictions. In Java 2, even applications can be subjected to the security policy of the local system.

A practical use of this restriction would be if you receive the bytecode of a Java application on a diskette or CD-ROM in the mail, or you get it from a remote site through the FTP protocol, and then you want to run it on your system. As far as you know, this application only has to initiate a print operation on the toolkit's platform, since this is what the application developer claims. However, you cannot be completely sure, since you did not have the opportunity to read the source code of the application. So it is possible that the application you are going to run on your system has some hidden agenda, and while it opens a pretty Print screen as the one shown in Figure 11 on page 26, it also attempts to read a file from your local file system, open a socket connection to a remote machine and send the contents of that file to a remote host. The file could contain sensitive information that you are not willing to share with other people. The application could write files on your system, install software you do not want, throw in a virus, or perform other terrible operations. For this reason, you do not want this application to be granted full permissions on your system.

The new Java security model offers you a way to limit the freedom of a Java local application installed on your system. The exact limits on the application's freedom depend as usual on the location of the application on your file system and/or the digital signatures that have been applied on the code.

1.4.2.1 The Java Code
Let's consider the following Java code, obtained by transforming the GetPrintJob applet, shown in Figure 1 on page 14 and Figure 2 on page 15, in the GetPrintJob Java application:

```
import java.awt.*;
import java.awt.event.*;

class GetPrintJob extends Frame implements ActionListener
{
    boolean p = true;

    GetPrintJob()
    {
```

Figure 12. (Part 1 of 2). GetPrintJob.java Application Source Code

```
        super("Toolkit.getPrintJob() test case");
        setSize(300, 100);
        setLocation(200, 200);
        Button b = new Button("getPrintJob");
        add(b, BorderLayout.CENTER);
        b.addActionListener(this);

        show();
    }

    public void actionPerformed(ActionEvent evt)
    {
        try
        {
            Toolkit.getDefaultToolkit().getPrintJob(null, "PrintJob", null);
        }

        catch(Exception e)
        {
            System.out.println("There was an exception, "+ e.toString());
            p=false;
        }
        if (p)
            System.out.println("No exception. Test is successful.");
    }

    public static void main(String[] args)
    {
        new GetPrintJob();
    }
}
```

Figure 13. (Part 2 of 2). GetPrintJob.java Application Source Code

What this application does is similar to what we have seen with the applet, except that it runs locally. Once run, it displays a button, and each time you press the button, it attempts to get a PrintJob object, which results in initiating a print operation on the toolkit's platform. This operation would have been allowed in JDK 1.0 and 1.1, since local applications were granted full access permissions on the underlying operating system.

In Java 2, according to the new security model, a security manager is not automatically installed when an application is running. In other words, an application has by default full access to resources, as was always the case in

JDK 1.0 and 1.1. However, by specifying a special parameter on the command line, `-Djava.security.manager`, you can invoke a security manager, and in this case the application would be subjected to the same security restrictions as a remote applet that has been downloaded on your system.

The Java source code shown above is compiled and transformed in Java bytecode through the Java compiler `javac`:

```
javac GetPrintJob.java
```

1.4.2.2 Running the Application without a Security Manager
The file produced after launching the above `javac` command is GetPrintJob.class and the application can be launched by entering:

```
java GetPrintJob
```

from the same directory where GetPrintJob.class resides. After launching the command above, the following graphical button is displayed:

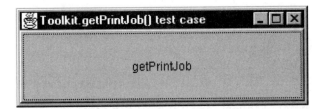

Figure 14. getPrintJob Button Displayed by the GetPrintJob Application

On pressing the **getPrintJob** button, you see that the application works correctly: a Print window similar to the one shown in Figure 11 on page 26 is brought up, and the Command Prompt window from which you launched the application displays the following message:

```
No exception. Test is successful.
```

The reason for this is that a local application is by default not subjected to any restrictions, and is allowed full access to system resources. A security manager is not automatically installed when an application is running.

1.4.2.3 Running the Application without the Necessary Permission
To apply the same security policy to an application found on the local file system as to downloaded applets, you can invoke the interpreter with the new `-Djava.security.manager` command line argument.

To execute the GetPrintJob application with the default security manager, type the following:

```
java -Djava.security.manager GetPrintJob
```

The application window this time displays a Warning yellow bar on the bottom, to remind you that the application is running under a security manager:

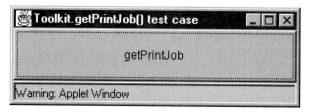

Figure 15. Executing the GetPrintJob Application with the Default Security Manager

However, on clicking on the **getPrintJob** button, you would see that the application does not work as expected: the Print window is not brought up and the Command Prompt window from which you launched the application registers the following security exception:

```
There was an exception, java.security.AccessControlException: access denied
(java.lang.RuntimePermission queuePrintJob )
```

The reason for this message is that the application is now running under the default security manager of the Java platform, and the security manager detects that the application does not have the proper permissions. This is a new feature implemented in the Java 2 security model, which was not implemented in the previous versions of Java, where local applications were automatically granted full permissions without the possibility to restrict their access to the system resources.

In order to run correctly, this application needs the permission to initiate a print operation on the toolkit's platform. The following sections show the steps to do this.

1.4.2.4 Packing the Application Class in a JAR File

First of all, the application class file GetPrintJob.class must be packed in a JAR file, called for instance GetPrintJob.jar. This could be done as explained in 1.4.1.3, "Packing the Applet Class in a JAR File" on page 18, by entering the command:

```
jar cvf GetPrintJob.jar GetPrintJob.class
```

However, the command above is not enough to produce a JAR file that could be run using the java command. In fact, when the java command runs against a JAR file, it needs to know the main class file contained in the JAR file itself. To do this, we create a text file called for example MainClass.txt, which contains the following line:

```
Main-Class: GetPrintJob
```

It is important that, when you edit this file, you hit Enter at the end of the line, so that an invisible end-of-line character is added at the end of this line and an empty new line is created.

After this, you can create the JAR file GetPrintJob.jar by using the `jar` command. However, this time, you should use the `m` option of the `jar` command and specify the file MainClass.txt on the command line, as follows:

```
jar cvfm GetPrintJob.jar MainClass.txt GetPrintJob.class
```

The `m` option forces the `jar` command to take into account the contents of the file MainClass.txt while producing the manifest file. So this time the file MANIFEST.MF of the GetPrintJob.jar file will contain the line:

```
Main-Class: GetPrintJob
```

This way the `java` command will know that GetPrintJob.class is the main Java class file that has to be run.

1.4.2.5 Code Signing

As we have explained, restricting access to local code makes particular sense in all the cases where we have received the bytecode of an application from a not completely trusted source and we have to run it on our system. In this example, we assume that the application has been written, compiled and signed on a machine called wtr05218.itso.ral.ibm.com, and then it has to run on a different machine, say wtr05366.itso.ral.ibm.com.

To sign the JAR file on wtr05218, we assume that we have already created the keystore file .keystore in the user home directory and that this file contains a key pair for the signer (see 1.4.1.4, "Creating a Keystore and a Signer's Key Pair" on page 18).

The signature on the JAR file is applied through the `jarsigner` command line tool, as explained in 1.4.1.5, "Signing the Code" on page 19.

The signer's certificate must be exported to a file on the machine wtr05218 (see 1.4.1.6, "Exporting the Signer's Certificate on the Server" on page 19), the file must be transferred to the machine wtr05366, for example using a diskette or via FTP, and then the certificate must be imported in the local keystore as a trusted certificate (see 1.4.1.7, "Importing the Signer's Certificate on the Client" on page 20).

1.4.2.6 Modifying the Security Policy

After saving the GetPrintJob.jar signed JAR file in the local directory D:\itso\ch01 of the machine wtr05366, the Java security system running on this machine must be informed that all the code signed by the signer marcokey and residing in the local directory D:\itso\ch01 must be granted permission to initiate a print operation on the toolkit's platform. If you do not modify the policy file properly, you will not be able to run the application correctly with the default security manager, because a security exception would be thrown.

The policy file configuration can be performed in a way very similar to the one we have shown in 1.4.1.8, "Modifying the Security Policy on the Client System" on page 20. The main difference now is that the system policy file that by default applies to Java applications, which is still called java.policy, is located in the directory *drive*:\Program Files\JavaSoft\JRE\1.2\lib\security. The Policy Tool can be used to modify this policy file:

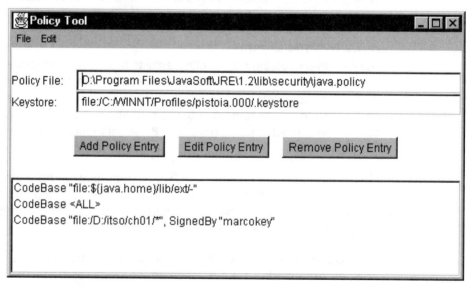

Figure 16. Policy Tool Window

This entry is automatically registered in the policy file after the Policy Tool configuration:

```
grant signedBy "marcokey",  codeBase "file:/D:/itso/ch01/*" {
  permission java.lang.RuntimePermission "queuePrintJob";
};
```

1.4.2.7 Running the Application with the Necessary Permission

The `java` command can be launched against a JAR file, provided that the `-jar` option is specified. After granting the code signed by marcokey and residing in the local directory D:\itso\ch01 permission to perform a print operation on the toolkit's platform, we launch the command:

```
javac -Djava.security.manager -jar GetPrintJob.jar
```

A button is shown similar to the one in Figure 15 on page 30. This time, the print operation can be performed. In fact, as soon as we click on the **getPrintJob** button, the Print window is brought up (see Figure 11 on page 26) and the Command Prompt window from which we launched the GetPrintJob application registers the following message:

```
No exception. Test is successful.
```

However, if the same application had attempted to read or write a file from the local file system, open a socket connection or perform another sensitive operation, a security exception would have been thrown, because such permissions were not granted to this code.

1.5 Summary

In this first chapter we have explained some basic concepts of Java and security and introduced the new Java 2 security model. We have also shown some basic examples to give you a better understanding of how Java can add a further security layer to the underlying operating system, without requiring particular programming efforts.

Although, in this first chapter, we did not explain all the details about the operations we performed and the underlying Java security architecture, you can rest assured that in the next chapters all these concepts will be explained in great detail.

Chapter 2. Attack and Defense

Many claims have been made for the security of Java. An underlying fact supporting such claims is that security was designed-in at an early stage in the development of the language. Saying that Java has strong security is like challenging the world to find the holes in it, which is exactly what has happened. Some very clever (and very devious) people have been applying their brain-power to the problem of breaking down the Java defenses.

In this chapter we give a high-level view of Java's built-in security features and then summarize the different ways in which it can be attacked.

2.1 Components of Java

For the reasons we have explained in 1.1, "Java Is Not Just a Language" on page 3, it is not surprising that Java has become so widely accepted, so quickly. Before we look at the security issues, let us review some Java fundamentals.

There are a number of different components to Java:

1. **Development environment**

   The Java 2 SDK contains the tools and executable code needed to compile and test Java programs. However, unlike a normal language, the Java 2 SDK includes object frameworks for creating graphical user interfaces, for networking and for complex I/O. Normally, in other programming languages, these things are provided as additions, either by the operating system or by another software package. Of course, fully-featured development environments do exist for Java, but the core language includes a lot of what they would normally have to provide.

2. **Execution environment**

   Java's execution environment is neither that of a compiled language nor an interpreted language. Instead it is a hybrid, implemented by the Java Virtual Machine (JVM). Java is often said to be platform-independent, but first the JVM must be ported to each platform to provide the environment it needs. The JVM implementation is responsible for all of the built-in security of Java, so it is important that it is done properly.

   The JVM is a subset of the Java Runtime Environment (JRE). JRE is the Java platform on which you can run, test and ship your own applications. It consists of the JVM, the Java platform core classes, and supporting files. It contains no development tools: no compiler, debugger, or other tools.

3. Interfaces and architectures

Java applications live in the real world. This means that they must be able to interact with non-Java applications. Some of these interactions are very simple (such as the way that a Java applet is invoked in a Web page). Others are the subject of more complex architectural definitions, such as the JDBC interface for relational database support. The mechanism for adding encryption to Java security, the Java Cryptography Architecture (JCA), falls into this latter category.

We will examine these components in the next three sections.

2.1.1 The Development Environment

Once you have installed the Java 2 SDK, you can start creating Java source code and compiling it. Java is like any other high-level programming language, in that you write the source code in an English-like form. The source code then has to be converted into a form that the machine can understand before it can be executed. To perform this conversion for a normal language, the code is usually either compiled (converted once and stored as machine code) or interpreted (converted and executed at run time).

Java combines these two approaches. The source code has to be compiled with a Java compiler, such as `javac`, before it can be used. This is a conventional compilation. However, the output that `javac` produces is not machine-specific code, but instead is *bytecode*, a system-independent format. We will take a closer look at how bytecode is constructed in 5.5, "Java Bytecode" on page 136.

In order to execute, the compiled code has to be processed by an interpreter, which is part of the Java execution environment known as the JVM. The JVM is a run-time platform, providing a number of built-in system services, such as thread support, memory management and I/O, in addition to the interpreter.

2.1.1.1 Class Consciousness

Java is an object-oriented language, meaning that a program is composed of a number of object classes, each containing data and methods. One result of this is that, although a program may consist of just a single class, when you have compiled it into bytecode, only a small proportion of the code that gets executed is likely to be in the resulting class file. The rest of the function will be in other classes that the main program references. The JVM uses *dynamic linking* to load these classes as they are needed. As an example, consider the simple applet contained in the following Java source file:

```
import java.awt.BorderLayout;
import java.awt.event.ActionEvent;
import java.awt.event.ActionListener;
import jamjar.examples.Button;

public class PointlessButton extends java.applet.Applet
    implements java.awt.event.ActionListener
{
   Button  donowt = new Button("Do Nothing");
   int count = 0;

/**
 * The button was clicked.
 */
   public void actionPerformed(java.awt.event.ActionEvent e)
   {
      donowt.setLabel("Did Nothing " + ++count + " time" + (count == 1 ? "" : "s"));
   }

   public void init()
   {
      setLayout(new BorderLayout());
      this.add("Center", donowt);
      donowt.addActionListener(this);
   }
}
```

Figure 17. PointlessButton.java

If the PointlessButton.java file was placed, say, in the C:\itso\ch02 directory,
then the following Java source file, Button.java, should be placed in the
C:\itso\ch02\jamjar\examples directory:

```
package jamjar.examples;

import java.awt.Color;
import java.awt.event.MouseEvent;
import java.awt.event.MouseListener;

/**
 * This class was generated by a SmartGuide.
 */
```

Figure 18. (Part 1 of 2). Button.java

```
public class Button extends java.awt.Button implements MouseListener
{

/**
 * @param title java.lang.String
 */
   public Button(String title)
   {
      super(title);
      addMouseListener(this);
      setBackground(Color.white);
   }

/**
 * Set the color of the button to red when the mouse enters
 */
   public void mouseEntered(MouseEvent m)
{
      setBackground(Color.yellow);
   }

/**
 * Reset the color of the button to white when the mouse exits
 */
   public void mouseExited(MouseEvent m)
   {
      setBackground(Color.white);
   }

/**
 * Three do nothing methods.
 * Needed to implement the MouseListener interface
 */
   public void mouseClicked(MouseEvent e) {}
   public void mousePressed(MouseEvent e) {}
   public void mouseReleased(MouseEvent e) {}
}
```

Figure 19. (Part 2 of 2). Button.java

The first listing, PointlessButton.java (see Figure 17 on page 37) is an applet that simply places a button on the Web page. Instead of using the standard AWT Button class, it uses a class of our own, also called Button (see Figure 18 on page 37 and Figure 19 on page 38), but available in a locally-written package. This works like a normal button, except that it changes color when you move the mouse pointer over it and registers how many times you clicked on it.

From the directory C:\itso\ch02, you should compile these files, by issuing the following command:

```
javac PointlessButton.java
```

Next, we show you the listing of an HTML file that includes two copies of the PointlessButton applet in the Web page:

```
<HTML>
    <HEAD>
        <TITLE>Pointless Button</TITLE>
    </HEAD>

    <BODY>
        <CENTER><H2>Pointless Button</H2>
        <HR>
        <BR>

        <APPLET Code="PointlessButton.class" Width=200 Height=50>
          <H4>This area contains a Java applet, but your browser is not Java-enabled</H4>
        </APPLET>

        <APPLET Code="PointlessButton.class" Width=200 Height=50>
          <H4>This area contains a Java applet, but your browser is not Java-enabled</H4>
        </APPLET>
    </BODY>
</HTML>
```

Figure 20. PointlessButton.html

The HTML file above is saved in the same directory where the Java class file PointlessButton.class resides.

You can load the PointlessButton.html file in your Web browser by pointing your browser to the URL where the HTML file resides. Figure 21 on page 40 shows the two copies of the applet running in the Web page:

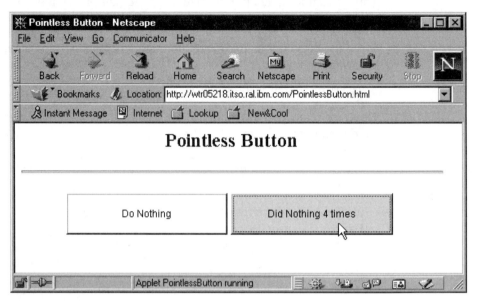

Figure 21. Running the pointlessButton Applet

The total size of the bytecode for this example is only 2 KB. However, the two classes cause a lot of other code to be dynamically installed, either as a result of inheritance (defined by the extends keyword in the class definition) or by instantiation (when a class creates an instance of another class with the new keyword). Figure 22 on page 41 shows the hierarchy of classes that could potentially be loaded to run our simple applet. Notice that this is a simplified view, because it does not consider classes that may be invoked by classes above the lowest level of the hierarchy:

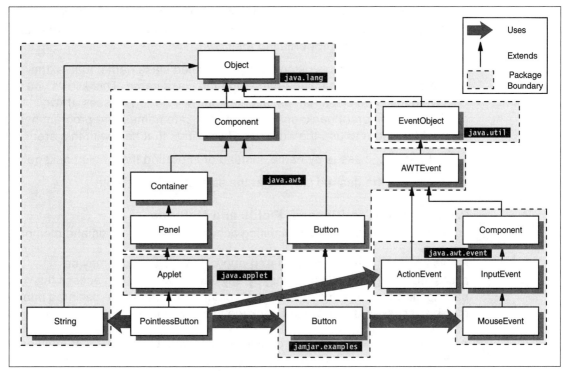

Figure 22. Classes Loaded for the PointlessButton Applet

This diagram illustrates a number of things about Java classes:

1. The classes are arranged in *packages*, which are collections of related classes. The language defines a large number of these, which have to be implemented by every JVM implementation. You can add your own class packages by defining new classes that inherit from one of the basic classes. In our example, all but two of the classes are provided as standard. Normally, Java class loaders impose a direct relationship between a package name and the location of the directory in which it expects to find the class files for the package. So, in our example, the classes contained in the jamjar.examples package will be found in directory ${codeBase}/jamjar/examples (codeBase is the base directory on the server from which the applet is loaded, specified in the <APPLET> tag).[1]

---

[1] In fact we are guilty of using an improper name construction here. If your package will be used together with packages from other sources, you should follow the naming standard laid down in the *Java Language Specification*, Gosling, Joy and Steele. In our case this would lead to a package name something like com.ibm.jamjar.examples. If you want to know more about the Java language specification, refer to http://java.sun.com/docs/books/jls/.

2. Classes are defined as *extending* existing classes. This means that they can inherit the properties (variables and methods) of the higher (or *super*) class. They can also selectively override the properties of the super class. They also add new properties of their own.

3. Java identifies classes using the fully-qualified class name, that is, the combination of the package name and the class name. This allows you to have duplicated class names, such as our two Button classes. If two classes in different packages do have duplicate names, the programmer must take care to use the right one. Two things that help with this are:

   - Importing classes by name, instead of importing the whole package

   - Placing the desired classes at the start of the class path

2.1.1.2 Access to Classes, Fields and Methods

Java provides mechanisms for limiting access to classes, fields and methods.

A class or interface may be declared *public*, in which case it may be accessed, using a qualified name, by any Java code that can access the package in which it is declared. A class or interface that is not declared public may be accessed only from the package in which it is declared.

A field, method, or constructor of a class may be declared using at most one of the `public`, `private`, or `protected` keywords:

- A *public* member may be accessed by any Java code.

- A *private* member may be accessed only from within the class that contains its declaration.

- A *protected* member of an object may be accessed only by the code responsible for the implementation of that object. To be precise, a protected member may be accessed from anywhere in the package in which it is declared and, in addition, it may be accessed from within any declaration of a subclass of the class type that contains its declaration.

- A member that is not declared public, protected, or private is said to have *default access* and may be accessed from, and only from, anywhere in the package in which it is declared.

Notice that every field or method of an interface must be public. Every member of a public interface is implicitly public, whether or not the keyword `public` appears in its declaration. If an interface is not public, then every one of its fields and methods must be explicitly declared public.

There are security implications when using these keywords to limit access to classes, fields and methods. We will see them in 7.4, "Avoiding Security Hazards" on page 204.

2.1.1.3 Visual Application Builders and Java Beans

Java is unusual in the breadth of function that its built-in class frameworks provide; however, for a project of any complexity you are likely to employ graphical tools, such as a *visual application builder* (VAB) to link together predefined components, thereby reducing the code you have to write to the core logic of the application. Examples of VABs include IBM VisualAge for Java, Lotus BeanMachine, NetObjects BeanBuilder and Sun Microsystems' JavaBeans Development Kit (BDK).

A *component* in this context is a package of Java classes that perform a given function. The JavaBeans definition describes a standard for components, known as *beans*. Basically a bean is a package of code containing both development and run-time components that:

- Allows a builder tool to analyze how it works (*introspection*)

- Allows a builder tool to customize its appearance and behavior

- Supports *events*, a simple communication metaphor than can be used to connect beans

- Supports *properties*, or settable attributes, used both when developing an application and programmatically when the application is running

- Supports *persistence*, so that a bean can be customized in an application builder and then have its customized state saved away and reloaded later

- Provides interfaces to other component architectures, such as ActiveX and LiveConnect

From this list you can infer that, although a bean is mostly made up of Java classes, it can also include other files, containing persistent information and other resources such as graphical elements, etc. These elements are all packed (or *pickled*) together in a Java Archive (JAR) file.

From a security viewpoint, VABs and beans do not affect the underlying strengths and weaknesses of Java. However, they may add more uncertainty, in that your application now includes sizeable chunks of code that you did not directly write. Their ability to provide interfaces to other component architectures may also cause problems, as we discuss in 2.1.3, "Interfaces and Architectures" on page 50.

2.1.1.4 Java 2 SDK Security Tools

The Java 2 development environment also contains a set of tools for managing the security features of the new Java platform:

- The Policy Tool creates and modifies the external policy configuration files that define your installation's security policy.

- The `jar` command line utility is used to create Java archives.

- The `keytool` utility creates key pairs and self-signed X.509 V1 certificates, and manages keystores. Keys and certificates are used to digitally sign your applications and applets. A *keystore* is a protected database that holds keys and certificates.

- The `jarsigner` command line tool signs JAR files, and verifies the signature(s) of signed JAR files. It accesses the keystore when it needs to find a key to sign a JAR file.

Notice that `keytool` and `jarsigner` replace `javakey`, which in Java Development Kit (JDK) 1.1 was the command line tool used to apply a digital signature to a JAR file.

We already saw a brief introduction on how to use the new security tools in 1.4, "Understanding Java 2 Security" on page 12. We will read more about these tools in detail in Chapter 9, "Java 2 SDK Security Tools" on page 259.

2.1.2 The Execution Environment

We have said that the JVM operates on the stream of bytecode as an interpreter. This means that it processes bytecode while the program is running and converts it to *real* machine code that it executes on the fly. You can think of a computer program as being like a railroad track, with the train representing the execution point at any given time. In the case of an interpreted program it is as if this train has a machine mounted on it, which builds the track immediately in front of the train and tears it up behind. It's no way to run a railroad.

Fortunately, in the case of Java, the JVM is not interpreting high-level language instructions, but bytecode. This is really machine code, written for the JVM instruction set, so the interpreter has much less analysis to do, resulting in execution times that are very fast. The JVM often uses just-in-time (JIT) compiler techniques to allow programs to execute faster, for example, by translating bytecode into optimized local code *once* and subsequently running it directly. Advances in JIT technology are making Java run faster all the time. IBM is one of many organizations exploring the technology.

Before the JVM can start this interpretation process, it has to do a number of things to set up the environment in which the program will run. This is the point at which the built-in security of Java is implemented. There are three parts to the process:

1. The first component of code checking is the *class loader*. This separates the classes it loads to avoid attack. Java built-in classes, specified in the *boot class path* (also known as *system class path* or *JVM class path*), are separated from extension classes, specified in the *extension class path*, and from other application classes, specified in the *user* or *application class path* variable. An *extension* is a group of Java packages that implement an API extending the Java platform, such as JavaServlet, Java3D, JavaManagement, etc. The search order is Java built-in classes first, extension classes and then application classes last. So, if, by accident or design, any application code contains a class of the same name as a built-in or extension class, the built-in or extension class will *not* be overwritten by the application code.

2. The second component is the *class file verifier*. This runs when the code is loaded, and confirms that the bytecode program is legal Java code and obeys the rules of the language. It is a multipass process which begins by making sure that the syntax is valid, checks for stack overflow or underflow, and runs a theorem prover that looks to see that access and type restrictions are observed.

3. The third component is the *security manager*, which checks sensitive accesses at run time. This is the component that enforces the security policy defined for the system and will not allow Java code illicit access to the file system, or to the network, or to the run-time operating system.

The Execution process can be summarized as shown in the following figure:

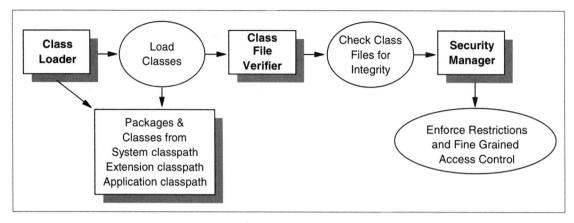

Figure 23. Execution Process

2.1.2.1 The Class Loader

Before the JVM can run a Java program, it needs to locate and load the classes which comprise that program into memory.

In a traditional execution environment, this service is provided by the operating system which loads code from the file system in a platform-specific way. The operating system has access to all of the low level I/O functions and has a set of locations on the file system that it searches for programs or shared code libraries. Depending on the operating system, this can be a list of directories to look in using environment variables, such as Path and CLASSPATH.

In the JRE things can get a little more complicated by the fact that not all class files are loaded from the same type of location and may not be under the local operating system's control to ensure integrity. The class loading mechanism plays a critical role in Java security since the class loader is responsible for locating and fetching the class files, consulting the security policy, and defining the class object with the appropriate permissions.

So how do classes get loaded? We answer this question taking as an example the PointlessButton applet, whose code is shown in Figure 17 on page 37. When the browser finds the <APPLET> tag in the HTML page (see Figure 20 on page 39), it starts the JVM which, in turn, invokes the applet class loader. This is, itself, a Java class which contains the code for fetching the bytecode of the applet and presenting it to the JVM in an executable form. The bytecode includes a list of referenced classes and the JVM works through the list, checks to see if the class is already loaded and attempts to load it if not. It first tries to load from the local disk, using a platform-specific function provided by the browser. In our example, this is the way that all of the core Java classes are loaded. If the class name is not found on the local disk, the JVM again tries to retrieve the class by searching for it in the extension class path. If this also fails, the JVM tries to retrieve the class from the Web server, as in the case of the jamjar.examples.Button class (see Figure 18 on page 37 and Figure 19 on page 38).

2.1.2.2 Where Class Loaders Come From

The class loader is just another Java class, albeit one with a very specific function. An application can declare any number of class loaders, each of which could be targeted at specific class types. The same is not true of an applet. The security manager prevents an applet from creating its own class loader. Clearly, if an applet can somehow circumvent this limitation, it can subvert the class loading process and potentially take over the whole browser machine.

The JVM keeps track of which class loader was responsible for loading any particular class. It also keeps classes loaded by different applets separate from each other.

You can create a specific class loader for your own application, if you wish to do so. Java 2 has simplified the development process by creating a subclass of ClassLoader, called SecureClassLoader. The distinguishing feature of SecureClassLoader is that it associates a sandbox for each class that it loads, which determines what accesses and rights the class can exercise in the client system. We will explain more details on this in 3.5, "Java 2 Class Loading Mechanism" on page 89 and 6.1, "Class Loaders" on page 145.

2.1.2.3 The Class File Verifier

At first sight, the job of the class file verifier may appear to be redundant. After all, isn't bytecode only generated by the Java compiler? So, if it is not correctly formatted and valid, surely the compiler needs to be fixed, rather than having to go through the overhead of checking each time a program is run.

Java divides the world into two parts, since it considers the Java core classes shipped as part of the JVM and installed on the local system as trusted, and therefore not subject to verification prior to execution. Sometimes other classes on the local disk are considered trusted as well – detailed implementation varies between vendors. Everything else is untrusted and therefore must be checked by the class file verifier. As we have seen, these are also the classes that the applet class loader is responsible for fetching.

The class loading process in the example of the PointlessButton applet is illustrated in the next figure:

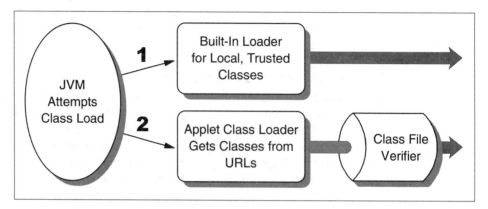

Figure 24. Where the Class File Verifier Fits

You can already see that, for an applet, the class loader and the class file verifier need to operate as a team, if they are to succeed in their task of making sure that only valid, safe code is executed.

From a security point of view the accuracy of the job done by the class file verifier is critical. There are a large number of possible bytecode programs, and the class file verifier has the job of determining the subset of them that are safe to run, by testing against a set of rules. There is a further subset of these verifiable programs: programs that are the result of compiling a legal Java program. Figure 25 on page 49 illustrates this. The rules in the class file verifier should aim to make the verifiable set as near as possible to the set of Java programs. This limits the scope for an attacker to create bytecode that subverts the safety features in Java and the protection of the security manager.

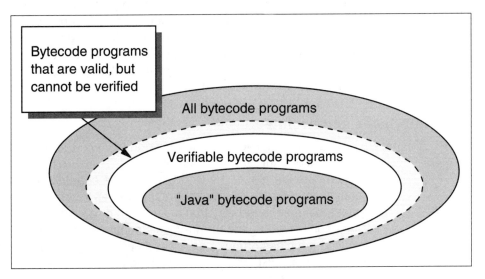

Figure 25. Decisions the Class File Verifier Has to Make

We will look in detail at how the class file verifier works in 6.2, "The Class File Verifier" on page 168.

2.1.2.4 The Security Manager

The third component involved in loading and running a Java program is the security manager. This is similar to the class loader in that it is a Java class (java.lang.SecurityManager) that any application can extend for its own purpose.

The verified code is further subjected to run-time restrictions. The security manager is responsible for enforcing these restrictions. Any flaw in the coding of the security manager, or any failure by the core classes to invoke it, could compromise the ability to run untrusted code securely.

Prior to Java 2, SecurityManager was an abstract class and a concrete implementation had to be provided by the application manufacturer as part of the application. Although any application could implement SecurityManager, it was most commonly found when executing an applet, that is, within a Web browser. The security manager built into your browser was wholly responsible for enforcing the *sandbox restrictions*: the set of rules that controlled what things an applet was allowed to do on your browser machine.

In Java 2, SecurityManager has been modified: now it is not abstract, and can be instantiated or subclassed. The manufacturer now has an alternative. He can choose to use the policy-based security manager implementation provided with the Java 2 platform and supply policy information to be added to the policy database. The manufacturer can still provide his own security manager, if he so chooses, adding to or replacing function supplied by the Java 2 SecurityManager. More details on this can be found in 3.5.1, "Run-Time Access Controls" on page 91 and in Chapter 7, "The Java 2 SecurityManager" on page 187.

2.1.3 Interfaces and Architectures

We have discussed two parts of the world of Java, the development environment and the execution environment. The third part is where the world of Java meets the rest of the world, that is, the capabilities it provides for extending Java functions and integrating with applications of other types. The simplest example is the way that a Java applet is created and integrated into a Web page by writing the program as a subclass of the Applet class and then specifying the class name in an <APPLET> HTML tag. In return, Java provides classes such as URL and a number of methods for accessing a Web server.

2.1.3.1 Don't Go Native! Seek Purity!

Another simple way to extend Java is by the use of *native methods*. These are sections of code written in some other, less exciting, language which provides access to native system interfaces. For example, imagine an organization with a *helpdesk* application which provides a C API for creating new problem records. You may well want to use this so that your new Java application can perform self-diagnosis and automatically report any faults it finds. One way to do so is to create a native method to interpret between Java and the helpdesk application's API. This provides simple extensibility, but at the cost of portability and flexibility, because:

- The native method has to be compiled for a specific system platform.
- It must be pre-installed and cannot be installed dynamically like a Java applet.

The Java purist will deprecate this kind of application. In fact, although the quest for *100% Pure Java*[2] sounds like an academic exercise, there are a number of real-world advantages to only using well-defined, architected interfaces, not the least of which is that the security aspects have presumably already been considered.

2.1.3.2 Some of the Roads to Purity

As projects using Java have matured from being interesting exercises in technology into mission-critical applications, so the need has arisen for more complex interactions with the outside world. The Java applet gives a very

[2] See http://www.javasoft.com/100percent/.

effective way to deliver client function without having to install and maintain code on every client. However, the application you create this way still needs access to data and function contained in existing *legacy systems*.

Legacy Systems

Legacy seems to be the current word-of-the-month to describe any computer system that does not fit the brave new architecture under discussion. It is an unfortunate choice, in that it implies a system that is outdated or inadequate. You may have a state-of-the-art relational database that is critical to the running of your business, but to the Web-based application that depends on the data it contains, it is still a legacy system.

With JDK 1.1, JavaSoft introduced a number of new interfaces and architectures for this kind of integration, which have been enhanced on the Java 2 platform. The objective is to enable applications to be written in 100% Pure Java, while still delivering the links to the outside world that real requirements demand.

Some of the more notable interfaces of this kind are:

- **JavaBeans**

  As we discussed above, the JavaBeans technology not only provides easier application development, but also provides integration with other distributed object architectures. From a security point of view this capability opens a back door which an attacker could exploit. The Java security manager provides strict and granular controls over what a Java program may do. But these controls are dependent on the integrity of the JVM and in particular the trusted classes it provides. A Java applet might not be able to meddle with the trusted classes directly, but a Bean can provide linkage to a different type of executable content, with less stringent controls. This could be used to corrupt the JVM trusted classes, thereby allowing an attack applet to take over.

- **Remote Method Invocation**

  Remote Method Invocation (RMI) allows a Java class running on one system to execute the methods of another class on a second system. This kind of remote function call processing allows you to create powerful distributed applications with a minimal overhead. For example, an applet running on a browser system could invoke a server-side function without having to execute a CGI program or provide its own sockets-based protocol.

The security concerns for RMI are, in general, similar to the CGI case. For example, consider a Java application that accesses a database of personal information, consisting of a server-side application communicating with a client applet. When writing the application, the programmers will naturally assume that the only code involved is what they write. However, the Java code that initiates the connection does not have to be their friendly applet, it could be the work of a cracker. The server application must be very careful to check the validity of any requests it gets and not rely on client-side validation.

RMI has several new enhancements on the Java 2 platform. Remote object activation introduces support for persistent references to remote objects and automatic object activation by using these references. Custom socket factories allow a remote object to specify the protocol that RMI will use for remote calls to that object. RMI over a secure transport – such as Secure Sockets Layer (SSL) – can be supported using custom socket factories. Minor API enhancements allow unexporting a remote object, obtaining the stub for an object implementation, and exporting an object on a specific port. We will read more about RMI in 14.6, "Distributed Object Architectures – RMI" on page 563 and 15.7, "Remote Method Invocation" on page 625.

- **Object Request Brokers**

  RMI provides a way to remotely execute Java code. However, for many years the O-O world has been trying to achieve a more generic form of remote execution. That is, a facility that allows a program to access the properties and methods of a remote object, regardless of the language in which it is implemented or the platform on which it runs. The facility that provides the ability to find and operate on remote objects is called *object request broker* (ORB). One of the most widely-accepted standards for ORBs is the Common Object Request Broker Architecture (CORBA), and packages are becoming available that provide a CORBA-compatible interface for Java. Figure 26 on page 53 illustrates the relationship between a Java application or applet and a remote object. Clearly, in an implementation of this kind the Java program relies on the security of the request brokers. It is the responsibility of the ORB and the inter-ORB communications to authenticate the endpoints and apply access control. The official standard for inter-ORB communications is the Internet Inter-ORB Protocol (IIOP).

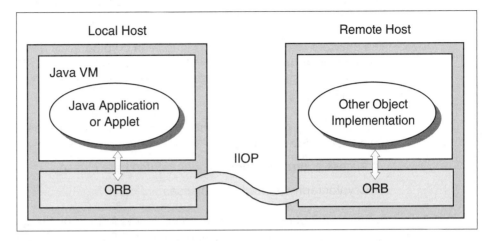

Local Host   Remote Host

Java VM

Java Application   Other Object
or Applet   Implementation

IIOP

ORB   ORB

Figure 26. Interacting with an ORB

- **JDBC**

  JDBC ought to stand for Java Database Connectivity, but actually it is a
  name in its own right. JDBC is an API for executing SQL statements from
  Java. Most relational databases implement the Open Database
  Connectivity (ODBC) API, originated by Microsoft. JBDC thoughtfully
  includes an ODBC bridge, thereby giving it instant usefulness. From a
  security point of view, there are some concerns. You should beware of
  giving access to more data than you intended. For example, imagine an
  applet which invokes JDBC on the Web server to extract information from
  a database. It is important that the server application is written to allow
  only the SQL requests expected from the applet, and not the more
  revealing requests that an attacker could make.

2.2 Java 2 and Cryptography

The interfaces that we have briefly described in 2.1.3, "Interfaces and
Architectures" on page 50, illustrate a big issue in Java. In the real world we
need to extend the security model to allow more powerful applications and
interfaces.

The security model needs to answer questions such as the following:

- Where did this piece of Java code come from?

- What type of things should the code be allowed to do?

- If someone appears to be using an applet I provide, how can I find out who
  they are?

- How can I protect the confidentiality of the data my Java application is handling?

The answers to questions of this kind lie in cryptography. The Java 2 platform significantly enhances the Java Cryptography Architecture (JCA), that was introduced in JDK 1.1 to define the way that cryptographic tools are made available to Java code.

From a security point of view, the set of security core classes shipped with the Java 2 SDK, Standard Edition, V1.2.*x* can be divided into two subsets:

- Access control and permissions related core classes
- Cryptography related core classes

In the Java 2 platform, the JCA framework is formed by the cryptography related core classes shipped with the Java 2 SDK, Standard Edition, V1.2. Support for encryption is provided by an extension package, called Java Cryptography Extension (JCE) 1.2. Details on cryptography can be found in Chapter 13, "Cryptography in Java 2" on page 475.

2.2.1 Cryptographic Tools in Brief

The derivation of the word *cryptography* is from Greek and means literally *secret writing*. Modern cryptography is still involved in keeping data secret, but the ability to authenticate a user (and hence apply some kind of access control) is even more important.

Although there are many cryptographic techniques and protocols, they mostly fall into one of three categories:

2.2.1.1 Bulk Encryption
This is the modern equivalent of *secret writing*. A *bulk encryption* algorithm uses a key to scramble (or *encrypt*) data for transmission or storage. It can then only be unscrambled (or *decrypted*) using the same key. Bulk encryption is so called because it is effective for securing large chunks of data. Some common algorithms are Data Encryption Standard (DES), Data Encryption Algorithm (DEA) and RC4. This is also called the symmetric encryption.

2.2.1.2 Public Key Encryption
This is also a technique for securing data but instead of using a single key for encryption and decryption, it uses two related keys, called *public key* and *private key*, which together form what is known as a *key pair*. As the word suggests, public keys are made available to everyone, but each entity that holds a key pair should keep the private key as secret. If data is encrypted

using one of the keys, it can only be decrypted using the other, and vice versa.

Public key encryption is a form of asymmetric encryption, because the key that is used to encrypt is different from the key used to decrypt. With this technology, the sender in a secure communication can use the receiver's public key to encrypt the data, because at that point in time only the receiver can decrypt the data, by using its own private key.

Notice that the public and the private keys are bound by a well known mathematical relationship, so that having one of the two keys it would be theoretically possible to obtain the other one. However, especially when the size of the building block of the keys is very long (for instance, 512 bits), the computational effort required makes the probability of breaking a key very small.

Compared to bulk encryption, public key encryption is more secure, because it does not require the transmission of a shared key that both the parties must hold. However, public key encryption is computationally expensive and is therefore not suited to large amounts of data. For this reason the most common solution, implemented for example in the SSL protocol, is for the two parties (sender and receiver) to use public key encryption to agree on and share a common key. After the common key has been shared using asymmetric encryption, so that only the two parties really know it, then bulk encryption is used. Notice that a common key is shared only for the time of a single connection. After a secure connection is closed, a new connection requires that the two parties agree on a new shared key.

The most commonly-used algorithm for public key encryption is the Rivest, Shamir and Adleman (RSA) system.

2.2.1.3 Hashing

A *secure hash* is an algorithm that takes a stream of data and creates a fixed-length digest of it. This digest is a *fingerprint* for the data. A digest has two main properties:

1. If even one single bit of data is changed, then the message digest changes as well. Notice, however, there is a very remote probability that two different arbitrary messages can have the same fingerprint.

2. Even if someone was able to intercept transmitted data and its fingerprint, that person would not be practically able to modify the original data so that the resulting data has the same digest as the original one.

Hashing functions are often found in the context of *digital signatures*. This is a method for authenticating the source of a message, formed by encrypting a hash of the source data. Public key encryption is used to create the signature, so it effectively ties the signed data to the owner of the key pair that created the signature.

2.2.2 Java Cryptography Architecture

JCA is described as a *provider architecture*. The primary principal in the design of the JCA has been to separate the cryptographic concepts from their algorithmic implementations. It is designed to allow different vendors to provide their own implementation of the cryptographic tools and other administrative functions. This makes a very flexible framework which will cater for future requirements and allow vendor independence.

The architecture defines a series of classes, called *engine classes*, that are representations of general cryptographic functions. So, for example, there are several different standards for digital signatures, which differ in their detailed implementation but which, at a high level, are very similar. For this reason, a single engine class, java.security.Signature, has been created that represents all of the variations in a digital signature. The actual implementation of the different signature algorithms is done by a provider class which may be offered by a number of vendors.

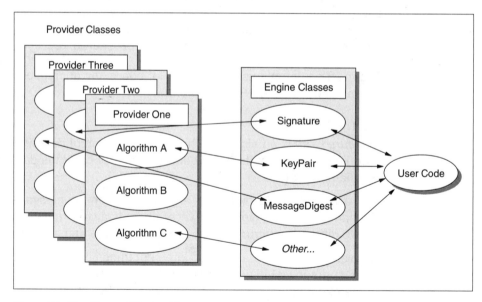

Figure 27. Provider and Engine Classes

The provider architecture has the virtue of offering a standard interface to the programmer who wants to use a cryptographic function, while at the same time having the flexibility to handle different underlying standards and protocols. The providers may be added either statically or dynamically.

Support for the management of keys and access control lists was not in the initial release of JDK 1.1, but has been provided in Java 2 SDK, Standard Edition, V1.2. Currently, Sun Microsystems' version of the JRE comes standard with a default provider, named SUN. Other Java Runtime Environments (JREs) may not necessarily supply the SUN provider. The SUN provider includes an implementation of the following algorithms:

- Digital Signature Algorithm (DSA)
- SHA[3]-1 and MD5[4] message digest algorithms
- SHA1PRNG pseudo-random number generation algorithm

Moreover, the SUN provider implements a DSA key factory, a certificate factory for X.509 certificates and certificate revocation list (CRLs), and a *keystore* implementation for the proprietary keystore type named Java Keystore (JKS).

2.2.3 United States Export Rules for Encryption

Unfortunately, only a subset of the cryptographic possibilities are implemented in Java 2 SDK, Standard Edition, V1.2. It includes all of the engine classes needed for digital signatures, plus a provider package, but nothing for bulk or public key encryption. The reason for this is the restrictions placed by the United States government on the export of cryptographic technology.

The National Security Agency (NSA) is responsible for monitoring communications between the United States and the rest of the world, aiming to intercept such things as the messages of unfriendly governments and organized crime. Clearly, it is not a good thing for such people to have access to unbreakable encryption, so the United States government sets limits on the strength of cipher that a United States company can export for commercial purposes.

---

[3] *Secure Hash Algorithm* (SHA) is a government-standardized algorithm that is used to construct a message authentication code that detects attempts to modify data while in transit.
[4] MD5 is the standard name for the RSA-MD5 Message Digest algorithm.

> **Cipher Strength**
>
> Cipher strength is controlled by the size of the key used in the encryption algorithm. Current export rules limit the key size for bulk encryption to 40 bits, which can now be cracked in a matter of hours with quite modest computing facilities. Each extra bit doubles the key space, so a key size of 64 bits is 16 million times tougher than 40 bits. A similar rule applies to public key encryption, where an export-quality 512-bit modulus is inadequate, but a 1024-bit modulus is expected to remain effective for the next ten years, at least for commercial use.

This applies to any software that can be used for *general purpose* encryption. So, the SUN provider package that comes with Java 2 SDK, Standard Edition, V1.2 can include the full-strength RSA public key algorithm, but it can only be used as part of a digital signature process and not for general encryption.

Finally, in 1996, the United States government relaxed the export rules. The promise is that any strength of encryption may be exported, so long as it provides a technique for *key recovery*, that is, a way for the NSA to retrieve the encryption key if they need to break the code.

The JavaSoft response to the current restrictions was to define two, related, packages for cryptography in Java. The exportable part of JCA is the one that contains the tools for signatures and is implemented in Java 2 SDK, Standard Edition, V1.2. The not-for-export part is the Java Cryptography Extension (JCE) 1.2, which includes the general purpose encryption capabilities. JCE 1.2 is a standard extension to the Java 2 platform. It supplements the cryptographic services defined in the Java 2 SDK by adding support for ciphers, key agreement, and message authentication codes (MACs). The eventual aim is to develop a full strength, exportable cryptographic toolkit.

The default provider that comes with JCE 1.2 is called SunJCE. We will see more details about JCE in 13.4, "Java Cryptography Extension" on page 493.

2.2.4 Signed Code

Using JCA, it is possible for a Java application or applet to create its own digital signatures. Now you can write more sophisticated programs, because the Java 2 security implementation allows you to let an applet do something that the sandbox permissions normally would forbid. In this case, the browser's user needs to be convinced that the applet is from a trustworthy source and belongs to a trusted entity.

The signature on an applet links the code to the programmer or administrator who created or packaged it. However, the user has to be able to check that the signature is valid. The signer enables this by providing a *public key certificate*.

2.2.5 The Other Side of the Coin – Access Control

When you receive an applet that has been digitally signed, you know where it comes from and who is the owner of the code, and you can make a judgment of whether or not it is trustworthy. Next, you want to exercise some *access control*.

For example, consider an applet that wants to use your hard disk to store some configuration information. You probably have no objection to it doing so, but that does not mean that you are happy for it to overwrite *any* file on the system. This is the difference between a *binary* trust model (*I trust you, do what you like* or *I don't trust you, don't do anything*) and a *fine-grained* trust model (*Tell me what you want to do and I'll decide whether I trust you or not*).

The security model implemented in JDK 1.1 was binary, while Java 2 offers the implementation of a fine-grained trust model, as we have already introduced in 1.4, "Understanding Java 2 Security" on page 12.

2.3 Attacking the World of Java

In general, security considerations have a low priority early in the software lifecycle. This makes Java very unusual, in that security has been an important consideration from the very beginning. No doubt, this is because the environment to which the infant language has been exposed in its formative years is a cruel and unforgiving one: the Internet. In this section we take a cracker's-eye view. What opportunities do we have to abuse a remote Java code, to make it do our dastardly deeds for us?

2.3.1 Perils in the Life of Remote Code

The remote Java code that runs in your Web browser has had an unusually long and interesting life history. Along the way it has passed through a number of phases, each of which is in some way vulnerable to attack. Figure 28 on page 60 illustrates the points of peril in the life of an applet:

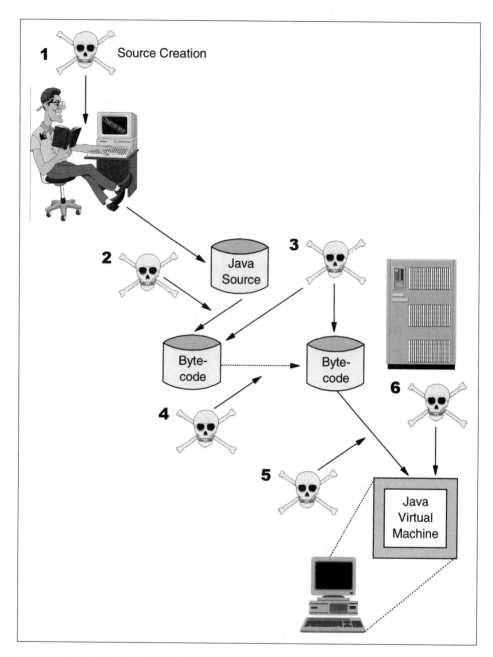

Figure 28. Perils in the Life of an Applet

Let us look at the points of vulnerability in some detail:

1. You may think that all of the programmers you know are angels, but there is no way to tell if really there is a devil inside. In the case of remote Java code, you are another step away from the person who wrote the code. So, when you buy a software product from a well-known company, you can be fairly sure that the contents of the shrink-wrap will not do you any harm (but even this is not 100% true, as we will see in the story of the JAR bug, described in 12.6, "The JAR Bug – Fixed In Java 2 SDK, Standard Edition, V1.2.1" on page 461). When you receive *any* code from the Internet you have to be wary of where it really comes from. In the case of a Java applet, the risk is in some ways worse, because you may not even be conscious that you have received the program at all. We will show some examples of the kind of things that a hostile applet can do in 7.3.2, "Malicious Applets" on page 195.

2. The Java compiler, javac, takes source code and compiles it into class files (in bytecode format) that can be executed by the JVM. It is quite common for a developer to have multiple versions of javac on his or her computer. For example, the Java 2 SDK for various system platforms is available for download from the JavaSoft Web site http://www.javasoft.com and other computer manufacturers. The Java compiler javac is also provided as part of many application development tools. Very often, a developer will have a current and one or more beta versions installed. It is also very common that developers have old versions installed too, especially when they are programming for platforms (such as Web browsers or Web servers) that have not picked up the current version of Java yet.

   Normally you expect that the bytecode generated by a compiler would reflect the source code you feed in. However, a compiler can easily be hacked so that it adds its own, nefarious, functions. Even worse, a compiler could produce bytecode output that *cannot* be a translation of normal Java source code. This would be a way to introduce code to exploit some frailty of the Java code verification process, for example.

   Although a hacked compiler is the most obvious example of a compromised programming tool, the same concern also applies to other parts of the programmer's arsenal, such as editors, development toolkits and pre-built components.

3. If an attacker can get update access to the class files, those files can be replaced by malicious code, which could then attack the system in harmful or annoying ways, for example, by modifying business data or by displaying rude messages. One obvious point of attack is where the class files are stored on the Web server. If an attacker can get update access to the directory they are in, they can be corrupted. Java class files should therefore be protected in much the same way as CGI programs, for example. Some basic principles for protection are:

   - Don't allow update permissions for the user ID that the Web server runs under. Many successful attacks on Web servers rely on finding holes in the logic or implementation of CGI programs and tricking them into executing arbitrary commands.

   - Make sure that the server has been properly hardened to reduce the risk of someone gaining access beyond the normal Web connection. You should remove unwanted network services and user IDs, enforce password restrictions and limit access using firewall controls. You should also make sure that you have the fixes for the latest security advisories installed.

4. One side-effect of Java's portability is that a webmaster can get remote code from any number of different sources. The code could just generate some entertaining animation or cool dialogs. Alternatively it could be a fully-fledged application, containing thousands of lines of source code.

   Any code you import in this way should be treated with suspicion. This raises a moral question: how responsible should you feel if your Web site somehow damages a client connecting to it, even if you are not ultimately responsible for the content that caused the damage? Most reasonable people will agree that there is a duty of care which should be balanced against your desire to build the world's most dynamic and attractive Web site. Indeed it would be a good idea to check whether your agreements with others mean that you have a formal *legal* duty of care. You do not want a thoughtlessly included applet to result in your being sued.

So, you are the administrator of a Web site and you want to include some applet code from somewhere else. You want to be sure that the applet is safe, but how can you check it?

For simple applets you should try to get the code in source form, so that you can inspect it and compile it yourself. This means that you need to understand the Java language. Your job already requires you to have a superhuman knowledge of computer systems and the Web; adding Java to your knowledge base must be a trivial matter for a person of such skill.

In fact the problem is not so great as it first appears. It is much easier to read a computer program and understand what it is doing than to write it in the first place. In 7.3.2, "Malicious Applets" on page 195, we will discuss some of the things that you should watch for.

Applets that are only provided in compiled form are more of a problem. Very often they are too large to do a practical visual check and anyway, if they are commercially-produced, the writer is unlikely to want to share his coding tricks with the world at large. You can, of course, check the external behavior, but that gives no clue to what browser holes it may be probing or background threads it may be spinning. There are tools like `javap` and Mocha which allow you to at least get an idea of what an applet is doing.

JDK 1.1 introduced signed applets which allow you to check who the real originator of an applet is and know that it has not been altered on its way to you. You still have to make a judgment of who to trust, but at least you are basing the judgment on sound data. With Java 2, the fine-grained access control mechanism helps you decide what resources should be accessed by whom and to what extent.

5. The next journey in the life of an applet is when it is loaded into the browser's JVM across the network from the server. Although it could, potentially, be intercepted in mid-flight and modified, a much more likely form of attack would involve some type of *spoofing*. What this means is that the attacker fools the browser into thinking that it is connecting to rocksolid.reliable.org, when really the applet is coming from nogood.badguys.com. The most sophisticated form of spoofing is the *Web spoof*, where the attacker acts as a filter for all of the traffic between the browser and anywhere else, passing most requests straight through, but intercepting particular requests and modifying them or replacing them with something more sinister (see Figure 29 on page 64). Note that it does not

have to be this way around. It is equally possible for a Web spoof to screen everything going to and from a server, rather than a client system.

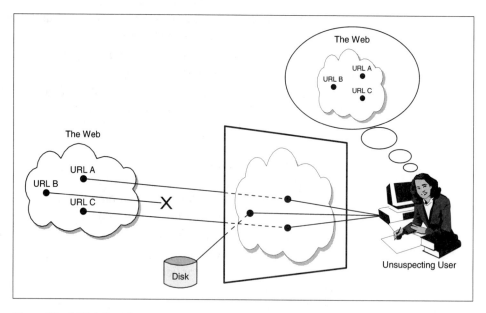

Figure 29. A Web Spoof

Spoofing is not just a problem for Java applets, of course. Any Web content can be attacked in this way. With Java this gives the attacker an opportunity to execute a malicious applet or try to exploit security holes in the browser environment. However, compared to the risk of downloading and installing a conventional program in this kind of environment, the risk is small. In fact, signed applets and servlets (see 14.5.7, "The Current Servlet Security Model" on page 556) can again help with this problem. An attacker may be able to substitute subversive class files to attack the browser, but it is much more difficult to forge the class signature.

6. Finally the applet arrives at the browser. Here, class files are loaded and verified and the JVM goes to work. If the installation is working as designed, the worst peril that can befall you as a user is that the applet may annoy you or eat excessive system resources (see 7.3.2, "Malicious Applets" on page 195). There are two other possible sources of security vulnerability:

   • The JVM, if there are bugs in its implementation

   • The browser itself, if a hacked version has been installed unknowingly

Of these two, the first is more likely. There have been a number of well-publicized security breaches found in the JVM components. The best description of how these operate can be found in *Java Security – Hostile Applets, Holes, and Antidotes*, by Felten and McGraw. The best way to protect yourself is to make sure you are aware of the latest breaches and install the fixes as they arrive.

The possibility of installing a browser that has been tampered with is a real one, although there are considerable practical hurdles for an attacker to overcome in creating such a thing. If you do as we recommend above and install the latest fixes, you will inevitably be running a downloaded version of the browser. There is some small risk that this could be a hacked version, but no examples of this have yet been detected.

The big question that all browser users ask about Java is this: "Should I allow it to run or not?" In the final analysis, this is a personal decision. As we have described, there is some peril in allowing Java applets to run in your system, unless you can be sure of where they have come from and who is the owner of the code. The Java 2 security model is a great help in this sense, because it allows you to grant specific permissions only to specific code. However, you may decide that the risk of having Java running on your system is too high to take.

If you take this view, you should also review your other Web usage. If you download any executable program from the Web it is potentially far more dangerous to the health of your system than any Java applet.

Notice that many companies and software producers are writing applications that use Java applets for their client component. These are usually designed for intranet, rather than Internet use, so the likelihood of attack is presumably much lower.

2.3.2 Vulnerabilities in Java Applications

A Java applet is an obvious vehicle to mount an attack from, because it could install itself uninvited and probe for weaknesses. A Java application, on the other hand, is a much less obvious threat. There are many ways in which such an application could be implemented, for example:

- On a Web server using CGI to interface with Web pages or applets

- As a stand-alone application on a server, interfacing with client code using socket connections

- As a stand-alone application on a server, using remote object request services (like RMI or CORBA) for communication

To a cracker, the fact that the application is written in Java rather than any other language is not really important. The strategies that he or she would use to search for vulnerabilities are the same. For example:

- Many successful attacks rely on driving the application with data that it is not equipped to handle. In particular, if the application uses a command line interface, it should be very careful to screen out escape sequences that an attacker could use to execute arbitrary commands.

- Applications frequently have to give themselves temporary higher privileges to use system functions or get special access (such as user IDs for database control). If an attacker can crash the application at this critical point, or link to it from another running program, he or she can use the special privileges illegally.

As we said earlier, vulnerabilities of this kind apply to applications written in Java the same as any other application programming environment. However, Java does include safety features that make it harder for an attacker to find a flaw. These safety features work at two levels:

- **Java source**

  The Java language uses strong *type* constraints to prevent the programmer from accessing data in an inconsistent way. You can cast objects from one type to another, but only if the two classes are related by inheritance; that is, one must be a superclass of the other. This does not operate symmetrically, which means you can always cast from a subclass to its superclass, but not always vice versa. Referring again to Figure 22 on page 41, you could access an instance of the Button class as an Object, but you could not access a Button as a Panel.

  Furthermore, Java prevents you from having direct access to program memory. In C it is common to use a pointer to locate a variable in memory and then to manipulate the pointer to process the data in it. This is a frequent source of coding errors, due to the pointer becoming corrupted or iterating beyond the end of the data. Java allows a variable to be accessed *only* through the methods of the object that contains it, thereby removing this class of error.

- **Bytecode**

  The JVM is *type-aware*. In other words, most of the primitive machine instructions are associated with a particular type. This means that the JVM also applies the type constraints that the compiler imposes on the Java source. In fact, this job is split between the class file verifier, which handles everything that can be statically checked, and the JVM, which deals with run-time exceptions. Contrast this with other languages, in which the compiler produces microprocessor machine code. In this case the program is just handled as a sequence of bytes, with no concept of the data types that are being represented.

  The JVM is also, at a basic level, strongly compartmentalized, mirroring the object orientation of the Java source. This means that each method in the code has its own execution stack and only has access to the memory of the class instance for which it was invoked.

2.4 Summary

In this chapter of the book we gave you an overview of the Java security architecture. You should now have a general idea of the Java development environment, the execution process and the relationship between Java and cryptography.

We also described the most common attacks to Java and the vulnerabilities in Java applications. We underlined how the final decision to permit Java on your client is up to you. However, the fine-grained security model implemented in the Java 2 platform greatly helps system and network administrators selectively manage security permissions to Java code downloaded and run on your system. Java 2 adds a further security layer to the security of the underlying system where your applications are to run.

Chapter 3. The New Java Security Model

This chapter describes the history of Java security, showing how Java security evolved from very basic and strict rules to powerful and flexible capabilities. Java has changed its security architecture according to its three main releases. For this reason, we show a technical comparison between the Java security model in JDK 1.0, JDK 1.1 and Java 2.

Moreover this chapter introduces all the main concepts related to the Java security architecture. The same concepts will be studied in detail in the rest of the book.

3.1 The Need for Java Security

From its inception, Java has shown that it was designed for the net. Java brought about, for the first time on a large scale, the concept of dynamic loading of code from a source outside the system. Though this is very powerful, and adds several features to the system using it, it is also a grave security threat. There are several risks associated with loading and running remote code. The remote code could steal memory, or CPU time; it could throw in a virus; it could read files on a local system and transmit them to another machine, etc. It is clear, then, that unlike other programming languages and systems, security mechanisms must be an integral part of Java.

Moreover, Java is not just for applets any more. Developers now use Java to build stand-alone, enterprise-class applications to enable disparate clients, such as workstations, PCs or Java-based network computers to access legacy databases and share applications across the network.

Java was designed to offer the following basic security measures:

- Language design features, such as legal type conversions only, no pointer arithmetic and bounds checking on arrays, provide strong memory protection.

- A sandbox mechanism controls what a Java program is permitted to do.

- Encryption and digital signatures are used by code owners to attach their certificate to Java classes. In this way, the end user can ascertain who the owner of the code is and whether the class file was altered after having been signed by the owner's certificate.

Java security builds upon three fundamental aspects of the Java Runtime Environment (JRE):

1. **Class loader**

   The class loader (see 2.1.2.1, "The Class Loader" on page 46 and 2.1.2.2, "Where Class Loaders Come From" on page 47) determines how and when Java programs can load codes, and ensures that system-level components within the run-time environment are not replaced.

2. **Class file verifier**

   The class file verifier (see 2.1.2.3, "The Class File Verifier" on page 47) ensures proper formatting of downloaded code. It verifies that the bytecode does not violate the type safety restrictions of the Java Virtual Machine (JVM), that internal stacks cannot over/underflow, and that the bytecode instructions will have correctly typed parameters.

3. **Security manager**

   The security manager (see 2.1.2.4, "The Security Manager" on page 49) performs run-time access controls on attempts to perform file I/O, network I/O, create a new class loader, manipulate threads and thread groups, start processes on the underlying operating system, terminate the JVM, load non-Java libraries (native code) into the JVM, perform certain types of windowing system operations and load certain types of classes into the JVM. For example, the Java applet *sandbox*, which severely constrains downloaded, untrusted applets to a limited set of functions that are considered to be relatively safe, is a function of the security manager.

Java security functionalities, even if built and designed in the language itself, have been changing their features over time, and their evolution has been dependent on the major Java language releases that have been developed until now: JDK 1.0, JDK 1.1 and Java 2 SDK, Standard Edition, V1.2.

3.2 Evolution of the Java Security Model

The Java programming language is one of the fastest-growing technologies in use on the Internet today. The principal reason why Java has scored over other languages is the promise that an application written once in Java can be run from any machine that has a JVM. From the early stages of Java development, it was realized that this feature poses the greatest challenge to Java security because code distribution is risky.

3.2.1 The JDK 1.0 Sandbox Security Model

The entire focus of the initial security model provided by Version 1.0 of the Java platform (known as the *sandbox model*) was to treat code downloaded from a remote location as *untrusworthy* and provide a restricted environment (the *sandbox*) to limit the resources that could be accessed by the alien code. At the same time local code was considered *trustworthy* and was allowed full access to all the system resources, as illustrated in the figure below:

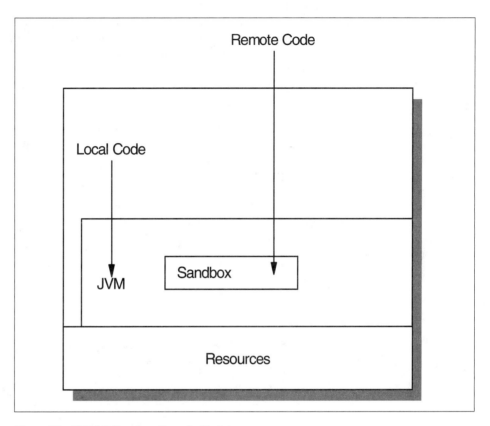

Figure 30. JDK 1.0 Sandbox Security Model

This was achieved by using the three components discussed in 3.1, "The Need for Java Security" on page 69, namely the class loader, the class file verifier and the security manager. However with the actions of the remote code constrained to a bare minimum, the *Write Once, Run Anywhere* benefit of Java could not be fully exploited.

Remote applets, though a powerful concept, were shackled by having to run inside a sandbox, and by not being able to perform several operations. They could not read local files and could not write to the disk. They had absolutely no access to the system resources. Moreover they could establish a network connection only with their servicing Web server. This heavily restricted the use of remote applets for all but cosmetic functions to decorate a Web page.

3.2.2 The Concept of Trusted Code in JDK 1.1

The next phase of evolution of Java security was based on an effort to increase the breathing space for remote code at the client location without compromising the safety of the client. The security architecture in JDK 1.1 introduced the concept of signed remote code. Remote codes, signed by a trusted entity, were permitted access to several of the system resources that were off limits for those remote programs without a trusted signature on them, as shown in the following figure:

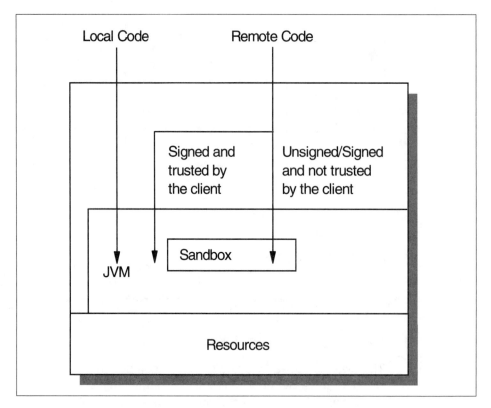

Figure 31. Trusted and Untrusted Code in JDK 1.1

A remote code (a remote applet or servlet, for example) with an *appropriate* digital signature was treated with the same respect as local code, and so it could be considered trusted. An appropriate digital signature was one that was recognized as trusted by the client.

On the other hand, unsigned remote code or remote code signed with a digital signature not recognized as trusted by the client, was still confined to the sandbox.

Though this opened up interesting possibilities, the system was still rather crude, with all local Java applications enjoying full access to the system resources and all remotely loaded code running inside a sandbox, unless signed by a trusted entity.

3.2.2.1 The jar and javakey Tools

Starting with JDK 1.1, the Java platform has offered the `jar` command line tool to pack and deliver remote codes together with their signatures, if any, in the Java Archive (JAR) format. The JAR file format (which we introduced in 1.4.1.3, "Packing the Applet Class in a JAR File" on page 18) is based on the ZIP file format and is used for aggregating and compressing many files into one. Although the `jar` utility can be used as a general archiving tool, the primary motivation for its development was so that Java applets and their requisite components (class files, images, sounds, etc.) could be downloaded to a browser in a single HTTP transaction, rather than opening a new connection for each piece. This greatly improves the speed with which an applet can be loaded onto a Web page and begin functioning. The JAR format, like a ZIP format, also supports compression, which reduces the size of the file and improves download time still further. Additionally, a JAR file may be digitally signed by the applet authors to authenticate the origin of the code.

The JAR format is cross-platform, handles audio and image files as well as class files and is backward-compatible with existing applet code. JAR consists of a ZIP archive, as defined by PKWARE, containing a manifest file and potentially signature files (see http://www.pkware.com). The `jar` tool is basically a Java application that combines multiple files into a single JAR file.

JDK 1.1 offered the `javakey` tool to sign JAR files.

3.2.2.2 JDK 1.1 Security API

The Java security API was built around the java.security package and its subpackages java.security.acl and java.security.interfaces. The first release for Java security, available in JDK 1.1, included primarily cryptography functions, which could be incorporated into Java-based applications. The cryptography framework in the Java security API was designed so that a new algorithm could be added later on without much difficulty and could be used in the same fashion as existing algorithms. For example, even if Digital Signature Algorithm (DSA) was the only built-in algorithm in this release, it was possible to use software from providers to help generate RSA signatures and key pairs for encryption.

The first release of Java security in JDK 1.1 included APIs for digital signatures, message digests, key management and access control lists (ACLs). APIs for data encryption and other functionalities, together with their implementations, were released separately in the Java Cryptography Extension (JCE) 1.1 as an add-on package to JDK, in accordance with United States export control regulations (see 2.2.3, "United States Export Rules for Encryption" on page 57). The JCE APIs included block and stream cipher, symmetric and asymmetric encryption and support for multiple modes of operation and multiple encryption.

3.2.3 The Fine-Grained Access Control of Java 2

An obvious handicap with the JDK 1.1 security architecture was no easy way of achieving fine-grained access control, with all local code enjoying unrestricted access to all the system resources and all remote code subjected to sandbox constraints unless signed in a way recognizable to the client as trusted. By *fine-grained access control*, we mean the ability to grant *specific permissions* to a *particular piece of code* about accessing *specific resources* of the client (say read and write permission on file *x*, but only read permissions on file *y* and no permissions on file *z*) depending on the signers of the code and/or the URL location from which the code was loaded. Thus, existence of a fine-grained access control would allow a user to specify access permissions on a case-by-case basis rather than a rigid classification of local code being fully trusted and remote code being untrusted and restricted to a sandbox, unless signed in a way recognizable to the client as fully trusted.

The new security architecture developed in Java 2 allows easy fine tuning of the access controls. The concept of signed code can now be extended to local code as well. With the new security model, all code, whether remotely downloaded or local, signed or unsigned, will have access to system resources based on what is defined in a *policy file*. This allows the client to explicitly specify the permissions to be granted to different signatories of code and different sources. This way the end user can download, install and run applications from the Web by granting them permissions for *only* those actions that are necessary. This will eliminate codes that have a hidden agenda, such as letting you play a nice game while sending your credit card information or your password file to a particular server at the same time.

Consider for example the following scenario, based on the JDK 1.1 security model. You download a little tic-tac-toe program from the Web. It is signed by an entity you trust, and you are sure that it will not crash your system. For this reason, you accept to run it. Nonetheless, this code reads your address book, and sends all the e-mail addresses you have to the database of the nearest junk mailer. Though not very malicious, this is something we all would like to avoid. This is a very likely situation, since more and more software is just being brought off the net, and this trend is likely to continue for a long time. This might lead to fly-by-night software vendors, some of whom might come up with very innovative software, but some of whom you cannot really trust. With JDK 1.1, you do not have an option to restrict access to code to do only certain things. You either install the software, or you make do without it.

However, if you are running Java 2-enabled software, you can instruct the JVM, through modifications in a policy file, that code loaded from a particular URL (local or remote) and/or signed by a particular entity is restricted to specific local resources. For example, you may specify in the policy file that the code in question may read files in one particular directory and can do nothing else – cannot open sockets, cannot write or delete any files, etc. This is the fine-grained control mechanism offered by Java 2. For more on this, see 1.4, "Understanding Java 2 Security" on page 12.

In versions of Java prior to Java 2, the JVM resource access was enforced by the sandbox security model, which was a function of the security manager. Extensions were usually limited to features implemented by the platform providers such as Web browsers and Web servers. When using Java 2, you can have full control over what each of your programs and applications is permitted to do – this was never possible until now. Similarly, you can now define the exact things an applet coming from a particular URL can do, or what any programs (applets, applications, servlets) signed by one or more particular entities can do. Further, in multi-user systems, the system administrator can define a default system policy, and each of the users of the system can have their own policy, which is combined with the system default.

Java programs now have the ability to define access restrictions on sensitive resources without having to write a new security manager or modify the underlying platform. For example, applets downloaded into a Java 2-enabled Web browser and servlets downloaded into a Java 2-enabled Web server can add resource access controls to a JVM without having to modify the underlying browser or server implementation. These new concepts of permission and policy enable the Java 2 platform to offer fine-grained, highly configurable, flexible, and extensible access control.

The Java 2 security model has been depicted in Figure 32 on page 76. As seen in the figure, a predetermined security policy of the client decides the security domains within which a specific piece of local or remote code can reside:

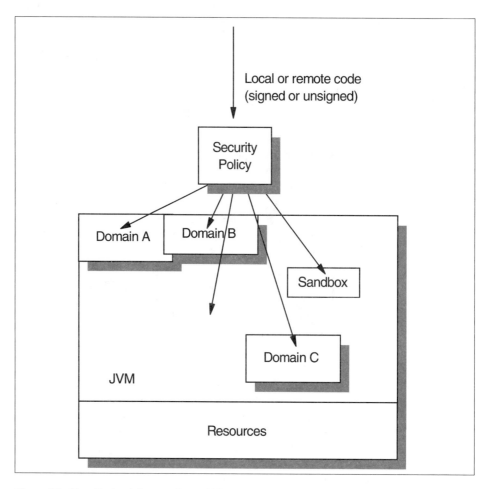

Figure 32. Fine-Grained Access Control Mechanism in Java 2 SDK

3.2.3.1 Lexical Scoping of Privilege Modifications

A new security feature implemented for the first time in Java 2 is the *lexical scoping of privilege modification*, which is a technique enforcing the least privileged mode. Using this technique, it is possible to enable only the execution of the piece of code that needs the privilege. All the sensitive code could therefore be added at one place and defined as privileged, by calling the doPrivileged() method, belonging to the java.security.AccessController class. The doPrivileged() method is discussed in 3.5.1, "Run-Time Access Controls" on page 91. But to get an idea in advance, basically, through the use of this method, Java 2 provides a facility to mark Java code as being privileged and temporarily grant it some permissions that it normally would not enjoy by itself by virtue of its location of origin and the identity of its signers.

3.2.3.2 Java 2 Security Tools

Java 2 provides four powerful security tools for ensuring confidentiality, integrity, authenticity of data and adequate control on access to various system and non-system resources. These are `jar`, `keytool`, `jarsigner` and Policy Tool.

The `jar` function is similar in Java 2 to what it was in JDK 1.1 (see 3.2.2.1, "The jar and javakey Tools" on page 73). JAR files acquire specific significance, since the old `javakey`, and its newer version `jarsigner`, can sign only JAR files.

The `keytool` command line utility creates key pairs – pairs of public and private keys – imports and exports X.509 V1, V2 and V3 certificates (see Appendix C, "X.509 Certificates" on page 683), generates self-signed X.509 V1 certificates and manages keystores. A *keystore* is a protected database that holds private keys as well as public keys and certificates. In the default implementation, a keystore is protected using a password and each private key stored in the keystore is protected with a possibly different password. The private keys are used to digitally sign applications and applets whereas public keys are used to verify signed data, and certificates are used to verify whether a public key indeed belongs to the person it is supposed to belong.

The `jarsigner` command line tool signs JAR files and verifies the signature(s) of signed JAR files. It accesses the keystore when it needs to find:

- A private key when signing a JAR file
- A public key when verifying a signature
- A certificate when verifying a public key

In the Java 2 platform, the `keytool` and `jarsigner` command line utilities replace the JDK 1.1 tool `javakey`. The `javakey` tool had several shortcomings, the most significant of them being the fact that both the public and private keys were stored in the same, unprotected location (often called an *identity database*). This allowed anyone with access to the identity database to determine all keys that were stored in the file. In contrast, private keys are now password protected in the keystore.

The Policy Tool utility, which is launched through the `policytool` command, creates and modifies the external policy configuration files that define the client's security policy.

All of these tools are discussed in detail later in this book (see Chapter 9, "Java 2 SDK Security Tools" on page 259).

3.2.3.3 Java 2 Security API

In Java 2 two new subpackages have been added to the java.security package, and they are java.security.cert and java.security.spec. These packages offer more features to deal with X.509 certificates and to create *certificate revocation lists* (CRLs) and *certificate signing requests* (CSRs). In particular, java.security.Certificate, that in JDK 1.1 was an interface of abstract methods for managing an identity certificate, is completely deprecated in Java 2, which offers the entire package java.security.cert to handle certificates. Moreover, the package java.security.cert adds X.509 V3 support to certificates.

Java 2 also provides an additional certificate interface: the X509Extension interface in the java.security.cert package. This is an interface for X.509 extensions. The extensions defined for X.509 V3 certificates and V2 CRLs provide methods for associating additional attributes with users or public keys, for managing the certification hierarchy, and for managing CRL distribution.

3.2.4 A Comparison of the Three Java Security Models

Table 1 on page 79 shows a comparison of the three Java security models based on seven parameters, which are:

- **Resource access to local unsigned code**

  This refers to the options provided by the security architecture to a client to determine access to local resources for local unsigned code.

- **Resource access to local signed code**

  This refers to the options provided by the security architecture to a client to determine access to local resources for local signed code.

- **Resource access to remote unsigned code**

  This refers to the options provided by the security architecture to a client to determine access to local resources for remote unsigned code.

- **Resource access to remote signed code**

  This refers to the options provided by the security architecture to a client to determine access to local resources for remote signed code.

- **Lexical scoping of privilege modification**

  This refers to the availability of the option in the security architecture to temporarily grant more privileges to a specific piece of code in an execution thread, which are additional to the privileges the code would have enjoyed by itself. This facility is available only with Java 2 and achieved with the help of the doPrivileged() method introduced in 3.2.3.1, "Lexical Scoping of Privilege Modifications" on page 76. This method actually internally modifies the way the run-time stack (for an execution thread) is checked for permissions.

- **Cryptographic services for data confidentiality/integrity**

  This refers to the availability of cryptographic services for data confidentiality and integrity. Such services became available only with JDK 1.1.

- **Digital signature services for code signing**

  This refers to the facility of digital signature services for signing code. Such services became available only with JDK 1.1.

Table 1. Evolution of the Java Security Model

	JDK 1.0	**JDK 1.1**	**Java 2 SDK**
Local unsigned code resource access	Unconstrained	Unconstrained	Policy based
Local signed code resource access	Not available	Unconstrained if trusted	Policy based
		Constrained by the Java sandbox if untrusted	
Remote unsigned code resource access	Constrained by the Java sandbox	Constrained by the Java sandbox	Policy based
Remote signed code resource access	Not available	Unconstrained if trusted	Policy based
		Constrained by the Java sandbox if untrusted	
Lexical scoping of privilege modification	Not available	Not available	Stack annotation based with doPrivileged()
Cryptographic services for data confidentiality/integrity	Not available	Java Cryptography Extension 1.1	Java Cryptography Extension 1.2
Digital signature services for code signing	Not available	Java Cryptography Architecture DSA signature	Java Cryptography Architecture DSA signature

This comparison shows the increasing flexibility and functionality provided by the evolving Java security model in determining a security policy.

3.3 Java 2 Protection Domain and Permissions Model

This section explains the concepts of protection domain, code source and security policy file which are the foundations of the new security model.

A *protection domain* can be scoped by a set of objects that are currently directly accessible by a principal, where a *principal* is an entity in the computer system to which *permissions* are granted. A principal can access objects in the protection domain by virtue of the permissions it enjoys over the objects in the protection domain. These permissions are specified explicitly in a security *policy file*, which is a text file that can be edited manually or through the Policy Tool. The Java 2 security architecture allows the combination of a system security policy, defined by the system administrator, with one or more user-defined security policies. A default system policy file comes with the installation of the Java 2 SDK (see 3.6, "The Policy File" on page 93).

Notice that, even if an arbitrary number of policy files can be specified, there is only one policy (meaning, one set of protection domains) in effect for the JVM at any given time. That policy might be the result of processing the information from many policy files. The default policy implementation, via the java.security.Policy class, has a public refresh() method that can be used to re-init the policy, eventually re-reading the policy file(s). However, there is no automatic policy change: refresh() must be called explicitly.

Using this security model, it is possible to grant specific access permissions to specific code whether local or remote. Local or remote code is now identified by its code source. The *code source* for a code is a combination of the URL location from which the code is loaded and the entity or entities that signed the code originating from that location. The code source is represented by the java.security.CodeSource class. The location from which the code is loaded is passed as an argument to the constructor of the CodeSource class in the form of a java.net.URL object. The identity of the signer(s) is passed as the second argument to the constructor of the CodeSource object in the form of a set of java.security.cert.Certificate objects. These certificates are for the public keys corresponding to the private keys that signed the code. The constructor of the CodeSource class therefore looks like the following line:

```
public CodeSource(URL url, Certificate[] certs)
```

The location from which the code is loaded is referred to as the *code base* in the policy file, as we have seen in the examples of 1.4, "Understanding Java 2 Security" on page 12. In the Java 2 security model, a policy file serves as a rule book, which lists what permission(s) can be granted to what type of code, depending on the location of origin of the code and the signer(s) for the code.

A policy file consists of a number of grant entries. The syntax of the grant entry is as follows:

```
grant [signedBy signers][, codeBase URL] {
permission permission_class [target][, action][, signedBy signers];
[permission ...]
};
```

Figure 33. The Syntax of a grant Entry in a Policy File

This syntax will be discussed in 3.6, "The Policy File" on page 93. For now, it should be noticed that, in the grant entry, *signers* will be replaced by the name of the entity or entities that have signed the code and *URL* will be replaced by the URL address of the location from where the code has originated. If the list of signers is omitted, code signed by any signers will be granted the specified permissions. If the code base is omitted, code coming from any location will be granted the specified permissions. In addition to this, a policy file can specify the URL location of the keystore.

Notice that, even if the default policy implementation is file-based, application developers can implement their own Policy subclass, providing an implementation of the abstract methods in the java.security.Policy class. There could be multiple instances of the Policy class, even if only one is in effect at any time. The currently installed Policy object can be obtained by calling the static getPolicy() method in the Policy class. Codes with permission to reset the policy can change the currently installed Policy object by calling the static setPolicy() method in the Policy class.

A protection domain is identified as an association of a code source and the permissions granted to that code source. A code source is composed of a URL (code's origination location) and optional signer(s). The permissions granted to a code source are specified in the policy file(s). When a non-system (non-trusted) class is loaded, it is mapped to a protection domain based upon its code source – where it was loaded from and any signers it may have. The grant entries in the policy file describe the permissions granted to a particular code source. Notice that classes that have the same permissions but are from different code sources belong to different protection domains.

Protection domains generally fall into two categories: *system domain* and *application domains*. We can think of the system domain as a single collection of all system code, which is not subjected to any policy restrictions and is granted all permissions. An application domain is specific to an application or applet and can include the domains of extensions as well, since even the standard extensions are subjected to the security policy specified in the policy file. The default java.policy file grants all extensions full access permissions to all system resources (java.security.AllPermission), provided the extension classes are stored as JAR files in the extensions directory ${java.home}\lib\ext or its subdirectories. On Windows systems, the default extensions directory is usually C:\Program Files\JavaSoft\JRE\1.2\lib\ext (see Figure 370 on page 676 and Figure 371 on page 677).

Notice that a thread of execution (which is often, but not necessarily, tied to a single Java thread, which in turn is not necessarily tied to the thread concept of the underlying operating system) may occur completely within a single protection domain or may involve an application domain and also the system domain. All protected resources, such as the file system, the networking facility, the screen and the keyboard, are accessible only via the system domains, as shown in the following figure:

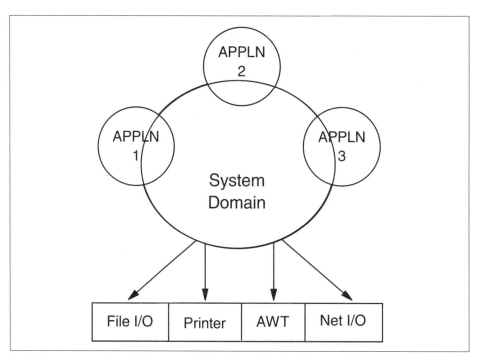

Figure 34. Domain Composition of a Java Application Environment

Each class file loaded into the JVM via a class loader is assigned to one and only one protection domain, as determined by the code source of the class. However, multiple classes may be assigned to the same protection domain, depending on the code source itself. In addition, a single protection domain may include one or more permissions, and the same permission can be part of different protection domains.

The Java application environment maintains a mapping from code (classes and instances) to their protection domains and then to their permissions as shown in the following figure:

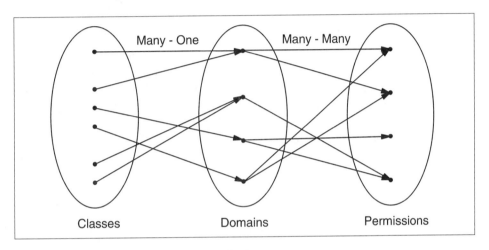

Figure 35. Mapping in the Java Application Environment

3.4 New Class Search Path

With JDK 1.1, the default class path value included the path where the Java system classes (compressed in the ZIP file classes.zip) resided, along with the current working directory, for instance:

```
CLASSPATH=.;C:\jdk1.1.7\classes;C:\jdk1.1.7\lib\classes.zip
```

Note that the default class path also included a path to a classes folder on the same directory level as lib. You could put your own class files (no JAR or ZIP files) in this classes folder that you had to create, and the Java executables would be able to find them with the default class path.

Either the `-classpath` and `-cp` flags of the `java` command line tool, or the CLASSPATH environment variable could be used to add a new library location to the class path, to expand upon the core set of class libraries provided by the JDK:

- If the CLASSPATH environment variable was set, the effective class path would still contain the classes.zip file (as in the default setting), but with the newly assigned value in place of the current working directory. So, when defining the CLASSPATH system environment variable, if you wanted the current working directory to be part of the class path, you had to explicitly specify it as part of the value of CLASSPATH.

- If, on the other hand, the `-classpath` or the equivalent `-cp` option was used, the value of this option specified on the command line had to contain both the original classes.zip reference, and the new application classes, for example:

```
java -classpath C:\jdk1.1.7\lib\classes.zip;\app\classes Application
```

The reason for this was that this option was used to override the search path for system classes.

This discrepancy between the two means of setting the class path caused a great deal of confusion, along with outright errors. Often, the explicitly specified version of classes.zip did not match the version of the `java` command being used.

This source of confusion has been eliminated in the Java 2 platform. The `-classpath` command line option now has the same functionality as the CLASSPATH environment variable. However, the single search path once specified by the class path has been broken down into three distinct areas which will be discussed in the following sections.

3.4.1 Boot Class Path

With the Java 2 platform, the system classes no longer reside in a ZIP file. They are now stored in JAR files: the run-time classes are found in the file rt.jar, while the SDK-supported tool classes are found in the tools.jar file. Both these files come with the default installation of the Java 2 SDK. Also, the *system class files* are no longer specified by either the CLASSPATH system environment variable or the `-classpath` command line option. Instead, the location of the system class files is specified automatically by the run-time environment as the value of the sun.boot.class.path variable, and takes the name of *boot class path*. Notice that the terms *JVM class path* and *system class path* are equivalent to boot class path. In beta releases of Java 2 SDK, Standard Edition, V1.2, the system class path was referred to by the value of a variable java.sys.class.path, which was replaced by sun.boot.class.path when Java 2 was officially released.

After the default installation of the Java 2 SDK on a Windows system, the boot class path is automatically configured to include the two files rt.jar and i18n.jar (both found in the directory lib under ${java.home}[1]) and the entire directory classes, which does not exist by default, but can be created by the user under the directory ${java.home}[2].

This default can be changed with the -bootclasspath compile time flag and the -Xbootclasspath run-time flag. For example, if temp.jar is a JAR file containing a different version of the system class files, the two following commands will use temp.jar to overwrite the default system class files:

```
javac -bootclasspath D:\temporary\temp.jar HelloWorld.java
java -Xbootclasspath:D:\temporary\temp.jar HelloWorld
```

Let's consider the following example. We have a simple program HelloWorld.java. We try to run it using the command:

```
java -Xbootclasspath:D:\temporary HelloWorld
```

We launch this command from the directory D:, which contains neither the HelloWorld class file, nor the rt.jar file. The directory D:\temporary contains the file HelloWorld.class, but does not contain the rt.jar file. In this case the JVM tries to find all the run-time classes in the directory D:\temporary only, but doesn't find them there. Hence we get an exception:

```
Can't find class java.lang.NoClassDefFoundError. (Wrong Class Path?)
```

This is a good response, because the JVM has detected that we might have made a mistake in specifying the system class path.

We now type the following command, again from the D: directory:

```
java -Xbootclasspath:D:\temporary;D:\jdk1.2\jre\lib\rt.jar HelloWorld
```

In this case, the HelloWorld program gets executed successfully.

This demonstrates that, in order to execute the program, the JVM is looking for mainly two things: the rt.jar file, containing the classes necessary for the JVM to execute any program, and the application class file being executed. After launching the above command line argument, the JVM finds the HelloWorld application class file in D:\temporary first (since it searches for classes in the order of the paths specified after -Xbootclasspath keyword in the command line) and then finds the rt.jar file in the D:\jdk1.2\jre\lib directory.

---

[1] For developing and testing reasons, a copy of rt.jar and i18n.jar is also found in the directory where the development environment is installed (for example, on Windows systems, C:\jdk1.2.x\jre\lib).
[2] ${java.home} translates into the directory where the JRE is installed. On Windows systems, by default, this directory is C:\Program Files\JavaSoft\JRE\1.2 (see A.2, "Program GetProperty" on page 678).

Next, we try to run the command:

```
java -Xbootclasspath:D:\temporary;d:\jdk1.2\jre\lib HelloWorld
```

This time we again get the error message:

```
Can't find class java.lang.NoClassDefFoundError. (Wrong Class Path?)
```

This is because the -Xbootclasspath option requires that the full path for the rt.jar file be given, including the name of the file rt.jar; just the name of the directory containing the rt.jar file is not sufficient. On the other hand, the application class is found either from the current working directory or any of the directories specified after the -Xbootclasspath keyword.

It is therefore important to remember, when using the -Xbootclasspath flag, to also include the default rt.jar file. With the Java 2 platform, the only classes trusted by the run-time are those on the boot class path. Thus, by explicitly adding something to the system class path, it becomes trusted. With JDK 1.1, anything loaded locally through the class path became trusted.

Two other JAR files are shipped with the Java 2 platform in the same directory as rt.jar:

- i18n.jar, which provides internationalization support classes and, as we already said, is part of the default boot class path

- jaws.jar, which provides capabilities such as JavaScript integration with Netscape's JSObject, along with JSException classes, and browser plug-in interoperability

---
The Compile-Time Flag

The -bootclasspath option is used to *cross-compile* against a specified set of boot classes. The Java 2 SDK javac command would by default compile against its own Java 2 bootstrap classes, and we may tell javac to compile against JDK 1.1 bootstrap classes instead, if needed at times. We do this with the -bootclasspath compile flag. Failing to do this allows compilation against a 1.2 API that might not be present on a 1.1 JVM and would fail at run time. The following command displays the use of the Java 2 SDK javac command to compile code that will run on a 1.1 JVM:

```
javac -target 1.1 -bootclasspath D:\jdk1.1.7\lib\classes.zip OldCode.java
```

3.4.2 Extensions Framework

Extensions are packages of classes written in the Java programming language (and any associated native code) that application developers can use to extend the functionality of the core part of the Java platform. Standard extensions are, for example, JavaServlet, Java3D and JavaManagement. The *extension framework* allows the JVM to use the extension classes in much the same way as the system classes.

The size of the core part of the Java platform has been growing steadily since the release of JDK 1.0. The first Java platform had eight core packages, in JDK 1.1 there were twenty-two packages, and in Java 2 there are over fifty! The extensions framework provides a standard means to add functionality to the Java platform for use when needed, without having to increase the size of the core API.

While the CLASSPATH system environment variable or -classpath command line option can still be used to add non-system libraries, this process, too, has been greatly simplified with Java 2 SDK, Standard Edition, V1.2. Simply place a JAR file in the extensions directory ${java.home}${/}lib${/}ext[3], and the library is added. JAR files placed in the extensions directory are called *installed extensions*.

An entry in the default system policy file shipped with the Java 2 SDK is devoted to the extensions directory and its subdirectories, as shown in the following screen:

```
grant codeBase "file:${java.home}/lib/ext/-" {
  permission java.security.AllPermission;
};
```

This means that all the classes placed in JAR files in the extensions directory and its subdirectories are automatically granted all permissions, irrespective of eventual signers.

Classes not contained in a JAR file can be added simply by placing them in the classes directory found under the JRE installation directory, ${java.home}. Note, however, that this directory does not exist by default, so it must be created by the user. However, as we have mentioned in 3.4.1, "Boot Class Path" on page 84, the classes directory is automatically considered part of the boot class path, while the ext directory is subjected to the security policy.

The locations of installed extensions can be overridden at compile time by using the -extdirs flag of the javac command, followed by a sequence of directories separated by semicolons (;).

---

[3] ${/} is the file separator variable. Its value is translated into the forward slash / on UNIX systems, and the back slash \ on Windows systems. Its use grants policy file portability across the platforms. More details about this are found in 3.6, "The Policy File" on page 93.

Notice that any native libraries that are installed with an extension are stored in the directory ${java.home}${/}bin.

The new extensions framework also supports downloadable extensions. To use a library within an applet, the library file can be specified in a special Class-Path: line in the manifest file MANIFEST.MF of the applet's JAR file (we already introduced the manifest file of a JAR file in 1.4.1.3, "Packing the Applet Class in a JAR File" on page 18). This is a handy alternative to either storing everything in one very large JAR file, or specifying multiple JAR files within the <APPLET> tag of the HTML page (both of which can still be done). Below is a sample Class-Path: manifest file entry, which shows how to add two JAR files to the normal class path as extensions:

```
Class-Path: milind.jar app/deepak.jar
```

Once the extension is found, it is downloaded and placed into a namespace in memory. Some differences between installed and downloaded extensions are:

- The classes in an installed extension are shared by all code in the same JVM. Classes for downloaded extensions are private to the session of the application or applet that uses the downloaded extension.

- An extension becomes an *installed extension* if the location of its JAR file is ${java.home}${/}lib${/}ext. The location of the JAR files that serve as downloaded extensions is irrelevant. A downloaded extension is an extension because it is referenced from the Class-Path: in the header of another JAR file's manifest.

- Only applets and applications bundled in a JAR file can make use of downloaded extensions. Applets and applications not bundled in a JAR file do not have a manifest from which to reference downloaded extensions. This limitation does not exist for installed extensions, which are shared by all code in the same JVM.

- Downloaded extensions are purely temporary. Also, they cannot use native code, and must be signed or loaded from a trusted source to gain permissions to perform system-level actions. These limitations do not exist for installed extensions, which may be permanently installed in the extensions directory and are granted all permissions by default.

3.4.3 Application Class Path

The property java.class.path is used by an application to specify the application's search path of URLs for loading application classes and resources. The CLASSPATH environment variable specifies the default value of the property java.class.path. If the CLASSPATH is not set, then the default value for java.class.path is set to the current directory. The option `-classpath` of the `java` command is now shorthand for setting the java.class.path property. Formerly, this option was used in JDK 1.0 and 1.1 to override the search path for the system classes, but in the new `java` command, there is no longer a need to set the system class path, and if you want to override the search path for the system classes, you have to use the command line option `-Xbootclasspath`.

The value of the variable java.class.path is called *application class path* or *user class path*.

3.4.4 Class Search Paths in Summary

In summary, three basic search paths are used to find classes in the Java 2 platform:[4]

1. The first location searched is the boot class path. This can be set using the `-Xbootclasspath` option. Its value can be examined by calling:

   `System.getProperty("sun.boot.class.path")`

2. The second location searched is the extensions directory, which by default is ${java.home}${/}lib${/}ext. The extensions directory can be examined by calling:

   `System.getProperty("java.ext.dirs")`

3. The third and final location searched is the application class path, set by either the `-classpath` option or the CLASSPATH system environment variable. The value of the application class path can be examined by calling:

   `System.getProperty("java.class.path")`

As with the user class path, boot class path entries are separated by semicolons (;) and can be directories, JAR archives, or ZIP archives.

In the case of a sealed JAR file (see 12.1.1, "Manifest File" on page 387 and 12.6, "The JAR Bug – Fixed In Java 2 SDK, Standard Edition, V1.2.1" on page 461), the search is limited to the JAR file only.

3.5 Java 2 Class Loading Mechanism

The class loading mechanism plays a critical role in Java security since the class loader is responsible for locating and fetching the class files, consulting

---

[4] The properties sun.boot.class.path, java.ext.dirs and java.class.path, mentioned in the list, can only be examined from a trusted program. See Appendix A, "Getting Internal System Properties" on page 675 for more details.

the security policy, and defining the appropriate permissions associated with the class object.

In JDK 1.1, local code and correctly signed remote code were generally trusted to have full access to all vital system resources, such as the file system itself, while unsigned remote code was not trusted and could access only limited resources. A security manager was responsible for determining which resource accesses were allowed. For this reason each application, such as a Web browser or a Web server, had to write its own subclasses of SecurityManager and ClassLoader.

Java 2 has simplified the development process:

- As discussed in 2.1.2.4, "The Security Manager" on page 49, SecurityManager is no longer an abstract class and can be instantiated or subclassed. Most of its methods now make calls to methods in class AccessController, which provides the access control functions in Java 2. This greatly simplifies the writing of new SecurityManager subclasses.

- A new powerful subclass of ClassLoader has been created in Java 2. It is called SecureClassLoader and is found in the package java.security (see 2.1.2.2, "Where Class Loaders Come From" on page 47). The distinguishing feature of a SecureClassLoader is that it associates a protection domain with each class that it loads. SecureClassLoader has a protected constructor, so its real use is to provide the basis for the development of other class loaders. When creating a custom class loader, one can subclass from the SecureClassLoader class or its subclasses, depending on the particular need.

To automatically invoke the security subsystem, a Java application is started from the command line of a native operating system with some additional command line arguments. We have shown one example of how applications can be subjected to security restrictions in Java 2 by specifying additional command line arguments (see 1.4.2, "An Example of Application Security in Java 2" on page 26). More details are discussed in 3.8.1, "Applying a Security Manager to Applets and Applications" on page 99.

When a Java code starts executing, the Java run time creates an instance of SecureClassLoader, which in turn is used to locate and load the class file of the code. A subclass of the security manager is created and installed in the Java run time. The main() method, in the case of an application, is then called with the command line arguments; the init() method is called in the case of an applet or a servlet.

SecureClassLoader is used to safely and correctly load classes into the Java run time. How does the SecureClassLoader ensure secure loading of classes?

1. First, SecureClassLoader searches for classes in the correct order. The correct order starts with the most trusted classes. Therefore, when the JVM needs a class, SecureClassLoader first looks for files referenced by the class path of the JVM, or the boot class path. This ensures that classes within the core Java API will not be superseded by classes loaded from the network or any other location.

2. If not found in the JVM class path, the locations of the installed extensions are searched.

3. Finally, the locations defined by the application class path are searched.

Once the class file has been loaded into the JVM, SecureClassLoader assigns the appropriate protection domain to the class file. The following list explains how SecureClassLoader does this:

1. When SecureClassLoader loads a class into the JVM, it also creates the code source for the class from the code base URL and any digital certificate(s) used to sign the code.

2. The code source is then used to locate the protection domain for the class. The protection domain contains the Permission objects that have been granted to the class. The information contained in the protection domain and the permissions granted to the code source are used in determining access control during run time.

3. Once a Java program starts to run, SecureClassLoader assists the JVM in loading other classes required to run the program. These classes are also assigned the appropriate protection domains based on their code source.

Notice that another new class, java.net.URLClassLoader, extends SecureClassLoader to provide a general purpose class loader to load class files from a list of local class file directories or HTTP-based URLs.

3.5.1 Run-Time Access Controls

At various points during a Java program's execution, access to protected resources is requested. This includes network I/O attempts, local file I/O, attempts to create a new ClassLoader or access to a program-defined resource. To verify whether the running program is allowed to perform the operation, the library routine makes a call to the method SecurityManager.checkPermission(). This method takes a Permission object argument and determines whether or not it is granted to the current thread.

Each thread in the JVM contains a number of *stack frames*. Simply stated, these frames contain the method instance variables for each method called in the current thread. The method checkPermission() walks back through the current thread's stack frames, getting the protection domain for each of the classes on the thread's stack. As each protection domain in the thread stack is located, the permission to check is compared to the Permission objects contained in the protection domain. For each stack frame, if the checked permission matches one of the Permission objects in the protection domain, testing of the permissions continues with the protection domain of the next stack frame (class) on the stack.

This testing repeats until the end of the stack is reached. That is, all of the classes in the thread have the permission to perform the operation. Thus, the access control check succeeds, typically meaning that the requested operation is able to proceed. If the checked permission is not granted to all classes on the stack (there is no appropriate Permission object in all of the class's ProtectionDomain objects), then a SecurityException is thrown, and access to the resource is denied.

A wrinkle in the above scenario is when a class has a set of permissions, and does not care who its callers may be. For example, a Java bean may be installed on a desktop computer needing to read files from the local disk drive. The ProtectionDomain of the bean's class has permission to read these local files. However, the program loaded from a Web server that calls the bean has a ProtectionDomain that does not have local file read permission. Normally, if the bean were called by the program loaded from the Web server, the bean would be denied access to the files on the local disk drive because the program from the Web server does not have a local file read permission. However, if the bean calls AccessController.doPrivileged(), an annotation is made on the thread's stack frame indicating that when the checkPermission() method searches for ProtectionDomains, the search stops at this stack frame. The bean may make any number of method calls, but when the checkPermission() method is called on another permission object, the search back through the stack frames to find ProtectionDomain objects stops at this stack frame.

Based on the above scenario, the ProtectionDomain objects for the bean will be checked, but the ProtectionDomain objects for the program from the Web server are not checked since the search stopped at the stack frame for the bean. Therefore, the file read operation will succeed.

A subtle aspect of the above doPrivileged() operation is that programs creating new threads would lose protection domain information when a new thread is created. That is, each new thread creates a new run-time stack. The classes on the stack of the parent thread are not present in the new thread. Important protection domain information is no longer available when a checkPermission() operation is performed, giving new threads more permissions than the threads that created them. This would give new threads more permissions than the threads that created them. To correct this apparent loss of security information, the ProtectionDomain objects of the parent thread are attached to (inherited by) a child thread when it is created. So, unless a doPrivileged() operation is performed in the child thread, the parent thread's ProtectionDomain objects are also checked during a checkPermission() operation.

3.6 The Policy File

As described in 3.5.1, "Run-Time Access Controls" on page 91, checkPermission() verifies that the protection domain of every class on the thread stack includes permission to perform the requested operation. Multiple policy files can define the overall policy; these policy files must be specified in the Java security properties file, java.security, by default located in the directory ${java.home}${/}lib${/}security. The default is to have a single system-wide policy file, and a user-defined policy file in the user's home directory.

A policy file contains a list of entries or directives. It may contain first of all a keystore entry and then must contain one or more grant entries. The keystore directive in the policy file is the URL to the keystore file. It is required if one of the grant entries in the policy file specifies signers whose certificate is stored in a keystore different from the default one. The keystore entry in the policy file can be an absolute URL or can be relative to the location of the policy file itself.

Let's talk now about the grant directives (see Figure 33 on page 81). In Java 2, you will notice several Permission classes. All these have the same ancestor, java.security.Permission. This is an abstract class, and is subclassed to represent specific accesses. The specific accesses are usually a part of the package where they are most likely to be used – for instance, the permission FilePermission is a part of the java.io package, thus making it java.io.FilePermission, and the SocketPermission class is part of the java.net package, so that you will find java.net.SocketPermission. Most of the permissions can be instantiated by giving two parameters, the first being the *target*, such as the name of the file, or the socket number, and the second being the permitted *action*, like read, write, open, listen. In most cases, a set of actions can be specified together as a comma-separated, composite string.

Notice, however, that not all of the Permission classes defined in the Java 2 platform have applicable actions yet and the second argument to the constructor would be null. The only system Permission classes that do have actions are FilePermission (read, write, execute, delete), PropertyPermission (read, write) and SocketPermission (resolve, accept, connect, listen).

A special permission class exists called java.security.AllPermission. This is a permission that implies all permissions. It is introduced to simplify the work to system administrators who might need to perform multiple tasks that require all or numerous permissions. Of course much caution is needed when granting this permission. In fact, the AllPermission class represents the permission to perform any operation. For this reason, this permission is usually given only to classes within the Java API and to classes in Java standard extensions, because granting this type of permission is potentially dangerous.

The permission policy that you set up is in a policy file. Each permission that you wish to grant must be a statement containing two parts: a code source and a list of permissions:

- The code source is also comprised of two parts:

  1. Code base URL

     The code base URL indicates where the classes originate from. This field is obtained by the keyword codeBase followed by a quoted string indicating the URL, for example:

     ```
     codeBase "http://www.redbooks.ibm.com"
     ```

     This field is optional. If omitted, the associated permissions are granted to code from any source.

  2. Digital certificate(s) used to sign the classes

     This field is obtained by the keyword signedBy followed by a quoted string indicating the name assigned to a digital certificate used to sign the classes. A comma-separated list of multiple signers is allowed. So, for example, correct entries could be:

     ```
     signedBy "Marco"
     ```

     or

     ```
     signedBy "Duane,Marco"
     ```

     This field is optional. If omitted, the associated permissions are granted to a signed or unsigned code. Also note that if there are multiple signers, the code must be signed by all of the signers in the list to be granted the permissions.

- Each permission of the list is comprised of five parts:

  1. The keyword `permission`

     This field is required.

  2. The fully qualified name of the Permission class

     This field is also required, and includes the package name, for example:

     `java.util.PropertyPermission`

  3. A quoted string naming the target of the Permission class

     For example, `"java.version"` could be the target for a PropertyPermission, while `"D:\\Works\\Stats.txt"` could be the target for a FilePermission. The only Permission class that this target field is not applicable to is the special java.security.AllPermission.

  4. A quoted string naming the actions requested

     As we said, a set of actions can be specified together as a comma-separated composite string. For example, `"read"` or `"read,write,delete,execute"` could be actions for a FilePermission, and `"resolve,accept"` or `"listen"` could be the actions for a SocketPermission. Action fields are not applicable to all Permission classes, but only to FilePermission, PropertyPermission and SocketPermission.

  5. Digital certificate used to sign the Permission class

     This field is obtained by the keyword `signedBy` followed by a quoted string indicating the name assigned to a digital certificate used to sign the Permission class. As we will see in 8.4.2, "grant Entries" on page 243, multiple signers are not allowed in this case.

     This field is optional. It may be necessary to prevent spoofing when the Permission class is not resident in the Java run time but is loaded from over the network.

Note that the syntax of the `grant` entries must be followed exactly; the omission of even a single comma results in rejection of the code by the JVM. An inadvertent mistake editing the policy file may cause unexpected changes in the Java security policy which, in turn, may compromise the security of the whole system. In future versions of Java, the default policy file may be encrypted, or may be stored in a format other than a flat file, which will make manual editing of the policy impractical. Today, the Policy Tool utility prevents errors likely in manual editing of the default text policy files. In the future, the Policy Tool will be essential in updating non-text policy data stored.

This is also a good point to discuss the ${/} file path separator we have been using. In a policy file, the strings for a file path must be written in a platform specific format. Strings are processed by java.io.StreamTokenizer, which considers a back slash (\) as an escape string. Therefore, in a policy file on a Windows system, we find two back slashes (\\) required to indicate one single back slash (for example, `C:\\milind\\file1` instead of `C:\milind\file1`). However, if the property policy.expandProperties in the java.security properties file is set to `true`, one can write portable policy files. The ${/} symbol can be used, which is automatically converted to an appropriate format, depending on the platform. For example, `C:${/}milind${/}file1` is converted to `C:/milind/file1` on UNIX systems and `C:\milind\file1` on Windows systems.

3.6.1 The Default System-Wide Policy File

This is the default system-wide policy file, java.policy, that comes with the Java 2 SDK installation in the directory ${java.home}${/}lib${/}security:

```
grant codeBase "file:${java.home}/lib/ext/-" {
      permission java.security.AllPermission;
};


// default permissions granted to all domains

grant {
      // Allows any thread to stop itself using the java.lang.Thread.stop()
      // method that takes no argument.
      // Note that this permission is granted by default only to remain
      // backwards compatible.
      // It is strongly recommended that you either remove this permission
      // from this policy file or further restrict it to code sources
      // that you specify, because Thread.stop() is potentially unsafe.
      // See "http://java.sun.com/notes" for more information.
      permission java.lang.RuntimePermission "stopThread";

      // allows anyone to listen on un-privileged ports
      permission java.net.SocketPermission "localhost:1024-", "listen";

      // "standard" properies that can be read by anyone

      permission java.util.PropertyPermission "java.version", "read";
      permission java.util.PropertyPermission "java.vendor", "read";
      permission java.util.PropertyPermission "java.vendor.url", "read";
```

Figure 36. (Part 1 of 2). The Default System Policy File

```
        permission java.util.PropertyPermission "java.class.version", "read";
        permission java.util.PropertyPermission "os.name", "read";
        permission java.util.PropertyPermission "os.version", "read";
        permission java.util.PropertyPermission "os.arch", "read";
        permission java.util.PropertyPermission "file.separator", "read";
        permission java.util.PropertyPermission "path.separator", "read";
        permission java.util.PropertyPermission "line.separator", "read";

        permission java.util.PropertyPermission "java.specification.version", "read";
        permission java.util.PropertyPermission "java.specification.vendor", "read";
        permission java.util.PropertyPermission "java.specification.name", "read";

        permission java.util.PropertyPermission "java.vm.specification.version", "read";
        permission java.util.PropertyPermission "java.vm.specification.vendor", "read";
        permission java.util.PropertyPermission "java.vm.specification.name", "read";
        permission java.util.PropertyPermission "java.vm.version", "read";
        permission java.util.PropertyPermission "java.vm.vendor", "read";
        permission java.util.PropertyPermission "java.vm.name", "read";
};
```

Figure 37. (Part 2 of 2). The Default System Policy File

As already noted (see 1.4.1.8, "Modifying the Security Policy on the Client System" on page 20), a copy of this file is also installed in the SDK home directory (on Windows systems, it comes by default in C:\jdk1.2.*x*\lib\security) for use with development tools, such as Applet Viewer.

As you can see from the default policy file shown above, in the first grant statement the code base is `"file:${java.home}/lib/ext/-"` and no signers are specified. This means that all the JAR files that are loaded from the Java extensions directory and its subdirectories will be granted all permissions. The second grant statement does not specify any code base or signer. This statement lists the standard permissions to be granted to all classes. All the non-system classes will have read access to the system properties listed. They will also be able to listen on a socket with a port number 1024 or greater (which implies that the class will be able to create a server socket on an unprivileged port).

Notice that any thread is allowed to stop itself using the java.lang.Thread.stop() method. As the comments in the policy file state, Thread.stop() is potentially unsafe. For this reason, you should remove this permission from this policy file or further restrict it to code sources that you specify.

3.7 Security Manager vs Access Controller

The access controller has been introduced in the Java 2 platform. Before the access controller existed, the security manager had to rely on its internal logic to determine the security policy needed to be in effect, and any change in the security policy meant changing the security manager itself.

Prior to Java 2, implementing customized security policies was possible with the security manager alone, but it took a great deal of effort. Starting with Java 2, the security manager can defer access control decisions to the access controller. Determining security policies is much more flexible now since the policy to be enforced by the security manager can be specified in a file. The access controller provides a simple procedure for giving specific permissions to specific code. The Java API still calls the methods of the security manager to enforce system security, but most of these methods call the access controller.

One of the reasons we still have both the security manager and the access controller is for backward compatibility. The security manager was the primary interface to the system security for Java programs prior to Java 2. The large body of Java programs built upon JDK 1.0 and 1.1 dictates that the security manager not be changed but supplemented by the access controller, which provides a simple method for implementing fine-grained access control.

Another role played by the access controller is allowing a program to determine that access to a resource must require explicit permissions. For instance, consider an online attendance marking system where each employee has to update his attendance record every day in the company's attendance database. Here, each employee should have access only to his records and not to records of others. While global access to the database might be controlled by the security manager (for instance if it is necessary to open a socket connection to access the database), access to a particular record is controlled by the access controller. Thus, a program can quite simply use the same security framework to specify access to general resources of the operating system as well as any specific resources of the program.

3.8 Security Management with Java 2

In this section we show you how to apply the security features of Java 2 to applets and applications running on your system.

3.8.1 Applying a Security Manager to Applets and Applications

The security manager is invoked by all the Java system code to perform access control checks based on the security policy currently in effect. A security manager (an implementation of the class SecurityManager) is typically installed when an applet is running (the Applet Viewer and most of the browsers install a security manager). A security manager is, however, not automatically installed when an application is running. To apply the same security policy to an application as is implemented by the security manager for an applet, there are two options available:

1. While running the application, the `java` command line option `-Djava.security.manager` should be provided. For instance, the JVM would invoke the security manager to apply the security policy to the application HelloWorld with the following command:

   ```
   java -Djava.security.manager HelloWorld
   ```

   An example of this was shown in 1.4.2, "An Example of Application Security in Java 2" on page 26, where we also demonstrated the differences that can be generated when running an application under the security manager and without it.

   Notice that the command line option `-Djava.security.manager` is a new flag introduced with Java 2 SDK, Standard Edition, V1.2. An application did not run under a security manager in JDK 1.0 or 1.1, since local code was considered trusted by default.

   A variant of the option above allows the user to specify a customized security manager, say the class MySecurityManager. In this case the syntax is the following:

   ```
   java -Djava.security.manager=MySecurityManager HelloWorld
   ```

   The default built-in security manager can be invoked by any of the following commands which are equivalent:

   ```
   java -Djava.security.manager HelloWorld
   java -Djava.security.manager="" HelloWorld
   java -Djava.security.manager=default HelloWorld
   ```

2. The application itself can call the setSecurityManager() method in the java.lang.System class. Examples of how to use the setSecurityManager() method are shown in 7.5, "Examples of Security Manager Extensions" on page 206.

3.8.2 Applying a User-Defined Security Policy

It is also possible to apply a user-defined security policy file in addition to or different from the security policy files specified in the security properties file java.security. This can be done by using the `-Djava.security.policy` command line argument. A command like:

```
java -Djava.security.manager -Djava.security.policy=MyPolicy HelloWorld
```

means that the security policy file MyPolicy will be used in addition to all the policy files specified in the security properties file. A command like:

```
java -Djava.security.manager -Djava.security.policy==MyPolicy HelloWorld
```

means that only the security policy file MyPolicy will be used and all others will be ignored.

Notice that the `java` command line option `-Djava.security.policy` allows you to specify the URL of MyPolicy, so that even remote policy files can be passed on to the command line.

3.8.3 Java Security Debugging

Security access can be monitored by setting the `java.security.debug` system property. A list of all debugging options can be viewed by typing:

```
java -Djava.security.debug=help
```

The following screen shows the results of typing the command above:

```
all         turn on all debugging
access      print all checkPermission results
jar         jar verification
policy      loading and granting
scl         permissions SecureClassLoader assigns

The following can be used with access:

stack       include stack trace
domain      dumps all domains in context
failure     before throwing exception, dump stack
            and domain that didn't have permission
```

We want to show now a concrete example of security debugging. Consider the following Java application:

```
class SomeProperties
{
    public static void main(String args[])
    {
        System.out.println("This program lists a few system properties");
        String S = System.getProperty("sun.boot.class.path");
        System.out.println("sun.boot.class.path = " + S);
        String S1 = System.getProperty("java.sys.class.path");
        System.out.println("java.sys.class.path = " + S1);
        String S2 = System.getProperty("user.home");
        System.out.println("user.home = " + S2);
    }
}
```

Figure 38. SomeProperties.java

The program above can be compiled by simply issuing the command:

`javac SomeProperties.java`

You can then run the Java class SomeProperties by launching:

`java SomeProperties`

The output produced is shown in the following screen:

```
This program lists a few system properties
sun.boot.class.path = D:\Program Files\JavaSoft\JRE\1.2\lib\rt.jar;D:\Program
Files\JavaSoft\JRE\1.2\lib\i18m.jar;D:\Program Files\JavaSoft\JRE\1.2\classes
java.sys.class.path = null
user.home = C:\WINNT\Profiles\pistoia
```

The program SomeProperties displays the value of the properties
sun.boot.class.path and user.home. It also attempts to print the value of the
property java.sys.class.path, which was the variable used with beta versions
of Java 2 SDK, Standard Edition, V1.2 to indicate the system class path. That
variable was then deprecated in the GA version of Java 2 SDK, Standard
Edition, V1.2, and replaced by sun.boot.class.path. Hence, the value of
java.sys.class.path is displayed as null in the output screen above.

Notice that the program above will not work with the option
`-Djava.security.manager`; it will throw an AccessControlException, unless it is
granted in one of the current policy files the permission to read system
properties. This can be done by adding the following lines to one of the policy
files currently in use:

```
grant codeBase "file:D:/itso/ch03/" {
    permission java.util.PropertyPermission "sun.boot.class.path", "read";
    permission java.util.PropertyPermission "user.home", "read";
    permission java.util.PropertyPermission "java.sys.class.path", "read";
};
```

where file:/D:/itso/ch03/ is the URL of the directory where
SomeProperties.class is installed.

Notice that permission to read the system property java.sys.class.path must
be granted although this system property does not exist, because the system
attempts to read it anyway; otherwise, an AccessControlException will be
thrown, as shown:

```
java.security.AccessControlException: access denied (java.util.PropertyPermission
java.sys.class.path read)
        at java.security.AccessControlContext.checkPermission(Compiled Code)
        at java.security.AccessController.checkPermission(AccessController.java:403)
        at java.lang.SecurityManager.checkPermission(SecurityManager.java:549)
        at java.lang.SecurityManager.checkPropertyAccess(SecurityManager.java:1222)
        at java.lang.System.getProperty(System.java:507)
        at SomeProperties.main(SomeProperties.java:8)
```

The following command, launched from the directory D:\itso\ch03 where the
SomeProperties class file resides, shows how it is possible to perform full
security debugging:

```
java -Djava.security.debug=all SomeProperties > Output.txt 2> SecurityDebug.txt
```

Launching this command will cause two text files to be created: Output.txt,
which will contain the normal output of the program as shown above, and
SecurityDebug.txt, which is the file containing all the security debugging
information. We show the contents of SecurityDebug.txt in the two following
figures:

```
scl:  getPermissions (file:/D:/itso/ch03/ <no certificates>)
policy: reading file:D:/Program Files/JavaSoft/JRE/1.2/lib/security/java.policy
policy: Adding policy entry:
policy:    signedBy null
policy:    codeBase file:D:/Program Files/JavaSoft/JRE/1.2/lib/ext/-
policy:
policy:    (java.security.AllPermission <all permissions> <all actions>)
policy:
policy: Adding policy entry:
policy:    signedBy null
```

Figure 39. (Part 1 of 3). Security Debug Information

```
policy:    codeBase null
policy:
policy:    (java.lang.RuntimePermission stopThread )
policy:    (java.net.SocketPermission localhost:1024- listen,resolve)
policy:    (java.util.PropertyPermission java.version read)
policy:    (java.util.PropertyPermission java.vendor read)
policy:    (java.util.PropertyPermission java.vendor.url read)
policy:    (java.util.PropertyPermission java.class.version read)
policy:    (java.util.PropertyPermission os.name read)
policy:    (java.util.PropertyPermission os.version read)
policy:    (java.util.PropertyPermission os.arch read)
policy:    (java.util.PropertyPermission file.separator read)
policy:    (java.util.PropertyPermission path.separator read)
policy:    (java.util.PropertyPermission line.separator read)
policy:    (java.util.PropertyPermission java.specification.version read)
policy:    (java.util.PropertyPermission java.spccification.vendor read)
policy:    (java.util.PropertyPermission java.specification.name read)
policy:    (java.util.PropertyPermission java.vm.specification.version read)
policy:    (java.util.PropertyPermission java.vm.specification.vendor read)
policy:    (java.util.PropertyPermission java.vm.specification.name read)
policy:    (java.util.PropertyPermission java.vm.version read)
policy:    (java.util.PropertyPermission java.vm.vendor read)
policy:    (java.util.PropertyPermission java.vm.name read)
policy:
policy: reading file:C:/WINNT/Profiles/pistoia.000/.java.policy
policy: error parsing file:C:/WINNT/Profiles/pistoia.000/.java.policy
policy: java.io.FileNotFoundException: C:\WINNT\Profiles\pistoia.000\.java.policy (The system cannot
    find the file specified)
java.io.FileNotFoundException: C:\WINNT\Profiles\pistoia.000\.java.policy (The system cannot find the
    file specified)
        at java.io.FileInputStream.open(Native Method)
        at java.io.FileInputStream.<init>(FileInputStream.java:68)
        at sun.security.provider.PolicyFile.getInputStream(PolicyFile.java:544)
        at sun.security.provider.PolicyFile.init(PolicyFile.java:508)
        at sun.security.provider.PolicyFile.initPolicyFile(PolicyFile.java:352)
        at sun.security.provider.PolicyFile.access$0(PolicyFile.java:285)
        at sun.security.provider.PolicyFile$1.run(PolicyFile.java:225)
        at java.security.AccessController.doPrivileged(Native Method)
        at sun.security.provider.PolicyFile.init(PolicyFile.java:223)
        at sun.security.provider.PolicyFile.getPermissions(PolicyFile.java:791)
        at sun.security.provider.PolicyPermissions.init(PolicyFile.java:1082)
        at sun.security.provider.PolicyPermissions.toString(PolicyFile.java:1101)
        at java.lang.String.valueOf(String.java:1911)
        at java.lang.StringBuffer.append(StringBuffer.java:365)
        at java.security.SecureClassLoader.getProtectionDomain(SecureClassLoader.java:148)
        at java.security.SecureClassLoader.defineClass(SecureClassLoader.java:101)
        at java.net.URLClassLoader.defineClass(URLClassLoader.java:248)
        at java.net.URLClassLoader.access$1(URLClassLoader.java:216)
        at java.net.URLClassLoader$1.run(URLClassLoader.java:197)
        at java.security.AccessController.doPrivileged(Native Method)
        at java.net.URLClassLoader.findClass(URLClassLoader.java:191)
        at java.lang.ClassLoader.loadClass(ClassLoader.java:280)
        at sun.misc.Launcher$AppClassLoader.loadClass(Launcher.java:275)
        at java.lang.ClassLoader.loadClass(ClassLoader.java:237)
policy: evaluate((file:/D:/itso/ch03/ <no certificates>))
policy:    granting (java.lang.RuntimePermission stopThread )
policy:    granting (java.net.SocketPermission localhost:1024- listen,resolve)
policy:    granting (java.util.PropertyPermission java.version read)
```

Figure 40. (Part 2 of 3). Security Debug Information

```
policy:    granting (java.util.PropertyPermission java.vendor read)
policy:    granting (java.util.PropertyPermission java.vendor.url read)
policy:    granting (java.util.PropertyPermission java.class.version read)
policy:    granting (java.util.PropertyPermission os.name read)
policy:    granting (java.util.PropertyPermission os.version read)
policy:    granting (java.util.PropertyPermission os.arch read)
policy:    granting (java.util.PropertyPermission file.separator read)
policy:    granting (java.util.PropertyPermission path.separator read)
policy:    granting (java.util.PropertyPermission line.separator read)
policy:    granting (java.util.PropertyPermission java.specification.version read)
policy:    granting (java.util.PropertyPermission java.specification.vendor read)
policy:    granting (java.util.PropertyPermission java.specification.name read)
policy:    granting (java.util.PropertyPermission java.vm.specification.version read)
policy:    granting (java.util.PropertyPermission java.vm.specification.vendor read)
policy:    granting (java.util.PropertyPermission java.vm.specification.name read)
policy:    granting (java.util.PropertyPermission java.vm.version read)
policy:    granting (java.util.PropertyPermission java.vm.vendor read)
policy:    granting (java.util.PropertyPermission java.vm.name read)
scl:    java.security.Permissions@f939d51d (
 (java.io.FilePermission \D:\SG24-2109-01\itso\ch03\- read)
 (java.net.SocketPermission localhost:1024- listen,resolve)
 (java.util.PropertyPermission java.specification.name read)
 (java.util.PropertyPermission java.version read)
 (java.util.PropertyPermission java.specification.version read)
 (java.util.PropertyPermission java.vm.vendor read)
 (java.util.PropertyPermission java.vm.specification.version read)
 (java.util.PropertyPermission os.arch read)
 (java.util.PropertyPermission java.vendor.url read)
 (java.util.PropertyPermission line.separator read)
 (java.util.PropertyPermission os.name read)
 (java.util.PropertyPermission java.vendor read)
 (java.util.PropertyPermission java.vm.specification.vendor read)
 (java.util.PropertyPermission java.specification.vendor read)
 (java.util.PropertyPermission java.vm.name read)
 (java.util.PropertyPermission java.vm.specification.name read)
 (java.util.PropertyPermission java.class.version read)
 (java.util.PropertyPermission os.version read)
 (java.util.PropertyPermission java.vm.version read)
 (java.util.PropertyPermission path.separator read)
 (java.util.PropertyPermission file.separator read)
 (java.lang.RuntimePermission stopThread )
 (java.lang.RuntimePermission exitVM )
)

scl:
```

Figure 41. (Part 3 of 3). Security Debug Information

As you can see, due to the `-Djava.security.debug=all` option given during the run-time command, an entire step-by-step security debug history is produced. This output would be printed on the screen if we had not redirected it to the SecurityDebug.txt file.

The output shown in the two figures above is produced with a security policy determined only by the default system-wide policy file, the same shown in Figure 36 on page 96 and Figure 37 on page 97.

The first step the system performs when running a program is to load classes. The sequence of loading classes was seen in 3.5, "Java 2 Class Loading Mechanism" on page 89. The classes in the system class path are first loaded without checking for their protection domains since these classes are shipped with the JVM and are supposed to be trusted. Next, in the sequence of class loading, are the classes in the extensions directories, specified by the java.ext.dirs system variable. Finally the classes specified by the value of java.class.path, which gives the application class path, are loaded.

These classes have to be assigned to their protection domains. Hence the getPermissions() method of SecureClassLoader is invoked. The argument passed to the getPermissions() method is the code source of the SomeProperties class.

In general, the getPermissions() method returns an object of type PermissionCollection, which is a list of all the permissions given to the code source supplied as argument to getPermissions(). To get the PermissionCollection object, the security policy files that specify the permissions to be granted to a given code source are examined. The security properties file used in this example is the same default properties file java.security that comes with the installation of the Java 2 SDK. The locations of the policy files in the preference order it gives are:

```
policy.url.1=file:${java.home}/lib/security/java.policy
policy.url.2=file:${user.home}/.java.policy
```

The policy file located at file:${java.home}/lib/security/java.policy is accessed first. Then the policy file specified at file:${user.home}/.java.policy is accessed. The second file, .java.policy, is a user-defined policy file, which can be written by the user to specify more information on permissions. Note that it is not installed by default; rather, users must create it explicitly.

In this case, the file has not been explicitly created. Therefore in the debug history, we see that the file ${user.home}/.java.policy is not found during run-time. Once the security policy file has been found, the permissions granted for different code sources are evaluated. The protection domain for the classes in the extensions directories and application class path are assigned, then the final set of permissions for those classes are listed.

The program is executed successfully because the classes in the application class path (which is the current directory D:\itso\ch03) have the permissions to access all the resources required to execute the program.

3.9 Summary

This first part of the book has been a tour through the many aspects of Java security. You should now have a good high-level understanding of the issues involved and the mechanisms that are at work. In the next section we look under the covers, at the detailed operation of the JVM and the security classes.

Part 2. Under the Hood

Chapter 4. The Java Virtual Machine

This part of the book is aimed primarily at people who wish to understand the inner workings of the Java 2 security model.

Understanding how the various components of the Java Virtual Machine (JVM) cooperate to provide a secure execution environment will enable you to understand how to administer your own security policy using the new features of Java 2 and to know when you should consider implementing your own extensions to provide a more tailored security policy.

4.1 The Java Virtual Machine, Close Up

Later chapters examine in detail the key components of the JVM involved in providing a secure environment. In this chapter we identify and introduce those components.

The following figure shows a simplified representation of the JVM:

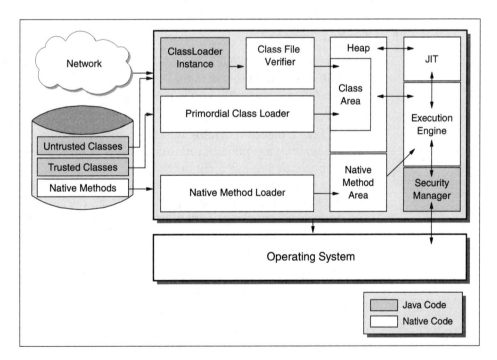

Figure 42. Components of the JVM

The JVM components that play a role in the security framework are the class loader, class file verifier and security manager.

4.1.1 The Class Loader

Before the JVM can run a Java program, it needs to locate and load the classes which comprise that program into memory. In a traditional execution environment, this service is provided by the operating system which loads code from the file system in a platform-specific way.

The operating system has access to all of the low level I/O functions and has a set of locations on the file system which it searches for programs or shared code libraries. Depending on the operating system, this can be a list of directories to look in using environment variables, such as Path and CLASSPATH, or a LINKLIST, which is included in each executable that specifies where to find components.

In the Java run-time environment things are more complicated by the fact that not all class files are loaded from the same type of location and may not be under the local operating system's control to ensure integrity. However, in general, classes can be divided into two categories, trusted and untrusted.

- **Trusted Classes**

  Trusted classes are class files that the JVM can assume are well behaved and safe. By making this assumption, the JVM can execute these classes more quickly because the verification and authorization steps can be skipped.

  On the Java 2 platform, where increased security is one of the main goals, the classes that are considered trusted have been restricted even further than in previous releases. By default, Java 2 considers only the Java Runtime Environment (JRE) classes to be fully trusted. These are the classes found in the boot class path. All others are subject to verification and permission checking. These are the classes that form the JVM's base functionality. They are shipped with the JVM implementation and are defined in the Java specification.

  In reality, Java 2 uses an internal list of directories (boot class path) to look in for these classes. We will look more at this in 6.1.1, "Loading Classes from Trusted Sources" on page 146.

  In previous releases, this list was the CLASSPATH environment variable and all classes found in this path setting were considered trusted and treated the same as the JRE core classes, unless, of course, an application explicitly changed this policy with its own SecurityManager implementation.

- **Untrusted Classes**

  With Java 2, all local files outside the boot class path are not automatically treated as trusted, neither are files loaded from a network source such as a remote Web server. This simply means these class files will be verified by the class file verifier upon loading and the code will be subjected to the security policy. The permission structure is quite granular in Java 2 (see 3.2.3, "The Fine-Grained Access Control of Java 2" on page 74). There are, in effect, levels, or more precisely groups, of trust (or untrust). This grouping is the foundation for protection domains (see 3.3, "Java 2 Protection Domain and Permissions Model" on page 80).

  For instance, Java 2 supports a new extension class framework. This framework allows the group of classes in the extensions directory (see 3.4.2, "Extensions Framework" on page 86 and 6.1.2, "Loading Classes from Untrusted Sources" on page 147) to be treated as extensions to the JVM core classes. These classes are subjected to verification and the security policy, but the default policy is AllPermission, as shown below in the lines extracted from the java.policy file that comes with the installation of the Java 2 SDK, Standard Edition, V1.2:

  ```
  grant codeBase "file:${java.home}/lib/ext/-" {
    permission java.security.AllPermission;
  };
  ```

With many possible sources for class files and the different checks required, different mechanisms are required to locate and load classes.

The ClassLoader class, in the package java.lang, is an abstract class and until Java 2 there was not a concrete implementation of a ClassLoader shipped with the JDK.

Prior to Java 2, application writers, such as Web browser manufacturers, were required to implement any class loading requirements beyond those the JVM's internal class loader would provide. This internal loader would have loaded classes from the local file system from locations specified by the CLASSPATH system environment variable.

Beginning with Java 2, the internal loader is restricted to handling only the JVM's core and extension classes. A new class, SecureClassLoader, in the package java.security, extends ClassLoader to provide function to build the protection domains for a class. Another new class, java.net.URLClassLoader, extends SecureClassLoader to provide a general purpose class loader to load class files from a list of local file directories or HTTP-based URLs.

Application developers using Java 2 still have a great deal of flexibility in implementing their class loading and security requirements, but can now also take advantage of a lot of function and a robust and flexible security model built into the JDK.

4.1.2 The Class File Verifier

Some of the class files loaded by the JVM will come from untrusted sources. These files need to be checked prior to execution to ensure that they do not threaten the integrity of the JVM. The class file verifier is invoked by the class loader to perform a series of tests on class files which are regarded as potentially unsafe.

These tests check all aspects of a class file from its size and structure down to its run-time characteristics. Only when these tests have been passed is the file made available for use.

4.1.3 The Heap

The heap is an area of memory used by the JVM to store Java objects during the execution of a program. Precisely how objects are stored on the heap is implementation specific and this adds another level of security since it means that a hacker can have no idea of how the JVM represents objects in memory. This in turn makes it far more difficult to mount an attack that depends on accessing memory directly.

One of the interesting features of the JVM design is that as objects are no longer needed, they are automatically marked for *garbage collection* and at some point the memory they occupied is freed up and made available for reuse.

4.1.4 The Class Area

The *class area* is where the JVM stores class-specific information such as static methods and static fields. When a class is loaded and has been verified, the JVM creates an entry in the class area for that class.

Often the class area is simply a part of the heap. In this case classes may also be garbage collected once they are no longer used. Alternatively, if the JVM implementation places the class area in a separate part of memory, it will require additional logic on the part of the JVM implementer to clean up classes which are not being used.

When a just-in-time (JIT) compiler is present, the native code generated for class methods is also stored in the class area.

4.1.5 The Native Method Loader

Many of the core Java classes, such as those classes representing GUI elements or networking features, require native-code implementations to access the underlying operating system functions. These native methods are composed of a Java wrapper – which specifies the method signature – and a native-code implementation – often a DLL or shared library.

The *native method loader* is responsible for locating and loading these shared libraries into the JVM. Note that it is not possible for the JVM to perform any validation or verification of native code.

Once native code has been loaded, it is stored in the native method area for speedy access when required.

4.1.6 The Security Manager

Even when untrusted code has been verified, it is still subject to run-time restrictions. The security manager is responsible for enforcing these restrictions. It is the security manager component, of a Web browser's JVM for instance, that prevents applets from reading or writing to the file system, accessing the network in an unsafe way, making inquiries about the run-time environment, printing and so on.

Prior to Java 2, in an application such as a Web browser, the security manager was provided by the application manufacturer as part of the application.

In Java 2, the manufacturer now has an alternative. He can choose to use the policy based SecurityManager implementation provided with the JDK and supply policy information to be added to the policy database. The manufacturer can still provide his own security manager, if he so chooses, adding to or replacing function supplied by the JDK's SecurityManager.

4.1.7 The Execution Engine

The *execution engine* is the heart of the JVM. It is the virtual processor which executes bytecode. Memory management, thread management and calls to native methods are also performed by the execution engine.

4.1.8 Just-in-Time Compilers

Since Java bytecodes are interpreted at run time in the execution engine, Java programs generally execute more slowly than the equivalent native platform code. This performance overhead occurs because each bytecode instruction must be translated into one or more native instructions each time it is encountered.

The performance of Java is still significantly better than that of other interpreted languages because the bytecode instructions were designed to be very low level – the simplest instructions have a one-to-one correlation with native machine code instructions.

Nevertheless, Sun saw that there would be a need to improve the execution performance of Java and to do so in a way which did not compromise the *Write Once, Run Anywhere* goal and did not undermine the security of the JVM.

Since all bytecode instructions are ultimately translated to native machine code by the JVM interpreter, the principal ways of speeding performance involve making this translation as quick as possible and performing it as few times as possible.

The security and portability of Java is dependent on the bytecode and class file format. This is what enables code to be run on any JVM and to be rigorously tested to ensure that it is safe prior to execution. Translating bytecode into native machine code and producing an executable file as happens with other programming languages would compromise the security and portability of Java. Thus, any translation must occur after a class file has been loaded and verified.

Two options present themselves:

1. Translate the whole class file into native code as soon as it is loaded and verified.

2. Translate the class file on a method-by-method basis as needed.

The first option seems quite attractive but it is possible that many of the methods in a class file will never be executed. Time to translate these methods is therefore wasted. The second option was the one selected by Sun. In this case, the first time a method is called, it is translated into native code, which is then stored in the class area. The class specification is updated so that future calls to the method run the native code rather than the original bytecode.

This meets our requirement that bytecode should be translated as few times as is necessary – once when the code is executed and not at all in the case of code which is not executed.

The process of translating the bytecode to native code on the fly is known as *JIT compilation* and performed by the JIT compiler. Sun provided a specification for how and when JIT compilers should execute and vendors were left to implement their own JIT compilers as they chose.

JIT-compiled code executes much more quickly than regular bytecode – between 10 to 50 times faster – without impacting portability or security.

4.2 Summary

You now have a good idea of how the various components of the JVM work together. The next chapters examine the principle elements of the Java security architecture – the class file structure, the class loader, the bytecode verifier and the security manager – in greater detail.

Chapter 5. Class Files in Java 2

In this chapter we explore a number of topics:

- The relationship between Java class files and conventional object and executable files
- The threat presented by the class file format
- How bytecodes aid security

In addition, we show you:

- A description of the contents of a Java class file
- A description of the ways to reduce the threat of decompilation

5.1 The Traditional Development Life Cycle

As you have seen earlier, Java is a compiled language. That is, source code is written in a high-level language and then converted through a process of compilation to a machine-level language, the Java bytecode, which then runs on the Java Virtual Machine (JVM). Before we look more closely at Java bytecode, we will quickly review the differences between high- and low-level languages, the compilation process and run-time behavior of a more traditional environment.

Program files are recognized in different ways depending on the operating environment. On most desktop operating systems, program files are recognized first by the file extension (such as exe or com) and secondly by the file format itself. Executable files contain information in a header which informs the operating system that this file is a program and has certain requirements in order to run. These requirements include such things as the address at which the program should be loaded, other supporting files which will be required and so on.

When the operating system attempts to run a program file, it loads the file and ensures that the header is legitimate, that is, that it describes a real program. The header also indicates where the starting point of the program itself is. The program is stored in the program file as machine code instructions. These instructions are numeric values which are read and interpreted by the processor as it executes. Having validated the header, the operating system starts executing the code at the indicated starting point.

From the above description, it should be clear that anyone with a good understanding of the header format and of the machine code for a particular operating system could construct a program file using little more than an editor capable of producing binary files.

Of course this is not how programs are produced. The closest that anyone gets to this is writing assembler code. Assembler language programming is very low-level. Its statements, after macro expansion, usually translate into one or at most two machine language instructions. The assembler source code is then fed through an assembler which converts the (almost) human readable code into machine code, generates the appropriate header and finally outputs an executable file.

Most programs, however, are written in a high-level language such as C, C++, COBOL and so forth. It is the task of the compiler to translate high-level instructions into low-level machine code in the most optimal way. The resultant machine code output is generally very efficient, although – depending on the compiler – it may be possible to write more efficiently in assembler language. Because different compilers manage the translation and optimization process in different ways, they will produce different output for the same source code. In general it is true to say that the higher level the source language, the more scope there is for variation in the resultant executable file since there will be more possible translations of each high-level statement into low-level machine code.

During the compilation process, high-level features such as variable and function names are replaced by references to addresses in memory and by machine code instructions, which cause the appropriate address to be accessed (in the case of variables) or jumped to (in the case of functions).

In the case of both assembler language and high-level language programming, the output of the assembler or compilation phase is generally not immediately executable. Instead, an intermediate file (known as an object module or object file[1]) is produced. One object file is produced for each source file compiled, regardless of the content or structure of the source code. These object modules are then combined using a tool called a linker which is responsible for producing the final executable file (or shared library). The linker ensures that references to a function or variable in one object module from another object module are correctly resolved.

---

[1] An unfortunate nomenclature and nothing at all to do with object-oriented programming. If the source file is the subject of the compilation process then the resultant file must be the object.

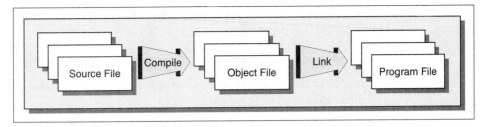

Figure 43. Program Compilation and Linking

In summary then:

- An object file contains the machine code which is the actual program plus some additional information describing any dependencies on other object files.

- An executable file is a collection of object files with all inter-file dependencies resolved, together with some header information which identifies the file as executable.

5.2 The Java Development Life Cycle

Moving back to the world of Java, we see that it is a high-level programming language and that bytecode is the low-level machine language of the JVM. Java is an object-oriented language; that is, it deals primarily with objects and their interrelationships. Objects are best thought of in this context as a collection of data (*fields*, in Java parlance) and the functions (*methods*) which operate on that data. Objects are created at run time based on templates (*classes*) defined by the programmer.

A Java source file may contain definitions for one or more classes. During compilation each of these classes results in the generation of a single class file. In some respects, the class file is the Java equivalent of an object module rather than an executable program file; that is, it contains compiled machine code, but may also contain references to methods and fields which exist in other classes and hence in other class files.

Class files are the last stage of the development process in Java. There is no separate link phase. Linking is performed at run time by the JVM. If a reference is found within one class file to another, then the JVM loads the referenced class file and resolves the references as needed.

The astute reader will deduce that this demand loading and linking requires the class file to contain information about other class files, methods and fields which it references, and in particular, the names of these files, fields and methods. This is in fact the case as we shall see in 5.3, "The Java 2 Class File Format" on page 124.

Even more astute readers may be pondering some of the following questions.

- Is it possible to compile Java source code to some machine language other than that of the JVM?
- Is it possible to compile some other high-level language to bytecode for the JVM?
- Is there such a thing as an assembler for Java?
- What is the relationship between the Java language and bytecode?

The simple answer to the first three questions is yes.

It is possible with the appropriate compiler (generally referred to as a native code compiler) to translate Java source code to any other low-level machine code, although this rather defeats the *Write Once, Run Anywhere* proposition for Java programs, since the resultant executable program will only run on the platform for which it has been compiled.

It is also possible to compile other high-level languages into Java bytecode, possibly via an interim step in which the source code is translated into Java source code which is in turn compiled. Bytecode compilers already exist for Ada, COBOL, BASIC and NetREXX (a dialect of the popular REXX programming language).

Finally, Jasmin is a freely available Java assembler which allows serious geeks to write Java code at a level one step removed from bytecode. Java Grinder[2] is a another freely available Java assembler and disassembler and is very simple to use. Let's consider the following Java code:

```
import java.io.*;

public class Count
{
    public static void main(String[] args) throws Exception
    {
        int count=0;
        if (args.length >= 1)
```

Figure 44. (Part 1 of 2). Count.java

[2] Java Grinder can be downloaded from http://www-personal.umich.edu/~mcafee/java/.

```
    {
        FileInputStream fis = new FileInputStream(args[0]);
        try
        {
            while (fis.read() != -1)
                count++;
            System.out.println("Hi! We counted " + count + " chars.");
        } // try{} block ends
        catch (Exception e)
        {
            System.out.println("No characters counted");
            System.out.println("Exception caught" + e.toString());
        } // catch(){} block ends
    } // if block ends
    else
        System.err.println("Usage: Count file_name");
    } // main() method ends
} // class Count ends
```

Figure 45. (Part 2 of 2). Count.java

We compile this code using the Java compiler:

`javac Count.java`

This command produces the Count.class file. This is a simple Java program that counts the number of characters in a file. The file name is given as an argument on the command line. If the Count program is able to count the characters in the file, it prints the number of characters counted, and if not, it prints the exception. We run this program against this sample text file, called itso.txt:

```
Marco Pistoia
Duane Reller
Deepak Gupta
Milind Nagnur
Ashok Ramani
```

Figure 46. itso.txt

Both the Count.class and itso.txt files are stored in the same directory, say D:\itso\ch05, and we launch the command:

`java Count itso.txt`

This is the output we receive:

```
Hi! We counted 70 chars
```

On disassembling the class file with the freely available software Java Grinder, we get an output file, which is shown in the following figures:

```
public class Count extends Object {
        public void <init>() {
                maxstack 1
                aload_0
                invokespecial void Object.<init>()
                return
        }
        public static void main(String[]) throws Exception {
                maxstack 4
                iconst_0
                istore_1
                aload_0
                arraylength
                iconst_1
                if_icmplt label4
                new FileInputStream
                dup
                aload_0
                iconst_0
                aaload
                invokespecial void FileInputStream.<init>(String)
                astore_2
                try // catch1
                goto label2
label1:         iinc 1 1
label2:         aload_2
                invokevirtual int FileInputStream.read()
                iconst_m1
                if_icmpne label1
                getstatic PrintStream System.out
                new StringBuffer
                dup
                ldc "Hi! We counted "
                invokespecial void StringBuffer.<init>(String)
                iload_1
                invokevirtual StringBuffer StringBuffer.append(int)
                ldc " chars."
```

Figure 47. (Part 1 of 2). Disassembled Count.class File

```
                    invokevirtual StringBuffer StringBuffer.append(String)
                    invokevirtual String StringBuffer.toString()
                    invokevirtual void PrintStream.println(String)
catch1:             catch Exception:label3
                    goto label5
label3:             astore_3
                    getstatic PrintStream System.out
                    ldc "No characters counted"
                    invokevirtual void PrintStream.println(String)
                    getstatic PrintStream System.out
                    new StringBuffer
                    dup
                    ldc "Exception caught"
                    invokespecial void StringBuffer.<init>(String)
                    aload_3
                    invokevirtual String Throwable.toString()
                    invokevirtual StringBuffer StringBuffer.append(String)
                    invokevirtual String StringBuffer.toString()
                    invokevirtual void PrintStream.println(String)
                    goto label5
label4:             getstatic PrintStream System.err
                    ldc "Usage: Count file_name"
                    invokevirtual void PrintStream.println(String)
label5:             return
          }
    }
```

Figure 48. (Part 2 of 2). Disassembled Count.class File

On assembling it again, we get the same functioning as the original class file.

Notice that even if someone changes your code by simply changing the message:

```
Hi! We counted count chars
```

to something undesirable like:

```
Hi! Guess what else I did to this program
```

the result can be disturbing. It is possible to manipulate it even further and add statements that can vary from serious things like reading files from your system to merely annoying things like throwing up continuous messages. Class files are most vulnerable when they are in transit along the information superhighway. There are ways to help prevent or at least detect this tampering. The Java 2 SDK provides tools for sealing classes in JAR files, as

we will see in 12.1.1, "Manifest File" on page 387 and 12.6, "The JAR Bug –
Fixed In Java 2 SDK, Standard Edition, V1.2.1" on page 461.

The following figure gives a pictorial model of how different languages, such
as COBOL, C++, NetREXX and Java, are compiled in different ways, as we
discussed in 5.1, "The Traditional Development Life Cycle" on page 117:

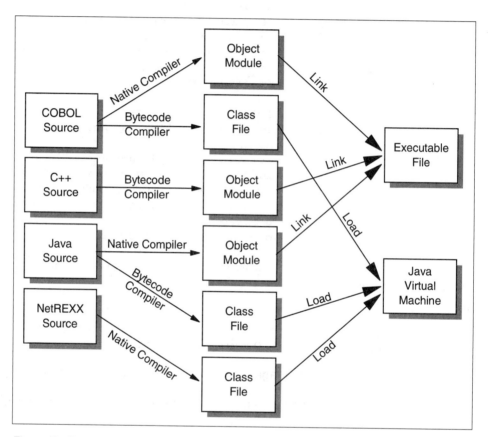

Figure 49. Compiler Models

5.3 The Java 2 Class File Format

The class file contains a lot more information than its cousin, the executable
file. Of course, it still contains the same type of information: program
requirements, an identifier indicating that this is a program and executable
code (bytecode, in this case). However, it also contains some very rich
information about the original source code.

The high level structure of a class file is shown in the following table:

Table 2. Class File Contents

Field	Description
Magic number	Four bytes identifying this file as a Java class file. Always set to 0xCAFEBABE
JVM minor version	The minor version number of the JVM on which this class file is intended to run
JVM major version	The major version number of the JVM on which this class file is intended to run
Constant pool count	Number of entries in Constant Pool Table
Constant pool	See 5.4, "The Constant Pool" on page 129
Access flags	Mask of modifiers used with class and interface declaration
Class name	The name of this class
Super class name	The name of the superclass in the Java class hierarchy
Interfaces count	Number of direct super interfaces
Interfaces	Description of the interfaces implemented for this class
Fields count	Number of structures in the fields table
Fields	Description of the class variables defined for this class
Methods count	Number of structures in the methods table
Methods	Description of the methods declared by this class
Attributes count	Number of attributes in the attributes table
Attributes	Attributes associated with the class file

Much here is as we would expect. There is information to identify the file as a Java class file, as well as the JVM on which it was compiled to run. In addition, there is information describing the dependencies of this class in terms of classes, interfaces[3], fields, and methods. There is much more information than this however, buried within the constant pool (see 5.4, "The Constant Pool" on page 129): information which includes variable and method names within both this class file and those on which it depends.

Let's explain in more detail the fields listed in Table 2:

---

[3] Each Java class has only a single *superclass*, and it inherits variables and methods from that superclass and all its superclasses. This limitation makes the relationship between classes easy to understand and design, but it can also be restrictive. To solve this problem, Java introduces the concept of interfaces, which collect method names (not implementations) into one place, and then allow you to add those methods as a group to the various classes that need them.

- The *magic number* is a hexadecimal number identifying the class format and is always 0xCAFEBABE[4].

- The values of *minor version* and *major version* are the minor and major versions of the compiler that produced this class.

- The *constant pool* is a table of variable length structures representing various string constants, class names, field names, and other constants that are referred to.

- The *access flag* is a mask of modifiers used with the class and interface declarations (for example, ACC_PUBLIC for public class or interface, ACC_FINAL for a final class etc. – see 2.1.1.2, "Access to Classes, Fields and Methods" on page 42).

- The *interfaces* field is an array of entries describing the interfaces implemented by the class.

- The *fields* field is an array of entries describing the class variables declared by this class or interface. It does not include those inherited.

- The *methods* field is an array of entries describing the methods declared by this class or interface.

- The only attribute defined for the *attributes* table is SourceFile, which indicates the name of the source file from which the class was created.

In addition to managing dynamic linking, the JVM must also ensure that class files contain only legal bytecode and do not attempt to subvert the run-time environment, and to do this, still more information is required in the class. More details of how this works are in Chapter 6, "The Class Loader and Class File Verifier" on page 145.

The main thing to understand at this point is that the inclusion of all of this information makes the job of a hacker much simpler in many ways. We discuss this in the next section.

5.3.1 Decompilation Attacks

One of the areas seldom discussed when considering security implications of deploying Java is that of securing Java assets. Often considerable effort is put into developing software and the resultant intellectual property can be very valuable to a company.

Hackers are a clever (although potentially misguided) bunch and there are many reasons why they might want to get *inside* your code. Here are a few:

---

[4] Just out of curiosity, 0xCAFEBABE corresponds to the decimal number 3405691582.

- To steal a valuable algorithm for use in their own code

- To understand how a security function works to enable them to bypass it

- To extract confidential information (such as hard-coded passwords and keys)

- To enable them to alter the code so that it behaves in a malicious way (such as installing Trojan horses or viruses)

- To demonstrate their prowess

- For their entertainment (much as other people might solve crosswords)

The chief tool in the arsenal of the hacker in these cases is the decompiler. A *decompiler*, as its name suggests, undoes the work performed by a compiler. That is, it takes an executable file and attempts to re-create the original source code.

Advances in compiler technology now make it effectively impossible to go from machine code to a high-level language such as C. Modern compilers remove all variable and function names, move code about to optimize its execution profile and, as was discussed previously, there are many possible ways to translate a high-level statement into a low-level machine code representation. For a decompiler, to produce the original source code is impossible without a lot of additional information which simply is not shipped in an executable file.

It *is*, however, very easy to recover an assembler language version of the program. On the other hand, the amount of effort required to actually understand what such a program does makes it far less worthwhile to the hacker to do.[5] So, it is fair to say that it is impossible to completely protect any program from tampering.

When the Java Development Kit (JDK) 1.0.2 was shipped, a decompiler named Mocha was quickly available which performed excellently. It was able to recover Java source code from a class file. It was so successful that at least one person used it as a way of formatting his source code! In fact the only information lost in the compilation process (and unrecoverable using Mocha) are the comments. However, if meaningful variable names are used in the code (such as `accountNumber`, or `password`), then it is readily possible to understand the function of the code, even without the comments.

---

[5] Nevertheless, it is done. Much pirated software is distributed in a *cracked* format, that is, with software protection disabled or removed.

Already, there are decompilers available, like SourceAgain[6], which can decompile Java codes including those programs written with the Java 2 SDK using new APIs.

Here is what a test decompiler returned for the same Count.class file we used in 5.2, "The Java Development Life Cycle" on page 119 (the originating source code Count.java was shown in Figure 44 on page 120 and Figure 45 on page 121):

```
import java.io.FileInputStream;
import java.io.PrintStream;
public class Count
{
    public static void main(String[] as) throws Exception
    {
        int i = 0;
        if (as.length >= 1)
        {
            FileInputStream fileinputstream1 = new FileInputStream (as[0]);
            try
            {
            while (fileinputstream1.read() != -1)
                ++i;
                System.out.println ("Hi! We counted " + i + " chars.");
            }
            catch(Exception exception1)
            {
                System.out.println("No characters counted");
                System.out.println("Exception caught" + exception1.toString());
            }
        }
        else
            System.err.println("Usage: Count file_name");
    }
}
```

Figure 50. Decompiled Count.class

You can see that the code has been successfully decompiled. Only small things like the name of the variables are changed.

There can be some advantages of having a decompiler:

1. Recovery of lost source code (by accident or otherwise)

[6] See http://www.ahpah.com/product.html.

2. Migration of applications to a new hardware platform

3. Translation of code written in obsolete languages not supported by compiler tools nowadays

4. Determination of the existence of viruses or malicious code in the program

5. Recovery of someone else's source code (to determine an algorithm for example)

As long as you are decompiling your own code with your own decompiler or a freely available one, you are safe. But once you decompile someone else's code, there may be legal and moral issues. Many programs are protected by copyright laws and license agreements.

Should You Have a Decompiler in Your Toolkit?

If you can read Java source code, it is a good idea to have a decompiler available, to check the function of Java class files that you receive, particularly if they come from an unknown origin.

The only problem with this is that you are stepping into a legal and moral mine field. Decompilers are downloadable from a number of sources and also are in some commercial Java development packages. However there have been strong attempts to prevent them being available in this way, because it allows unscrupulous people to steal the source code of proprietary products.

The authorsí view is that, until verifiable Java is more generally available, there is a place for the decompiler as a tool for checking what is really going on inside a class file.

5.4 The Constant Pool

We said earlier that the constant pool contains a great deal of information. In fact it contains an interesting mixture of items. The constant pool combines the function of a symbol table for linking purposes as well as a repository for constant values and string literals present in the source code. It may be considered as an array of heterogeneous data types which are referenced by index number from other sections of the class file such as the Field and Method sections. In addition, many Java bytecode instructions take as arguments numbers which are in turn used as indexes into the constant pool.

The following table shows the types of entries in the constant pool, as defined by the current JVM:

Table 3. Constant Pool Entry Types

Type names	Used for...	Contains...
UTF8	String in UTF8 format[a]	An array of bytes making up the string
Integer	A constant 32-bit signed integer value	The numeric value of the integer
Long	A constant 64-bit signed integer value	The numeric value of the long
Float	A constant 32-bit floating point value	The numeric value of the float
Double	A constant 64-bit double precision floating point value	The numeric value of the double
String	A Java string literal	Reference to the UTF8 representation of the string
ClassRef	Symbolic reference to a class	Reference to a UTF8 representation of the class name
FieldRef	Symbolic reference to a field	Reference to a ClassRef for the class in which the field occurs and a NameAndType for this field
MethodRef	Symbolic reference to a method	Reference to a ClassRef for the class in which the method occurs and a NameAndType for this method
InterfaceMethodRef	Symbolic reference to an interface method	Reference to a ClassRef for the interface in which the field occurs and a NameAndType for this method
NameAndType	Shorthand representation of a field or method signature and name	Reference to a UTF8 representation of the name and another to the signature[b]

a. A shorthand for writing Unicode strings.
b. The *signature of a field* is simply its type. The *signature of a method* is both its return type and the types of any parameters which it takes. Method signatures are represented by a pair of parentheses with the parameter types enclosed and separated by semicolons. The parentheses are followed by the return type of the method. See Appendix B, "Signature Formats" on page 681, for a full description of Java type representations.

As an example of a constant pool, let's take a look at the PointlessButton example we met in Appendix 2.1.1.1, "Class Consciousness" on page 36 (the source code PointlessButton.java is shown in Figure 17 on page 37). The following table shows a dump of the constant pool for the PointlessButton class:

Table 4. Constant Pool Example

Index	Type	Value
1	UTF8	`bytes = "PointlessButton"`
2	Class	`name = (1) "PointlessButton"`
3	UTF8	`bytes = "java/applet/Applet"`
4	Class	`name = (3) "java/applet/Applet"`
13	NameAndType	`name = (8) "donowt", type = (7) "Ljamjar/examples/Button;"`
14	FieldRef	`class = (2) "PointlessButton", name and type = (13) "donowt", "Ljamjar/examples/Button;"`
17	UTF8	`bytes = "Did Nothing "`
18	String	`value = (17) "Did Nothing "`
24	MethodRef	`class = (20) "java/lang/String", name and type = (23) "valueOf", "(Ljava/lang/Object;)Ljava/lang/String;"`
25	UTF8	`bytes = "<init>"`
33	NameAndType	`name = (31) "append", type = (32) "(I)Ljava/lang/StringBuffer;"`
34	MethodRef	`class = (16) "java/lang/StringBuffer", name and type = (33) "append", "(I)Ljava/lang/StringBuffer;"`
52	MethodRef	`class = (49) "java/awt/Button", name and type = (51) "setLabel", "(Ljava/lang/String;)V"`
53	UTF8	`bytes = "Code"`
54	UTF8f	`bytes = "()V"`
55	NameAndType	`name = (25) "<init>", type = (54) "()V"`
56	MethodRef	`class = (4) "java/applet/Applet", name and type = (55) "<init>", "()V"value = (37) " times"`

The full table has 83 entries, not bad for such a simple program. Looking at this data you can see that there is a wealth of information here.

As an example of how a method is represented, let's look at entry number 56. This is a MethodRef entry and as such it has two further references to track down:

1. The first is the Class entry (4), which in turn references a UTF8 entry (3) for the class name: java.applet.Applet.

2. The second is the NameAndType entry, which identifies the method name and the type of the method. The NameAndType entry (55) references a UTF8 entry (25) for the method name <init>, and another UTF8 entry (54) for the type ()v.

   The name used here is a little special: <init> is not a valid name in itself, but it is used by the JVM to represent a constructor for a class. The type entry ()v indicates a method which takes no parameters (empty parentheses) and returns no value (v following the parentheses indicates a return type of void - Java's term for no value). These details are explained in Appendix B, "Signature Formats" on page 681.

From this little jaunt through the constant pool we see that the PointlessButton class calls the java.applet.Applet default constructor. Following a similar process, we can identify all of the other fields and methods utilized in this class. Furthermore, by finding where entry number 56 is referenced in the bytecode, we can build a clear picture of what this code does.

This is precisely what the javap utility, shipped with the Java 2 SDK, does. By examining the constant pool and other parts of the class file structure, it is able to produce a high-level picture of the class file. Here's the output of javap when run against PointlessButton.class with the command:

javap PointlessButton

```
Compiled from PointlessButton.java
public class PointlessButton extends java.applet.Applet implements
java.awt.event.ActionListener {
    jamjar.examples.Button donowt;
    int count;
    public PointlessButton();
    public void actionPerformed(java.awt.event.ActionEvent);
    public void init();
}
```

As we already knew, PointlessButton extends java.applet.Applet and as such it must call the Applet constructor – the method reference we saw by tracing through the constant pool.

If this were all that javap did, then it would still be a useful tool for examining class files for which we didn't have the source code in an attempt to reuse them or work out what they were doing. But it is not all. By using additional option switches it is possible to get richer information, including even the disassembled bytecode. The following is the result of running `javap` with the -c (disassemble the code) and -private (show all classes and members) options enabled:

```
Compiled from PointlessButton.java
public class PointlessButton extends java.applet.Applet implements java.awt.event.ActionListener {
    jamjar.examples.Button donowt;
    int count;
    public PointlessButton();
    public void actionPerformed(java.awt.event.ActionEvent);
    public void init();
}

Method PointlessButton()
   0 aload_0
   1 invokespecial #15 <Method java.applet.Applet()>
   4 aload_0
   5 new #8 <Class jamjar.examples.Button>
   8 dup
   9 ldc #5 <String "Do Nothing">
  11 invokespecial #17 <Method jamjar.examples.Button(java.lang.String)>
  14 putfield #24 <Field jamjar.examples.Button donowt>
  17 aload_0
  18 iconst_0
  19 putfield #23 <Field int count>
  22 return

Method void actionPerformed(java.awt.event.ActionEvent)
   0 aload_0
   1 getfield #24 <Field jamjar.examples.Button donowt>
   4 new #14 <Class java.lang.StringBuffer>
   7 dup
   8 ldc #4 <String "Did Nothing ">
  10 invokespecial #18 <Method java.lang.StringBuffer(java.lang.String)>
  13 aload_0
  14 dup
  15 getfield #23 <Field int count>
  18 iconst_1
  19 iadd
  20 dup_x1
  21 putfield #23 <Field int count>
  24 invokevirtual #21 <Method java.lang.StringBuffer append(int)>
  27 ldc #2 <String " time">
  29 invokevirtual #22 <Method java.lang.StringBuffer append(java.lang.String)>
  32 aload_0
  33 getfield #23 <Field int count>
  36 iconst_1
  37 if_icmpne 45
  40 ldc #1 <String "">
  42 goto 47
  45 ldc #6 <String "s">
  47 invokevirtual #22 <Method java.lang.StringBuffer append(java.lang.String)>
  50 invokevirtual #27 <Method java.lang.String toString()>
  53 invokevirtual #25 <Method void setLabel(java.lang.String)>
  56 return
```

Figure 51. (Part 1 of 2). Output of the javap Command with Options -c and -p

```
Method void init()

   0 aload_0
   1 new #10 <Class java.awt.BorderLayout>
   4 dup
   5 invokespecial #16 <Method java.awt.BorderLayout()>
   8 invokevirtual #26 <Method void setLayout(java.awt.LayoutManager)>
  11 aload_0
  12 ldc #3 <String "Center">
  14 aload_0
  15 getfield #24 <Field jamjar.examples.Button donowt>
  18 invokevirtual #19 <Method java.awt.Component add(java.lang.String, java.awt.Component)>
  21 pop
  22 aload_0
  23 getfield #24 <Field jamjar.examples.Button donowt>
  26 aload_0
  27 invokevirtual #20 <Method void addActionListener(java.awt.event.ActionListener)>
  30 return
```

Figure 52. (Part 2 of 2). Output of the javap Command with Options -c and -p

Here we have the complete code for all of the methods albeit in a language that we could define as *Java assembler*. By appropriate use of a binary editor it would be a relatively simple matter for a hacker to subvert the function of this code. For example, simply changing the value of the string Did Nothing in the constant pool, we could cause the button to print a rude message when pressed. This is a trivial example but hopefully illustrates the vulnerability of class files.

5.4.1 Beating the Decompilation Threat

The very real threat of decompilation is not going to go away. Decompilers work by recognizing patterns in the generated bytecode which can be translated back into Java source code statements. The field and method names required to make this source code more readable are readily available in the constant pool as we have seen.

To date, there have been two main approaches to thwarting would-be decompilers: *code obfuscation* and *bytecode hosing*[7]:

1. The principle of obscuring (or obfuscating) source code to make it more difficult to read is not new. In the UNIX world – where incompatibilities between platforms and implementations make it necessary to distribute many applications in source format – *shrouding* is common. This is the process of replacing variable names with meaningless symbols, removing comments and white space and generally leaving as little human readable content in the source code without impacting its compilability. The end result of obfuscation is that although a class file will decompile into valid

[7] For the benefit of non-US readers, if something is *hosed*, it is seriously damaged, in this case deliberately.

Java, that valid Java will not be very readable by humans. Note that although obfuscation certainly makes decompilation more difficult and the Java file not readable, it might not protect your code against a determined adversary. You can think of copyrighting your code, although it is not an ideal solution, but it is better than nothing.

After the release of Mocha, the author released Crema, a further appalling coffee pun, which was designed to thwart Mocha. It did this by replacing names in the constant pool with illegal Java variable names and reserved words (such as `if` and `class`). This had no affect on the JVM, which merely used the names as tags to resolve references without attributing any meaning to them. Nor did it actually prevent decompilation. It did however mean that the decompiled code was more difficult to read and understand and also would not recompile as the Java compiler would object to the illegal names.

2. Bytecode hosing is more subtle and is aimed at preventing the decompiler from recognizing patterns within the bytecode from which it could recover valid source. It does this by breaking up recognizable patterns of bytecodes with *do-nothing* instruction sequences (such as the NOP code or a PUSH followed by a POP). A good example of a bytecode hoser is HoseMocha.

Of course, this approach can be defeated, since once a hacker has established what types of do-nothing sequences are being generated by a bytecode hoser, he or she can modify the behavior of the decompiler to ignore such sequences. Furthermore, attempts to decompile hosed bytecode will generally result in broadly readable code interspersed with unintelligible passages rather than completely unreadable code.

In addition to this, bytecode hosers present a more insidious problem to Java users. As we have already seen in Appendix 2.1.2, "The Execution Environment" on page 44, the principal method of optimizing Java performance is in the JVM and in particular through the use of just-in-time (JIT) compilation. And how do JIT compilers work? Yes, you guessed it, they recognize patterns in the generated bytecode that can be optimized into native code. Breaking up these patterns through the use of a bytecode hoser can seriously impact the performance of JIT compilers.

For this reason, it is safe to assume that Java compilers will not follow the same evolutionary path as their native compiler cousins in terms of generating wildly differing output for the same source code since this too would thwart JIT compilers.

This is a well understood dilemma in security circles: the trade off between security and performance/price/ease-of-use.

The only safe course of action is to assume that *all* Java code will at some point be decompiled.

For developers this means ensuring that no sensitive information, like passwords or cryptographic keys, is distributed in the class file either algorithmically or as hard-coded values. This can be accomplished by building client/server type applications with a Java presentation layer which can be run anywhere and a secured server side where sensitive information or algorithms can be stored. This may also involve extending the development and testing process to ensure that distributed Java code is *safe*.

Also note that if a hacker is able to decompile your program, he can look for weaknesses in its security. This will help him in attacking your system more efficiently. Browser JVMs may become targets of such attacks.

Finally you may decide that the existing method of protecting distributed code, that of legal sanction under copyright laws, is sufficient to deal with any serious threat to Java-based intellectual property. However, in a networked environment, these assumptions cannot be made so lightly.

5.5 Java Bytecode

In the next chapter we look at how the Java class loader and class file verifier provide a level of security against rogue class files. This section prepares us for that chapter by looking more closely at bytecode.

5.5.1 A Bytecode Example

Though you may not realize it, you have already seen an example of bytecode or at least its human readable format. The output generated by the `javap` command when we ran it with the `-c` flag (see Figure 51 on page 133 and Figure 52 on page 134) contained a disassembly of each of the methods in the class file.

Let's consider now the actionPerformed() method of the PointlessButton class:

```
public void actionPerformed(java.awt.event.ActionEvent e)
{
    donowt.setLabel("Did Nothing " + ++count + " time" + (count == 1 ? "" : "s"));
}
```

We compile the PointlessButton.java file with the Java compiler `javac` and subsequently disassemble the class file with the command:

```
javap -c -private PointlessButton
```

In this process, the actionPerformed() method generates the code snippet in the following figure:

```
Method void actionPerformed(java.awt.event.ActionEvent)
   0 aload_0
   1 getfield #24 <Field jamjar.examples.Button donowt>
   4 new #14 <Class java.lang.StringBuffer>
   7 dup
   8 ldc #4 <String "Did Nothing ">
  10 invokespecial #18 <Method java.lang.StringBuffer(java.lang.String)>
  13 aload_0
  14 dup
  15 getfield #23 <Field int count>
  18 iconst_1
  19 iadd
  20 dup_x1
  21 putfield #23 <Field int count>
  24 invokevirtual #21 <Method java.lang.StringBuffer append(int)>
  27 ldc #2 <String " time">
  29 invokevirtual #22 <Method java.lang.StringBuffer append(java.lang.String)>
  32 aload_0
  33 getfield #23 <Field int count>
  36 iconst_1
  37 if_icmpne 45
  40 ldc #1 <String "">
  42 goto 47
  45 ldc #6 <String "s">
  47 invokevirtual #22 <Method java.lang.StringBuffer append(java.lang.String)>
  50 invokevirtual #27 <Method java.lang.String toString()>
  53 invokevirtual #25 <Method void setLabel(java.lang.String)>
  56 return
```

Figure 53. Disassembled actionPerformed() Method

Notice the #*n* references in the bytecode such as instruction 45:

```
45 ldc #6 <String "s">
```

The #6 reference here refers to entry number 6 in the constant pool, while the text after the #6 reference is a comment for the benefit of the reader showing that entry #36 in the constant pool is a String with value s.

The next thing that you should notice about this code is that even at this level, there are still references made to methods and fields. From this you may infer that Java is object-oriented even at the bytecode level and you would be correct.

We are not going to analyze all of this code, there are other books which serve to teach bytecode. Instead we will compare this code fragment with 80x86 equivalent code and draw some conclusions about the measures that exist within bytecode itself to protect the JVM against subversion.

Let's look at the following fragment:

```
13 aload_0
14 dup
15 getfield #23 <Field int count>
18 iconst_1
19 iadd
20 dup_x1
21 putfield #23 <Field int count>
```

The following table explains what each of these instructions does:

Table 5. Bytecode Byte-by-Byte

Instruction	Effect	Stack after instruction
aload_0	Push a copy of local variable 0 onto the stack. This variable is equivalent to the this keyword in Java source code; it holds a reference to the current object. In this case, that object is an instance of PointlessButton.	this (PointlessButton) [end of stack]
dup	Duplicates the item on the top of the stack.	this (PointlessButton) this (PointlessButton) [end of stack]
getfield #23	Pops the top item from the stack. Checks that it is a PointlessButton reference. Gets the count field with type I (integer) from it. Pushes the count field onto the stack.	this.count (int) this (PointlessButton) [end of stack]
iconst_1	Pushes the integer constant 1 onto the stack.	1 (int) this.count (int) this (PointlessButton) [end of stack]
iadd	Pops the top two values from the stack. Adds them. Pushes the result (as an integer).	this.count + 1 (int) this (PointlessButton) [end of stack]

Instruction	Effect	Stack after instruction
dup_x1	Duplicates the value on top of the stack and inserts it under the second item from the top.	this.count + 1 (int) this (PointlessButton) this.count + 1 (int) [end of stack]
putfield #23	Store the value on top of the stack in the PointlessButton.count field of the object second from the top of the stack.	this.count + 1 (int) [end of stack]

The net of this sequence of operations is to have incremented the count field of the current object by one and left a copy of it on the stack (for use in the next instruction which prints the count).

The equivalent 80x86 code looks like this:

```
MOV BX, thisPointlessButton   ; Set BX to the base address of this button
MOV SI, count_field           ; Set SI to the offset of the count in button class
MOV CX, [ BX + SI ]           ; Get the count field in register CX
INC CX                        ; increment the CX register
MOV [ BX + SI ], CX           ; Store the result in BX+SI (the count field)
```

There are a few differences here, which we will examine in turn:

- **Stack-based architecture vs register-based architecture**

  The JVM has a *stack-based* architecture. This means that its instructions deal with pushing values onto, popping values from, and manipulating values on a stack.

  The 80x86 processor range from Intel are *register-based*. They have a number of temporary storage areas (registers) some of which are general purpose, others of which have a particular function.

  The advantage of making the JVM stack-based is that it is easier to implement a stack-based architecture using registers than vice versa. Thus, porting the JVM to Intel platforms is easy compared with porting a register-based virtual machine to a stack-based hardware platform.

  In addition, there are benefits in a stack-based architecture when it comes to establishing what code actually does – more of this in the next chapter.

- **Object-oriented vs non-object-oriented**

  As we have already mentioned, the Java bytecode is object-oriented. This makes for safer code since the JVM checks at run time that the type of fields being accessed or methods invoked for an object are genuinely applicable to that object.

In the 80x86 code snippet, we have variable names to make it clearer what the code is doing, but there are no checks to make sure that the value loaded into the base register really is a pointer to an object of type PointlessButton and that the offset loaded into SI represents the count field of that object.

There is no object-level information at all stored in 80x86 machine code, regardless of the high-level language from which it was compiled!

This is so important we will restate it: even if you write programs in Java, once you compile them to 80x86 machine code, all object information is lost and with it a degree of security, since the run-time engine cannot test for the validity of method and/or field accesses.

- **Type Safety**

While on the subject of type information, a difference to notice is the inclusion of type information in JVM bytecode instructions. The instruction iadd, for example, pops the top two values from the stack, adds them and pushes the return value. The i prefix indicates that the instruction operates on and returns an integer value. The JVM will actually check that the stack contains two integers when the iadd instruction is to be executed. In fact this check is performed by the bytecode verifier, prior to run-time execution.

Contrast this with the 80x86 instructions, which contain no type information. In this case, it is possible that the data loaded into the cx register for incrementing is an integer. However, it is also possible that it is part of a telephone number, an address, or anything different. There are simply no checks performed on data type. This is fine if you can trust your compiler and there is no likelihood of programs being attacked *en route* to their execution environment. As we have seen, however, in a networked environment, these assumptions cannot be made so lightly.

Not all bytecodes are typed; with a maximum of 256 distinct bytecode values, there are simply not enough to go around. Where a bytecode instruction is typed, the type on which it can operate is indicated by the prefix of the instruction. Table 6 lists the type prefixes and Table 7 shows the bytecodes in detail:

Table 6. Type Prefixes for Bytecode

Prefix	Bytecode type
i	Integer
f	Floating point
l	Long
d	Double precision floating point
b	Byte
s	Short
c	Character
a	Object reference

Table 7. Bytecode Table

Bytecode	int	long	float	double	byte	char	short	object ref	Function
?2c	X								Convert value of type ? to character.
?2d	X	X	X						Convert value of type ? to double.
?2i		X	X	X					Convert value of type ? to integer.
?2f	X	X		X					Convert value of type ? to float.
?2l	X		X	X					Convert value of type ? to long.
?2s	X								Convert value of type ? to short.
?add	X	X	X	X					Add two values of type ?.
?aload	X	X	X	X	X	X	X	X	Push an element of type ? from an array onto the stack.
?and	X	X							Perform logical AND on two values of type ?.
?astore	X	X	X	X	X	X	X	X	Pop a type ? from the stack and store in an array of type ?.
?cmp		X							Compare two long values. If they're equal push 0, if the first is greater push 1, else push -1.

Bytecode	int	long	float	double	byte	char	short	object ref	Function
?cmpg			X	X					Compare two IEEE values of type ? from the stack. If they're equal push 0, if the first is greater push 1 if the second is greater push -1. If either is not-a-number (NaN) push 1.
?cmpl			X	X					Compare two IEEE values of type ? from the stack. If they're equal push 0, if the first is greater push 1 if the second is greater push -1. If either is NaN push 1.
?const	X	X	X	X				X	Push constant value n of type ? onto the stack.
?div	X	X	X	X					Perform a division using two values of type ? and store the quotient.
?inc	X								Increment the top of the stack (possibly by a negative value).
?ipush					X		X		Push sign extender byte or short value onto stack.
?load	X	X	X	X					Push a value of type ? from a local variable.
?mul	X	X	X	X					Perform multiplication of two values of type ?.
?neg	X	X	X	X					Negate a value of type ?.
?newarray								X	Create a new array of object references.
?or	X	X							Perform logical OR on two values of type ?.
?rem	X	X	X	X					Perform a division using two values of type ? and store the remainder.
?return	X	X	X	X				X	Return a value of type ? to the invoking method.
?shl	X	X							Perform arithmetic shift left on type ?.
?shr	X	X							Perform arithmetic shift right on type ?.
?store	X	X	X	X				X	Pop a value of type ? and store in a local variable.
?sub	X	X	X	X					Perform a subtraction using two values of type ?.

There are a few seeming anomalies about this table. For example, the ?cmp
and ?newarray instructions are typed and yet only apply to a single type (long

in the case of ?cmp and object references in the case of ?newarray).
Interestingly enough there is no equivalent of the ?cmp instruction for integers.
These oddities can be explained away in terms of future expansions to the
instruction set. However there are other peculiarities which are not as easily
explained.

Consider the fact that there are no typed arithmetic instructions for byte or
short values. This, coupled with the lack of support for short and byte values
in the constant pool, might lead you to believe that the underlying support in
the JVM for these types is less than full. You would be right.

The JVM's processor stack is 32 bits wide. Values which are longer (doubles
or longs) or shorter (bytes or shorts) than this are treated specially within the
JVM. Double and long values occupy two spaces each on the stack and thus
require special instructions to deal with them. Bytes and shorts on the other
hand are treated as integers within the JVM for arithmetic and logical
operations. If you are dealing with pure Java source code then this is not a
problem as the Java compiler will take care of generating the appropriate
instructions on your behalf. If you start to work with bytecode which has not
been generated from the Java compiler then things become a little different
and it is quite possible that variables of byte or short types may end up
containing values larger than their maximum permissible ones.

This is a symptom of one of the general difficulties with the JVM. There is no
one-to-one relationship between Java source code and bytecode.

On the one hand, the lack of a tight binding between the source language and
bytecode enables cross-compilation from other source languages, as we
discussed previously. On the other hand it does mean that there has to be a
lot more work performed to ensure that the bytecode being executed is safe.
There is some concern that the lack of a rigid relationship between the Java
language and Java bytecode may be the source of some as yet undiscovered
nastiness which could emerge to overthrow the entire Java security model.
The next chapter looks at some of the measures which have been taken to
prevent this type of nastiness.

Chapter 6. The Class Loader and Class File Verifier

In this chapter we explore two topics:

1. How class files are located and loaded by the class loader

2. How the class file verifier ensures that class files are legal prior to execution

The following discussion assumes a Java Virtual Machine (JVM) that is running with a security manager. This is the wrong book to be running without one.

6.1 Class Loaders

Class loaders are the gatekeepers of the JVM, controlling what bytecode may be loaded and what should be rejected. As such they have a number of responsibilities:

1. To separate name spaces, thus preventing intentional and unintentional code corruption and limiting name clash problems to class files from one source.

2. To protect the boundaries of the core Java class packages (trusted classes) by refusing to load classes into these restricted packages.

3. Starting in Java 2, establish the protection domain (set of permissions) for a loaded class. This is the basis for run-time authorization checking for access to resources.

4. To enforce a search order that will prevent core and local classes from being replaced by classes from less trusted sources.

The class loader has another, useful, side effect. By controlling how the JVM loads code, all platform-specific file I/O is channelled through one part of the JVM, thus making porting the JVM to different platforms a much simpler task.

Let's look a little more closely at these responsibilities and why they are necessary.

First, Java code can be loaded from a number of different sources. Some of the more common sources are:

- The trusted core classes that ship with the JVM (java.lang.*, java.applet.* etc.)

- Any installed JVM extensions

- Classes stored in the local file system (usually found using the CLASSPATH system environment variable)

- Classes retrieved from external sources such as from a Web server

Clearly, we would not want to overwrite a trusted JVM class with an identically named class from a Web server since this would undermine the entire Java security model. For instance, the SecurityManager class is responsible for a large part of the JVM run-time security and is a trusted local class; consider what would happen to security if the SecurityManager could be replaced by a class loaded from a remote site. The class loader must therefore ensure that trusted local classes are loaded in preference to remote classes where a name clash occurs.

Secondly, where classes are loaded from Web servers, it is possible that there could be a deliberate or unintentional collision of names (although the Sun Java naming conventions exist to prevent unintentional name collisions). If two versions of a class exist and are used by different applets from different Web sites, then the JVM, through the auspices of the class loader, must ensure that the two classes can coexist without any possibility of confusion occurring.

The class loader must protect the boundaries of the trusted class packages. The core Java class libraries that ship with the JVM reside in a series of packages. Within the Java programming language, it is possible to give special access privileges to classes that reside in the same package; thus, a class which is part of the java.lang package, for instance, has access to methods and fields within other classes in the java.lang package which are not accessible to classes outside of this package.

If it were possible for a programmer to add his or her own classes to the java.lang package, then those classes would also have privileged access to the core classes. This would be an exposure of the JVM and consequently must not be allowed. The class loader must therefore ensure that classes cannot be dynamically added to the various core language packages.

The JVM may have many class loaders operating at any point in time, each of which is responsible for locating and loading classes from different sources.

6.1.1 Loading Classes from Trusted Sources

There is one class loader, the *primordial* class loader, which is a built-in part of the JVM; that is, its code is written in the same language the JVM is written in (typically C) and is an integral part of the JVM. It is also known as the *internal*, or *null*, or *default* class loader. The primordial class loader is the root of the class loader delegation hierarchy (see 6.1.4.2, "How the Design Is Implemented" on page 152 for details on delegation) and *is responsible for loading the trusted classes of the Java run time.*

Classes loaded by the primordial class loader are regarded as special insofar as they are not subject to verification prior to execution; that is, they are assumed to be well formed, safe Java classes. In the Java Development Kit (JDK) 1.1, these are the JVM core classes plus any classes which can be found using the CLASSPATH system environment variable. Obviously, if would-be attackers could somehow introduce a malicious class into the CLASSPATH of a JVM they could cause serious damage[1].

In Java 2, this exposure is minimized by removing the core class path information from the CLASSPATH environment variable and subjecting all but the core classes to verification and the security policy. It is also possible to subject the core classes to verification using the -verify option of the java command or the -J-verify option of the appletviewer command, for example. Of course, this does not affect that part of the JVM implemented in the native language.

The core classes in Java 2 are located by using a JVM internal property, sun.boot.class.path. The value of this property is called the *boot class path* and is formed internally from install information or can be specified by the java command option -Xbootclasspath, which becomes -J-Xbootclasspath for the appletviewer command (see 3.4.1, "Boot Class Path" on page 84).

6.1.2 Loading Classes from Untrusted Sources

Along with bounding the scope of implicitly trusted classes to just the Java core classes, Java 2 removed the responsibility for the loading of local user classes from the primordial loader. Now, at JVM startup, the application class path information is copied from the CLASSPATH environment variable into the JVM internal property java.class.path and this is used to start an instance of java.net.URLClassLoader, a new class loader class extending the new class java.lang.SecureClassLoader (described in 6.1.3, "Beyond What the JVM Provides" on page 148). This instance is given a list of file-based URLs generated from CLASSPATH, which it will use to locate and load local user classes. This class loader instance will also verify the class file and set up the associated protection domain. The value of java.class.path can also be set on the command line using the option -classpath (or -cp). This will override the CLASSPATH environment setting.

---

[1] This was the basis of one of the attacks discovered by the Secure Internet Programming team at Princeton University. Their attack, *Slash and Burn*, is described more fully in *Java Security, Hostile Applets, Holes and Antidotes,* Gary McGraw and Ed Felten.

From a trust viewpoint, logically in between the fully trusted core classes (no policy file permission entries required) and the completely untrusted application classes (explicit policy file permissions required) are classes of the new extension class framework (see 3.4.2, "Extensions Framework" on page 86). This framework allows for the installation of Java archive files in a specific *extensions directory* pointed to by the JVM internal property java.ext.dirs. The default setting for java.ext.dirs is ${java.home}/lib/ext and can be set using the -Djava.ext.dirs=*somevalue* command line option. A Java class called ExtClassLoader is responsible for loading installed extensions. ExtClassLoader is an inner class of the sun.misc.Launcher class. ExtClassLoader is also know as *extensions class loader*.

These classes are in the search order after core classes, but before application classes. They are subjected to verification and policy, but the default policy is AllPermissions (see 4.1.1, "The Class Loader" on page 110).

6.1.3 Beyond What the JVM Provides

Application writers (including JVM implementers) are at liberty to build more class loaders to handle the loading of classes from different sources such as the Internet, an intranet, local storage or perhaps even from ROM in an embedded system. These class loaders are not a part of the JVM; rather, they are part of an application running on top of the JVM.

In JDK 1.1, application implementers were required to implement any class loading requirements beyond what the primordial loader would provide by extending the java.lang.ClassLoader abstract class. The most obvious example of this is in the context of a Web browser which must load classes from an HTTP server. The browser's class loader that does this is generally known as the *applet class loader* and is itself a Java class which knows how to request and load other Java class files from a Web server across a TCP/IP network. The JDK's Applet Viewer includes a reference implementation called AppletClassLoader, which is shipped with the JDK in the sun.applet package and has been the basis for most browsers' class loaders.

Starting with Java 2, the Java run time includes an implementation of ClassLoader called SecureClassLoader. SecureClassLoader implements the basic security related requirements of class loading. It handles checking with the security manager, calling the class file verifier, linking of the class and setting up the protection domain. Its constructor is protected. SecureClassLoader is meant to be the basis for the development of other class loaders. To extend this, there is also a general purpose loader included in the SDK, called URLClassLoader, in the java.net package, which is a subclass of SecureClassLoader. URLClassLoader adds the ability to find and load class files from a list of file and HTTP-based URLs. URLClassLoader should meet most of the requirements an application may have for loading class files. And if not, developers should now develop their own loaders by subclassing one of these two classes, instead of the ClassLoader abstract class, to benefit from the function and security built into SecureClassLoader.

It should be clear that there can be many types of class loaders within a Java environment at any one time. In addition, there may be many instances of a particular type of class loader operating at once.

To summarize:

- There will always be one and only one *primordial* class loader. It is part of the JVM, like the execution engine.
- There will be one instance of the URLClassLoader which was created at JVM initialization. This instance is responsible for loading user classes from the local file system specified in the java.class.path property, which is set from the CLASSPATH environment variable.
- In a Web browser environment, there will be at least one additional class loader, which is responsible for loading the applet classes.
- There will be zero or more additional class loader types. These should extend one of the class loader classes: URLClassLoader, SecureClassLoader, or least desirably the ClassLoader abstract class. There are, of course, other choices.
- For each additional ClassLoader type, there will be zero or more instances of that type created as Java objects.

Let's look at this last point more closely.

Why would we want to have multiple instances of the same class loader running at any one time?

To answer this question we need to examine what class loaders do with a class once it has been loaded.

Every class present in the JVM has been loaded by one and only one class loader. For any given class, the JVM *remembers* which class loader was responsible for loading it. If that class subsequently requires other classes to be loaded, the JVM uses the same class loader to load those classes.

This gives rise to the concept of a *name space*, the set of all classes which have been loaded by a particular instance of a class loader. Within this name space, duplicate class names are prohibited. More importantly, there is no cross name space visibility of classes; a class in one name space (loaded by a particular class loader instance) cannot access a class in another name space (loaded by a different class loader instance).

Returning to the question *Why would we want to have multiple instances of the same class loader running at any one time?*, consider the case of the applet class loader. It is responsible for loading classes from a Web server across the Internet or intranets. On most networks (and certainly the Internet) there are many Web servers from which classes could be loaded and there is nothing to prevent two webmasters from having different classes on their sites with the same name.

Since a given instance of a class loader cannot load multiple classes with the same name, if we didn't have multiple instances of the applet class loader, we would very quickly run into problems when loading classes from multiple sites. Moreover, it is essential for the security of the JVM to separate classes from different sites so that they cannot inadvertently or deliberately cross reference each other. This is achieved by having classes from separate Web sites loaded into separate name spaces, which in turn is managed by having different instances of the applet class loader for each site from which applets are loaded.

6.1.4 The Class Loading Process

We now look at the class loading process. First, we will look at it from a design viewpoint. Second, we show how the design is implemented in Java 2 class loaders and how it should be implemented by an application needing to develop a class loader in Java 2. Keep in mind, we are assuming a security manager.

6.1.4.1 What Is Supposed to Happen

In this section, we look at some of the design aspects of the class loading architecture in Java 2. In other words, we describe what is supposed to happen from the viewpoint of the Java architects.

1. When a class is referenced, the JVM execution environment invokes the instance of the class loader associated with the requesting program to locate and load the referenced class.

2. The class loader first checks to see if the requested class has been previously loaded by itself.

   - If so, the loader checks with the security manager to see if the program has permission to access the requested class.

     - If it does not have permission, a security exception is generated.

- If the program has permission, the loader returns a reference to the existing class object.

- If not already loaded, the class loader checks with the security manager to see if this program has permission to create the requested class.

  - If it does not, a security exception is generated.

  - If the program has permission, the loader first tries to find the requested class in the core Java API followed by any JVM extensions. The difference between the core and extension classes is that the extension classes are subject to verification and the security policy in effect. This step prevents the JVM's core and extension classes from being replaced by classes from another location. If the class is found, the class is loaded into the class area and a reference to the class object is returned. The core and extension classes should be loaded using the JVM's built-in class loader, the primordial class loader.

3. If we have come to this point without finding the requested class, this means that the requested class has not been found in a trusted location. Therefore, the class loader will load the class as an array of bytes to be verified by the class file verifier before constructing a class object. The loader will look through the application class path before going to the network to locate the class. The application class path is found in the JVM internal property java.class.path, which is set from the CLASSPATH environment variable, or the -classpath (or -cp) argument of the java command.

4. The class file verifier is responsible for making sure that class files contain only legal Java bytecodes and that they behave properly (for example, they do not attempt to underflow or overflow the stack, forge illegal pointers to memory or in any other way subvert the JVM). Details of this are in 6.2, "The Class File Verifier" on page 168. If verification fails, a security exception is generated.

5. If the bytecodes pass verification, a class object is created and a protection domain is associated with the class for subsequent resource authorization checking. The class is then linked by resolving any references to other classes within it. This may result in additional calls to the class loader to locate and load other classes.

6. Next, static initialization of the class is performed; that is, static variables are defined and static initializers are run.

7. Finally, the class is available to be executed.

6.1.4.2 How the Design Is Implemented

Every class loader, being just another Java class itself, is loaded by a class loader, with one exception, the primordial class loader. This forms a run-time parent-child hierarchical relationship between class loader objects with the primordial class loader at the root. This relationship is the basis for the *delegation model*, which is the recommended implementation model for all class loaders starting with Java 2. That is, every class loader upon entry should immediately invoke (delegate the request to) the class loader which loaded it, its *parent* class loader. This will cause a call back all the way to the JVM's internal loader which will stop this apparent foolishness and attempt to load the class from the bootstrap class path or the extension class path. Only if all ancestors fail should the child try to locate and load the class.

To illustrate how this works, consider the PointlessButton applet (see Figure 17 on page 37). As a reminder, PointlessButton uses a second class, jamjar.examples.Button, which represents a push button on the browser display. Pushing the button results in nothing happening except a display is updated to inform you how many times nothing has happened to date.

In this example, we will work on a Web browser, called MyFavoriteWebBrowser. MyFavoriteWebBrowser just happens to implement a Java 2 style class loader, which extends URLClassLoader and is called Java2StyleAppletClassLoader. When MyFavoriteWebBrowser encounters the PointlessButton applet in a Web page the following sequence of events occurs:

1. MyFavoriteWebBrowser finds the <APPLET> tag in the Web page and determines that it needs to load PointlessButton.class. It creates an instance of MyFavoriteWebBrowser's Java2StyleAppletClassLoader, with the URL of the Web page, and invokes its findClass() method with the class name from the <APPLET> tag.

2. Java2StyleAppletClassLoader first delegates this request to its parent. As it turns out, the parent in this case is an instance of URLClassLoader. This is because the JVM for Java 2 creates an instance of URLClassLoader during JVM startup. In fact the JVM's internal loader no longer handles user class files. This instance of URLClassLoader loads the initial class file in a user program and any subsequent user classes found using the CLASSPATH environment variable. This instance of URLClassLoader has as its list of URLs the directories and files specified in the CLASSPATH variable. Of course, URLClassLoader will first ask its parent to handle the request, which is the primordial class loader.

3. The primordial class loader, which only knows about the core classes, fails to locate PointlessButton and returns control to the child that called it, in this case, the JVM-created instance of URLClassLoader.

An Observation on the sun.boot.class.path Property

This is a good time to bring up an observation. The locations the primordial class loader will search are specified by the JVM internal property values sun.boot.class.path and java.ext.dirs. The boot class path identified in property sun.boot.class.path on our test system (determined using the System.getProperty() method), has the value:

```
drive:\Program Files\JavaSoft\JRE\1.2\lib\rt.jar;
drive:\Program Files\JavaSoft\JRE\1.2\lib\i18n.jar;
drive:\Program Files\JavaSoft\JRE\1.2\classes
```

This tells us a couple of things. First, the core APIs are contained in two JAR files, rt.jar and i18n.jar. But, what is the last entry? This does not exist by default. There is no file or directory with this name. However, it would appear that if we create a directory with this name, the JVM would look in it for class files and, would consider them core classes. Indeed, this is the case. This is very powerful, but one should take care in granting the ability to create directories or files within the Java run-time directory structure, especially creating a directory named classes and the ability to place files in it.

We also found that only class files are recognized in this classes directory. Other files, such as JAR files, are ignored.

---

4. This instance of URLClassLoader attempts to find PointlessButton in the application class path, specified by the java.class.path property. For this example, PointlessButton does not exist on the local system, so URLClassLoader returns to Java2StyleClassLoader failing to find a PointlessButton class.

5. Java2StyleClassLoader now knows it must find and load the requested class itself. Since Java2StyleClassLoader extends URLClassLoader and uses as much of the URLClassLoader function as possible, we are at this point really executing the same findClass() logic as was just executed in the JVM created URLClassLoader, except the list of places to look is different. The URL list is not from the CLASSPATH, it is the URL of the Web page. So, the loader connects to the Web site specified by the URL using the HTTP protocol and downloads the PointlessButton class. The last thing findClass() does is to call defineClass() which runs the class file through the verifier, links it and sets up the protection domain for the class.

6. The JVM begins executing the PointlessButton applet.

7. PointlessButton needs to create an instance of jamjar.examples.Button, a class which currently has not been loaded. PointlessButton requests the JVM to load the class.

8. The JVM locates the instance of Java2StyleAppletClassLoader which loaded PointlessButton and invokes it to load jamjar.examples.Button.

9. The same steps that were described above for locating and loading PointlessButton are now executed looking for jamjar.examples.Button and the jamjar.examples.Button is executed.

10. jamjar.examples.Button creates a java.lang.String object for the title of the button. The String class has not yet been loaded, so again the JVM is requested to load the class.

11. The class loader which loaded both PointlessButton and jamjar.examples.Button (the same instance of Java2StyleClassLoader we are now getting tired of hearing about) is now invoked to load the java.lang.String class.

12. Java2StyleAppletClassLoader again delegates the request, only this time the primordial class loader is able to locate and load the class since it is part of the trusted classes package. Since the primordial class loader was successful, both URLClassLoader and Java2StyleAppletClassLoader have nothing to do but return the reference to the String class created by the primordial class loader.

There are a few interesting points to note here:

• In this example, Java2StyleClassLoader really offered no additional function beyond what URLClassLoader provides except to give us a meaningful name to use during the discussion and to provide a place holder for future potential changes to the browser's loading needs without affecting the browser's mainline code. So, for this example, the browser could have just created an instance of URLClassLoader.

• At Step 3 on page 153, if we had been using a regular java.awt.Button class then the primordial class loader would have been able to find the class in the trusted packages and the search would have stopped.

• There are actually many references to the java.lang.String class in the code. However, only the first reference results in the class being loaded from disk. Subsequent requests to the class loader will result in it returning the class already loaded. Since it is the primordial class loader which loads the String class, if there are multiple applets on a single page, only the first one to request a String class will result in the primordial class loader loading the class from disk.

Note also the order in which the applet class loader Java2StyleClassLoader searches for classes. An applet class loader could decide not to follow the delegation model and search the Web server from which it loaded the applet first for any subsequent classes and this would cut out some calls to the primordial class loader. This would be incredibly bad practice for two reasons:

- Most of the class load requests for an applet will be for trusted classes from the SDK packages, so searching the Web server for each of the classes encountered would be very expensive and wasteful in terms of network traffic.

- More importantly, if classes were sought on the Web server before being sought in the trusted package, it would allow subversion of built-in types, enabling malicious programmers to substitute their own implementations of core, trusted classes such as the SecurityManager or even the applet class loader itself.

For this reason, even prior to Java 2, all commercially available browsers have applet class loaders which implement the following search strategy[2]:

1. Ask the primordial class loader to load the class from the trusted packages.

2. If this fails, request the class from the Web server from which the original class was loaded.

3. If this fails, report the class as not locatable by throwing a ClassNotFound exception.

This search strategy is effectively the same as the delegation model advocated in Java 2 and ensures that classes are loaded from the most trusted source in which they are available. Java 2 makes implementing this strategy much easier through the delegation model and the functions now provided by URLClassLoader and SecureClassLoader.

6.1.5 Should You Build Your Own Class Loader

The ability to create additional class loaders is a very powerful feature of Java and places a heavy responsibility on the class loader implementer. This becomes particularly apparent when you realize that user-written class loaders have the choice of following the delegation model or not. They get first choice on whether to load a class or not. They can even take priority over the primordial class loader. This enables a user-written class loader to replace any of the system classes, including the SecurityManager. In other words, since the class loader is *Cerberus* to the JVM's *Hades*, you had better

---

[2] This is common practice but note that it is *not* enforced by the JVM architecture. Class loader writers are at liberty to implement any search strategy they choose for locating classes.

be sure that when you replace it, you don't inadvertently install a lap dog in its place.

We have already stated that a class loader which has loaded a particular class is invoked to load any dependent classes. We also know that a class loader generally has responsibility for loading classes from one particular source such as Web servers.

What if the class first loaded requires access to a class from the trusted core classes such as java.lang.String? This class needs to be loaded from the local core class package, not from across a network. It would be possible to write code to handle this within the application's class loader but it is unnecessary. We already have a class loader in the shape of the primordial class loader which knows how to load classes from the trusted packages.

With the Java 2 enhancements to security and class loading, there is much less reason to implement your own class loader.

URLClassLoader can load classes from a list of file-based and HTTP-based URLs. It knows how to process class files, Java Archive (JAR) files and signed JAR files. It handles setting up the protection domains and handles the questions for the security manager during class loading.

If you are on a 1.1 system, the JDK includes the class RMIClassLoader, which is still available in the Java 2 platform. Its methods are static, so they can be called directly to load individual unsigned class files from a single URL and define a class from the loaded file. Its name is misleading, since it is much more general purpose than its name implies and can be used to just load class files. It can support HTTP, Internet Inter-ORB Protocol (IIOP) and other protocols.

If, after all this, you still have reason to build your own class loader, such as one that performs class access auditing, or work across a network protocol other than HTTP, you can still benefit from subclassing one of the provided classes. For instance, if you are not using HTTP, but everything else is the same, implement your own XYZClassLoader based on SecureClassLoader and model it after URLClassLoader.

The next two sections show application class loaders. They both demonstrate how to extend the class loading functions of the SDK by simply adding the logic to record in a file all classes it is asked to load:

1. The first is a class loader written JDK 1.1 style, although it also runs on Java 2 SDK, Standard Edition, V1.2.x; It extends the abstract class ClassLoader and implements all steps in the class loading process.

2. The second is Java 2 style, extending URLClassLoader. This requires much less work on our part and provides the protection domain for the class allowing for run-time authorization checking by the security manager.

6.1.5.1 Program AuditClassLoader (JDK 1.1 Style)

AuditClassLoader (shown in Figure 54 on page 157 through Figure 58 on page 161) is an implementation of a class loader based on the abstract class ClassLoader. It first puts an entry in a log file, auditclasses.log, and then locates and loads a class file. It then defines and resolves a class from the class file. It is pretty much what a JDK 1.1 application developer had to do to implement a class loader. It works fine in Java 2, but *does not follow the delegation hierarchy*. It assumes all core class names start with `java.` and calls the primordial class loader (via the findSystemClass() method) for these; otherwise, it loads all classes itself using the `java.class.path` (which if you will remember is set from CLASSPATH) to locate the class file. It does check to see if the class is already loaded. *It does not have an access control scheme.*

```
/**
 * AuditClassLoader
 * Extends ClassLoader to record loading of classes
 *
 */
import java.util.*;
import java.util.zip.*;
import java.io.*;
import java.net.*;

public class AuditClassLoader extends ClassLoader
{
    private Hashtable loadedClasses = new Hashtable();
    private Hashtable resolvedClasses = new Hashtable();
    private Socket sock;
    private DataOutputStream auditlog;

    /**
     * constructor.
     */
    public AuditClassLoader()
    {
        super();
```

Figure 54. (Part 1 of 5). AuditClassLoader.java

```
        try
        {
            auditlog = new DataOutputStream(new FileOutputStream("auditclasses.log"));
            auditlog.writeBytes("Audit Started:\n");
        }
        catch (IOException e)
        {
            System.err.println("Audit file not opened properly\n" + e.toString());
        }
    }


/**
 * @return byte[]
 * @param name java.lang.String
 * @exception java.io.IOException The exception description.
 */
    private byte[] getClassFile(String className) throws java.io.IOException
    {
        InputStream is;
        byte classBytes[];

        is = locateClass(className);

        classBytes = new byte[is.available()];
        is.read(classBytes);

        return classBytes;
    }


/**
 * The method which actually loads a class file
 * The loadClass method is invoked to load a new class.
 * The steps which it must carry out are:
 * - Check to see if the class requested has already been loaded.
 * - Check to see if the class is a "system" class.
 * - Retrieve the bytes for the class
 * - Resolve the class if instructed
 * - Return the class to the caller.
 *
 * @param java.lang.String name The fully qualified name of the class to load
 * @param boolean resolve If true then the class is resolved
 */
    public Class loadClass(String name, boolean resolve) throws ClassNotFoundException
```

Figure 55. *(Part 2 of 5). AuditClassLoader.java*

```
{
    Class theClass = null;

    try
    {
        /*
         * Write the name of the class being loaded to the log file
         */
        auditlog.writeBytes("loading class: " + name + "\n");

        /*
         * Only attempt to load the class if it's not in the cache
         */
        if( !loadedClasses.containsKey(name))
        {

            /*
             * If the class is a system class, invoke the primordial class loader
             */
            if (name.startsWith("java."))
            {
                theClass = findSystemClass(name);
            }
            else
            {
                /*
                 * Otherwise, get the class as a bytearray and define it
                 */
                byte[] classBytes = getClassFile(name);
                theClass = defineClass(name, classBytes, 0, classBytes.length);
            }
        }

        /*
         * Store the class in the local cache
         */
        if (theClass != null) loadedClasses.put(name, theClass);
    }
    catch(IOException ioe)
    {
        throw new ClassNotFoundException();
    }
    catch(ClassFormatError cfe)
```

Figure 56. (Part 3 of 5). AuditClassLoader.java

```
    {
      throw new ClassNotFoundException();
    }

    /*
     * Resolve the class if it's
     * a) not resolved
     * b) the resolve flag is set
     */
    if (resolve && !resolvedClasses.containsKey(name))
    {
      resolveClass((Class) loadedClasses.get(name));
      resolvedClasses.put(name, "true");
    }

    return (Class) loadedClasses.get(name);
  }

  /**
   * A utility method used to locate a class file from it's name
   * this method searches the class path, including ZIP archives
   * @param className the fully qualified class name
   * @return an InputStream for the class file
   */
  private InputStream locateClass(String className) throws IOException
  {
    String fileName = className.replace('.', File.separatorChar) + ".class";
    String searchPath = System.getProperty("java.class.path").toUpperCase();
    String classPathEntry;

    while ( searchPath != "" )
    {
      int scIndex = searchPath.indexOf(File.pathSeparatorChar);
      if ( scIndex == -1 )
      {
        classPathEntry = searchPath;
        searchPath = "";
      }
      else
      {
        classPathEntry = searchPath.substring(0, scIndex);
        searchPath = searchPath.substring(scIndex + 1);
      }
```

Figure 57. (Part 4 of 5). AuditClassLoader.java

```
        if (classPathEntry.endsWith(".ZIP"))
        {
            ZipFile zf;
            ZipEntry ze;
            zf = new ZipFile(classPathEntry);
            ze = zf.getEntry(fileName);
            if (ze != null)
                return zf.getInputStream(ze);
        }
        else
        {
            String fullName = classPathEntry + File.separatorChar + fileName;
            File f = new File( fullName );
            if ( f.exists() ) return new FileInputStream( fullName );
        }
    }
    throw new IOException( className + " not found" );
}
}
```

Figure 58. (Part 5 of 5). AuditClassLoader.java

TestAuditClassLoader (see Figure 59 on page 161 and Figure 60 on page 162) is a program that can be used to invoke AuditClassLoader. It takes as a single parameter the name of a class, so the correct way to launch it is:

```
java TestAuditClassLoader ClassName
```

It creates an instance of AuditClassLoader and asks it to load the class name it received as a parameter. It then checks to see if the class is abstract. If it is, it asks the class to print information about itself. If it is not abstract, it creates a new instance of the class and asks the instance to print information about itself.

```
/**
 * Test AuditClassLoader
 *    Expects a class name as input
 *
 */
import java.lang.reflect.Modifier;

public class TestAuditClassLoader
```

Figure 59. (Part 1 of 2). TestAuditClassLoader.java

```
{

    /**
     * main entrypoint - starts the application
     * @param args java.lang.String[]
     */
    public static void main(java.lang.String[] args) throws Exception
    {
      if ( args.length != 0 )
      {
        AuditClassLoader loader = new AuditClassLoader();
        Class myself = loader.loadClass(args[0], true);
        int mods = myself.getModifiers();
        if (!Modifier.isAbstract(mods))
        {
          Object o = myself.newInstance( );
          System.out.println("New instance created:");
          System.out.println(o);
        }
        else
        {
          System.out.println("Abstract class loaded:");
          System.out.println(myself);
        }
      }
    }
}
```

Figure 60. (Part 2 of 2). TestAuditClassLoader.java

We show now the results of running TestAuditClassLoader, first against a concrete class and second, against an abstract class.

On running TestAuditClassLoader against a concrete class, for example the GetPrintJob applet class obtained from the code in Figure 1 on page 14 and Figure 2 on page 15, the output produced is:

- On the console:

```
New instance created:
GetPrintJob[panel0,0,0,0x0,invalid,layout=java.awt.FlowLayout]
```

- In the auditclasses.log file:

```
Audit Started:
loading class: GetPrintJob
loading class: java.applet.Applet
loading class: java.awt.event.ActionListener
loading class: java.lang.Throwable
loading class: java.lang.Exception
loading class: java.awt.Button
loading class: java.awt.Container
```

Upon running TestAuditClassLoader against an abstract class, for example java.util.TimeZone, we would see the following:

- On the console:

```
Abstract class loaded:
class java.util.TimeZone
```

- In the auditclasses.log file:

```
Audit Started:
loading class: java.util.TimeZone
```

6.1.5.2 Program Audit2ClassLoader (Java 2 Style)

Audit2ClassLoader (shown in Figure 61 on page 163 through Figure 63 on page 165) is based on the Java 2 URLClassLoader, which extends the new SecureClassLoader class. It extends URLClassLoader by overriding the loadClass() method. It simply records class load requests in a file hard-coded as auditclasses.log and then asks its parent to load the class. By using all of URLClassLoader's function, Audit2ClassLoader is very short. But, it offers a more elegant implementation than AuditClassLoader because *it implements the delegation model and associates a protection domain with the class.*

```
/**
 * Audit2ClassLoader
 * Extends java.net.URLClassLoader to record the loading
 * of classes
 *
 */

import java.io.*;
import java.net.*;
```

Figure 61. (Part 1 of 3). Audit2ClassLoader.java

```
import java.lang.*;

public class Audit2ClassLoader extends URLClassLoader
{
    private DataOutputStream auditlog;

    /**
     * Audit2ClassLoader constructor
     * Calls URLClassLoader's constructor and
     * opens a file for recording class load messages
     *
     */
    public Audit2ClassLoader(URL[] urls)
    {
        super(urls);
        try
        {
            auditlog = new DataOutputStream(new FileOutputStream("auditclasses.log"));
            auditlog.writeBytes("Audit Started:\n");
        }
        catch (IOException e)
        {
            System.err.println("Audit file not opened properly\n" + e.toString() );
        }
    }


    /**
     * The method which actually loads a class file
     * The findClass method is invoked to load a new class.
     * The steps which it must carry out are:
     * - Write message to log file.
     * - Call parent findClass method to load, verify, resolve and
     *   set up protection domains.
     *
     * @param java.lang.String name The fully qualified name of the class to load
     */
    public Class loadClass(String name) throws ClassNotFoundException
    {
        try
        {
            auditlog.writeBytes("loading class: " + name + "\n");
        }
        catch (IOException ioe)
```

Figure 62. (Part 2 of 3). Audit2ClassLoader.java

```
        {
            System.err.println("Could not write to audit file\n" + ioe.toString());
        }

        try
        {
            return super.loadClass(name);
        }
        catch (Exception e)
        {
            throw new ClassNotFoundException(name);
        }
    }
}
```

Figure 63. (Part 3 of 3). Audit2ClassLoader.java

Figure 64 on page 166 shows TestAudit2ClassLoader, a program which can be used to try out Audit2ClassLoader. The significant difference here from TestAuditClassLoader is that Audit2ClassLoader requires a list of URLs to be passed to its constructor. This is really a requirement of URLClassLoader. This limits the scope of where Audit2ClassLoader will look for user class files. In this test case, it will only look in the current directory. Note the creation of the URL using `file:./`. The / character is very important. It says this is a directory; otherwise, it is assumed the URL points to a file. However, files in java.class.path (application class path) and sun.boot.class.path (core classes) will be found and loaded during delegation by the appropriate class loader instance. In this example the result is the same as our JDK 1.1 style class loader (AuditClassLoader) except that AuditClassLoader has two tiers, system classes (a class starting with `java.`) and all others (found via CLASSPATH), whereas AuditClass2Loader uses delegation (not a naming convention) and has three tiers, as follows:

- AuditClass2Loader will handle the files not found by delegation and will only look in the URL list passed on to its constructor. In our example, using TestClass2Loader, this is just the current directory.

- The URLClassLoader instance created at JVM startup will handle the classes not found by the primordial loader and that it can find via java.class.path

- The primordial loader will find all core classes found using sun.boot.class.path, which can be more than just `java.`, as in AuditClassLoader.

```
/**
 * Test Audit2ClassLoader
 * Expects a class name as input.
 *
 */
import java.net.*;
import java.lang.reflect.Modifier;

public class TestAudit2ClassLoader
{
   /**
    * main entrypoint - starts the application
    * @param args java.lang.String[]
    */
   public static void main(java.lang.String[] args) throws Exception
   {
      if (args.length != 0)
      {
         URL dirs[] = new URL[1];
         dirs[0] = new URL("file:./");
         Audit2ClassLoader loader = new Audit2ClassLoader(dirs);
         Class myself = loader.loadClass(args[0]);
         int mods = myself.getModifiers();
         if (!Modifier.isAbstract(mods))
         {
            Object o = myself.newInstance();
            System.out.println("New instance created:");
            System.out.println(o);
         }
         else
         {
            System.out.println("Abstract class loaded:");
            System.out.println(myself);
         }
      }
   }
}
```

Figure 64. TestAudit2ClassLoader.java

Here are the results of running TestAudit2ClassLoader using the same classes as we used for trying out TestAuditClassloader.

On running TestAudit2ClassLoader against the concrete class GetPrintJob (see again Figure 1 on page 14 and Figure 2 on page 15), the results are:

- On the console:

```
New instance created:
GetPrintJob[panel0,0,0,0x0,invalid,layout=java.awt.FlowLayout]
```

- In the auditclasses.log file:

```
Audit Started:
loading class: GetPrintJob
```

On running TestAudit2ClassLoader against an abstract class, such as java.util.TimeZone, the output would be:

- On the console:

```
Abstract class loaded:
class java.util.TimeZone
```

- In the auditclasses.log file:

```
Audit Started:
loading class: java.util.TimeZone
```

6.1.5.3 In Summary

Obviously, Audit2ClassLoader is much simpler to implement and adds access control using Java 2's new security mechanism. There is, however, a small price we paid for this. We saw that TestAuditClassLoader recorded a message in the log file for the class being loaded and for each class loaded during the resolve step, that is for each class the subject class referenced. This is not true for TestAudit2ClassLoader. In fact we saw that in this case there is only a message for the class requested. This is because Audit2ClassLoader asks its parent to do all the real work by delegating the request. The parent, URLCLassLoader, happily handles the resolve step for Audit2ClassLoader. We could do a little more of the work in Audit2ClassLoader and handle this, if it were necessary.

6.2 The Class File Verifier[3]

Once a class has been located and loaded by a class loader (other than the primordial class loader), it still has another hurdle to cross before being available for execution within the JVM. At this point we can be reasonably sure that the class file in question cannot supplant any of the core classes, cannot inveigle its way into the trusted packages and cannot interfere with other safe classes already loaded.

We cannot, however, be sure that the class itself is safe. There is still the safety net of the SecurityManager which will prevent the class from accessing protected resources such as network and local hard disk, but that in itself is not enough. The class might contain illegal bytecode, forge pointers to protected memory, overflow or underflow the program stack, or in some other way corrupt the integrity of the JVM.

As we have said in earlier chapters, a well behaved Java compiler produces well behaved Java classes and we would be quite happy to run these within the JVM since the Java language itself and the compiler enforce a high degree of safety. Unfortunately we cannot guarantee that everyone is using a well behaved Java compiler. Nasty devious hacker types may be using homemade compilers to produce code designed to crash the JVM or worse, subvert the security thereof. In fact, as we saw in Chapter 5, "Class Files in Java 2" on page 117, we cannot even be sure that the source language was Java in the first place!

In addition to this there is the problem of release-to-release binary compatibility. Let's say that you have built an applet which uses a class called TaxCalculator from a third party. You have constructed your applet with great care and have purchased and installed the TaxCalculator class on the server with your applet code.

At this point you are certain that the methods you call in TaxCalculator are present and valid but what happens if/when you upgrade TaxCalculator? Of course you *should* make sure that the API exposed by TaxCalculator hasn't changed and that your class will still work, but what if you forget? In practice it is quite possible that TaxCalculator has changed between versions and methods or fields which were previously accessible have become inaccessible, been removed or changed type from dynamic to static fields. In this case, when your applet is downloaded to a browser and it tries to make method calls or access fields within TaxCalculator those calls may fail.

---

[3] *Important note* – The class file verifier is sometimes referred to as the bytecode verifier, but as we show in this section, running the bytecode verifier is only one part of the class file verification process.

This is because the binary code compatibility between the classes has been broken between releases. These problems exist with *all* forms of binary distributable libraries. On most systems this results in at best a system message and the application refusing to run; at worst the entire operating system could crash. The JVM has to perform at least as well as other systems in these circumstances and preferably better.

For all of the above reasons, an extra stage of checking is required before executing Java code and this is where the class file verifier comes in.

After loading an untrusted class via a ClassLoader instance, the class file is handed over to the class file verifier which attempts to ensure that the class is fit to be run. The class file verifier is itself a part of the Java Virtual Machine and as such cannot be removed or overridden without replacing the JVM itself.

6.2.1 An Example of Class File Verification

As a very simple example to show the affects of class file verification and to see when classes are subjected to verification, we wrote a Java class, TestVerify.java, which adds two integers initialized to the values 3 and 4 and displays the answer 7.

```
/**
 * TestVerify.java
 * Used to create an invalid class file to
 * test when verification occurs
 */

import java.awt.*;
import java.applet.*;

public class TestVerify extends Applet
{
    public static void main(String[] args)
    {
        System.out.println("3 + 4 = " + add());
    }

    static int add()
    {
        int a,b,c;
        a = 3;
```

Figure 65. (Part 1 of 2). TestVerify.java

```
        b = 4; // use hex editor to change to "a = 4" in class file
        return (a+b);
    }

    public void paint(Graphics g)
    {
        g.drawString("3 + 4 = " + add(), 10, 20);
    }
}
```

Figure 66. (Part 2 of 2). TestVerify.java

- The class above can be launched as a Java application, through the command:

```
java TestVerify
```

This is the output produced:

```
3 + 4 = 7
```

- Or, TestVerify can be launched as a Java applet using Applet Viewer or a Java-enabled Web browser. The following is the code of TestVerify.html, a simple HTML page that invokes the TestVerify applet:

```
<HTML>

    <HEAD>
        <TITLE>TestVerify Applet</TITLE>
    </HEAD>

    <BODY>

        <H3>TestVerify Applet</H3>

        <APPLET Code="TestVerify" Width=250 Height=50>
        </APPLET>

    </BODY>
</HTML>
```

Figure 67. TestVerify.html

Below, in Figure 68 on page 171, is the output of the command:

```
appletviewer TestVerify.html
```

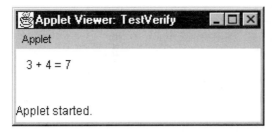

Figure 68. TestVerify Class Running as an Applet

TestVerify was used to determine when verification of classes occurs. In the TestVerify.class file, the initialization of variable b in method add() was modified using a hexadecimal editor to re-initialize variable a, so that variable b is never initialized.

Below, in Figure 69 on page 171 and Figure 70 on page 172, is the output of the command:

```
javap -c TestVerify
```

```
Compiled from TestVerify.java
public class TestVerify extends java.applet.Applet {
    public TestVerify();
    static int add();
    public static void main(java.lang.String[]);
    public void paint(java.awt.Graphics);
}

Method TestVerify()
   0 aload_0
   1 invokespecial #9 <Method java.applet.Applet()>
   4 return

Method int add()
   0 iconst_3
   1 istore_0
   2 iconst_4
   3 istore_1
   4 iload_0
   5 iload_1
   6 iadd
   7 ireturn
```

Figure 69. (Part 1 of 2). Disassembling TestVerify.class Using javap

```
Method void main(java.lang.String[])
    0 getstatic #14 <Field java.io.PrintStream out>
    3 new #7 <Class java.lang.StringBuffer>
    6 dup
    7 ldc #2 <String "3 + 4 == ">
    9 invokespecial #10 <Method java.lang.StringBuffer(java.lang.String)>
   12 invokestatic #11 <Method int add()>
   15 invokevirtual #12 <Method java.lang.StringBuffer append(int)>
   18 invokevirtual #16 <Method java.lang.String toString()>
   21 invokevirtual #15 <Method void println(java.lang.String)>
   24 return

Method void paint(java.awt.Graphics)
    0 aload_1
    1 new #7 <Class java.lang.StringBuffer>
    4 dup
    5 ldc #1 <String "3 + 4 = ">
    7 invokespecial #10 <Method java.lang.StringBuffer(java.lang.String)>
   10 invokestatic #11 <Method int add()>
   13 invokevirtual #12 <Method java.lang.StringBuffer append(int)>
   16 invokevirtual #16 <Method java.lang.String toString()>
   19 bipush 10
   21 bipush 20
   23 invokevirtual #13 <Method void drawString(java.lang.String, int, int)>
   26 return
```

Figure 70. (Part 2 of 2). Disassembling TestVerify.class Using javap

If you look at method add(), instruction 3, you will see an istore_1 instruction. This is the initialization of variable b and has the bytecode 3C. As you can see in Figure 71 on page 173, we changed this via a hexadecimal editor to 3B, the bytecode for istore_0, which is the same as instruction 1 and re-initializes variable a, thereby eliminating the initialization of variable b.

```
TestVerify.class                                                    _ □ ×
000001B0 0100 126A 6176 612F 6170 706C 6574 2F41  ...java/applet/A
000001C0 7070 6C65 7401 0011 6A61 7661 2F61 7774  pplet...java/awt
000001D0 2F47 7261 7068 6963 7301 0013 6A61 7661  /Graphics...java
000001E0 2F69 6F2F 5072 696E 7453 7472 6561 6D01  /io/PrintStream.
000001F0 0016 6A61 7661 2F6C 616E 672F 5374 7269  ..java/lang/Stri
00000200 6E67 4275 6666 6572 0100 106A 6176 612F  ngBuffer...java/
00000210 6C61 6E67 2F53 7973 7465 6D01 0004 6D61  lang/System...ma
00000220 696E 0100 036F 7574 0100 0570 6169 6E74  in...out...paint
00000230 0100 0770 7269 6E74 6C6E 0100 0874 6F53  ...println...toS
00000240 7472 696E 6700 2100 0300 0400 0000 0000  tring.!.........
00000250 0400 0100 2300 1B00 0100 2400 0000 1D00  ....#.....$.....
00000260 0100 0100 0000 052A B700 09B1 0000 0001  .......*........
00000270 0025 0000 0006 0001 0000 0009 0008 002A  .%.............*
00000280 0019 0001 0024 0000 0028 0002 0002 0000  .....$...(......
00000290 0008 063B 023E 1A1B 60AC 0000 0001 0025  ...;.>..`......%
000002A0 0000 000E 0003 0000 0013 0002 0014 0004  ................
000002B0 0015 0009 0032 0020 0001 0024 0000 0035  .....2. ...$...5
000002C0 0004 0001 0000 0019 B200 0EBB 0007 5912  ..............Y.
000002D0 02B7 000A B800 0BB6 000C B600 10B6 000F  ................
000002E0 B100 0000 0100 2500 0000 0A00 0200 0000  ......%.........
000002F0 0E00 1800 0C00 0100 3400 1D00 0100 2400  ........4.....$.
00000300 0000 3700 0400 0200 0000 1B2B BB00 0759  ..7........+...Y
00000310 1201 B700 0AB8 000B B600 0CB6 0010 100A  ................
00000320 1014 B600 0DB1 0000 0001 0025 0000 000A  ...........%....
00000330 0002 0000 0018 001A 0017 0001 0027 0000  .............'..
00000340 0002 0029                                         ...)
```

Figure 71. Edit of TestVerify.class with istore_1 Instruction Changed to istore_0

We then ran the modified class file in a JDK 1.1.6 system as an application and as an applet:

- As a local application, a user class can only be found by searching the CLASSPATH system environment variable. Since the current directory is always front appended to CLASSPATH, a program runs as a trusted class and, therefore, is not subject to verification. The modified version of our program ran and produced the following erroneous results:

```
3 + 4 = 26246588
```

- Using the JDK 1.1.6 Applet Viewer, which forces all user classes to be verified, produced the following results:

```
java.lang.VerifyError
        at java.lang.ClassLoader.resolveClass(ClassLoader.java:237)
        at sun.applet.AppletClassLoader.loadCode(AppletClassLoader.java:299)
        at sun.applet.AppletClassLoader.loadCode(AppletClassLoader.java:375)
        at sun.applet.AppletPanel.createApplet(AppletPanel.java:456)
        at sun.applet.AppletPanel.runLoader(AppletPanel.java:392)
        at sun.applet.AppletPanel.run(Compiled Code)
        at java.lang.Thread.run(Thread.java:466)
```

As you can see, the file failed verification and was not allowed to run.

We then tried this on our Java 2 system. Since now, in Java 2, the primordial class loader loads only the core classes using the property sun.boot.class.path, this class always fails verification and does not run, with one exception. We will talk about this in a moment.

- When run as an application, it produced the following output:

```
Exception in thread "main" java.lang.VerifyError: (class: TestVerify,
method: add signature: ()I) Accessing value from uninitialized register 1
```

- When run as an applet, the output produced is the following:

```
java.lang.VerifyError: (class: TestVerify, method: add signature: ()I)
Accessing value from uninitialized register 1
        at java.lang.Class.newInstance0(Native Method)
        at java.lang.Class.newInstance(Class.java:239)
        at sun.applet.AppletPanel.createApplet(AppletPanel.java:532)
        at sun.applet.AppletPanel.runLoader(AppletPanel.java:468)
        at sun.applet.AppletPanel.run(Compiled Code)
        at java.lang.Thread.run(Thread.java:479)
```

As you can see, the code we have shown fails as an application and as an applet in a normal mode of operation.

However, we just said there was an exception. If you will remember, in the Box "An Observation on the sun.boot.class.path Property" on page 153, we showed that there was a non-existent directory called classes in the java.home directory which, if created, provided a place to put classes to be considered core. Well, we placed the TestVerify class in this directory (after creating it) and ran the class as an application and as an applet. As suspected it ran without being verified in both cases. Here are the results:

- As an application:

  `3 + 4 = 26284364`

- As an applet using Applet Viewer:

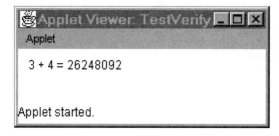

Figure 72. TestVerify Running as an Applet from ${java.home}${/}classes Directory

One last thing to note: the results when TestVerify was not verified are different each time. This is because the memory for integer b was never initialized and the add operation just added 3 to whatever value happened to be left from some previous usage of that memory location.

6.2.2 The Duties of the Class File Verifier

Before discussing what the class file actually does, we look at the possible ways in which a class file might be *unsafe*. By understanding a threat, we can understand better how the Java architecture guards against it.

The following are some of the things that a class file could do which could compromise the integrity of the JVM:

- **Forge illegal pointers**

  If a Java class can obtain a reference to an object of one type and treat it as an object of a different type then it effectively circumvents the access modifiers (private, protected, etc.) on the fields of that object. This type of attack is known as a *class confusion attack* since it relies on confusing the JVM about the class of an object.

- **Contain illegal bytecode instructions**

  The JVM's execution engine is responsible for running the bytecode of a program in the same way as a conventional processor runs machine code.

  When a conventional processor encounters an illegal instruction in a program, there is nothing that it can do other than stop execution. You may have seen this in Windows systems, where the operating system can at least identify that an illegal instruction has been found and display a message.

  Similarly, if the execution engine finds a bytecode instruction that it cannot execute, it is forced to stop executing. In a well written execution engine this would not be good, but in a poorly written version it is possible that the entire JVM, or the Web browser in which it is embedded or even the underlying operating system might be halted. This is obviously unacceptable.

- **Contain illegal parameters for bytecode instructions**

  Passing too many or too few parameters to a bytecode instruction, or passing parameters of the wrong type, can lead to class confusion or errors in executing the instruction.

- **Overflow or underflow the program stack**

  If a class file could underflow the stack (by attempting to pop more values from it than it had placed on it) or overflow the stack (by placing values on it that it did not remove) then it could at best cause the JVM to execute an instruction with illegal parameters or at worst crash the JVM by exhausting its memory.

- **Perform illegal casting operations**

  Attempting to convert from one data type to another – for example, from an integer to a floating point or from a String to an Object – is known as casting. Some types of casting can result in a loss of precision (such as converting a floating point number to an integer) or are simply illegal (such as converting a String to a DataInputStream).

  The legality of other types of casts is less clear; for example, all Strings are Objects (since the String class is derived from the Object class) but not all Objects are Strings. Trying to cast from an Object to a String is legal only if the Object is originally a String or a String derivative. Allowing illegal casts to be performed will result in class confusion and thus must be prevented.

- **Attempt to access classes, fields or methods illegally**

  As discussed above, a class file may attempt to access a nonexistent class. Even if the class does exist, it may attempt to make reference to methods or fields within the class which either do not exist or to which it has no access rights. This may be part of a deliberate hacking attempt or as a result of a break in release-to-release binary compatibility.

By tagging each object with its type, the JVM could check for illegal casts. By checking the size of the stack before and after each method call, stack overflows and underflows can be caught. The JVM could also test the stack before each bytecode is executed and thus avoid illegal or wrongly numbered parameters.

In fact, all of these tests could be made at run time but the performance impact would be significant. Any work that the class file verifier can do in advance of run time to reduce the performance burden is welcome. With some idea of the magnitude of the task before the class file verifier, we now look at how it meets this challenge.

6.2.3 The Four Passes of the Class File Verifier

Before we go into any detail on how the class file verifier works it is important to note that the Java specification requires the JVM to behave in a particular way when it encounters certain problems with class files, which is usually to throw an error and refuse to use the class.

The precise implementation varies from one vendor to the next and is not specified. Thus some vendors may make all checks prior to making a class file available; others may defer some or all checks until run time. The process described below is the way in which Sun's HotJava Web browser works; it has been adopted by most JVM writers, not least because it saves the effort of reinventing a complex process.

The class file verifier makes four passes over the newly loaded class file, each pass examining it in closer detail. Should any of the passes find fault with the code then the class file is rejected. For reasons which we explain below, not all of these tests are performed prior to executing the code. The first three passes are performed prior to execution and only if the code passes the tests here will it be made available for use.

The fourth pass, really a series of *ad hoc* tests, is performed at execution time, once the code has already started to run.

6.2.3.1 Pass 1 – File Integrity Check
The first and simplest pass checks the structure of the class file. It ensures that the file has the appropriate signature (first four bytes are 0xCAFEBABE) and that each of the structures within the file is of the appropriate length. It checks that the class file itself is neither too long nor too short and that the constant pool contains only valid entries. Of course class files may have varying lengths but each of the structures (such as the constant pool) has its length included as part of the file specification.

If a file is too long or too short, the class file verifier throws an error and refuses to make the class available for use.

6.2.3.2 Pass 2 – Class Integrity Check
The second pass performs all other checking which is possible without examining the actual bytecode instructions themselves. Specifically, it ensures that:

- The class has a superclass (unless this class is Object).
- The superclass is not a final class, and this class does not attempt to override a final method in its superclass.
- Constant pool entries are well formed, and all method and field references have legal names and signatures.

Note that in this pass, no check is made as to whether fields, methods or classes actually exist, merely that their names and signatures are legal according to the language specification.

6.2.3.3 Pass 3 – Bytecode Integrity Check

This is the pass in which the *bytecode verifier* runs and is the most complex pass of the class file verifier. The individual bytecodes are examined to determine how the code will actually behave at run time. This includes data-flow analysis, stack checking and static type checking for method arguments and bytecode operands.

It is the bytecode verifier which is responsible for checking that the bytecodes have the correct number and type of operands, that datatypes are not accessed illegally, that the stack is not over or underflowed and that methods are called with the appropriate parameter types.

The precise details of how the bytecode verifier operates may be found in 6.3, "The Bytecode Verifier in Detail" on page 180. For now, it is important to state two points:

1. The bytecode verifier analyzes the code in a class file *statically.* It attempts to reconstruct the behavior of the code at run time, but does not actually run the code.

2. Some very important work has been done, which demonstrates that it is *impossible* for static analysis of code to identify all of the problems which may occur at run time. We include this proof in 6.4, "An Incompleteness Theorem for Bytecode Verifiers" on page 183.

To restate this in simple terms, any class file falls into one of three categories:

- Run-time behavior is demonstrably safe.

- Run-time behavior is demonstrably unsafe.

- Run-time behavior is neither demonstrably safe nor demonstrably unsafe.

Clearly the bytecode verifier should accept those class files in the first category and reject those in the second category. The problem arises with class files in the third category.

These class files *may or may not* contain code that will cause a problem at run time, but it is impossible from static analysis of the code to determine which.

The more complex the bytecode verifier becomes, the more it can reduce the number of cases which fall into the third category but no matter how complex the verifier, it can never completely eliminate the third category and for this reason there will always be bytecode programs which pass verification, but which may contain illegal code.

This means that simply having the bytecode verifier is not enough to prevent run-time errors in the JVM and that the JVM must perform some run-time checking of the executable code.

Lest you begin panicking at this stage you should comfort yourself with the thought that the level of verification performed by the JVM prior to executing bytecode is significantly higher than that performed by traditional run-time environments for native code (that is, none at all).

6.2.3.4 Pass 4 – Run-Time Integrity Check

As we have hinted, the JVM must make a trade-off between security and efficiency. For that reason, the bytecode verifier does not exhaustively check for the existence of fields and classes in pass 3. If it did, then the JVM would need to load all classes required by an applet or application prior to running it. This would result in a very heavy overhead which is not strictly required.

We will examine the following case with three classes, MyClass, MyOtherClass and SubclassOfMyClass, which is derived from MyClass. MyOtherClass has two public methods:

- methodReturningMyClass(), which returns an instance of MyClass

- methodReturningSubclassOfMyClass(), which returns an instance of SubclassOfMyClass.

Against this background, consider the following code snippet:

```
MyOtherClass x = new MyOtherClass();
MyClass y = x.methodReturningMyClass();
```

In 6.2.3.3, "Pass 3 – Bytecode Integrity Check" on page 178, the class file verifier has ascertained that the method methodReturningMyClass() is listed in the constant pool as a method of MyOtherClass which is public (and therefore reachable from this code).

It also checks that the return type of methodReturningMyClass() is MyClass. Having made this check and assuming that the classes and methods in question *do* exist, the assignment statement in the second line of code is perfectly legal. The bytecode verifier does not in fact need to load and check the class MyClass at this point.

Now consider this similar code:

```
MyOtherClass x = new MyOtherClass();
MyClass y = x.methodReturningSubclassOfMyClass();
```

In this case, the return type of the method call does not return an object of the same class as y, but the assignment is still legal since the method returns a subclass of MyClass. This is not, however, obvious from the code alone: the verifier would need to load the class file for the return type SubclassOfMyClass and check that it is indeed a subclass of MyClass.

Loading this class involves a possible network access and running the class file verifier for the class and it may well be that these lines of code are never executed in the normal course of the program's execution in which case loading and checking the subclass would be a waste of time.

For that reason, class files are only loaded when they are required, that is when a method call is executed or a field in an object of that class is modified. This is determined at run time and so that is when the fourth pass of the verifier is executed.

6.3 The Bytecode Verifier in Detail

The first stage of the bytecode verifier process is the identifying of bytecode instructions and their arguments. This operation is completed in two passes. The first pass locates the start of each instruction and stores it in a table. Having found the start of each instruction, the verifier makes a second pass, parsing the instructions. This involves building a structure for each instruction, storing the instruction and its arguments. These arguments are checked for validity at this point. Specifically:

- All arguments to flow-control instructions must cause branches to the start of a valid instruction.

- All references to local variables must be legal. That is, an instruction may not attempt to read or write to a local variable beyond those that a method declares.

- All references to the constant pool must be to an entry of the appropriate type.

- All opcodes must have the correct number of arguments.

- Each exception handler must have start and end points at the beginning of valid instructions with the start point before the end point. In addition, the offset of the exception handler must be the start of a valid instruction.

6.3.1 The Data Flow Analyzer

Having established that the bytecodes are syntactically correct, the bytecode verifier now has the task of analyzing the run-time behavior of the code (within the limitations examined in 6.4, "An Incompleteness Theorem for Bytecode Verifiers" on page 183).

To perform this analysis, the bytecode verifier has to keep track of two pieces of information for each instruction:

- The status of the stack prior to executing that instruction in the form of the number and type of items on the stack.

- The contents of local variables prior to executing that instruction. Only the type of each local variable is tracked. The value is ignored.

Where types are concerned, the analyzer does not need to distinguish between the various normal integer types (byte, short, char) since, as we discuss in 5.5, "Java Bytecode" on page 136, they all have the same internal representation.

The first stage is the initialization of the data flow analyzer:

- Each instruction is marked as unvisited. That is, the data flow analyzer has not yet examined that instruction.

- For the first instruction, the stack is marked as empty and the local variables corresponding to the method's arguments are initialized with the appropriate types.

- All other local variables declared as used by the method are marked as containing illegal values.

- The *changed* bit of the first instruction is set, indicating that the analyzer should examine this instruction.

Finally, the data flow analyzer runs, looping through the following steps:

1. Find a virtual machine instruction whose changed bit is set.

2. If no instruction remains whose changed bit is set, the method has successfully been verified; otherwise turn off the changed bit of the instruction found and proceed to Step 3.

3. Emulate the effect of this instruction on the stack and local variables:

   - If the instruction uses values from the stack, ensure that there are sufficient elements on the stack and that the element(s) on the top of the stack are of the appropriate type.

- If the instruction pushes values onto the stack, ensure that there is sufficient room on the stack for the new element(s) and update the stack status to reflect the pushed values.

- If the instruction reads a local variable, ensure that the specified variable contains a value of the appropriate type.

- If the instruction writes a value to a local variable, change the type of that variable to reflect that change.

4. Determine the set of all possible instructions which could be executed next. These are:

- The next instruction in sequence, if the current instruction is not an unconditional `goto`, a `return`, or a `throw`.

- The target instruction of a conditional or unconditional branch.

- The first instruction of all exception handlers for this instruction.

5. For each of the possible following instructions, merge the stack and local variables as they exist after executing the current instruction with the state prior to executing the following instruction. In the exception-handler case, change the stack so that it contains a single object of the exception type indicated by the exception handler information. Merging proceeds as follows:

- If the stacks are of different sizes then this is an error. *Stop!*

- If the stacks contain exactly the same types, then they are already merged.

- If the stacks are identical other than having differently typed object references at corresponding places on the stacks then the merged stack will have this object reference replaced by an instance of the first common superclass or common superinterface of the two types. Such a reference type always exists because the type Object is a supertype of all class and interface types.

- If this is the first time the successor instruction has been visited, set up the stack and local variable values using those calculated in Step 2 and set the changed bit for the successor instruction. If the instruction has been seen before, merge the stack and local variable values calculated in Step 2 and Step 3 into the values already there; set the changed bit if there is any modification.

6. Go to Step 1.

If the dataflow analyzer runs on the method without reporting any failures, then the method has been successfully verified by Pass 3 of the class file verifier (see 6.2.3.1, "Pass 1 – File Integrity Check" on page 177).

6.4 An Incompleteness Theorem for Bytecode Verifiers

The bytecode verifier is a key component of Java security. Practical bytecode verifiers divide bytecode programs into three classes:

1. Those that will not cause problems when they run

2. Those that will cause problems when they run

3. Those where the verifier is not certain.

You can improve a bytecode verifier by reducing its area of uncertainty. Can you eliminate uncertainty completely? Can you build a complete bytecode verifier that determines whether a program is safe or not before it runs?

The answer is *no*, you cannot. It is mathematically impossible. This short section shows why.[4]

To demonstrate this, we focus on one aspect of bytecode verification, stack-underflow checking. This involves determining whether a bytecode program will underflow the stack, by removing more items from it than were ever placed on it. Then we use the argument known as *reductio ad absurdum*. We assume that there is a complete stack-underflow checker and show that this assumption leads to a contradiction. This means that the assumption must have been false – a complete stack-underflow checker is impossible. Since a complete bytecode verifier must contain a complete stack-underflow checker, a complete bytecode verifier is impossible too.

Suppose then that there is such a thing as a complete stack-underflow checker. We write a method in standard Java bytecode which takes as its argument the name of a class file and returns:

• The value `true` if the specified class file does not underflow the stack

• The value `false` if it does

We call this method doesNotUnderflow().[5]

---

[4] The problem has been deliberately stated in terms that mathematicians may recognize as being similar to the halting problem. The proof, a diagonalization argument, follows the flow of Christopher Strachey's halting-problem proof (Computer Journal 1967).

[5] We have here used Church's Thesis, which states that a programming language (such as the Java bytecode language) which can code a Turing machine can code *any* computable function.

We now consider the bytecode program Snarl, whose main method contains the following code lines:

```
if doesNotUnderflow(classFile)
    while true pop();          // thus underflowing Snarl's stack
else
    {}                        // exiting gracefully
```

The pop() method – which removes the top element from the stack – may not be pure Java, but can certainly be written in bytecode. The bytecode program Snarl is compiled into the class file Snarl.class.[6]

What happens if we give Snarl itself as a parameter? The first thing it does is to invoke the method doesNotUnderflow on Snarl.class:

- If doesNotUnderflow(Snarl.class) is `true`, then Snarl immediately underflows the stack.
- If doesNotUnderflow(Snarl.class) is `false`, then Snarl exits safely, without underflowing the stack.

This contradiction means that there could never have been a method doesNotUnderflow() which worked for all class files. The quest for a way of determining statically that a class would behave itself at run time was doomed. Complete checking for stack underflow *must* be done at run time if it is to be done at all.

This result can be generalized and applied to any aspect of bytecode verification where you try to determine statically something that happens at run time. So all bytecode verifiers are incomplete. This does not, of course, mean that they are not useful – they contribute significantly to Java security – nor that they cannot be improved. It does mean, however, that some checking has to be left until run time.

6.5 Summary

You have now seen the types of checking which take place before a class file from an untrusted source can be loaded and run inside the JVM and the improvements in this area Java 2 offers.

---

[6] Snarl is a pretty nasty piece of programming, and most practical bytecode verifiers would reject it out of hand. The reason for this is that while true pop (); is disastrous if executed and has no practical purpose; a good rule of thumb is to leave it out. But there's nothing invalid about Snarl – if we really have finite bytecode for the method doesNotUnderflow(), then we can readily construct the bytecode for Snarl – and doesNotUnderflow(), being complete, has no need for rules of thumb.

Once it is running, code from untrusted sources is subject to further checking at the hands of the *security manager* which we have mentioned briefly here. Chapter 7, "The Java 2 SecurityManager" on page 187 describes how the security manager works and looks at ways in which it is possible to reduce the burden placed on the class loader and class file verifier by extending the range of classes which the JVM regards as trusted.

Chapter 7. The Java 2 SecurityManager

As we said in 1.3.3, "Java as a Threat to Security" on page 9, we can imagine four levels of attack to which a Java environment can be subjected:

1. System modification, in which a program gets read/write access and makes some changes to the system

2. Privacy invasion, in which a program gets read access and steals restricted information from your system

3. Denial of service, in which a program uses system resources without being invited

4. Impersonation, in which a program masquerades as the real user of the system

The Java security manager enforces restrictions based on policy statements that are designed to prevent the first two of these and, with Java 2, to some extent the last. In this chapter we look at what the security manager does, and how it does it.

Along the way, we will look at some of the loopholes (now closed) in which security has been circumvented in previous releases of the Java Development Kit (JDK). Finally we briefly consider the tricks that an applet can use to perform the *nuisance* attacks – denial of service and impersonation.

7.1 What SecurityManager Does

Beginning with Java 2, the class java.lang.SecurityManager is no longer abstract and its implementation supports the new policy driven security model.

Before Java 2, SecurityManager was an abstract class that application developers, such as Web browser manufacturers, extended to implement a set of access controls. These controls placed applets in the so-called sandbox. Although the class was abstract, it did implement a set of methods with names starting with check, for example checkWrite() and checkConnect(). The intent was for the application developer to override these methods with something that answered the question *Is the applet allowed to do this?* either by quietly returning to the caller (an implicit *Yes*) or by throwing a security exception (an emphatic *No*). As shipped, each method did have a default behavior in case the application did not override the method. Each method simply said no by throwing a security exception.

With Java 2, SecurityManager is a fully functional resource level access control facility. Application developers need only call one method, checkPermission(), which takes a permission object as a parameter. For compatibility, the other check methods are still available, but now answer the question using the new permission and policy file model by turning the request into a permission and calling checkPermission(). All of the check methods can still be overridden, if necessary.

Table 8 summarizes the checks, the default policy (based on the java.policy file that comes with the installation of Java 2 SDK, Standard Edition, V1.2.*x*) and the permission type which is passed to checkPermission() by each check method. This is also the permission type to pass to checkPermission() when you call it directly.

Note that, if running an applet using the Java 2 SDK, Standard Edition, V1.2.*x* Applet Viewer, Applet Viewer will add socket permissions to connect, accept, and resolve to the local host and the host the applet is loaded from, including the host name of the local system, if loaded locally.

Table 8. Security Manager Controls

Area of Control	Check Method	"Is program allowed to..."	Permission Type Passed to checkPermission()
Network connections	checkAccept()	... accept a socket connection?	`java.net.SocketPermission "host:port", "accept";`
	checkConnect()	... request a socket connection?	`java.net.SocketPermission "host", "resolve";`
			`java.net.SocketPermission "host:port", "connect";`
	checkListen()	... listen for connection?	`java.net.SocketPermission "localhost:1024-", "listen";`
			`java.net.SocketPermission "localhost:port", "listen";`
	checkMulticast()	... use multicast?	`java.net.SocketPermission maddr.getHostAddress(), "accept,connect";`
	checkSetFactory()	... set socket factory?	`java.lang.RuntimePermission "setFactory"`
Threads	checkAccess()	... modify thread arguments?	`java.lang.RuntimePermission "modifyThread";`
			`java.lang.RuntimePermission "modifyThreadGroup";`

Area of Control	Check Method	"Is program allowed to..."	Permission Type Passed to checkPermission()
File system	checkDelete()	... delete a specified file?	`java.io.FilePermission "file", "delete";`
	checkRead()	... read from a specified file?	`java.lang.RuntimePermission "readFileDescriptor";`
			`java.io.FilePermission "file", "read";`
	checkWrite()	... write to a specified file?	`java.lang.RuntimePermission "writeFileDescriptor";`
			`java.io.FilePermission "file","write";`
Operating system	checkExec()	... execute a system command?	`java.io.FilePermission "command", "execute";`
	checkPrintJobAccess()	... create a print job?	`java.lang.RuntimePermission "queuePrintJob";`
	checkSystemClipboardAccess()	... access the system clipboard?	`java.awt.AWTPermission "accessClipboard";`
	checkLink()	... link to a system library?	`java.lang.RuntimePermission "loadLibrary.lib";`
	checkTopLevelWindow()	... display a window without also displaying a banner warning that the window was created by an applet?	`java.awt.AWTPermission "showWindowWithoutWarningBanner";`
JVM control	checkExit()	... kill the JVM?	`java.lang.RuntimePermission "exitVM";`
	checkPropertyAccess()	... access specified system properties?	`java.lang.PropertyPermission "key", "read,write";`
	checkPropertiesAccess()	... access system properties?	`java.lang.PropertyPermission "*", "read,write";`
	checkAwtEventQueueAccess()	... access the AWT event queue?	`java.awt.AWTPermission "accessEventQueue";`
	checkCreateClassLoader()	... create a new class loader?	`java.RuntimePermission "createClassLoader";`
Packages and classes	checkPackageAccess()	... access a specified Java class package?	`java.lang.RuntimePermission "accessClassInPackage.package";`

Area of Control	Check Method	"Is program allowed to..."	Permission Type Passed to checkPermission()
	checkPackageDefinition()	... define a specified Java class package?	`java.lang.RuntimePermission "defineClassInPackage.package";`
	checkMemberAccess()	... access declared members of a class?	`java.lang.RuntimePermission "accessDeclaredMembers";`
Security functions	checkSecurityAccess()	... execute a specified security function?	`java.security.SecurityPermission "action";`

7.2 Operation of the Security Manager

Although any Java program, applet, servlet, bean or application, can extend java.lang.SecurityManager, the JVM will allow only one security manager to be active at a time. To make a security manager active you have to call the static system method java.System.setSecurityManager() or set the property java.security.manager as an option on the `java` command. The command line option `-Djava.security.manager` will make the Java 2 SDK, Standard Edition, V1.2.*x* default security manager (java.lang.SecurityManager) active. The option `-Djava.security.manager=MySecurityManager` will load and make MySecurityManager.class the active security manager.

Once a security manager is active, by either method above, it cannot be replaced unless the program has the authority to do the two following things:

1. Create an instance of SecurityManager.

2. Set a security manager instance as active.

In order for an application stored in the local directory D:\itso\ch07 to replace the active security manager, this is what you should set in the current policy file:

```
grant codeBase "file:/D:/itso/ch07" {
  permission java.lang.RuntimePermission "createSecurityManager";
  permission java.lang.RuntimePermission "setSecurityManager";
};
```

In fact, if there is a security manager already installed:

1. Invoking a new security manager constructor first calls the SecurityManager's checkPermission() method with the RuntimePermission createSecurityManager permission to ensure the calling thread has permission to create a new security manager. This may result in throwing a SecurityException.

2. Invoking the java.lang.System.setSecurityManager() method first calls the security manager's checkPermission() method with a RuntimePermission setSecurityManager permission to ensure it is permitted to replace the existing security manager. This may result in throwing a SecurityException.

The installed security manager is only really active on request; it does not check anything unless it is called by other system functions. Figure 73 illustrates the flow for a specific restricted operation, establishing a network connection. The calling code creates a new Socket class, using one of the constructor methods it provides. This method invokes the checkConnect() method of the local SecurityManager subclass instance.

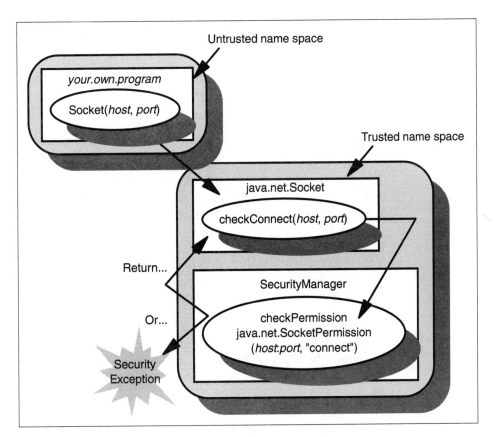

Figure 73. Secuirty Manager Operation

The security manager has a very simple question to answer: *Is this program allowed to perform the subject operation?* In Figure 73, *can your.own.program connect to host:port?* In order to answer this question, the security manager checks that each class in the stack has a permission entry to connect to *host:port*.

7.2.1 Interdependence of the Three JVM Security Elements

Although the three elements of JVM security – class loader, class file verifier and security manager – each have unique functions, they are interdependent. The security manager relies on the class loader to keep untrusted classes and local classes in separate name spaces and protection domains and to prevent the local trusted classes from being overwritten (for example, by a Socket class that failed to invoke the checkConnect() method).

Conversely, the class loader relies on the security manager to prevent an applet from loading its own class loader, which could flag untrusted code as trusted. And everything relies on the class file verifier to make sure that class confusion is avoided and that class protection directives are honored.

The bottom line is this: if an attacker can breach one of the three defenses, the security of the whole system is usually compromised.

7.3 Attacking the Defenses of Java

We have now seen how the different parts of the Java defense act together to create a secure environment in which programs can run. If everything is working correctly, you should be safe from programs that try to attack your system or use your system to mount attacks on other systems, in theory...

In practice, a number of holes were found in previous releases of the implementation of the Java defense, and a variety of attack applets were demonstrated that exploited them. Luckily for all of us, most of these holes were discovered by researchers in a lab environment and quickly plugged.

Although the security framework is much more robust in Java 2, we should not expect it to be without holes. The JVM is a large piece of code and, inevitably, there will be bugs in it. Some of the attacks have exploited bugs, but most of them rely on finding ambiguities: using JVM facilities in a way that the original writers did not envision. The new security model is much more rigorous and much less prone to ambiguities and has benefited from the experience of earlier releases. However, attack techniques do not stand still, so you should regularly monitor the JavaSoft Web site at http://www.javasoft.com to find out if security bugs have been discovered and download the latest release of the SDK containing the necessary fixes.

7.3.1 Types of Attack

Although we do not describe any attacks in detail, it is worth summarizing some of the techniques that have been successfully used by hackers or researchers in previous releases:

- **Infiltrating local classes**

  Prior to Java 2, David Hopwood, once a student at Oxford and then a Netscape employee, discovered an implementation bug in a vendor implementation of the JVM that allowed an applet to load a class from *any* directory on the browser system. This bug was quickly fixed. But, there will always be opportunities for the industrious cracker to exploit.

  Downloading code packages from the Internet has become a part of everyday life for many people. Any of those packages could have been modified to plant a Trojan horse class file along with their legitimate payload. Of course, this is not just a Java problem, but more like a new form of computer virus. One solution lies in signed content, so that you know that the package you download has not been tampered with.

  Fully trusted classes are those that the JVM assumes and depends upon being correct and well behaved. Prior to Java 2, any class pointed to by the CLASSPATH environment variable was considered trusted. Therefore, changing the trusted class set could be accomplished simply by changing the value of CLASSPATH. In Java 2, the fully trusted classes are limited to those on the boot class path, which is internally specified in the JVM by the sun.boot.class.path property; all other classes are subject to verification and security policy. Protecting the trusted classes in Java 2 is a matter of limiting access to the directories and files on the boot class path.

- **Type confusion**

  Java goes to great lengths to ensure that objects of a particular type are dealt with consistently. We see this both in the compiler and later in the third pass of the class file verifier (see 6.2.3.3, "Pass 3 – Bytecode Integrity Check" on page 178).

  It is crucial that the class of an object and level of access it allows (as specified by the `private`, `protected` or `public` keywords) are preserved. In the JVM, objects are referenced by entries in the constant pool. As shown in 5.4, "The Constant Pool" on page 129, each entry includes the type of the referenced object.

  If, somehow, an attacker can create an object reference that is *not* of the type it claims to be, there is a possibility of breaking down the protection. Several examples have shown ways to achieve type confusion, by taking advantage of various implementation flaws, such as:

- A bug that allowed a class loader to be created but avoided calling the ClassLoader constructor that normally invokes checkCreateClassLoader() (see Table 8 on page 188)

- Flaws in JVM access checking which allowed a method or object defined as private in one class to be accessed by another class as public

- A bug in the JVM that failed to distinguish between two classes with the same name but loaded by different class loaders

These bugs were discovered in vendor implementations of the JVM.

- **Network loopholes**

  The first security-related JVM flaw to get worldwide attention was a failure to check the source IP address of an applet rigorously enough. This was exploited by abusing the Domain Name System (DNS), a network service responsible for resolving names to addresses and vice versa, to fool the security manager into allowing the applet to connect to a host that would normally have been invisible to the server from which the applet was loaded. In this way the attacker could access a system that would normally be safe behind a firewall.

- **JavaScript backdoors**

  There was a series of JavaScript exploits that allowed a script to persist after the Web page it was invoked from had been exited. This was used to track the user's Web accesses. The flaw was fixed, but then reappeared when Netscape introduced LiveConnect, which allows a JavaScript script to create Java objects and invoke Java methods. Both languages have strict limitations on what they are allowed to do, but the limitations are *different* limitations. By combining them you effectively get a union of the two protection schemes.

If application developers use the fully functional security manager in Java 2 as a base for their work, the number and variations of security implementations, and therefore possibilities for error, will be greatly reduced.

Flaws and the security exposures they might create are inevitable. However, Java receives a great deal of attention by a wide audience. An encouraging thing about this is that most of the flaws found to date were identified by researchers in the field attempting to find and close all holes. Fixes were provided rapidly by Sun and application vendors. All of this experience has influenced the evolution of the Java Security Architecture now available in Java 2.

7.3.2 Malicious Applets

So far we have talked about system modification and privacy invasion (see Point 1 and Point 2 on page 187). What about the last two categories of exposure – the things that *are* allowed by the framework (see 3 and 4 on page 187), but which can still be annoying or damaging?

Setting the rules for a program's environment is always a question of striking a balance. The program needs some system and/or network resources; otherwise, it will not be useful at all. On the other hand, it must not be allowed to have free reign over the system, especially if this program has been downloaded from a remote site.

We have said that there are two types of malicious programs, denial of service and impersonation. There is also another type of malice that is not Java-specific. This is based on deception, that is, to try to trick the user into entering information that they would not normally give away. This sort of thing is not specific to Java, in fact there are much easier ways to do the same thing using scripting languages or simple HTML forms, so we won't consider them further here.[1]

7.3.2.1 Cycle Stealing

Denial of service attacks have, for a long time, been a scourge of the Internet. Normally you think of them taking down a server or even a whole site. A denial of service applet is unusual in that it normally only affects a single system or user.

Denial of service implies that the user can no longer use the system. *Cycle stealing* is much more subtle; by this we mean any program that consumes resources, whether computer or human, without the user's permission. The most extreme form of these *are* denial of service programs, but the most insidious ones may not be detected by their victim at all.

There are obvious denial of service attacks. For example a program could try to create an infinite number of windows, or it could sit in a tight loop, using up CPU cycles. These are very annoying and they can have a real impact, for example if the user has to reboot the machine to recover. However, if they are tied to a particular Web page, the user will quickly realize where the problem is coming from and simply not go there. A program that is not so easily traced back to its source is more effective.

The key to this kind of program lies in persistent, background, threads. Every implementation of the Java Virtual Machine (JVM) supports threads, and the language makes it very easy to use them. Normally, when you leave a Web

---

[1] The Hostile Applets home page is at http://www.rstcorp.com/hostile-applets/index.html.

page in a browser containing an applet, the applet will stop any threads it created. However, there is nothing to assist the applet in this task nor to enforce that this is done. Indeed, if the applet fails (intentionally or unintentionally) to explicitly stop any threads it created, they will continue to run until they end on their own or the application (the Web browser for instance) ends.

Program AppletThread, shown in Figure 74 on page 196 and Figure 75 on page 197, demonstrates this. It starts a thread which prints out a message every 5 seconds that proclaims it is still alive and for how long it has been alive and gives its thread identification information.

```java
import java.util.Calendar;
import java.text.SimpleDateFormat;
import java.util.Date;

public class AppletThread extends Applet implements Runnable
{
    public void start()
    {
        Thread aThread = new Thread(this);
        aThread.start();
        System.out.println("Applet start.");
    }

    public void run()
    {
        int i = 1;
        System.out.println("Thread started, id: " + Thread.currentThread().toString());
        while (true)
        {
            try
            {
                Thread.sleep(5000);
            }
            catch (InterruptedException e)
            {
                e.printStackTrace();
            }

SimpleDateFormat formatter = new SimpleDateFormat("HH:mm:ss");
Date currentTime = new Date();
String AppletTime = formatter.format(currentTime);
```

Figure 74. (Part 1 of 2). AppletThread.java

```
        System.out.println(Thread.currentThread().toString() + ": Alive at " +
            AppletTime + " for " + 5*i + " seconds.");
        i++;
      }
  }

  public void paint(Graphics g)
  {
      g.drawString("Applet with a thread running, see console for messages", 10, 30);
  }
}
```

Figure 75. (Part 2 of 2). AppletThread.java

The following HTML file, called AppletThread.html, simply invokes the
AppletThread applet and displays the results on a Web page:

```
<HTML>

  <BODY>
      <APPLET Code="AppletThread" Width=400 Height=60>
      </APPLET>
  </BODY>

</HTML>
```

Figure 76. AppletThread.html

Another applet, AppletClock (see Figure 77 on page 198), is used to help
demonstrate the malicious functionality of AppletThread. AppletClock merely
posts the time it started on the browser's window.

This way, when we switch pages in the browser, we can see if the time
messages from AppletThread are time stamped after we have left the
AppletThread page and gone on to AppletClock's page, thereby showing the
thread is still around and running, instead of stopped.

```
/**
 * Applet to post its birth time on browser window
 * It is used to help demonstrate a point about threads
 */

import java.awt.*;
import java.applet.*;
import java.util.Calendar;
import java.text.SimpleDateFormat;
import java.util.Date;

public class AppletClock extends Applet
{
    String AppletStartTime;
    public void start()
    {
        SimpleDateFormat formatter = new SimpleDateFormat("HH:mm:ss");
        Date currentTime = new Date();
        AppletStartTime = formatter.format(currentTime);
    }

    public void paint(Graphics g)
    {
        g.drawString("Applet Started at " + AppletStartTime, 10, 30);
    }
}
```

Figure 77. AppletClock.java

The following lines of code belong to the HTML file AppletClock.html
necessary to invoke the AppletClock applet:

```
<HTML>

    <BODY>
        <APPLET Code="AppletClock" Width=400 Height=60>
        </APPLET>
    </BODY>

</HTML>
```

Figure 78. AppletClock.html

Because we wanted to travel from one page to another, we used Netscape Communicator Version 4.5 as the browser environment instead of the Java 2 SDK Applet Viewer. In each of the following figures you will see the Netscape Navigator browser window, the Netscape browser's Java console window and the Windows NT Task Manager's performance window.

In Figure 79, we see that AppletThread has started and has spawned a thread which has printed out its identification and is happily pronouncing its well-being every 5 seconds. This is our starting point and we take note of the number of threads in the system and the memory and CPU usage information on the Task Manager display.

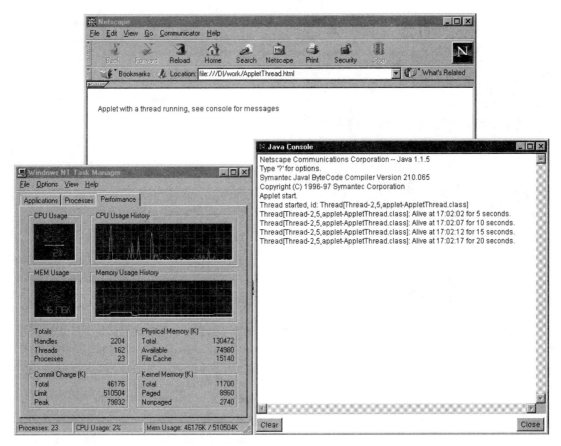

Figure 79. AppletThread after Just Starting

Now that we have set the stage, let's see what happens when we leave this page and travel on to another. Figure 80 on page 200 shows the results of going to the Web page hosting the AppletClock applet and staying there for a short period of time. AppletClock started at 17:02:30. We can also see that the thread that AppletThread spawned is still running happily along at 17:03:03 and has been alive now for 65 seconds. Notice that the thread count has increased (albeit by 1) and that the memory usage has increased as well.

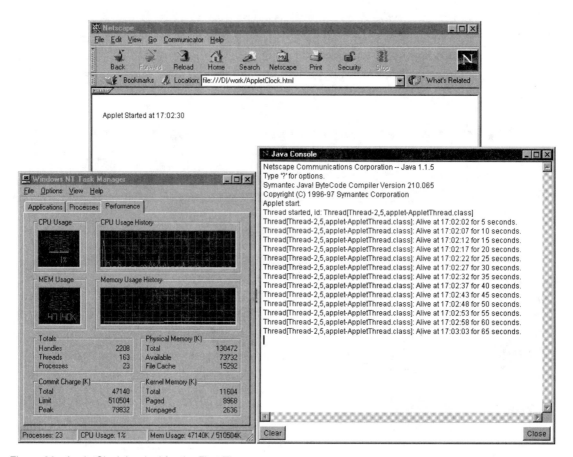

Figure 80. AppletClock Invoked for the First Time

At this point, we can already see the effect of applets not properly cleaning up after themselves. But, let's carry this out just a little bit further to point out a couple more interesting affects.

Next, we press the **Back** button to return to the AppletThread.html page. When the browser returns to the AppletThread page it re-runs the applet's start() method. This causes AppletThread to spawn a second thread. Figure 81 on page 201 shows that the original thread and a new thread are now both running happily along. You can see that the new thread, having ID

3,5,applet-AppletThread.class, is much younger, only 10 seconds old, while the one with ID 2,5,applet-AppletThread.class is 80 seconds old. This time the Task Manager doesn't show an increase in threads, but the memory and CPU usage have increased. The thread count stays the same because the main thread for AppletClock stopped, and AppletThread started the new one.

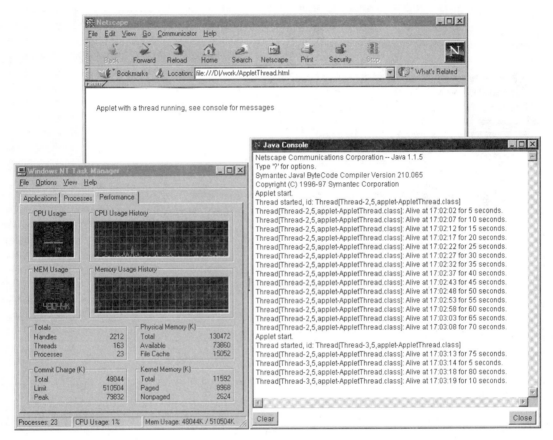

Figure 81. Upon Using the Back Button to Return to the AppletThread Page

The last thing we do for this exercise is to press the **Forward** and **Back** buttons several more times to toggle between AppletThread and AppletClock to better illustrate the affect. Figure 82 on page 202 shows the results: seven threads are now running in the background and the memory, CPU usage and thread count have increased significantly. Imagine the effect of surfing the Internet for an hour if all of the applets you encountered behaved this way. Not only could your system's performance degrade, but there is a potential for more serious misuse of your system's resources and even unauthorized gathering of information from your system.

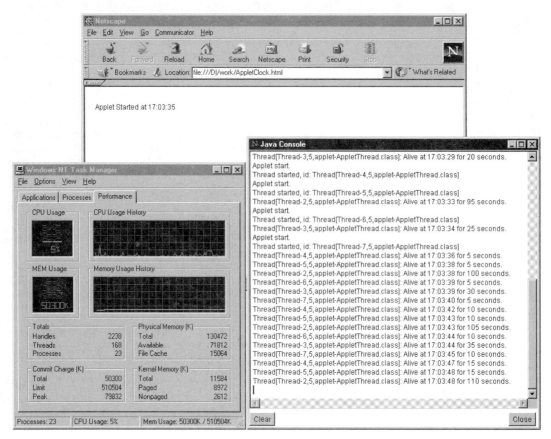

Figure 82. AppletClock after Several Iterations of the Back and Forward Buttons

Alternatively, we can also press the **Reload** button, while possibly holding the Shift key, in order to force the browser to retrieve a new copy of the Web contents. Doing an experiment like this, we were able to generate 50 threads, with consequent increase of CPU and memory usage.

Another thing to say is that, with a simple modification, the AppletThread applet could be transformed into an invisible applet. It would be enough to remove from its code the line:

```
g.drawString("Applet with a thread running, see console for messages", 10, 30);
```

The result would be that the applet runs on your system and generates multiple threads, and you could be totally unaware of this.

Another modification of the AppletThread applet could make the applet not only reside in memory even when another Web page is displayed, but it could even generate additional threads by itself, without the need to reload the page hosting it. However, we did not want to show how to write such a malicious applet in this book. The applet we have described here is fairly benign. What has really happened here is that the attacker has obtained free use of machine cycles on your system. What sort of thing might he or she want to do with them?

One example might be to do *brute force* cipher cracking. A feature of any good symmetric key encryption algorithm is a uniform key space. That is, if you want to crack the code, there is no mathematical shortcut to finding the key, you just have to try all possible keys until you find one that works. Several recent encryption challenges have been solved by using spare cycles on a large number of computers working as a loosely-coupled complex, each being delegated a range of keys to try, under the direction of a central coordinator.

This sort of effort depends on the cooperation and goodwill of a lot of people who donate machine time and access. But, if we replaced the AppletThread URL in the above example with, for example, getNextKeyRange, it would be possible to do the same thing without having to ask anybody. A number of other applets along the same lines have been demonstrated, such as applets that kill the threads of other applets executing concurrently.

7.3.2.2 Impersonation

Internet e-mail is based on the Simple Mail Transfer Protocol (SMTP). Mail messages are passed from one SMTP gateway to another using sessions on TCP/IP port 25. Abusing these connections to send bogus e-mail is an established nuisance of the Internet. A hacker can create mail messages that appear to come from someone else, which can be used to embarrass or annoy the receiver of the mail and the apparent sender.

Mail that has been forged in this way is not impossible to tell from the real thing, however. The SMTP gateways keep track of the original IP address, so you can trace the message back, if not to a person, at least to a machine (unless the originator was also using a spoofed IP address).

A Java applet allows this kind of errant behavior to go one stage further. Until Java 2, there was nothing to prevent an applet from connecting to port 25 and appearing to be a mail client. However, the only system it could connect to was the one that it was originally loaded from, because of the sandbox restrictions. So, if an attacker had control over a Web page, he or she could cause an applet to be sent to a client machine, which connected back to the server and sent e-mail to the target of the attack. When the recipient checks the IP address, it belongs to a complete stranger, who has no idea that anything has happened.

Java 2 enforces and refines the security model and now we can restrict access by individual resource, including the port number.

7.4 Avoiding Security Hazards

An attack in Java is likely to come through the front door, meaning through public methods on your applet's class and public static methods on any public class (see 2.1.1.2, "Access to Classes, Fields and Methods" on page 42). Therefore, to reduce security risks in your Java applet, all public methods should be examined and classified as follows:

1. The method is declared public but does not need to be, so it could be changed to private, protected or default access.

2. The method is absolutely safe or, in other words, it does not use directly or indirectly any extra-sandbox privileges and does not reveal private data.

3. The method is reasonably safe in that it uses extra-sandbox privileges in a limited fashion, constrained so as to be, in practice, safe.

4. The method allows malicious use directly.

After classifying your applet's public methods, you may be able to take specific measures to close security holes they may introduce.

You can use the `javap` command line utility from the Java 2 SDK, with the option `-public`, to generate a list of all public methods on your applet's class. An example is shown in the following session screen:

```
D:\itso\ch02>javap -public PointlessButton
Compiled from PointlessButton.java
public class PointlessButton extends java.applet.Applet implements java.awt.event.ActionListener {
    public PointlessButton();
    public void actionPerformed(java.awt.event.ActionEvent);
    public void init();
}

D:\itso\ch02>
```

This example is generated by running the `javap` command against the PointlessButton class, whose code is shown in Figure 17 on page 37.

Most applets have too many public methods. Potential security holes can be plugged by simply changing the methods to private, protected or default access, whenever possible.

In Java bean development, the BeanInfo interface is used to list all the methods that your bean advertises to a builder, and so these methods must be public. You may be able to reduce your security exposure by constraining access to the remaining, non-advertised methods.

Next, identify the public methods that run in the sandbox and only call methods that also run in the sandbox. These may be considered absolutely safe if these additional conditions are met:

- The method does not return sensitive data, such as the user's name, the machine's IP address or any other personal information.
- The method does not return an object, unless all of the object's public methods are also absolutely safe.
- The method does not trust its input parameters in security-sensitive contexts, since the input may come from untrusted sources.

Methods that have been deemed absolutely safe require no further treatment. For the remaining public methods, you will need to estimate the overall security risk of allowing unrestricted access to them by untrusted users. A security guideline could be the following: a method is reasonably safe if it uses extra-sandbox permissions, but it can do nothing malicious, regardless of the state of the applet as configured through input parameters to that method, or via other public methods.

Once the reasonably safe methods have been addressed, evaluate the remaining potentially dangerous methods. Do not make calls to enable privileges in these methods; instead, require that the method's caller do the enabling. Any method that could be used maliciously in a rather transparent manner should be treated in this way. For example, as we have already discussed, a setFileName() method that takes the name of a file and saves to it is dangerous and falls in this category.

7.4.1 How to Test

In the process of making these changes, you must ensure that the applet's functionality has not been broken. You should verify the following:

- In a trusted environment, all functionality should work from the user interface with no security exceptions.

- In an untrusted environment, all methods assessed as absolutely safe should work.

- In a trusted environment, all methods assessed as absolutely or reasonably safe should work.

- In a trusted environment, all methods, including the dangerous ones, should work when called from another trusted applet on the page.

You also need to define exactly what, if anything, your applet does in an untrusted environment. Once you have a functionality definition, then you will need to verify that your applet can provide this functionality and handle user requests for functionality that cannot be done in the sandbox.

The first step is to verify that all attempts to acquire a guarded resource are done in a `try{}` block, with a security exception being caught and handled. The rest is user interface work, targeted at how well you communicate to the user, through the user interface, what functionality is available in an untrusted environment.

7.5 Examples of Security Manager Extensions

The Java 2 permission structure allows for granting a code source (code from some source) the right to perform some action (such as read, write, connect, etc.) on a resource (file, port, etc.). The structure is very flexible and most applications will find that the new security manager will give them all the function they need. However, there will be cases where an application developer will want to extend or limit the default security manager's capabilities. Several examples come to mind:

- You may want to prevent access to a file even if someone explicitly gives that permission by entering a `grant` statement in a policy file.

- You may want to keep track of requests for access to certain resources.

- You may want to prompt users with a special password before accessing files in the local file system.

- If this is a multi-user system, such as a server, you may want to extend the security model to incorporate the concept of a user by adding principal-based access control.

7.5.1 First Example – Overriding checkWrite()

For our first example, we will take an easy task and continue with our theme from 6.1.5, "Should You Build Your Own Class Loader" on page 155, by implementing a simple audit log of permission requests to write to files.

Our example creates a log file during construction of the security manager and overrides the checkWrite() method. Whenever a checkWrite() is received, it will log (in file writerequests.log) that a check is being made for write access to a file and the file's name, and then will call the parent SecurityManager's checkWrite() method. Figure 83 on page 207 and Figure 84 on page 208 show MySecurityManager.java, which implements this extension to the SecurityManager class.

```java
/**
 *  MySecurityManager.java
 *  Extends SecurityManager
 *  Simple extension to log write permission requests
 */

import java.io.*;
import java.net.*;
import java.lang.*;
import java.security.Permission;
import java.security.AccessController;

public class MySecurityManager extends SecurityManager
{
    private DataOutputStream auditlog;

    public MySecurityManager()
    {
        super(); /* initilize using parent constructor */

        try
        {
            auditlog = new DataOutputStream(new FileOutputStream("writerequests.log"));
            auditlog.writeBytes("Write Requests Log Started:\n");
        }
        catch (IOException e)
        {
            System.err.println("Write requests log file not opened properly\n" +
                e.toString());
        }

        System.out.println("MySecurityManager constructed");
    }

    public void checkWrite(String f)
```

Figure 83. (Part 1 of 2). MySecurityManager.java

```
    {
        try
        {
            auditlog.writeBytes("Write Request file: " + f + "\n");
        }
        catch(IOException ioe)
        {
            System.err.println("Could not write to log file\n" + ioe.toString());
        }

        super.checkWrite(f);   /* Go do real checkWrite */
    }
}
```

Figure 84. (Part 2 of 2). MySecurityManager.java

In Figure 85 on page 208 and Figure 86 on page 209 is TestSM.java. This
program sets MySecurityManager as the current security manager and asks
it whether it has write permission to a file name passed to it on the command
line. You can actually pass it any number of file names to check.

```
/**
 *   Test MySecurityManager
 */

import java.io.*;
import java.security.*;

public class TestSM
{
    /**
     * main entrypoint - starts the application
     * @param args java.lang.String[]
     */
    public static void main(java.lang.String[] args)
    {
        if (args.length > 0)
        {
            System.setSecurityManager(new MySecurityManager());

            for (int i = 0; i < args.length; i++)
            {
```

Figure 85. (Part 1 of 2). TestSM.java

```
            try
            {
                System.getSecurityManager().checkWrite(args[i]);
            }
            catch(SecurityException se)
            {
                System.out.println("Write request for: " + args[i] +
                    " denied. Message:");
                System.out.println(se.toString());
                break;
            }

            System.out.println("Write request for: " + args[i] + " permitted");
        }
      }
    }
}
```

Figure 86. (Part 2 of 2). TestSM.java

Before we can run this test case, we have to consider the permissions
required for it. The TestSM application creates a security manager instance
and then sets it as the active security manager by using the method
java.lang.System.setSecurityManager(). Alternatively, we could have set a
security manager by the command line option -Djava.security.manager. In any
case, supposing that D:\itso\ch07 is the directory where the file TestSM.class
is stored, the following statements must exist in either a user policy file or the
system policy file:

```
grant codeBase "file:/D:/itso/ch07/" {
  permission java.lang.RuntimePermission "createSecurityManager";
  permission java.lang.RuntimePermission "setSecurityManager";
};
```

On the other hand, it makes sense for a security manager to be completely
trusted, and not subjected to security checks. For this reason, the class file
MySecurityManager.class should be stored in a separate directory and its
code be granted AllPermission. The most correct way to do this is probably to
store MySecurityManager in the classes directory under ${java.home}. This
directory does not exist by default, but once you create it, each class file that
is stored in that directory becomes part of the boot class path (see 3.4.1,
"Boot Class Path" on page 84, Figure 370 on page 676 and Figure 371 on
page 677); thus it is completely trusted.

Next, we need to decide on a couple of tests. Since we are just checking permissions, the files do not actually have to exist, but the permissions must. So the previous statements are not enough. In fact, the JVM, by default, gives our applications permission to read files in the current directory, not to write them, so we should set appropriate write permissions even if the files that we pass to TestSM on the command line are in the same directory.

The following screen shows our user policy file, which by default is called .java.policy and is specified by the policy.url.2 property. This property is set in the java.security file, found in the ${java.home}/lib/security directory. You can see that classes found in our working directory D:\itso\ch07 have permission to create and set a security manager and to write the file testFile1, stored in the same directory:

```
grant codeBase "file:/D:/itso/ch07/" {
  permission java.lang.RuntimePermission "createSecurityManager";
  permission java.lang.RuntimePermission "setSecurityManager";
  permission java.io.FilePermission "D:${/}itso${/}ch07${/}testFile1", "write";
};
```

We are now ready to run the test case. We run the program as follows:

```
java TestSM testFile1 testFile2
```

Write access to testFile1 should be permitted and write access to testFile2 should be denied. The results of this are shown next:

- The output on the console:

```
MySecurityManager constructed
Write request for: testFile1 permitted
Write request for: testFile2 denied. Message:
java.security.AccessControlException: access denied (java.io.FilePermission testFile2 write)
```

- The resultant contents of the writerequests.log file:

```
Write Requests Log Started:
Write Request file: testFile1
Write Request file: testFile2
```

With this example complete you should have a good idea what it takes to add function to the SecurityManager provided with Java 2 without losing the function provided by SecurityManager. We have also shown how to catch a security exception and handle it in a proper way.

7.5.2 Second Example – Overriding checkPermission()

We want to show you now the use of the new checkPermission() method which takes a Permission object as an argument. However, if you test this example on Java 2 SDK, Standard Edition, V1.2 and V1.2.1, you will run into a problem, which prevents you from completing the test successfully. On these two platforms, overriding SecurityManager.checkPermission() causes the JVM to overflow its stack when calling System.setSecurityManager(), or during JVM initialization if the option -Djava.security.manager is used. This does not occur if you choose to override one of the other check methods (see 7.5.1, "First Example – Overriding checkWrite()" on page 206). We reported this problem and a fix was implemented in the maintenance release Java 2 SDK, Standard Edition, JDK V1.2.2. So, if you have a need to extend SecurityManager and wish to override checkPermission(), you must run with a minimum of Java 2, Standard Edition, V1.2.2.

In Figure 87 on page 211 through Figure 90 on page 213 are the SecurityManager extension, CPSecurityManager.java and the test program, TestCheckPerm.java respectively. They show you how to create a permission from the file name argument and how to call checkPermission().

```
/**
 *   CPSecurityManager.java
 *   Extends SecurityManager
 *   Simple extension to log write permission requests
 */

import java.io.*;
import java.net.*;
import java.lang.*;
import java.security.Permission;
import java.security.AccessController;

public class CPSecurityManager extends SecurityManager
{
    private DataOutputStream auditlog;

    public CPSecurityManager()
    {
        super(); /* initilize using parent constructor */

        try
        {
```

Figure 87. (Part 1 of 2). CPSecurityManager.java

```
                auditlog = new DataOutputStream(new FileOutputStream("CPwriterequests.log"));
                auditlog.writeBytes("Write Requests Log Started:\n");
            }
            catch (IOException e)
            {
                System.err.println("Write requests log file not opened properly\n" +
    e.toString());
            }

            System.out.println("CPSecurityManager constructed");
        }

        public void checkPermission(Permission perm)
        {
            String s = perm.getActions();
            if (s.indexOf("write") != -1)
            {
                try
                {
                    auditlog.writeBytes("Request: " + perm.toString() + "\n");
                }
                catch (IOException ioe)
                {
                    System.err.println("Could not write to log file\n" + ioe.toString());
                }
            }

            super.checkPermission(perm);  /* Go do real checkPermission */
        }
    }
```

Figure 88. (Part 2 of 2). CPSecurityManager.java

```
/**
 *  Test CPSecurityManager
 */

import java.io.*;
import java.security.*;

public class TestCheckPerm
{
```

Figure 89. (Part 1 of 2). TestCheckPerm.java

```
/**
 * main entrypoint - starts the application
 * @param args java.lang.String[]
 */
public static void main(java.lang.String[] args)
{
  if (args.length > 0)
  {
    FilePermission fp;
    System.setSecurityManager(new CPSecurityManager());
    for (int i = 0; i < args.length; i++)
    {
      fp = new FilePermission(args[i], "write");

      try
      {
        System.getSecurityManager().checkPermission(fp);
      }
      catch (SecurityException se)
      {
        System.out.println("Write request for: " + args[i] + " denied. Message:");
        System.out.println(se.toString());
        break;
      }
      System.out.println("Write request for: " + args[i] + " permitted");
    }
  }
}
```

Figure 90. (Part 2 of 2). TestCheckPerm.java

7.5.2.1 The Bug and the Fix

In order to understand why this program caused the Java 2 JVM to overflow, we must show the lines of code of the method java.lang.System.setSecurityManager(), as reported in the src.jar file after installing Java 2 SDK, Standard Edition, V1.2 and V1.2.1:

```
public static synchronized void setSecurityManager(SecurityManager s)
{
   if (security != null)
   {
      // ask the currently installed security manager if we can replace it.
      security.checkPermission(new RuntimePermission("setSecurityManager"));
   }

   security = s;
   InetAddressCachePolicy.setIfNotSet(InetAddressCachePolicy.FOREVER);
}
```

Figure 91. setSecurityManager() in Java 2 Standard Edition SDK V1.2 and V1.2.1

What this method does is the following:

- If there is a security manager already installed, setSecurityManager() first calls the security manager's checkPermission() method with a `RuntimePermission("setSecurityManager")` permission, to ensure it is permitted to replace the existing security manager. This may result in throwing a SecurityException.

- Otherwise, the argument is established as the current security manager. If the argument is null and no security manager has been established, then no action is taken and the method simply returns.

Essentially, the problem that causes the JVM to overflow in the 1.2 and 1.2.1 platforms is that when the JVM first tries to initialize the policy, it generates security checks to be invoked, which causes the JVM to try to initialize the policy, which causes security checks to be invoked... This way a loop is generated. The program could still be launched by entering the following command:

```
javac TestCheckPerm fileTest1 fileTest2
```

However, a severe problem would occur and the following error window would be displayed instantly:

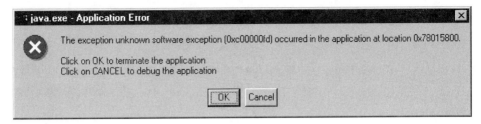

Figure 92. JVM Overflow Error Message

The loop does not occur if there is only system code on the stack, but when you set a security manager, which is *not* on system code, you run into the looping problem.

As we said, this bug has been fixed in the java.lang.System.setSecurityManager() implementation of the maintenance release Java 2 SDK, Standard Edition, V1.2.2[2], as shown in the following figure:

```
public static synchronized void setSecurityManager(final SecurityManager s)
{
  if (security != null)
  {
    // ask the currently installed security manager if we can replace it.
    security.checkPermission(new RuntimePermission("setSecurityManager"));
  }

  if (s.getClass().getClassLoader() != null)
  {
    // New security manager class is not on bootstrap classpath.
    // Cause policy to get initialized before we install the new
    // security manager, in order to prevent infinite loops when
    // trying to initialize the policy (which usually involves
    // accessing some security and/or system properties, which in turn
    // calls the installed security manager's checkPermission() method
    // which will loop infinitely if there is a non-system class
    // (in this case: the new security manager class) on the stack).
    AccessController.doPrivileged(new PrivilegedAction()
    {
      public Object run()
      {
```

Figure 93. (Part 1 of 2). setSecurityManager() in Java 2 SDK, Standard Edition, V1.2.2

[2] Java 2 SDK, Standard Edition, V1.2.2 was not yet released when this book went to print. So you should consider that this understanding is based on a not-yet-released level of the Java 2 SDK.

```
            s.getClass().getProtectionDomain().implies(new AllPermission());
            return null;
        }
    });
}

security = s;
InetAddressCachePolicy.setIfNotSet(InetAddressCachePolicy.FOREVER);
}
```

Figure 94. (Part 2 of 2). setSecurityManager() in Java 2 SDK, Standard Edition, V1.2.2

This fix essentially forces the policy to get initialized when we call:

```
s.getClass().getProtectionDomain().implies(new AllPermission());
```

This time, the initialization is done in a privileged block, and completes without further looping.

7.5.2.2 Installing and Running the Program

Assuming that D:\itso\ch07 is the directory where the file TestCheckPerm.class is stored, the following statements must exist in either a user policy file or the system policy file:

```
grant codeBase "file:/D:/itso/ch07/" {
  permission java.lang.RuntimePermission "createSecurityManager";
  permission java.lang.RuntimePermission "setSecurityManager";
};
```

On the other hand, as we mentioned in 7.5.1, "First Example – Overriding checkWrite()" on page 206, it makes sense for a security manager to be completely trusted, and not subjected to security checks. For this reason, the class file CPSecurityManager.class should be stored in a separate directory and its code be granted AllPermission. We have already said that the most correct way to do this is probably to store CPSecurityManager in the classes directory under ${java.home}. This directory does not exist by default, but once you create it, each class file that is stored in that directory becomes part of the boot class path (see 3.4.1, "Boot Class Path" on page 84, Figure 370 on page 676 and Figure 371 on page 677), thus it is completely trusted.

Next, we want to implement a couple of tests, very similar to what we did when overriding the checkWrite() method. Since we are just checking permissions, the files do not actually have to exist, but the permissions must.

So the previous statements are not enough and we have to set appropriate write permissions. The same user policy file .java.policy shown in 7.5.1, "First Example – Overriding checkWrite()" on page 206 can still be applied, without any modification:

You can see that classes found in our working directory, D:\itso\ch07, have permission to create and set a security manager and to write the file testFile1:

```
rant codeBase "file:/D:/itso/ch07/" {
    permission java.lang.RuntimePermission "createSecurityManager";
    permission java.lang.RuntimePermission "setSecurityManager";
    permission java.io.FilePermission "D:${/}itso${/}ch07${/}testFile1", "write";
};
```

You can see that classes found in our working directory D:\itso\ch07 have permission to create and set a security manager and to write the file testFile1, stored in the same directory.

We are now ready to run the test case. We run the program as follows:

```
java TestCheckPerm testFile1 testFile2
```

Write access to testFile1 should be permitted and write access to testFile2 should be denied. The results of this are shown next and they confirm what we expected:

- The output on the console:

```
CPSecurityManager constructed
Write request for: testFile1 permitted
Write request for: testFile2 denied. Message:
java.security.AccessControlException: access denied (java.io.FilePermission testFile2 write)
```

- The resultant contents of the CPwriterequests.log file:

```
Write Requests Log Started:
Request: (java.io.FilePermission testFile1 write)
Request: (java.io.FilePermission testFile2 write)
```

With this example you should now have a good idea of how to override the checkPermission() method of the default security manager.

7.5.3 Third Example – Overriding checkRead() and checkWrite()

In this example we show you how to implement a security manager which asks the user for a password whenever a simple file read or write is attempted. This security manager overrides the default one provided by the Java 2 SDK APIs, java.lang.SecurityManager. Here is the code:

```java
import java.io.*;

public class RWSecurityManager extends SecurityManager
{
    private String rpasswd;   // We have a private read password
    private String wpasswd;   // We have a private write password

    public RWSecurityManager(String rpwd, String wpwd)
    {
        super();

        // The class using this security manager will give the read password
        this.rpasswd = rpwd;

        // The class using this security manager will give the write password
        this.wpasswd = wpwd;
    }

    public void checkRead(FileDescriptor filedescriptor)
    {
    }

    public void checkRead(String filename)
    {
        String pwdgiven;

        // Ask if the user has the required password
        System.out.println("What's the secret password for reading the file?");
        try
        {
            pwdgiven = new BufferedReader(new InputStreamReader(System.in)).readLine();
            if (pwdgiven.equals(rpasswd))
                System.out.println("Granted permission to read files");
            else
                throw new SecurityException("You do not have access to read the file!");
        }
        catch (IOException e)
```

Figure 95. (Part 1 of 2). RWSecurityManager.java

```
        {
            throw new SecurityException("You do not have access to read the file!");
        }

        // Uncomment the line below if you want to call
        // SecurityManager.checkRead() at this time

        // super.checkRead(filename);
    }

    public void checkRead(String filename, Object executionContext)
    {
    }

    public void checkWrite(FileDescriptor filedescriptor)
    {
    }

    public void checkWrite(String filename)
    {
        String pwdgiven;

        // Ask if the user has the required password
        System.out.println("What's the secret password for writing the file?");
        try
        {
            pwdgiven = new BufferedReader(new InputStreamReader(System.in)).readLine();
            if (pwdgiven.equals(wpasswd))
                System.out.println("Granted the permission to write to files");
            else
                throw new SecurityException("You do not have access to write to a file!");
        }
        catch (IOException e)
        {
            throw new SecurityException("You do not have access to write to a file!");
        }

        // Uncomment the line below if you want to call
        // SecurityManager.checkWrite() at this time

        // super.checkWrite(filename);
    }
}
```

Figure 96. (Part 2 of 2). RWSecurityManager.java

The code above implements a security manager, called RWSecurityManager, that overrides the checkRead() and checkWrite() methods of java.lang.SecurityManager. What the code really does is easy to understand by reading the comments embedded in the code.

Next, we write the code of the application that uses this security manager. We create a class called TestRWSecMgr, which invokes RWSecurityManager passing two String arguments to it, corresponding to the fields rpasswd (password for reading files on the system) and wpasswd (password for writing to files on the system). Whenever an application tries to read any file, the checkRead() method of the RWSecurityManager class is called. Hence this asks the user for the password and checks the user input against the read password supplied by the application. The same happens for writing, the only difference being that in this case the checkWrite() method is called.

The full code for the TestRWSecMgr application is shown in the following figure:

```java
import java.io.*;

public class TestRWSecMgr
{
    public static void main(String[] args) throws Exception
    {
        int count=0;
        if (args.length != 2)
            System.out.println("Usage: java TestSecMgr FILENAME OUTPUTFILENAME");
        else
        {
            try
            {
                System.setSecurityManager(new RWSecurityManager("redbook", "ibm"));
            }
            catch (SecurityException e)
            {
                System.err.println("SecurityManager could not be set!");
            }

            try
            {
                //Reading from a file
                FileInputStream fis = new FileInputStream(args[0]);
                while (fis.read() != -1)
```

Figure 97. (Part 1 of 2). TestRWScrMgr.java

```
                count++;
            fis.close();

            //Writing to a file
            DataOutputStream fos = new DataOutputStream(new FileOutputStream(args[1]));
            fos.flush();
            fos.writeBytes("Hi! We counted ");
            fos.writeBytes(new Integer(count).toString());
            fos.writeBytes(" chars.");
            fos.close();
        }
        catch (Exception e)
        {
            System.err.println("Exception caught: " + e);
        }
    }
  }
}
```

Figure 98. (Part 2 of 2). TestRWScrMgr.java

As you can see, this application sets the security manager to
RWSecurityManager. This is done by calling the method
setSecurityManager() for the class java.lang.System, which we discussed in
7.5.2, "Second Example – Overriding checkPermission()" on page 211:

```
System.setSecurityManager(new RWSecurityManager("redbook","ibm"));
```

Notice that the passwords passed to the security manager are `redbook` for
reading and `ibm` for writing.

The class RWSecurityManager can be compiled with the command:

```
javac RWSecurityManager.java
```

This command is supposed to be launched from the same directory where
RWSecurityManager.java resides. As we discussed in 7.5.2, "Second
Example – Overriding checkPermission()" on page 211, it makes sense for a
security manager class to be trusted by the Java system. The proper location
for a security manager is the classes directory under the directory
${java.home}. As we have already explained, this directory does not exist by
default. It must be explicitly created by the user. Once created, all the class
files that are stored in that directory automatically become part of the boot
class path. For this reason, we copy RWSecurityManager.class to the classes
directory.

When we compile TestRWSecMgr.java, we need to specify where RWSecurityManager.class is, because this class must be found at compile time. The proper way to compile TestRWSecMgr.java is through the following command, launched from the same directory where TestRWSecMgr.java resides:

```
javac -classpath .;"D:\\Program Files\\JavaSoft\\JRE\\1.2\\classes" TestRWSecMgr.java
```

Now, if you run this program specifying the -Djava.security.manager command line option, you will see that the TestRWSecMgr application is not allowed to set or create a security manager. The default security manager, which is called first, does not give this application the permission to set and create a different security manager. It is therefore necessary to modify the current security policy configuration, adding the following lines to one of the current policy files:

```
grant codeBase "file:/F:/itso/ch07/" {
  permission java.lang.RuntimePermission "setSecurityManager";
  permission java.lang.RuntimePermission "createSecurityManager";
};
```

We assume here that the TestRWSecMgr class is located in the directory F:\itso\ch07.

Then we run the program and we see that it works as expected, as shown in the following session screen:

```
F:\itso\ch07>java -Djava.security.manager TestRWSecMgr TestRWSecMgr.java results.txt
What's the secret password for reading the file?
redbook
Granted permission to read files
What's the secret password for writing the file?
ibm
Granted the permission to write to files

F:\itso\ch07>
```

The parameters passed on the command line are the Java source code of the TestRWSecMgr class, TestRWSecMgr.java, and a file called results.txt that is automatically created by the application in the same directory. In this file, the application writes the number of characters it counts in the TestRWSecMgr.java file. On opening results.txt with a normal text editor, we find the following contents:

```
Hi! We counted 1206 chars.
```

Notice that it has not been necessary to grant the code source of the TestRWSecMgr class the permission to read and write files. This is because we have completely overridden the methods checkRead() and checkWrite() of the superclass java.lang.SecurityManager, which in turn would have called checkPermission() in AccessController. Our security manager bases its policy decision on a password. If you want to keep the behavior of SecurityManager, which requires specific read and write permissions enabled through the policy file, you have to call super.checkRead() and super.checkWrite(). The code in Figure 95 on page 218 and Figure 96 on page 219 shows the calls to these two methods commented out. Just uncomment those lines if you want to enable the default security manager functions. At that point, you will need to modify one of the current policy files of your system in order to have the application work correctly. What you should add to it is the following:

```
grant codeBase "file:/F:/itso/ch07/" {
  permission java.lang.RuntimePermission "setSecurityManager";
  permission java.lang.RuntimePermission "createSecurityManager";
  permission java.io.FilePermission "<<ALL FILES>>", "read, write";
};
```

This example illustrates how to implement a security manager that does more than a simple access logging, as the others seen in 7.5.1, "First Example – Overriding checkWrite()" on page 206 and 7.5.2, "Second Example – Overriding checkPermission()" on page 211. In fact this shows how to overwrite the default security manager and base the access verification on passwords. We have also seen how it is possible to combine the password-based control to the policy-based access control of the default security manager.

We also want to bring your attention to the fact that the two passwords are hardcoded in the TestRWSecMgr class file. This could be a security risk, as we underlined in 5.3.1, "Decompilation Attacks" on page 126. The passwords we used would appear in the clear after decompiling the program or even after opening the class file with a hexadecimal editor or a simple text editor. The purpose of this example, once again, was to demonstrate how to use the Java 2 APIs to implement a customized security manager. However, for serious applications, we recommend that you build a client/server type application with a Java presentation layer that can be run anywhere and a secured server side where sensitive information can be stored.

7.6 Summary

The security manager is a class that allows applications to implement a security policy. It allows an application to determine, before performing a possibly unsafe or sensitive operation, what the operation is and whether it is being attempted in a security context that allows the operation to be performed. The application can allow or disallow the operation.

In this chapter, we explained the unique role that the security manager plays in Java 2. You should now have a clear idea of the main functions of the security manager and its relationship with the class loader and class file verifier.

This chapter has also demonstrated a security attack that can affect your system when browsing the Internet: an invisible applet can install itself on your system, generate a number of new threads, and steal CPU cycles and memory.

Finally, we demonstrated how to write simple extensions of the default Java 2 security manager java.lang.SecurityManager. Those examples are useful especially when you want to add new functions to the default security manager, such as logging or password protection, without losing the basic features of the security manager that comes with the Java 2 platform.

Chapter 8. Security Configuration Files in the Java 2 SDK

The security aspects of Java have changed drastically from the Java Development Kit (JDK) 1.1 to Java 2 SDK, Standard Edition, V1.2. In this section, we show you how you can configure Java 2 security on your system.

After the installation of the Java 2 SDK, you will see two files located in the directory ${java.home}${/}lib${/}security: the *security file*, java.security, and the *policy file*, java.policy. These are the primary security configuration files of the Java Virtual Machine (JVM) running on your system, and they are used to define security properties and manage access permissions. After the installation, you can modify or rewrite these default files.

Notice that a copy of these files is also installed in the Java 2 SDK development security directory (by default, on Windows systems, C:\jdk1.2.x\jre\lib\security), for use only with the development tools, such as the Applet Viewer and the Java compiler javac.

8.1 A Note on java.home and the JRE Installation Directory

An interesting thing to note is that when you install the Java 2 SDK, Standard Edition, V1.2.*x*, you have the option to install the Java Runtime Environment (JRE) 1.2.*x* as one of its components, as shown in the following figure:

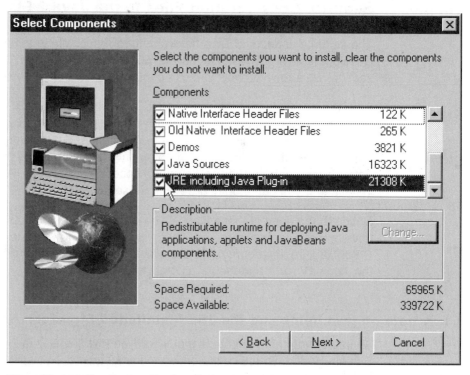

Figure 99. Installing the Java Runtime Environment and Java Plug-in

If you install the Java 2 SDK while the JRE box is checked, you will have in fact two JREs on your system: one is installed with the SDK and the other is a separate JRE. You can uncheck the option to install the JRE at the very beginning of the install process but later you cannot do that.

On Windows systems, Java 2 SDK, Standard Edition, V1.2.*x* installs by default in the C:\jdk1.2.*x* directory and JRE in the directory C:\Program Files\JavaSoft\JRE\1.2. If you keep the default settings, you will find two pairs of the security configuration files: one in the directory C:\jdk1.2.*x*\jre\lib\security and the other in the directory C:\Program Files\JavaSoft\JRE\1.2\lib\security. The configuration files which are effective are in the second directory. In this case, the value of the variable java.home is C:\Program Files\JavaSoft\JRE\1.2, as demonstrated in Appendix A, "Getting Internal System Properties" on page 675.

However, if you uncheck the option to install the JRE at the beginning, you get only one set of security configuration files. The value of the variable java.home in this case is C:\jdk1.2.*x*\jre and the configuration files are located in C:\jdk1.2.*x*\jre\lib\security. Interestingly, if you do not uncheck the option at the beginning, and later on, during the JRE installation, you change the installation directory of the JRE to C:\jdk1.2.*x*\jre, then the previous files are overwritten. In such a case the installation routine does not install the JRE again and the value of java.home is C:\jdk1.2.*x*\jre, which is the JRE development directory.

The value of java.home takes effect for all the Java programs you run on your system, including the applets you run in a Web browser that make use of the Java Plug-in (see Chapter 11., "The Java Plug-In" on page 359); the system uses the value of that variable to search for system libraries and configuration files. However, for all the development tools, such as the Java compiler and the Applet Viewer, the system always considers java.home as C:\jdk1.2.*x*\jre, irrespective of whether JRE is installed again or not. This is because test tools are used for development only. So, in this way, Java helps you separate the development environment from the run-time environment. This is demonstrated by the following applet:

```java
import java.applet.*;
import java.awt.Graphics;

public class PropertyApplet extends Applet
{
    public void paint(Graphics g)
    {
        try
        {
            String s1 = System.getProperty("java.home");
            String s2 = System.getProperty("user.home");
            g.drawString("java.home has the following value: " + s1, 20, 20);
            g.drawString("user.home has the following value: " + s2, 20, 40);
        }
        catch (Exception e)
        {
            System.out.println("Exception caught" + e.toString());
        }
    }
}
```

Figure 100. PropertyApplet.java

This applet is compiled through the command:

```
javac PropertyApplet.java
```

We invoke it from within the following HTML page:

```
<HTML>
   <HEAD>
      <TITLE>PropertyApplet Applet</TITLE>
   </HEAD>

   <BODY>
      <CENTER><h2>PropertyApplet Applet</h2>
      <HR>
      <BR>

      <APPLET Code="PropertyApplet.class" Width=400 Height=50>
         <H4>This area contains a Java applet, but your browser is not Java-enabled</H4>
      </APPLET>

   </BODY>
</HTML>
```

Figure 101. PropertyApplet.html

Next, we invoke this HTML page with the Java 2 SDK Applet Viewer:

`appletviewer PropertyApplet.html`

In order for the command above to work without throwing any exception, it is necessary to grant the Java class PropertyApplet, residing in the directory D:\itso\ch08, the permission to read the Java system properties java.home and user.home. This is done by adding the following lines to one of the current policy files, as we will see in 8.4, "Security Policy Files" on page 242:

```
grant codeBase "file:/D:/itso/ch08/" {
   permission java.util.PropertyPermission "java.home", "read";
   permission java.util.PropertyPermission "user.home", "read";
};
```

The `appletviewer` command brings up the following Applet Viewer window:

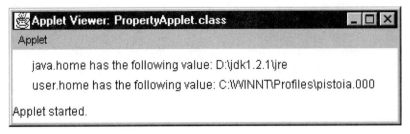

Figure 102. PropertyApplet Running

This demonstrates that for a development tool, such as the Applet Viewer, the java.home directory changes to become the JRE development directory, while another system property, such as user.home, still has the same value.

Notice that, whenever you have two JRE environments installed on your machine, you need to be very careful and must know where your library and configuration files are being picked up from. For example when you compile a Java program using the command:

```
javac MyClass.java
```

then the core Java classes and the extensions are picked up from the JRE development directory (typically C:\jdk1.2.*x*\jre) and its subdirectories. However, when you run the program with:

```
java MyClass
```

then they are picked up from the separate JRE run-time directory (typically C:\Program Files\JavaSoft\JRE\1.2) and its subdirectories. The same holds true for the security and policy files, which are the security configuration files.

When the JRE is installed, a copy of the java executable file (java.exe on Windows systems) is also put in a location that is on the operating system's default system Path. For example, on a Windows NT system, it is typically put in C:\WINNT\system32. Hence, when you install the Java 2 SDK, you will be able to run the `java` command without setting the Path variable. However, to run the `javac` command, you will have to include the appropriate path to the javac executable file (javac.exe on Windows systems) in the Path variable. All SDK development tools, including the `javac` compiler, are installed in the same directory, typically C:\jdk1.2.*x*\bin, on Windows systems.

You are probably wondering how the system can know the value of the java.home property. If you install Java 2 SDK, Standard Edition, V1.2 on AIX and you run the program GetProperty shown in A.2, "Program GetProperty" on page 678 to find out the value of java.home, you see the following output:

```
property value is: J1.2/bin/..
```

This means that to define java.home, Java finds the directory where the Java executable files are and then goes one level up: that is the java home directory. This, at least, seems to happen on AIX. We repeat the same experiment on Windows NT.

If we move all the Java executables to the D:\itso\bin directory, java.home becomes D:\itso, as the following output demonstrates:

```
java.home property value is: D:\itso
```

If we put them in D:\ all programs return an error as there is no directory one level up from the root directory.

Note that in order to verify the java.home directory when moving the executables, the Path variable must be manually set to include the new directory where the executables are and the boot class path must be specified on the command line using the -Xbootclasspath option.

In the rest of this section we describe the two security configuration files of the Java system. However, before examining them, we first need to introduce the concept of a keystore.

8.2 Keystores

A *keystore* is a database of private keys and their associated certificates or certificate chains, which authenticate the corresponding public keys.

The default keystore implementation, provided by Sun Microsystems, is a flat file, utilizing a proprietary keystore type or format, named *Java Keystore* (JKS). This format protects the integrity of the entire keystore with a keystore password. A hash value of the entire keystore is used to protect the keystore from alteration. Each private key in the keystore is also protected with a separate password (though this password may be identical to the keystore password). In different keystore implementations that can make use of encryption, such as the keystore implementation that comes with JCE 1.2 (see Point 2 on page 492), private keys can be stored encrypted using one of the encryption algorithms provided.

Notice that a KeyStore class is provided in the package java.security. It supplies methods to access and modify the information in the keystores (see 10.1.6, "Key Management" on page 305).

On a Windows NT system, the keystore is created by default with the `keytool` command as the file .keystore in the directory ${user.home}. It is possible to change both the implementation and the location of the keystore that comes by default with the Java 2 SDK installation, but the system must be aware of what implementation and location have been selected:

- The implementation of the keystore is specified, as we are going to see, in the security properties file, defined by the value of the property named keystore.type.

- The location of the keystore is specified in the policy file, defined by the `keystore URL` entry.

If you so desire, you can create a new keystore implementation. You might want to do so to, say, store keys and certificates in a database. Then you need to refer to your own keystore implementation in the security properties file and to the location of the keystore in the policy file.

In a keystore you can store your own certificates or certificates of CAs and trusted entities. As we have said, Java 2 provides the `keytool` command line utility for storing your private keys and viewing or listing public information about a certificate in a JKS keystore. Since a keystore is password-protected, you need to enter a password to access the private information stored in the keystore. Each private key may also be protected by a separate password which also needs to be provided by the user.

Notice that public information can be accessed without the password. However, in that case, as the `keytool` utility is unable to verify the integrity of the keystore, a warning message is displayed on the screen, as shown here:

```
*****************  WARNING WARNING WARNING  *****************
* The integrity of the information stored in your keystore  *
* has NOT been verified!  In order to verify its integrity, *
* you must provide your keystore password.                  *
*****************  WARNING WARNING WARNING  *****************
```

You will notice that if you register the public information of a certificate as trusted and then try to run an applet signed by that certificate, the JVM automatically retrieves the public key from the keystore, *without* your intervention and *without* asking for the keystore password. The reason for this is that all public information, such as public key and certificate, is stored unencrypted in the keystore, and only the private key is stored password-encrypted, so that it is protected from unauthorized users. The keystore password is used for an integrity check only, so you are prompted to verify that the keystore has not been tampered with.

A demonstration of this can be obtained in the following way. When you open the keystore with a text editor, amidst all the junk, you can see the value of a certificate you know existed in the keystore in plain text:

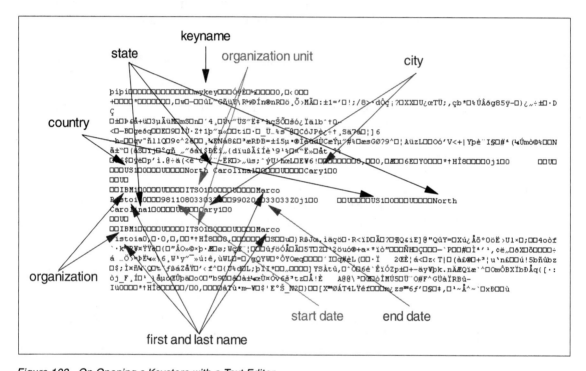

Figure 103. On Opening a Keystore with a Text Editor

Notice also that all keys or certificates stored in the keystore are identified by aliases.

Users can have as many keystores as they wish. Users can create additional keystores if they want to:

1. Generate a public-private key pair for themselves.

2. Sign a code with their private key and export their certificates to send to others for verification along with the signed code.

3. Import others' certificates to verify signatures.

4. Create a certificate request to be signed by a certification authority (CA).

All these activities are facilitated by the `keytool` command line utility. Notice that each different keystore can be protected with a different password.

8.2.1 The Certificates KeyStore File cacerts

The cacerts file is a system-wide keystore for storing trusted CA certificates. It is implemented in the JKS format, is located in the ${java.home}${/}lib${/}security directory and can be manipulated with the `keytool` command line utility.

Currently, the cacerts file ships with five VeriSign root CA certificates. You can view these certificates using the `-list` command associated with the `keytool` utility:

```
keytool -list -keystore cacerts
```

The output of this command is shown in the following figure:

```
Keystore type: jks
Keystore provider: SUN
Your keystore contains 5 entries:

verisignclass3ca, Mon Jun 29 13:05:51 EDT 1998, trustedCertEntry,
Certificate fingerprint (MD5):
78:2A:02:DF:DB:2E:14:D5:A7:5F:0A:DF:B6:8E:9C:5D
verisignclass1ca, Mon Jun 29 13:06:17 EDT 1998, trustedCertEntry,
Certificate fingerprint (MD5):
51:86:E8:1F:BC:B1:C3:71:B5:18:10:DB:5F:DC:F6:20
verisignserverca, Mon Jun 29 13:07:34 EDT 1998, trustedCertEntry,
Certificate fingerprint (MD5):
74:7B:82:03:43:F0:00:9E:6B:B3:EC:47:BF:85:A5:93
verisignclass4ca, Mon Jun 29 13:06:57 EDT 1998, trustedCertEntry,
Certificate fingerprint (MD5):
1B:D1:AD:17:8B:7F:22:13:24:F5:26:E2:5D:4E:B9:10
verisignclass2ca, Mon Jun 29 13:06:39 EDT 1998, trustedCertEntry,
Certificate fingerprint (MD5):
EC:40:7D:2B:76:52:67:05:2C:EA:F2:3A:4F:65:F0:D8
```

Figure 104. Default CA Certificates in the Java 2 Platform

On launching this command you will be asked for the password. However, a password is not mandatory to display the contents of a keystore; if you do not enter the right password, the output shown in the figure above is displayed anyway, but you will be informed that the integrity of the information stored in the keystore has not been verified. On the contrary, you will not be allowed to import a new certificate in the keystore file if you do not enter the exact password. By default, the initial password is `changeit`. As the name itself suggests, it is recommended you change the default password, as this keystore is very important for the simple reason that it contains the certificates of the CAs that are considered trusted. A keystore password can be changed using the `-storepasswd` command associated with the `keytool` command line utility (see 9.1.3, "Commands and Options Associated with keytool" on page 262).

Since CAs are entities that are trusted by users for signing and issuing certificates to other entities, the cacerts file should be managed only by system administrators. With the `keytool` utility, it is possible to add new CA certificates or remove old CA certificates from the cacerts file. Utmost care should be taken while importing any trusted certificate into the cacerts keystore, as it should only contain certificates of the CAs that the system administrators trust.

8.3 The Security Properties File, java.security

This is a configuration file in which you set the Java security properties for the system. These security properties are used by classes in the java.security package. The following figure shows the default properties file installed with Java 2 SDK, Standard Edition, V1.2.1, except for the fact that the comments that explain each entry have been removed here:

```
security.provider.1=sun.security.provider.Sun
policy.provider=sun.security.provider.PolicyFile
policy.url.1=file:${java.home}/lib/security/java.policy
policy.url.2=file:${user.home}/.java.policy
policy.expandProperties=true
policy.allowSystemProperty=true
policy.ignoreIdentityScope=false
keystore.type=jks
system.scope=sun.security.provider.IdentityDatabase
package.access=sun.
#package.definition=
```

Figure 105. Default Security Properties File

As we have said, the directory where this file is installed is ${java.home}${/}lib${/}security, and a copy of it is found also in the JRE development directory for use with the development tools.

The java.security file, amidst all the comments and explanations, contains important directives, which are all of the form:

```
property_variable=value
```

Notice that by default the last entry is commented out.

In the following list we explain all the entries of the default security properties file:

- **Security provider**

    The first entry specifies the cryptography package providers, their locations, and their precedence orders. The term *provider* refers to a package or set of packages that supply a concrete implementation of a subset of the cryptography aspects of the Java Security API. A provider may, for example, implement one or more digital signature algorithms or message digest algorithms.

    There must be at least one provider specification in java.security. If an alternative provider has to be added, it must be specified in the security properties file as:

    ```
    security.provider.n=className
    ```

    This adds the provider with the preference order *n*. The provider order is 1-based. If an implementation is supplied by multiple providers, the implementation of the provider with the higher preference (that is, lower serial number *n*) is chosen. This means that the JVM looks for the implementation required in the first provider. If it is found, it stops and uses that; otherwise, it looks in the next provider, and continues until it gets the implementation.

    `className` must specify the subclass of the java.security.Provider abstract class whose constructor sets the values of various properties that are required for the Java security API to look up the algorithms or other facilities implemented by the provider.

    The Provider class has methods for accessing the provider name, version number, and other information about the implementations of the algorithms for key generation, conversion and management facilities, signature generation, and message digest generation.

    Provider subclasses statically registered through the security properties file are instantiated when the system is initialized. Providers may also be registered dynamically. To do so, you should call either the addProvider() or insertProviderAt() static methods in the java.security.Security class. However, such a configuration is not persistent and can only be done by *trusted* programs. This may be done if only specific applications need a particular provider. Note that by *trusted programs* we mean applications that have been granted a specific SecurityPermission by the user. See 8.4, "Security Policy Files" on page 242 and 10.7, "The Permission Classes" on page 339 for more details.

The default provider that comes standard with the Java 2 SDK is called SUN, and its Provider subclass, named Sun, appears in the sun.security.provider package. The SUN provider offers:

- An implementation of the Digital Signature Algorithm (DSA)

  Signature algorithms are used to create a signature of a particular file using the message digest and the private key of the signer.

- An implementation of the MD5 and Secure Hash Algorithm (SHA)-1 message digest algorithms

  Message digest algorithms are used to create the message digests of files using the file itself and the constant *chaining variable* defined in the digest algorithm.

- A DSA key pair generator for generating a pair of public and private keys suitable for the DSA algorithm

- A DSA algorithm parameter generator

- A DSA algorithm parameter manager

- A DSA *key factory* providing bi-directional conversions between opaque DSA private and public key objects and their underlying key material

- An implementation of the proprietary SHA1PRNG pseudo-random number generation algorithm

- A *certificate factory* for X.509 certificates and certificate revocation Lists (CRLs)

- The JKS keystore implementation for the proprietary keystore type

- **Policy provider**

  The second entry in the security policy file specifies the class to instantiate as the system policy. This is the name of the class that will be used as the Policy object, in order to determine which permissions are available for code from various sources. The code source includes the

URL location of the code and the certificates of the entities that have signed the code.

The default value defined for the policy provider is the class PolicyFile in the package sun.security.provider. This class defines the default Java 2 SDK policy implementation, which uses static policy files to configure security on the JVM.

- **Policy file URL location**

  If the Policy object instantiated is constructed from policy files, you can specify in the security properties file an ordered list of URLs for the policy files to load and utilize. The default is to have a system-wide policy file having URL location file:/${java.home}/lib/security/java.policy and a user-defined policy file in the user's home directory, having URL location file:${user.home}/.java.policy. To discover the value of java.home and user.home on your system, you can use either of the two programs shown in Appendix A, "Getting Internal System Properties" on page 675.

  The policy order is 1-based. This means that the `policy.url.1` file is read first and the subsequent files later. Note that the precedence numbers must be serial and continuous. In other words, if `policy.url.1` and `policy.url.3`, are present, but `policy.url.2` is missing, then `policy.url.3` is ignored and only `policy.url.1` is considered. So by default, when the Policy class is initialized, the system policy is loaded first and the user policy is added to it. If neither is present, a built-in policy is used, and this is the original sandbox policy. However you can change this implementation by editing the java.security file and modifying the policy file URL location entries according to the following syntax:

  ```
  policy.url.n=URL
  ```

  where n is the precedence number of the policy file to be considered and URL points to the path of the corresponding policy file.

  For instance:

  ```
  policy.url.3=file:/C:/itso/ibm/ibmpolicy
  ```

  The fact that the location of a policy file is specified as a URL implies that policy files do not need to be local, but can be retrieved from a remote system through the HTTP protocol. This opens up interesting possibilities; for example, system administrators can install a system-wide policy file on a policy server and users can use it from their client machines, combining it with a local user-defined policy file.

- **Property expansion**

  This entry specifies whether or not property expansion should be allowed in policy files. The syntax for this entry is the following:

```
policy.expandProperties=boolean
```

where `boolean` can be either `true` (the default) or `false`.

- When this security property is set to `true`, all the system property variables, such as ${java.home} or ${user.home} will be automatically translated into their value each time they appear in a policy file. For example, ${java.home} would be expanded to the value of the java.home property (see Appendix A, "Getting Internal System Properties" on page 675).

- If this security property is set to `false`, property variables will not be expanded in the policy files and must be explicitly hard coded. For example, instead of `${java.home}`, you will have to type the full path, something similar to `C:\Program Files\JavaSoft\JRE\1.2`.

This security property, if set to `true`, makes policy files portable across platforms. In fact, as we said when we spoke about the policy file URL location, system administrators can install a system-wide policy file on a policy server and users can retrieve it from client machines. The possibility to expand system property variables in policy files makes it possible to use the same policy file regardless of the operating system. For example if this property is set to true, `${/}` will be exploded to the appropriate file separator used on the local operating system: a forward slash (/) on UNIX systems and a backslash (\) on Windows systems. Even machines with the same operating system could have differences limiting portability. For example, on one Windows machine the JRE could have been installed in the C drive, and on another machine on the D drive, making the value of java.home C:\Program Files\JavaSoft\JRE\1.2 and D:\Program Files\JavaSoft\JRE\1.2 respectively. Another example is given by the system property user.home: two different users, even working on the same machine, have different home directories, each one containing different security entities, such as the keystores. The possibility to translate `${user.home}` into the actual value of the user home directory makes policy files more general. Expanding the system properties in the policy files solves this kind of problem and applies the concept of *Write Once, Run Anywhere*, which is typical of Java.

On the other hand, if this property is set to `false`, you must specify the system properties explicitly, which means that you will rarely be able to port a policy file from one machine to another.

- **Extra policy**

  In the security property file, you can specify whether or not an extra policy file can be passed on the `java` command line with the option:

```
-Djava.security.policy=policyFile
```

The syntax for this security property is as follows:

```
policy.allowSystemProperty=boolean
```

where `boolean` can be either `true` (the default) or `false`. If this security property is set to `true`, users can specify an additional policy file on the `java` command line for specific applications, as shown in the following example:

```
java -Djava.security.manager -Djava.security.policy=ibmpolicy Count
```

This implies that besides the policy files mentioned in the security file, an *additional* ibmpolicy file is used.

A double equal sign (==), instead of a single one (=), can be specified after the `-Djava.security.policy` flag, as shown in the following example:

```
java -Djava.security.manager -Djava.security.policy==ibmpolicy Count
```

This implies that the policy file specified on the command line (in this example, ibmpolicy) is the *only* policy file used for this application.

Since the same flags used for the `java` command apply also to the `appletviewer` command, provided they are preceded by `-J`, this would be the way to specify an *additional* policy file for use with the Applet Viewer:

```
appletviewer -J-Djava.security.policy=ibmpolicy Count.html
```

This example shows how to specify an *exclusive* extra policy file for use with Applet Viewer:

```
appletviewer -J-Djava.security.policy==ibmpolicy Count.html
```

If this property is set to `false` or is commented out in the security properties file, users will not be able to specify a policy file on the command prompt using the option above, and only the policy files mentioned in the properties file will be used. System administrators can set it to `false` if they wish to strictly check all security permissions and do not want users to set their own permissions thus overriding the system-wide settings. However, setting this to `true` will grant more flexibility as users can define their own policy files according to their applications as and when required.

- **Identity scope**

  The security properties file allows you to set whether or not to look into the identity scope for trusted identities when a JDK 1.1 signed Java Archive (JAR) file is encountered. The security property to configure this is the following:

  ```
  policy.ignoreIdentityScope=boolean
  ```

  where boolean can be either `false` (the default) or `true`.

If this property is set to `true`, the identity scope is ignored and the Java 2 security policy is enforced. If it is set to `false`, the identity scope for trusted identities is looked into and if identity is found and is trusted it is granted AllPermission.

- **Keystore type**

  The security properties file allows you to specify the keystore type to use in your Java security system. The syntax for this property is:

  ```
  keystore.type=type
  ```

  This property is by default set to `jks`, corresponding to the proprietary keystore type, named JKS and created by Sun Microsystems. The features of this keystore implementation are described in 8.2, "Keystores" on page 230.

- **System identity scope**

  Each JVM has a system identity scope that manages a repository of keys, certificates and trust levels. That repository is available to applications that need it for authentication or signing purposes.

  The class to instantiate as the system identity scope is set in the security properties file java.security through the following property:

  ```
  system.scope=className
  ```

  A default identity scope class for a persistent database is supplied by the provider named SUN. This class is sun.security.provider.IdentityDatabase (a subclass of the IdentityScope class). An instance of this class is created every time a Java program is run or an Applet Viewer is started.

  By default, the value of this property is set to the class IdentityDatabase, found in the package sun.security.provider.

- **Packages causing a security exception when passed to checkPackageAccess()**

  In the security properties file, you are allowed to specify a comma-separated list of packages that will cause a security exception to be thrown when passed to SecurityManager.checkPackageAccess(), unless the corresponding RuntimePermission has been granted. Instead of full package names, you can specify a comma-separated list of strings, and all packages that start with one of those strings will also cause a security exception to be thrown.

  The syntax for this entry is as follows:

  ```
  package.access=string1,string2,...,stringN
  ```

  By default, this entry is set to the string `sun`.

The checkPackageAccess() method takes as argument a String representing a package name, and throws a security exception if the calling thread is not allowed to access the package specified by the argument. This method is used by the loadClass() method of class loaders. If the package is restricted, then a call is made to checkPermission() with the permission:

```
java.lang.RunTimePermission("accessClassInPackage.packageName")
```

If it does not have a permission, then the calling thread is not allowed to access classes in that package and a security exception is thrown.

- **Packages causing a security exception when passed to checkPackageDefinition()**

  In the security properties file, you are allowed to specify a comma-separated list of packages that will cause a security exception to be thrown when passed to SecurityManager.checkPackageDefinition(), unless the corresponding RuntimePermission has been granted. Instead of full package names, you can specify a comma-separated list of strings, and all packages that start with one of those strings will also cause a security exception to be thrown.

  The syntax for this entry is as follows:

  ```
  package.definition=string1,string2,...,stringN
  ```

  The checkPackageDefinition() method takes as argument a String representing a package name, and throws a security exception if the calling thread is not allowed to define classes in the package specified by the argument.

  This method is used by the loadClass() method of class loaders. If the package is restricted, then a call is made to checkPermission() with the permission

  ```
  java.lang.RunTimePermission("defineClassInPackage.packageName")
  ```

  If it does not have a permission, then the calling thread is not allowed to define classes in that package and a security exception is thrown.

  However, by default the package.definition entry in the security property files is not set to anything and is commented out:

  ```
  #package.definition=
  ```

  This means that, by default, no packages are restricted for definition. Moreover, none of the class loaders supplied with the Java 2 SDK call checkPackageDefinition().

8.4 Security Policy Files

Security policy files are used to grant permissions to various Java codes depending upon the code base and/or the digital signatures applied to the code.

We introduced the policy files in 3.6, "The Policy File" on page 93, and in 3.6.1, "The Default System-Wide Policy File" on page 96, we described all the entries that appear in the default system-wide policy file that comes with the installation of the Java 2 SDK. In this section, we give more details about how you can configure security on your system through the use of policy files.

As we explained in 8.3, "The Security Properties File, java.security" on page 234, multiple policy files can be simultaneously installed and take effect on your system. Their URL locations and order numbers must be specified in the security properties file java.security.

A policy file contains a list of entries. There may be a `keystore` entry and zero or more `grant` entries. Each `grant` entry contains zero or more `permission` entries, and can contain a `signedBy` entry and a `codeBase` entry.

> **Case in Policy Files**
>
> In policy files, case is unimportant for the identifiers (`grant`, `keystore`, `permission`, `signedBy` and `codeBase`) but is significant for any string that is passed in as a value.

8.4.1 keystore Entry

The `keystore` entry is necessary in the policy file if a signer is specified in any of the `grant` entries. There can be only one `keystore` entry per policy file. If there are multiple `keystore` entries, only the first one is considered and the rest are ignored.

The `keystore` entry line can appear anywhere in the file and it looks like:

```
keystore "URL" "type"
```

where `URL` represents the URL location of the keystore, and `type` refers to the type of the keystore.

The `type` specification is optional. If `type` is missing, the type is taken from the keystore.type property of the Java security properties file (see 8.3, "The Security Properties File, java.security" on page 234). As you remember, that property is by default set to JKS, the proprietary keystore implementation supplied by Sun Microsystems.

In general, a keystore type defines the storage and data format of the keystore information, and the algorithms used to protect private keys in the keystore and the integrity of the keystore itself.

The URL location of the keystore can be absolute or relative to the location of the policy file in question. For example, let's say that in the security properties file java.security, the entry defining the policy file in question is:

```
policy.url.2=file:/C:/itso/ibm/ibmpolicy
```

If the keystore entry in this policy file is:

```
keystore ".keystore"
```

then the keystore URL location is considered relative to the location of the policy file, and the keystore is loaded from file:/C:/itso/ibm/.keystore.

If the keystore entry in the policy file is:

```
keystore "file:/C:/.keystore"
```

then the URL is considered absolute and the keystore is loaded from file:/C:/.keystore.

The fact that the keystore location can be specified as a URL allows you to retrieve a keystore not only from the local file system, but also from a remote location, using the HTTP protocol.

8.4.2 grant Entries

These entries are used to grant permissions to codes from various sources and/or signed by various entities.

As shown in Figure 33 on page 81, the syntax for a grant entry is as follows:

```
grant [signedBy "signers"][, codeBase "URL"] {
permission permission_class ["target"][, "action_list"][, signedBy "signer"];
[permission permission_class ["target"][, "action_list"][, signedBy "signer"];
...
permission permission_class ["target"][, "action_list"][, signedBy "signer"];]
};
```

The entry begins with the word grant, which can be followed by the signedBy and codeBase name-value pairs. A list of zero or more permission entries follows. A grant entry always terminates with a semicolon (;).

- **signedBy entry**

  The value followed by the signedBy keyword is a double-quoted string containing names of one or more signers. Multiple signers are separated by commas. A signer entity is indicated through the alias of its certificate stored in the keystore. The permissions granted are for the code that has been signed by the private key corresponding to the public key in the certificate indicated by the alias.

  When multiple signers are specified, the code must be signed by *all* of them. This is because the relationship between multiple signers is a logical AND, and not a logical OR. For an OR relationship, you need to duplicate the same grant permission with different signers.

  If this optional name-value pair is absent, then the permissions in the grant entry are valid for code signed by anyone or code that is not signed.

- **codeBase entry**

  The URL value followed by the codeBase keyword is the originating location of the code to which permissions are to be granted. The value of the codeBase entry must be represented as a double-quoted string, formatted as a URL. This means that it should always contain forward slashes (/) even if the platform is a Windows system, since backslashes (\) are not allowed in a URL. Absence of this optional name-value pair indicates that the specified permissions are to be granted to all code, regardless of its originating location.

  Let's see some examples of valid code bases:

  - To grant the permissions to all class files in a specific directory, the codeBase entry must be similar to the following:

    ```
    codeBase "file:/C:/ibm/itso/"
    ```

    This is equivalent to:

    ```
    codeBase "file:/C:/ibm/itso"
    ```

  - To grant the permissions to all the class files as well as JAR files in the specified directory, a wildcard (*) is required at the end of the URL[1]:

    ```
    codeBase "file:/C:/ibm/itso/*"
    ```

[1] This is as per the documentation. However, this was not the case in Java 2 SDK, Standard Edition, V1.2. In fact, by putting a wildcard (*) at the end of the URL, not only the JAR files were being excluded from the protection domain, but the class files were also not given the permissions. In effect, the permissions were totally disregarded. The reason for this bug is that some modifications were made to the method java.io.File.getCanonicalPath(), which on Win32 systems threw an IOException when canonicalizing a file with a wildcard (*) in its name. This bug is fixed in V1.2.1.

- To grant the permissions to only a particular JAR file, the `codeBase` entry must be similar to the following:

  ```
  codeBase "file:/C:/ibm/itso/redbook.jar"
  ```

  The JAR file must be specifically mentioned in the codeBase URL. However, this does not work for a class file.

- To grant the permissions to all the class files as well as JAR files in the specified directory and in all its subdirectories recursively, a minus sign (-) is required at the end of the URL:

  ```
  codeBase "file:/C:/ibm/itso/-"
  ```

- **permission entries**

  Each `permission` entry specifies a permission that is granted to a specific code source.

  A `permission` entry begins with the keyword `permission`, followed by the fully qualified permission class name, such as java.io.FilePermission, java.util.PropertyPermission, etc. (see 3.6, "The Policy File" on page 93). The `target` field refers to the target of the permission if any, and is represented as a double-quoted string, such as `"java.home"` for PropertyPermission. A double-quoted list of one or more actions can follow, such as `"read"` or `"write"` or `"read,write"` (multiple actions are separated by commas). This refers to the actions that are allowed.

  As we observed in 3.6, "The Policy File" on page 93, not all of the Permission classes defined in the Java 2 platform have applicable actions yet. The only system Permission classes that do have actions are FilePermission (read, write, execute, delete), PropertyPermission (read, write) and SocketPermission (resolve, accept, connect, listen).

  A `permission` entry always terminates with a semicolon (`;`).

  The last item in the `permission` statement is composed of the `signedBy` keyword, followed by a double-quoted string indicating a signer. Each signer entity is indicated by the corresponding alias in the keystore. A signed permission is granted to the specified code source only if the permission class itself is in JAR format and is signed by the private key corresponding to the public key in the certificate referred to by the signer's alias. This is useful for permission classes that are not part of the Java core API; these non-standard permission classes are often remotely loaded, and signing by a trusted entity is one way to ensure code authenticity.

  When it comes to signing applets and applications, multiple signers are allowed, and this means that the code must be signed by *all* of these and not a subset. However, this is not true for Permission classes. The JAR file of a Permission class can be signed by a single entity. If multiple entities apply their digital signatures to the JAR file of a Permission class, only the first signature takes effect, and the others are disregarded.

Absence of the optional `signedBy` specification means that the permission in question is granted to the specified code source regardless of any digital signature applied to the permission class file.

Let's look at some examples of syntactically correct `grant` entries:

- The following `grant` entry allows *all* code (irrespective of the code base and eventual signers) to read the property java.version from the system:

```
grant {
  permission java.util.PropertyPermission "java.version", "read";
};
```

- The following `grant` entry in a valid policy file would give JAR files signed by IBM and residing in the directory D:\ibm or its subdirectories recursively read and write file permissions to all the files in the system:

```
grant signedBy "IBM", codeBase "file:/D:/ibm/-" {
  permission java.io.FilePermission "<<ALL FILES>>", "write,read";
};
```

- We modify the `signedBy` entry above by specifying a new signer, ITSO:

```
grant signedBy "IBM, ITSO", codeBase "file:/D:/ibm/-" {
  permission java.io.FilePermission "<<ALL FILES>>", "write,read";
};
```

Now the JAR files in the local directory D:\ibm and signed only by IBM will not have access. Only if signed by both IBM and ITSO they will be granted permission.

- Here is another interesting example for a `grant` entry:

```
grant signedBy "itso" codeBase "file:/${user.home}/*" {
  permission java.io.FilePermission "${user.home}${/}*", "read,write";
  permission java.io.FilePermission "${user.myhome}${/}*", "read";
};
```

Assuming that a system property user.myhome is not defined, the above means that only JAR files present in the home directory of the user and signed by the private key corresponding to the public key present in the certificate referred to by the alias itso in the keystore are allowed to read and write all files in the home directory of the user.

There are some points to note in this example:

1. `${user.home}` is expanded to its value, which is the user's home directory, only if the security properties file, java.security, sets the property policy.expandProperties to `true` (see 8.3, "The Security Properties File, java.security" on page 234). Property expansion is allowed in a policy file anywhere a double-quoted string is used.

2. `${/}` or `${file.separator}` indicates the file separator specific to the platform. The value of this variable is the file separator used on the system, but again, this requires that property expansion is allowed in the java.security file. However, the file separator variable should not be used in the `codeBase` entry as this requires a URL-formatted string as its value, so only forward slashes (/) are allowed, and backslashes (\) are forbidden, irrespective of the platform.

   Other property variables, such as `${user.home}`, can be used in the `codeBase` statement, but if they include a file separator, this would explode to a forward slash (/) and not to a backslash (\). This would happen even on a Windows system, because the value for a `codeBase` must be URL-formatted. So, even if the value of user.home is something like C:\WINNT\Profiles\pistoia.000 (see Figure 370 on page 676 and Figure 371 on page 677), in a `codeBase` entry `${user.home}` would explode to `C:/WINNT/Profiles/pistoia.000`.

3. `${user.home}${/}` is allowed in the `permission` entry, but `${user.${abcd}}` is not, even though `${abcd}` might expand to `home`. In other words, *nested variables cannot be used*. The reason for this limitation is that the property parser does not recognize nested properties; it simply looks for the first `${`, and then keeps looking until it finds the first `}` and tries to interpret the result. In this case, it would try to interpret `${user.${abcd}` as a single property, but fails if there is no such property.

4. If not using the file separator variable `${/}`, on a Windows system a single backslash (\) should be replaced by a double backslash (\\) every time a file separator is written in a `permission` entry of a policy file. So, for example, C:\WINNT\Profiles\pistoia.000 would be written as C:\\WINNT\\Profiles\\pistoia.000. The double backslashes (\\) are necessary to represent a single backslash (\) because in a policy file the strings are processed by a tokenizer (java.io.StreamTokenizer), which allows a single backslash (\) to be used as an escape character (for example, \n indicates a new line). Thus, two backslashes (\\) are required to indicate a single backslash (\). After the tokenizer has

processed the above FilePermission target string, converting double backslashes (\\) to single backslashes (\), the end result is the actual path.

5. If a property cannot be expanded in a `keystore` entry, `grant` entry or `permission` entry, that specific entry is totally ignored. So, assuming that a system property user.myhome is not defined, the `permission` entry:

```
permission java.io.FilePermission "${user.myhome}${/}*", "read";
```

is completely disregarded.

The Concept of Negative Permission in Java 2

From the discussion above, it is clear that the Java 2 platform lacks the concept of *negative permission*. That is, according to the Java 2 security architecture, you cannot specifically deny a permission. Everything is restricted by default, and you must grant specific permissions to specific codes, as explained above.

8.5 An Example of Security Settings in the Java 2 Platform

Let's see now an example of how a policy affects the functioning of a simple application.

8.5.1 The Count Application Source Code

We consider again the simple Count application shown in Figure 44 on page 120 and Figure 45 on page 121. The purpose of this application is to count the characters in a text file, whose name is passed on the command line. The code Count.java is shown in the following figure:

```
import java.io.*;

public class Count
{
    public static void main(String[] args) throws Exception
    {
        int count=0;
        if (args.length >= 1)
        {
            FileInputStream fis = new FileInputStream(args[0]);
```

Figure 106. (Part 1 of 2). Count.java

```
        try
        {
           while (fis.read() != -1)
               count++;
           System.out.println("Hi! We counted " + count + " chars.");
        }
        catch (Exception e)
        {
           System.out.println("No characters counted");
           System.out.println("Exception caught" + e.toString());
        }
     }
     else
        System.err.println("Usage: Count file_name");
   }
}
```

Figure 107. (Part 2 of 2). Count.java

We save the Count.java file in the directory D:\itso\ch08.

8.5.2 A Sample Text File

Then we write a sample text file to use in our scenario. We consider the file itso.txt, shown in Figure 46 on page 121. We save it in the directory D:\itso\textFile. The contents of this file are shown again in the following figure:

```
Marco Pistoia
Duane Reller
Deepak Gupta
Milind Nagnur
Ashok Ramani
```

Figure 108. itso.txt

8.5.3 Compiling the Application

Then, we compile Count.java:

```
javac Count.java
```

This command creates a file called Count.class in the same directory, D:\itso\ch08, as is the Java file Count.java.

8.5.4 Running the Application without a Security Manager

At this point, we can run Count against the text file itso.txt. This can be done through the following command, launched from the directory D:\itso\ch08:

```
java Count D:\itso\textFile\itso.txt
```

Although the Count application attempts to read to a file in the local file system, and no read permissions have been granted to its code source yet, we get the output as expected, as all applications have by default full access to all the system resources, unless a security manager is invoked:

```
Hi! We counted 70 chars.
```

8.5.5 Running the Application with the Default Security Manager

Now, let's run this program with restricted permissions, by invoking the default security manager, java.lang.SecurityManager. The command to do so is the following:

```
java -Djava.security.manager Count D:\itso\textFile\itso.txt
```

The output is shown in the following screen:

```
Exception in thread "main" java.security.AccessControlException: access denied
(java.io.FilePermission D:\itso\textFile\itso.txt read)
        at java.security.AccessControlContext.checkPermission(Compiled Code)
        at java.security.AccessController.checkPermission(AccessController.java:403)
        at java.lang.SecurityManager.checkPermission(SecurityManager.java:549)
        at java.lang.SecurityManager.checkRead(SecurityManager.java:864)
        at java.io.FileInputStream.<init>(FileInputStream.java:65)
        at Count.main(Compiled Code)
```

As you can see, we got an AccessControlException. This is because we have invoked the default security manager, and without the adequate permission the Count application is by default denied read access to the local file system.

8.5.6 Policy File Modification

Now we want to demonstrate how an adequate modification to one of the policy files in effect can modify the behavior of the Count application when run under the default security manager.

Keeping the default java.security file, shown in Figure 105 on page 234, we see that a user-defined policy file, called .java.policy and placed in the user home directory, will be added and combined to the system-wide policy file. It is recommended to modify the user-defined policy file, rather than the system-wide one. The user-defined policy file does not exist by default, so we create it with a text editor, and insert in it the following grant entry:

```
grant codeBase "file:/D:/itso/ch08/" {
  permission java.io.FilePermission "D:${/}itso{/}textFile${/}itso.txt", "read";
};
```

The grant entry above gives permission to all the class files stored in the local directory D:\itso\ch08 to access the file D:\itso\textFile\itso.txt in read mode.

We can then run the program again and see that this time it works as expected. The code is now able to read the input file.

In this example, we added the policy in the .java.policy user-defined policy file. Another possibility would have been to create a new policy file, say, newpolicy, stored for example in the same directory where the Count.class file is. Then the Count application could have been run using the -Djava.security.policy command line option, as shown:

```
java -Djava.security.manager -Djava.security.policy=newpolicy Count D:\itso\textFile\itso.txt
```

As we explained in 8.3, "The Security Properties File, java.security" on page 234, an extra policy can be passed on the command line with the option -Djava.security.policy flag only if in the java.security file the policy.allowSystemProperties entry is set to true.

Alternatively, if you are a system administrator, you can modify the java.security file and specify the policy file newpolicy in addition to the system-wide and user-defined policy files. The entries to do this in the java.security file are:

```
policy.url.1=file:${java.home}/lib/security/java.policy
policy.url.2=file:${user.home}/.java.policy
policy.url.3=file:D:/itso/ch08/newpolicy
```

In this section we showed how to add a policy by manually editing a policy file. Care should be taken when manually editing a policy file, since a mistake in the syntax could compromise the policy of your system. We already saw in other parts of this book that the Java 2 SDK provides a utility that helps you create or modify a policy file through a graphical user interface (GUI), limiting the possibilities of inadvertent syntax errors. This utility is called Policy Tool, and we will see more details about it in 9.4, "Policy File Creation and Management Tool" on page 288.

8.6 File Read Access to Files in the Code Base URL Directory

Although the default security manager prevents untrusted code from having read access to the system files, there is an exception to this rule: a class file is automatically granted, by the default security manager, read access to all files contained in the class' directory and all its subdirectories recursively. So a class file does not need explicit permission to read a file from the same URL location directory it is in, or recursively from a subdirectory of that directory, because this permission is automatically granted. Notice, however, that this property is not valid for JAR files, which still require an explicit permission.

8.7 Security Properties and Policy File Protection

One thing to keep in mind is that the Java 2 SDK does not provide any protection to the security properties file or to the policy files. They are stored without any password protection and they are not encrypted. Moreover, by default, they are not even protected by the operating system on which the Java 2 SDK has been installed. So anyone having physical access to your machine can tamper with these files. For this reason, it is important to manually protect these files once the Java 2 SDK has been installed. Access to the machine should be granted to authorized users only, and directory/file protection should be activated, depending upon the underlying operating system.

8.8 How to Implement a Policy Server

A *policy server* is a Web server machine that provides access to a system-wide policy file for all the client machines connected to the same network. As discussed in 8.3, "The Security Properties File, java.security" on page 234, there are two features of the Java security implementation that allow the creation of a policy server:

1. The fact that the java.security file can specify policy files using the HTTP protocol makes it possible to configure the local system's policy using a policy file retrieved from a remote system.

2. The ability to expand system properties in policy files makes it possible to use the same policy file on different operating systems.

This way system administrators can set up an environment where a system-wide policy file is globally accessible on a policy server machine and shared among all the clients in the network. Users can add their own policy restrictions by editing local user-defined policy files or by dynamically adding a policy from the command line, if this is allowed in the Java configuration in the java.security file.

In the next scenario, we describe a policy server running on a Win Server Version 4.0 machine, on which a Web server is installed. The system-wide policy file, java.policy, is stored on this machine, in the di lib/security under the JRE development directory D:\jdk1.2.x\jre. As discussed in 8.1, "A Note on java.home and the JRE Installation Directory" page 225, the Java security configuration files found in this directory affect all the development tools, such as the Applet Viewer and the Java compiler javac.

In order to make the system-wide policy file global and accessible from remote machines, we add the following Pass statement to the HTTP configuration file of the Web server:

```
Pass /security/* D:\jdk1.2\jre\lib\security\*
```

Assuming that the host name of the policy server machine is WTR05218.itso.ral.ibm.com, the above statement means that a user on a remote machine who wants to access the system-wide policy file simply has to access the URL http://WTR05218.itso.ral.ibm.com/security/java.policy.

In this scenario, two machines have the role of policy clients: one is another Windows NT Server Version 4.0 machine, the other one is a RISC/6000 running AIX Version 4.3.2. This scenario is graphically shown in the following figure:

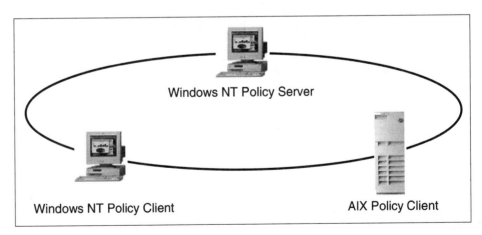

Figure 109. Policy Server Multiplatform Scenario

icy client machines, we modify the java.security file in the ...y directory under the JRE development directory so that the ...L statements appear as follows:

```
file:${java.home}/lib/security/java.policy
file:${user.home}/.java.policy
p://WTR05218.itso.ral.ibm.com/security/java.policy
```

...n other words, we comment out the default entries, and we add a new entry, which tells the system to retrieve the system-wide policy file from the remote policy server WTR05218.

Next, we write the code for the following Java applet:

```java
import java.io.*;
import java.applet.*;
import java.awt.Graphics;

public class CountApp extends Applet
{
    public void paint(Graphics g)
    {
        int count=0;
        try
        {
            String s1 = System.getProperty("user.home");
            String s2 = System.getProperty("file.separator");
            FileInputStream fis = new FileInputStream(s1 + s2 + "itso.txt");
            while (fis.read() != -1)
                count++;
            g.drawString("File was accessed.  We counted " + count + " chars.", 20, 20);
        }
        catch (Exception e)
        {
            System.out.println("No characters counted");
            System.out.println("Exception caught" + e.toString());
        }
    }
}
```

Figure 110. CountApp.java

We compile the Java applet file with the following command:

```
javac CountApp.java
```

This command produces the applet class file CountApp.class.

As you can see, the code above is the applet-version of the Count application, shown in Figure 106 on page 248 and Figure 107 on page 249. This applet, which we save in the JRE development directory of the two policy client machines, attempts to read the contents of the file itso.txt, shown in Figure 108 on page 249. However, this time the location of the file is the user home directory. The user home directory is different on the various platforms, but rather than hard coding it in the applet code, we can make use of the Java system properties user.home and file.separator to write an applet that is really portable across the platforms.

Notice that the applet class file is physically saved in all the policy client machines. We could have used the Web server running as the policy server to distribute the applet via HTTP, but in this case the code base URL for the applet would have been the URL of the Web server. Instead, we prefer in this case to use the local JRE development directory as the code base to show you an example of policy file portability.

In the system-wide policy file that appears under the JRE development directory policy server machine, we add the following grant entry to the default contents:

```
grant codeBase "file:/${java.home}/-" {
  permission java.io.FilePermission "${user.home}${/}itso.txt", "read";
  permission java.util.PropertyPermission "user.home", "read";
  permission java.util.PropertyPermission "file.separator", "read";
};
```

This means that we are granting all the class and JAR files stored in the Java home directory and all its subdirectories permission to read the file itso.txt in the user home directory. We are also granting the same code source permission to read the system properties of user.home and file.separator. Since this scenario is run using the Applet Viewer, ${java.home} is translated into the JRE development directory, as demonstrated in Figure 102 on page 229. This is also the directory where the applet CountApp is stored.

In order to run, the applet needs to be invoked from within an HTML page. This is the HTML page we wrote for it:

```
<HTML>
   <HEAD>
      <TITLE>CountApp Applet</TITLE>
   </HEAD>

   <BODY>
      <CENTER><H2>CountApp Applet</H2></CENTER>
      <HR>
      <BR>

      <APPLET Code="CountApp.class" Width=300 Height=50>
         <H4>This area contains a Java applet, but your browser is not Java-enabled</H4>
      </APPLET>

   </BODY>
</HTML>
```

Figure 111. CountApp.html

The program works as expected on all platforms. In fact, on running the command:

```
appletviewer CountApp.html
```

the following Applet Viewer window is brought up:

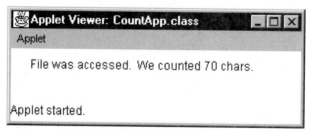

Figure 112. CountApp Applet Running

This demonstrates that the policy file on the policy server can be accessed by the policy clients and the policies defined in it are effective. This is possible because the Java 2 platform enables the specification of the policy file through the HTTP protocol. Also notice how we make use of the variables ${java.home}, ${user.home} and ${/}, so that the same file can be used on UNIX as well as on Windows systems. As discussed in 8.3, "The Security Properties File, java.security" on page 234, the value of policy.expandProperties in the java.security file must be `true` *on the client machines* to make this happen.

Chapter 9. Java 2 SDK Security Tools

As we introduced in Chapter 3, "The New Java Security Model" on page 69, the Java 2 SDK provides four security-related tools. These are:

1. The `keytool` command line utility for key and certificate management
2. The `jar` command line tool to compress and archive Java class files
3. The `jarsigner` command line tool to sign and verify Java Archive (JAR) files
4. The GUI-based Policy Tool for creating and managing policy files

We now describe how to use these tools.

9.1 Key and Certificate Management Tool

The `keytool` command line utility is used to manage keystores. With this tool, you can:

1. Create key pairs and self-signed certificates.
2. Export certificates to send to others along with the signed code.
3. Issue certificate signing requests (CSRs) to be sent to certification authorities (CAs) for signing.
4. Import other peoples' certificates to verify signatures.
5. Designate trusted certificates and also import trusted root CA certificates in the CA keystore cacerts.
6. Manage your own keystores.

9.1.1 keytool Syntax

The basic format of the `keytool` is:

```
keytool command [option] ... [option]
```

To get help for this tool, just enter `keytool` on the command line, with or without the `-help` flag. You will get an output similar to the following:

```
keytool usage:

-certreq     [-v] [-alias <alias>] [-sigalg <sigalg>]
             [-file <csr_file>] [-keypass <keypass>]
             [-keystore <keystore>] [-storepass <storepass>]
             [-storetype <storetype>]

-delete      [-v] -alias <alias>
             [-keystore <keystore>] [-storepass <storepass>]
             [-storetype <storetype>]

-export      [-v] [-rfc] [-alias <alias>] [-file <cert_file>]
             [-keystore <keystore>] [-storepass <storepass>]
             [-storetype <storetype>]

-genkey      [-v] [-alias <alias>] [-keyalg <keyalg>]
             [-keysize <keysize>] [-sigalg <sigalg>]
             [-dname <dname>] [-validity <valDays>]
             [-keypass <keypass>] [-keystore <keystore>]
             [-storepass <storepass>] [-storetype <storetype>]

-help

-identitydb  [-v] [-file <idb_file>] [-keystore <keystore>]
             [-storepass <storepass>] [-storetype <storetype>]

-import      [-v] [-noprompt] [-trustcacerts] [-alias <alias>]
             [-file <cert_file>] [-keypass <keypass>]
             [-keystore <keystore>] [-storepass <storepass>]
             [-storetype <storetype>]

-keyclone    [-v] [-alias <alias>] -dest <dest_alias>
             [-keypass <keypass>] [-new <new_keypass>]
             [-keystore <keystore>] [-storepass <storepass>]
             [-storetype <storetype>]

-keypasswd   [-v] [-alias <alias>]
             [-keypass <old_keypass>] [-new <new_keypass>]
             [-keystore <keystore>] [-storepass <storepass>]
             [-storetype <storetype>]

-list        [-v | -rfc] [-alias <alias>]
             [-keystore <keystore>] [-storepass <storepass>]
```

Figure 113. (Part 1 of 2). keytool Commands and Options

```
              [-storetype <storetype>]

-printcert    [-v] [-file <cert_file>]

-selfcert     [-v] [-alias <alias>] [-sigalg <sigalg>]
              [-dname <dname>] [-validity <valDays>]
              [-keypass <keypass>] [-keystore <keystore>]
              [-storepass <storepass>] [-storetype <storetype>]

-storepasswd [-v] [-new <new_storepass>]
              [-keystore <keystore>] [-storepass <storepass>]
              [-storetype <storetype>]
```

Figure 114. (Part 2 of 2). keytool Commands and Options

Figure 113 on page 260 and Figure 114 on page 261 show the possible commands that can be entered with the `keytool` utility and the options that are associated with those commands.

9.1.2 Store and Private Key Password

The default implementation of the keystore that comes with the Java 2 SDK protects the keystore with a *store password* to verify integrity. A private key in the keystore is stored encrypted and is protected with a *private key password*, which should be different from the store password.

Most commands operating on a keystore require the store password. Some commands require a private key password. Passwords can be specified on the command line (in the `-storepass` and `-keypass` options, respectively). However, we recommend you not put the password on the command prompt, because it then becomes visible in the command history; anyone can see it by examining the history, for example by using the arrow keys on the command prompt of Windows systems (if doskey is installed) or the Esc-K key sequence on AIX systems (if the Korn shell is running).

If you do not specify a required password option on a command line, you will be prompted for it. When typing in a password at the password prompt, the password is currently echoed; this means that it is displayed exactly as typed, and not masked by a sequence of asterisks (*), so be careful not to type it in front of anyone and remember to close the Command Prompt window as soon as you are done with that specific `keytool` command. On Windows systems, there is yet another reason for closing the Command Prompt window; if you type the full `keytool` command from the same window again, you can still use the arrow keys from the `keytool` prompt to retrieve a password previously typed in. So, anyone can know your store and private key passwords if he gets access to your machine and your Command Prompt window is still open where you accessed your keystore.

9.1.3 Commands and Options Associated with keytool

We now explain the meaning of the commands and options shown in Figure 113 on page 260 and Figure 114 on page 261.

In the `keytool` command line, *command* can be one of the following:

- `-certreq`

  This is used to generate a CSR using the PKCS#10 format. A CSR is intended to be sent to a CA. The CA will authenticate the certificate requestor (usually offline) and will return a certificate or certificate chain, used to replace the existing certificate chain (which initially consists of a self-signed certificate) in the keystore. The private key and X.500 distinguished name[1] associated with the alias of the certificate are used to create the PKCS#10 certificate request. In order to access the private key, the appropriate password must be provided, since private keys are protected in the keystore with a password. If `-keypass` is not provided at the command line, and the key password is different from the password used to protect the integrity of the keystore, the user is prompted for it.

  `sigalg` specifies the algorithm that should be used to sign the CSR. The CSR is stored in the file `csr_file`. If no file is given, the CSR is output to standard output.

  Use the `-import` command to import the response from the CA.

- `-delete`

  Deletes the entry identified by `alias` from the keystore. The user is prompted for the alias, if no alias is provided at the command line.

- `-export`

  Reads (from the keystore) the certificate associated with `alias`, and stores it in the file `cert_file`. If no file is given, the certificate is output to standard output. By default, the certificate is output in binary encoding, but will be output in the printable encoding Base 64 format[2] if the `-rfc` option is specified.

---

[1] X.500 *distinguished names* are used to identify entities, such as those which are named by the subject and issuer (signer) fields of X.509 certificates (see Appendix C, "X.509 Certificates" on page 683). The `keytool` utility supports the following subparts: `commonName`, `organizationUnit`, `organizationName`, `localityName`, `stateName`, and `country`.

[2] The *Base 64 format* is a commonly used Internet standard. You could encode binary data in Base 64 by rearranging the bits of the data stream in such a way that only the 6 least significant bits are used in every byte. For more details, see the Request for Comments (RFC) 1421 at http://info.internet.isi.edu/in-notes/rfc/files/rfc1421.txt.

If `alias` refers to a trusted certificate, that certificate is output. Otherwise, `alias` refers to a key entry with an associated certificate chain. In that case, the first certificate in the chain is returned. This certificate authenticates the public key of the entity addressed by `alias`.

- `-genkey`

  Generates a key pair and wraps the public key in an X.509 V1 self-signed certificate, which is stored as a single-element certificate chain. This certificate chain and the private key are stored in a new keystore entry, identified by `alias`.

  `keyalg` specifies the algorithm to be used to generate the key pair, and `keysize` specifies the size of each key to be generated. `sigalg` specifies the algorithm that should be used to sign the self-signed certificate; this algorithm must be compatible with `keyalg`. Finally, `dname` specifies the X.500 distinguished name to be associated with `alias`, and is used as the issuer and subject fields in the self-signed certificate. If no distinguished name is provided at the command line, the user will be prompted for one.

  `keypass` is a password used to protect the private key of the generated key pair. If no password is provided, the user is prompted for it. If you press Enter at the prompt, the key password is set to the same password as that used for the keystore. `keypass` must be at least 6 characters long.

  `valDays` is the number of days for which the certificate should be considered valid.

- `-help`

  Lists all the commands and their options.

- `-identitydb`

  This command reads the Java Development Kit (JDK) 1.1.*x*-style identity database from the file `idb_file`, and adds its entries to the keystore. If no file is given, the identity database is read from standard input. If a keystore does not exist, it is created. Only identity database entries that were marked as trusted will be imported into the keystore. All other identities will be ignored. For each trusted identity, a keystore entry will be created. The identity's name is used as the `alias` for the keystore entry.

  The private keys from trusted identities will all be encrypted under the same password, `storepass`. This is the same password that is used to protect the keystore's integrity. Users can later assign individual passwords to those private keys by using the `-keypasswd` keytool command option.

  An identity in an identity database may hold more than one certificate, each certifying the same public key. But a keystore key entry for a private key has that private key and a single certificate chain (initially just a single certificate), where the first certificate in the chain contains the public key corresponding to the private key. When importing the information from an identity, only the first certificate of the identity is stored in the keystore. This is because an identity's name in an identity database is used as the alias for its corresponding keystore entry, and alias names are unique within a keystore.

- -import

  This command reads the certificate or certificate chain (where the latter is supplied in a PKCS#7 formatted reply) from the file cert_file, and stores it in the keystore entry identified by alias. If no file is given, the certificate or PKCS#7 reply is read from standard input. keytool can import X.509 V1, V2, and V3 certificates, and PKCS#7 formatted certificate chains consisting of certificates of that type. The data to be imported must be provided either in binary encoding format, or in printable encoding Base 64 format. In the latter case, the encoding must be bounded at the beginning by a string that starts with -----BEGIN, and bounded at the end by a string that starts with -----END.

  When importing a new trusted certificate, the alias you assign to it must not yet exist in the keystore. Before adding the certificate to the keystore, keytool tries to verify it by attempting to construct a chain of trust from that certificate to a self-signed certificate (belonging to a root CA), using trusted certificates that are already available in the keystore.

  If the -trustcacerts option has been specified, additional certificates are considered for the chain of trust, namely the certificates in the file named cacerts that we introduced in 8.2.1, "The Certificates KeyStore File cacerts" on page 233. The cacerts file represents a system-wide keystore with CA certificates. System administrators can configure and manage that file using keytool, specifying jks as the keystore type. The cacerts keystore file ships with five VeriSign root CA certificates whose X.500 distinguished names are shown in Figure 104 on page 233.

  If keytool fails to establish a trust path from the certificate to be imported up to a self-signed certificate (either from the keystore or the cacerts file), the certificate information is printed out, and the user is prompted to verify it, for example, by comparing the displayed certificate fingerprints with the fingerprints obtained from some other (trusted) source of information, which might be the certificate owner. Be very careful to ensure the certificate is valid prior to importing it as a trusted certificate! The user then has the option of aborting the import operation. If the -noprompt option is given, however, there will be no interaction with the user.

When importing a certificate reply, the certificate reply is validated using trusted certificates from the keystore, and optionally using the certificates configured in the cacerts keystore file (if the -trustcacerts option was specified). If the reply is a single X.509 certificate, keytool attempts to establish a trust chain, starting at the certificate reply and ending at a self-signed certificate (belonging to a root CA). The certificate reply and the hierarchy of certificates used to authenticate the certificate reply form the new certificate chain of alias.

If the reply is a PKCS#7 formatted certificate chain, the chain is first ordered (with the user certificate first and the self-signed root CA certificate last), before keytool attempts to match the root CA certificate provided in the reply with any of the trusted certificates in the keystore or the cacerts keystore file (if the -trustcacerts option was specified). If no match can be found, the information of the root CA certificate is printed out, and the user is prompted to verify it, for example, again, by comparing the displayed certificate fingerprints with the fingerprints obtained from some other (trusted) source of information, which might be the root CA itself. The user then has the option of aborting the import operation. If the -noprompt option is given, however, there will be no interaction with the user.

The new certificate chain of alias replaces the old certificate chain associated with this entry. The old chain can only be replaced if a valid keypass, the password used to protect the private key of the entry, is supplied. If no password is provided, and the private key password is different from the keystore password, the user is prompted for it.

- -keyclone

  This command creates a new keystore entry, which has the same private key and certificate chain as the original entry. The original entry is identified by alias (which defaults to mykey if not provided). The new (destination) entry is identified by dest_alias. If no destination alias is supplied at the command line, the user is prompted for it.

  If the private key password is different from the keystore password, then the entry will only be cloned if a valid keypass is supplied. This is the password used to protect the private key associated with alias. If no key password is supplied at the command line, and the private key password is different from the keystore password, the user is prompted for it. The private key in the cloned entry may be protected with a different password, if desired. If no -new option is supplied at the command line, the user is prompted for the new entry's password (and may choose to let it be the same as for the cloned entry's private key).

This command can be used to establish multiple certificate chains corresponding to a given key pair, or for backup purposes.

- keypasswd

  This password changes the password under which the private key identified by `alias` is protected, from `old_keypass` to `new_keypass`.

  If the `-keypass` option is not provided at the command line, and the private key password is different from the keystore password, the user is prompted for it. If the `-new` option is not provided at the command line, the user is prompted for it.

- -list

  This command prints to standard output the contents of the keystore entry identified by alias. If no alias is specified, the contents of the entire keystore are printed.

  This command by default prints the MD5 fingerprint of a certificate:

  - If the `-v` option is specified, the certificate is printed in human-readable format, with additional information such as the owner, issuer, and serial number, and looks similar to the following screen:

```
Owner: CN=Marco Pistoia, OU=ITSO, O=IBM Corporation, L=Cary, ST=North Carolina,
C=US
Issuer: CN=Marco Pistoia, OU=ITSO, O=IBM Corporation, L=Cary, ST=North Carolina,
 C=US
Serial number: 371cdccd
Valid from: Tue Apr 20 16:00:13 EDT 1999 until: Mon Jul 19 16:00:13 EDT 1999
Certificate fingerprints:
         MD5:  D2:FC:81:5B:EE:39:D1:79:01:AC:1F:90:59:E3:FF:5B
         SHA1: A2:1C:11:3B:E2:6F:A2:46:80:F5:B4:19:62:D9:C5:3C:19:91:34:93
```

  - If the `-rfc` option is specified, certificate contents are printed using the printable encoding Base 64 format. An example is shown in the following screen:

```
-----BEGIN CERTIFICATE-----
MIIDITCCAt4CBDcc3M0wCwYHKoZIzjgEAwUAMHYxCzAJBgNVBAYTAlVIMRcwFQYDVQQIEw5Ob3J0
aCBDYXJvbGluYTENMAsGA1UEBxMEQ2FyeTEYMBYGA1UEChMPSUJNIENvcnBvcmF0aW9uMQ0wCwYD
VQQLEwRJVFNPMRYwFAYDVQQDEw1NYXJjbyBQaXN0b2lhMB4XDTk5MDQyMDIwMDAxM1oXDTk5MDcx
OTIwMDAxM1owdjELMAkGA1UEBhMCVVMxFzAVBgNVBAgTDk5vcnRoIENhcm9saW5hMQ0wCwYDVQQH
EwRDYXJ5MRgwFgYDVQQKEw9JQk0gQ29ycG9yYXRpb24xDTALBgNVBAsTBElUU08xFjAUBgNVBAMT
DU1hcmNvIFBpc3RvaWEwggG3MIIBLAYHKoZIzjgEATCCAR8CgYEA/X9TgR11EilS30qcLuzk5/YR
t1I870QAwx4/gLZRJmlFXUAiUftZPY1Y+r/F9bow9subVWzXgTuAHTRv8mZgt2uZUKWkn5/oBHsQ
IsJPu6nX/rfGG/g7V+fGqKYVDwT7g/bTxR7DAjVUE1oWkTL2dfOuK2HXKu/yIgMZndFIAccCFQCX
YFCPFSMLzLKSuYKi64QL8Fgc9QKBgQD34aCF1ps93su8q1w2uFe5eZSvu/o66oL5V0wLPQeCZ1FZ
V4661F1P5nEHEIGAtEkWcSPoTCgWE7fPCTKMyKbhPBZ6i1R8jSjgo64eK7QmdZFuo38L+iE1YvH7
YnoBJDvMpPG+qFGQiaiD3+Fa5Z8GkotmXoB7VSVkAUw7/s9JKgOBhAACgYBLonLwYk+FBPFgQq8b
CxLk1nsxfzy/W+PfIpo6EWNVxVj6FUDktBAGpx/ZElsgd3PMKaAPauqG3LXMFHmVLOyGtjPGGbFW
/n9A0JMC7OKZ3aJWKYow9rbIvYU5AqJnM0HJy1OOZijZ0LgJzdJ0QQomgEN7zVN2CicSweN6+IfV
sTALBgcqhkjOOAQDBQADMAAwLQIVAIkqKqc+7f0r84DRqx9NMWZFMCJFAhQaDCKtP6V60ygtuG8W
ijdzP5qFag==
-----END CERTIFICATE-----
```

Notice that you cannot specify both -v and -rfc.

- -printcert

  This command, which can be used independently of a keystore, reads the certificate from the file cert_file, and prints its contents in a human-readable format. If no file is given, the certificate is read from standard input.

  The certificate may be either binary encoded or in printable encoding Base 64 format.

- -selfcert

  Generates an X.509 V1 self-signed certificate, using keystore information including the private key and public key associated with alias. If dname is supplied at the command line, it is used as the X.500 distinguished name for both the issuer and subject of the certificate. Otherwise, the X.500 distinguished name associated with alias (at the bottom of its existing certificate chain) is used.

  The generated certificate is stored as a single-element certificate chain in the keystore entry identified by alias, where it replaces the existing certificate chain.

  sigalg specifies the algorithm that should be used to sign the certificate.

  In order to access the private key, the appropriate password must be provided, since private keys are protected in the keystore with a password. If keypass is not provided at the command line, and is different from the password used to protect the integrity of the keystore, the user is prompted for it.

valDays is the number of days for which the certificate should be considered valid.

- -storepasswd

  This command changes the password used to protect the integrity of the keystore contents. The new password is new_storepass, which must be at least 6 characters long.

The commands above that require the presence of a keystore create it if one is not already present.

There are three options that are valid for all the above commands, except -help and -printcert. One of these is the -storepass option, which we have already commented on. The two others are:

- -storetype

  This specifies the type of keystore to be instantiated. The default keystore type is the one that is specified as the value of the keystore.type property in the security properties file. This value is returned by the static getDefaultType() method in java.security.KeyStore.

- -keystore

  This option specifies the keystore location. It defaults to the file .keystore in the user's home directory, as determined by the user.home system property. The value of the user.home system property can be found by using one of the two applications described in Appendix A, "Getting Internal System Properties" on page 675.

Finally, the -v option can be used with all the commands above, except -help. If it appears, it signifies *verbose mode*, and detailed certificate information will be output.

Notice also that:

- The -alias option refers to the alias of an entry present in the keystore. If the alias is not present, the keystore throws the appropriate warning and exits. On the other hand, the -genkey exits and an error message is seen on the screen if the alias is already present.

- The -validity option refers to the length of time a certificate is valid and corresponds to the number of days the certified entity can rely on the public value, if the associated private key has not been compromised. In general, the validity period chosen depends on a number of factors, such as the strength of the private key used to sign the certificate or the amount one is willing to pay for a certificate. By default, if a validity value is not explicitly specified, it is set to 90 days.

An interesting thing to note here is that the `keytool` allows the validity to be set to 0 or even a negative number. This is because for testing purposes any date is assumed to be valid.

- The `-file` option refers to the file from which to import the certificate or export the certificate to.

- The `-keysize` option refers to the modulus length of the key to be generated.

Some options have default values, shown in the following table:

Table 9. Default Values for keytool Options

Option	Default Value
-alias	mykey
-keyalg	DSA
-keysize	1024
-validity	90
-keystore	${user.home}${/}.keystore
-file	stdin if reading
	stdout if writing

The signature algorithm, specified with the `-sigalg` option, is derived from the algorithm of the underlying private key; if the underlying private key is of type DSA, the `-sigalg` option defaults to SHA1withDSA, and if the underlying private key is of type RSA, `-sigalg` defaults to MD5withRSA.

9.1.4 An Example of keytool Usage

The session shown in the following figure is an example of how to use the `-genkey` command associated with the `keytool` utility to generate a key pair and wrap the public key in a self-signed certificate:

```
D:\itso>keytool -genkey -keystore deepakstore -alias TestKey
Enter keystore password:  deepak
What is your first and last name?
  [Unknown]:  Deepak Gupta
What is the name of your organizational unit?
  [Unknown]: ITSO
```

Figure 115. (Part 1 of 2). Usage of the -genkey Command Associated with the keytool Utility

```
What is the name of your organization?
  [Unknown]: IBM
What is the name of your City or Locality?
  [Unknown]: Cary
What is the name of your State or Province?
  [Unknown]: NC
What is the two-letter country code for this unit?
  [Unknown]: US
Is <CN=MyName, OU=MyOrgUnit, O=MyOrg, L=City, ST=State, C=IN> correct?
  [no]:  Y
Enter key password for <TestKey>
        (RETURN if same as keystore password):

D:\itso>
```

Figure 116. (Part 2 of 2). Usage of the -genkey Command Associated with the keytool Utility

Note that if you enter N when you are prompted to confirm the correctness of the information you typed in, or enter a carriage return or type anything junk, the tool will ask you for all the information again. You can simply press Enter for all the correct information and change the one you want.

Several other examples in later sections will show how to use all the commands and options associated with the keytool command line utility.

9.2 Java Archive Tool

One characteristic of the dynamic loading of class files is that a typical applet may involve a number of small network transfers. It may also involve the retrieval of other files, such as graphic images. Given the indifferent performance of many World Wide Web (WWW) connections, this can be a serious performance hit. JDK 1.1 provided relief for this by introducing the JAR format for packing everything into a single file. A JAR file can be created and managed by using the Java Archive command line tool jar. This utility, also a part of the Java 2 SDK, allows for compression, which can further improve performance. The compression is done based on the ZIP and the ZLIB compression format[3]. This is also the only archive format (that we know of) which is cross platform.

In addition to a number of files packed together and possibly compressed, a JAR file can contain a special text file, called *JAR manifest* or simply *manifest*, which is a description of each file contained in the JAR file itself.

[3] More information on the ZLIB format can be seen on the site http://www.cdrom.com/pub/infozip/zlib/.

The manifest file includes the name of each file and other information used to identify particular classes or beans.

9.2.1 Options of the jar Command

We now describe more details about the `jar` command. If you know the UNIX `tar` command, `jar` will be very familiar. In fact, these two commands have almost the same syntax. The syntax for a `jar` command is:

```
jar {ctxu}[vfmOM] [jar-file] [manifest-file] [-C dir] files ...
```

Notice that at least one of the options `ctxu` *must* be specified.

The meaning of the available command flags is explained in the following table:

Table 10. jar Command Options

Flag	Function
c	Create a new JAR file
t	List the table of contents for a JAR file
x	Extract named (or all) files from a JAR file
u	Update an existing JAR file
v	Generate a verbose output on standard output
f	Specify the JAR file name, else it is written to stdout
m	Include manifest information from a specified manifest file
0	Store files in a JAR file without any compression
M	Do not create a manifest file for the entries
C	Change to the following directory and include the following file

If any file is a directory then it is processed recursively.

We now show, through some examples, how to use the `jar` command line tool:

- To archive two class files, say itso.class and javasec.class, and one text file, say ibmreadme.txt, into an archive called ibmclasses.jar, enter:

```
jar cvf ibmclasses.jar itso.class javasec.class ibmreadme.txt
```

Notice that the options of the `jar` command can be preceded by a minus sign or not, so the command above could have been typed as:

```
jar -cvf ibmclasses.jar itso.class javasec.class ibmreadme.txt
```

- To extract all these files from this archive, enter:

```
jar xvf ibmclasses.jar
```

- To view the contents of the JAR file, the command is:

```
jar tvf ibmclasses.jar
```

- To update the contents of the JAR file ibmclasses.jar with another file called file.txt, enter:

```
jar uvf ibmclasses.jar file.txt
```

- Note that if you do not specify the f option, jar writes the output to standard output. For example, after entering:

```
jar cv test.txt
```

the following would be displayed on standard output:

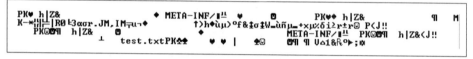

Figure 117. Output of the jar Command Displayed on stdout

No JAR file is created in this case. However, if you redirect the output to a file, say myJar.jar, then the command:

```
jar cv test.txt > myJar.jar
```

is equivalent to:

```
jar cvf myJar.jar test.txt
```

- The v option is for verbose output on the screen. For example, when creating the JAR file myJar.jar with the command:

```
jar cvf myJar.jar test.txt
```

the following information is displayed on standard output while the command is executing:

```
added manifest
adding: test.txt (in=13) (out=15) (deflated -15%)
```

If the v option is not specified, the command is executed without any user acknowledgment.

- The 0 option is used when you do not wish to compress the single files that are part of the JAR file. In other words, using this option, the files are packed together, but they are not compressed.

  Using this flag is a trade off between speed and download time. Uncompressed JAR files will take a longer time to download over the network. However, once downloaded, classes can be extracted from it faster.

- The command:

  ```
  jar cvf ibm.jar ibm.class java\redbook.class
  ```

  creates the JAR file ibm.jar including the two files ibm.class and redbook.class, which are located in the java directory. Because the directory tree is respected by the `jar` command, you would see the same files and same directory structure when extracting the JAR file ibm.jar.

  Instead of typing `java\redbook.class`, you could have used the -C option of the `jar` command, and typed:

  ```
  jar cvf ibm.jar ibm.class -C java redbook.class
  ```

  The -C option is used to specify the directory where a file is located. However, in this case the directory hierarchy is not maintained. Upon extracting the JAR file ibm.jar, the two files ibm.class and redbook.class are located in the same directory.

- The wildcard character (*) is allowed in the syntax of the `jar` command and can be used to archive all files in a directory. For example:

  ```
  jar cvf myJarFile.jar *
  ```

- The manifest uses the RFC822 ASCII format[4], so it is easy to view and process the manifest file contents. Using the `m` option of the `jar` command, you can include manifest information from a specified existing file. For example, if you want to produce a JAR file, say myJarFile.jar, from the class file MyClass.class, but you want to provide your own manifest file, or at least a subset of the information a manifest file should contain, then the right command would be something like:

  ```
  jar cvmf myManifestInfo myJarFile.jar MyClass.class
  ```

  where MyManifestInfo is the file containing the manifest file information. The `jar` tool takes the information from that file, and builds a manifest file. Notice that the order with which you entered the information in the manifest information file might be rearranged by the `jar` tool according to specific syntax rules.

---

[4] See http://info.internet.isi.edu:80/in-notes/rfc/files/rfc822.txt.

- The -M option of the `jar` command is used to create a JAR file without the manifest file. For example the command:

```
jar cvMf myJarFile.jar MyClass.class YourClass.class
```

would produce a JAR file, called myJarFile.jar, from the class files MyClass and YourClass. However, this file would not contain the manifest file. This way, the `jar` tool is only acting as a mere compressing tool and it would be equivalent to other archiving and compressing tools such as WinZip.

- If both the `m` and `M` options are present, the `m` option is ignored and the resulting JAR file will not have a manifest file.

We will give you more details about the `m` and `M` options and their usage in 12.1, "JAR Files and Applet Signing" on page 385.

9.2.2 Running a JAR File

Java class files inside JAR files can be run like uncompressed and unpacked class files:

- The applet files inside a JAR file can be used by an HTML file specifying an `<APPLET>` tag with the `Archive` attribute. The syntax of that tag should be something similar to the following:

```
<APPLET Code="itso.class" Archive="ibm.jar">
```

- To run a class file in a JAR file on the command prompt, the `-jar` option of the `java` command has to be used. The syntax is as shown next:

```
java -jar [-options] jar_file [args ...]
```

Note here that `java` looks at the manifest file for the `Main-Class:` parameter and runs the class file specified by it. By default, when a JAR file is created, this information is not added in the JAR manifest and there is no prompting by the tool to ask for this class name. So, assuming that MyClass is the main class of the program that has to be archived and compressed, these are the steps you should follow:

1. Create a text file, called say, MyManifestInfo.txt, which only contains the following:

```
Main-Class: MyClass
```

In other words, this file should contain the line:

```
Main-Class: MyClass
```

followed by an empty line. Notice that after the class name, you should type Enter, in order to create an end-of-line character, or this file will be ignored by the `jar` tool.

A point to note here is that the extension .class must not be specified in this manifest information file.

2. From the directory where MyClass.class is, run the following command:

```
jar cvfm MyClass.jar META-INF\MyManifestInfo.txt MyClass.class
```

For detailed information about this process, refer to 12.1, "JAR Files and Applet Signing" on page 385.

9.3 JAR Signing and Verification Tool

The JAR signing and verification tool offered by Java 2 SDK is called `jarsigner`. This is a command line tool, used to sign JAR files and to verify signatures and the integrity of signed JAR files. As we will see in 12.1, "JAR Files and Applet Signing" on page 385, a signed JAR file includes a *signature file*, with extension SF, and a *signature block file*, with extension DSA:

- For each source file included in the JAR file, the SF file has three lines, just as in the manifest file, listing the following:

  1. The file name
  2. The name of the digest algorithm used (SHA)
  3. SHA digest value

  In the manifest file, the Signature Hash Algorithm (SHA) digest value for each source file is the digest of the binary data in the source file. In the SF file, on the other hand, the digest value for a given source file is the hash of the three lines in the manifest file for the source file. The signature file also, by default, includes a header containing a hash of the whole manifest file. This is an example of an SF file:

```
Signature-Version: 1.0
SHA1-Digest-Manifest: i/yxbIQglNG2IVL/bL9Idh85TYM=
Created-By: 1.2.1 (Sun Microsystems Inc.)

Name: Count.class
SHA1-Digest: e3V355tfsF1jVzzkKy3cas3bazk=
```

- The SF file is signed and the signature is placed in the DSA file. The DSA file also contains, encoded inside it, the certificate or certificate chain from the keystore which authenticates the public key corresponding to the private key used for signing.

Inside the JAR file, both the SF and DSA files are found in the directory META-INF. This directory was previously created by the `jar` tool and already contains the manifest file MANIFEST.MF.

The basic format for the `jarsigner` command for JAR file signing purposes is:

```
jarsigner [options] jar-file alias
```

If you want a JAR file to be signed by the private key of a particular entity, `alias` should indicate the name with which the corresponding public key has been aliased in the keystore. The tool might prompt for the password of the keystore and the key, if any, and if not already provided as part of the options.

The syntax of the `jarsigner` command, when used for signature and integrity verification purposes, is the following:

```
jarsigner -verify [options] jar-file
```

Quick help on this command can be obtained by entering `jarsigner` on the command prompt, with or without the `-help` flag. The output of this is shown in the next figure:

[-keystore <url>]	keystore location
[-storepass <password>]	password for keystore integrity
[-storetype <type>]	keystore type
[-keypass <password>]	password for private key (if different)
[-sigfile <file>]	name of .SF/.DSA file
[-signedjar <file>]	name of signed JAR file
[-verify]	verify a signed JAR file
[-verbose]	verbose output when signing/verifying
[-certs]	display certificates when verbose and verifying
[-internalsf]	include the .SF file inside the signature block
[-sectionsonly]	don't compute hash of entire manifest

Figure 118. jarsigner Help on the Command Line

We now explain the meaning of the options shown in Figure 118 on page 276:

- `-keystore`

  This option specifies the URL of the keystore location. This defaults to the file .keystore in the user's home directory, as determined by the user.home system property (see Appendix A, "Getting Internal System Properties" on page 675).

  A keystore is required when signing, so you must explicitly specify one if the default keystore does not exist (or you want to use one other than the default).

  A keystore is not required when verifying, but if one is specified, or the default exists, and the `-verbose` option was also specified, additional information is output regarding whether or not any of the certificates used to verify the JAR file are contained in that keystore.

  Note that the `-keystore` argument can actually be a file name (and path) specification rather than a URL, in which case it is treated the same as a `file:` URL. That is,

  `-keystore D:\itso\myKeystore`

  is equivalent to:

  `-keystore file:/D:/itso/myKeystore`

- `-storepass`

  This option specifies the password which is required to access the keystore. This is only needed when signing (not verifying) a JAR file. In that case, if a `-storepass` option is not provided at the command line, the user is prompted for the password.

  See 9.1.2, "Store and Private Key Password" on page 261 for recommendations on providing passwords to command line utilities.

- `-storetype`

  This option specifies the type of keystore to be instantiated. The default keystore type is the one that is specified as the value of the keystore.type property in the java.security properties file. That value is also returned by the static getDefaultType() method in java.security.KeyStore.

- `-keypass`

  This option specifies the password used to protect the private key of the keystore entry addressed by the alias specified on the command line. The password is required when using `jarsigner` to sign a JAR file. If no password is provided on the command line, and the required password is different from the store password, the user is prompted for it.

See 9.1.2, "Store and Private Key Password" on page 261 for recommendations on providing passwords to command line utilities.

- `-sigfile`

  This option specifies the base file name to be used for the generated SF and DSA files. For example, if `file` is `mySign`, the generated SF and DSA files will be named MYSIGN.SF and MYSIGN.DSA, and will be placed in the META-INF directory of the signed JAR file, where the manifest file also resides.

  The characters in `file` can be only letters, numbers, the underscore (_) and hyphen (-) characters. However, note that all lowercase characters will be converted to uppercase for the SF and DSA file names.

  If no `-sigfile` option appears on the command line, the base file name for the SF and DSA files will be the first 8 characters of the alias name specified on the command line, all converted to uppercase. If the alias name has fewer than 8 characters, the full alias name is used. If the alias name contains any characters that are not legal in a signature file name, each such character is converted to an underscore (_) character in forming the file name.

  As an example, the command:

  ```
  jarsigner test.jar ibm
  ```

  creates the files IBM.SF and IBM.DSA in the JAR file test.jar. By using the `-sigfile` option, you can specify a different file name. So, the command:

  ```
  jarsigner -sigfile itso test.jar IBM
  ```

  creates the files ITSO.SF and ITSO.DSA in the JAR file test.jar.

- `-signedjar`

  This option specifies the name to be used for the signed JAR file. If no name is specified on the command line, the name used is the same as the input JAR file name; in other words, the unsigned JAR file is overwritten with the signed JAR file.

Signed JAR File Extension

In JDK 1.1, digital signatures were applied by using the javakey command, whose functionality in the Java 2 SDK has been replaced and enhanced by keytool and jarsigner. The javakey tool added a sig extension to the jar extension of the JAR file to be signed. So, for example, after signing test.jar with javakey, you would have found a file called test.jar.sig.

In the Java 2 SDK this naming convention has been simplified, and jarsigner does not add any extension to the jar extension of the JAR file. By default, signing test.jar with jarsigner, produces another file that is still called test.jar, and that contains also the digital signature information. Therefore, this file overwrites the unsigned JAR file, unless you use the -signedjar option to specify a different name for the signed JAR file.

- -verify

  If this option appears on the command line, the specified JAR file will be verified, but not signed. If the verification is successful, the following message will be displayed:

  `jar verified.`

  If you try to verify an unsigned JAR file, or a JAR file signed with an unsupported algorithm (for example, RSA when you do not have an RSA provider installed), the following is displayed:

  `jar is unsigned. (signatures missing or not parsable)`

  It is possible to verify JAR files signed using either `jarsigner` or the JDK 1.1 `javakey` tool, or both.

- -verbose

  If this appears on the command line, it indicates *verbose mode*, which causes `jarsigner` to output extra information on the progress of the JAR signing or verification.

- -certs

  If this option appears on the command line, along with the `-verify` and `-verbose` options, the output includes certificate information for each signer of the JAR file.

- -internalsf

  In the past, the DSA file generated when a JAR file was signed included a complete encoded copy of the SF file also generated. This behavior has been changed. To reduce the overall size of the output JAR file, the DSA file by default does not contain a copy of the SF file. If `-internalsf` appears on the command line, the old behavior is utilized.

This option is used mainly for testing; in practice, it should not be used, since using it eliminates an optimization.

- `-sectionsonly`

If this option appears on the command line, the SF file generated when a JAR file is signed does not include a header containing a hash of the whole manifest file. It contains only information and hashes related to each source file included in the JAR file.

For example, without this option, the SF file looks like the following:

```
Signature-Version: 1.0
SHA1-Digest-Manifest: 6nvtQTd+OCb9m0xIEQcg3lzjuUw=
Created-By: 1.2 (Sun Microsystems Inc.)

Name: itso.txt
SHA1-Digest: HZxJifZphtKVJLL75v060Hx7ZWE=

Name: redbook.class
SHA1-Digest: AzHPdtYGvpHDSvHd6YCpQ/ifZa4=
```

On the other hand, if the option `-sectionsonly` is specified, the SF file looks like the following:

```
Signature-Version: 1.0
Created-By: 1.2 (Sun Microsystems Inc.)

Name: itso.txt
SHA1-Digest: HZxJifZphtKVJLL75v060Hx7ZWE=

Name: redbook.class
SHA1-Digest: AzHPdtYGvpHDSvHd6YCpQ/ifZa4=
```

Notice that the `SHA1-Digest-Manifest:` header information is not included in the file generated with the `-sectionsonly` option.

By default, this header is added as an optimization, so it is generally not advisable to use the `-sectiononly` option.

9.3.1 jarsigner Scenario

Using `jarsigner` and `keytool` together you can send signed code or even data to another person and he can verify the signature ensuring authenticity and integrity. To illustrate this, consider an example where a sender Deepak creates a JAR file and a key pair with an associated certificate, signs the JAR file, exports his certificate and sends the JAR file along with his certificate to the receiver named Ashok. Ashok imports the certificate sent by Deepak into his keystore and verify the signature on the JAR file.

The scenario above requires the following steps:

- At the sender's end:

1. Create a key pair and the associated self-signed certificate.

   This is done using the `-genkey` command of the `keytool` utility, as shown in the following session screen:

```
D:\deepak>keytool -genkey -keystore deepakstore -alias deepak
Enter keystore password:  deepak
What is your first and last name?
  [Unknown]:  Deepak Gupta
What is the name of your organizational unit?
  [Unknown]:  ITSO
What is the name of your organization?
  [Unknown]:  IBM
What is the name of your City or Locality?
  [Unknown]:  Raleigh
What is the name of your State or Province?
  [Unknown]:  NC
What is the two-letter country code for this unit?
  [Unknown]:  US
Is <CN=Deepak Gupta, OU=ITSO, O=IBM, L=Raleigh, ST=NC, C=US> correct?
  [no]:  Y

Enter key password for <deepak>
        (RETURN if same as keystore password):

D:\deepak>
```

The keystore, deepakstore, is created only if it is not already present. A public-private key pair and a self-signed certificate are generated and associated with the alias deepak.

2. Sign the JAR file with the private key generated.

   Assuming we have a JAR file called myjar.jar, this step is performed by using the `jarsigner` utility, as illustrated in the following session screen:

```
D:\deepak>jarsigner -keystore deepakstore myjar.jar deepak
Enter Passphrase for keystore: deepak

D:\deepak>
```

The `jarsigner` tool would have prompted us for the key password of the deepak alias, if this password had been different from the keystore password.

3. Export the self-signed certificate created to a file.

To do this, the `-export` option of the `keytool` utility is used. Assuming we want to export the certificate to the file deepak.crt, this step is illustrated in the following session screen:

```
D:\deepak>keytool -export -keystore deepakstore -file deepak.crt -alias deepak
Enter keystore password:  deepak
Certificate stored in file <deepak.crt>

D:\deepak>
```

4. Send the certificate along with the code.

The files deepak.crt and myjar.jar can be sent to the receiver, who can use the contents in myjar.jar after verifying the signature.

- At the receiver's end:

1. Verify the received certificate and import it into the receiver's keystore.

Assume that the receiver has a keystore called ashokstore with store password ashokr. Then the import operation can be performed by using the `-import` command associated with the `keytool` utility option, as shown in the following session screen:

```
D:\ashok>keytool -import -file deepak.crt -keystore ashokstore
Enter keystore password:  ashokr
Owner: CN=Deepak Gupta, OU=ITSO, O=IBM, L=Raleigh, ST=NC, C=US
Issuer: CN=Deepak Gupta, OU=ITSO, O=IBM, L=Raleigh, ST=NC, C=US
Serial number: 369e614d
Valid from: Thu Jan 14 16:27:41 EST 1999 until: Wed Apr 14 17:27:41 EDT 1999
Certificate fingerprints:
        MD5:  C2:BE:02:C9:33:48:60:55:5E:6B:66:87:A9:E7:42:27
        SHA1: CA:15:8E:6B:28:A9:EB:6E:B9:B8:65:A3:68:77:5C:3F:33:11:10:2C
Trust this certificate? [no]:  y
Certificate was added to keystore

D:\ashok>
```

Note that the tool shows you the certificate information and asks whether to trust the certificate or not.

Since the default for alias is mykey, when we import a certificate in a local keystore it gets stored in the keystore with the alias mykey, if such an alias does not exist already. If you wish to specify another alias you should use the `-alias` option of the `keytool` utility. If you attempt to import a certificate with an alias that already exists in the local keystore, you will receive an error message and the operation will abort:

```
keytool error: Certificate not imported, alias <mykey> already exists
```

It is very important that you verify the certificate fingerprints before agreeing to trust it. Contact the person who sent the certificate, and ask him to provide you with the certificate fingerprints, for example by attaching them to an encrypted e-mail. The sender should use the `-printcert` command associated with the `keytool` utility to display the information related to his certificate:

```
D:\deepak>keytool -printcert -file deepak.crt
Owner: CN=Deepak Gupta, OU=ITSO, O=IBM, L=Raleigh, ST=NC, C=US
Issuer: CN=Deepak Gupta, OU=ITSO, O=IBM, L=Raleigh, ST=NC, C=US
Serial number: 369e614d
Valid from: Thu Jan 14 16:27:41 EST 1999 until: Wed Apr 14 17:27:41 EDT 1999
Certificate fingerprints:
         MD5:  C2:BE:02:C9:33:48:60:55:5E:6B:66:87:A9:E7:42:27
         SHA1: CA:15:8E:6B:28:A9:EB:6E:B9:B8:65:A3:68:77:5C:3F:33:11:10:2C

D:\deepak
```

Then, you should compare the two sets of fingerprints. Only if the fingerprints are equal is it guaranteed that the certificate has not been replaced in transit with somebody else's (for example, an attacker's) certificate. If such an attack took place, and you did not check the certificate before you imported it, you would end up trusting anything the attacker has signed (for example, a JAR file with malicious class files inside).

2. Verify the digital signature.

   This is done by using the `jarsigner` command with the `-verify` option, as shown in the following session screen:

```
D:\ashok>jarsigner -verify -keystore ashokstore myjar.jar
jar verified.

D:\ashok>
```

Alternatively, to obtain further details, you can use the `-verbose` option:

```
D:\ashok>jarsigner -verify -verbose -keystore ashokstore myjar.jar

           188 Thu Jan 14 16:30:44 EST 1999 META-INF/DEEPAK.SF
          1004 Thu Jan 14 16:30:44 EST 1999 META-INF/DEEPAK.DSA
             0 Thu Jan 14 16:30:28 EST 1999 META-INF/
  smk        6 Thu Jan 14 16:30:24 EST 1999 myownclass.class

    s = signature was verified
    m = entry is listed in manifest
    k = at least one certificate was found in keystore
    i = at least one certificate was found in identity scope

  jar verified.

D:\ashok>
```

This verifies the signature.

If the JAR file is not signed, the above verification command will throw the message that we have already described:

```
jar is unsigned. (signatures missing or not parsable)
```

If the files in the JAR were modified, we would see an error message. For example, if someone has exploded a signed JAR file, has modified one of its files, and has rebuilt the JAR file, when we try to verify the signature using jarsigner, we get the following error message:

```
jarsigner: java.lang.SecurityException: SHA1 digest error for
itso.class
```

where itso.class is the name of the modified file.

9.3.2 Observations on the jarsigner Verification Process

A successful JAR file verification occurs if the signatures are valid, and none of the files that were in the JAR file when the signatures were generated have been changed since then. JAR file verification through the jarsigner tool involves the following steps:

1. Verify the signature of the SF file itself.

   That is, the verification ensures that the signature stored in each DSA file was in fact generated using the private key corresponding to the public key whose certificate (or certificate chain) also appears in the DSA file. It also ensures that the signature is a valid signature of the corresponding signature SF file, and thus the SF file has not been tampered with.

2. Verify the digest listed in each entry in the SF file with each corresponding section in the manifest.

The SF file by default includes a header containing a hash of the entire manifest file. When the header is present, then the verification can check to see whether or not the hash in the header indeed matches the hash of the manifest file.

- If that is the case, verification proceeds to the next step.
- If that is not the case, a less optimized verification is required, to ensure that the hash in each source file information section in the SF file equals the hash of its corresponding section in the manifest file.

One reason the hash of the manifest file that is stored in the SF file header may not equal the hash of the current manifest file could be because one or more files were added to the JAR file (using the `jar` tool) after the signature (and thus the SF file) was generated. When the `jar` tool is used to add files, the manifest file is changed (sections are added to it for the new files), but the SF file is not. A verification is still considered successful if none of the files that were in the JAR file when the signature was generated have been changed since then, which is the case if the hashes in the non-header sections of the SF file equal the hashes of the corresponding sections in the manifest file.

3. Read each file in the JAR file that has an entry in the SF file. While reading, compute the file's digest, and then compare the result with the digest for this file in the manifest section.

The digests should be the same, or verification fails.

If any serious verification failures occur during the verification process, the process is stopped and a security exception is thrown. It is caught and displayed.

From the above description, you can see that `jarsigner` only verifies the signature present on the JAR file and in fact does not verify if that signature has been made by some trusted entity, whose certificate is present in the user's keystore. It only ensures that the files inside the JAR file have not been modified since the signature was put on it.

For all practical purposes, this is actually as good as not verifying at all, because if a person (a hacker that is) modifies the files inside the JAR file, he or she can just as well remove the SF and DSA signature files and sign the modified JAR file with his or her own keys. The JAR file will still be verified. Therefore, note that when you see the message:

```
jar verified.
```

this only implies that the *signature* on the JAR file has been verified and not that it has been signed by the entity whose certificate you just imported. So, even if the receiver did not follow Step 1 on page 282, he would see the same results when performing Step 2 on page 283. However, this does not mean that the step of verifying the sender's certificate and importing it into the local keystore can be skipped. On the contrary, the receiver should perform both the steps we have listed, and then, to verify that the JAR file came from the person he trusts, run the JAR file under a protection domain with a `signedBy` parameter pointing to the certificate just imported.

9.3.3 Tampering with a Signed JAR File

Let's see now what happens when a signed JAR file has been tampered with and we run the `jarsigner` command with the `-verify` option to verify the signature.

In this scenario, we initially take two files, redbook.class and itso.txt. We run the `jar` command to produce a JAR file, which we call test.jar, in the following way:

```
jar cvf test.jar redbook.class itso.txt
```

Then we assume that two different signers, ibm and test, apply their digital signatures:

```
jarsigner test.jar ibm
jarsigner test.jar test
```

At this point, the contents of the JAR file test.jar are:

- redbook.class
- itso.txt
- META-INF\MANIFEST.MF
- META-INF\IBM.SF
- META-INF\IBM.DSA
- META-INF\TEST.SF
- META-INF\TEST.DSA

These are possible scenarios:

1. We change one of the content files, for example itso.txt.

   This can be done by modifying the original itso.txt file (for example, deleting a few characters from it and saving the new version with the same name again) and updating the JAR file using the following command:

   ```
   jar -uf test.jar itso.txt
   ```

   Next, we run the following command:

```
jarsigner -verify test.jar
```

and we get the following exception:

```
jarsigner: java.lang.SecurityException: SHA1 digest error for itso.txt
```

2. We change the manifest file by modifying the SHA-1 digest of one of the content files, for example the redbook.class file.

To do this, we have to explode the JAR file first:

```
D:\>jar -xvf test.jar
 extracted: META-INF/MANIFEST.MF
 extracted: META-INF/IBM.SF
 extracted: META-INF/IBM.DSA
 extracted: META-INF/TEST.SF
 extracted: META-INF/TEST.DSA
   created: META-INF/
 extracted: redbook.class
 extracted: itso.txt

D:\>
```

At this point, the SHA-1 digest for the redbook.class file can be modified in the manifest file with a text editor. After this, the new, tampered version of the JAR file can be created as shown in the following session screen:

```
D:\>jar -cvfM test.jar META-INF/MANIFEST.MF META-INF/IBM.SF META-INF/IBM.DSA
META-INF/TEST.SF META-INF/TEST.DSA redbook.class itso.txt
 adding: META-INF/MANIFEST.MF (in=196) (out=168) (deflated 14%)
 adding: META-INF/IBM.SF (in=249) (out=200) (deflated 19%)
 adding: META-INF/IBM.DSA (in=972) (out=737) (deflated 24%)
 adding: META-INF/TEST.SF (in=249) (out=200) (deflated 19%)
 adding: META-INF/TEST.DSA (in=971) (out=740) (deflated 23%)
 adding: redbook.class (in=6) (out=8) (deflated -33%)
 adding: itso.txt (in=70) (out=68) (deflated 2%)

D:\>
```

Notice the use of the M option for the jar command. As we said in 9.2.1, "Options of the jar Command" on page 271, this option prevents jar from creating a new manifest file. We use it because we are already passing the manifest information META-INF\MANIFEST.MF on the command line.

We then attempt to verify the signature information:

```
jarsigner -verify test.jar
```

And as a result, we obtain an error message:

```
jarsigner: java.lang.SecurityException: invalid SHA1 signature file
digest for redbook.class
```

3. We change some other information in the manifest file, for example we add the following line:

```
Main-Class: redbook
```

This can be done again as indicated in Step 2 on page 287. Interestingly and as expected, if we try to verify the JAR file, it verifies:

```
jar verified.
```

4. We change the SF file by modifying the SHA-1 digest of one of the content files, for example redbook.class.

This can be done again with a procedure similar to Step 2 on page 287. The result of the verification test is the following:

```
jarsigner: java.lang.SecurityException: cannot verify signature block
file META-INF/TEST
```

5. We add another file, say ibm.class, to the JAR file.

This can be done using the `jar` command with options `uf`, as indicated in Step 1 on page 286. This operation automatically updates the manifest file as well, with information on the new file. We then try to verify the JAR file and it verifies as expected:

```
jar verified.
```

6. Another point to note here is that `jarsigner`, while verifying, does not check for the validity of the certificate. That is, it does not check if the certificate with which the files were signed has expired or not.

- We create a certificate with validity -1 (which for testing purposes is allowed by the `keytool` utility, as explained in 9.1.3, "Commands and Options Associated with keytool" on page 262). With this certificate, we sign a JAR file and then attempt to verify the digital signature.

- We sign a JAR file with a certificate that has already expired and then attempt to verify the digital signature.

- We sign a JAR file with an active certificate and then try to verify the signature after the certificate has expired.

The JAR file verifies in all cases:

```
jar verified.
```

9.4 Policy File Creation and Management Tool

The Policy Tool is a GUI-based utility for creating and managing policy files.

You can open this tool by typing `policytool` on the command prompt. According to the default security properties file java.security, the Policy Tool expects to find a policy file called .java.policy in the user home directory. If the .java.policy file in the user home directory exists, the tool will open it by default as soon as you enter the `policytool` command. If it does not exist, you will receive an error message similar to the following one:

Figure 119. Policy Tool Error

Just click **OK** in this case.

The following window shows what the Policy Tool looks like:

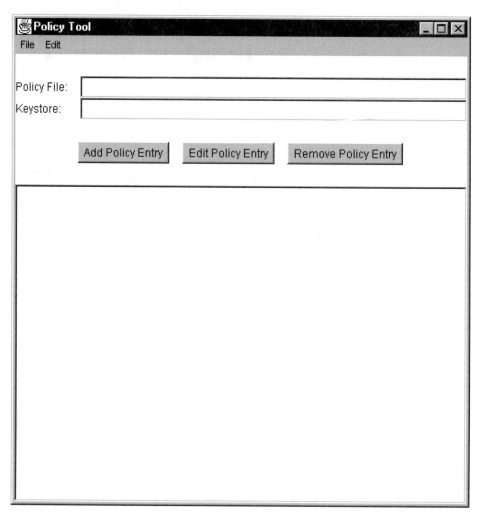

Figure 120. Policy Tool Initial Screen

The functions you can perform are:

1. Create a new policy file.

   To do this, you simply have to add policy entries and then save the new security policy configuration to a policy file, using the **Save As** option from the File menu. If a policy file is already under construction, and you want to start the creation of a new one, select **New** from the File menu.

2. Modify an existing policy file.

   To do this, open the policy file using the **Open** item from the File menu and make the modifications you want to the policy configurations.

Then, save the file by selecting **Save** from the File menu.

3. View the warning log.

   The Policy Tool maintains a warning log where it registers all the warning messages that have been displayed during a policy configuration session. This log can be accessed by clicking on **View Warning Log** from the File menu.

4. Exit the Policy Tool.

   Just select **Exit** from the File menu.

The following modifications can be made to policy files:

1. Add a new policy entry.
2. Modify a policy entry.
3. Remove a policy entry.
4. Change the keystore.

All these can be done using the Edit menu option. For the first three, buttons are also provided.

To add a new entry, click on the **Add Policy Entry** button and the following Policy Entry dialog will be brought up:

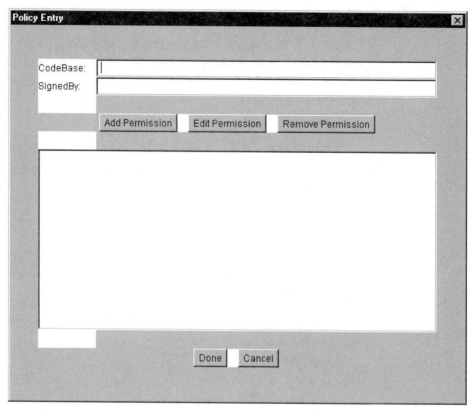

Figure 121. Policy Entry Dialog

The same box is displayed by clicking on **Edit Policy Entry** after selecting a policy entry that had been previously defined.

At this stage, you can specify a code source by entering a code base and a comma-separated string of signers in the CodeBase and SignedBy fields respectively. Then you can add, edit or remove permissions; specific buttons are provided for these operations. For example, on clicking on **Add Permission**, we get the following Permissions window:

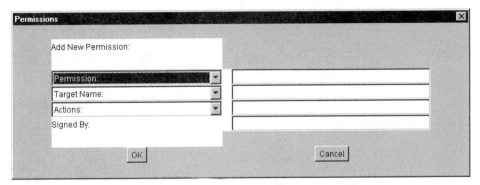

Figure 122. Permissions Screen

Drop-down lists allow you to choose among the various options already provided in the Java 2 security implementation. Notice that you can also type in the text box provided in the Permissions window to specify non-standard permissions (see 10.7.1, "How to Create New Permissions" on page 344). However, if you add a permission that is not part of the Java core APIs, a warning message appears when you press the **OK** button:

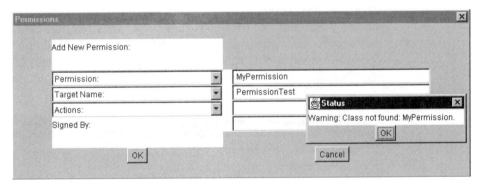

Figure 123. Warning Message with a Custom Permission

For editing permissions, the same window opens. You must select the permission to be edited and then click on **Edit Permission**.

To remove a permission, select the permission and click **Remove Permission**.

To change the keystore to which the policy configuration should apply, click on **Change KeyStore** from the Edit menu. The following window opens:

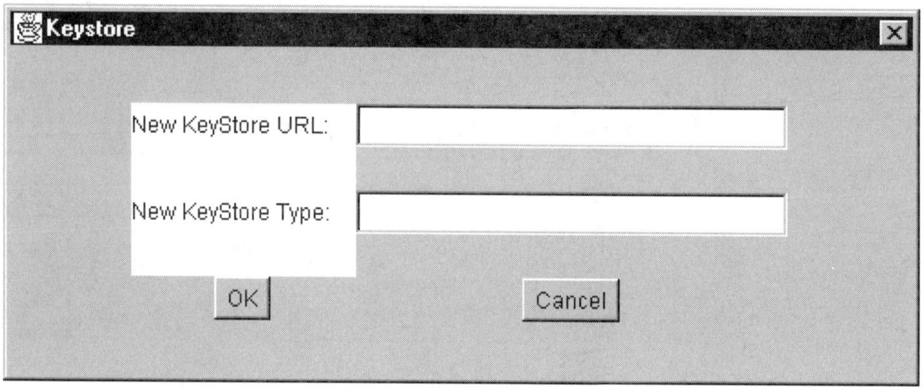

Figure 124. Keystore Dialog Box

Here you can specify the URL location and type of the keystore you want to use in this policy configuration. If you do not enter anything in the New KeyStore Type field, the system will take the default keystore type from the java.security file (see 8.3, "The Security Properties File, java.security" on page 234).

Note that, if you change the keystore, the previous keystore is no longer valid, since a policy file can only refer to a single keystore at a time. Hence, if you had permissions with a signedBy name-value pair related to an alias in the previous keystore, the Policy Tool may no longer be able to find that and will register an error. The exact nature of the error is explained in the warning log:

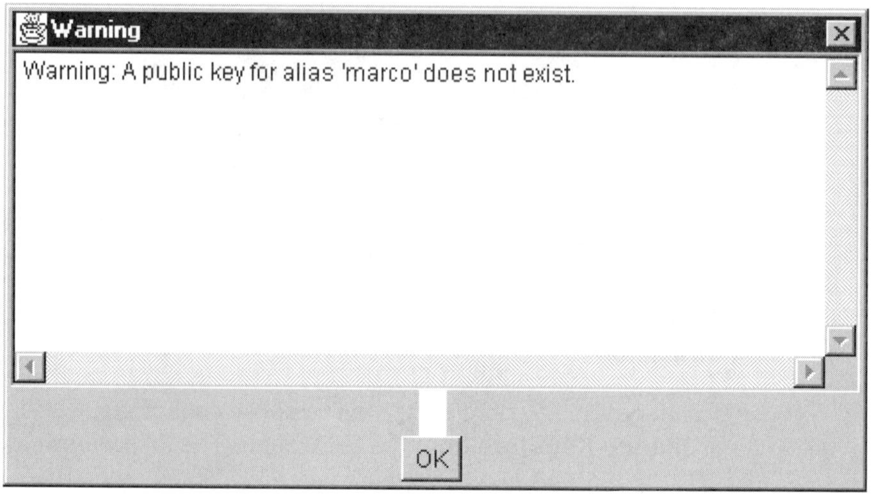

Figure 125. Warning Log

Several scenarios in this book make use of the Policy Tool to configure the security policy in the Java system. See for example 1.4.1.8, "Modifying the Security Policy on the Client System" on page 20 and 1.4.2.6, "Modifying the Security Policy" on page 32.

9.4.1 Observations on the Use of the Policy Tool

There are some things to consider when using the Policy Tool:

1. If you are modifying an *existing* policy file and try to exit the tool without saving the updated configuration, the Policy Tool will prompt you with the option to save it:

Figure 126. Option to Save an Updated Configuration

However, this is the case only if you make a change in the Permissions panel (see Figure 122 on page 293) or if you modify the keystore (see Figure 124 on page 294). If you modify the code base URL or the list of signers in the Policy Entry dialog box (see Figure 121 on page 292), the Policy Tool does not prompt you to save before exiting.

2. If you are creating a *new* policy file and exit the Policy Tool before saving the new configuration, the tool simply exits regardless of the changes you have made. It does not prompt you to save before closing.

Also, you cannot open the File menu and click on **Save** if the policy file is new, in which case the Policy File text box is still empty. In place of switching to the **Save As** option automatically, as most applications do, this tool throws a java.io.FileNotFoundException in a pop-up window on the screen:

Figure 127. FileNotFoundException Thrown by the Policy Tool

You must select **Save As** from the File menu and only then, on further changes, can you select **Save**.

Chapter 10. Security APIs in Java 2

In addition to the features and the security tools discussed, Java 2 provides several class packages that can be used for writing secure applications. The package java.security, and its subpackages java.security.acl and java.security.interfaces were provided in Java Development Kit (JDK) 1.1. The Java 2 platform adds two new subpackages, java.security.cert and java.security.spec, which provide more flexibility and functionality. These packages together form the Java Cryptography Architecture (JCA), which provides Java programs with cryptographic capabilities. Java also provides a cryptographic package called javax.crypto and its two subpackages javax.crypto.interfaces and javax.crypto.spec. However, these are sold and distributed separately as part of the Java Cryptography Extension (JCE) 1.2, due to the United States export regulations (see 2.2.3, "United States Export Rules for Encryption" on page 57).

In this chapter we present the Java 2 security APIs. Several examples are provided to demonstrate how to use the Java 2 security libraries to build secure applications.

10.1 The Package java.security

This package contains classes and interfaces for the general security framework. It includes classes that mainly cover security concepts such as access control and permissions, keys, key pairs and keystores, message digests, signatures, secure random generation, etc. Many classes and interfaces in this package are abstract and provider-based. You can supply your own implementations by using providers other than the defaults (see 10.1.3, "Providers" on page 299).

10.1.1 Principals

With respect to security, a *principal* represents an entity such as an individual user or a company. To represent this concept, the java.security package defines an interface called Principal. This interface is used to grant a particular type of access to a resource. Notice that there is no implementation for principals in Java 2 SDK, Standard Edition, V1.2.

A group of principals is represented by the Group interface, discussed in 10.5, "The Package java.security.acl" on page 324.

10.1.2 Guard Interface and GuardedObject Class

The Guard interface is provided to create an object used to guard a protected resource. The *supplier of the resource* can create an object representing the resource, encapsulate it into a GuardedObject, and keep the resource inside this GuardedObject. In creating the GuardedObject, the supplier also specifies the Guard object. The *consumer of the resource* can access the resource object only if the security checks inside the Guard object are satisfied.

The relationship between the GuardedObject, the Object and the Guard can be seen in the constructor of the GuardedObject class:

```
public GuardedObject(Object object, Guard guard)
```

The only method in the Guard interface is called checkGuard(). It takes an Object as its argument and it performs security checks to determine whether or not to allow access to that object.

The Permission class in java.security implements the Guard interface. For example, suppose a system thread is asked to open a file D:\itso\redbook.lwp for read access, but the system thread does not know who the requester is or under what circumstances the request is being made. Therefore, the system thread can use the GuardedObject class to delay the access control checking, as follows:

```
FileInputStream fis = new FileInputStream("D:\\itso\\redbook.lwp");
FilePermission fperm = new FilePermission("D:\\itso\\redbook.lwp", "read");
GuardedObject guardFile = new GuardedObject(fis, fperm);
```

Now the system thread can pass the guardFile object to the consumer thread. For that thread to obtain the file input stream, it must call:

```
FileInputStream finps = (FileInputStream) guardFile.getObject();
```

The getObject() method in turn invokes the checkGuard() method on the Guard object fperm, and because fperm is a Permission, its checkGuard() method is:

```
public void checkGuard(Object object) throws SecurityException
{
    SecurityManager sm = System.getSecurityManager();
    if (sm != null)
        sm.checkPermission(this);
}
```

This ensures that a proper access control check takes place within the consumer context.

10.1.3 Providers

The java.security package also supplies a Provider class. The term *cryptographic service provider* (*provider* for short) is used to refer to a package or set of packages that supply a concrete implementation of a subset of the cryptography aspects of the Java security API. The Provider class is the interface to such a package or set of packages.

As we will see in 13.3.1, "The Provider Concept in the JCA" on page 484, for each engine[1] class in the API, a particular implementation is requested and instantiated by calling a getInstance() method on the engine class, specifying the name of the desired algorithm and, optionally, the name of the provider whose implementation is desired. If no provider is specified, getInstance() searches the registered providers for an implementation of the requested cryptographic service associated with the named algorithm. In any Java Virtual Machine (JVM), providers are installed in a given preference order specified in the java.security file. That order is the order in which they are searched when no specific provider is requested. If the implementation is found in the first provider, it is used. If it is not found, it is searched for in the second provider and so on. If it is not found in any provider, an exception is raised. The getInstance() methods that include a Provider argument enable developers to specify which provider they want an algorithm from. A program can also obtain a list of all the installed Providers using the getProviders() method in the Security class and choose one from the list.

Each provider class instance has a (currently case-sensitive) name, a version number and a string description of the provider and its services. These three pieces of information can be obtained by calling the methods getName(), getVersion() and getInfo(), respectively.

10.1.3.1 Installing and Configuring Providers

Providers can be installed by first copying the package in the system and then configuring the provider itself:

1. To install the provider classes, you can simply place the JAR file(s) containing the classes anywhere on the user class path (see 3.4.3, "Application Class Path" on page 88) or even on the boot class path (see 3.4.1, "Boot Class Path" on page 84). However, the best solution is to supply the provider library as an installed or bundled extension, by placing

---

[1] *Engine* is a term used to depict an abstract representation of a cryptographic service without a concrete implementation.

the JAR file(s) in the extensions directory, as explained in 3.4.2, "Extensions Framework" on page 86.

For example, to install JCE 1.2 on your Java 2 SDK, Standard Edition, V1.2 system, you can copy the JAR file jce1_2-do.jar in the extensions directory. This directory is indicated as the value of the java.ext.dirs system variable (see Appendix A, "Getting Internal System Properties" on page 675).

Following these directions, you will be able to *run* all the programs that use this particular provider. If you also need to *develop* and *compile* programs using this provider, then the JAR file containing the provider classes must be also copied in the extensions directory under the JRE development directory (see 8.1, "A Note on java.home and the JRE Installation Directory" on page 225).

2. Next, you need to configure the provider. For this you simply need to add it to your list of approved providers.

   • This is done statically by adding the provider to the security provider list in the java.security file (see 8.3, "The Security Properties File, java.security" on page 234).

   For example, to configure JCE 1.2 on your Java 2 SDK, Standard Edition, V1.2 system, the security provider called SunJCE must be provided together with the SUN provider in the java.security file, as shown:

   ```
   security.provider.1=sun.security.provider.Sun
   security.provider.2=com.sun.crypto.provider.SunJCE
   ```

   As we have mentioned, the order number with which the provider is added to the list is very important, in that if an implementation is supplied in multiple providers, the implementation of the provider with the higher preference (corresponding to the lower order number) is chosen by the JVM.

   In the same way, a provider is removed by simply deleting the entry corresponding to it in the java.security file.

   • Providers may also be registered dynamically. To do so, call either the addProvider() or insertProviderAt() static method in the java.security.Security class.

   For example, to add the JCE 1.2 provider SunJCE dynamically, you can use the following two lines of code:

```
Provider sunJce = new com.sun.crypto.provider.SunJCE();
int pos = Security.addProvider(sunJce);
```

The addProvider() method adds a new provider at the end of the list of the installed providers.

On the other hand, the insertProviderAt() method adds a new provider at a specified position in the array of providers. If the given provider is installed in the requested position, the provider that used to be at that position, and all the providers with a position greater than that, are shifted up one position, toward the end of the list of the installed providers.

Both the methods return the preference position in which the provider was added, or -1 if the provider was not added because it was already installed.

If the preference position of a provider has to be changed, the provider must be first removed, and then inserted in back at the new preference position.

A provider can be removed by calling the removeProvider() method of the java.security.Security class.

Notice that the dynamic provider registration is not persistent and can only be done by trusted programs or, in other words, programs that have been granted the necessary permissions:

- To add a provider, or insert it in a specified position in the list, the permission required is:

  ```
  permission java.security.SecurityPermission "insertProvider.name"
  ```

- To remove a provider, the permission required is:

  ```
  permission java.security.SecurityPermission "removeProvider.name"
  ```

Note that the SunJCE provider relies on some of the algorithm implementations supplied by the SUN provider, which is the default provider of the Java 2 SDK platform. This means that when you install the SunJCE provider, you need to make sure that the SUN provider is also installed. We will see more details on this in Chapter 13, "Cryptography in Java 2" on page 475.

10.1.4 The Security Class

As we mentioned in 10.1.3, "Providers" on page 299, the package java.security also provides a Security class to manage installed providers and security-related properties. It only contains static methods and is never instantiated. Its methods fall into two categories:

1. Methods used to get the installed providers, and also to add, delete, and insert providers

   - The method getProviders() can be used to get the list of all installed providers. They are returned in a Provider array in the order of their preference.

   - The method getProvider() returns the Provider object specified in the argument.

   - The method addProvider() is used to add a provider to the end of the list of installed providers, as shown in Step 2 on page 300. These methods returns the preference position in which the provider was added, or –1 if the provider was not added because it was already installed.

   - The method insertProviderAt() is used to add a new provider at a specified position. This method returns the actual preference position in which the Provider was added, or –1 if the provider was not added because it was already installed, as shown in Step 2 on page 300. You cannot install a provider that is already installed. If you need to change the preference order, you must first remove the provider and then insert it in the specified position.

   - To remove a provider, use the removeProvider() method (see Step 2 on page 300).

2. Methods used to get and set system-wide properties

   The Security class also has methods to manage security properties. A security property is accessible with the getProperty() method and can be set with the setProperty() method. However, only trusted programs, or programs with specific permissions, can use these methods.

The following program shows how to get the information about a provider:

```
import java.security.*;

class ProviderInformation
{
    public static void main(String[] args)
    {
        String providername;
```

Figure 128. (Part 1 of 2). ProviderInformation.java

```
    try
    {
        providername = args[0];
        Provider myprov = Security.getProvider(providername);

        if (myprov != null)
        {
            String info = myprov.getInfo();
            System.out.println("\n\n" + info + "\n\n");
        }
        else
            System.out.println("No provider with the speicified name is installed");
    }
    catch (Exception e)
    {
        System.out.println("There was an exception.  The exception was " +
            e.toString());
    }
  }
}
```

Figure 129. (Part 2 of 2). ProviderInformation.java

Compile this program with the command:

```
javac ProviderInformation.java
```

Then you can run it and pass it a provider name on the command line. By default, the only security provider that comes with the installation of Java 2 SDK, Standard Edition, V1.2 is SUN, the provider supplied by Sun Microsystems (see 8.3, "The Security Properties File, java.security" on page 234). By launching the command:

```
java ProviderInformation SUN
```

you would see the following output:

```
SUN (DSA key/parameter generation; DSA signing; SHA-1, MD5 digests;
SecureRandom; X.509 certificates; JKS keystore)
```

The information above shows the features of the SUN provider, listed in 8.3, "The Security Properties File, java.security" on page 234.

Assuming that you have installed JCE 1.2 on your Java 2 SDK, Standard Edition, V1.2 system, as indicated in Step 1 on page 299 and Step 2 on page

300, you can invoke the above program and pass the SunJCE provider name on the command line, as shown:

```
java ProviderInformation SunJCE
```

The output in this case is:

```
SunJCE Provider (implements DES, Triple DES, Blowfish, PBE, Diffie-Hellman,
HMAC-MD5, HMAC-SHA1)
```

The information above shows the features of the SunJCE provider, listed in Point 2 on page 492.

10.1.5 Access Control APIs

The java.security package provides the AccessController class used to make access control decisions based on the security policy in effect. It is also used to mark code in the execution stack as privileged (see 3.2.3.1, "Lexical Scoping of Privilege Modifications" on page 76), thus affecting subsequent access determinations. Finally, this class is used to obtain a snapshot of the current calling context, so that access control decisions from a different context can be made with respect to the saved context.

A thread's security context is based upon the classes on its execution stack. Each class is associated with a single protection domain which, in turn, specifies the permissions granted to that class (see 3.3, "Java 2 Protection Domain and Permissions Model" on page 80). So a security context can be thought of as a stack of protection domains corresponding to the classes on the stack. When an access control decision is made, this stack of protection domains is examined; only if every protection domain possesses the necessary permission does the access control check pass. If a protection domain is examined that does not possess the necessary permission, an AccessControlException is thrown.

Consider the following two lines of code:

```
FilePermission perm = new FilePermission("file", "read");
AccessController.checkPermission(perm);
```

This fragment of code checks whether the calling thread has permission to read the given file. That is, each class on this thread's execution stack must belong to a protection domain that includes the requested permission.

Assume that this thread creates a new thread. This new child thread has a new stack with a new security context. If the parent's security context was not retained, then security decisions made in the child thread would be based solely on the child's security context. This would enable less trusted code (in the parent) to access protected resources by calling more trusted code (in the child). To prevent this, Java ensures that a child thread automatically inherits its parent's security context. This inheritance continues down a thread-creation hierarchy, so that whenever a resource access is attempted, the security context of the executing thread, and those of all its ancestors, must permit the access.

Typically, each class in a thread's security context must possess the requested permission in order for an access check to pass. However, this top-to-bottom stack crawl can be short-circuited by using the AccessController.doPrivileged() method to mark a class on the stack as privileged. Once a privileged frame is encountered, no further protection domains are examined. This means that code that would otherwise lack permission to access a resource may do so if it calls (directly or indirectly) code that possesses the permission and calls doPrivileged(). Note that if the class that calls doPrivileged() does not possess the requested permission, an AccessControlException is thrown as usual. The doPrivileged() method enables trusted code to perform operations on behalf of callers that may or may not have the necessary permission themselves.

An implementation of the PrivilegedAction interface is passed as an argument to doPrivileged() to define the operation to be performed with privileges enabled. This interface is used only for operations that do not throw checked exceptions; operations that throw checked exceptions must be implemented as a PrivilegedExceptionAction instead.

The AccessControlContext class in java.security is used to make access control decisions based on the security context defined by an AccessControlContext object. An AccessControlContext object is created by calling AccessController.getContext(), which takes a snapshot of the current calling context and places it in the AccessControlContext returned. The AccessControlContext.checkPermission() method makes access control decisions based upon the encapsulated context, rather than the context of the current execution thread.

10.1.6 Key Management

The package java.security offers several interfaces and classes to provide key generation and management.

- The Key interface is the top-level interface for all cryptographic keys and defines the functionality shared by all keys. All keys have three characteristics:

1. An *algorithm*

   This is the key algorithm for that key. The key algorithm is usually an encryption or asymmetric operation algorithm (such as DSA or RSA). The name of the algorithm of a key is obtained using the getAlgorithm() method.

2. An *encoded form*

   This is an external encoded form for the key used when a standard representation of the key is needed outside the JVM, as when transmitting the key to some other party. The key is encoded according to a standard format (such as X.509 or PKCS#8), and is returned using the getEncoded() method.

3. A *format*

   This is the name of the format of the encoded key. It is returned by the getFormat() method.

- PrivateKey and PublicKey are interfaces that extend the Key. These interfaces contain no methods or constants. They merely serve to group (and provide type safety for) all public and private key interfaces. The specialized public and private key interfaces, such as the DSAPublicKey and DSAPrivateKey interfaces in the java.security.interfaces package, extend PublicKey and PrivateKey respectively.

- The java.security package also contains classes to manage keys and key pairs, such as the KeyFactory class, which is used to convert keys into key specifications (and vice versa), and the KeyFactorySpi class, which is used to define the Service Provider Interface (SPI) for the KeyFactory class. As we will see in 10.2, "The Package java.security.spec" on page 322, a representation of key material is *opaque* if it does not give you any direct access to the key material fields.

  Key factories are *bi-directional*. This means that they allow you to build an opaque key object from given key material (*specification*), or to retrieve the underlying key material of a key object in a suitable format. A KeyFactory object can be created using the static KeyFactory.getInstance() method. From a key specification, you can generate the keys using the generatePublic() and generatePrivate() methods. To get the key specification from a KeyFactory, you can use the getKeySpec() method.

- The KeyPair class is used to hold a public key and a private key. It provides getPrivate() and getPublic() methods to get the private and the public keys respectively.

- The KeyPairGenerator class is used to generate key pairs, while the KeyPairGeneratorSpi class is used to define the SPI for the KeyPairGenerator class.

  A KeyPairGenerator object can be created using the getInstance() static method for the KeyPairGenerator class. A KeyPairGenerator object must be initialized before it can generate keys. To do this, four methods are provided, all of them called initialize(), but each having a different signature. The four initialize() methods allow you to:

  - Generate a key pair in an algorithm-independent manner or in an algorithm-specific manner.

  - Provide a specific source of randomness or use the SecureRandom implementation of the highest-priority installed provider as the source of randomness.

  When you initialize a key pair in an algorithm-independent manner, you specify the key size. If you initialize in an algorithm-specific way, you supply the AlgorithmParameterSpec to the generator.

  In the algorithm-independent case, it is up to the provider to determine the algorithm-specific parameters to be associated with each of the keys. The provider may use pre-computed parameter values, or may generate new values. For example:

```
KeyPairGenerator keyGen = KeyPairGenerator.getInstance("DSA");
SecureRandom random = SecureRandom.getInstance("SHA1PRNG", "SUN");
random.setSeed(userSeed);
keyGen.initialize(1024, random);
```

  In the algorithm-specific case, the user supplies the parameters to initialize a key pair:

```
KeyPairGenerator keyGen = KeyPairGenerator.getInstance("DSA");
DSAParameterSpec dsaSpec = new DSAParameterSpec(p, q, g);
SecureRandom random = SecureRandom.getInstance("SHA1PRNG", "SUN");
random.setSeed(userSeed);
keyGen.initialize(dsaSpec, random);
```

- The KeyStore class is used to represent an in-memory collection of keys and certificates, while the KeyStoreSpi class defines the SPI for the KeyStore class. You can generate a KeyStore object using the static getInstance() method. To load a KeyStore object from an InputStream, the load() method is provided. The store() method can be used to store the keystore to an OutputStream.

The KeyStore class provides methods to get and set keys and certificates from the keystore. For instance, aliases() lists all the alias names in the keystore, deleteEntry() deletes the entry identified by a specific alias from the keystore, and getKey() gets the key associated with a given alias from the keystore.

10.1.6.1 An Example of Keystore Management

The following program loads a KeyStore object, gets a key with alias marco from it and stores it into another KeyStore object. In other words, this code performs exactly the same function as the -export and -import commands associated with the keytool utility (see 9.1, "Key and Certificate Management Tool" on page 259).

The code comments explain the operations in detail:

```
class KeyStoreManagement
{
    public static void main(String[] args)
    {
        try
        {
            // create the Keystore object
            KeyStore ks = KeyStore.getInstance("JKS", "SUN");
            String keypass = "marcop";
            char[] pwd = new char[6];
            for (int i = 0; i < pwd.length; i++)
                pwd[i] = keypass.charAt(i);

            // load the keystore from the system
            FileInputStream fisk = new
                FileInputStream("D:\\itso\\ch10\\keystore1\\marcostore");
            ks.load(fisk, pwd);

            // get the certificate from the keystore with alias marco
            // similar to keytool -export
            X509Certificate certs = (X509Certificate)ks.getCertificate("marco");

            // Storing the same certificate in other keystore.
            // create the keystore object
            KeyStore itsostore = KeyStore.getInstance("JKS", "SUN");
            FileInputStream fisk1 = new
                FileInputStream("D:\\itso\\ch10\\keystore2\\marcostore");
```

Figure 130. (Part 1 of 2). KeyStoreManagement.java

```
        // load the keystore
        itsostore.load(fisk1, pwd);

        // insert the certificate in the keystore
        // similar to keytool -import
        itsostore.setCertificateEntry("marco", certs);

        // And finally store the keystore
        FileOutputStream outputstore = new
            FileOutputStream("D:\\itso\\ch10\\keystore2\\marcostore");
        itsostore.store(outputstore, pwd);
    }
    catch (Exception e)
    {
        System.out.println("There was an exception.  The exception was " +
            e.toString());
    }
    }
  }
}
```

Figure 131. (Part 2 of 2). KeyStoreManagement.java

This program is compiled by running the following command:

`javac KeyStoreManagement.java`

Since our purpose here is to show how to use the Java security API to manage keystores, for simplicity, we have assumed the following:

1. Both keystores are called marcostore although they are located in two different directories: D:\itso\ch10\keystore1 and D:\itso\ch10\keystore2. These file names are hardcoded.

2. All passwords are set to `marcop`, and this password is hardcoded.

3. Both keystores have been created using the `keytool` utility.

4. In the keystore D:\itso\ch10\keystore1\marcostore, the key pair and the certificate wrapping the public key are associated with an alias called marco.

5. In the keystore D:\itso\ch10\keystore2\marcostore, the key pair and the certificate wrapping the public key are associated with an alias called mykey.

Therefore, before launching the KeyStoreManagement program, the keystore D:\itso\ch10\keystore2\marcokeystore contains only one keystore entry, that related to the alias mykey, as shown in the following session screen:

```
D:\itso\ch10\keystore2>keytool -list -keystore marcostore
Enter keystore password:  marcop

Keystore type: jks
Keystore provider: SUN

Your keystore contains 1 entry:

mykey, Sat Apr 24 01:16:51 EDT 1999, keyEntry,
Certificate fingerprint (MD5): 26:33:61:BA:0E:39:CC:38:30:5E:74:76:55:A9:D7:92

D:\itso\ch10\keystore2>
```

Then we launch the KeyStoreManagement program through the following command:

```
java KeyStoreManagement
```

At this point, the program loads the marcostore keystore from the directory D:\itso\ch10\keystore1, gets the certificate associated with the alias marco, inserts this certificate into the marcostore destination keystore in the directory D:\itso\ch10\keystore2 and stores the destination keystore.

```
D:\itso\ch10\keystore2>keytool -list -keystore marcostore
Enter keystore password:  marcop

Keystore type: jks
Keystore provider: SUN

Your keystore contains 2 entries:

mykey, Sat Apr 24 01:16:51 EDT 1999, keyEntry,
Certificate fingerprint (MD5): 26:33:61:BA:0E:39:CC:38:30:5E:74:76:55:A9:D7:92
marco, Sat Apr 24 01:42:05 EDT 1999, trustedCertEntry,
Certificate fingerprint (MD5): 6E:66:0C:C5:24:F5:36:1F:27:EE:10:4C:9B:E3:7D:B7

D:\itso\ch10\keystore2>
```

Note that the keystore APIs require the keystore password to be passed to the specific APIs accessing the keystore and the key password to the specific APIs accessing the private key. However, security holes may be created if the program is not coded with caution. For example, in the above example, the password has been hardcoded in the program. As explained in 5.3.1, "Decompilation Attacks" on page 126, the password could be easily recovered from class files. Therefore, in real life, you should take these parameters as input from the user. Our purpose here was to demonstrate how to use the Java security APIs to manage keystores, and for this reason we have kept things simple.

10.1.7 Message Digests and Digital Signatures

The package java.security provides APIs for message digests and digital signatures:

- The MessageDigest class provides applications with the functionality of the message digest algorithms, such as MD5 and SHA1, while the MessageDigestSpi class defines SPIs for the MessageDigest class.

- The Signature class provides applications with the functionality of the signature algorithms, such as SHA-1/DSA, MD2/RSA, MD5/RSA or SHA-1/RSA, while the SignatureSpi class defines SPIs for the Signature class.

In both the MessageDigest and the Signature class you can generate an object using a getInstance() method. You must supply the algorithm or the algorithm and the provider. Notice that:

- A MessageDigest object starts out initialized.

- A Signature object must be initialized by a private key using initSign() if it is for signing, and by a public key using initVerify() if it is for verification.

Both the classes MessageDigest and Signature provide an update() method that you can use to update MessageDigest objects and Signature objects with the data to be digested or signed/verified respectively. Lastly you can digest the data using the digest() method of the MessageDigest class and you can sign or verify the data using the sign() or verify() method in the Signature class respectively.

The package java.security also offers DigestInputStream and DigestOutputStream classes for reading and writing to I/O.

10.1.7.1 An Example of Message Digest Generation

The following example creates a message digest of the file D:\itso\textFile\itso.txt and stores it in the file D:\itso\textFile\itsodigest.txt. What the program really does is explained in the comments embedded in the code.

```
import java.security.*;
import java.io.*;

class MessageDigestGeneration
{
   public static void main(String[] args)
   {
      try
      {
         // generate a Message Digest objects
         MessageDigest classMD = MessageDigest.getInstance("SHA1");

         // get the file to be digested
         File inputTextFile = new File("D:\\itso\\textFile\\itso.txt");
         FileInputStream cfis = new FileInputStream(inputTextFile);
         BufferedInputStream cbis = new BufferedInputStream(cfis);
         byte[] cbuff = new byte[1024];

         while (cbis.available() != 0)
         {
            int len = cbis.read(cbuff);

            // update the digest with the data to be digested
            classMD.update(cbuff, 0, len);
         }

         cbis.close();
         cfis.close();

         // finally calculate the digest
         byte[] classdigest = classMD.digest();

         // write the digest information to a file
         File outputTextFile = new File("D:\\itso\\textFile\\itsodigest.txt");
         FileOutputStream cfos = new FileOutputStream(outputTextFile);
         BufferedOutputStream cbos = new BufferedOutputStream(cfos);
         cbos.write(classdigest);
         cbos.close();
         cfos.close();
      }
      catch(Exception e)
      {
         System.out.println("There was en exception.  The exception was " +
```

Figure 132. (Part 1 of 2). MessageDigestGeneration.java

```
            e.toString());
        }
    }
}
```

Figure 133. (Part 2 of 2). MessageDigestGeneration.java

This Java file is compiled to a class file by launching the following command:

`javac MessageDigestGeneration.java`

The contents of the file itso.txt are shown in Figure 108 on page 249. We run the MessageDigestGeneration program by launching the command:

`java MessageDigestGeneration`

and then we see that a new file, called itsodigest.txt, is created in the same directory D:\itso\textFile where itso.txt is. This file contains the digest information of itso.txt, and its contents can be displayed with a normal text editor:

Figure 134. Digest Information Displayed with a Text Editor

10.1.7.2 An Example of Signature Generation
The following example creates a signature of the file D:\itso\textFile\itso.txt and stores it in the file D:\itso\textFile\itsosignature.txt. Again, what this program really does is explained in the comments embedded in the code.

```
import java.security.*;
import java.io.*;

class SignatureGeneration
{
```

Figure 135. (Part 1 of 3). SignatureGeneration.java

```java
public static void main(String[] args)
{
    try
    {
        // generate the KeyPair
        KeyPairGenerator KPG = KeyPairGenerator.getInstance("DSA");
        SecureRandom r = new SecureRandom();
        KPG.initialize(1024, r);
        KeyPair KP = KPG.genKeyPair();

        // get the private key to sign the data
        PrivateKey priv = KP.getPrivate();
        System.out.println("Algorithm is " + priv.getAlgorithm() + "\n");

        // generate the signature object
        Signature dsasig = Signature.getInstance("SHA1withDSA", "SUN");

        // initialize the signature object for signing with the private key
        dsasig.initSign(priv);

        // get the file to be signed
        File inputTextFile = new File("D:\\itso\\textFile\\itso.txt");
        FileInputStream fis = new FileInputStream(inputTextFile);
        BufferedInputStream bis = new BufferedInputStream(fis);
        byte[] buff = new byte[1024];
        int len;

        while (bis.available() != 0)
        {
            len=bis.read(buff);

            // update the signature object with the data to be signed
            dsasig.update(buff, 0, len);
        }
        bis.close();
        fis.close();

        // sign the data and create the signature
        byte[] realsignature = dsasig.sign();

        // write the digital signature to a file
        File outputTextFile = new File("D:\\itso\\textFile\\itsosignature.txt");
        FileOutputStream cfos = new FileOutputStream(outputTextFile);
```

Figure 136. (Part 2 of 3). SignatureGeneration.java

```
        BufferedOutputStream cbos = new BufferedOutputStream(cfos);

        cbos.write(realsignature);
        cbos.close();
        cfos.close();
    }
    catch(Exception e)
    {
        System.out.println("There was en exception.  The exception was " +
            e.toString());
    }
  }
}
```

Figure 137. (Part 3 of 3). SignatureGeneration.java

This Java file is compiled to a class file by launching the following command:

`javac SignatureGeneration.java`

The contents of the file itso.txt are shown in Figure 108 on page 249. We run the SignatureGeneration program by launching the command:

`java SignatureGeneration`

The following message is displayed on the command line:

`Algorithm is DSA`

and then we see that a new file, called itsosignature.txt, is created in the same directory D:\itso\textFile where itso.txt is. This file contains the signature of itso.txt, and its contents can be displayed with a normal text editor:

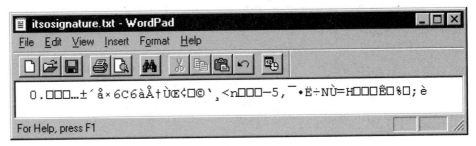

Figure 138. Signature Displayed with a Text Editor

10.1.8 Secure Random Number Generation

In the code of the SignatureGeneration class, shown in Figure 135 on page 313 through Figure 137 on page 315, the class java.security.SecureRandom is used. This class provides a cryptographically strong Pseudo-Random Number Generator (PRNG). The package java.security also offers the class SecureRandomSpi, which defines the SPI for SecureRandom.

Let's consider the following instruction:

```
SecureRandom r = new SecureRandom();
```

This obtains a SecureRandom object containing the implementation from the highest-priority installed security provider (SUN, in our case) that has a SecureRandom implementation. You will remember that the list of providers is in the java.security file (see 8.3, "The Security Properties File, java.security" on page 234).

Another way to instantiate a SecureRandom object is via the static method getInstance(), supplying the algorithm and optionally the provider implementing that algorithm:

```
SecureRandom random = SecureRandom.getInstance("SHA1PRNG", "SUN");
```

10.1.9 The SignedObject Class

SignedObject is a class for the purpose of creating authentic run-time objects whose integrity cannot be compromised without being detected. More specifically, a SignedObject contains another serializable object and its signature.

The signed object is a *deep copy* (in serialized form) of an original object. Once the copy is made, further manipulation of the original object has no side effect on the copy.

A typical usage for signing is the following:

```
Signature signingEngine = Signature.getInstance(algorithm, provider);
SignedObject so = new SignedObject(myobject, signingKey, signingEngine);
```

A typical usage for verification is the following:

```
Signature verificationEngine = Signature.getInstance(algorithm, provider);
if (so.verify(publickey, verificationEngine))
    try
    {
        Object myobj = so.getObject();
    }
    catch (ClassNotFoundException e)
    {
    };
```

Potential applications of SignedObject include:

- It can be used internally to any Java run time as an *unforgeable authorization token* – one that can be passed around without the fear that the token can be maliciously modified without being detected.

- It can be used to sign and serialize data/object for storage outside the Java run time (for example, storing critical access control data on disk).

- Nested SignedObject objects can be used to construct a logical sequence of signatures, resembling a chain of authorization and delegation.

10.1.10 Permission APIs

The permission classes represent access to the system resources. The java.security package provides the abstract class Permission, which is subclassed to represent specific accesses. Several subclasses of this class are available in the Java core API. You can define your own specific permission classes by subclassing this class or by using available subclasses like java.security.BasicPermission.

Although each permission class subclasses, directly or indirectly, the Permission class in the package java.security, specific accesses are represented by permission classes that are generally part of the package where they are most likely to be used. For example, the permission class FilePermission is part of the java.io package, and SocketPermission class belongs to the package java.net.

Permissions may have a *target* and an optional list of *actions*. For example, the target for FilePermission can be the file D:\itso\textFile\itso.txt and the actions can be read and write. We have discussed the use of permissions and their associated targets and actions when managing policy files (see 3.6, "The Policy File" on page 93 and 8.4.2, "grant Entries" on page 243).

Besides the Permission class, the built-in permission classes found in the java.security package are AllPermission, BasicPermission,

SecurityPermission and UnresolvedPermission. Associated with the Permission class, there are also the abstract class java.security.PermissionCollection and final class java.security.Permissions class. The former represents a collection of homogeneous permissions, such as a set of file permissions. The latter is for a collection of heterogeneous Permission objects.

When implementing a subclass of the Permission class, it is crucial to implement the abstract method implies(). Here *a implies b* means that giving an application permission *a* automatically grants it permission *b* too. For example, giving some code permission AllPermission implies giving all the rest of the permissions. Of course, much caution is needed when granting this permission.

In 10.7, "The Permission Classes" on page 339 we will:

- Study all the permission classes that are part of the Java core API

- See which permission classes require a target or a list of actions to be specified

- Explain how to implement custom permissions

10.1.11 Code Source

The CodeSource class extends the HTML concept of code base to encapsulate not only the URL location of the code, but also the certificates containing the public keys that should be used to verify signed code originating from that location. The code base is represented as a java.net.URL object and the list of signers as an array of java.security.cert.Certificate objects. This is the constructor for the CodeSource class:

```
CodeSource(URL url, Certificate[] certs)
```

The URL location is then extracted using the getLocation() method and the certificates with the getCertificates() method.

The CodeSource class also provides an implies() method which returns whether or not the CodeSouce specified as argument is implied by this CodeSource. For example, say that we have two CodeSource objects, codeSource1 and codeSource2, with the following features:

- codeSurce1 specifies file:/D:/- as the code base URL and has certificates corresponding to the signers marco and deepak.

- codeSource2 specifies file:/D:/itso/- as the code base URL and has certificates corresponding to the signers marco, duane and deepak.

Then codeSource2 is implied by codeSource1, but not vice versa.

The example we have just described is implemented through the CodeSourceTest class, whose code is shown in the following figure. Notice that what the code below exactly does is explained in the comments embedded in the code itself.

```java
import java.security.*;
import java.security.cert.*;
import java.net.*;
import java.io.*;

class CodeSourceTest
{
    public static void main(String[] args)
    {
        try
        {
            // create code base URLs
            URL codeBase1 = new URL("file:/D:/-");
            URL codeBase2 = new URL("file:/D:/itso/-");

            // create the Keystore object
            KeyStore ks = KeyStore.getInstance("JKS", "SUN");
            String keypass = "javakeys";
            char[] pwd = new char[8];
            for (int i = 0; i < pwd.length; i++)
                pwd[i] = keypass.charAt(i);

            // load the keystore from the system
            FileInputStream fisk = new
                FileInputStream("D:\\itso\\ch10\\keystore\\localstore");
            ks.load(fisk, pwd);

            // get the certificates from the keystore with aliases marco, deepak and duane
            // similar to keytool -export
            X509Certificate marco = (X509Certificate)ks.getCertificate("marco");
            X509Certificate deepak = (X509Certificate)ks.getCertificate("deepak");
            X509Certificate duane = (X509Certificate)ks.getCertificate("duane");

            // create certificate arrays
            X509Certificate[] signers1 = {marco, deepak};
            X509Certificate[] signers2 = {marco, deepak, duane};
```

Figure 139. (Part 1 of 2). CodeSourceTest.java

```
            // create code sources
            CodeSource codeSource1 = new CodeSource(codeBase1, signers1);
            CodeSource codeSource2 = new CodeSource(codeBase2, signers2);

            // display the answer
            if (codeSource1.implies(codeSource2))
            System.out.println("codeSource1 implies codeSource2");
            else
                System.out.println("codeSource1 does not imply codeSource2");
        }

        catch(Exception e)
        {
            System.out.println("There was an exception: " + e.toString());
        }
    }
}
```

Figure 140. (Part 2 of 2). CodeSourceTest.java

The code shown in the figure above assumes that a JKS keystore file, called localstore, will be stored in the directory D:\itso\ch10\keystore\localstore. The X.509 certificates for the aliases marco, deepak and duane must be stored in this keystore. The keystore password is assumed to be javakeys and for simplicity it is hardcoded in the example above. However, in general, it is recommended that passwords not be hardcoded, since a simple decompilation attack could expose them (see 5.3.1, "Decompilation Attacks" on page 126).

Compile the CodeSourceTest class with the command:

```
javac CodeSourceTest.java
```

Then run it by entering:

```
java CodeSourceTest
```

This message will be displayed on the Command Prompt window:

```
codeSource1 implies codeSource2
```

This confirms what we said about the implies() method for the CodeSource class.

10.1.12 Protection Domain

This ProtectionDomain class is used to represent a unit of protection within a Java application environment. The arguments for its constructors are a CodeSource object and a PermissionCollection object representing the set of permissions granted to the CodeSource object itself:

```
ProtectionDomain(CodeSource codesource, PermissionCollection permissions)
```

Notice that:

- Classes that have the same permissions but are from different code sources belong to different protection domains.

- Each class belongs to one and only one protection domain, depending on its code source and the permissions granted to the code source.

- All the classes in the same code source belong to the same protection domain.

The method getCodeSource() returns the code source of the domain and the method getPermissions() returns the permissions of the domain. Moreover, given a particular Permission object, a method implies() is provided to check and see if a specific ProtectionDomain implies the permission expressed in the Permission object.

10.1.13 Policy

The package java.security provides an abstract class called Policy for representing the system security policy for a Java application environment. The purpose of this class is to specify which permissions are available for code from various sources. The security policy is represented by a Policy subclass providing an implementation of the abstract methods in this Policy class.

There is only one Policy object in effect at any given time. It is consulted by a ProtectionDomain when it initializes its set of permissions.

The source of the policy information used to construct the Policy object depends upon the Policy implementation. The policy configuration may be stored, for example, as a flat ASCII file (like the default policy implemented by Sun), as a serialized binary file of the Policy class, or as a database.

The currently installed Policy object can be obtained by calling the getPolicy() static method, and it can be changed by a call to the setPolicy() static method. However, only code with permission to reset the Policy can call setPolicy(). The refresh() method causes the Policy object to refresh/reload its current configuration. This is implementation dependent. For example, if the Policy object stores its policy in configuration files, calling refresh() will cause it to re-read the configuration policy files.

The getPermissions() method takes a CodeSource object as argument, evaluates the global policy and returns a Permissions object specifying the set of permissions allowed for code from the specified CodeSource.

10.1.14 Secure Class Loader

The java.security package offers the SecureCLassLoader class, which extends java.lang.ClassLoader. SecureClassLoader provides additional support for defining classes with an associated code source and permissions which are retrieved by the system policy by default.

10.1.15 Algorithm Parameters

The AlgorithmParameters class is an engine class that provides an opaque representation of cryptographic parameters. An *opaque representation of cryptographic parameters* is one in which you have no direct access to the parameter fields; you can only get the name of the algorithm associated with the parameter set and some kind of encoding for the parameter set itself. This is in contrast to a *transparent representation of cryptographic parameters*, in which you can access each value individually, through one of the get methods defined in the corresponding specification class. However, you can call the AlgorithmParameters.getParameterSpec() method to convert an AlgorithmParameters object to a transparent specification.

The package java.security also provides the AlgorithmParameterGenerator and AlgorithmParameterGeneratorSpi classes:

- The AlgorithmParameterGenerator class is used to generate a set of parameters to be used with a certain algorithm. Parameter generators are constructed using the getInstance() factory methods[2].

- The AlgorithmParameterGeneratorSpi class defines the SPI for the AlgorithmParameterGenerator class.

10.2 The Package java.security.spec

This package contains classes and interfaces for key specifications and algorithm parameter specifications. Key specifications are transparent representations of the key material that constitutes a key. A *transparent representation of key material* means that you can access each key material value individually, through one of the get methods defined in the

---

[2] *Factory methods* are static methods that return instances of a given class.

corresponding specification class. For example, DSAPrivateKeySpec, which is a specification class for keys using the DSA algorithm, defines getX(), getP(), getQ() and getG() methods to access the private key x, and the DSA algorithm parameters used to calculate the key: the prime p, the sub-prime q and the base g. This is contrasted with an *opaque representation of key material* (as defined by the Key interface discussed in 10.1.6, "Key Management" on page 305), in which you have no direct access to the key material fields.

This package contains key specifications for DSA public and private keys, RSA public and private keys, PKCS#8 private keys in DER-encoded format, and X.509 public and private keys in DER-encoded format. It also provides an algorithm parameter specification class DSAParameterSpec, which specifies the set of parameters used with the DSA algorithm.

The interfaces provided are AlgorithmParameterSpec and KeySpec:

- The AlgorithmParameterSpec interface is a specification of cryptographic parameters. It groups all parameter specifications. All parameter specifications, such as the DSAParameterSpec class provided in the same package, must implement it.

- The KeySpec interface is a specification of the key material that constitutes a cryptographic key. This interface also groups all key specifications. All key specifications must implement this interface.

Neither of these interfaces contain any methods or constants.

10.3 The Package java.security.cert

This package provides classes to manage and handle digital certificates and certificate revocation lists (CRLs), and provides separate classes for managing X.509 certificates and X.509 CRLs.

- The abstract Certificate class can be used to manage different types of identity certificates, while the abstract X509Certificate class, which extends Certificate and implements the X509Extension interface, is specifically for X.509 certificates.

- The CRL class is an abstraction of CRLs, which have different formats but important common uses. For example, all CRLs share the functionality of listing revoked certificates, and can be queried on whether or not they list a given certificate. Specialized CRL types can be defined by subclassing this abstract class. An example is the X509CRL class, which extends CRL and implements the X509Extension interface. An X509CRLEntry class is provided for a revoked certificate entry in an X.509 CRL.

- The java.security.cert package also provides a CertificateFactory class to generate certificates and CRL objects from their encodings, and a CertificateFactorySpi class to define the SPI for the CertificateFactory class. CertificateFactory objects can be instantiated using the getInstance() method. Then, the generateCertificate() and generateCRL() methods can be used to create a certificate and a CRL object, respectively.

An example of Java code importing and using the java.security.cert package is provided by the class CodeSourceTest, whose code is shown in Figure 139 on page 319 and Figure 140 on page 320.

10.4 Package java.security.interfaces

This package contains only interfaces, which are used for generating DSA and RSA keys. The RSA key generation interfaces are as defined in the RSA Laboratory Technical Note PKCS#1, while those for DSA are as defined in the NIST FIPS 186 (see 2.2.2, "Java Cryptography Architecture" on page 56).

The DSAKey, DSAPrivateKey and DSAPublicKey interfaces provide the standard interfaces to DSA keys. The package also provides a DSAKeyPairGenerator interface for generating DSA key pairs and a DSAParams interface for generating a DSA-specific set of key parameters, which define a DSA key family.

The RSAPublicKey and RSAPrivateKey interfaces are for RSA keys. The package also contains a class named RSAPrivateCrtKey, which is the interface to an RSA private key, as defined in the PKCS#1 standard, using the Chinese Remainder Theorem (CRT) information values.

10.5 The Package java.security.acl

This package offers a set of interfaces to manage access control lists (ACLs).[3] An *access control list* is a data structure used to guard access to resources. These are the interfaces provided:

- The Acl interface represents an ACL.

- The AclEntry interface represents an entry in an ACL.

- The Group interface represents a group of principals. This interface extends the Principal interface in the java.security package (see 10.1.1, "Principals" on page 297).

---

[3] JavaSoft states that the java.security.acl APIs have been superseded by classes in the java.security package.

- The Owner interface is used to manage owners of ACLs or ACL configurations.

- The Permission interface is used to represent a permission, such as that used to grant a particular type of access to a resource.

10.6 Examples Using the Java 2 Security APIs

We have shown several examples of code that makes use of the Java 2 security APIs. This section provides other interesting examples.

10.6.1 Signature and Signature Verification

In this section we demonstrate how to use the Java 2 APIs to sign a document and then verify the signature. First we write a program, SignFile.java, in which we create a key pair, use this to sign a document and store the signature and the public key in two separate files:

```java
import java.io.*;
import java.security.*;

class SignFile
{
    public static void main(String arg[])
    {
        if (arg.length != 3)
            System.out.println("Usage: java signFile DATAFILE SIGNATUREFILE
                PUBLICKEYFILE");
        else
            try
            {
                // We create the keypair - Key strength can be 1024 inside the United States
                KeyPairGenerator KPG = KeyPairGenerator.getInstance("DSA", "SUN");
                SecureRandom r = new SecureRandom();
                KPG.initialize(1024, r);
                KeyPair KP = KPG.generateKeyPair();

                // We get the generated keys
                PrivateKey priv = KP.getPrivate();
                PublicKey publ = KP.getPublic();

                // We intialize the signature
                Signature dsasig = Signature.getInstance("SHA1withDSA", "SUN");
```

Figure 141. (Part 1 of 2). SignFile.java

```
            dsasig.initSign(priv);

            // We get the file to be signed
            FileInputStream fis = new FileInputStream(arg[0]);
            BufferedInputStream bis = new BufferedInputStream(fis);
            byte[] buff = new byte[1024];
            int len;

            // We call the update() method of Signature class ->
            // Updates the data to be signed
            while (bis.available() != 0)
            {
                len=bis.read(buff);
                dsasig.update(buff, 0, len);
            }

            // We close the buffered input stream and the file input stream
            bis.close();
            fis.close();

            // We get the signature
            byte[] realsignature = dsasig.sign();

            // We write the signature to a file
            FileOutputStream fos = new FileOutputStream(arg[1]);
            fos.write(realsignature);
            fos.close();

            // We write the public key to a file
            byte[] pkey = publ.getEncoded();
            FileOutputStream keyfos = new FileOutputStream(arg[2]);
            keyfos.write(pkey);
            keyfos.close();
        }
        catch (Exception e)
        {
            System.out.println("Caught Exception: " + e);
        }
    }
}
```

Figure 142. (Part 2 of 2). SignFile.java

The comments embedded in the code explain what the code does. A detailed explanation follows:

In this program, we get a key pair generator to generate keys for the DSA signature algorithm. The KeyPairGenerator class is used to generate pairs of public and private keys. Key pair generators are constructed using one of the two getInstance() factory methods provided in the KeyPairGenerator class. A key pair generator for a particular algorithm creates a public/private key pair that can be used with this algorithm. It also associates algorithm-specific parameters with each of the generated keys. We generate a KeyPairGenerator object by implementing the DSA algorithm provided by the SUN provider of Sun Microsystems:

```
KeyPairGenerator KPG = KeyPairGenerator.getInstance("DSA", "SUN");
```

Then we initialize the KeyPairGenerator with a random number. The source of randomness is an instance of the SecureRandom class. This class provides a cryptographically strong PRNG. To get an instance of this class, you can use the getInstance() method specifying the PRNG algorithm and the provider that supplies it:

```
SecureRandom r = SecureRandom.getInstance("SHA1PRNG", "SUN");
```

Another option, which is the option selected for this example, is to call the SecureRandom constructor directly:

```
SecureRandom r = new SecureRandom();
```

This obtains a SecureRandom object containing the implementation from the highest-priority installed provider (SUN, in our case) that has a SecureRandom implementation. The list of providers is available in the java.security file (see 8.3, "The Security Properties File, java.security" on page 234).

We can now create the key pair using the generateKeyPair() method. The key size is set to 1024:

```
KPG.initialize(1024, r);
KeyPair KP = KPG.generateKeyPair();
```

The private and the public keys can be retrieved using the getPrivateKey() and the getPublicKey() methods of the KeyPair class respectively:

```
PrivateKey priv = KP.getPrivate();
PublicKey publ = KP.getPublic();
```

The Signature object is generated using the getInstance() factory method of the Signature class. We need to provide the signing algorithm and the provider name. Then we associate the private key to be used for signing using the initSign() method:

```
Signature dsasig = Signature.getInstance("SHA1withDSA", "SUN");
dsasig.initSign(priv);
```

Next we get the file to be signed. The signature can be generated using the sign() method after all the data has been updated.

In fact, once generated, a Signature object has three phases. For signing data, it must be initialized using the initSign() method as done above. Then, it must be updated with the data to be signed using the update() method:

```
dsasig.update(buff, 0, len);
```

The final phase is to actually sign the data using the sign() method:

```
byte[] realsignature = dsasig.sign();
```

Signature verification consists of similar phases. The initializing is done with the public key rather than the private key. The update is done by the data to be verified rather than the data to be signed. Lastly, the sign() method is replaced by the verify() method.

The final step is to save the signature generated and the public key to two files. We need to get the public key in its encoded format before writing it to the file. This can be done using the getEncoded() method provided in the Key interface:

```
byte[] pkey = publ.getEncoded();
```

Notice that the names of the three files used in this program should be passed by the user on the command line. They are:

1. Input file to be signed
2. File where the signature will be written
3. File where the public key will be written

This program is compiled with the following command:

```
javac SignFile.java
```

It is executed by using the Java interpreter java and passing the names of the three files on the command line. For instance:

```
java SignFile itso.txt sign pub
```

Notice that it is not necessary that the sign signature file and the pub public key file exist. The program creates them automatically. These are their contents after the execution of the SignFile class:

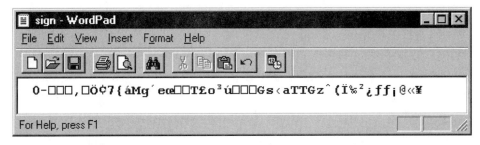

Figure 143. sign Signature File

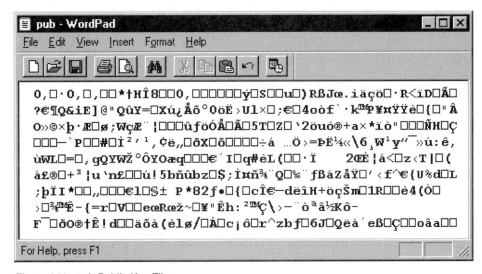

Figure 144. pub Public Key File

The contents of the file itso.txt are shown in Figure 108 on page 249.

At this point, the three files can be sent to the receiver who will execute the following program to verify the signature:

```
import java.io.*;
import java.security.*;
import java.security.spec.*;

class VerifyFile
{
    public static void main(String args[])
```

Figure 145. (Part 1 of 3). VerifyFile.java

```
{
    if (args.length != 3)
        System.out.println("Usage: java VerifyFile DATAFILE SIGNATUREFILE
            PUBLICKEYFILE");
    else
        try
        {
            FileInputStream fis = new FileInputStream(args[0]);
            FileInputStream sfis = new FileInputStream(args[1]);
            FileInputStream pfis = new FileInputStream(args[2]);

            //Get the public key of the sender
            byte[] encKey = new byte[pfis.available()];
            pfis.read(encKey);
            pfis.close();
            X509EncodedKeySpec pubKeySpec = new X509EncodedKeySpec(encKey);
            KeyFactory KeyFac = KeyFactory.getInstance("DSA", "SUN");
            PublicKey pubkey = KeyFac.generatePublic(pubKeySpec);

            // Get the signature on the file - This will be verified
            byte[] sigToVerify = new byte[sfis.available()];
            sfis.read(sigToVerify);
            sfis.close();

            // Initialize the signature
            // update() method used to update the data to be verified
            Signature dsasig = Signature.getInstance("SHA1withDSA", "SUN");
            dsasig.initVerify(pubkey);
            BufferedInputStream buf = new BufferedInputStream(fis);
            byte[] buff = new byte[1024];
            int len;
            while(buf.available() != 0)
            {
                len = buf.read(buff);
                dsasig.update(buff, 0, len);
            }
            buf.close();
            fis.close();

            // Verify the signature
            boolean verifies = dsasig.verify(sigToVerify);
            if (verifies)
                System.out.println("Verified: The signature on the file is correct.");
```

Figure 146. (Part 2 of 3). VerifyFile.java

```
        else
            System.out.println("Warning: The signature on the file has been tampered
                with.");
    }

    catch (Exception e)
    {
        System.out.println("Caught Exception: " + e);
    }
  }
}
```

Figure 147. (Part 3 of 3). VerifyFile.java

The comments embedded in the code explain what the code does. A detailed explanation follows.

First, notice that we must import the encoded public key bytes from the file containing the public key and convert them to a PublicKey. Hence, we read the key bytes, instantiate the DSA publickey using the KeyFactory class, and generate the key from it:

```
byte[] encKey = new byte[pfis.available()];
pfis.read(encKey);
pfis.close();
X509EncodedKeySpec pubKeySpec = new X509EncodedKeySpec(encKey);
KeyFactory KeyFac = KeyFactory.getInstance("DSA", "SUN");
PublicKey pubkey = KeyFac.generatePublic(pubKeySpec);
```

The X509EncodedKeySpec class represents the DER encoding of a public or private key, according to the format specified in the X.509 standard. The public key can be created from it using the KeyFactory class. This class is used to convert keys (opaque cryptographic keys of type Key) into key specifications (transparent representations of the underlying key material), and vice versa. We specify the key algorithm (DSA) and the provider (SUN) and use the generatePublic() method to generate the public key.

The rest of the program is similar to SignFile. The only difference is that the signature is initialized with this public key in place of the private key, and the sign() method is replaced by the verify() method.

The program is compiled by simply entering:

```
javac VerifyFile.java
```

To run it, the user should specify three files on the command line:

1. Input file on which a signature has been applied
2. File where the signature has been written
3. File where the public key has been written

Notice that this time all three files must exist in advance. We run this program passing to it the file itso.txt as the file on which the signature was applied (see Figure 108 on page 249), and the signature and public key files generated by SignFile. This way, we are simulating a scenario in which a sender generates a signature and then sends the original file to a receiver along with the signature and the public key.

Run the program by entering:

```
java VerifyFile itso.txt sign pub
```

The output is as expected:

1. If none of the three files has been altered after the signature was applied, the program displays the following:

   ```
   Verified: The signature on the file is correct.
   ```

2. If you change the contents of *any* of the three files, the program displays the following message:

   ```
   Warning: The signature on the file has been tampered with.
   ```

3. If you modify the signature file, so that it no longer respects the signature format, this is the message displayed:

   ```
   Caught Exception: java.security.SignatureException:
           invalid encoding for signature
   ```

This example demonstrates how you can successfully use the Java 2 APIs to send documents with proof of data integrity and authenticity.

10.6.2 Using Keystores

In the SignFile.java program, if you wish to load the keys from a keystore rather than generating them, you can use the following program:

```
import java.io.*;
import java.security.*;
import java.security.cert.*;
```

Figure 148. (Part 1 of 3). SignFileKS.java

```
class SignFileKS
{
    public static void main(String arg[])
    {
        if (arg.length != 5)
            System.out.println("Usage: java signFileKS DATAFILE SIGNFILE CERTFILE ALIAS
                KEYSTOREPWD");
        else
            try
            {
                // Access the default keystore in the user home directory
                String s1 = System.getProperty("user.home");
                String s2 = System.getProperty("file.separator");
                FileInputStream fisk = new FileInputStream(s1 + s2 + ".keystore");
                KeyStore ks = KeyStore.getInstance("JKS", "SUN");

                // Access the private key and the certificate of the signer alias
                String keypass = arg[4];
                char[] pwd = new char[keypass.length()];
                keypass.getChars(0, keypass.length(), pwd, 0);
                ks.load(fisk, pwd);
                String alias = arg[3];
                PrivateKey priv = (PrivateKey)ks.getKey(alias, pwd);
                X509Certificate certs = (X509Certificate)ks.getCertificate(alias);

                // Intialize the signature
                Signature dsasig = Signature.getInstance("SHA1withDSA", "SUN");
                dsasig.initSign(priv);

                // Get the file to be signed
                FileInputStream fis = new FileInputStream(arg[0]);
                BufferedInputStream bis=new BufferedInputStream(fis);
                byte[] buff = new byte[1024];
                int len;

                // update() method of Signature class -> Updates the data to be signed
                while (bis.available() != 0)
                {
                    len=bis.read(buff);
                    dsasig.update(buff, 0, len);
                }

                // Close the buffered input stream and the file input stream
```

Figure 149. (Part 2 of 3). SignFileKS.java

```
                    bis.close();
                    fis.close();

                    // Get the signature
                    byte[] realsignature = dsasig.sign();

                    // Write the signature to a file
                    FileOutputStream fos = new FileOutputStream(arg[1]);
                    fos.write(realsignature);
                    fos.close();

                    // Write the certificate to a file
                    byte[] cert = certs.getEncoded();
                    FileOutputStream certfos = new FileOutputStream(arg[2]);
                    certfos.write(cert);
                    certfos.close();
                }
                catch (Exception e)
                {
                    System.out.println("Caught Exception: " + e);
                }
        }
    }
}
```

Figure 150. (Part 3 of 3). SignFileKS.java

The comments embedded in the code explain what the code really does. You can see that this program is very similar to SignFile. The only difference here is that, in place of generating keys, we load an existing keystore and use keys already created and present in it. The program is configured to retrieve the keystore from the user home directory. System variables are used to grant code portability across the platforms.

You can generate a keystore by using the -genkey option of the keytool command line utility.

This program also gets the certificate associated with the alias passed by the user on the command line and saves it into a file so that it can be sent to the receiver for verification.

We generate the KeyStore object using the getInstance() factory method for the KeyStore class. The implementation we use is JKS and the provider is SUN, which is the default provider supplied by Sun Microsystems:

```
String s1 = System.getProperty("user.home");
```

```
String s2 = System.getProperty("file.separator");
FileInputStream fisk = new FileInputStream(s1 + s2 + ".keystore");
KeyStore ks = KeyStore.getInstance("JKS", "SUN");
```

When you run this sample, ensure that you have generated a keystore called
.keystore on your user home directory. This file name and location are the
default for the keystore creation performed by the -genkey command of the
keytool utility.

Next we load the keystore using the load() method, and we supply the
keystore password, which is also required as a command line argument:

```
ks.load(fisk, pwd);
```

Finally, we get the private key (with the getKey() method) and the certificate
(with the getCertificate() method) associated with the intended alias.

```
PrivateKey priv = (PrivateKey)ks.getKey(alias, pwd);
X509Certificate certs = (X509Certificate)ks.getCertificate(alias);
```

This program is compiled with the command:

```
javac SignFileKS.java
```

Notice that five pieces of information should be provided by the user on the
command line. They are:

1. Input file to be signed
2. File where the signature will be written
3. File where the certificate will be written
4. Alias associated with the entity signing the file
5. Keystore password

The program is executed by using the Java interpreter java and passing this
information on the command line. For instance:

```
java SignFileKS itso.txt signKS certKS marco javakeys
```

Notice that it is not necessary that the signature file or the file to which the
certificate is exported exist. The program creates them automatically. These
are the contents after the execution of the SignFile class:

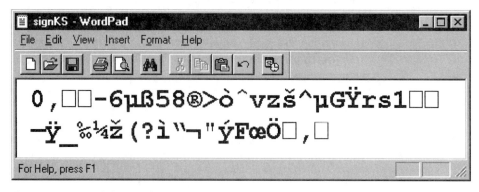

Figure 151. signKS Signature File

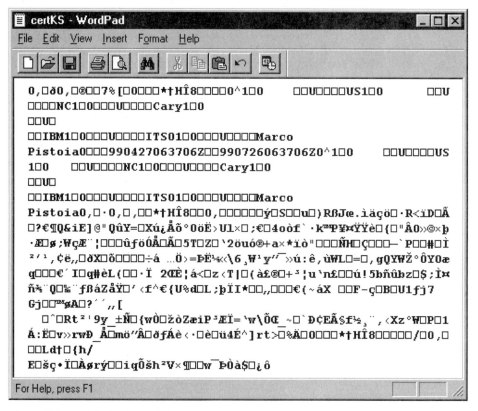

Figure 152. certKS Certificate File

The contents of the file itso.txt are shown in Figure 108 on page 249.

At this point, the three files can be sent to the receiver who will execute the following program to verify the signature:

```java
import java.io.*;
import java.security.*;
import java.security.spec.*;
import java.security.cert.*;


class VerifyFileKS
{
    public static void main(String args[])
    {
        if (args.length != 3)
            System.out.println("Usage: java VerifyFileKS DATAFILE SIGNFILE CERTFILE");
        else
            try
            {
                FileInputStream fis = new FileInputStream(args[0]);
                FileInputStream sfis = new FileInputStream(args[1]);
                InputStream cfis = new FileInputStream(args[2]);

                // Get the certificate from the file
                CertificateFactory mycf = CertificateFactory.getInstance("X.509");
                X509Certificate cert = (X509Certificate) mycf.generateCertificate(cfis);
                cfis.close();

                // Get the public key from the certificate
                PublicKey pubkey = cert.getPublicKey();

                // Get the signature on the file - This will be verified
                byte[] sigToVerify = new byte[sfis.available()];
                sfis.read(sigToVerify);
                sfis.close();

                // Initialize the signature
                // update() method used to update the data to be verified
                Signature dsasig = Signature.getInstance("SHA1withDSA","SUN");
                dsasig.initVerify(pubkey);
                BufferedInputStream buf = new BufferedInputStream(fis);
                byte[] buff = new byte[1024];
                int len;
                while (buf.available() != 0)
                {
```

Figure 153. (Part 1 of 2). VerifyFileKS.java

```
            len = buf.read(buff);
            dsasig.update(buff, 0, len);
        }
        buf.close();
        fis.close();

        // Verify the signature
        boolean verifies = dsasig.verify(sigToVerify);
        if (verifies)
            System.out.println("Tested: The signature on the file is correct.");
        else
            System.out.println("Warning: The signature on the file has been tampered
                with.");
    }
    catch (Exception e)
    {
        System.out.println("Caught Exception: " + e);
    }
  }
}
```

Figure 154. (Part 2 of 2). VerifyFileKS.java

The comments embedded in the code explain what the code does. A detailed explanation follows.

The difference between this program and VerifyFile is only in the way they generate the public key object. In the VerifyFile.java code, we retrieve the public key from a file. Here, in the VerifyFileKS.java code, we simply take it from the certificate provided; we generate an X509Certificate object using the certificate received and use its getPublicKey() method to get the public key.

```
CertificateFactory mycf = CertificateFactory.getInstance("X.509");
X509Certificate cert = (X509Certificate)mycf.generateCertificate(cfis);
cfis.close();
PublicKey pubkey = cert.getPublicKey();
```

The program above is compiled with the command:

```
javac VerifyFileKS.java
```

To run it, the user should specify on the command line the names of the following files:

1. Input file on which a signature has been applied
2. File where the signature has been written

3. File where the certificate has been exported

Notice that all three files must exist in advance. We run this program passing to it the file itso.txt as the file on which the signature was applied (see Figure 108 on page 249), and the signature and certificate files generated by SignFileKS. This way, we are simulating a scenario in which a sender generates a signature and then sends the original file to a receiver along with the signature and the public key.

We run the program by entering:

```
java VerifyFileKS itso.txt signKS certKS
```

The output is as expected:

1. If none of the three files has been altered after the signature was applied, the program displays the following:

```
Verified: The signature on the file is correct.
```

2. If you change the contents of *any* of the three files, the program displays the following message:

```
Warning: The signature on the file has been tampered with.
```

3. If you modify the signature file, so that it no longer respects the signature format, this is the message displayed:

```
Caught Exception: java.security.SignatureException:
invalid encoding for signature
```

This example demonstrates how you can successfully integrate the Java 2 APIs with local security structures, such as keystores, to send documents with proof of data integrity and authenticity.

10.7 The Permission Classes

As we discussed in 10.1.10, "Permission APIs" on page 317, the permission classes represent access to the System resources. The built-in permissions classes are:

- **java.security.Permission**

  This is an abstract class, which is the ancestor of all permissions; it defines the essential functionality required for all permissions. An important abstract method that must be implemented by each subclass is the implies() method to compare Permissions. Basically, *permission p1 implies permission p2* means that if one is granted permission *p1*, one is also granted permission *p2*. Thus, this is not an equality test, but rather more of a subset test.

The built-in permission classes that subclass Permission directly are AllPermission, FilePermission, SocketPermission, UnresolvedPermission and BasicPermission.

- **java.security.AllPermission**

This is a class that *implies* all permissions, including any new permissions that may be defined later on.

As we cautioned earlier, granting AllPermission should be done with extreme care, as it implies all other permissions. In other words, it grants code the ability to run with security disabled. This permission should be used only during testing, or in extremely rare cases where an application or applet is completely trusted and adding the necessary permissions to the policy is prohibitively cumbersome.

- **java.io.FilePermission**

This class represents access to a file or directory. A FilePermission consists of a *path name* and a set of *actions* valid for that path name.

The path name indicates the file or directory subject to the specified actions. Notice that:

- A path name that ends in `/*` (where `/` is the file separator character) indicates all the files and directories contained in that directory.

- A path name that ends with `/-` indicates (recursively) all files and subdirectories contained in that directory.

- A path name consisting of the special token `<<ALL FILES>>` matches any file or directory.

The actions to be granted are passed to the constructor in a string containing a list of one or more comma-separated keywords. The possible keywords are `read` (for read permission), `write` (for write permission), `execute` (for execute permission), and `delete` (for delete permission).

Be careful when granting FilePermission. Think about the implications of granting read and especially write access to various files and directories. The `<<ALL FILES>>` path name token with write action is especially dangerous. This grants permission to write to the entire file system, and one thing this effectively allows is replacement of the system binaries, including the JVM run-time environment.

Note that the code will always have permission to read files from its originating URL location, and all subdirectories of that location; it does not need explicit permissions to do so (see 8.6, "File Read Access to Files in the Code Base URL Directory" on page 252).

- **java.net.SocketPermission**

This class represents access to a network via sockets. A SocketPermission consists of a *host specification* and a set of *actions* specifying ways to connect to that host. The possible ways to connect to the host are `accept`, `connect`, `listen` and `resolve`.

Granting code permission to accept or make connections to remote hosts may be dangerous because malevolent code can then more easily transfer and share confidential data among parties who may not otherwise have access to the data.

- **java.security.UnresolvedPermission**

This class is used to hold permissions that were unresolved when the policy was initialized. An *unresolved* permission is one whose actual Permission class does not yet exist at the time the policy is initialized.

Whenever a policy is initialized or refreshed, Permission objects of appropriate classes are created for all permissions allowed by the policy. However, some permission classes may not yet exist during policy initialization. For example, a referenced permission class may be in a JAR file that will later be loaded. For each such class, an UnresolvedPermission is instantiated. Thus, an UnresolvedPermission is essentially a *placeholder* containing information about the permission. Later, when code calls AccessController.checkPermission() on a permission of a type that was previously unresolved, but whose class has since been loaded, previously unresolved permissions of that type are resolved. That is, for each such UnresolvedPermission, a new object of the appropriate class type is instantiated, based on the information in the UnresolvedPermission. This new object replaces the UnresolvedPermission, which is removed.

- **java.security.BasicPermission**

This is a fully implemented abstract class. It extends the Permission class and can be used as the base class for other permissions that want to follow the same naming convention as BasicPermission. The name for a BasicPermission is the name of the given permission (for example, `exitVM`, `setFactory`, `queuePrintJob`, etc.).

BasicPermission is commonly used as the base class for *named* permissions (ones that contain a name but no actions list; you either have the named permission or you don't.) Subclasses may implement actions on top of BasicPermission, if desired. The built-in permission classes that subclass Permission through BasicPermission are AWTPermission, NetPermission, PropertyPermission, ReflectPermission, RuntimePermission, SecurityPermission and SerializablePermission.

- **java.io.AWTPermission**

  This class is for Abstract Windowing Toolkit (AWT) permissions. An AWTPermission contains a target name, but no actions list; you either have the named permission or you don't.

  The target name is the name of the AWT permission. The possible AWTPermission target names are: `accessClipboard`, `accessEventQueue`, `listenToAllAWTEvents`, `showWindowWithoutWarningBanner` and `readDisplayPixels`.

- **java.net.NetPermission**

  This class is for various network permissions. A NetPermission contains a target name, but no actions list; you either have the named permission or you don't.

  The target name is the name of the network permission. The possible NetPermission target names are `requestPasswordAuthentication`, `setDefaultAuthenticator` and `specifyStreamHandler`.

- **java.util.PropertyPermission**

  This class is for property permissions. A property permission consists of a *name* and a set of *actions*.

  The name is the name of the property (`java.home`, `os.name`, etc.). The actions to be granted are passed to the constructor in a string containing a list of zero or more comma-separated keywords. The possible keywords are `read` (for read permission) and `write` (for write permission).

  Care should be taken before granting code permission to access certain system properties. For example, granting permission to access the java.home system property gives potentially malevolent code sensitive information about the system environment (the Java installation directory). Also, granting permission to access the user.name and user.home system properties gives potentially malevolent code sensitive information about the user environment (the user's account name and home directory).

- **java.lang.reflect.ReflectPermission**

  This is the permission class for reflective operations. A ReflectPermission is a named permission and has no actions. The only name currently defined is `suppressAccessChecks`, which allows suppressing the standard Java language access checks – for public, default (package) access, protected, and private members – performed by reflected objects at their point of use.

- **java.lang.RuntimePermission**

  This class is for run-time permissions. A RuntimePermission contains a target name, but no actions list; you either have the named permission or you don't. The target name is the name of the run-time permission, for example `setSecurityManager`, `createSecurityManager` (see 7.5, "Examples of Security Manager Extensions" on page 206) and `queuePrintJob` (see 1.4.1.8, "Modifying the Security Policy on the Client System" on page 20 1.4.2.6, "Modifying the Security Policy" on page 32).

- **java.security.SecurityPermission**

  This class is for security permissions. A SecurityPermission contains a target name, but no actions list; you either have the named permission or you don't. The target name is the name of a security configuration parameter.

  Currently the SecurityPermission object is used to guard access to the Policy, Security, Provider, Signer, and Identity objects.

- **java.io.SerializablePermission**

  This class is for serializable permissions. A SerializablePermission contains a target name, but no actions list; you either have the named permission or you don't.

  The target name is the name of the serializable permission. Two are the possible SerializablePermission target names: `enableSubclassImplementation` and `enableSubstitution`.

The Java 2 platform also offers two other permission classes that do not subclass java.security.Permission. These are PermissionCollection and Permissions, and they also are found in the java.security package:

- **java.security.PermissionCollection**

  The PermissionCollection class is an abstract class that can be used to hold a homogenous collection of permissions. Each instance will hold permissions of the same kind.

- **java.security.Permissions**

  The Permissions class generally holds a heterogeneous collection of permissions, organized into PermissionCollection objects. Thus, this class represents a collection of PermissionCollections.

10.7.1 How to Create New Permissions

Custom permissions can be created when the built-in permissions in the Java 2 core APIs are not sufficient to meet the needs of a specific program. In such cases, we can create a new class that extends, directly or indirectly, the java.security.Permission class. Care should be taken when implementing this permission's implies() method.

This new class must then be included in the application package. When the application's resource management code makes an access control decision, it calls the AccessController.checkPermission() static method passing a new Permission object as parameter.

The default SecurityManager class' checkPermission() method invokes AccessController.checkPermission(). Therefore, if our program uses the default SecurityManager class, we can use the SecurityManager.checkPermission() method instead of AccessController.checkPermission(). In other words, we can use:

```
sm.checkPermission(p)
```

where sm is the SecurityManager object, as shown below:

```
sm = System.getSecurityManager();
if (sm != null)
   sm.checkPermission(new MyPermission("target","action_list"));
```

Code should always invoke a permission check by calling the security manager's checkPermission() method. Note that, with this mechanism, you can create a new Permission class without needing to add a new method to the security manager. In the previous versions of Java, in order to enable checking of a new type of access, you had to add a new method to the security manager.

We now see an example of how to implement our own permission class. In the main program, we check for our custom permission and then try to read the file D:\itso\textFile\itso.txt, whose contents are shown in Figure 108 on page 249. We then execute the program with a Policy file that contains permission entries for MyPermission and FilePermission.

First, we code the Java source files MyPermission.java (that implements MyPermission, extended from the BasicPermission class) and PermissionTest.java (that contains the main() method). The following figure shows the code for the class MyPermission:

```
import java.security.*;

public class MyPermission extends BasicPermission
{
    public MyPermission(String name)
    {
        super(name);
        System.out.println("Constructor MyPermission(String name) called");
    }
    public MyPermission(String name, String actions)
    {
        super(name);
        System.out.println("Constructor MyPermission(String name, String actions)
            called");
    }
}
```

Figure 155. MyPermission.java

This Java file is compiled to the class file MyPermission.class with the following command:

```
javac MyPermission.class
```

When creating a new Permission class we extend java.security.Permission or java.security.BasicPermission. The difference is that java.security.Permission defines more complex permissions that require targets and actions, like a file name and the actions to execute on that file, for example read or write. The java.security.BasicPermission is much simpler in that we just need to define the target. This is why BasicPermission is known as the base class for *named permissions*, which are the permissions that contain a name but no actions list. Subclasses may implement actions on top of BasicPermission, if desired. Another advantage of the BasicPermission class is that, in extending Permission, it provides an implementation for the Permission.implies() abstract method.

As you can see in Figure 155, MyPermission extends BasicPermission. Note that we have called the parent class's constructor using a call to the super() method in both our permission class constructors. It is mandatory that both the constructors be defined. If we defined only one constructor, we would get an access control exception.

After calling the constructor of the super class, we insert a call to the System.out.println() method to log the call to the constructor. This way we can verify that both the constructors are being called. The println() statement must be introduced after the super() call, because the call to super(), if present, should be the first line in the constructor. The interesting thing here is that, when this program is run, it executes the println() statement in both the constructors even though we used only one of the constructors to instantiate the object MyPermission. We require the second constructor for use by the Policy object to instantiate new Permission objects. The source code of the PermissionTest class shows the instantiation of a MyPermission object:

```java
import java.io.*;
import java.security.*;

public class PermissionTest
{
    public static void main(String args[])
    {
        try
        {
            SecurityManager sm = System.getSecurityManager();
            if (sm != null)
                sm.checkPermission(new MyPermission("PermissionTest"));

            File inputFile = new File("D:\\itso\\textFile\\itso.txt");
            FileInputStream fis = new FileInputStream(inputFile);
            InputStreamReader isr = new InputStreamReader(fis);
            BufferedReader br = new BufferedReader(isr);

            String lineRead;
            while ((lineRead = br.readLine()) != null)
                System.out.println(lineRead);
        }

        catch(Exception e)
        {
            e.printStackTrace();
        }
    }
}
```

Figure 156. PermissionTest.java

This code is compiled to the class PermissionTest.class through the command:

```
javac PermissionTest.java
```

We define the main() method in the PermissionTest.java file. We also get the SecurityManager, and if the SecurityManager is not null, we check for our custom permission. The default implementation of the SecurityManager calls the AccessController.checkPermission() method. Note that the checkPermission() method accepts a single permission argument and always performs security checks within the current execution context. The checkPermission() method determines if the calling thread has permission to perform the requested operation, based on the security policy currently in effect. This method quietly returns if the access request is permitted, or throws a suitable AccessControlException otherwise.

We assume that both the class files PermissionTest.class and MyPermission.class are stored in the directory D:\itso\ch10. If they were stored in two different directories, the -classpath option of the java command could be used when running PermissionTest, in order for the application class path to include both the directories where these files are.

As you can see in Figure 156 on page 346, the PermissionTest class attempts to read the file itso.txt, stored in D:\itso\textFile.

At this point, we can run PermissionTest without invoking a security manager. The command to do this is simply:

```
java PermissionTest
```

This command produces the following output:

```
Marco Pistoia
Duane Reller
Deepak Gupta
Milind Nagnur
Ashok Ramani
```

This output confirms that, without a security manager, the program works even if no special permissions have been granted. Notice that none of the two constructors for the class MyPermission have been called. The reason for this is that MyPermission would be instantiated only if the current security manager is not null.

Now we want to run PermissionTest with the default security manager. The command to do this is:

```
java -Djava.security.manager PermissionTest
```

The default security manager requires that a FilePermission be granted to the code source of PermissionTest, so that read access to the file itso.txt is allowed. It also requires that MyPermission be granted to PermissionTest. Without these permissions, the system would throw an AccessControlException. For this reason, we add the following permissions in the user-defined policy file, which by default is ${user.home}${/}.java.policy[4]:

```
grant codeBase "file:/D:/itso/ch10/" {
  permission java.io.FilePermission "D:\\itso\\textFile\\itso.txt", "read";
  permission MyPermission "PermissionTest";
};
```

Now, upon running PermissionTest with the default security manager, the program works as expected and displays the following output:

```
Constructor MyPermission(String name) called
Constructor MyPermission(String name, String actions) called
Marco Pistoia
Duane Reller
Deepak Gupta
Milind Nagnur
Ashok Ramani
```

This also demonstrates that, when invoking the default security manager, both the constructors for the class MyPermission are called.

10.7.2 Working with Signed Permissions

In this section we repeat the example shown in 10.7.1, "How to Create New Permissions" on page 344, but we also demonstrate Java's capability to recognize a digital signature applied to a permission class file. As discussed in 8.4.2, "grant Entries" on page 243, the ability to digitally sign permission class files is useful for non-standard permissions that are remotely loaded. The digital signature of a trusted entity ensures that a class has not been replaced by an imposter class.

Let's consider the following modification to the user-defined policy file:

---

[4] To find out the value of the system properties, such as user.home and /, refer to Appendix A, "Getting Internal System Properties" on page 675. Notice that / is a shortcut for file.separator (see Figure 370 on page 676 and Figure 371 on page 677).

```
keystore ".keystore";

grant codeBase "file:/D:/itso/ch10/" {
    permission java.io.FilePermission "D:\\itso\\textFile\\itso.txt", "read";
    permission MyPermission "PermissionTest", signedBy "marco";
};
```

The rest is the same as in 10.7.1, "How to Create New Permissions" on page
344. Again, we run the PermissionTest class under the default security
manager:

```
java -Djava.security.manager PermissionTest
```

However, this time, an exception is thrown on the command line and the
program exits without completing:

```
Constructor MyPermission(String name) called
java.security.AccessControlException: access denied (MyPermission PermissionTest )
        at java.security.AccessControlContext.checkPermission(Compiled Code)
        at java.security.AccessController.checkPermission(Compiled Code)
        at java.lang.SecurityManager.checkPermission(Compiled Code)
        at PermissionTest.main(Compiled Code)
```

The reason for this error is that this time the policy now in effect requires that
the permission class MyPermission be signed by the trusted entity marco.

Consider a new scenario. The first part of the scenario is similar to the
process described in 9.3.1, "jarsigner Scenario" on page 280. You may refer
to that section for details.

On a remote machine, the code for MyPermission is written and compiled as
indicated in 10.7.1, "How to Create New Permissions" on page 344. The class
file MyPermission.class is then put into a JAR file, say MyPermission.jar:

```
jar cvf MyPermission.jar MyPermission.class
```

A signer, whose alias is marco, applies his digital signature on the JAR file
MyPermission.jar. To do this, a key pair for marco must have been defined in
a keystore residing in the remote machine, and the public key must have been
wrapped in a certificate. This can be done by using the –genkey command
associated with the keytool utility (see 9.3.1, "jarsigner Scenario" on page
280).

The signature is applied to the JAR file on the remote machine by entering
the following command:

```
jarsigner MyPermission.jar marco
```

The signer on the remote machine then sends the signed JAR file MyPermission.jar to the client machine where PermissionTest is to be run. The signer also sends his digital certificate exported to a file.

On the local machine, the receiver verifies the received certificate and imports it into a local keystore. As recommended in 9.3.1, "jarsigner Scenario" on page 280, the receiver should verify the certificate fingerprints before accepting to trust it. The receiver should also verify the digital signature on the JAR file MyPermission.jar. This can be done by using the jarsigner command with the -verify option.

At this point, the receiver installs the signed JAR file MyPermission.jar in the local file system, for example in the same directory where the PermissionTest.class file is. However, this time it is necessary to add MyPermission.jar to the application class path, in order for the Java run-time to find it. The full command to run the PermissionTest program this time is:

```
java -classpath .;MyPermission.jar -Djava.security.manager PermissionTest
```

This time, the test runs to completion because the class MyPermission is signed correctly and the PermissionTest code has the required permissions.

10.8 How to Write Privileged Code

In 10.1.5, "Access Control APIs" on page 304, we explained why in Java 2, whenever a resource access is attempted, each class in the execution stack is checked for permission for that resource access. The security policy would be ineffective if code with no permissions was able to invoke code with more permissions and access system resources that it should not access by virtue of its own protection domain. If any caller in a thread execution stack does not have permission to the requested resource, the AccessController.checkPermission() method throws an AccessControlException.

However, the Java 2 security architecture permits an exception to this rule. If some code on the thread is granted the requested permission and is marked as *privileged*, then none of the previous callers are checked for the permission. To mark a code as privileged, it is necessary to make a call to the AccessController.doPrivileged() method[5]. A piece of trusted code that is

---

[5] In beta versions of Java 2 SDK, Standard Edition, V1.2, the AccessController class did not define a doPrivileged() method for marking a code segment as privileged. Instead, it implemented two methods, beginPrivileged() and endPrivileged(), that encapsulated the privileged code. These two methods were deprecated in the final release and replaced by the doPrivileged() method.

marked as privileged is enabled to temporarily grant other codes in the thread stack permissions that otherwise would not have been granted by virtue of their protection domains.

In this section we examine how to make use of the doPrivileged() method.

10.8.1 First Case – No Return Value, No Exception Thrown

If you do not need to return a value from within the privileged block, and if the privileged block is not supposed to throw any exceptions, your call to doPrivileged() will look like the following:

```
somemethod()
{
    // some normal code here...

    AccessController.doPrivileged(new PrivilegedAction()
    {
        public Object run()
        {
            // privileged code goes here, for example:
            System.loadLibrary("awt");
            return null; // nothing to return
        }
    });

    // some normal code here...
}
```

We can also separate the privileged code, calling doPrivileged() without using an anonymous inner class, as shown next:

```
class MyPrivilegedAction implements PrivilegedAction
{
    public Object run()
    {
        // privileged code goes here, for example:
        System.loadLibrary("awt");
        return null; // nothing to return
    }
}

somemethod()
{
    // some normal code here...

    AccessController.doPrivileged(new MyPrivilegedAction());

    // some normal code here...
}
```

As you can see, in order to write privileged code you must use the
PrivilegedAction interface from the package java.security. This interface has a
single method, named run(), which returns an Object. Once implemented, the
run() method contains the code that needs the privilege.

The AccessController.doPrivileged() method takes an object of type
PrivilegedAction as an argument and invokes its run() method in privileged
mode.

In the above skeleton, when the call to doPrivileged() is made, an instance of
the PrivilegedAction implementation is passed to it. In general, the
doPrivileged() method calls the run() method from the PrivilegedAction
implementation after enabling privileges, and returns the run() method's
return value as the doPrivileged() return value. In this particular case, the
return value is ignored as there is nothing to return.

10.8.2 Second Case – Return Value, No Exception Thrown

In this case we assume that the privileged block does need to return a value,
but no exceptions are supposed to be thrown.

If a return value is required, we can write the code in the following way:

```
somemethod()
{
   // some normal code here...

   String user = (String) AccessController.doPrivileged(new PrivilegedAction()
   {
      public Object run()
      {
         // privileged code goes here, for example:
         return System.getProperty("user.name");
      }
   });

   // some normal code here...
}
```

For this case, the same considerations apply as in 10.8.1, "First Case – No
Return Value, No Exception Thrown" on page 351; the doPrivileged() method
calls the run() method from the PrivilegedAction implementation after
enabling privileges, and returns the run() method's return value as the
doPrivileged() return value. The only difference is that in this case the return
value is not null. For example, in the skeleton above, the return value is a
String object. Note that we must cast the value returned by doPrivileged() to
convert it to a String object.

10.8.3 Third Case – Return Value, Exception Thrown

The last case to consider is if the sensitive action performed in the run() method could throw a checked exception. A *checked exception* is one of those exceptions listed in the `throws` clause of a method. In this case, you must use the PrivilegedExceptionAction interface instead of the PrivilegedAction interface and you must also catch a PrivilegedActionException in the `try{}catch(){}` block, as shown in the following example:

```
somemethod() throws FileNotFoundException
{
   // some normal code here...

   try
   {
      FileInputStream fis = (FileInputStream) AccessController.doPrivileged(new PrivilegedExceptionAction
      {
         public Object run() throws FileNotFoundException
         {
            // privileged code goes here, for example:
            return new FileInputStream("someFile");
         }
      });
   }
   catch(PrivilegedActionException e)
   {
      throw (FileNotFoundException) e.getException();
   }

   // some normal code here...
}
```

Notice that the getException() method for PrivilegedActionException returns an Exception object. Therefore, you must cast this Exception object to the specific exception to be thrown, as only checked exceptions (those in the `throws` clause of the method) will be wrapped in a PrivilegedActionException. In effect, PrivilegedActionException is a wrapper for an exception thrown by a privileged action. In this example, the exception that needs to be thrown is a FileNotFoundException.

10.8.4 Accessing Local Variables

If you are using an anonymous inner class, any local variables you access must be final. For example:

```
somemethod()
{
    // some normal code here...

    final String lib = "awt";
    AccessController.doPrivileged(new PrivilegedAction()
    {
        public Object run()
        {
            // privileged code goes here, for example:
            System.loadLibrary(lib);
            return null;
        }
    });

    // some normal code here...
}
```

The variable lib used must be declared final if it is to be used inside the privileged block. For those cases in which a variable cannot be declared final (because it gets modified, for example) a final variable can be set to the non-final variable's value and then used immediately within the privileged block. For example:

```
somemethod()
{
    // some normal code here...

    String lib;

    // We can't make lib final because it gets set multiple times
    // So, we create a final String that we can use inside of the run() method
    final String fLib = lib;
    AccessController.doPrivileged(new PrivilegedAction()
    {
        public Object run()
        {
            // privileged code goes here, for example:
            System.loadLibrary(flib);
            return null;
        }
    });

    // some normal code here...
}
```

10.8.5 An Example of Privileged Blocks Usage

Let's see an example of how to use privileged blocks.

We modify the sample program Count (see Figure 106 on page 248 and Figure 107 on page 249) so that the sensitive action it performs is encapsulated within a privileged block. This new program is called CountFile, and its function is to count the characters of a file and print them to standard output. The file we give it as input is itso.txt (see Figure 108 on page 249), stored in the directory D:\itso\textFile. This file name is hardcoded in the Java file, but it would be very easy to modify the code of the program so that the user is prompted to enter the file name on the command line.

```java
import java.io.*;
import java.security.*;

class MyPrivilegedExceptionAction implements PrivilegedExceptionAction
{
    public Object run() throws FileNotFoundException
    {
        FileInputStream fis = new FileInputStream("D:\\itso\\textFile\\itso.txt");

        try
        {
            int count = 0;
            while (fis.read() != -1)
                count++;
            System.out.println("Hi! We counted " + count + " chars.");
        }
        catch (Exception e)
        {
            System.out.println("Exception " + e);
        }
        return null;
    }
}

public class CountFile
{
    public CountFile() throws FileNotFoundException
    {
        try
        {
            AccessController.doPrivileged(new MyPrivilegedExceptionAction());
        }
        catch (PrivilegedActionException e)
        {
```

Figure 157. (Part 1 of 2). CountFile.java

```
            throw (FileNotFoundException) e.getException();
        }
    }
}
```

Figure 158. (Part 2 of 2). CountFile.java

Next we create a class file in a separate directory D:\itso\newdir which just
instantiates the CountFile class. The name of this class file is
CountFileCaller.class, and its code is shown in the following figure:

```
public class CountFileCaller
{
    public static void main(String[] args)
    {
        try
        {
            System.out.println("Instantiating CountFile...");
            CountFile cf = new CountFile();
        }
        catch(Exception e)
        {
            System.out.println("" + e.toString());
            e.printStackTrace();
        }
    }
}
```

Figure 159. CountFileCaller.java

We compile CountFile.java in the directory D:\itso\ch10 and
CountFileCaller.java in the directory D:\itso\newdir. These are the commands
we issue, respectively:

```
javac CountFile.java
javac -classpath .;D:\itso\ch10 CountFileCaller.java
```

CountFileCaller invokes CountFile, but the two files are not in the same
directory. Hence it is necessary to specify the local directory and the path to
CountFile in the application class path.

Notice also that compiling CountFile.java produces two class files:
CountFile.class and MyPrivilegedExceptionAction.

CountFileCaller indirectly attempts to read the file D:\itso\textFile\itso.txt. To do so, it would need a special FilePermission. However, we are going to demonstrate to you that only the CountFile class needs the specified read permission. Since CountFile invokes the doPrivileged() method, CountFileCaller is enabled to access the file itso.txt in read mode as well.

The read permission to CountFile is granted by adding the following lines to one of the current policy files:

```
grant codeBase "file:/D:/itso/ch10/" {
  permission java.io.FilePermission "D:${/}itso${/}textFile${/}itso.txt", "read";
};
```

Then, from the directory D:\itso\newdir, we run CountFileCaller. Of course, we invoke the default security manager, through the option -Djava.security.manager. Without this option, the program would work regardless of permissions and privileges, because it is local, and it would not make sense to use privileged blocks. However, it is also necessary to specify an application class path on the command line, because the file CountFile, which is invoked by the CountFileCaller class, is located on a different directory. So the full command to launch this application is:

```
java -classpath D:\itso\ch10 -Djava.security.manager CountFileCaller
```

The results are as expected:

```
Instantiating CountFile...
Hi! We counted 70 chars.
```

This demonstrates that the CountFileCaller class has been temporarily granted the read permission it would not have had by virtue of its own protection domain.

If the doPrivileged() method in the CountFile class had not been called, when the CountFile class tried to access the itso.txt file, the security manager would have checked that CountFile as well as the calling class CountFileCaller had the permission to read the file and would have thrown an exception. This can easily be verified by replacing the call to CountFile with a call to Count (see Figure 106 on page 248 and Figure 107 on page 249) in the code of CountFileCaller. Count does not make use of the doPrivileged() method.

However, since the CountFile class calls the doPrivileged() method, the security manager only checks if CountFile has permission to read the file, and the permission checking stops at this point in the thread stack. Whether or not the CountFileCaller class is granted read permission to the file itso.txt does not matter when CountFile calls doPrivileged().

Notice if the above permission to the CountFile class is removed from the policy file, CountFile itself would not be able to read the file and consequently CountFileCaller would be denied the read access. The output in this case would be as shown:

```
Instantiating CountFile...
java.security.AccessControlException: access denied (java.io.FilePermission
D:\itso\textFile\itso.txt read)
java.security.AccessControlException: access denied (java.io.FilePermission
D:\itso\textFile\itso.txt read)
        at java.security.AccessControlContext.checkPermission(Compiled Code)
        at java.security.AccessController.checkPermission(Compiled Code)
        at java.lang.SecurityManager.checkPermission(Compiled Code)
        at java.lang.SecurityManager.checkRead(SecurityManager.java:864)
        at java.io.FileInputStream.<init>(FileInputStream.java:65)
        at MyPrivilegedExceptionAction.run(Compiled Code)
        at java.security.AccessController.doPrivileged(Native Method)
        at CountFile.<init>(CountFile.java:30)
        at CountFileCaller.main(CountFileCaller.java:8)
```

10.8.6 General Recommendations on Using the Privileged Blocks

Be very careful in your use of the privileged construct, and remember to make the privileged code segment as small as possible.

Also note that the call to doPrivileged() should be made in the code that has direct need to enable its privileges. Do not be tempted to write a utility class that itself calls doPrivileged() as that could create security holes.

Chapter 11. The Java Plug-In

The Java Plug-in enables developers and users to direct Java applets or JavaBeans components on their Web pages to use the Sun's Java Runtime Environment (JRE) in place of the browser's default Java Virtual Machine (JVM). This software can be downloaded for free from the Java Soft Web site http://www.javasoft.com, and it comes also with the installation of JRE 1.2.x and Java 2 SDK, Standard Edition, V1.2.x.

The Java Plug-in can be used with the following browsers:

- Netscape Navigator 3.0 or higher on Windows 95, Windows 98, Windows NT and Solaris

- Microsoft Internet Explorer 3.02 or higher on Windows 95, Windows 98 and Windows NT

Sun Java 2 SDK, Netscape Communicator and Microsoft Internet Explorer follow different methods for distributing signed Java code over the Web:

- If the applet is to run on Netscape's JVM implementation, then the code should be put in a Java Archive (JAR) file, signed using a VeriSign Certificate for Object Signing.

  The signature format for Netscape is RSA, and the message digest algorithm used is Secure Hash Algorithm (SHA)-1.

- If the applet is to run in a pure Sun Java 2 SDK environment, the code must be put in a JAR file as well, but it is signed using a self-signed certificate created by the `keytool` utility. The signature format in this case would be Digital Signature Algorithm (DSA) and not RSA, unless you add the providers to support RSA.

  The message digest algorithms supported on this platform by default are SHA-1 and MD5.

- If the applet is to run on Microsoft Internet Explorer, the code is put in a CAB file for Internet Explorer and is signed using a VeriSign Certificate for Authenticode. Note that this certificate is different from the one used with Netscape.

  The signature format in this case is RSA, while the message digest algorithm used on this platform is MD5.

These differences generate several problems for applet developers who want to write code that is portable across the platforms. Developers must sign and package their code in three different ways. They often have to deploy three different versions of any page hosting a trusted (or even untrusted) Java applet.

Moreover, each platform has its own way of determining policies and permissions:

- Sun Java 2 SDK uses keystore files for storing users' private keys and certificates (see 8.2, "Keystores" on page 230). Certificates of certification authorities (CAs) are located in a file called cacerts (see 8.2.1, "The Certificates KeyStore File cacerts" on page 233).
- Netscape Navigator uses a cert7.db certificate database file and a certificate server.
- Microsoft Internet Explorer uses Microsoft system and user stores.

All of these implementations are incompatible with each other. Signatures applied by one cannot be verified by another. Hence, developers must also support three different types of certificate databases and security policy configurations.

The Java Plug-in solves these problems by allowing the codes signed with the Java 2 method to be used with Netscape Communicator and Microsoft Internet Explorer. This implies that you can implement your signed code only using the Java 2 SDK methods and distribute your code to everyone.

This has some disadvantages:

- It supports the Java 2 SDK methods only. The signature algorithm must be DSA. Internet Explorer and Communicator use the RSA algorithm to produce signatures, and this is stronger than the DSA algorithm used by the Java 2 SDK.
- Netscape Communicator and Microsoft Internet Explorer certificate and key databases are not supported. A user will have to configure a Java 2 SDK certificate and key database.

However, these appear as minor problems compared to the benefits in portability and ease of implementation when using the Java Plug-in. Overall, the Java Plug-in is a very useful tool, which enables you to use the same signed applet on the three major platforms: Navigator, Internet Explorer and Java 2 SDK.

11.1 Main Features of Java Plug-In

The Java Plug-in delivers several key capabilities to people using Internet Explorer and Navigator:

1. It provides the full Java 2 SDK, Standard Edition, V1.2 support to the applets running on Netscape and Internet Explorer. It allows developers to use the features of the Java 2 SDK, such as JavaBeans enhancements, security, graphical support, etc. For example, the Java Plug-in allows Java 2 SDK signed classes to be loaded into the browser and be subject to the Java 2 security model. This is important, because historically, after JavaSoft's publication of a new version of Java, browser vendors have taken several months to incorporate the changes in their browsers' JVM platforms. The result was that many applet developers had to continue to code programs in an old-style fashion that was compatible with the browsers' old JVM platforms.

2. It provides an architecture that makes it easy for new Java features and functionality to be incorporated. With the Java Plug-in, as soon as JavaSoft produces a new version of the Java 2 SDK with new features, the new capabilities become immediately available on the browser systems.

3. It provides free public download and easy installation. When browsers encounter a Web page that specifies that the Java Plug-in is required, if the Plug-in is not yet installed the browser will immediately prompt the user to download and install it from the Web site http://java.sun.com/products/jdk/1.2/jre/download-windows.html, as shown in the next figure:

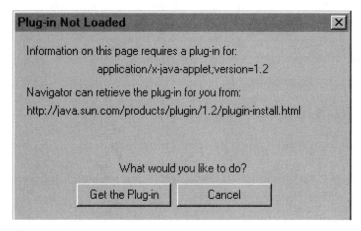

Figure 160. Plug-in Not Loaded Message

On clicking the **Get the Plug-in** button, a download page is opened in a new window. Once the Java Plug-in is downloaded and installed, any time a Web site requires the Java Plug-in, this window will not appear and the Java Plug-in will start immediately.

Similarly, on opening a Web page requiring the Java Plug-in with Internet Explorer, the user will be asked whether to download an ActiveX control that is digitally signed by Sun Microsystems, Inc. and verifiable by the associated VeriSign Class 3 certificate:

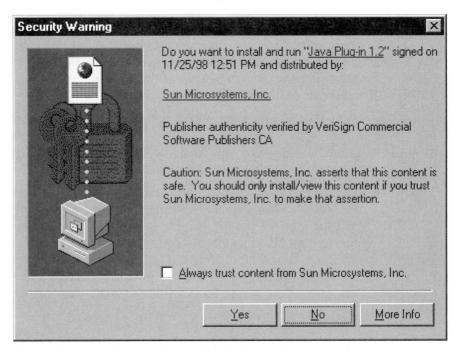

Figure 161. Internet Explorer Security Warning for Java Plug-in

You can view the details on Sun Microsystems by clicking on the button **More Info**. If you click on **Yes**, this means that you accept to download the code and install it. The following window appears:

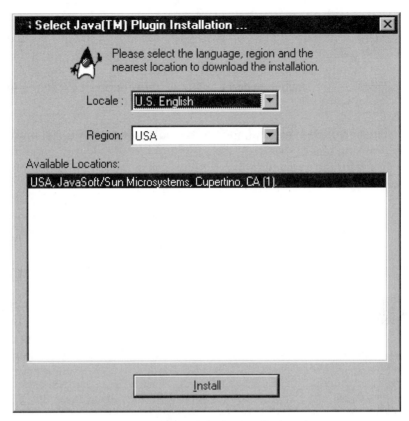

Figure 162. Java Plug-in Install Screen by Internet Explorer

If the user clicks on **Install**, Internet Explorer will quickly download a small ActiveX control from Sun's Web site. This will handle downloading the main Java Plug-in ActiveX control and Sun's JRE. It will then download the files automatically and install them. Once the Java Plug-in is downloaded, any time a Web site requires the Java Plug-in, none of these windows will appear and the Java Plug-in will start immediately.

4. To use the Java Plug-in, Web pages need to be modified a little, as explained in 11.3, "Java Plug-In HTML Changes" on page 364. The Java Plug-in HTML Converter is a new tool available for this purpose; it is quite easy to use and helps you do the changes automatically, as we will see in 11.3.5, "Java Plug-in Software HTML Converter" on page 369.

11.2 What Does the Java Plug-In Do?

The Java Plug-in enables Web page authors to specify Sun's JRE in place of the default browser JRE for a given Web page. However, it does not replace or modify the browser's underlying JVM. This allows the developers to execute the Java 2 based applets with full support for all the features of Java 2.

In Netscape Navigator, the Java Plug-in runs its JRE inside the browser making use of Netscape's plug-in architecture. A Web page must use the <EMBED> tag in place of the <APPLET> tag to indicate that the applet should run with the Java Plug-in.

In Microsoft Internet Explorer, the Java Plug-in runs inside the browser through the browser's extension mechanisms using Microsoft's COM/ActiveX technology. A Web page must use the <OBJECT> tag in place of the <APPLET> tag to indicate that the applet should run with the Java Plug-in.

11.3 Java Plug-In HTML Changes

To make the browsers run the Java Plug-in, some Web page changes are required. Normally we use an HTML <APPLET> tag in the following form:

```
<APPLET Code="XYZApp.class" Codebase="html/" Align="baseline"
   Width="200" Height="200">
   <PARAM Name="redbook" Value="JavaSecurity">
</APPLET>
```

An <APPLET> tag specifies the information about the applet, while the <PARAM> tags between the <APPLET> and </APPLET> tag pair store the applet information.

The <APPLET> tag is inadequate to use Java Plug-in, because it would force the browser itself to render the applet, and the browser would not use the Java Plug-in to do this. For this reason, new tags are necessary. We must use the <OBJECT> or the <EMBED> tag – the former being for Internet Explorer and the latter for Netscape Navigator – in place of the <APPLET> tag.

11.3.1 Changes Supported by Navigator

As stated, when the Java Plug-in must be used on Netscape Navigator, the <APPLET> tag must replaced by the <EMBED> tag in order for the browser to recognize that the Java Plug-in is required.

For example, let's say that the HTML code using the <APPLET> tag is:

```
<APPLET Code="IBM.class" Codebase="html/" Width="200" Height="200">
   <PARAM Name="redbook" Value="JavaSecurity">
   No Java 2 support for APPLET
</APPLET>
```

Figure 163. HTML Code Using the <APPLET> Tag

Then the corresponding code using the <EMBED> tag will be:

```
<EMBED Type="application/x-java-applet;version=1.2" Width="200" Height="200"
   Code="IBM.class" Codebase="html/" redbook="JavaSecurity"
   Pluginspage="http://java.sun.com/products/plugin/1.2/plugin-install.html">
   <NOEMBED>
      No Java 2 support for APPLET
   </NOEMBED>
</EMBED>
```

Figure 164. HTML Code Using the <EMBED> Tag

As you can see, the parameters remain essentially the same. However they all are now defined inside the <EMBED> tag itself.

Note that there are new attributes inside the <EMBED> tag:

- The Type attribute defines the type of application (applet or bean).
- The Pluginspage attribute points to the Java Plug-in download page on the JavaSoft Web site. The value of the Pluginspage attribute is used when the Java Plug-in is not installed on a particular system.

The <PARAM> tags that were inside the <APPLET> tag are also put inside the new <EMBED> tag.

11.3.2 Changes Supported by Internet Explorer

The <APPLET> tag is replaced by the <OBJECT> tag in Microsoft Internet Explorer, in order for the browser to recognize that the Java Plug-in is required.

Let's consider again an <APPLET> tag shown in Figure 163. Then the corresponding <OBJECT> tag will be:

```
<OBJECT Classid="clsid:8AD9C840-044E-11D1-B3E9-00805F499D93" Width="200" Height="200"
Codebase="http://java.sun.com/products/plugin/1.2/jinstall-12-win32.cab#Version=1,2,0,0">
    <PARAM Name="Code" Value="IBM.class">
    <PARAM Name="Codebase" Value="html/">
    <PARAM Name="Type" Value="application/x-java-applet;version=1.2">
    <PARAM Name="redbook" Value="JavSecurity">
    No Java 2 support for APPLET
</OBJECT>
```

Figure 165. HTML Code Using the <OBJECT> Tag

The Classid attribute indicates the class identifier of the Java Plug-in and
should be the same in every HTML page. The Codebase attribute inside the
<OBJECT> tag points to the Java Plug-in download page. The Codebase
parameter of the <APPLET> tag is now provided inside the <PARAM> tags. In
addition, all the parameters that were initially inside the <APPLET> tag are now
defined in the <PARAM> tags.

Note that if the original <APPLET> tag already has attributes like Type,
Codebase, Code, Object or Archive in the <PARAM> tags, mapping it to the
<OBJECT> tag will cause problems, because duplicate parameter names will
occur. To avoid this, Java Plug-in also supports another set of param names,
as follows:

Table 11. Parameter Names When Using the <OBJECT> Tag

Original Parameter Names	New Parameter Names
Type	java_type
Codebase	java_codebase
Code	java_code
Object	java_object
Archive	java_archive

11.3.3 Changes Supported by Both Navigator and Internet Explorer

Most pages on the Web are meant to be launched by both browsers Netscape
Navigator and Microsoft Internet Explorer. In that case, you want your HTML
code to be compatible with both platforms. This is possible, as shown by the
following HTML code:

```
<OBJECT Classid="clsid:8AD9C840-044E-11D1-B3E9-00805F499D93" Width="200" Height="200"
Codebase="http://java.sun.com/products/plugin/1.2/jinstall-12-win32.cab#Version=1,2,0,0">
    <PARAM Name="Code" Value="IBM.class">
    <PARAM Name="Codebase" Value="html/">
    <PARAM Name="Type" Value="application/x-java-applet;version=1.2">
    <PARAM Name="redbook" Value="JavaSecurity">
    <COMMENT>
        <EMBED Type="application/x-java-applet;version=1.2" width="200" height="200"
            code="IBM.class"
        Codebase="html/" redbook="JavaSecurity"
        Pluginspage="http://java.sun.com/products/plugin/1.2/plugin-install.html">
            <NOEMBED>
    </COMMENT>
            No Java 2 support for APPLET
        </NOEMBED>
    </EMBED>
</OBJECT>
```

Figure 166. HTML Code Supported by Both Navigator and Internet Explorer

Notice that the <COMMENT> tag is a special HTML tag understood only by
Internet Explorer. Whatever is encapsulated between the <COMMENT> and
</COMMENT> tag pair is considered as a comment by Internet Explorer and
therefore ignored. On the other hand, Navigator does not understand the
<OBJECT> and <COMMENT> tags. So effectively both browsers are able to read the
information they need.

11.3.4 All the Web Browsers

If a different browser loads this page, the Java Plug-in should not be
activated, because it would not be supported. Therefore, we need to put
some checks in the HTML code, as shown next:

```
<!-- The following code to be specified at the beginning of the <BODY> tag. -->
<SCRIPT LANGUAGE="JavaScript"><!--
    var _info = navigator.userAgent; var _ns = false;
    var _ie = (_info.indexOf("MSIE") > 0 && _info.indexOf("Win") > 0
        && _info.indexOf("Windows 3.1") < 0);
//--></SCRIPT>
<COMMENT><SCRIPT LANGUAGE="JavaScript1.1"><!--
    var _ns = (navigator.appName.indexOf("Netscape") >= 0
        && ((_info.indexOf("Win") > 0 && _info.indexOf("Win16") < 0
        && java.lang.System.getProperty("os.version").indexOf("3.5") < 0)
        || _info.indexOf("Sun") > 0));
```

Figure 167. (Part 1 of 2). HTML Code Supported by All the Web Browsers

```
//--></SCRIPT></COMMENT>

<!-- The following code should be repeated for each APPLET tag -->
<SCRIPT LANGUAGE="JavaScript"><!--
    if (_ie == true) document.writeln('
<OBJECT
   Classid="clsid:8AD9C840-044E-11D1-B3E9-00805F499D93" Width="200" Height="200"

Codebase="http://java.sun.com/products/plugin/1.2/jinstall-12-win32.cab#Version=1,2,0,0">
   <NOEMBED><XMP>');
    else if (_ns == true) document.writeln('
<EMBED Type="application/x-java-applet;version=1.2" Width="200" Height="200"
Code="IBM.class" Codebase="html/" redbook="JavaSecurity"
Pluginspage="http://java.sun.com/products/plugin/1.2/plugin-install.html">
<NOEMBED><XMP>');
//--></SCRIPT>
<APPLET code="IBM.class" codebase="html/" Width="200" Height="200">
</XMP>
    <PARAM Name="java_code" Value="IBM.class">
    <PARAM Name="java_codebase" Value="html/">
    <PARAM Name="java_type" Value="application/x-java-applet;version=1.2">
    <PARAM Name="redbook" Value="JavaSecurity">
    No Java 2 support for APPLET
</APPLET></NOEMBED></EMBED>
</OBJECT>

<!--
    <APPLET Code="IBM.class" Codebase="html/" Width="200" Height="200">
    <PARAM Name="redbook" Value="JavaSecurity">
    No Java 2 support for APPLET
    </APPLET>
-->
```

Figure 168. (Part 2 of 2). HTML Code Supported by All the Web Browsers

The initial section is provided at the beginning of the <BODY> HTML tag. It is used to determine the browser type and the client platform. This operation is performed by using JavaScript. Based on the browser and the platform, only one among the <EMBED>, <OBJECT> and <APPLET> tags is considered:

- Netscape Navigator will consider only the <EMBED> tag.

- Microsoft Internet Explorer will consider only the <OBJECT> tag.

- Any other browser will consider only the <APPLET> tag.

11.3.5 Java Plug-in Software HTML Converter

The Java Plug-in Software HTML Converter is a free tool that can be downloaded from the JavaSoft Web site http://www.javasoft.com. It is used to convert traditional HTML files to HTML files that incorporate the use of the Java Plug-in. This tool is first downloaded as a ZIP file, which must then be extracted. You run it with the command:

```
java HTMLConverter
```

This opens a GUI-based tool which can be used to convert HTML files. This is what the original screen looks like:

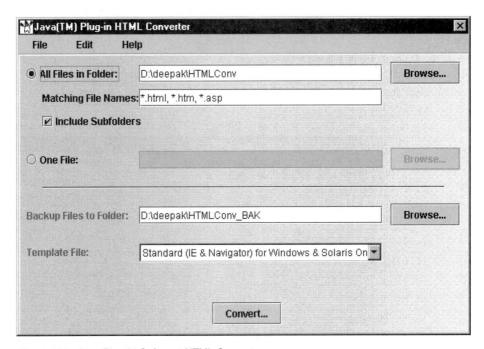

Figure 169. Java Plug-in Software HTML Converter

This tool gives you the option of changing a particular file or an entire directory (including its subdirectories). It also has four templates to change for Netscape Navigator, Microsoft Internet Explorer, both of them or for all browsers, as explained in the previous sections. You also have an option to use your own templates.

The converter backs up your original file in the directory you specify so that you can revert back to your original copy. It also keeps a log of the operations in a log file.

11.4 Java Plug-In Control Panel

The Java Plug-in Control Panel enables you to change the default settings used by the Java Plug-in at startup. All applets running inside an instance of the Java Plug-in will use these settings. On a Windows system, the icon for the Java Plug-in Control Panel is by default created in the Start menu when it is installed.

Once you launch the Java Plug-in Control Panel, you will see three tabs in the Control Panel labeled Basic, Advanced and Proxies. You can use them to enter different panels, and configure the Java Plug-in. Once you have made all the changes, you can save your settings by clicking on the **Apply** button. The **Reset** button restores the original settings.

11.4.1 The Basic Panel

The Basic panel is brought up by default and it is shown in the following figure:

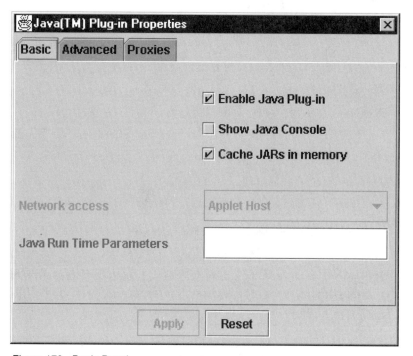

Figure 170. Basic Panel

The Basic panel has the following settings:

- **Enable Java Plug-in**

  This enables the Java Plug-in to run applets and JavaBeans components. If this box is unchecked, the Java Plug-in will not be activated during any browser session and it will not be allowed to run any applets or beans. In that case, when a page that requires the Java Plug-in is loaded, a message appears saying:

  ```
  Java is not enabled
  ```

- **Show Java Console**

  When this option is selected, the Java Plug-in Java Console is automatically brought up each time the Java Plug-in is activated. The Java Console is a very useful tool, especially for debugging purposes, because it displays the information sent to System.out and System.err.

  Notice that the Java Plug-in Java Console is different from the browser Java console, because the browser Java Console is associated with the browser JVM, while the Java Plug-in Java Console is associated with the JVM used by the Java Plug-in.

- **Cache JARs in memory**

  This option is used to cache and reuse applet JAR files that have previously been loaded, in order to ensure an efficient use of memory. You should leave this option unchecked if you are debugging an applet or are always interested in loading the latest applet classes.

- **Network Access**

  This sets the network access you want to grant your running applets. For example, you can restrict network access so the applet cannot make any network calls, you can restrict the access only to the host that served the applet itself or you can grant an applet unrestricted access to the network. This last option would be a security exposure.

- **Java Run Time Parameters**

  You can override the Java Plug-in default startup parameters by specifying custom options. The syntax is the same as the parameters to the `java` command line invocation, with some restrictions. For example, the `-Xbootclasspath` option is not supported (as it is a non-standard option of the `java` command), but you can use the `-cp` option to alter the class path (see 3.4, "New Class Search Path" on page 83).

11.4.2 The Advanced Panel

The Advanced panel has the following appearance:

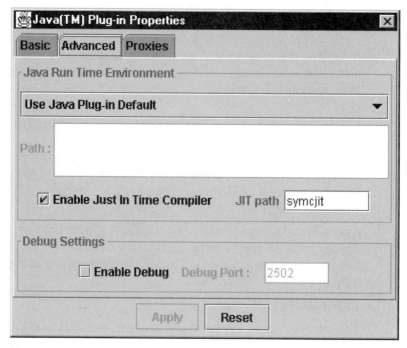

Figure 171. Advanced Panel

It offers several configuration options:

- **Java Plug-in Default**

  This is a list box which lists all the JREs installed; you can force the Java Plug-in to run with any of them by choosing it here. By default, the Java Plug-in has JRE 1.2.*x* selected. This is the first option in the list box. There is also an option **Other...**, in which you can specify JVMs not detected by the Java Plug-in. In this case, the Path text box is enabled and you must specify the Path to the JRE you want the Plug-in to use.

- **Enable Just In Time Compiler**

  This option is available for the Win32 platform only. It enables the just-in-time (JIT) compiler. If you select this option, a path must also be specified; as you can see in Figure 171 on page 372, the default JIT path is symcjit. The JIT compiler must be located in the bin directory for the JRE selected in the Java Plug-in Default list box.

- **Enable Debug**

  This option is available on Internet Explorer only. It enables debugging if Internet Explorer is being used. The debug port must be specified in the

Debug Port text box; the default is port 2502. When you run the debugger inside Internet Explorer, a window will pop up with the debugger password.

11.4.3 Proxies Panel

The Proxies panel has the following appearance:

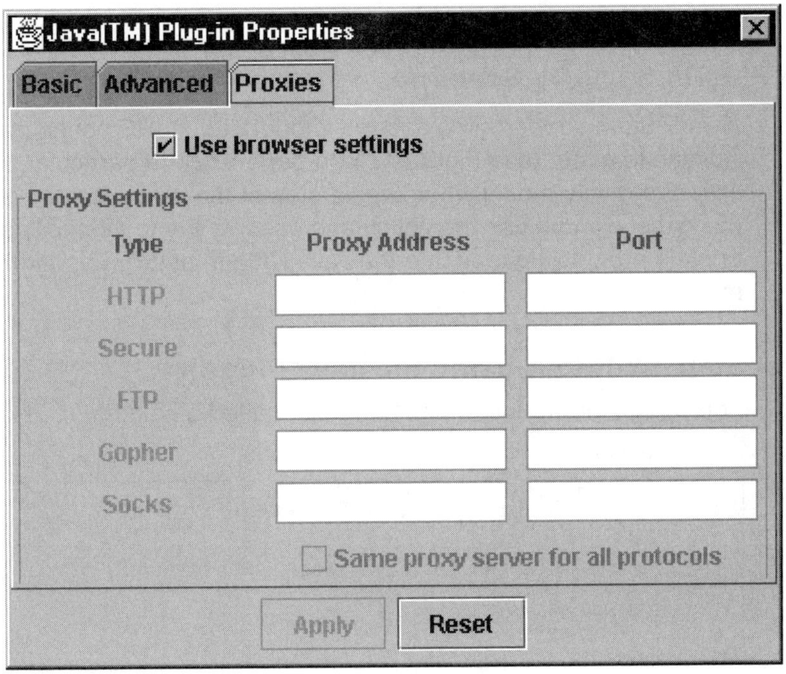

Figure 172. Proxies Panel

This panel has the following settings:

- **Use browser settings**

  If this box is checked, the Java Plug-in uses the browser proxy settings. You can override the default settings by unchecking this check box, then completing the proxy information beneath the check box. You can enter the proxy address and port for each of the supported protocols[1].

  Certain situations, such as mobile users connecting to the company through a modem, require a direct connection to the intranet environment. Proxies should not be used in these cases. Both Internet Explorer and Navigator support direct connection in the browser. Java Plug-in

---

[1] Currently, the Java Plug-in only supports HTTP, FTP, Gopher and SOCKS V4 protocols through the proxy server and does not support SSL.

recognizes and supports direct connection when you choose it in the browser.

- **Same proxy server for all protocols**

  If you want to override the proxy settings of the browser and use the same address and port for all the protocols, then enter the address and port once and check this box.

11.5 Java Plug-In Security Scenario

Java Plug-in supports the security model of the JRE configured in the Advanced panel (see Figure 171 on page 372). In particular, it supports the Java 2 security model when the version of the JRE selected is 1.2 or later. In this case, we can use the policy and security file to monitor permissions. The applets are downloaded into the Java Plug-in and run under the security manager.

11.5.1 First Step – Without Using the Java Plug-in

Let's consider the following HTML file, called plugin.html:

```
<HTML>
    <HEAD>
        <TITLE>Testing for Java Plug-in</TITLE>
    </HEAD>

    <BODY>
        OK, Hereís the applet that should run.
    <BR>
    <APPLET Code="App.class" WIDTH=150 HEIGHT=25></APPLET>
    <BR>
        And was it successful?
    <BR>
    </BODY>
</HTML>
```

Figure 173. plugin.html – Basic Version

Before running this HTML file, we need to provide the App.class file, which is required by the <APPLET> tag. We write the App.java code, shown in Figure 174 on page 375. The class file it defines attempts to access a file in read mode. The file in question is itso.txt, stored in the directory D:\itso\textFile (see Figure 108 on page 249). If this access is successful, it prints the following message on the browser screen:

```
File was accessed
```

Otherwise, an error message is printed on the browser's Java Console. The code for the App applet is shown in the following figure:

```
import java.io.*;
import java.applet.*;
import java.awt.Graphics;

public class App extends Applet
{
   public void paint(Graphics g)
   {
      try
      {
         FileInputStream fis = new FileInputStream("D:\\itso\\textFile\\itso.txt");
         g.drawString("File was accessed", 10,10);
      }
      catch (Exception e)
      {
         System.out.println("Exception caught: " + e.toString());
      }
   }
}
```

Figure 174. App.java

This code is compiled by launching the command:

```
javac App.java
```

We store the HTML file and the associated applet class file in the home directory of a test Web server machine, and then invoke the HTML file from a client machine running Netscape Navigator. The output is as expected: the applet is not allowed to access the file and the successful message is not displayed:

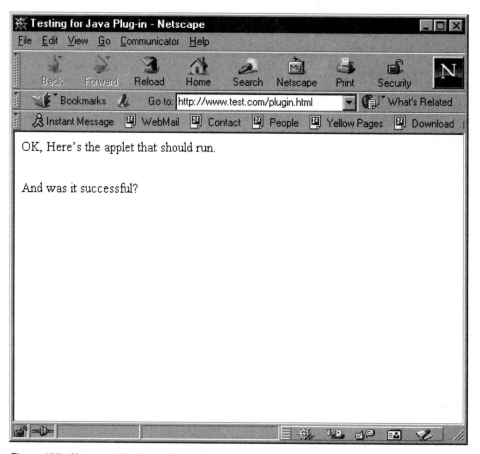

Figure 175. Netscape Navigator Output Screen

It is possible to understand the reason for this failure by opening the Java Console, which registers a netscape.security.AppletSecurityException:

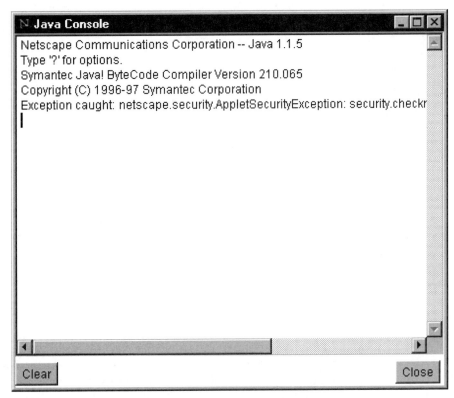

Figure 176. AppletSecurityException on the Java Console

What happens here is that we have tried to run this applet on the JVM 1.1.5 provided by Netscape Communicator V4.5. In the Java Development Kit (JDK) 1.1 security model, a remote applet is not allowed to read files in the local file system, hence an AppletSecurityException is thrown.

11.5.2 Second Step – Using the Java Plug-in

Next, we modify the HTML file plugin.html to enable the Java Plug-in, as shown:

```
<HTML>
    <HEAD>
        <TITLE>Testing for Java Plug-in</TITLE>
    </HEAD>
```

Figure 177. (Part 1 of 2). plugin.html – Java Plug-in Version

```
<BODY>
    OK, Here's the applet that should run.
    <BR>
    <EMBED Type="application/x-java-applet;version=1.2" java_code = "App.class"
    Width = 150 Height = 25
    pluginspage="http://java.sun.com/products/plugin/1.2/plugin-install.html">
    <NOEMBED>
    </NOEMBED>
    </EMBED>

    <!--
      <APPLET  CODE = "App.class" WIDTH = 150 HEIGHT = 25 >
      </APPLET>
    -->
    <BR>
        And was it successful? <br>
    </BODY>
</HTML>
```

Figure 178. (Part 2 of 2). plugin.html – Java Plug-in Version

If we load this Web page in the Netscape Navigator browser, the results we
get are still the same: the applet is not allowed to access the file and the Java
Console registers an exception. However, there are some differences. This
time the applet is running in the JRE 1.2 invoked by the Java Plug-in, and the
reason why the applet is not allowed to access the file is because we have not
granted it the necessary permission. This is demonstrated also by the
exception registered on the Java Console:

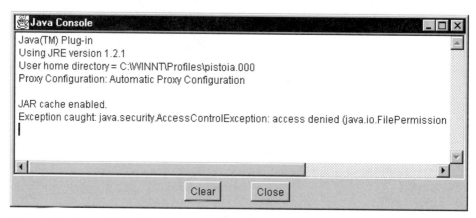

Figure 179. AccessControlException on the Java Plug-in Console

Since we selected the **Show Java Console** check box in the Basic panel of the Java Plug-in Control Panel (see 11.4.1, "The Basic Panel" on page 370), the Java Console brought up this time is the one associated with the JRE used by the Java Plug-in. In this case, the Plug-in is running with JRE 1.2.1, and the Netscape Navigator Java Console is not activated. The Java Plug-in Java Console displays a security exception of a different nature: it is a java.security.AccessControlException.

The Netscape Communicator and Microsoft Internet Explorer JVM implementations offer a dynamic permission prompting, as we will see in 12.4, "Signed Code Scenario in Netscape Communicator" on page 409 and 12.5, "Signed Code Scenario in Microsoft Internet Explorer" on page 437. On the contrary, as we have just seen, the Java Plug-in does not offer any dynamic permission prompting. Therefore, on this platform, if the policy is not set up correctly, the applet will fail.

Notice that in the Java 2 security model an applet is not necessarily prevented from accessing a file in the local file system; its permissions depend upon the policy in effect at a given time. For this reason, we add the following entry to the user-defined policy file:

```
grant codeBase "http://www.test.com/" {
  permission java.io.FilePermission "D:${/}itso${/}textFile${/}itso.txt", "read";
};
```

Then, we open the HTML file again, and we can see that the applet is allowed to access the file indicated:

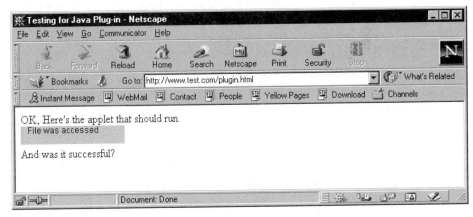

Figure 180. Accessing the Local File with the Right Permission

This confirms that the Java Plug-in supports the Java 2 security model, allowing you to incorporate the advanced Java 2 security in applets and JavaBeans components that will be distributed across the net.

11.5.2.1 Java Plug-in and Code Signed with jarsigner

A similar test can be run successfully using JAR files. In this case, you must specify the JAR file name in the <EMBED> and <APPLET> tags of the HTML file, using the java_archive attribute for the <EMBED> tag and the Archive attribute for the <APPLET> tag. For example, after running the jar utility against the App.class file, we produce a JAR file called App.jar. Then it is necessary to add the following:

- java_archive="App.jar" in the <EMBED> tag

- Archive="App.jar" in the <APPLET> tag

Next, we sign the App.jar file with the private key of a signer marco, using the jarsigner utility. The certificate for this entity is stored in the keystore .keystore, located in the user's home directory. Finally, the policy file must contain the following:

```
keystore ".keystore";
grant signedBy "marco", codeBase "http://www.test.com/" {
  permission java.io.FilePermission "D:${/}itso${/}textFile${/}itso.txt", "read";
};
```

After loading the HTML file in the Netscape Navigator browser, we can see that the applet is allowed to access the file.

11.5.2.2 Java Plug-In and Code Signed with javakey

The Java Plug-in is compatible with the Java 2 security model as long as the version of the JRE selected in the Advanced configuration panel (see Figure 171 on page 372) is 1.2 or later. As we mentioned in 8.3, "The Security Properties File, java.security" on page 234, the Java 2 platform is backward compatible with signatures applied with the old JDK 1.1 javakey tool. For this reason, the Java Plug-in must be compatible as well. This is what we demonstrate now.

We want to sign the applet JAR file using the javakey tool shipped with JDK 1.1.7B and then run it in a Java 2 system using the Java Plug-in. We install JDK 1.1.7B on a separate machine and proceed with the following steps:

1. We create a trusted signer called duke, as shown in the following session screen:

```
D:\deepak\deepak\plugin>javakey -cs duke true
Created identity [Signer]duke[identitydb.obj][trusted]

D:\deepak\deepak\plugin>
```

2. We generate a DSA key pair of strength 1024 for duke, as shown in the following session screen:

```
D:\deepak\deepak\plugin>javakey -gk duke DSA 1024
Generated DSA keys for duke (strength: 1024).

D:\deepak\deepak\plugin>
```

3. Next we create a certificate directive file for duke, called dukeCertDirFile, whose contents are shown in the following screen:

```
issuer.name=duke
subject.name=duke
subject.real.name=Duke Duke
subject.org.unit=ITSO
subject.org=IBM
subject.country=US
start.date=1 Jan 1999
end.date=31 Jan 1999
serial.number=1
out.file=duke.cer
```

4. Using the certificate directive file above, we can create a certificate for duke, as shown in the following screen:

```
D:\deepak\deepak\plugin>javakey -gc dukeCertDirFile
Generated certificate from directive file dukeCertDirFile.

D:\deepak\deepak\plugin>
```

5. We verify the results so far using the -ld and -dc options of the javakey command, as shown in the following session screen:

```
D:\deepak\deepak\plugin>javakey -ld

Scope: sun.security.IdentityDatabase, source file: C:\\identitydb.obj

[Signer]duke[identitydb.obj][trusted]
        public and private keys initialized
        certificates:
        certificate 1    for  : CN=Duke Duke, OU=ITSO, O=IBM, C=US
                         from : CN=Duke Duke, OU=ITSO, O=IBM, C=US


        No further information available.

D:\deepak\deepak\plugin>javakey -dc duke.cer
[
  X.509v1 certificate,
  Subject is CN=Duke Duke, OU=ITSO, O=IBM, C=US
  Key:   Sun DSA Public Key
parameters:
p: fd7f53811d75122952df4a9c2eece4e7f611b7523cef4400c31e3f80b6512669455d402251fb5
93d8d58fabfc5f5ba30f6cb9b556cd7813b801d346ff26660b76b9950a5a49f9fe8047b1022c24fb
ba9d7feb7c61bf83b57e7c6a8a6150f04fb83f6d3c51ec3023554135a169132f675f3ae2b61d72ae
ff22203199dd14801c7
q: 9760508f15230bccb292b982a2eb840bf0581cf5
g: f7e1a085d69b3ddecbbcab5c36b857b97994afbbfa3aea82f9574c0b3d0782675159578ebad45
94fe67107108180b449167123e84c281613b7cf09328cc8a6e13c167a8b547c8d28e0a3ae1e2bb3a
675916ea37f0bfa213562f1fb627a01243bcca4f1bea8519089a883dfe15ae59f06928b665e807b5
52564014c3bfecf492a

y: 5f552e40c064cca092099c5ca89460d9a06a8458d315243f1e8be5e9d745d6c7345dc45694a4c
bc666563b84d4238f8cc47f5dde308fed7486e915e5bfabdb3066317ddb9c039b8f1bc183f1c078f
274ad18f1956284b5d30552deaa0c921b89f2ee8a11ccd8c91dfc403a2383d09a050373e24a3c450
452d476eb57993918d2
  Validity <Fri Jan 01 00:00:00 EST 1999> until <Sun Jan 31 00:00:00 EST 1999>
  Issuer is CN=Duke Duke, OU=ITSO, O=IBM, C=US
  Issuer signature used [SHA1withDSA]
  Serial number =      01
]

D:\deepak\deepak\plugin>
```

6. Next we create the JAR file App.jar from the class file App.class. To do this, we apply the `jar` utility, as shown in the following session screen:

```
D:\deepak\deepak\plugin>jar -cvf App.jar App.class
adding: App.class (in=944) (out=593) (deflated 37%)

D:\deepak\deepak\plugin>
```

7. To sign the App JAR file, we first have to prepare a signature directive file, which we call dirfile and whose contents are shown in the following screen:

```
signer=duke
cert=1
chain=0
signature.file=Duke
out.file=App.jar
```

8. Then, using the JDK 1.1 `javakey` utility, we apply the signature to App.jar, as shown in the following screen:

```
D:\deepak\deepak\plugin>javakey -gs dirfile AppU.jar
Adding entry: META-INF/MANIFEST.MF
Creating entry: META-INF/DUKE.SF
Creating entry: META-INF/DUKE.DSA
Adding entry: App.class
Signed JAR file AppU.jar using directive file dirfile.

D:\deepak\deepak\plugin>
```

After this process, we load the plugin.html HTML file (shown in Figure 177 on page 377 and Figure 178 on page 378) in the Netscape Navigator browser. As expected, the Java Plug-in is activated and the applet is loaded, but the permission to access the itso.txt file in the local file system is denied to the applet, and the browser window appears as in Figure 175 on page 376. This is because we have not yet imported the identity database into the Java 2 keystore, which we do in the next step.

9. We import the identity database generated with the older JDK 1.1.7B into the Java 2 keystore .keystore being used in the user-defined policy file, as shown in the following session screen:

```
D:\deepak\work>keytool -identitydb -file identitydb.obj
Enter keystore password:  javakeys
Creating keystore entry for <duke> ...

D:\deepak\work>
```

10. We verify the results with the -list command associated with the keytool utility, as shown in the following screen:

```
D:\deepak\work>keytool -list
Enter keystore password:  javakeys

Keystore type: jks
Keystore provider: SUN

Your keystore contains 2 entries:

marco, Mon Jan 25 19:18:46 EST 1999, keyEntry,
Certificate fingerprint (MD5): CD:B2:98:F3:9B:8B:32:55:2A:CE:6B:14:1B:0D:D7:AD
duke, Tue Jan 26 13:36:57 EST 1999, keyEntry,
Certificate fingerprint (MD5): 17:82:9D:31:6C:8E:06:2A:F6:BF:49:E0:7A:E2:8B:AA
```

11.We add the following in the user-defined policy file:

```
keystore ".keystore";
grant signedBy "duke", codeBase "http://www.test.com/" {
  permission java.io.FilePermission "D:${/}itso${/}textFile${/}itso.txt", "read";
};
```

Now, when we run the HTML file, the applet is able to access the file on the local file system successfully.

The above example demonstrates how applets signed with the JDK 1.1 javakey tool can be integrated in the Java 2 platform and subjected to the Java 2 security model. In particular, this demonstration has been done using the Java Plug-in environment.

Chapter 12. Java Gets Out of Its Box

We have seen in previous chapters that the Java Development Kit (JDK) 1.1 applet sandbox is a very safe place where all untrusted applets can run. However, one person's *safe* can be another person's *boring* or *useless*. Creating effective client/server applications using Java often requires us to give the applet some freedom from the confines of the sandbox.

The Java 2 access control security model is built around the concept of a *protection domain*. The applet sandbox was a protection domain with very tight controls. By contrast the Java application environment was a protection domain with no controls at all, other than those imposed by the underlying operating system. What we really need is a protection domain lying somewhere between the two, one that provides certain well-defined permissions that can be changed depending upon the needs at the time.

That was provided for the first time in JDK 1.1, where remotely loaded applets were granted full permissions, provided that code was signed and the signature was considered trusted. As we have discussed, JDK 1.1 offered signed applets as a way to escape from the sandbox restrictions. Java 2 SDK, Standard Edition, V1.2 has enhanced the security model provided by the previous release, and now permissions granted to local or remote, signed or unsigned code are all policy-based. In this sense, the Java 2 security model provides fine-grained access control.

What about Web browser security? There are different philosophies in the way that signed Java Archive (JAR) files are used to elicit extra permissions from the client. In the Sun case, the browser is configured in advance to allow a signed applet to do certain things that are normally forbidden by the security manager. In the Netscape case, the applet must request the permissions it wants, using a special API. Microsoft has taken yet another approach, not using JAR files at all.

In this chapter we look at examples of the different implementations.

12.1 JAR Files and Applet Signing

In 9.2, "Java Archive Tool" on page 270, we introduced the JAR file format and showed all the details related to the `jar` command line utility, which was shipped for the first time with JDK 1.1 to create and manage JAR files. In this section we describe the details of the JAR format.

First of all, let's consider the command below, which creates an archive for the PointlessButton applet (see Figure 17 on page 37):

```
jar cvf pbutton.jar PointlessButton.class jamjar\examples\Button.class
```

Figure 181 shows the format of the pbutton.jar file that the command above creates:

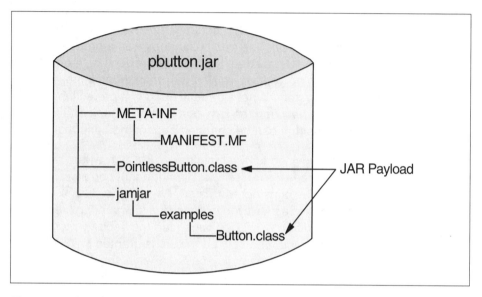

Figure 181. The pbutton Archive

The files that make up the *payload* of the JAR are packed into a copy of the original directory structure. The MANIFEST.MF file, also known as the *manifest* file, contains details of the payload of the JAR. The manifest file is created under a directory META-INF. This is what the manifest looks like in this case:

```
Manifest-Version: 1.0
Created-By: 1.2 (Sun Microsystems Inc.)
```

Figure 182. Manifest File Created by the jar cvf Command

JAR files can be digitally signed. A digital signature on a JAR file guarantees the sender's identity to the receiver, but it also vouches for the integrity of the JAR file itself – that is, the JAR file was not altered after signing. JAR signing allows you to generate digital signatures for any of the files in the archive. In fact, files can be signed by more than one signer. So, for example, an applet could be signed by the developer who created it and then also signed by the IT department of the company that uses it. When the user loads the applet, he or she not only knows that the applet comes from a trustworthy source, but also knows that it has been approved for corporate use.

As we can see in Figure 181 on page 386, the manifest file is created by the `jar` command in the META-INF directory. However, when you sign a file in a JAR archive with the Java 2 SDK `jarsigner` tool, two new files are added to the META-INF directory; we will call them the *signature file* and *signature block* file.

Let's discuss in detail these files one by one.

12.1.1 Manifest File

A manifest file, MANIFEST.MF, is created by default in the META-INF directory whenever a new JAR file is created. According to the specifications (see http://java.sun.com/products/jdk/1.2/docs/guide/jar/manifest.html), the manifest file must include as a minimum the following line:

```
Manifest Version: 1.0
```

Figure 182 on page 386 shows the sample manifest file created by using the `jar` command with the option `cvf`. However, you have the possibility to include your own manifest information from a specified text file.

A customized manifest file can be manually edited, but this is a risky operation, because you must be sure that you respect the syntax. Another option you have is to let the `jar` tool create a default manifest file while compressing the files. Then you should extract the JAR file, modify the manifest, customizing it according to your needs, and then compress the JAR file again including the manifest file you modified. This operation also requires editing the manifest file, but at least you can use part of the manifest information produced by default by the `jar` tool. A customized manifest can be packed with a JAR file by using the M or m option provided with the `jar` utility:

- The M option does not create the manifest file at all. So the command:

```
jar cvfM jarFile file1 file2 ... fileN
```

compresses all the files in a single JAR file, without adding any manifest information file. This can be useful if you wish to include your own manifest file. In this case, in fact, you can use the M option and your predefined manifest file will appear as one of the regular files that must be compressed, as shown:

```
jar cvfM jarFile file1 file2 ... fileN META-INF\MANIFEST.MF
```

where `META-INF\MANIFEST.MF` is the manifest file you previously created. Remember that there can be only one manifest file in the archive. It must be called MANIFEST.MF and it is required to be in the directory META-INF, otherwise it will not be recognized as the manifest file during signing, updating, verifying, etc. and will be treated as a normal file in the JAR. The names META-INF and MANIFEST.MF should be generated as uppercase, but they will be recognized in any case. Also, if you manually edited the manifest file, be sure you respect the syntax.

- The `m` option is probably the most useful one. It can be applied as follows:

```
jar cvfm jarFile manifestInput file1 file2 ... fileN
```

or:

```
jar cvmf manifestInput jarFile file1 file2 ... fileN
```

Using the `m` option, a new manifest file is created taking the information contained in an existing manifest input text file, specified on the command prompt.

Note the order of the files to be specified on the command prompt. If the option `f` is specified before `m`, then `jarFile` must come before `manifestInput`; otherwise the order will have to be `manifestInput jarFile`. The files to be compressed, `file1 file2 ... fileN`, are always specified last.

Another important thing to notice is that, with the `m` option, the file you pass on the command line as the manifest file does not need to be called MANIFEST.MF and does not need to reside in the directory META-INF. The `jar` utility will create a file called MANIFEST.MF and will place it in a directory called META-INF, as you can see by extracting the resulting JAR file.

There are several reasons why you might want to create a JAR file with a specific manifest. These reasons depend on what role you want your JAR file to play. If you're interested only in the ZIP-like features of JAR files, such as compression and archiving, you do not have to worry about the manifest file. The manifest doesn't really play any role in those situations. However, for other purposes, you will need to change the default manifest file. For example, you can add special-purpose name-value attribute headers to the manifest file that are not contained in the default manifest. Examples of such headers would be those for vendor information, package sealing, downloaded extensions, and headers to make JAR-bundled applications executable.

For applications bundled in a JAR file, you have to add the following line to your manifest file:

```
Main-Class: ClassName
```

An example of this can be found in 1.4.2.4, "Packing the Application Class in a JAR File" on page 30.

For downloaded extensions, which are JAR files referenced by other JAR files (see 3.4.2, "Extensions Framework" on page 86), you need to add the following line to your manifest file:

```
Class-Path: extensionJarName
```

A package within a JAR file can be optionally *sealed*, which means that all classes defined in that package must be archived in the same JAR file. Package sealing is a new feature introduced for the first time with Java 2 SDK, Standard Edition, V1.2. You might want to seal a package, for example, to ensure version consistency among the classes in your software or as a security measure. To seal a package, you need to add a Name header for the package, followed by a Sealed header, similar to this:

```
Name: myCompany/myPackage/
Sealed: true
```

The Name header's value is the package's relative path name. Note that it ends with a forward slash (/) to distinguish it from a file name. Any headers following a Name header, without any intervening blank lines, apply to the file or package specified in the Name header. In the above example, because the Sealed header occurs after the Name header, with no blank lines between, the Sealed header will be interpreted as applying (only) to the package myCompany/myPackage/.

Another new feature introduced only with Java 2 SDK, Standard Edition, V1.2 is package versioning. The *package versioning* specification defines several manifest headers to hold versioning information. One set of such headers can be assigned to each package. The versioning headers should appear directly beneath the Name header for the package. This example shows all the versioning headers:

```
Name: java/util/
Specification-Title: "Java Utility Classes"
Specification-Version: "1.2"
Specification-Vendor: "Sun Microsystems, Inc.".
Implementation-Title: "java.util"
Implementation-Version: "build57"
Implementation-Vendor: "Sun Microsystems, Inc."
```

Header information, such as vendor information, package sealing, downloaded extensions, and headers to make JAR-bundled applications executable, is not inserted in the default manifest file created by the `jar` utility. Therefore you must provide those headers in a manifest input file and then use the `m` option, or in alternative you have to edit a manifest file with the information you need and include it in the JAR file using the `M` option, to prevent `jar` from creating the default manifest.

Notice that the default manifest has the Created-By and Manifest-Version information (see Figure 182 on page 386). If you use the `m` option and either or both of these two pieces of information are also present in the manifest input file you pass on the command line, the same values will be present in the new manifest file, although the order of the entries might be rearranged.

For example if your manifest input file is:

```
Manifest-Version: 1.0
Created-By: DEEPAK GUPTA
Main-Class: GetProps
```

then the manifest file created is:

```
Manifest-Version: 1.0
Main-Class: GetProps
Created-By: DEEPAK GUPTA
```

As you can see, the `jar` utility has rearranged the order of the entries in the manifest file.

On the other hand, if your original manifest file contained only the line:

```
Main-Class: GetProps
```

then the manifest file that is created is:

```
Manifest-Version: 1.0
Main-Class: GetProps
Created-By: 1.2 (Sun Microsystems Inc.)
```

So, in this case, the `jar` utility has provided the missing manifest information.

Also, note that the manifest file entries must have the syntax:

```
Name: value
```

When the `jar` utility encounters incorrect syntax, the following error is returned in the Command Prompt window:

```
java.io.IOException: invalid header field
        at java.util.jar.Attributes.read(Compiled Code)
        at java.util.jar.Manifest.read(Compiled Code)
        at java.util.jar.Manifest.<init>(Manifest.java:55)
        at sun.tools.jar.Main.run(Main.java:87)
        at sun.tools.jar.Main.main(Main.java:760)
```

As we said also in Step 1 on page 274, the last line of the manifest input file must be empty. That is, there should be a new line character at the end of the file. If this is missing, the `jar` utility simply ignores the manifest file. Therefore, when you are manually editing the manifest file, make sure to press the Enter key after the last line.

When a manifest file is signed, the digest values of the files in the JAR are added to the manifest file. Note that this behavior is different from what happened with the JDK 1.1 `jar` utility, which always computed the digests, regardless of whether or not the JAR file was signed. In other words, in JDK 1.1, the digests were calculated and added to the manifest file when the JAR file was created. In Java 2 SDK, Standard Edition, V1.2, this operation is done only when the JAR file is signed for the first time. This is to speed up the creation of unsigned JAR files, for which you do not need any digests.

The following lines are present in the manifest of a signed JAR file:

```
Name: dirpath/whatever.class
Algorithm-Digest: base-64_representation_of_digest
```

So after a JAR file is signed, the manifest should look like the following:

```
Manifest-Version: 1.0
Created-By: 1.2 (Sun Microsystems Inc.)

Name: PointlessButton.class
SHA1-Digest: Sj15dptWhrZhiIFRNU27WRY1brc=

Name: jamjar/examples/Button.class
SHA1-Digest: Fo6pYkn6ZR17eessxEiN7fK5xpE=
```

The digest values recorded in the manifest are calculated from the contents of the payload files they refer to. They are used to validate the payload files when they are verified.

Notice that by default only the SHA-1 digest is present.

12.1.2 Signature File

A signature file is automatically generated and placed in the META-INF directory each time a JAR file is signed. This file looks very similar to the manifest file shown above, except that the digests in it are calculated from the manifest file entries, not from the actual contents of the payload files.

The name of this file is *signerID*.SF, where *signerID* is an arbitrary name for the creator of the signature. If the JAR has been signed by more than one signer, each signer will generate a separate SF file. The signature file looks like the following:

```
Signature-Version: 1.0
SHA1-Digest-Manifest: 3jdG5UfTfZHcBQxGCBWSnCRb0p4=
Created-By: 1.2 (Sun Microsystems Inc.)

Name: jamjar/examples/Button.class
SHA1-Digest: WuhnnW3v9MiVHl0z1T8qnwFDYOo=

Name: PointlessButton.class
SHA1-Digest: L1S9Bcrbn4ZGAOflam1Cwn9qDFw=
```

The SHA1-Digest-Manifest header gives the digest of the complete manifest file. The SHA1-Digest header for the different file entries in the SF file give the digests of the entries of the respective files in the manifest file. By default, the digest is calculated using the SHA-1 algorithm.

12.1.3 Signature Block File

In addition to the signature file, a signature block file is automatically placed in the META-INF directory each time a JAR file is signed. Unlike the manifest file or the signature file, which are ASCII files, signature block files are binary, so they are not human-readable.

The signature block file is in PKCS#7 format[1]. It contains two elements essential for verification:

1. The digital signature for the JAR file, generated with the signer's private key

2. The certificate containing the signer's public key, to be used by anyone wanting to verify the signed JAR file

---

[1] Public Key Cryptography Standards (PKCS) is a set of rules for encoding various cryptographic structures. PKCS#7 defines a general-purpose signature format, including the signed digest, the certificate of the signer and the certification authority (CA) certificates that support it.

Signature block file names typically will have a .DSA extension indicating that they were created by the default Digital Signature Algorithm (DSA). Other file name extensions are possible if keys associated with some other standard algorithm are used for signing. For example, .RSA is the extension if the signature is obtained from an algorithm that uses RSA encryption, and .PGP is the extension with a Pretty Good Privacy (PGP) signature.

12.2 Signed Code Scenario in JDK 1.1 and Sun HotJava

In this section we show how to use the commands to create three key databases:

1. A certificate authority database
2. A database for a Web server
3. A database for a Web client

We then use these keys to sign a JAR file containing an applet that attempts to read a file on the browser system.

12.2.1 Creating the CA Key Database

The certificate authority is a principal in its own key database, with a self-signed certificate. We create it as follows:

1. The first thing to do is to create a new key database. The key database is created implicitly when you add the first principal to it:

```
D:\work\sun_signed_jar>javakey -cs "JamJar CA" true
Created identity [Signer]JamJar CA[identitydb.obj][trusted]

D:\work\sun_signed_jar>
```

This creates the key database identitydb.obj in your home directory.

2. Next, generate a key pair for the CA principal. We choose to use a 1024-bit key:

```
D:\work\sun_signed_jar>javakey -gk "JamJar CA" DSA 1024
Generated DSA keys for JamJar CA (strength: 1024).

D:\work\sun_signed_jar>
```

This can take a while to do. We ran it on a 75 MHz 486 machine and the command ran for 2 minutes and 40 seconds (the time is related to the key size).

3. We use the list option of `javakey` to check the results so far:

```
D:\work\sun_signed_jar>javakey -ld
Scope: sun.security.IdentityDatabase, source file: C:\users\default\identitydb.obj
[Signer]JamJar CA[identitydb.obj][trusted]
        public and private keys initialized
        certificates:
        No further information available.

D:\work\sun_signed_jar>
```

4. The key pair allows the CA to sign certificates, but we also need to generate a certificate for the CA itself, so that others can accept the CA's signatures. The first thing to do is to create a certificate information file, containing the distinguished name information for the CA and the certificate issuer. In this case, the certificate is self-signed, so the issuer and the subject are the same:

```
issuer.name=JamJar CA
issuer.cert=1
subject.name=JamJar CA
subject.real.name=Project JamJar Certificate Authority
subject.org.unit=ISL
subject.org=IBM
subject.country=UK
start.date=12 Sep 1997
end.date=12 Sep 1998
serial.number=1
out.file=cert.jamjar
```

We save this file as certinfo.jamjar.

5. Finally we can generate the CA's certificate:

```
D:\work\sun_signed_jar>javakey -gc certinfo.jamjar
Generated certificate from directive file certinfo.jamjar.
D:\work\sun_signed_jar>javakey -ld
Scope: sun.security.IdentityDatabase, source file: C:\users\default\identitydb.o
bj
[Signer]JamJar CA[identitydb.obj][trusted]
        public and private keys initialized
        certificates:
        certificate 1   for  : CN=Project JamJar Certificate Authority, OU=ISL,O=IBM, C=UK
                        from : CN=Project JamJar Certificate Authority, OU=ISL,O=IBM, C=UK
        No further information available.

D:\work\sun_signed_jar>
```

12.2.2 Creating the Server Key Database

Now we want to create a key database for our server:

1. If we use `javakey` to create the principal for the server, it will add it to the CA database. So first we must choose to use a different key database, by setting the identity.database directive in the main security properties file, ${java.home}\lib\security\java.security, where ${java.home} in this case is the directory where JDK 1.1 was installed. We add the following line:

   ```
   identity.database=D:/work/sun_signed_jar/serverdb.obj
   ```

2. The server has to know about the CA that signed its own certificate, so first we add the CA principal to the key database and import the CA certificate:

```
D:\work\sun_signed_jar>javakey -cs "JamJar CA" true
Created identity [Signer]JamJar CA[D:/work/sun_signed_jar/serverdb.obj][trusted]

D:\work\sun_signed_jar>javakey -ic "JamJar CA" cert.jamjar
Imported certificate from cert.jamjar for JamJar CA.

D:\work\sun_signed_jar>javakey -ld
Scope: sun.security.IdentityDatabase, source file: D:/work/sun_signed_jar/serverdb.obj
Signer]JamJar CA[D:/work/sun_signed_jar/serverdb.obj][trusted]
        no keys
        certificates:
        certificate 1   for  : CN=Project JamJar Certificate Authority, OU=ISL,O=IBM, C=UK
                        from : CN=Project JamJar Certificate Authority, OU=ISL,O=IBM, C=UK

D:\work\sun_signed_jar>
```

Notice that in this case the list command shows a key database with no keys in it, just a public key certificate. This is slightly misleading, because the certificate contains the public key; the display should really say that there are no key pairs.

3. We create the principal and generate a key pair for our server:

```
D:\work\sun_signed_jar>javakey -cs "Robusta"
Created identity [Signer]Robusta[D:/work/sun_signed_jar/serverdb.obj][not trusted]
D:\work\sun_signed_jar>javakey -gk "Robusta" DSA 512
Generated DSA keys for Robusta (strength: 512).

D:\work\sun_signed_jar>
```

4. Next we want to use the CA key pair to sign the server's public key. First we export the public key to a file:

```
D:\work\sun_signed_jar>javakey -ek Robusta pubkey.robusta
Public key exported to pubkey.robusta.

D:\work\sun_signed_jar>
```

5. We need to import this key into the CA's key database. To do this we
   comment out the identity.database entry that we added to java.security
   (see Step 1 on page 395), create the server's principal in the CA database
   and import the public key:

```
D:\work\sun_signed_jar>javakey -cs "Robusta"
Created identity [Signer]Robusta[D:/work/sun_signed_jar/serverdb.obj][not trusted]
D:\work\sun_signed_jar>javakey -ik Robusta pubkey.robusta
Set public key from pubkey.robusta for Robusta.

D:\work\sun_signed_jar>
```

6. Now we can sign the server's certificate. The process is the same as for
   the CA certificate. First we create the certificate information file:

```
issuer.name=JamJar CA
issuer.cert=1
subject.name=Robusta
subject.real.name=All Java is secure but signed Java is Robusta
subject.org.unit=ISL
subject.org=IBM
subject.country=UK
start.date=12 Sep 1997
end.date=12 Sep 1998
serial.number=2
out.file=cert.robusta
```

7. Then we sign the certificate:

```
D:\work\sun_signed_jar>javakey -gc certinfo.robusta
Generated certificate from directive file certinfo.robusta.

D:\work\sun_signed_jar>
```

8. To use the certificate, we have to import it into the server's key database,
   which means that we first have to find out the number assigned to the
   certificate in the CA database and export the certificate to a file:

```
D:\work\sun_signed_jar>javakey -li Robusta
Identity: Robusta
[Signer]Robusta[identitydb.obj][not trusted]
        no keys
        certificates:
        certificate 1   for  : CN=All Java is secure but signed Java is Robusta
OU=ISL, O=IBM, C=UK
                        from : CN=Project JamJar Certificate Authority, OU=ISL,O=IBM, C=UK
D:\work\sun_signed_jar>javakey -ec Robusta 1 cert.robusta
Certificate 1 exported to cert.robusta.

D:\work\sun_signed_jar>
```

9. Finally, we switch the active key database back to the server, by restoring the identity.database entry in java.security (see Step 5 on page 394). Then import the certificate:

```
D:\work\sun_signed_jar>javakey -ic Robusta cert.robusta
Imported certificate from cert.robusta for Robusta.

D:\work\sun_signed_jar>javakey -ld

Scope: sun.security.IdentityDatabase, source file: D:/work/sun_signed_jar/serverdb.obj
[Signer]JamJar CA[D:/work/sun_signed_jar/serverdb.obj][trusted]
        no keys
        certificates:
        certificate 1   for  : CN=Project JamJar Certificate Authority, OU=ISL,O=IBM, C=UK
                        from : CN=Project JamJar Certificate Authority, OU=ISL,O=IBM, C=UK
        No further information available.
[Signer]Robusta[D:/work/sun_signed_jar/serverdb.obj][not trusted]
        public and private keys initialized
        certificates:
        certificate 1   for  : CN=All Java is secure but signed Java is Robusta OU=ISL, O=IBM, C=UK
                        from : CN=Project JamJar Certificate Authority, OU=ISL,O=IBM, C=UK

D:\work\sun_signed_jar>
```

12.2.3 Creating and Signing a JAR File

To illustrate the use of the key databases we have a simple Java applet that attempts to perform an action normally prohibited by the sandbox; it reads a local file and displays the contents on screen. We need to package this in a JAR archive and then sign it.

1. We create the jar file and display its contents using the `jar` command:

```
D:\work\sun_signed_jar>jar -cvf jam.jar GetFile.class
adding: GetFile.class (in=2239) (out=1201) (deflated 46%)
D:\work\sun_signed_jar>jar -tf jam.jar
META-INF/MANIFEST.MF
GetFile.class

D:\work\sun_signed_jar>
```

2. We have to tell `javakey` which key pair to use for the signature (in fact, the key database only has one key pair in it, but `javakey` does not know that). To do this we create a signature directive file, as follows:

```
signer=Robusta
cert=1
chain=0
signature.file=ROBUSTA
```

The signature.file directive does not define a real file, but the file name part of the signer and signature files that are placed in the META-INF directory of the JAR.

3. Now we can sign the JAR:

```
D:\work\sun_signed_jar>javakey -gs sign_directive.robusta jam.jar
Adding entry: META-INF/MANIFEST.MF
Creating entry: META-INF\ROBUSTA.SF
Creating entry: META-INF\ROBUSTA.DSA
Adding entry: GetFile.class
Signed JAR file jam.jar using directive file sign_directive.robusta.

D:\work\sun_signed_jar>
```

Notice the conflicting use of forward slash (/) and back slash (\) in the metadata files. In theory a JAR should use forward slashes only, but this mixed use does not seem to cause a problem.

4. The result of performing the signature is a file named jam.jar.sig. Now we can put that on the Web server and reference it in a Web page using the `<APPLET>` tag:

```
<APPLET CODE=GetFile.class archive=jam.jar.sig WIDTH=600 HEIGHT=600>
   <PARAM NAME=FileToTry VALUE="c:\thingy">
</APPLET>
```

12.2.4 Running the Applet

We can finally try to load the HTML page that invokes a Web browser (or, for testing purposes, the JDK 1.1 Applet Viewer). However, when we do so we get the same error as if it was a normal applet running under the sandbox restrictions:

```
sun.applet.AppletSecurityException: checkread
        at sun.applet.AppletSecurity.checkRead(AppletSecurity.java:384)
        at sun.applet.AppletSecurity.checkRead(AppletSecurity.java:346)
        at java.io.FileInputStream.<init>(FileInputStream.java:58)
        at GetFile.init(GetFile.java:15)
        at sun.applet.AppletPanel.run(AppletPanel.java:287)
        at java.lang.Thread.run(Thread.java:474)
```

You can see that the checkRead() method of the applet security manager is throwing an exception. Why is this? The reason is that the client does not have the certificate that it needs to decrypt the JAR's signature, and hence establish trust in the signer.

12.2.5 Creating the Client Key Database

According to the signature hierarchy the client should only need the JamJar CA certificate to authenticate the server, because JamJar CA signed the server's certificate. However, this did not work as expected for JDK 1.1. We found we had to add the server certificate to the client's key database, as follows:

1. We set the key database to a new one for the client, by changing the identity.database directive in the java.security file:

   identity.database=d:\work\sun_signed_jar\clientdb.obj

2. Then we create the entry for the server and import the certificate:

```
D:\work\sun_signed_jar>javakey -cs "Robusta" true
Created identity [Signer]Robusta[D:/work/sun_signed_jar/clientdb.obj][trusted]
D:\work\sun_signed_jar>javakey -ic "Robusta" cert.robusta
Imported certificate from cert.robusta for Robusta.

D:\work\sun_signed_jar>
```

3. Now, at last, the applet runs as we want it to:

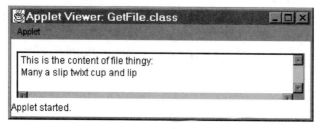

Figure 183. Running the Signed Applet

The Applet Viewer gives full access to any signed applet, which is acceptable because it is a test tool. A real browser should provide more control over access. HotJava, for example, allows you to set a range of different trust levels:

- **Untrusted**

  This is like the normal sandbox environment, except that it is even more restricted because the applet cannot make any network connections.

- **High Security**

  This is similar to the sandbox, with the addition of the ability for an applet to listen on network ports above 1024.

- **Medium Security**

  Prompts the user whenever the applet tries to do something that is normally not allowed, so that the user can permit or deny it.

- **Low Security**

  Allows the applet to do anything, without prompting the user.

12.3 Signed Code Scenario in Java 2 SDK, Standard Edition, V1.2

JDK 1.1 provided the `javakey` and `jar` commands for managing databases of public keys and for creating, signing and manipulating JAR archives (this process is described in 11.5.2.2, "Java Plug-In and Code Signed with javakey" on page 380).

Java 2 SDK, Standard Edition, V1.2 provides the `keytool`, `jar` and `jarsigner` tools to manage key databases and for creating, signing, verifying, updating and manipulating JAR files.

12.3.1 Creating a Keystore for Certification Authorities

By default, Java 2 SDK, Standard Edition, V1.2 comes with a keystore file, called cacerts, which contains five VeriSign root certification authority (CA) certificates (see 8.2.1, "The Certificates KeyStore File cacerts" on page 233). Here, we create a new CA keystore called CAStore. We will work in the D:\CA directory for the CA.

1. We create the CAStore keystore and the keys for it. This process, which automatically creates a self-signed certificate, is shown in the following session screen:

```
D:\CA>keytool -genkey -alias CAkey -keystore CAStore
Enter keystore password:  CertAuth
What is your first and last name?
  [Unknown]:  ITSO Certificate Authority
What is the name of your organizational unit?
  [Unknown]:  ITSO
What is the name of your organization?
  [Unknown]:  IBM
What is the name of your City or Locality?
  [Unknown]:  Cary
What is the name of your State or Province?
  [Unknown]:  NC
What is the two-letter country code for this unit?
  [Unknown]:  US
Is <CN=ITSO Certificate Authority, OU=ITSO, O=IBM, L=Cary, ST=NC, C=US> correct? [no]:  Y
Enter key password for <CAkey>
        (RETURN if same as keystore password):  ibmitsojava

D:\CA>
```

2. We export the certificate to the file CAcert.crt:

```
D:\CA>keytool -export -keystore CAStore -alias CAkey -file CAcert.crt
Enter keystore password:  CertAuth
Certificate stored in file <CAcert.crt>

D:\CA>
```

3. We print the certificate to standard output to view its contents:

```
D:\CA>keytool -printcert -file CAcert.crt
Owner: CN=ITSO Certificate Authority, OU=ITSO, O=IBM, L=Cary, ST=NC, C=US
Issuer: CN=ITSO Certificate Authority, OU=ITSO, O=IBM, L=Cary, ST=NC, C=US
Serial number: 36aa4592
Valid from: Sat Jan 23 16:56:34 EST 1999 until: Fri Apr 23 17:56:34 EDT 1999
Certificate fingerprints:
        MD5:   24:0A:0E:3D:AC:20:7F:97:A1:31:95:25:95:F5:84:8F
        SHA1: 7E:74:32:0B:20:9C:45:74:BD:3B:88:AB:CE:C7:DD:CB:BF:70:D0:C5

D:\CA>
```

12.3.2 Creating the Server Certificate

We work in the D:\server directory for the tasks related to creating the server certificate. We create the server certificate as follows:

1. We create the server key pair:

```
D:\server>keytool -genkey -alias Serverkey -keystore ServerStore
Enter keystore password:  Server
What is your first and last name?
  [Unknown]:  Java security Redbook
What is the name of your organizational unit?
  [Unknown]:  ITSO
What is the name of your organization?
  [Unknown]:  IBM
What is the name of your City or Locality?
  [Unknown]:  Cary
What is the name of your State or Province?
  [Unknown]:  NC
What is the two-letter country code for this unit?
  [Unknown]:  US
Is <CN=Java security Redbook, OU=ITSO, O=IBM, L=Cary, ST=NC, C=US> correct?
  [no]:  Y
Enter key password for <Serverkey>
        (RETURN if same as keystore password):  ibmitsojava

D:\server>
```

2. We export the certificate to the file Servercert.crt:

```
D:\server>keytool -export -keystore ServerStore -alias Serverkey -file Servercert.crt
Enter keystore password:  Server
Certificate stored in file <Servercert.crt>

D:\server>
```

3. We print the certificate to standard output to view its contents:

```
D:\server>keytool -printcert -file Servercert.crt
Owner: CN=Java security Redbook, OU=ITSO, O=IBM, L=Cary, ST=NC, C=US
Issuer: CN=Java security Redbook, OU=ITSO, O=IBM, L=Cary, ST=NC, C=US
Serial number: 36aa4730
Valid from: Sat Jan 23 17:03:28 EST 1999 until: Fri Apr 23 18:03:28 EDT 1999
Certificate fingerprints:
         MD5:  D0:34:8B:6F:A6:C1:A0:0C:4C:6A:20:F8:EE:CB:B2:40
         SHA1: BD:F9:E8:98:DB:93:50:5A:68:D7:7F:B5:0B:19:3E:38:5F:A6:83:BB

D:\server>
```

4. Next, we need to sign this server certificate using the CA private key.

   This is rather complex. Although in JDK 1.1 we could use the `javakey` tool to sign a certificate with a CA signer, in Java 2 SDK, Standard Edition, V1.2, only self-signed certificates can be created using the tools provided. In future versions of the Java 2 SDK this limitation will probably be removed. However, the Java 2 APIs enable us to apply a digital signature on a certificate request by writing an appropriate Java application, as shown in the following figures:

```java
import java.io.*;
import java.security.*;
import sun.security.x509.*;
import sun.security.util.*;


class Sign
{
   public static void main(String arg[])
   {
      try
      {
         FileInputStream fisk = new FileInputStream("D:\\CA\\CAStore");
         KeyStore ks = KeyStore.getInstance("JKS", "SUN");
         String storepass = "CertAuth";
         char[] pwd = new char[storepass.length()];
         for (int i = 0; i < pwd.length; i++)
            pwd[i] = storepass.charAt(i);

         String keypass = "ibmitsojava";
         char[] kpwd = new char[keypass.length()];
         for (int i = 0; i < kpwd.length; i++)
            kpwd[i] = keypass.charAt(i);
```

Figure 184. (Part 1 of 2). Sign.java

```
        ks.load(fisk, pwd);
        PrivateKey priv = (PrivateKey)ks.getKey("CAKey", kpwd);
        X509Cert certs = new X509Cert();
        certs.decode(new FileInputStream("D:\\CA\\CAcert.crt"));
        AlgorithmId SHAalg = new AlgorithmId(AlgorithmId.DSA_oid);
        X500Signer CA = certs.getSigner(SHAalg, priv);

        FileInputStream bis = new FileInputStream("D:\\server\\Servercert.crt");
        X509Cert srvrCert = new X509Cert();
        srvrCert.decode(bis);

        BigInt i = srvrCert.getSerialNumber();
        byte[] signedcert = srvrCert.encodeAndSign(i, CA);

        FileOutputStream certfos = new FileOutputStream("D:\\server\\signedcert.crt");
        certfos.write(signedcert);
        certfos.close();
    }
    catch (Exception e)
    {
        System.out.println("Exception: " + e);
    }
  }
}
```

Figure 185. (Part 2 of 2). Sign.java

In this application, in particular, we have made use of the sun.security APIs, which allow you to sign a server certificate with a CA certificate.

The classes that JavaSoft includes with the Java 2 SDK fall into at least two packages: java.* and sun.*. Only classes in java.* packages are a standard part of the Java platform and will be supported into the future. JavaSoft states that:[2]

- API outside of java.* can change at any time without notice, and so cannot be counted on either across platforms (Sun, Microsoft, Netscape, Apple, etc.) or across Java versions.

- Programs that contain direct calls to the sun.* API are not 100% Pure Java. In other words a Java program that directly calls any API in sun.* packages is not guaranteed to work on all Java-compatible platforms. In fact, such a program is not guaranteed to work even in future versions on the same platform.

[2] General information on the sun.* packages can be found at http://java.sun.com/products/jdk/faq/faq-sun-packages.html.

For these reasons, there is no documentation available for the sun.*
classes.[3] Therefore, if you want to use the Sign program shown in Figure
184 on page 403 and Figure 185 on page 404, do it at your own risk.

The program above is compiled by issuing:

```
javac Sign.java
```

Then, it can be launched by entering:

```
java Sign
```

The program outputs the signed certificate to the file signedcert.crt, in the
directory D:\server.

5. We print the CA-signed certificate to standard output to check out its
contents:

```
D:\server>keytool -printcert -file signedcert.crt
Owner: CN=Java security Redbook, OU=ITSO, O=IBM, L=Cary, ST=NC, C=US
Issuer: CN=ITSO Certificate Authority, OU=ITSO, O=IBM, L=Cary, ST=NC, C=US
Serial number: 36aa4730
Valid from: Sat Jan 23 17:03:28 EST 1999 until: Fri Apr 23 18:03:28 EDT 1999
Certificate fingerprints:
        MD5:  D0:34:8B:6F:A6:C1:A0:0C:4C:6A:20:F8:EE:CB:B2:40
        SHA1: BD:F9:E8:98:DB:93:50:5A:68:D7:7F:B5:0B:19:3E:38:5F:A6:83:BB

D:\server>
```

Notice the difference between this output and the one obtained in Step 3
on page 402, where the issuer and the owner of the certificate were the
same entity, because the certificate was self-signed. In this case, instead,
the owner of the certificate is still the server, but the issuer is the CA.

6. Next, we try to import this certificate back to our server keystore:

```
D:\server>keytool -import -file signedcert.crt -alias Serverkey -keystore ServerStore
Enter keystore password:  Server
Enter key password for <Serverkey>:  ibmitsojava
keytool error: Failed to establish chain from reply

D:\server>
```

Oops! We get an error because the keystore does not recognize the entity
who has signed the certificate as trusted. So we first have to import the
CA's certificate as a trusted root[4]:

---

[3] Nonetheless, we found the documentation we needed to implement the Sign class at
http://jserv.javasoft.com/products/java-server/documentation/webserver1.0.2/apidoc/Package-sun.security.x509.html.
[4] A *trusted root* is the certificate of a widely-accepted CA.

```
D:\server>keytool -import -trustcacerts -file D:\CA\CAcert.crt -alias CA -keystore ServerStore
Enter keystore password:  Server
Owner: CN=ITSO Certificate Authority, OU=ITSO, O=IBM, L=Cary, ST=NC, C=US
Issuer: CN=ITSO Certificate Authority, OU=ITSO, O=IBM, L=Cary, ST=NC, C=US
Serial number: 36aa4592
Valid from: Sat Jan 23 16:56:34 EST 1999 until: Fri Apr 23 17:56:34 EDT 1999
Certificate fingerprints:
        MD5:   24:0A:0E:3D:AC:20:7F:97:A1:31:95:25:95:F5:84:8F
        SHA1: 7E:74:32:0B:20:9C:45:74:BD:3B:88:AB:CE:C7:DD:CB:BF:70:D0:C5
Trust this certificate? [no]:  Y
Certificate was added to keystore

D:\server>
```

Then we try importing the CA-signed server certificate again:

```
D:\server>keytool -import -file signedcert.crt -alias Serverkey -keystore ServerStore
Enter keystore password:  Server
Enter key password for <Serverkey>:  ibmitsojava
Certificate reply was installed in keystore

D:\server>
```

And this operation finally succeeds.

Notice that the system recognizes when a server certificate is signed with the private key of a trusted CA. In fact, upon importing the CA-signed server certificate, we have not been prompted with the question:

```
Trust this certificate? [no]:
```

12.3.3 Creating and Signing a JAR file

Now we create a JAR file signed by the server. We will use the CountApp applet that we implemented in 8.8, "How to Implement a Policy Server" on page 252. We save the class file CountApp.class and the HTML file CountApp.html invoking the applet (see Figure 111 on page 256) in the directory D:\server.

1. We create a JAR file CountApp.jar from the class file CountApp.class:

```
D:\server>jar cvf CountApp.jar CountApp.class
added manifest
adding: CountApp.class (in=948) (out=595) (deflated 37%)

D:\server>
```

2. We sign the CountApp.jar file with the server's private key:

```
D:\server>jarsigner -keystore ServerStore CountApp.jar Serverkey
Enter Passphrase for keystore: Server
Enter key password for Serverkey: ibmitsojava

D:\server>
```

3. Assuming that we have a client keystore in the directory D:\client, we import the CA's certificate into the client's keystore as a trusted CA with alias CA:

```
D:\client>keytool -import -trustcacerts -keystore ClientStore -file D:\CA\CAcert.crt -alias CA
Enter keystore password:  Client
Owner: CN=ITSO Certificate Authority, OU=ITSO, O=IBM, L=Cary, ST=NC, C=US
Issuer: CN=ITSO Certificate Authority, OU=ITSO, O=IBM, L=Cary, ST=NC, C=US
Serial number: 36aa4592
Valid from: Sat Jan 23 16:56:34 EST 1999 until: Fri Apr 23 17:56:34 EDT 1999
Certificate fingerprints:
        MD5:  24:0A:0E:3D:AC:20:7F:97:A1:31:95:25:95:F5:84:8F
        SHA1: 7E:74:32:0B:20:9C:45:74:BD:3B:88:AB:CE:C7:DD:CB:BF:70:D0:C5
Trust this certificate? [no]:  Y
Certificate was added to keystore

D:\client>
```

According to the signature hierarchy, even if the JAR file has been signed with the server's private key, the client should only need the CA certificate to authenticate the server, because the CA signed the server's certificate. For this reason, we do not import the server's certificate into the client's keystore.

12.3.4 Granting the Permissions and Running the Applet

If you go back to 8.8, "How to Implement a Policy Server" on page 252, you will see that the CountApp applet needs the following permissions in order to run correctly:

```
permission java.io.FilePermission "${user.home}${/}itso.txt", "read";
permission java.util.PropertyPermission "user.home", "read";
permission java.util.PropertyPermission "file.separator", "read";
```

The same permissions must be granted to the code source of the CountApp.jar file, or it will throw an AccessControlException when we launch it.

1. We add the following entries to one of the current policy files:

```
keystore "file:/D:/client/ClientStore";

grant signedBy "CA",  codeBase "file:/D:/server/-" {
  permission java.io.FilePermission "${user.home}${/}itso.txt", "read";
  permission java.util.PropertyPermission "user.home", "read";
  permission java.util.PropertyPermission "file.separator", "read";
};
```

As we said in Step 3 on page 407, the client should not grant any
particular permissions to the server, although it was the server that signed
the JAR file. In fact, the client does not even have the server certificate in
the keystore. The client only has the CA certificate registered as a trusted
root, and this should be enough because the CA signed the server's
certificate. This is the reason for the entry

```
signedBy "CA"
```

in the policy file above.

2. At the time of writing this book, the signature hierarchy did not work as
   expected for Java 2 SDK, Standard Edition, V1.2.1. In fact we found that it
   was necessary to add the server's certificate to the client's keystore, as
   follows:[5]

```
D:\client>keytool -import -keystore ClientStore -file D:\server\signedcert.crt -alias server
Enter keystore password:  Client
Certificate was added to keystore

D:\client>
```

The screen above shows that the server is added with alias server.

Also, the entry in the policy file must explicitly indicate that the signer is
server:

```
keystore "file:/D:/client/ClientStore";

grant signedBy "server",  codeBase "file:/D:/server/-" {
  permission java.io.FilePermission "${user.home}${/}itso.txt", "read";
  permission java.util.PropertyPermission "user.home", "read";
  permission java.util.PropertyPermission "file.separator", "read";
};
```

3. Only at this point, after the server's certificate is also imported in the
   client's keystore and the server signer is given the right permissions, the
   applet is able to run without any exceptions.

---

[5] Notice that this is not a bug, but the way the signature hierarchy has been implemented in the Java 2 platform.

12.4 Signed Code Scenario in Netscape Communicator

While JavaSoft was working on developing the security model for the Java 2 platform, the major browser manufacturers were also wrestling with ways to relax the access control applied to signed applets.

Netscape has embraced the JAR format and the opportunities that signing offers. In fact, they are using the format for other types of Web content, such as JavaScript programs, plug-ins and Web pages. However, at the time of writing, you could not simply use a Netscape Communicator V4.5 browser to access a JAR file that was signed using the `jarsigner` or the old `javakey` command.

There are two reasons for this:

1. Netscape browsers require that the CA that signs a JAR file be predefined as a trusted root. The self-signed certificates used by `jarsigner` and `javakey` cannot be loaded into the browser.

2. The trust model implemented by HotJava works on an exception basis; the applet tries to do something that is forbidden, which causes a prompt to ask the user if it is acceptable. Netscape has implemented a more sophisticated model, in which the applet code requests the permissions it needs and in which it can control the period for which each permission is active.

In other words, the programmer decides in advance what permissions are needed, instead of trying to use the permissions and relying on the browser to handle the exception. Although this may seem like a small distinction, it does allow a more natural style of application. For example, if an applet attempts several privileged actions, the user can be prompted to allow access to all of them at once, instead of being repeatedly interrupted each time one of them is encountered in the code.

The ability to turn permissions on and off within the code is also important, because it reduces the exposure to an attack where another applet invokes the trusted applet's methods, thereby using the JAR signature improperly.

The Netscape access control request mechanism is implemented as a Java class package named netscape.security.[6] We illustrate the security model with an example of an applet that requests permission to read system properties and also to read a file on the browser disk. There are three parts to the setup:

1. Writing the applet to use the netscape.security extensions

[6] The Netscape JVM implementation does not provide the package java.security.

2. Installing and configuring the key pairs and certificates

3. Signing the JAR and running the applet

12.4.1 Using the netscape.security Package

The Netscape security mechanism is based on *privilege targets*. These are definitions of operations that the applet may want to perform. Control over whether they should or should not be permitted lies with a new security function, the *privilege manager*. This places indicators on the JVM stack to show what privileges the applet has been allowed. The Netscape version of the security manager then refers to the indicators when performing its authorization checking.

The netscape.security package includes a large number of predefined privilege targets and also allows the programmer to register new targets. You will find the netscape.security package in the JAR file java40.jar, located in the directory C:\Program Files\Netscape\Communicator\Program\java\classes (provided you followed the default installation of Netscape Communicator V4.5) or in a similar tree inside the directory where you installed Netscape. The applet we are going to show you requests access to two of the standard targets:

- Read access to system properties

- Read access to a local file

This applet is called GetFileNS. We split its source code in two parts, so that it is easier to comment on what the applet does. The first part of the applet code, containing the import statements, the class declaration and the init() method, is shown in Figure 186 on page 410 and Figure 189 on page 414:

```
import java.awt.*;
import java.io.*;
import netscape.security.*;

public class GetFileNS extends java.applet.Applet implements Runnable
{
   String filename;
   Thread t;
   TextArea ta = new TextArea("", 10, 50);
   public boolean granted = false;
   PrivilegeManager privMgr;
   protected Principal li101Me;
```

Figure 186. (Part 1 of 4). GetFileNS.java

```
public void init()
{
    filename = getParameter("FileToTry");
    add(ta);

    // Find out what operating system we are on
    try
    {
        PrivilegeManager.enablePrivilege("UniversalPropertyRead");
        String osName = System.getProperty("os.name");
        ta.appendText("\nI see you are running " + osName);
        PrivilegeManager.revertPrivilege("UniversalPropertyRead");
    }
    catch (netscape.security.ForbiddenTargetException e)
    {
        ta.appendText("\nPermission to read system properties denied by user.");
    }

    // Request permission to read a specific file
    lilOlMe = PrivilegeManager.getMyPrincipals()[0];
    privMgr = PrivilegeManager.getPrivilegeManager();

    try
    {
        Target freadTgt = Target.findTarget("FileRead");
        privMgr.enablePrivilege(freadTgt , lilOlMe, (Object) filename);
        granted = true ;
    }
    catch(ForbiddenTargetException e)
    {
        ta.appendText("\nUser won't let me read " + filename);
    }

    // Start the thread running
    if (t == null)
    {
        t = new Thread(this);
        t.start();
    }
}
```

Figure 187. (Part 2 of 4). GetFileNS.java

The following are some comments on this first part of the applet code:

- **Requesting the permissions to read system properties**

  Here we request permission to read system properties:

  ```
  PrivilegeManager.enablePrivilege("UniversalPropertyRead");
  ```

  The enablePrivilege() method causes a dialog box to pop up asking for permission. If the user refuses, it throws an exception. Otherwise the applet goes on to read the property, which in this case is the type of operating system on which the browser is running.

- **Reverting the privilege**

  Note that we revert the privilege immediately:

  ```
  PrivilegeManager.revertPrivilege("UniversalPropertyRead");
  ```

  This minimizes the time during which the applet is open to abuse.

- **Requesting permission to read a specific file**

  The second example is more complex:

  ```
  lilOlMe = PrivilegeManager.getMyPrincipals()[0];
  privMgr = PrivilegeManager.getPrivilegeManager();

  try
  {
     Target freadTgt = Target.findTarget("FileRead");
     privMgr.enablePrivilege(freadTgt , lilOlMe, (Object) filename);
     granted = true ;
  }
  catch(ForbiddenTargetException e)
  {
     ta.appendText("\nUser won't let me read " + filename);
  }
  ```

  In this case the privilege is not universal (*view any system property*) but specific (*read file X*). We therefore cannot just refer to the privilege target by name, but have to pass a netscape.security.Target object to enablePrivilege(). This could be a target that we created ourselves, or, as in this case, a target provided by the package. The file name is passed to enablePrivilege(). This version of the method also requires details of the applet signer, contained in a Principal object.

Now you are probably wondering why we requested access to read the local file but then did not do so. In fact we are going to need the file access later in the applet, in another thread.

Figure 188 on page 413 and Figure 189 on page 414 show the second half of the applet code, in which the FileRead privilege is used. This illustrates an oddity of the mechanism: the privilege manager grants privileges for the life of the applet, but the indicators are placed on the program stack, which is unique to each method and the methods it invokes. This means that you have to re-issue the enablePrivilege() request from the method where the privilege is actually exercised. However, as the privilege manager has kept track of what permissions have been granted, it will not ask the user again.

```java
public void run()
{
    // Did we get the permission we wanted?
    if (granted == true)
    {
        try
        {
            Target freadTgt = Target.findTarget("FileRead");
            privMgr.enablePrivilege(freadTgt , lilOlMe, (Object) filename);
            ta.appendText("\nThis is the content of file " + filename + ":\n"
                readTheFile(filename).toString());
        }
        catch(ForbiddenTargetException e)
        {
            ta.appendText("\nShould never reach here...");
        }
    }
}

private StringBuffer readTheFile(String filename)
{
    DataInputStream dis;
    String line;
    StringBuffer buf = new StringBuffer();
    FileInputStream theFile;

    try
    {
        theFile = new FileInputStream(filename);
        try
        {
            dis = new DataInputStream(new BufferedInputStream(theFile));
            while ((line = dis.readLine()) != null)
            {
                buf.append(line + "\n");
            }
        }
```

Figure 188. (Part 3 of 4). GetFileNS.java

```
                }
            }
        catch (IOException e)
        {
            System.out.println("IO Error:" + e.getMessage());
        }
        }
        catch (FileNotFoundException e)
        {
            System.out.println("File not found: " + filename);
        }

        return (buf);
    }
}
```

Figure 189. (Part 4 of 4). GetFileNS.java

Now we can make some comments on the second part of the applet:

- **Requesting the FileRead privilege again**

  Here is where we request again the privilege to read a specific file. As you can see, this time, we actually read the file:

```
try
{
    Target freadTgt = Target.findTarget("FileRead");
    privMgr.enablePrivilege(freadTgt , lilOlMe, (Object) filename);
    ta.appendText("\nThis is the content of file " + filename + ":\n" +
        readTheFile(filename).toString());
}
catch(ForbiddenTargetException e)
{
    ta.appendText("\nShould never reach here...");
}
```

- **The method that reads the data**

  The method readTheFile() is the one that reads the data. It is a general-purpose function, so we do not request privileges within it. If we did, an attack applet could invoke it using inter-applet communication and get privileges without a signature. It is also private, which protects the run() method from a similar attack.

  When you start to ease the restrictions in your browser you have to be aware that you may be opening yourself to attack. The applet itself is signed by someone you trust, based on the signature in the certificate, so it should not do anything dangerous directly. However, as we mentioned in the example above, another applet could get a free ride on the signature by using inter-applet communications to invoke methods that have had privileges granted to them. Such an attack can be launched only from an applet within the same context (that is, contained within the same document). This highlights an important point about signed applets: *the signature implies a trustworthy programmer, not a trustworthy site.*

How to Use Privileges with Care

The GetFileNS applet illustrates a number of techniques for reducing the risk of a second applet abusing your privileges. In summary the techniques are:

- Enable privileges for as short a time as possible.

- Place privileged accesses within private or protected methods.

- When creating general-purpose methods – like readTheFile() in the example – enable privileges in the calling code, not the method itself.

Further discussion can be found at http://developer.netscape.com/library/documentation/signedobj/capabilities.

12.4.1.1 Compiling the Applet Code

The full code of the GetFileNS applet can be obtained by concatenating the code shown in Figure 186 on page 410 through Figure 189 on page 414.

Before compiling an applet that imports the netscape.security package, you will need to copy the JAR file java40.jar in the extensions directory under the JRE development directory (see 8.1, "A Note on java.home and the JRE Installation Directory" on page 225). This way the Java compiler javac will be able to find the classes you imported. After doing this, the GetFileNS applet code can be compiled by entering:

```
javac GetFileNS.java
```

This command generates the class file GetFileNS.class.

12.4.2 Installing Keys and Certificates in Netscape Communicator

Now that we have written the code that will request and use special privileges, we need to install it in a signed JAR. But before we can generate a signature, we need a key pair and a certificate.

Public key signatures rely on a *web of trust*. That is, anyone receiving a signed message needs to have the certificates of CAs that establish the trustworthiness of the signer. This does not only apply to signed Java, of course. One of the most widespread uses of digital signatures is in the Secure Sockets Layer (SSL), a general-purpose protocol for encrypting Web data and authenticating the server and client (see Chapter 16, "Java and SSL" on page 629).

To get around the problem of establishing the web of trust needed by SSL, the browser manufacturers provide key databases containing *trusted roots* as part of the browser installation. This allows a browser to accept any signature that is supported by a certificate from one of the known CAs. But signed Java poses other problems:

1. If you are creating a signed JAR for general use, you can purchase a certificate from one of the well-known CAs. But if you are creating a local, intranet application with a limited web of trust, you need a way for the signer and the browser to install the local CA certificate as a trusted root.

2. As the signer of the code, you need the facility to generate a key pair and then acquire a certificate for your own public key and install it into your own key database.

Netscape has developed mechanisms to solve both of these problems. They are based on messages with special MIME types that trigger key management functions in the browser. The MIME types are:

- **application/x-x509-ca-cert**

  This message delivers a new CA certificate. When it is received, the browser pops up a dialog in which the user can check the details of the certificate before installing it as a trusted root (see Figure 191 on page 418).

- **application/x-x509-user-cert**

  This message delivers a new personal certificate. This does not make sense unless the browser has previously generated a key pair and provided distinguished name information to place in the certificate. Netscape uses a special HTML tag, <KEYGEN>, which causes the browser to generate the key pair. Figure 190 on page 417 shows how this works.

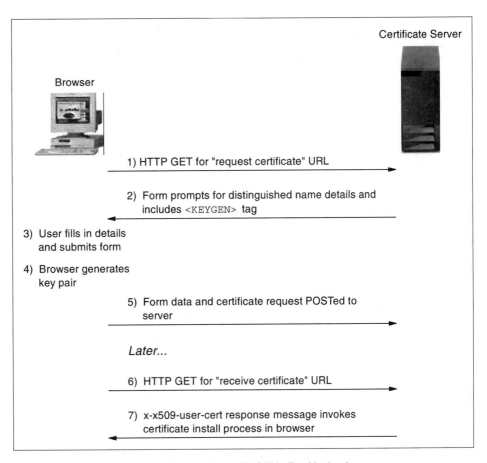

Figure 190. Requesting a Certificate – The <KEYGEN> Tag Mechanism

In our example we used the Netscape Certificate Server product to generate and install a new CA key and a personal key for code signing. Any suitable key management software could be used, as long as it supports the special MIME types and <KEYGEN> tag. The IBM Registry product has this capability.

In order to use the key pair for signing JAR files, it must be a X.509 V3 certificate with a special attribute set to indicate that it is suitable for code signing.

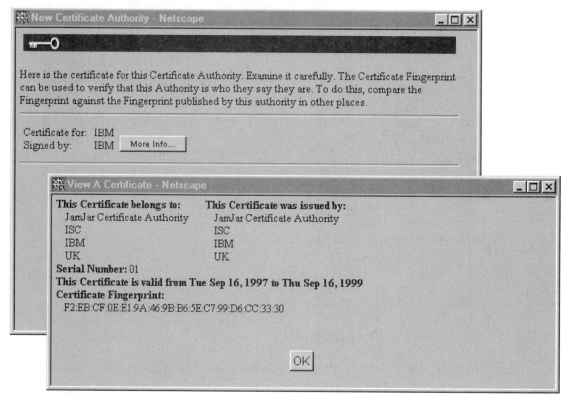

Figure 191. Receiving a New CA Certificate

12.4.3 Signing JAR Files with Netscape Signing Tool

Now everything is in place to store the applet in a JAR and to sign it. Netscape provides a command line utility called Netscape Signing Tool[7], which makes this operation easy to do and compatible with the standards used by Netscape.

Netscape Signing Tool replaces the older Netscape tools, Zigbert and JAR Packager, which are no longer supported. Netscape Signing Tool can be launched from the command prompt by entering the `signtool` command. This command has several options, and now we show you how to use it on a concrete example.

First of all, we create a signing certificate for ourselves using Netscape Signing Tool.

---

[7] Netscape Signing Tool can be downloaded from http://developer.netscape.com/software/signedobj/index.html. Documentation on this tool is available at http://developer.netscape.com/docs/manuals/signedobj/signtool/index.htm.

Before running this utility, it is necessary to set a password with which Communicator will protect your private key. The window to set this password can be accessed by clicking on the Netscape Security lock icon and selecting **Passwords** in the Security Info page. This will bring up a window where you will be prompted for entering the password twice, as shown in the following figure:

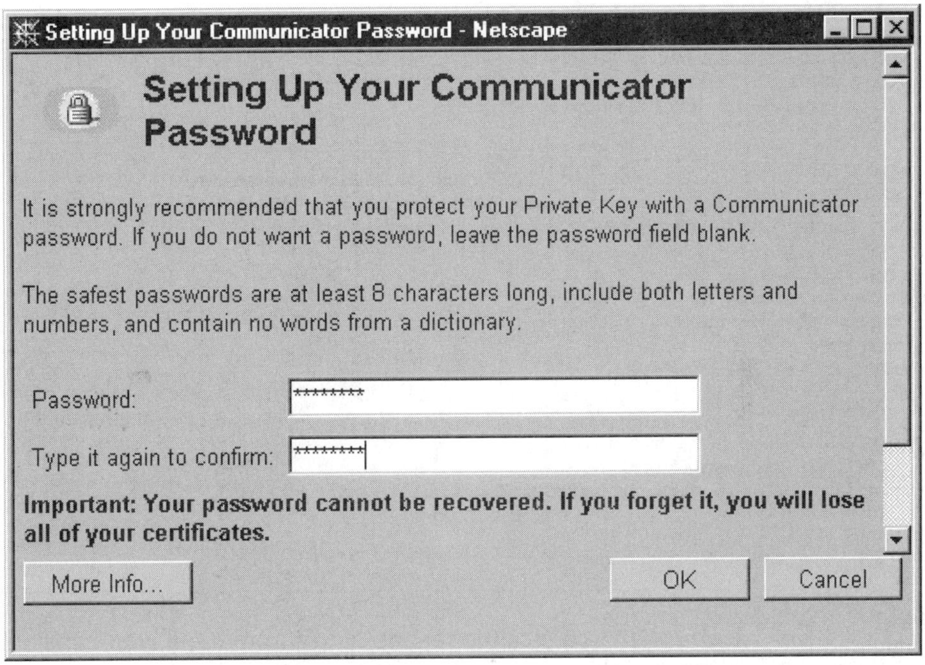

Figure 192. Setting up Your Communicator Password

A few precautions should be taken about the Netscape certificate database files cert7.db and key3.db. These are database files used by Netscape to store trusted certificates and user certificates respectively. They are located in the directory
C:\Program Files\Netscape\Users*user_name*, provided you followed the default installation of Netscape Communicator. Chances exist that these two files may get corrupted during the use of Netscape Signing Tool. Therefore, we recommend that you back them up before running the signtool command. Also note that you should close all the Netscape windows before launching Netscape Signing Tool, as there might be interactions with the database files and, again, they could get corrupted.

The signtool command has an option -G, which creates an object signing certificate with a specified alias. In our case, the alias we use is

PistoiaSignCert. When running this command, you also have to use the -d option, to specify the directory where the Netscape database files are located. An example of the full command is shown in the following session screen:

```
F:\itso\ch12>signtool -G "PistoiaSignCert" -d "D:\\Program Files\\Netscape\\Users\\pistoia"
using certificate directory: D:\\Program Files\\Netscape\\Users\\pistoia

WARNING: Performing this operation while Communicator is running could cause
corruption of your security databases. If Communicator is currently running,
you should exit Communicator before continuing this operation. Enter
"y" to continue, or anything else to abort: y


Enter certificate information.  All fields are optional. Acceptable
characters are numbers, letters, spaces, and apostrophes.
certificate common name: Marco Pistoia
organization: IBM Corporation
organization unit: ITSO
state or province: NC
country (must be exactly 2 characters): US
username: pistoia
email address: pistoia@us.ibm.com
Enter Password or Pin for "Communicator Certificate DB":
generated public/private key pair
certificate request generated
certificate has been signed
certificate "PistoiaSignCert" added to database
Exported certificate to x509.raw and x509.cacert.

F:\itso\ch12>dir
```

If you wish to check the results of this command, you can list the object signing certificates installed on your Netscape Communicator system by using the -l option of the signtool command, as shown next:

```
F:\itso\ch12>signtool -l -d "D:\\Program Files\\Netscape\\Users\\pistoia"
using certificate directory: D:\\Program Files\\Netscape\\Users\\pistoia

Object signing certificates
---------------------------------------
PistoiaSignCert
    Issued by: PistoiaSignCert (Marco Pistoia)
    Expires: Thu Aug 05, 1999
---------------------------------------
For a list including CA's, use "signtool -L"

F:\itso\ch12>
```

Another possibility is for you to use the -L option, and see the certificates of all the CAs installed on your Netscape Communicator system. In particular, all the certificates that can be used to sign objects will be marked with an asterisk (*). In our example, only the certificate with alias PistoiaSignCert, which we have just created, is enabled to sign objects. This is shown in the following session screen:

```
F:\itso\ch12>signtool -L -d "D:\\Program Files\\Netscape\\Users\\pistoia"
using certificate directory: D:\\Program Files\\Netscape\\Users\\pistoia

S Certificates
- ------------
  Thawte Personal Premium CA
  Verisign/RSA Commercial CA
  TC TrustCenter, Germany, Class 2 CA
  BelSign Secure Server CA
  American Express Global CA
  Equifax Premium CA
  TC TrustCenter, Germany, Class 3 CA
  Thawte Personal Freemail CA
  Thawte Server CA
  VeriSign Class 3 Primary CA
  VeriSign Class 4 Primary CA
  GTE CyberTrust Root 5
  GTE CyberTrust Japan Root CA
  GlobalSign Class 1 CA
  GlobalSign Partners CA
  TC TrustCenter, Germany, Class 0 CA
  TC TrustCenter, Germany, Class 4 CA
  Verisign/RSA Secure Server CA
  VeriSign Class 1 Primary CA
  GTE CyberTrust Root CA
  GTE CyberTrust Root 4
  Thawte Personal Basic CA
  American Express CA
  BelSign Object Publishing CA
  VeriSign Class 2 Primary CA
  GTE CyberTrust Root 2
  TC TrustCenter, Germany, Class 1 CA
  Thawte Premium Server CA
* PistoiaSignCert
  Equifax Secure CA
  GTE CyberTrust Global Root
  GTE CyberTrust Root 3
  GTE CyberTrust Japan Secure Server CA
- ------------
Certificates that can be used to sign objects have *'s to their left.

F:\itso\ch12>
```

Netscape Communicator immediately reflects the presence of the new object signing certificate that has been added. This can be verified in the following way:

1. Open Netscape Communicator, and click on the Security lock icon on the tool bar. In the Certificates menu of the Security Info page, click on **Yours**.

The certificate you have just created will appear as one of your personal certificates, as shown in Figure 193:

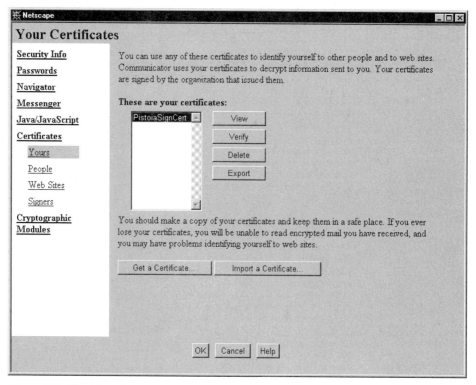

Figure 193. User Certificates on Netscape Communicator after Using Netscape Signing Tool

You can use this certificate to identify yourself to other entities and also to decrypt information that is sent to you.

2. Highlight the certificate you have just created, as shown in Figure 193, and then click on **View**. All the details about the certificate will be displayed, and you will see that they reflect what you entered with the Netscape Signing Tool:

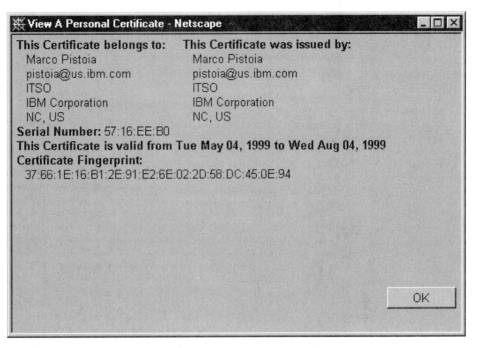

Figure 194. User's Certificate Generated by the Netscape Signing Tool

Click **OK** in the window above.

3. In the Certificates menu of the Security Info page, this time click on **Signers**. The certificate you have just created will appear as one of the CA certificates installed, as shown in the following figure:

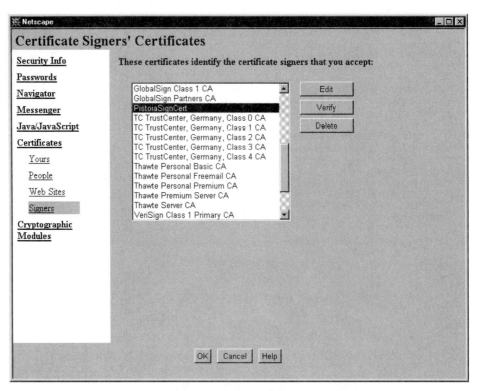

Figure 195. Trusted Roots on Netscape Communicator after Using Netscape Signing Tool

4. Highlight the CA certificate you have just created, as shown in Figure 195, and then click on **Edit**. All the details about the certificate will be displayed, and you will see that they reflect what you entered with the Netscape Signing Tool:

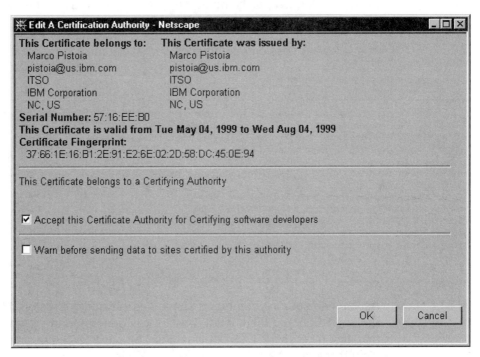

Figure 196. Signer's Certificate Generated with Netscape Signing Tool

The next step is to produce a signed JAR file from the class file GetFileNS.class, produced in 12.4.1.1, "Compiling the Applet Code" on page 415. In Java 2 SDK, Standard Edition, V1.2, we use the `jar` tool to produce the JAR file, and the `jarsigner` utility to sign it. On the Netscape Communicator platform, you can do this with one single command line by using Netscape Signing Tool.

Netscape Signing Tool works with directory trees. So we need to create a specific directory where we put the class file we want to package and sign. Our working directory in this scenario is F:\itso\ch12. We create a subdirectory called NSsign under our working directory. In NSsign, we copy the class file GetFileNS.class. The path to the directory NSsign must be specified on the `signtool` command line.

In addition, we will have to use:

- The `-d` flag to specify the location of the Netscape certificate database files (in our case, D:\Program Files\Netscape\Users\pistoia)

- The `-k` flag to specify the alias of the signer whose key we want the JAR file to be signed by (in this example, PistoiaSignCert)

- The -z flag to specify the name of the signed JAR file (in this example, we choose to use the name GetFileNS_sign.jar).

The following session screen shows what the full command and its output look like:

```
F:\itso\ch12>signtool -d "D:\\Program Files\\Netscape\\Users\\pistoia" -k PistoiaSignCert
-Z GetFileNS_sign.jar NSsign
using certificate directory: D:\\Program Files\\Netscape\\Users\\pistoia
Generating NSsign/META-INF/manifest.mf file..
--> GetFileNS.class
adding NSsign/GetFileNS.class to GetFileNS_sign.jar...(deflated 46%)
Generating zigbert.sf file..
Enter Password or Pin for "Communicator Certificate DB":
adding NSsign/META-INF/manifest.mf to GetFileNS_sign.jar...(deflated 14%)
adding NSsign/META-INF/zigbert.sf to GetFileNS_sign.jar...(deflated 27%)
adding NSsign/META-INF/zigbert.rsa to GetFileNS_sign.jar...(deflated 43%)
tree "NSsign" signed successfully

F:\itso\ch12>
```

As you can see, the command above has created a directory META-INF under NSsign and then, in META-INF, has generated the manifest file manifest.mf (see 12.1.1, "Manifest File" on page 387), the signature block file zigbert.rsa (see 12.1.3, "Signature Block File" on page 392) and the signature file zigbert.sf (see 12.1.2, "Signature File" on page 392). Then all these files, plus the class file GetFileNS.class, have become part of the GetFileNS_sign.jar JAR archive, which is stored in the working directory F:\itso\ch12.

It is interesting to look at the three files generated by the command above:

1. The contents of the manifest.mf file are shown in the following screen:

```
Manifest-Version: 1.0
Created-By: Signtool (signtool 1.1)
Comments: PLEASE DO NOT EDIT THIS FILE. YOU WILL BREAK IT.

Name: GetFileNS.class
Digest-Algorithms: MD5 SHA1
MD5-Digest: 63pNwecdstHKXrJzZDq2Qw==
SHA1-Digest: nXl/EjnqRYoqB/uuS3NpQnLrqrA=
```

2. The following figure shows the signature block file opened with a text editor:

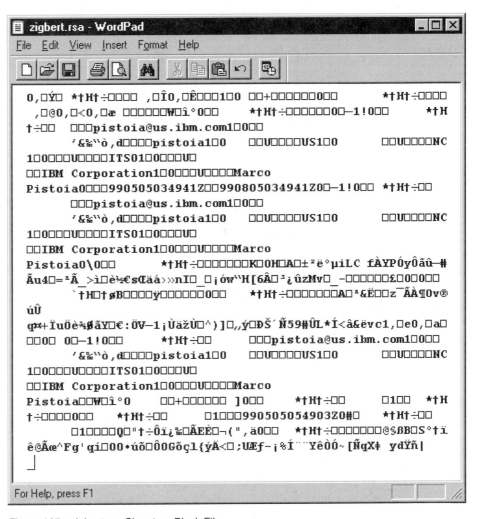

Figure 197. zigbert.rsa Signature Block File

3. These are the contents of the signature file zigbert.sf:

```
Signature-Version: 1.0
Created-By: Signtool (signtool 1.1)
Comments: PLEASE DO NOT EDIT THIS FILE. YOU WILL BREAK IT.
Digest-Algorithms: MD5 SHA1
MD5-Digest: eJVyFB+9CfJ/Nq3pbjx13w==
SHA1-Digest: Xk/TCdWyhWx4oLwUWUqYZneXn6A=

Name: GetFileNS.class
Digest-Algorithms: MD5 SHA1
MD5-Digest: pCKJNzo9Shf2aigBJZR/yA==
SHA1-Digest: bFHtqrC297IrCiSZpsz2ttCjpE0=
```

At this point, you might want to use the -v option of the signtool command.
This option displays the contents of an archive and verifies the cryptographic
integrity of the digital signatures it contains and the files with which they are
associated. This includes checking that the certificate for the issuer of the
object-signing certificate is listed in the certificate database, that the CA's
digital signature on the object-signing certificate is valid and that the relevant
certificates have not expired. The following session screen shows the
verification of our signed JAR file:

```
F:\\itso\ch12>signtool -v GetFileNS_sign.jar -d "D:\\Program Files\\Netscape\\Users\\pistoia"
using certificate directory: D:\\Program Files\\Netscape\\Users\\pistoia
archive "GetFileNS_sign.jar" has passed crypto verification.

        status      path
    ------------    ------------------
      verified     GetFileNS.class

F:\itso\ch12>
```

The final step is to access the signed applet from the Netscape
Communicator Web browser. We copy the signed JAR file GetFileNS_sign.jar
in the home directory of a Web server machine, and in the same directory we
save the following HTML file, called GetFileNS.html, from which the applet is
invoked:

```
<HTML>

    <HEAD>
        <TITLE>GetFileNS Applet</TITLE>
    </HEAD>
```

Figure 198. (Part 1 of 2). GetFileNS.html

```
<BODY>

    <H3>GetFileNS Applet</H3>

    <APPLET Archive="GetFileNS_sign.jar" Code="GetFileNS.class" Width=500 Height=500>
        <PARAM Name="FileToTry" Value="F:\itso\textFile\secret.txt">
    </APPLET>

</BODY>
</HTML>
```

Figure 199. (Part 2 of 2). GetFileNS.html

As you can see, the HTML file sets the value for the variable FileToTry to the file name F:\itso\textFile\secret.txt. This file is stored in the local file system of the Web browser machine, and is the file that the applet attempts to read. Its contents are shown in the following figure:

```
My Credit Card number is
1234 5678 9012
This information is secret.
Only trusted entities should read it.
```

Figure 200. secret.txt

Finally, we can access the HTML page GetFileNS.html from the Netscape Communicator Web browser machine where we have previously generated and installed the certificate. When we point the Web browser to the URL of the GetFileNS.html file, the browser recognizes the presence of the <APPLET> tag and immediately activates Java. At that point, the following window is brought up:

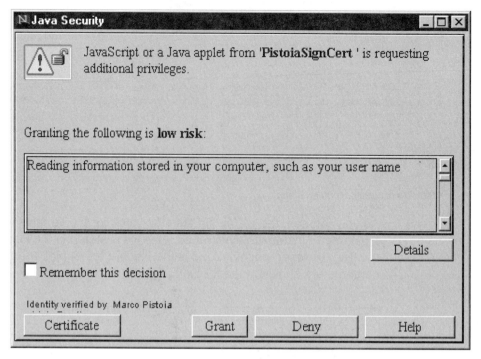

Figure 201. Java Security Warning – Low Risk

As you can see, Netscape Communicator informs us that the applet is attempting to execute a sensitive action, which is marked as a low-risk access. If we want to know something more about the additional privilege requested by the applet, we can click on **Details**, and the following window will be displayed:

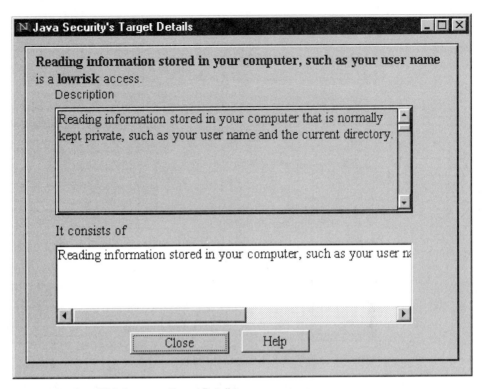

Figure 202. Low Risk Access – Target Details

Now we know that the applet is trying to read private information related to the computer environment, such as the user name or the current directory. In reality, if we go back and read the source code for the GetFileNS applet, shown in Figure 186 on page 410 through Figure 189 on page 414, we see that the information the applet attempts to read first is the operating system name of the Web browser machine.

We click on **Close** on the above window and then, before granting the additional privilege to the applet, we click on **Certificate** in the Java Security window shown in Figure 201 on page 430, to find out something more about the entity that signed the applet. The following Certificate window is displayed:

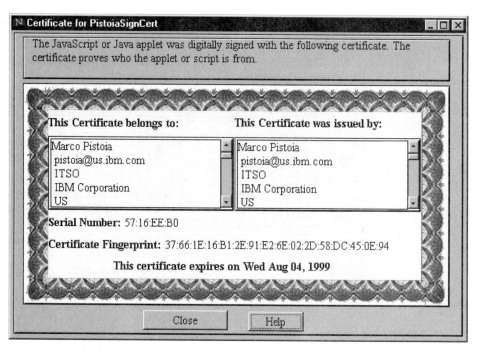

Figure 203. Certificate Information Window

We decide to trust this entity, so we click on **Close** in the window above, and then we press **Grant** in the Java Security window, shown in Figure 201 on page 430.

However, this is not enough to allow the applet to run on Netscape Communicator. In fact, according to the source code of the applet, there is another sensitive action that the applet attempts to do now: to read a specific file from the local file system of the Web browser machine. For this reason, a new Java Security warning window is brought up:

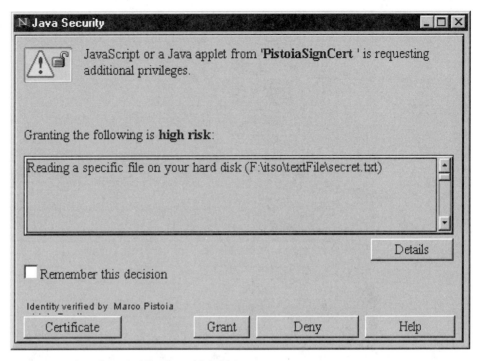

Figure 204. Java Security Warning – High Risk

As you can see, Netscape Communicator informs us about the specific action the applet is attempting to do and we can also know which file the applet will read if we grant it the additional privilege it requests. This time the sensitive action is classified as a high-risk access. In fact Netscape Communicator categorizes privileges by the damage they could do to your system. We can click on **Details** to know something more about a high-risk access:

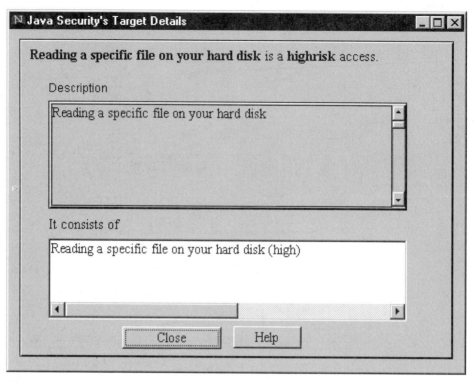

Figure 205. High-Rsk Access – Target Details

The applet has already asked permission to read one of the system properties: the operating system name of the Web browser machine. That information can be considered private, but sharing it with an entity on the network is not really a security exposure. This is the reason why that action was classified as a low-risk access. Things are different now; reading a file from the local file system can be dangerous. The applet can communicate that information back to the Web server machine, and sensitive data could get into the wrong hands. However, we trust the entity that signed the applet, and after closing the above window, we click on **Grant** in the Java Security warning window shown in Figure 204 on page 433. Notice that clicking on **Certificate** would show the same certificate information seen in Figure 203 on page 432.

At this point, the applet can access the system property information and can read the file secret.txt from our local file system. These are the results displayed in the HTML page:

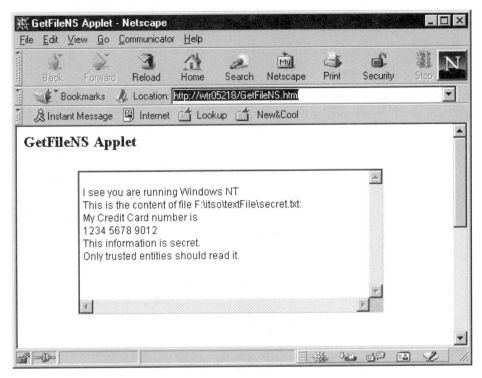

Figure 206. GetFileNS Applet Running on Netscape Communicator

The additional privileges we have granted to the code signer are valid only for the current session of the Web browser. If we had wanted to grant the same privileges on a permanent basis, we should have selected the **Remember this decision** check box in Figure 201 on page 430 and Figure 204 on page 433. If we had wanted to deny the same permissions, we should have pressed the **Deny** button, and in that case, clicking **Remember this decision** would have denied those permissions persistently.

These configuration settings can be edited very easily, and you can modify a decision you made. To do this, you should click on the Security lock icon in the Netscape Communicator tool bar, and then, in the menu on the left, you should select **Java/JavaScript**. A list of all the signers to which additional privileges have been granted will appear, as shown in the following figure:

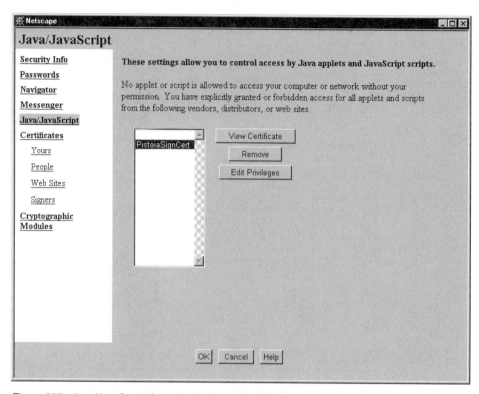

Figure 207. Java/JavaScript Security Configuration Window

Here, you can select the particular signer to which you have granted additional privileges, and then you can view the certificate, remove it from the list or edit the privileges you have granted to it. Clicking on **Edit Privileges**, you can review the privileges you have granted and modify them, if you wish to do so:

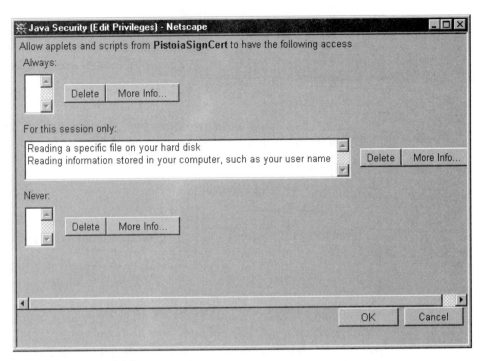

Figure 208. Editing Privileges

As you can see, the particular privileges we granted apply only to the current session of Netscape Communicator. You can use this window to remove any of the privileges you granted before.

12.5 Signed Code Scenario in Microsoft Internet Explorer

Externally, the most distinctive thing about the Microsoft approach is that it uses *cabinets* (particular files with extension .cab, also known as CAB files) to contain the applets and other data, instead of JAR files. This is not to say that Internet Explorer will not handle JAR archives, but it does not deal with signed JAR files in any special way.

CABs are also used for packaging the installation images of other Microsoft software. And, just as Netscape is using signed JAR files to deliver many types of Web content, CAB files are used by Microsoft to install ActiveX controls and other platform-specific code.

The Internet Explorer security model is built around *security zones*. These are groupings of applet sources, based on URLs. By default, four zones are defined:

- **Intranet**

    This security zone contains Web sites that are within the local, secure network or are only accessed via SSL connections. Sites in this category may be defined by URL or by other attribute, for example, sites that are not reached through a proxy server.

- **Trusted sites**

    A list of sites that are trustworthy, but which don't quite give the same level of reassurance that the intranet sites do.

- **Internet**

    The great mass of Web sites.

- **Restricted sites**

    Sites that you have reason to believe are actually dangerous.

Each of these zones has a *security level* associated with it of low, medium, high or custom. These apply to all sorts of Web elements, such as ActiveX controls, cookies, and user IDs as well as Java. The first three are related to a very specific set of permissions. The high security level is equivalent to the sandbox restrictions. The medium level adds the ability for an applet to use a scratchpad directory on the browser disk for storing and retrieving persistent data. The low level allows an applet unrestricted access. The custom level allows you (or an administrator) to set specific controls for different types of Web content.

Of course, a protection scheme based solely on URLs and IP addresses would be very risky. To be effective, the security model requires Java code to be delivered in signed CABs. Functionally, a signed CAB is like a signed JAR with one, important, exception: in addition to identifying the originator of the code, the signature on a CAB *also defines the permissions that the code is requesting*. These permissions are defined when the CAB file itself is being signed. You have to mention whether you are requesting high, medium, or low permissions. Note that an applet signed with low permission value is requesting for all permissions. So we should be careful when we grant such an applet the privileges it requires.

12.5.1 First Example with Signed CAB Files

The best way to understand how to use CAB files is to illustrate it with an example. To develop this example, we make use of the Microsoft Software Development Kit (SDK) for Java V3.2[8]. By default, this product gets installed in the directory C:\Program Files\Microsoft SDK for Java 3.2. To simplify the

---

[8] The Microsoft SDK for Java can be downloaded from http://www.microsoft.com/java/download.htm.

use of this product, it is important to set the Path system environment variable to include the directory Bin under the installation directory.

Here we use the App applet that we developed in 11.5, "Java Plug-In Security Scenario" on page 374. The App applet uses basic Java I/O stream classes and will therefore normally fail with a security exception. We show you here how that applet can receive additional privileges and run on Microsoft Internet Explorer.

The applet class file must be put into a signed CAB file. This operation involves three steps.

12.5.1.1 Step 1 – Creating a Signing Certificate

The Microsoft SDK for Java provides a command line tool, makecert, for generating a software developer certificate. An example of how to use it is shown in the following session screen:

```
D:\deepak\IE>makecert -sk deepakkey -n "CN=Deepak Gupta" Deepak.cert
Succeeded

D:\deepak\IE>
```

The command above generates a key pair called deepakkey and places it in the Windows registry under HKEY_Current_User/Software/Microsoft/Cryptography/UserKeys. It also creates a certificate request file, using the public key and the distinguished name information from the command.

Normally, the next step would be to send this to a CA for authentication and signing.[9] However, in our case we are only signing the applet for test purposes, so we can use another tool from the SDK, cert2spc, to convert the certificate request file into a test certificate:

```
D:\deepak\IE>cert2spc Deepak.cert Deepak.crt
Succeeded

D:\deepak\IE>
```

12.5.1.2 Step 2 – Creating and Signing the CAB File

CAB files are potentially much more complex than JAR archives, but for our purposes we can create a simple CAB using the cabarc tool:

[9] Internet Explorer defines just one root CA, the Microsoft Authenticode Root CA, for software signing, but there is a technique to update the list, using ActiveX controls.

```
D:\deepak\IE>cabarc N App.cab App.class

Microsoft (R) Cabinet Tool - Version 1.00.602.2 (08/14/97)
Copyright (c) Microsoft Corp 1994-1997. All rights reserved.

Creating new cabinet 'App.cab' with compression 'MSZIP':
  -- adding App.class

Completed successfully

D:\deepak\IE>
```

This creates a CAB file called App.cab with just one file, our applet, in it. To sign this as a Java archive we use the `signcode` tool, again from Microsoft SDK for Java. At this point we must decide what level of security the applet will ask for – low, medium or high. Since this applet is going to read a file from the local file system, which can be a sensitive operation, we sign it specifying a low level of security for now:

```
D:\deepak\IE>signcode -j JavaSign.dll -jp low -spc Deepak.crt -k deepakkey App.cab
Warning: This file is signed, but not timestamped.
Succeeded

D:\deepak\IE>
```

This means that this applet will request a lot of additional privileges, some of which may not really be needed. We will see in 12.5.1.4, "Permission INI Files" on page 446 how to limit the requests of additional privileges based on what is really necessary.

When the applet is downloaded to an Internet Explorer Web browser machine, it will pop up a message box, informing the user that the applet has requested all permissions.

12.5.1.3 Step 3 – Using the CAB File in a Web Page
The format for coding an `<APPLET>` tag using a CAB file is different from the JAR version. This is the tag for our example:

```
<APPLET CODE=App.class  WIDTH=100 HEIGHT=20>
   <PARAM NAME="cabbase" VALUE="App.cab">
</APPLET>
```

For the rest, the Web page will be very similar to the one shown in Figure 173 on page 374.

When we first select the URL for the HTML page from Internet Explorer, the following pop-up dialog appears:

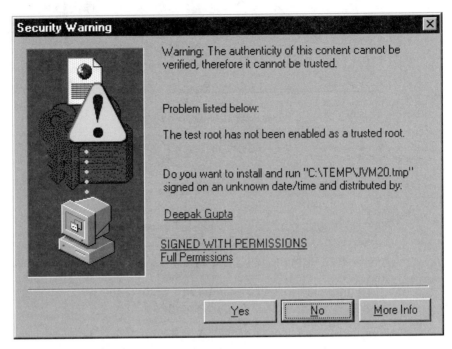

Figure 209. Security Warning – Full Permissions

Why does this appear? The reason is that Internet Explorer is warning the user that the signer Deepak Gupta may not be trustworthy, because it does not own a valid software developer's certificate. Note here that the browser is informing the user that the applet is requesting full permissions. Throwing caution to the winds, we click on **Yes** and the applet runs as intended:

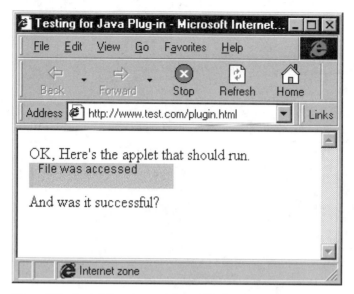

Figure 210. Applet Running on Internet Explorer

If we had signed with medium permissions, the Security Warning window would have been like the following one:

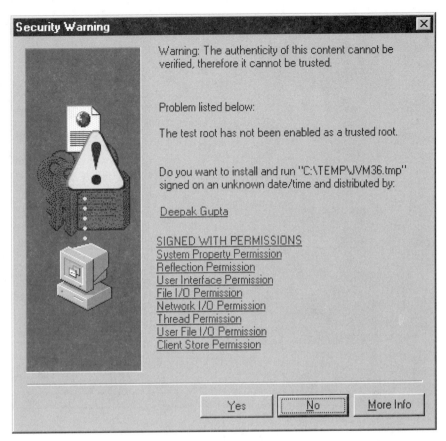

Figure 211. Security Warning – Medium Permissions

And for a high-permission signed CAB file, the Security Warning window would be:

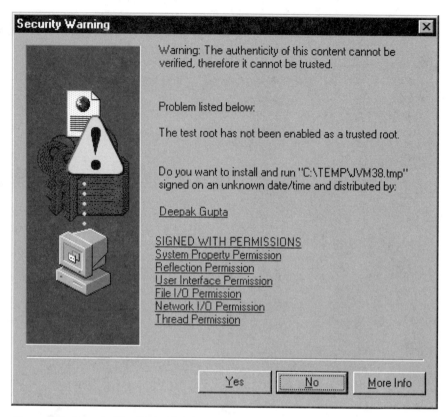

Figure 212. Security Warning – High Permissions

The difference is only in what permissions the applet is requesting. You can click on these permissions and see the details, and then decide on whether you wish to grant them or not.

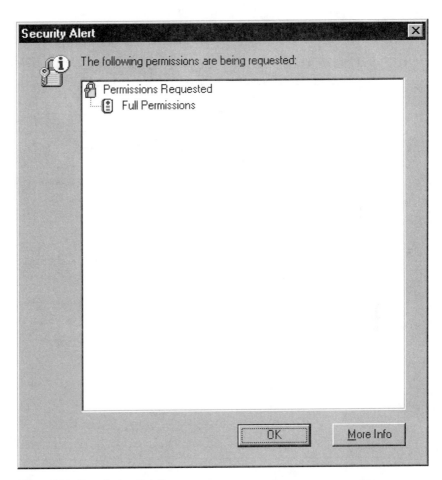

Figure 213. Permission Details

You will see a different set of permissions for applets signed with a high or medium permission request. Depending upon what your applet tries to do on the client machine, you should sign accordingly. You can also view the certificate of the signer by clicking on the distinguished name of the signer.

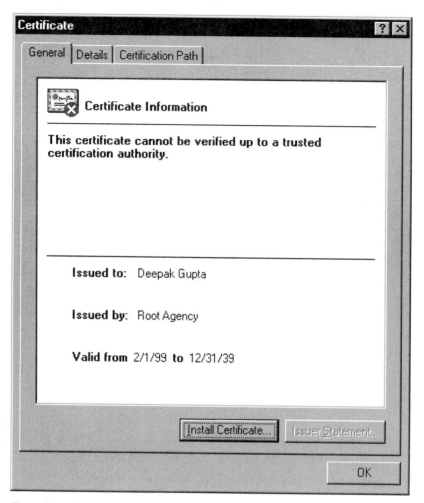

Figure 214. Certificate Information

Notice that, in this example, although the applet needed only a
FilePermission, we signed it with a low security tag, granting it full
permissions. This was done for ease of explanation only.

12.5.1.4 Permission INI Files

Microsoft SDK for Java also provides the ability to sign only with the particular
permissions requested, using a permission INI file, which is a textual security
configuration file. In this case, the signing command is the following:

```
D:\deepak\IE>signcode -j JavaSign.dll -jp App.ini -spc Deepak.crt -k deepakkey App.cab
Warning: This file is signed, but not timestamped.
Succeeded

D:\deepak\IE>
```

Notice that our input INI file is named App.ini. Here is what it looks like:

```
[com.ms.security.permissions.FileIOPermission]
IncludeRead=;D:\\deepak\\itso.txt
ExcludeRead=
IncludeWrite=
ExcludeWrite=
IncludeDelete=
ExcludeDelete=
ReadFileURLCodebase=false
```

Figure 215. App.ini

As you can see, the INI file technique allows us to select only the specific permission the applet really needs: in this case, read permission to the file D:\deepak\itso.txt. The security warning appears in the following figure:

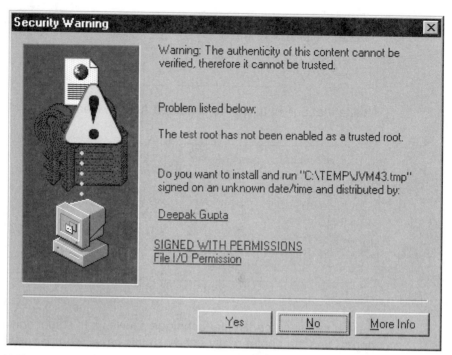

Figure 216. Warning from IE for Only Specified Permission

Clicking the highlighted permission, the user can view details about the applet request: the applet is attempting to read the file D:\deepak\itso.txt.

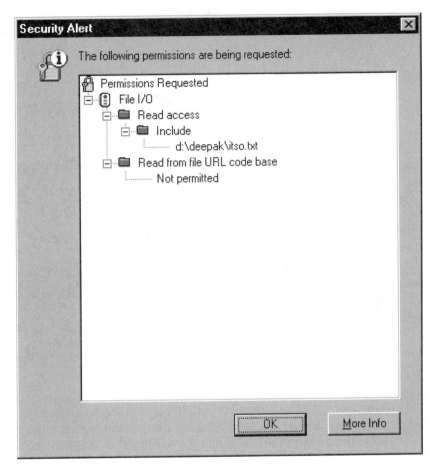

Figure 217. Permissions Requested by the Applet

If we grant this permission and then run the applet, we get the same window as the one shown in Figure 210 on page 442.

The syntax of the INI file can be very complicated, and does not allow mistakes. You can also use the GUI-based Permission INI File Editor to edit an INI file. It is simpler than manually editing an INI file and you do not need to worry about the syntax. Figure 218 on page 450 shows the Permission INI File Editor window:

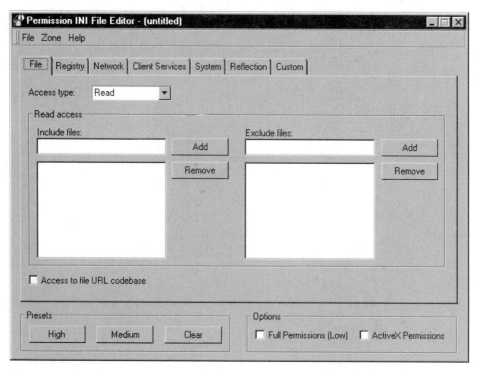

Figure 218. Permission INI File Editor Window

This tool, which is launched from the command line with the `PIniEdit`
command, allows you to choose the permission type and the access type you
want the applet to request, and the tool itself will create the file for you.

12.5.2 A More Complex Signed CAB File Example

In addition to creating a method for delivering signed applets and requesting
permissions, Microsoft has also produced classes that allow an applet to
store and recover data from a limited disk cache on the browser. The
rationale behind this is that for many developers the really irksome restriction
imposed by the sandbox is the inability to store local configuration and state
information. The data caching function is in a class package called
com.ms.io.clientstorage.

12.5.2.1 The Applet Source Code

The code in Figure 219 on page 451 and Figure 220 on page 452 is an
example of an applet, GetFileMS, that uses the package to write information
into a file and then read it:

```
import java.awt.*;
import java.io.*;
import java.util.* ;
import com.ms.io.clientstorage.*;

public class GetFileMS extends java.applet.Applet implements Runnable
{
   Thread t;
   TextArea ta = new TextArea("", 10, 50);
   public boolean granted = false;

   public void init()
   {
      add(ta);

      // Start the thread running
      if (t == null)
      {
         t = new Thread(this);
         t.start();
      }
   }

   public void yikes(Exception e, String msg)
   {
      ta.appendText(msg + ": " + e.toString());
      System.exit(1);
   }

   public void run() {
   String line;
   ClientStore harrods;

      try
      {
         harrods = ClientStorageManager.getStore();
         PrintWriter pw = new PrintWriter(harrods.openWritable("preserve.log",
            ClientStore.OPEN_FL_APPEND));
         pw.println("JamJar was here! " + new Date().toString());
         pw.close() ;
      }
      catch (IOException e)
      {
```

Figure 219. (Part 1 of 2). GetFileMS.java

```
        yikes(e, "Could not create or update our file");
    }

    try
    {
        harrods = ClientStorageManager.getStore();
        BufferedReader br = new BufferedReader(new
            InputStreamReader(harrods.openReadable("preserve.log")));
        ta.appendText("This is the contents of clientstore file preserve.log:\n");
        while ((line = br.readLine()) != null)
        {
            ta.appendText(line + "\n");
        }
        br.close() ;
    }
    catch (IOException e)
    {
        yikes(e, "Could not read our file");
    }
    }
}
}
```

Figure 220. (Part 2 of 2). GetFileMS.java

Let's now look more closely at the operations the applet performs:

- **Import the com.ms.io.clientstorage package**

  This is done with the following line of code:

  ```
  import com.ms.io.clientstorage;
  ```

- **Get access to the client store**

  This is obtained by calling the getStore() method for the
  ClientStorageManager class:

  ```
  harrods = ClientStorageManager.getStore();
  ```

- **Open a file in the client store and update it**

  This operation is obtained with the following instruction:

  ```
  PrintWriter pw = new PrintWriter(harrods.openWritable("preserve.log",
      ClientStore.OPEN_FL_APPEND));
  ```

Notice that the store is persistent, so we can read it later, but the maximum
size of the store allocated to a given code signer is fixed, so the applet cannot
fill the hard disk.

12.5.2.2 Compiling the Applet

Compiling the GetFileMS applet is not different from compiling every other Java program. You simply have to enter:

```
javac GetFileMS.java
```

However, this applet imports the package com.ms.io.clientstorage, which is not part of the standard Java 2 SDK libraries. For this reason, the command above generates an error unless you, before compiling, copy a JAR file containing that package into the extensions directory under the JRE development directory (see 8.1, "A Note on java.home and the JRE Installation Directory" on page 225).

After the default installation of Microsoft Internet Explorer V5, we found a ZIP file, Ff7h75v3.zip, located in the directory C:\WINNT\Java\Packages. This file contained the package needed by our applet. In previous installations of Internet Explorer, another ZIP file contained that package. It was called classes.zip, and came into the directory C:\WINNT\Java\Classes. Whatever version of Internet Explorer you have installed on your system, you should take the corresponding ZIP file and copy it in the extensions directory under the JRE development directory. Notice that the installed extensions must be JAR files. However, it is not necessary to extract the ZIP file and then use the `jar` utility to produce a JAR file. In fact, since the JAR format is based on the ZIP format, a JAR file is obtained by simply changing the extension of the Microsoft Java library file from .zip to .jar, and the system will recognize the class files inside it without any problems.

12.5.2.3 Placing the Applet Class File in a Signed CAB file

The procedure to place a Java class file in a signed CAB file has already been explained in 12.5.1, "First Example with Signed CAB Files" on page 438. We list here the operations involved and the related session screens:

1. We create a key pair, marcokey, and a certificate request file, Marco.cert, with X.500 distinguished name Marco Pistoia:

```
D:\itso\ch12>makecert -sk marcokey -n "CN=Marco Pistoia" Marco.cert
Succeeded

D:\itso\ch12>
```

2. We convert the certificate request file into a test certificate, stored in the file Marco.crt:

```
D:\itso\ch12>cert2spc Marco.cert Marco.crt
Succeeded

D:\itso\ch12>
```

3. We create a CAB file, GetFileMS.cab, containing the class file
   GetFileMS.class:

```
D:\itso\ch12>cabarc N GetFileMS.cab GetFileMS.class

Microsoft (R) Cabinet Tool - Version 1.00.602.2 (08/14/97)
Copyright (c) Microsoft Corp 1994-1997. All rights reserved.

Creating new cabinet 'GetFileMS.cab' with compression 'MSZIP':
  -- adding GetFileMS.class

Completed successfully

D:\itso\ch12>
```

4. We sign the CAB file with the private key of the signer Marco Pistoia, and
   we assign level of security medium:

```
D:\itso\ch12>signcode -j JavaSign.dll -jp medium -spc Marco.crt -k marcokey GetFileMS.cab
Warning: This file is signed, but not timestamped.
Succeeded

D:\itso\ch12>
```

Next, we save the signed CAB file in an accessible directory of a Web server
machine.

12.5.2.4 Accessing the Applet with Microsoft Internet Explorer

The signed CAB file GetFileMS.cab can be accessed from the Internet
provided it is invoked by an HTML page. GetFileMS.html is a simple HTML file
that invokes the applet:

```
<HTML>

   <HEAD>
      <TITLE>GetFileMS Applet</TITLE>
   </HEAD>
```

Figure 221. (Part 1 of 2). GetFileMS.html

```
    <BODY>

        <H3>GetFileMS Applet</H3>

        <APPLET Code="GetFileMS.class" Width=500 Height=500>
            <PARAM Name="cabbase" Value="GetFileMS.cab">
        </APPLET>

    </BODY>
</HTML>
```

Figure 222. (Part 2 of 2). GetFileMS.html

If you compare Figure 222 with Figure 199 on page 429, you will notice that the <APPLET> tag has a different syntax when it is targeted to Microsoft Internet Explorer.

When the user invokes the HTML page and the applet gets loaded, it requests many permissions that, in fact, it does not need:

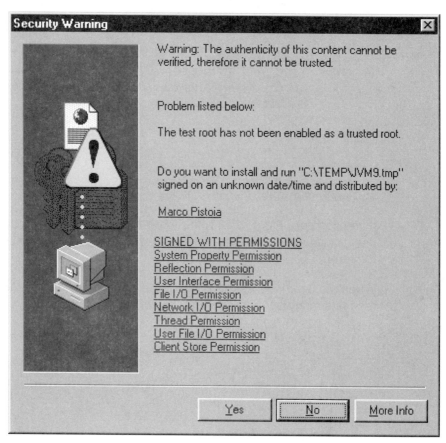

Figure 223. Medium Level of Security for the GetFileMS Applet

This is because we specified a security level of medium in the `signcode` command (see Step 4 on page 454). It would be friendlier to ask for only the permissions needed.

The way to do this is to create a permission INI file (see 12.5.1.4, "Permission INI Files" on page 446). This file must specify the requested permissions. Once we build an appropriate INI file, we pass it to the `signcode` command. The INI file for this applet, JamJar.ini, is shown in the following figure:

```
[com.ms.security.permissions.UIPermission]
Version=2
ClipboardAccess=false
```

Figure 224. (Part 1 of 2). JamJar.ini

```
TopLevelWindows=true
NoWarningBanners=false
FileDialogs=false
EventQueueAccess=false

[com.ms.security.permissions.ClientStoragePermission]
Version=2
Limit=1048576
RoamingFiles=false
GlobalExempt=false

[com.ms.security.permissions.ThreadPermission]
Version=2
AllThreadGroups=false
AllThreads=false
```

Figure 225. (Part 2 of 2). JamJar.ini

As you can see, the JamJar.ini permission INI file does not look very simple. However, it is not necessary to edit it manually. As we said in 12.5.1.4, "Permission INI Files" on page 446, it is possible to use the Permission INI File Editor tool that comes with Microsoft SDK for Java. The permission INI file above is generated by saving to a file JamJar.ini the security configuration represented in the following figure:

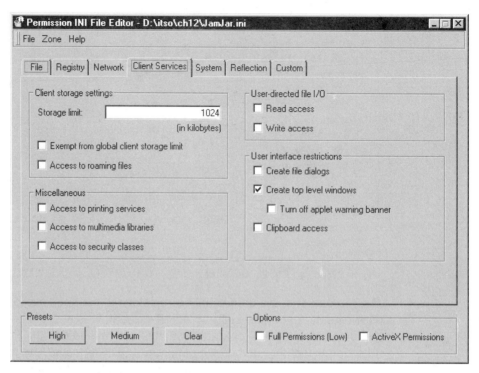

Figure 226. Permission INI File Editor for JamJar.ini

As you can see, we just select a limit of 1024 kilobytes for the client store, so that, as we said, an applet cannot fill the hard disk, and also we give the applet the permission to create top level windows. These two permissions are the lower set of privileges that the GetFileMS applet requires, as you can easily verify by excluding either of them and noticing that the applet is no longer allowed to run correctly.

Once the JamJar.ini file has been generated, it must be passed on the command line of the `signcode` command when the GetFileMS applet class is signed:

```
D:\itso\ch12>signcode -j JavaSign.dll -jp JamJar.ini -spc Marco.crt -k marcokey GetFileMS.cab
Warning: This file is signed, but not timestamped.
Succeeded

D:\itso\ch12>
```

This way, we have demonstrated how the applet developer can sign an applet CAB file targeted to an Internet Explorer platform using a customized security classification, without necessarily using the strict categorization of high, medium and low security.

Now, when the applet gets loaded in the HTML page, a Security Warning window is still displayed, asking the user to grant additional privileges to the applet:

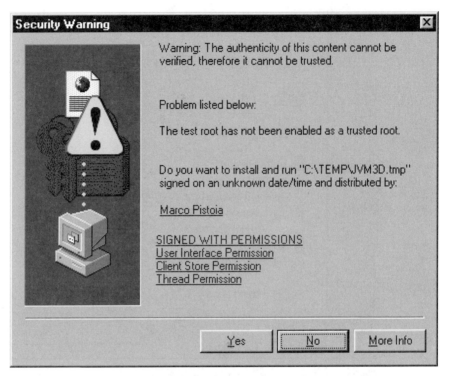

Figure 227. Security Warning – Privileges Requested by the GetFileMS Applet

However, this time, the privileges being requested are exactly the privileges necessary. This is clear if we click on the privilege list, and we explode the permission tree in the window that is brought up:

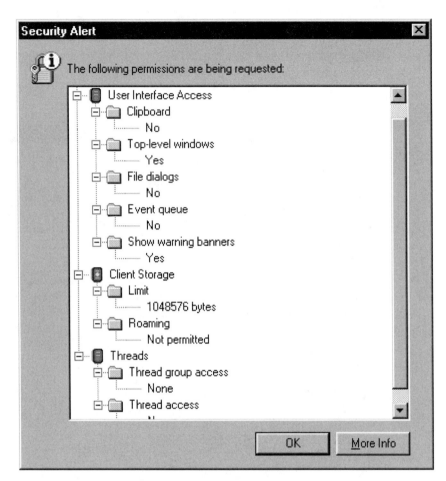

Figure 228. Permissions Being Requested

The user on the browser machine can now make a decision. The signer of the applet is not a trusted entity, because it is not recognized by any certification authority. However, the privileges the applet is requesting are limited, and the risk of compromising the system is limited. It is true that the applet will read and write on the hard disk of the browser machine, but it will be allowed to use only a specific area of the disk.

Figure 229 on page 461 shows what the user will see if he or she decides to grant the applet the privileges it requests:

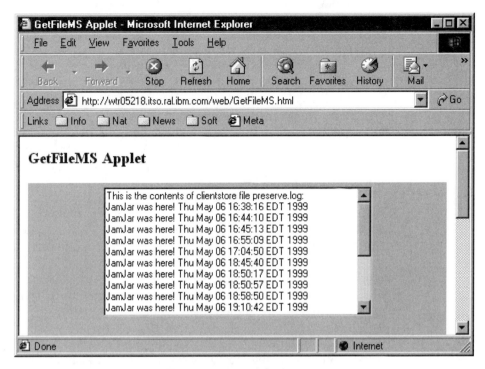

Figure 229. GetFileMS Applet Running on Internet Explorer

As you can see, the client store has permanently registered all the times the applet has been granted the permissions to run on the system. This information is displayed in the text area of the HTML page.

12.6 The JAR Bug – Fixed In Java 2 SDK, Standard Edition, V1.2.1

In 12.1, "JAR Files and Applet Signing" on page 385, we have illustrated the JAR format and the modifications a JAR file passes through when it is signed. Applying a digital signature to a JAR file automatically generates digest values for each of the files that are part of the archive. These digest values are stored in the manifest file. Therefore the manifest file of a signed JAR file contains much more information than the manifest file of an unsigned JAR file. Moreover, when a JAR file is signed, a signature file is also generated, containing a digest for each entry of the manifest file, plus a digest of the manifest file itself. A signed JAR file contains also a signature block file, which stores the digital signature of the JAR file, along with the digital certificate of the signing entity.

JAR signing should be a method to guarantee the sender's identity to the receiver, and also the integrity of the JAR file itself. In other words we expect to be able to verify whether or not a signed JAR file has been altered since signing.

Unfortunately, an implementation bug has recently been discovered that makes it possible to modify the contents of a JAR file without generating any exception. This means that anyone could alter the contents of a JAR file, but the signature on the JAR file would still be from the original signer, and the JVM would not able to detect that the JAR file has been tampered with. Ideally, it is desirable that the hash values of the files contained in the JAR file are dynamically checked whenever a file from the JAR is to be used.

Actually, it is very simple to modify one of the files that are part of the JAR payload without affecting either the manifest file or the signature and signature block files. In fact, a JAR file has its own content format based on the industry-standard ZIP file format, and you could use the jar tool itself (or a graphical tool like WinZip) to extract a JAR file, modify or remove one of the files of the JAR payload, and package the file again, producing a new JAR file with the same name as the previous one.

The implementation bug has demonstrated that if you open a signed JAR file with WinZip and delete some files, you will still be able to use the corrupted JAR file in a Web browser, at least until a class that was deleted is needed. Another malicious attack consists of replacing a Java class file in a signed JAR file – again using WinZip. The applet still works, but its functionality of course has changed.

In Java 2 SDK, Standard Edition, V1.2, the concept of a sealed package inside a JAR file has been introduced to fix this problem (see 12.1.1, "Manifest File" on page 387), but this also has not been enough. If a package is *sealed*, all classes defined in that package must originate from the same JAR file; otherwise, a SecurityException is thrown. A sealed JAR specifies that all packages defined by that JAR file are sealed, unless overridden specifically for a package.

For example, suppose that a JAR file contains a couple of packages: xyz/mypackage/package_1/ and xyz/mypackage/package_2/. If we want to seal xyz/mypackage/package_1/ but not xyz/mypackage/package_2/, our archive-level sealed header will look like the following:

```
Manifest-Version: 1.0

Name: xyz/mypackage/package_1/
Sealed: true

Name: xyz/mypackage/package_2/
Sealed: false.
```

On the other hand, if we want to seal the entire JAR file, we specify:

```
Manifest-Version: 1.0
Sealed = true
```

This seals all the packages inside the JAR file, which is equivalent to saying that the JAR file itself has been sealed. Sealing of a package ensures that all the classes defined in the package must originate from the same JAR file.

However, this concept does not solve the problem for which it has been introduced. In fact, since the JAR file itself is not in the signature context, a change in the JAR file does not invalidate the signature. An attacker therefore can put his malicious class in a signed JAR file which can call any package-scope classes and methods of the trusted classes. There has to be some mechanism to check if an alien class has been added to a package contained in a signed and sealed JAR file.

Let's consider the following scenario, obtained by modifying the example described in 12.4, "Signed Code Scenario in Netscape Communicator" on page 409. First, we create a very simple class called NormalClass:

```java
import java.awt.Graphics;

public class NormalClass
{
    public static String giveString()
    {
        return "Thank you for your visit";
    }
}
```

Figure 230. NormalClass.java – Original Version

This class has a static method, giveString(), which simply returns the string:

Thank you for your visit

Then, we rename the Java applet file GetFileNS.java (shown in Figure 186 on page 410 through Figure 189 on page 414) as GetFileNS2.java. In the new file, we change the run() method of the GetFileNS class as shown in the following figure:

```
public void run()
    {
        // Did we get the permission we wanted?
        if (granted == true)
        {
            try
            {
                Target freadTgt = Target.findTarget("FileRead");
                privMgr.enablePrivilege(freadTgt , lilOlMe, (Object) filename);
                ta.appendText("\nThis is the content of file " + filename + ":\n" +
                    readTheFile(filename).toString());
                ta.appendText(NormalClass.giveString());
            }
            catch(ForbiddenTargetException e)
            {
                ta.appendText("\nShould never reach here...");
            }
        }
    }
```

Figure 231. run() method in GetFileNS2.java

As you can see, the only difference here is that we have added the line:

```
ta.appendText(NormalClass.giveString());
```

This line calls the giveString() method for the class NormalClass and displays in the applet text box the string returned by it.

Next we compile the two Java files NormalClass.java and GetFileNS2.java:

```
javac NormalClass.java
javac GetFileNS2.java
```

We obtain the two class files NormalClass.class and GetFileNS2.class. From these two files, we generate a signed JAR file, by using Netscape Signing Tool, as explained in 12.4.3, "Signing JAR Files with Netscape Signing Tool" on page 418. We call this JAR file GetFileNS2_sign.jar, and we put it in the home directory of a Web server. Then we invoke it using the following HTML file:

```
<HTML>

   <HEAD>
      <TITLE>GetFileNS2 Applet</TITLE>
   </HEAD>

   <BODY>

      <H3>GetFileNS2 Applet</H3>

      <APPLET Archive="GetFileNS2_sign.jar" Code="GetFileNS2.class" Width=500
Height=500>
         <PARAM Name="FileToTry" Value="F:\itso\textFile\secret.txt">
      </APPLET>

   </BODY>
</HTML>
```

Figure 232. GetFileNS2.html

The result is as expected; the applet displays an additional string in its text area, as shown in the following figure:

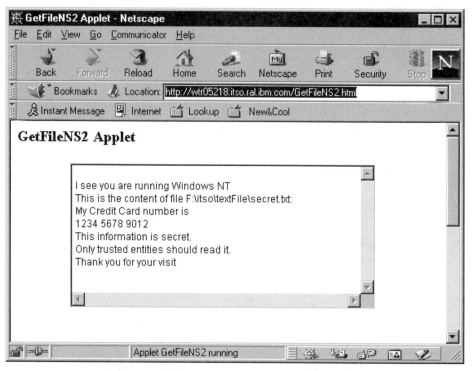

Figure 233. GetFileNS2 Applet on Netscape Communicator

Of course, before displaying this window, the Web browser prompted us to accept or deny granting this applet the additional privileges it requests, as shown in Figure 201 on page 430 and Figure 204 on page 433, and we granted the requested privileges. The classes in the package are allowed to access outside the Java sandbox. For more information on this process, refer to 12.4, "Signed Code Scenario in Netscape Communicator" on page 409.

Now, if someone sets a man-in-the-middle attack, so that one of the original classes in the official package is replaced by a modified class, then Netscape Communicator will load the modified class, regardless of the signature applied.

To show you how simply this attack can be performed, we copy the JAR file GetFileNS2_sign.jar in a directory D:\BUG, and here we extract it using WinZip. Then we modify the original version of the Java file NormalClass. A man-in-the-middle attack could be obtained with a decompiler, which would give the attacker the source code of the NormalClass, or with a hexadecimal editor, which would allow an attacker to edit the class file directly. This is how we modify the source code of the class NormalClass:

```
import java.awt.Graphics;

public class NormalClass
{
    public static String giveString()
    {
        return "Ah ah! You didn't expect me, did you?";
    }
}
```

Figure 234. NormalClass.java – Corrupted Version

As you can see, the message printed on the text area has been modified (it could have been something even worse than that). We compile this class again, and we re-create the JAR file keeping the same manifest and signature information as before. This can be done by issuing the following command from the directory D:\BUG, where the JAR file had been extracted:

`jar cvfM GetFileNS2_sign.jar *`

Notice that the M option prevents the jar tool from creating a new manifest file, while the asterisk (*) forces the jar command to compress all the files in the local directory and in all the subdirectories recursively, and in this case, the only subdirectory generated by extracting the JAR file is META-INF.

After this, the JAR file is saved again in the Web server machine, and when a client machine accesses the HTML page GetFileNS2.html, this is what the Web browser shows:

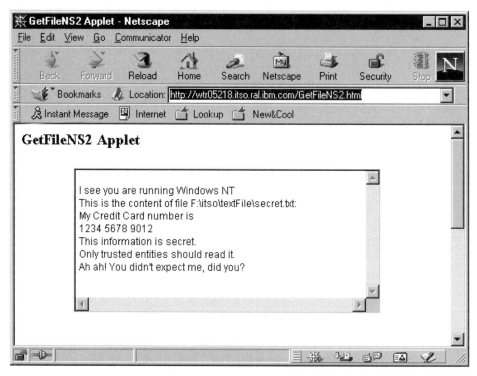

Figure 235. Corrupted Version of the GetFileNS Applet

Of course, this applet is not really a security threat; what this applet does is not dangerous for the integrity of the system. However, we would have expected that, if any class in a signed JAR file is changed, the entire JAR file would be treated as corrupted. Instead, if someone changes the content of a JAR file by replacing a class file, as we did, the user downloading the JAR file does not even get a warning message from the browser.

The situation is not so terrible, though. In fact it turns out that each class file that has been changed or replaced will be treated as unsigned, while unchanged classes continue to be treated as signed. The reason why the Web browser has permitted NormalClass to execute is because that class does not try to access outside the sandbox. If a modified class tries to access outside the sandbox, then the browser security manager would prevent that class from executing, because each class, once altered, is treated as unsigned.

Let's demonstrate this last statement. The class GetFileNS2 attempts to access outside the sandbox. So, if we corrupt the signed JAR file modifying GetFileNS2 instead of NormalClass, we should see an exception; the browser security manager should prevent the class from gaining the additional privileges it requests. Indeed, this is exactly what happens.

We proceed as in the previous example, but this time, after extracting the signed JAR file, we modify the run() method of GetFileNS2.java, adding the following line of code to it:

```
ta.appendText("\nThis line is new");
```

Then we recompile the Java file and run the `jar` tool with the M option, as explained previously. The corrupted JAR file is finally copied to the Web server home directory, and when the Netscape Communicator client machine, with the proper certificate installed, accesses the HTML file that invokes the applet, this is the result that the user sees:

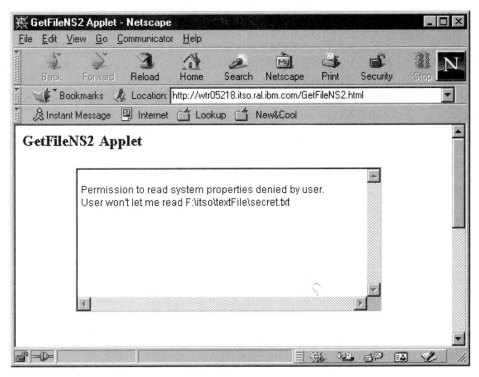

Figure 236. Forbidden Access for the Corrupted Applet Class

Even though this could seem acceptable from a *protection* point of view, because the security manager is not bypassed, it is unacceptable from an *integrity* point of view, because JAR signing is no longer a guarantee that you are using what the developer originally wrote.

12.6.1 The Solution in Java 2 SDK, Standard Edition, V1.2.1

The root of the vulnerability for the *package join attack* (the process of adding a malicious class to a package, thereby allowing it access to package-scope classes and methods of trusted classes) was identified in the absence of a *same package – same principal* check during class loading. The same package – same principal rule ensures that the class loader does not load trusted and untrusted classes into a single package, by verifying that all classes in a package have the same principal. A *principal* for a class refers to the identity of the signer(s) in case of signed code (see 10.1.1, "Principals" on page 297). An attempt to add a class to a package by an attacker would result in the principal for that class being different from the principal of the rest of the classes in the package and would therefore throw an exception with the new class loader available in Java 2 SDK, Standard Edition, V1.2.1.

The ClassLoader class now maintains a hashtable package2certs that maps packages to certificates. While loading any package, the class loader adds an entry in the hashtable that contains the name of the package and the set of certificates of signers that signed the first class contained in the package. For loading subsequent classes in the package, the class loader checks whether the principal for the class is the same as that found in the hashtable entry for that package. If not, an exception is thrown.

The bug shown in this section can be recreated with all the JVMs that still use a ClassLoader version prior to Java 2. SDK, Standard Edition, V1.2.1. We recreated it on Netscape Communicator, whose JVM level has not been ported to 1.2 yet. This bug cannot be recreated on the Java 2 SDK, Standard Edition, V1.2.1 Applet Viewer; a security exception is thrown to standard output.

12.7 Future Developments

In this chapter we have seen examples of three different approaches to the use of digital signatures for authenticating applet code and relaxing the constraints of the sandbox. The Java 2 SDK uses basic security tools (we have also shown the old approach used in JDK 1.1, since it still applies on all the systems that use the JDK 1.1 security architecture). The Netscape and Microsoft approaches are, as you would expect, strongly browser-centric. They both seek to reduce the impact of cryptography on the end user, not only for Java but also for other active Web content.

The following table summarizes the differences between the three approaches.

Table 12. Comparison of JavaSoft, Netscape and Microsoft Signed Applet Support

Function	Java 2 SDK	Netscape Communicator	Microsoft Internet Explorer
Delivery mechanism	Java 2-signed JAR files	Netscape-signed JAR files	Microsoft-signed CAB files
Signing	Command-line tools shipped with the Java 2 SDK	Command-line downloadable toolkit	Command-line downloadable toolkit
Signature Verification Algorithm	DSA/SHA1	RSA/SHA1	RSA/MD5
Certificate handling	Uses keystores to handle keys and certificates	Uses the standard key and certificate management capabilities of Netscape Communicator	Uses command-line tools for signer key creation and certificate requests – Standard key and certificate management capabilities of Internet Explorer for client side
Request for privileges	By exception – Applet attempts privileged action and an exception is thrown if it is not permitted	Programmer defines the privileges required by calling PrivilegeManager methods	Code signer defines the privileges required as part of CAB signature
Configuration of permissions granted	Policy configuration file maps code origin (URL plus signer) to privileges	User prompted the first time privileges are requested – Granted permissions can be perpetual or per session	Basic security zone preset by user – More complex permission scheme can be defined by administrator

Clearly, there are some basic incompatibilities between the different mechanisms. This is not to say that the development of competing extensions to the security framework is a bad thing; just that there should be a base level of function at which they should all interoperate.

It may be that by the time you read this book, the differences described above will have been resolved by the vendors and a common base will have emerged. IBM is already looking at this problem and is working on a solution. One thing that is clear from the discussion is that any solution cannot simply concentrate on the mechanics of code-signing and requests for privileges. The problems of the end user are equally important. Solutions must answer such questions as how to tell the user, in a clear way, the permissions an applet requires, and how to install and maintain certificates for signers and CAs.

Part 3. Beyond the Island of Java – Surfing into the Unknown

Chapter 13. Cryptography in Java 2

From Java Development Kit (JDK) 1.1 onwards, Java provides general purpose APIs for cryptographic functions, collectively known as the Java Cryptography Architecture (JCA) and Java Cryptography Extension (JCE). Signed applets, discussed in Chapter 12, "Java Gets Out of Its Box" on page 385, are one specialized use of the JCA capabilities. JDK 1.1 introduced the *provider architecture* that allows for multiple and interoperable cryptography implementations. The Java 2 platform significantly extends the JCA. The certificate management infrastructure has been augmented to support X.509 V3 certificates.

In this chapter we describe the sort of problems for which cryptography can provide solutions and then look in more detail at JCA and JCE. Notice that the general concepts of Java 2 and cryptography have already been introduced in 2.2, "Java 2 and Cryptography" on page 53. Moreover, Chapter 10, "Security APIs in Java 2" on page 297, contains several examples that demonstrate how the Java security APIs can be used to implement cryptographic services, such as keystore management (see 10.1.6, "Key Management" on page 305 and 10.6.2, "Using Keystores" on page 332), message digests and digital signatures (see 10.1.7, "Message Digests and DIgital Signatures" on page 311), and signature verification (see 10.6.1, "Signature and Signature Verification" on page 325). Additional examples and scenarios are provided in this chapter to give you a better understanding of the technology involved.

13.1 Security Questions, Cryptographic Answers

We want to create secure applications, but *secure* means different things, depending on what the application does and the environment in which it operates. In each case we need to understand what the requirements are, based on the following categories:

- **Authentication**

  How sure does the client need to be that the server really is who it claims to be? And does the server need to identify the client, or can the client remain anonymous? Normally, authentication is based on either *something you know* (such as a password), or *something you have* (such as an encryption key or card).

  A developing form of authentication is based on *something you are*, including biometric measurements such as retinal scans or voice recognition.

- **Access control**

  Having found out who is at the other end of the session, the next step is to decide whether they are allowed to do what they want to do.

- **Data integrity**

  You want to be sure that data has not been altered between what was sent and what was received. This is especially true if the application crosses an non-secure network, such as the Internet, where a man-in-the-middle attack may be easily mounted.

- **Confidentiality**

  If any of the data that you are sending is sensitive, you do not want an attacker to be able to read it in transit. To prevent this, it needs to be encrypted.

- **Non-repudiation**

  An important security measure that the user or the application environment can require is a non-repudiation service. The goal of a non-repudiation service is to prove that a particular transaction took place. A non-repudiation service establishes accountability of information about a particular event or action to its originating entity.

If we measure applet sandbox security against these requirements we find that the only one it helps us with is access control. The control is very strict: if the security manager cannot authenticate the owner of the applet, it will allow it to only do safe things.

We have a trio of tools to answer the questions that these requirements pose, namely:

- Symmetric key encryption
- Public key encryption
- Hashing/digital signatures

Encryption is the process of taking data, called *cleartext*, and a cryptographic key, and producing *ciphertext*, which is encrypted data, or data meaningless to anybody who does not know the key. A *cryptographic key* is actually a mathematical function which operates on the data. If the original data is represented by x, and the cryptographic key by the function f, then the encrypted data is nothing but $f(x)$.

Decryption is the inverse of encryption; it is the process of taking ciphertext and a cryptographic key, and producing the original cleartext. The cryptographic key which is used for decryption is a mathematical function which, when operated on f(x), gives x back. This means that, if the encrypting key is function f, the corresponding decrypting key is function f^{-1}.

Notice that:

- f is equal to f^{-1} in the case of symmetric keys.
- f is *not* equal to f^{-1} in the case of asymmetric keys.

Symmetric key, or *bulk*, *encryption* provides confidentiality, by making sure that a message can be read only if the recipient has the same key as the sender. But how to share the key in a secure manner? A common answer is to use *public key*, or *asymmetric*, *encryption*. This is too inefficient for general encryption of the whole data stream, but it is ideal for encrypting a small item, such as a bulk encryption key. The sender uses the receiver's public key to encrypt it, knowing that only the owner of the private half of the key pair, that is to say the receiver, will be able to decrypt it. Having secretly shared the bulk encryption key in this way, they can then use it to encrypt the real data that they want to keep private.

Digital signatures also use public key encryption, but the other way around. The following figure illustrates how they work:

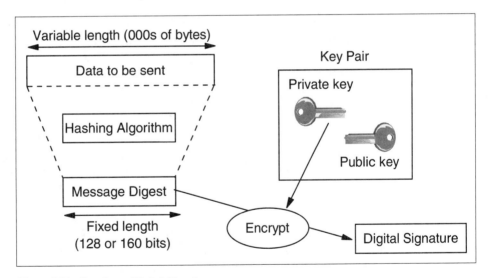

Figure 237. Creating a Digital Signature

The sender generates a digest from the data and then encrypts it with its private key. It then sends the result, together with the public key, along with the data. The receiver uses the sender's public key to decrypt the signature and then performs the same hashing function on the data. If the digest obtained matches the result of the decryption, the receiver knows:

1. That the data has not been changed in transit (data integrity)
2. That it really was sent by the owner of the key pair (authentication)

13.1.1 Public Key Certificates

Whenever public key encryption is used, the owner of the key pair has to make the public key available to the session partner. But how can the session partner be sure of where the key really came from? The answer lies in *public key certificates*. Instead of sending a naked key, the owner sends a certificate, which is a message containing:

- The public key

- Detailed information about the owner of the key. This is known as the *distinguished name*. It is a formatted string that contains the name, address, network information and other information about the entity that owns the key pair (see Appendix C, "X.509 Certificates" on page 683).

- The expiration date of the certificate

- Optionally, additional application-specific data

Typically, the whole message is digitally signed by a *trusted third party*. This is an organization that is trusted by both sender and receiver, and it is usually known as a certificate authority (CA). The resulting certificate electronically ties the real identity of the user to the public key.

The following scenario explains why digital certificates are needed. We saw in 10.6.1, "Signature and Signature Verification" on page 325 and 10.6.2, "Using Keystores" on page 332 an example where the sender of data, say Duane, generates a key pair, signs the data to be sent with the private key portion of the key pair, and sends the public key, along with the signed data, to the receiver, say Marco. Marco would use Duane's public key to verify that the signer of the data was indeed Duane.

Unfortunately, it is quite likely that somebody, say Ashok, has intercepted the signed data as well as the public key while in transit from Duane to Marco. Ashok can modify the data, sign the corrupted data with his own private key, replace Duane's signature with his own signature and replace Duane's public key with his own public key. When the signed data reaches Marco, Ashok's signature would get verified as that of Duane's with the help of Ashok's public key.

This explains the need for some means to ensure the receiver of signed data that the public key arriving with the signed data indeed belongs to a particular signer. Certificates were introduced to satisfy this need. An identity certificate is a binding of a principal to a public key which is vouched for by another principal. A *principal* represents an entity such as an individual user, a group, or a corporation (see 10.1.1, "Principals" on page 297). A *public key certificate* is a digitally signed statement from one entity, saying that the public key (and some other information) of another entity has some specific value.

Consider in the above example that there is another party, say Milind, whom Marco trusts. Marco already has Milind's public key which he has obtained *directly* from Milind (hence Marco is confident that this public key indeed belongs to Milind). Marco will therefore be comfortable with anything signed by Milind. In fact Marco holds Milind's public key, and can verify that the digital signature was really applied by Milind.

What Duane does is to send a request to Milind to verify that the public key that accompanies data signed by Duane indeed belongs to Duane. Milind writes a certificate vouching for the fact that the public key accompanying the data indeed belongs to Duane, signs the certificate and sends the signed data along with the public key and certificate to Duane. After this, Duane sends the data, the signature he applied, his public key as well as the certificate issued by Milind to Marco. Seeing the certificate, Marco can be assured that the sender of the data was indeed Duane.

The international standard for public key certificates is called X.509. This has evolved over time and the latest version is V3 (see again Appendix C, "X.509 Certificates" on page 683). The most significant enhancement in X.509 V3 is the ability to add other, arbitrary, data in addition to the basic identity fields of the distinguished name. This is useful when constructing certificates for specific purposes (for example, a certificate could include a bank account number, or credit card information).

13.1.1.1 Certificate Hierarchies

In the scenario described in 13.1.1, "Public Key Certificates" on page 478, the principal Milind acts as a CA. In real-life situations, there are chains of CAs, where each successive CA verifies and vouches for the public key of the next identity in the chain.

In this case, a public key certificate embodies a chain of trust. Consider the situation shown in Figure 238 on page 480. A system has received a request containing a chain of certificates, each of which is signed by the next higher CA in the chain. The system also has a collection of root certificates from

CAs that it views as trusted. It can match the top of the chain in the request with one of these root certificates, say Ham's. If the chain of signatures is intact, the receiver can infer that Nimrod is trustworthy and has inherited its trustworthiness from Ham.

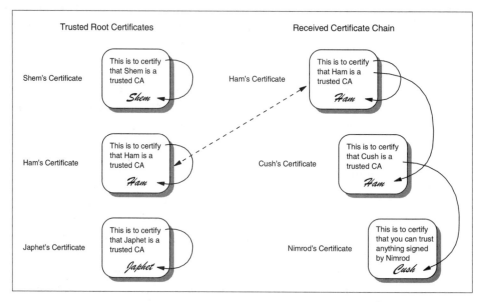

Figure 238. Certificate Hierarchy

Note that one of the implications of a certificate chain is that the certificate at the top of the chain is *self-signed*.

13.2 The Java Cryptography Architecture Framework

The JCA is a framework for accessing and developing cryptographic functionality for the Java platform. It encompasses the parts of the Java 2 security API related to cryptography. The JCA was designed around the following two principles:

- **Implementation independence and interoperability**

  - *Implementation independence* is achieved using a provider-based architecture. As we said in 10.1.3, "Providers" on page 299, the term *cryptographic service provider* (*provider* for short) refers to a package or a set of packages that supply a concrete implementation of a subset of the cryptography aspects of the Java security API. In other words, these packages must implement one or more cryptography services, such as digital signature algorithms, message digest algorithms, and key conversion services. Providers may be updated transparently to the application, for example when faster or more secure versions are available.

- *Implementation interoperability* means that various implementations can work with each other, use each other's keys, or verify each other's signatures. This would mean, for example, that for the same algorithms, a key generated by one provider would be usable by another, and a signature generated by one provider would be verifiable by another.

- **Algorithm independence and extensibility**

  - *Algorithm independence* is achieved by defining types of cryptographic services, and defining classes that provide the functionality of these cryptographic services. These classes are called *engine classes*, and examples are the MessageDigest, Signature, and KeyFactory classes.

  - *Algorithm extensibility* means that new algorithms that fit in one of the supported engine classes can easily be added.

13.2.1 JCE and United States Export Considerations

As we discussed in 2.2.3, "United States Export Rules for Encryption" on page 57, the security-related classes shipped with the Java 2 SDK only provide for the message digest and digital signature part of the cryptographic spectrum. This allows us to perform reliable authentication which, in turn, can be used as a basis for implementing access controls that relax the sandbox restrictions. However, it does not provide the general purpose encryption needed to send confidential data.

This function is provided by the JCE, which is an extension to the cryptography-related classes shipped with the Java 2 SDK. The JCE package uses the same structure of the JCA, being composed of engine classes that expose the algorithms in a generic way. The JCE provides engine classes for symmetric key encryption and for generating and manipulating the secret keys that such algorithms require.

The primary principle in the design of the JCA has been to separate the cryptographic concepts from their algorithmic implementations. Before we explain how JCA achieves this separation, it is worthwhile to review the types of classes supplied by the Java 2 SDK, the APIs that are part of the JCA and the API extensions supplied by the JCE.

13.2.2 Relationship between Java 2 SDK, JCA and JCE APIs

The Java 2 SDK APIs consist of the core classes that are shipped with the Java Virtual Machine (JVM), as we have seen in previous chapters of the book. The set of core classes in the Java 2 platform can be divided into two subsets:

- Security-related core classes
- Other core classes

The security-related core classes can be further subdivided as:

- Access control and permission related core classes
- cryptography-related core classes

Of these, only the cryptography-related core classes are part of the JCA APIs. The JCE extends the JCA API to include APIs for encryption, key exchange, and message authentication code (MAC). Together, the JCE and the cryptography aspects of the Java 2 SDK provide a complete, platform-independent cryptography API. The JCE is released separately as an extension to the Java 2 SDK, in accordance with United States export control regulations. The following figure offers a graphical representation of the relationship between the Java 2 SDK APIs, the JCA APIs and the extension APIs provided by JCE:

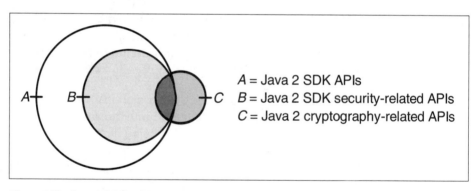

Figure 239. Java 2 SDK, JCA and JCE APIs

Referring to the above figure we can see that we have three circles that overlap each other. The circles graphically represent sets *A*, *B* and *C* respectively:

- *A* represents the APIs supported by the Java 2 SDK, Standard Edition, V1.2.

- *B*, which is a subset of *A*, represents the security-related core classes in the Java 2 SDK.

- C represents the cryptography-related classes in the Java 2 platform.

The diagram above shows that:

- The intersection $B \cap C$ represents all the cryptography classes that come with the standard installation of the Java 2 SDK.

- The difference $C - (B \cap C)$ represents the cryptography extension APIs that come with the JCE.

- The difference $B - (B \cap C)$ represents the access control and permission classes that are shipped with the Java 2 SDK.

Having understood how the Java 2 SDK, JCA and JCE APIs are related, we now define some basic terms that are commonly used in cryptography.

13.3 JCA Terms and Definitions

In order to become familiar with the JCA, a few terms need to be explained. These terms are *engine*, *algorithm* and *provider*.

1. *Engine* is the term used to depict an abstract representation of a cryptographic service that does not have a concrete implementation. A *cryptographic service* is always associated with a particular algorithm or type, and it can have one of the following functions:

   - To provide cryptographic operations (like those for digital signatures or message digests)

   - To generate or supply the cryptographic material (keys or parameters) required for cryptographic operations

   - To generate data objects (keystores or certificates) that encapsulate cryptographic keys (which can be used in a cryptographic operation) in a secure fashion

   Message digests and signatures are examples of engines. The JCA encompasses the cryptography-related classes of the Java 2 security package, including the engine classes. Users of the JCA API request and utilize instances of the engine classes to carry out corresponding operations.

2. An *algorithm* can be looked upon as an implementation of an engine. For instance, the MD5 algorithm is one of the implementations of the message digest engine. The internal implementation of the MD5 algorithm can differ depending on the source that provides the MD5 algorithm class.

3. A *provider* does not know the actual implementation of the cryptographic algorithms. However, a provider knows which algorithm class can provide

a particular algorithmic implementation. Each set of algorithm classes from a particular source is managed by an instance of the java.security.Provider class. Installed providers are listed in the java.security properties file present in the ${java.home}${/}lib${/}security directory (see 8.1, "A Note on java.home and the JRE Installation Directory" on page 225 and 8.3, "The Security Properties File, java.security" on page 234). The only default provider entry found in this file is:

```
security.provider.1=sun.security.provider.Sun
```

The provider that comes as a part of JCE 1.2 is SunJCE, and it is implemented by the class com.sun.crypto.provider.SunJCE. Several providers can be installed in the system, together with a preference order number.

The provider architecture of JCA aims to allow *algorithm independence*. The provider infrastructure permits implementations of various classes in the security package to be found at runtime, without any changes to the code. Representing all functions of a given type by a generic engine class masks the idiosyncrasies of the algorithm behind standardized Java class behavior. *Vendor independence* is supported in the same way, by allowing any number of vendors to register their own implementations of the algorithms.

An engine class defines API methods that allow applications to access the specific type of cryptographic service it provides. The actual implementations (from one or more providers) are those for specific algorithms. The MessageDigest engine class, for example, provides access to the functionality of a message digest algorithm.

From the brief discussion above, one can see that cryptographic solutions require a whole collection of tools and functions, which include not only the encryption algorithms themselves, but functions for message digests, certificate management and key generation. And of course, life would be too simple if there were only one way to do each of these functions. So, for example, there are two different message digest algorithms in common use: the MD5 algorithm from RSA and the United States government-standardized Secure Hash Algorithm (SHA) (see 2.2.2, "Java Cryptography Architecture" on page 56).

13.3.1 The Provider Concept in the JCA

The JCA offers the Provider class in the java.security package to define the concept of provider. This is an abstract class, which must be subclassed by specific provider classes. The constructor of a provider class sets the values of various properties that are required for the Java security API to look up the algorithms or other facilities implemented by the provider.

The Provider class has methods for accessing the provider name, version number, and other information about the implementations of the algorithms for key generation, conversion and management facilities, signature generation, and message digest generation.

If an application needs an implementation of the message digest algorithm MD5, it will typically create an instance of the message digest engine and pass the string MD5 as the argument to the getInstance() method:

```
MessageDigest m = MessageDigest.getInstance("MD5");
```

Internally, the getInstance() method asks the java.security.Security class to supply the required object. Since no specific provider has been specified, the Security class in turn asks all the providers in the sequence they are listed in the java.security file, until a provider implementing the requested algorithm is found. The default entry in the java.security file is:

```
security.provider.1=sun.security.provider.Sun
```

The class sun.security.provider.Sun implements SUN, the default provider shipped by Sun Microsystems with the Java 2 SDK, Standard Edition, V1.2. As you can see, by default, the SUN provider is installed with precedence number 1. A provider manages the individual algorithm classes. In this case, the SUN provider will receive the request first since it is listed as the first provider in the java.security file. The SUN provider replies to the Security class that the requested algorithm class is sun.security.provider.MD5. If the SUN provider had not had an implementation for the message digest algorithm MD5, or if it were not listed as the first provider, the Security class would have asked the second provider in the list, and so on, until a provider with the requested implementation was found, if any. The java.security.Security class passes this reply to the getInstance() method of the MessageDigest class. The object m can now be created by the getInstance() method using the MD5 algorithmic implementation provided by the sun.security.provider.MD5 class.

Notice that if the Security class cannot find any implementation of the message digest algorithm MD5, it throws a NoSuchAlgorithmException.

When an array of bytes, say inputData, is to be hashed into a digest using the MD5 algorithm, the update() method for the object m will be used. To find out the digest value, the digest() method for the object m will be used:

```
m.update(inputData);
```

```
byte[] digest = m.digest();
```

This way we have demonstrated how the provider architecture allows for vendor and algorithm independence. The same procedure is adopted with any other cryptographic service, such as digital signature and key pair generation. The following figure shows how vendor and algorithm independence is achieved when a particular Java application requests the implementation of a key pair generation algorithm:

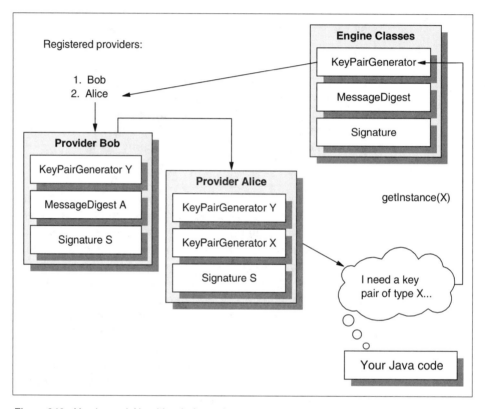

Figure 240. Vendor and Algorithm Independence

13.3.1.1 Managing Providers

It is important to note that the order in which the providers are listed in the java.security file is the order in which the java.security.Security class asks the providers for a requested service, unless a particular provider is specified. The first available algorithmic class that satisfies the requirements of the application and is supplied by one of the providers listed in the java.security file is accepted.

Each JVM installation has one or more provider packages installed. Providers may be added and removed statically or dynamically. In order to statically add or remove a provider, you have to edit the java.security file and respectively add or remove the security provider entry. To do the same operations dynamically, you have to call the addProvider() or insertProviderAt() methods for the java.security.Security class if you want to add a provider; otherwise, if your purpose is to remove a provider, you should use the removeProvider() method instead. This process is described in detail in 10.1.3, "Providers" on page 299, and you can refer to that section also to see what permissions are needed for a Java program running under the default security manager to add and remove providers dynamically.

The JCA also offers a set of APIs that allow users to query which providers are installed and what services they support. A couple of methods in the suite of provider management methods with the Security class can be used to obtain information on currently installed providers:

- The getProvider() method returns the provider with the name specified in the argument or null if the specified provider is not found.

- The getProviders() method returns an array of the currently installed security providers.

13.3.2 Engine Classes

The provider architecture of JCA has been designed to allow algorithm and vendor independence, as we have shown in 13.3.1, "The Provider Concept in the JCA" on page 484. This way implementations of various classes in the security package can be found at run-time, without any changes to the code. For this reason, abstract representations of cryptographic services are offered by generic *engine classes*.

The engine classes shown in the following table are defined in the Java 2 SDK core APIs as part of the JCA framework:

Table 13. Engine Classes in Java 2 SDK, Standard Edition, V1.2

Java 2 SDK engine class	Function
java.security.MessageDigest	Used to calculate the message digest (hash) of specified data
java.security.Signature	Used to sign data and verify digital signatures
java.security.KeyPairGenerator	Used to generate a pair of public and private keys suitable for a specified algorithm
java.security.KeyFactory	Used to convert opaque cryptographic keys of type Key into key specifications (transparent representations of the underlying key material), and vice versa

Java 2 SDK engine class	Function
java.security.certificate.CertificateFactory	Used to create public key certificates and certificate revocation lists (CRLs)
java.security.KeyStore	Used to create and manage a keystore (see 8.2, "Keystores" on page 230)
java.security.AlgorithmParameters	Used to manage the parameters for a particular algorithm, including parameter encoding and decoding
java.security.AlgorithmParameterGenerator	Used to generate a set of parameters suitable for a specified algorithm
java.security.SecureRandom	Used to generate random or pseudo-random numbers

The following list shows the engine classes defined in JCE 1.2:

Table 14. Engine Classes in JCE 1.2

JCE 1.2 engine class	Function
javax.crypto.Cipher	Provides the functionality of a cryptographic cipher for encryption and decryption
javax.crypto.KeyAgreement	Provides the functionality of a key agreement (or key exchange) protocol
javax.crypto.KeyGenerator	Provides the functionality of a (symmetric) key generator
javax.crypto.Mac	Provides the functionality of a MAC algorithm
javax.crypto.SecretKeyFactory	Represents a factory for secret keys

The above engine classes can be instantiated by using the getInstance() static method. If you pass this method a single argument, it must be the name of the algorithm to be used. In this case, the getInstance() method will ask the Security class to find the first provider in the preference list offering an implementation of that method, as discussed in 13.3.1, "The Provider Concept in the JCA" on page 484. Otherwise, you can force this decision and specify two arguments; in this case, along with the algorithm, you will explicitly pass in the provider.

An engine class provides the methods to enable applications to access the specific cryptographic service it provides, independent of the particular type of cryptographic algorithm. The MessageDigest engine class, for example, provides access to the functionality for *all* message digesting algorithms. The application interfaces supplied by an engine class are implemented in terms of a service provider interface (SPI). That is, for each engine class, there is a corresponding abstract SPI class, which defines the methods that cryptographic service providers must implement. The name of each SPI class is the same as that of the corresponding engine class, followed by Spi. For example, the SPI class corresponding to the Signature engine class is the SignatureSpi class. Each SPI class is abstract.

To supply the implementation of a particular type of service, for a specific algorithm, a provider must subclass the corresponding SPI class and supply implementations for all the abstract methods. By convention, the abstract methods in the SPI class all begin with `engine`. For example, the SignatureSpi class defines abstract methods like engineInitVerify() and engineInitSign(). An instance of an engine class, the *API object*, encapsulates (as a private field) an instance of the corresponding SPI class, the *SPI object*. All API methods of an API object are declared final, and their implementations invoke the corresponding SPI methods of the encapsulated SPI object. For instance, while writing an implementation of a specific type of signature algorithm, when the initVerify() method of the Signature class is called, it calls the engineinitVerify() method of the SignatureSpi class.

An instance of an engine class (and of its corresponding SPI class) is created by a call to the getInstance() factory method of the engine class itself. Notice that a factory method is always static.

13.3.3 Algorithms

The following program lists all the providers installed on your Java 2 SDK system, and shows for each of them the name, version number and general information on the cryptographic services supported and the algorithms implemented:

```
import java.security.*;
import java.util.*;

class GetProviderInfo
{
   public static void main(String[] args)
   {
      System.out.println("Providers installed on your system:");
      System.out.println("----------------------------------");
      Provider[] providerList = Security.getProviders();
      for (int i = 0; i < providerList.length; i++)
      {
         System.out.println("[" + (i + 1) + "] - Provider name: " +
            providerList[i].getName());
         System.out.println("Provider version number: " +
            providerList[i].getVersion());
```

Figure 241. (Part 1 of 2). GetProviderInfo.java

```
            System.out.println("Provider information:\n" + providerList[i].getInfo());
            System.out.println("----------------------------------");
        }
    }
}
```

Figure 242. (Part 2 of 2). GetProviderInfo.java

As you can see, the GetProviderInfo Java program uses the getProviders() method for the java.security.Security class, and builds an array of Provider objects with all the providers installed on the system. Then, for each provider, it invokes the methods getName(), getVersion() and getInfo() of the Provider class to get the provider's name, version number and general information respectively.

This Java application is compiled with the command:

```
javac GetProviderInfo.java
```

To launch it, just enter the command:

```
java GetProviderInfo
```

On a system where the provider SUN is installed with precedence number 1 and the provider SunJCE is installed with precedence number 2, the output of the command above is:

```
Providers installed on your system:
----------------------------------
[1] - Provider name: SUN
Provider version number: 1.2
Provider information:
SUN (DSA key/parameter generation; DSA signing; SHA-1, MD5 digests; SecureRandom; X.509 certificates;
JKS keystore)
----------------------------------
[2] - Provider name: SunJCE
Provider version number: 1.2
Provider information:
SunJCE Provider (implements DES, Triple DES, Blowfish, PBE, Diffie-Hellman, HMAC-MD5, HMAC-SHA1)
----------------------------------
```

You can discover some more information by adding the following lines of code to the `for` cycle of the GetProviderInfo.java program:

```
Enumeration properties = providerList[i].propertyNames();
while (properties.hasMoreElements())
{
    String key, value;
    key = (String)properties.nextElement();
    value = providerList[i].getProperty(key);
    System.out.println("Key: " + key + " - Value: " + value);
}
```

These additional lines of code make use of the fact that the Provider class extends java.util.Properties, so it inherits the propertyNames() method, which returns an Enumeration object. The `while` cycle goes through all the properties of the Provider objects installed on the system, and prints a list of the keys and values, from which you can understand the cryptographic services supported by the providers installed on your system and the algorithms implemented. If SUN and SunJCE are the two providers installed on your system, the output is composed of a large number of lines, and we recommend that you redirect it to a file. Reading the file generated, you can verify that:

1. The SUN provider offers:

   - An implementation of the Digital Signature Algorithm (DSA), described in NIST FIPS[1] 186

   - An implementation of the MD5 (RFC[2] 1321) and SHA-1 (NIST FIPS 180-1) message digest algorithms (see 2.2.2, "Java Cryptography Architecture" on page 56).

   - A DSA key pair generator for generating a pair of public and private keys suitable for the DSA algorithm

   - A DSA algorithm parameter generator

   - A DSA algorithm parameter manager

   - A DSA key factory providing bidirectional conversions between opaque DSA private and public key objects and their underlying key material

   - An implementation of the proprietary SHA1PRNG pseudo-random number generation algorithm, following the recommendations in the IEEE P1363 standard

   - A certificate factory for X.509 certificates and certificate revocation lists (CRLs)

---

[1] Federal Information Processing Standards (FIPS) algorithm conformance certification by the National Institute of Standards and Technology (NIST).
[2] A list of all the Requests for Comments (RFCs) can be found at http://info.internet.isi.edu/in-notes/rfc/files/.

- A keystore implementation for the proprietary keystore type named Java Keystore (JKS)

2. The SunJCE provider offers:

- An implementation of the Data Encryption Standard (DES) (FIPS PUB[3] 46-1), Triple DES[4], and Blowfish[5] encryption algorithms in the Electronic Code Book (ECB), Cipher Block Chaining (CBC), Cipher Feedback (CFB), Output Feedback (OFB), and Propagating Cipher Block Chaining (PCBC) modes

- Key generators for generating keys suitable for the DES, Triple DES, Blowfish, HMAC-MD5, and HMAC-SHA1 algorithms

- An implementation of the MD5 with DES-CBC password-based encryption (PBE)[6] algorithm defined in PKCS#5

- Secret-key factories providing bidirectional conversions between opaque DES, Triple DES and PBE key objects and transparent representations of their underlying key material

- An implementation of the Diffie-Hellman (DH) key agreement[7] algorithm between two or more parties

- A Diffie-Hellman key pair generator for generating a pair of public and private values suitable for the Diffie-Hellman algorithm

- A Diffie-Hellman algorithm parameter generator

- A Diffie-Hellman key factory providing bidirectional conversions between opaque Diffie-Hellman key objects and transparent representations of their underlying key material

- Algorithm parameter managers for Diffie-Hellman, DES, Triple DES, Blowfish, and PBE parameters

- An implementation of the HMAC-MD5 and HMAC-SHA1 keyed-hashing algorithms defined in RFC 2104

- An implementation of the padding[8] scheme described in PKCS#5

---

[3] Federal Information Processing Standards (FIPS) Publication (PUB).

[4] *Triple DES* is the particular block cipher that is the United States Data Encryption Standard (DES), performed three times, with two or three different keys.

[5] Blowfish is a symmetric block cipher. It takes a variable-length key, from 32 bits to 448 bits, making it ideal for both domestic and exportable use. Blowfish was designed in 1993 by Bruce Schneier as a fast, free alternative to existing encryption algorithms. Since then it has been analyzed considerably, and it is slowly gaining acceptance as a strong encryption algorithm. Blowfish is unpatented and license-free, and is available free for all uses.

[6] PBE derives an encryption key from a password. In order to make the task of getting from password to key very time-consuming for an attacker, most PBE implementations will mix in a random number, known as a salt, to create the key.

[7] *Key agreement* is a protocol by which two or more parties can establish the same cryptographic keys, without having to exchange any secret information.

- A keystore implementation for the proprietary keystore type named Java Cryptography Extension Keystore (JCEKS)

13.4 Java Cryptography Extension

JCE has been provided as an extension to the Java platform. JCE 1.2 provides a framework and implementations for encryption, key generation, key agreement, and MAC to supplement the interfaces and implementations of message digests and digital signatures provided by Java 2 SDK, Standard Edition, V1.2.

The provider architecture of the JCA aims to allow algorithm independence. The design principles behind JCE also share the same philosophy of implementation and algorithm independence by the use of the provider architecture. In addition to making it possible to use newer algorithms for generating keys, JCE also introduces some very new interfaces and classes that facilitate the implementation of these concepts.

JCE provides for symmetric bulk key encryption through the use of secret keys – the same key is shared by the sender and receiver to encrypt as well as to decrypt data. Associated concepts of MAC and key agreements support symmetric bulk encryption and symmetric stream encryption.

13.4.1 JCE – Packages and Their Contents

The SunJCE provider consists of the main package javax.crypto and its two subpackages javax.crypto.spec and javax.crypto.interfaces.

The javax.crypto package forms the main body of the JCE 1.2 class structure. The package primarily consists of classes which represent the new concepts

---

[8] Before encrypting, the length of plaintext packets must be a multiple of the cipher block size. If necessary, packets are expanded to become that length; this operation is known as *padding*.

of ciphers, key agreements, and message authentication codes and their SPI classes.

Table 15. The javax.crypto Package

Interfaces	Classes	Exceptions
SecretKey	Cipher CipherInputStream CipherOutputStream CipherSpi KeyAgreement KeyAgreementSpi KeyGenerator KeyGeneratorSpi Mac MacSpi NullCipher SealedObject SecretKeyFactory SecretKeyFactorySpi	BadPaddingException IllegalBlockSizeException NoSuchPaddingException ShortBufferException

The javax.crypto.spec package consists of various key specification and algorithm parameter specification classes.

Table 16. The javax.crypto.spec Package

Interfaces	Classes	Exceptions
	DESedeKeySpec DESKeySpec DHGenParameterSpec DHParameterSpec DHPrivateKeySpec DHPublicKeySpec IvParameterSpec PBEKeySpec PBEParameterSpec RC2ParameterSpec RC5ParameterSpec SecretKeySpec	

The javax.crypto.interfaces package consists of the DHKey interface and a couple of its subinterfaces – DHPrivateKey and DHPublicKey. These are the interfaces for the keys based on the Diffie-Hellman algorithms.

Table 17. The javax.crypto.interfaces Package

Interfaces	Classes	Exceptions
DHKey DHPrivateKey DHPublicKey		

13.4.2 The Cipher Class

The javax.crypto.Cipher engine class forms the core of the JCE 1.2 framework. This class provides the implementation of a cryptographic cipher used for encryption and decryption.

Like other engine classes, the cipher class is instantiated using the getInstance() factory method. This method takes as argument a String object that represents a transformation. A *transformation* is a string that describes the operation (or set of operations) to be performed on the given input, to produce some output. A transformation always includes the name of a cryptographic algorithm (for example, DES), which may be followed by a feedback mode and padding scheme:

- A Cipher object obtained from getInstance() must be initialized for either *encryption* or *decryption mode*. These modes are defined as final integer constants in the Cipher class. The two modes can be referenced by their symbolic names ENCRYPT_MODE and DECRYPT_MODE

- Algorithms usually operate on blocks having a predefined size. Plain text packets which are of a length not a multiple of that size must be *padded* prior to encrypting according to a specified *padding scheme*.

From what we said, a transformation is of the form `algorithm/mode/padding` or `algorithm`. If mode and padding are not specified, provider-specific default values are used.

For example, the following is a valid way to create a Cipher object:

```
Cipher c = Cipher.getInstance("DES/CBC/PKCS5Padding");
```

Optionally, getInstance() can accept a second argument after the transformation, and this is the name of the provider.

A Cipher object is initialized by calling the init() method. When this happens, it loses all previously acquired states. In other words, initializing a Cipher is equivalent to creating a new instance of that Cipher, and initializing it.

Data can be encrypted or decrypted in one step (*single-part* operation) or in multiple steps (*multiple-part* operation). You will encrypt or decrypt data in a single step or in multiple steps depending on whether you call the doFinal() or update() method respectively. A multiple-part operation is useful if the exact length of the data is not known in advance, or if the data is too long to be stored in memory all at once.

13.4.3 The Cipher Stream Classes

JCE 1.2 introduces the concept of secure streams, which combine an InputStream or OutputStream with a Cipher object. Secure streams are provided by the CipherInputStream and CipherOutputStream classes:

- The javax.crypto.CipherInputStream class is a FilterInputStream that encrypts or decrypts the data passing through it. It is composed of an InputStream, or one of its subclasses, and a Cipher. CipherInputStream represents a secure input stream into which a Cipher object has been interposed. The read methods of CipherInputStream return data that are read from the underlying InputStream but have additionally been processed by the embedded Cipher object.

  Notice that the Cipher object must be fully initialized before being used by a CipherInputStream. For example, if the embedded Cipher has been initialized for decryption, the CipherInputStream will attempt to decrypt the data it reads   from the underlying InputStream before returning it to the application.

- The javax.crypto.CipherOutputStream class is a FilterOutputStream that encrypts or decrypts the data passing through it. It is composed of an OutputStream, or one of its subclasses, and a Cipher. CipherOutputStream represents a secure output stream into which a Cipher object has been interposed. The write methods of CipherOutputStream first process the data with the embedded Cipher object before writing it out to the underlying OutputStream.

  The Cipher object must be fully initialized before being used by a CipherOutputStream. For example, if the embedded Cipher has been initialized for encryption, the CipherOutputStream will encrypt its data, before writing it out to the underlying output stream.

13.4.3.1 Encrypting and Decrypting Using the JCE 1.2 APIs

Here is a simple program, EncryptDecrypt.java, that reads data from an input file, encrypts it using a Cipher object itsocipher1 initialized for the DES algorithm in the ENCRYPT_MODE, then decrypts it using another Cipher object itsocipher2 initialized for the DES algorithm in the DECRYPT_MODE and prints the output to a file. The output file name is also specified on the command line.

```java
import java.io.*;
import java.security.*;
import javax.crypto.*;

class EncryptDecrypt
{
    public static void main(String args[])
    {
        if (args.length != 2)
            System.out.println("Usage: java EncryptDecrypt inputFileName outputFileName");
        else
        {
            try
            {
                // generate Cipher objects for encoding and decoding
                Cipher itsocipher1 = Cipher.getInstance("DES");
                Cipher itsocipher2 = Cipher.getInstance("DES");

                // generate a KeyGenerator object
                KeyGenerator KG = KeyGenerator.getInstance("DES");
                System.out.println("Using algorithm " + KG.getAlgorithm());

                // generate a DES key
                Key mykey = KG.generateKey();

                // initialize the Cipher objects
                System.out.println("Initializing ciphers...");
                itsocipher1.init(Cipher.ENCRYPT_MODE, mykey);
                itsocipher2.init(Cipher.DECRYPT_MODE, mykey);

                // creating the encrypting cipher stream
                System.out.println("Creating the encrypting cipher stream...");
                FileInputStream fis = new FileInputStream(args[0]);
                CipherInputStream cis1 = new CipherInputStream(fis, itsocipher1);
```

Figure 243. (Part 1 of 2). EncryptDecrypt.java

```
            // creating the decrypting cipher stream
            System.out.println("Creating the decrypting cipher stream...");
            CipherInputStream cis2 = new CipherInputStream(cis1, itsocipher2);

            // writing the decrypted data to output file
            System.out.println("Writing the decrypted data to output file " + args[1]);
            FileOutputStream fos = new FileOutputStream(args[1]);
            byte[] b2 = new byte[1024];
            int i2 = cis2.read(b2);
            while (i2 != -1)
            {
                fos.write(b2, 0, i2);
                i2 = cis2.read(b2);
            }

            fos.close();
            cis1.close();
            cis2.close();
        }
        catch (Exception e)
        {
            System.out.println("Caught exception: " + e);
        }
    }
  }
}
```

Figure 244. (Part 2 of 2). EncryptDecrypt.java

We compile the program above with the command:

```
javac EncryptDecrypt.java
```

In order for the above command to work, the SunJCE provider must be installed on your system. This means that you have to follow the directions explained in Step 1 on page 299 and Step 2 on page 300.

Then we launch the program, passing on the command line the name of an existing input text file, itso.txt (see Figure 108 on page 249), and the name of an output file where the EncryptDecrypt program writes the data that it has encrypted and decrypted:

```
java EncryptDecrypt itso.txt itso_out.txt
```

The output is shown below:

```
Using algorithm DES
Initializing ciphers...
Creating the encrypting cipher stream...
Creating the decrypting cipher stream...
Writing the decrypted data to output file itso_out.txt
```

On opening the itso_out.txt file with a text editor, we can verify that its contents are exactly the same as the contents of the original file itso.txt.

13.4.4 Secret Key Interfaces and Classes

JCE 1.2 offers a set of classes and interfaces to manage secret keys:

- The javax.crypto.SecretKey interface contains no methods or constants. Its only purpose is to group (and provide type safety for) secret (symmetric) keys. Provider implementations of this interface must overwrite the equals() and hashCode() methods inherited from java.lang.Object, so that secret keys are compared based on their underlying key material and not based on reference. Since it extends the Key interface (see 10.1.6, "Key Management" on page 305), this interface is an opaque representation of a symmetric key.

- The javax.crypto.SecretKeyFactory class represents a factory for secret keys. Key factories are bidirectional, which means that they allow building an opaque Key object from a given key specification (key material), or retrieving the underlying key material of a Key object in a suitable format.

  In general, key factories are used to convert keys (opaque cryptographic keys of type Key) into key specifications (transparent representations of the underlying key material), and vice versa. In particular, secret key factories operate only on secret (symmetric) keys.

- The javax.crypto.spec.SecretKeySpec class specifies a secret key in a provider-independent fashion. It can be used to construct a SecretKey from a byte array, without the need to go through a provider-based SecretKeyFactory. This class is only useful for raw secret keys that can be represented as a byte array and have no key parameters associated with them, for example DES or Triple DES keys. This class is a transparent representation of a symmetric key (see also 10.2, "The Package java.security.spec" on page 322).

13.4.5 The KeyGenerator Class

The javax.crypto.KeyPairGenerator class, which is part of the Java 2 SDK, Standard Edition, V1.2 APIs, is used to generate a pair of public and private keys. JCE 1.2 provides for a KeyGenerator engine class which is used to generate secret keys for symmetric algorithms. KeyGenerator objects are created using the getInstance() factory method of the KeyGenerator class. Notice that a factory method is by definition static.

The getInstance() method takes as its argument the name of a symmetric algorithm for which a secret key is to be generated. Optionally, a package provider name may be specified. If just an algorithm name is specified, the system will determine if there is an implementation of the requested key generator available in the environment, and if there is more than one, the preferred one will be selected. If both an algorithm name and a package provider are specified, the system will determine if there is an implementation of the requested key generator in the package requested, and throw an exception if there is not. A key generator for a particular symmetric-key algorithm creates a symmetric key that can be used with that algorithm. It also associates algorithm-specific parameters (if any) with the generated key.

13.4.6 The KeyAgreement Class

Whenever two or more parties decide to initiate a secure conversation over a non-secure communication channel, they need to use the same secret key (which is called the *session key*), without transmitting it in the clear over the channel. To achieve this, public key encryption can be used to transmit the session key securely.

Another solution is to use a key agreement. A *key agreement* is a protocol that allows two or more parties to calculate the same secret value without exchanging it directly. Therefore, the parties share the same secret key and can encrypt the communication using symmetric encryption. The most famous of these protocols is the Diffie-Hellman (DH) algorithm, whose implementation is provided by JCE 1.2 (see 13.3.3, "Algorithms" on page 489).

The javax.crypto.KeyAgreement class provides the functionality of a key agreement protocol. The keys involved in establishing a shared secret key are created by one of the key generators (KeyPairGenerator or KeyGenerator), a key factory, or as a result from an intermediate phase of the key agreement protocol.

Each party involved in the key agreement has to create a KeyAgreement object. This can be done using the getInstance() factory method of the KeyAgreement class. This method accepts as its argument a string representing a key agreement algorithm as parameter. Optionally you can specify a provider as the second argument:

- If just an algorithm name is specified, the system will determine if there is an implementation of the requested key agreement available in the environment, and if there is more than one, the preferred one will be selected.

- If both an algorithm name and a package provider are specified, the system will determine if there is an implementation of the requested key agreement in the package requested, and throw an exception if there is not.

If the Diffie-Hellman algorithm is used, a Diffie-Hellman private key is used to initialize the KeyAgreement object. Additional initialization information may contain a source of randomness and/or a set of algorithm parameters.

Every key agreement protocol consists of a number of phases that need to be executed by each party involved in the key agreement. The doPhase() method is used to execute the next phase in the key agreement. This method takes two arguments: a Key and a boolean.

- The Key argument contains the key to be processed by that phase. In most cases, this is the public key of one of the other parties involved in the key agreement, or an intermediate key that was generated by a previous phase. The doPhase() method may return an intermediate key that you may have to send to the other parties of this key agreement, so they can process it in a subsequent phase.

- The boolean parameter specifies whether or not the phase to be executed is the last one in the key agreement:

  - A value of `false` indicates that this is not the last phase of the key agreement, and there are more phases to follow.

  - A value of `true` indicates that this is the last phase of the key agreement and the key agreement is completed.

After each party has executed all of the required key agreement phases, it can compute the shared secret by calling the generateSecret() method.

13.4.7 The SealedObject Class

Using the javax.crypto.SealedObject class, it is possible to encrypt and seal any serializable object using an appropriately initialized Cipher object. This provides a way of storing a serializable object safely. A sealed object is created that encapsulates the original object, in serialized format, and seals (encrypts) the serialized contents using a cryptographic algorithm, such as DES, to protect the object's confidentiality.

This class provides a variety of options for decrypting the sealed object and recovering it in its original form. The sealed object can be recovered by either passing the same Cipher object appropriately initialized with the same key and algorithm parameters as used for encryption, or by passing just the decryption key (and in this case the appropriate Cipher object is automatically created with the decryption key and the same algorithm parameters that were stored in the sealed object).

The following program illustrates the use of the SealedObject class:

```
import java.io.*;
import java.security.*;
import javax.crypto.*;

class Seal
{
    public static void main(String args[])
    {
        try
        {
            // generate Cipher objects for encoding and decoding
            Cipher itsocipher1 = Cipher.getInstance("DES");
            Cipher itsocipher2 = Cipher.getInstance("DES");

            // generate a KeyGenerator Object
            KeyGenerator KG = KeyGenerator.getInstance("DES");
            System.out.println("The algorithm is " + KG.getAlgorithm());

            // generate a DES key
            Key mykey = KG.generateKey();

            // initialize the Cipher to encrypt mode
            itsocipher1.init(Cipher.ENCRYPT_MODE, mykey);
            itsocipher2.init(Cipher.DECRYPT_MODE, mykey);

            // seal a String object
            SealedObject s = new SealedObject("Credit card number 1234 5678 9012",
                itsocipher1);

            // recover the sealed String object
            String s1 = (String)s.getObject(itsocipher2);
            System.out.println ("The sealed object is\n: " + s1);
        }
```

Figure 245. (Part 1 of 2). Seal.java

```
        catch (Exception e)
        {
            System.out.println("Caught Exception " + e);
        }
    }
}
```

Figure 246. (Part 2 of 2). Seal.java

This Java file is compiled with the command:

```
javac Seal.java
```

Then it can be launched by issuing the following command:

```
java Seal
```

The output is shown in the following screen:

```
The algorithm is DES
The sealed object is:
Credit card number 1234 5678 9012
```

13.5 Java Cryptography in Practice

In this section we describe a couple of examples of the kinds of applications that the JCA can be used for.

In 13.4.3.1, "Encrypting and Decrypting Using the JCE 1.2 APIs" on page 497, we saw an example where we encrypted and then decrypted a text file in the same class. But real-life situations are more complex. A realistic situation would be when two persons are situated at two different locations and want to exchange data safely by encrypting the data during transmission. In this case, there will be two different programs for encryption and decryption.

13.5.1 First Scenario

In the first example, we will consider the following scenario. Two persons, named Bob and Alice, want to exchange data. Bob wants to send some data to Alice and wants to encrypt the data to maintain its safety in transit. For this reason, Bob writes a program called Encrypt1.java which does the following:

1. Reads data from a text file JavaTeam.txt

2. Encrypts the data using a Cipher object initialized by the DES algorithm and a DES secret symmetric key

3. Stores the encrypted data in a file bob.enc

4. Stores the secret key in another file bob.key

The following figure shows the file JavaTeam.txt read and encrypted by the Encrypt1 Java program:

```
Anthony Nadalin
Julianne Yarsa
Bruce Rich
Larry Koved
```

Figure 247. JavaTeam.txt

Bob runs his program and then sends Alice the two files bob.enc and bob.key. This is not very realistic, since it is like locking the jewels in a box and sending the key along with the locked box of jewels. However, in 13.5.2, "Second Scenario" on page 509, we will demonstrate how to implement encryption and decryption by remote parties without actually transmitting the key.

Alice, at the receiving end, writes a program named Decrypt1.java that does the following:

1. Reads the data from the encrypted file bob.enc

2. Reads the key from the bob.key file

3. Initiates a Cipher object using this key and decrypts the data from bob.enc

4. Writes the decrypted data into a file bob.dec

13.5.1.1 Bob's Program
The program Encrypt1.java written by Bob looks as shown in the following two figures:

```
import java.io.*;
import java.security.*;
import javax.crypto.*;

class Encrypt1
{
    public static void main(String args[])
```

Figure 248. (Part 1 of 3). Encrypt1.java

```
{
    if (args.length != 3)
        System.out.println("Usage: java Encrypt1 inputFileName encryptedFile
            keyFile");
    else
        try
        {
            // generate a Cipher object
            Cipher itsocipher = Cipher.getInstance("DES/ECB/NoPadding");

            // generate a KeyGenerator object
            KeyGenerator KG = KeyGenerator.getInstance("DES");

            // generate a DES key
            SecretKey mykey = KG.generateKey();

            // initialize the Cipher object to encrypt mode
            itsocipher.init(Cipher.ENCRYPT_MODE, mykey);

            // accessing the input file
            FileInputStream fis = new FileInputStream(args[0]);
            BufferedInputStream bis = new BufferedInputStream(fis);
            int len = bis.available();
            byte[] buff = new byte[len];
            byte[] encText = new byte[len];

            // update the cipher with the data to be encrypted
            while (bis.available() != 0)
            {
                len = bis.read(buff);
                int bytecount = itsocipher.update(buff, 0, len, encText);
            }
            bis.close();
            fis.close();
            itsocipher.doFinal();

            // write the output file containing the encrypted data
            FileOutputStream encfile = new FileOutputStream(args[1]);
            encfile.write(encText);
            encfile.close();

            // write the encoded key to a file
            FileOutputStream keyfile = new FileOutputStream(args[2]);
```

Figure 249. (Part 2 of 3). Encrypt1.java

```
                keyfile.write(mykey.getEncoded());
                String s1;
                s1 = mykey.getFormat();
                keyfile.close();
            }
            catch (Exception e)
            {
                System.out.println("Caught Exception: " + e);
            }
        }
    }
}
```

Figure 250. (Part 3 of 3). Encrypt1.java

Bob issues the `javac` command to compile this program:

```
javac Encrypt1.java
```

Next, he launches it by passing the names of the following files on the command line:

- The input file that he wants to encrypt

- The output file containing the encrypted data

- The output file containing the encoded key

This is the full command launched by Bob:

```
java Encrypt1 F:\itso\textFile\JavaTeam.txt bob.enc bob.key
```

The program runs successfully and two files are generated: the file bob.enc containing the encrypted data and the file bob.key containing the encoded key.d and the key file milind.key. The file bob.enc, opened with a text editor, is shown in the following figure:

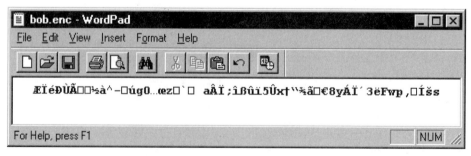

Figure 251. The Contents of the bob.enc File

13.5.1.2 Alice's Program

Alice receives the two files bob.enc and bob.key and wants to decrypt the encrypted data contained in bob.enc using the key contained in bob.key. For this reason, she writes a program that retrieves the key from the bob.key file, uses the key to initialize a Cipher object, and uses the Cipher object to decrypt the message contained in the file bob.enc. The decrypted message is stored in a file called bob.dec.

Alice's program, called Decrypt1.java, is shown in the following two figures:

```
import java.io.*;
import java.security.*;
import javax.crypto.*;
import javax.crypto.spec.*;

class Decrypt1
{
    public static void main(String args[])
    {
        if (args.length != 3)
            System.out.println("Usage: java Decrypt1 inputEncryptedFile keyFile
                outputFile");
        else
            try
            {
                // get the key to decrypt
                FileInputStream kfis =  new FileInputStream(args[1]);
                byte[] encKey = new byte[kfis.available()];
                kfis.read(encKey);
                kfis.close();
                SecretKeyFactory mykeyfac1 = SecretKeyFactory.getInstance("DES");
                DESKeySpec dk = new DESKeySpec(encKey);
                SecretKey mykey1 = mykeyfac1.generateSecret(dk);

                // generate a Cipher object
                Cipher itsoCipher = Cipher.getInstance("DES/ECB/NoPadding");

                // initialize the Cipher object to decrypt mode
                itsoCipher.init(Cipher.DECRYPT_MODE, mykey1);

                // access the file to be decrypted
                FileInputStream data = new FileInputStream(args[0]);
                BufferedInputStream bis = new BufferedInputStream(data);
```

Figure 252. (Part 1 of 2). Decrypt1.java

```
            int len1 = bis.available();
            byte[] encText1 = new byte[len1];
            byte[] buff = new byte[len1];

            // update the cipher with the data to be decrypted
            while (bis.available() != 0)
            {
                len1 = bis.read(buff);
                int countjlt = itsoCipher.update(buff, 0, len1, encText1);
            }

            bis.close();
            data.close();
            itsoCipher.doFinal();

            // write the output file containing the decrypted data
            FileOutputStream encfile = new FileOutputStream(args[2]);
            encfile.write(encText1);
            encfile.close();
        }
        catch (Exception e)
        {
            System.out.println("Caught Exception: " + e);
        }
    }
}
```

Figure 253. (Part 2 of 2). Decrypt1.java

Alice compiles the program above by entering the following command:

```
javac Decrypt1.java
```

Then she launches the program by passing the following file names on the command line:

- The encrypted file to be decrypted
- The file containing Bob's key
- The output file where the decrypted data must be saved

This is the full command launched by Alice:

```
java Decrypt1 bob.enc bob.key bob.dec
```

The program executes successfully and as a result it produces the bob.dec file, containing the decrypted text. On opening bob.dec with a text editor, it shows the same contents as the file JavaTeam.txt (see Figure 247 on page 504), which means that, using Bob's key, Alice has successfully decrypted the message sent by Bob.

13.5.2 Second Scenario

In this second example, again two persons are involved – say Bob and Alice again. This time they will not send the key along with the message but instead will generate the same secret key independently. These two parties want to establish a secret key between themselves, without actually transmitting the secret key over the network:

- Bob writes a program Bob.java that accepts data at the command line, encrypts that data using the secret key and sends the encrypted data over the network to Alice.

- Alice writes a program that, with the help of the shared secret key, decrypts this encrypted data and writes it in a file alice.dat.

The main steps involved in the process are:

1. Both parties generate a key pair using the Diffie-Hellman algorithm. The private key in this key pair is used to initiate a KeyAgreement object by either party.

2. The public key generated in the key pair is encoded and stored in a file by both parties. Both parties now send this file to one another.

3. Using the public key belonging to Alice and Bob's own private key, the Bob's KeyAgreement object generates a secret key using the DES algorithm.

4. Similarly, using the public key belonging to Bob and Alice's own private key, Alice's KeyAgreement object generates a secret key also using the DES algorithm.

5. Using his secret key, Bob encrypts the data read from the command line and stores the encrypted data in a file called bob.cip. The encryption is done using a Cipher object, which is initialized in the ENCRYPT_MODE. The file bob.cip is then transmitted over the network to Alice.

6. Using her secret key, Alice decrypts the data in the file bob.cip, and stores the decrypted data in a file called alice.dat. The decryption is done using the Cipher object at Alice's end, which is initialized in the DECRYPT_MODE.

13.5.2.1 Bob's Program
The following figures show the program written by Bob:

```java
import java.io.*;
import java.security.*;
import java.security.spec.*;
import javax.crypto.*;
import javax.crypto.spec.*;

public class Bob
{
    public static void main(String arg[])
    {
        if (arg.length != 1)
        {
            System.out.println("Usage: java Bob testString");
        }
        else
            try
            {
                // generate the AlgorithmParameterGenerator object
                AlgorithmParameterGenerator paramalgo =
                    AlgorithmParameterGenerator.getInstance("DH");
                paramalgo.init(512);

                // generate the algorithm parameters
                AlgorithmParameters parameters = paramalgo.generateParameters();
                DHParameterSpec myParamSpec =
                    (DHParameterSpec)parameters.getParameterSpec(DHParameterSpec.class);

                // generate and initialize the key pair
                KeyPairGenerator kpg = KeyPairGenerator.getInstance("DH");
                kpg.initialize(myParamSpec);
                KeyPair kp = kpg.generateKeyPair();

                // write the public key to a file
                byte[] pubKeyEnc = kp.getPublic().getEncoded();
                FileOutputStream fos = new FileOutputStream("F:\\itso\\ch13\\bob.pub");

                fos.write(pubKeyEnc);
                fos.close();

                // generate and initialize the key agreement object
                KeyAgreement keyAgree = KeyAgreement.getInstance("DH");
                keyAgree.init(kp.getPrivate());
```

Figure 254. (Part 1 of 3). Bob.java

```
          // wait for Alice's public key
          boolean read = false;

          while(!read)
              try
              {
                  FileInputStream pfistry = new
                      FileInputStream("F:\\itso\\ch13\\alice.pub");
                  pfistry.close();
                  read = true;
              }
              catch(Exception e)
              {
              }

          // get Alice's public key
          FileInputStream pfis = new FileInputStream("F:\\itso\\ch13\\alice.pub");
          byte[] encKey = new byte[pfis.available()];
          pfis.read(encKey);
          pfis.close();

          // generate the secret key
          X509EncodedKeySpec pubKeySpec = new X509EncodedKeySpec(encKey);
          KeyFactory KF = KeyFactory.getInstance("DH");
          PublicKey peerpubkey = KF.generatePublic(pubKeySpec);
          keyAgree.doPhase(peerpubkey, true);
          byte[] SharedSecret = keyAgree.generateSecret();
          keyAgree.doPhase(peerpubkey, true);
          SecretKey seckey = keyAgree.generateSecret("DES");

          // generate and initialize the Cipher object
          Cipher itsoCipher = Cipher.getInstance("DES/ECB/PKCS5Padding");
          itsoCipher.init(Cipher.ENCRYPT_MODE, seckey);

          // store the encrypted data in a file
          byte[] mydata = arg[0].getBytes();
          byte[] cipherdata = itsoCipher.doFinal(mydata);
          FileOutputStream cfos = new FileOutputStream("F:\\itso\\ch13\\bob.cip");
          cfos.write(cipherdata);
          cfos.close();
      }
      catch(Exception e)
      {
```

Figure 255. (Part 2 of 3). Bob.java

```
                System.out.println(e);
            }
        }
    }
}
```

Figure 256. (Part 3 of 3). Bob.java

This program is compiled by entering the following command:

`javac Bob.java`

Notice that the above program uses F:\itso\ch13 as its working directory, where it stores the encrypted file and the file containing Bob's public key, and where it looks for Alice's public key file.

13.5.2.2 Alice's Program
The program written by Alice to interact with Bob is shown in the following two figures:

```
import java.io.*;
import java.security.*;
import java.security.spec.*;
import javax.crypto.*;
import javax.crypto.spec.*;
import javax.crypto.interfaces.*;

public class Alice
{
    public static void main(String args[])
    {
        // wait for Bob's public key
        boolean over = false;
        while(!over)
            try
            {
                FileInputStream pfis1 = new FileInputStream("F:\\itso\\ch13\\bob.pub");
                pfis1.close();
                over=true;
            }
            catch(Exception e)
            {
            }
```

Figure 257. (Part 1 of 3). Alice.java

```
try
{
    // get Bob's public key
    FileInputStream pfis = new FileInputStream("F:\\itso\\ch13\\bob.pub");
    byte[] mencKey = new byte[pfis.available()];
    pfis.read(mencKey);
    pfis.close();
    X509EncodedKeySpec mpubKeySpec = new X509EncodedKeySpec(mencKey);
    KeyFactory mKeyFac = KeyFactory.getInstance("DH");
    PublicKey mpeerpubkey = mKeyFac.generatePublic(mpubKeySpec);

    // use the parameters of the public key
    DHParameterSpec mmyParamSpec = ((DHPublicKey)mpeerpubkey).getParams();

    // generate the key pair
    KeyPairGenerator mKPG = KeyPairGenerator.getInstance("DH");
    mKPG.initialize(mmyParamSpec);
    KeyPair mKP = mKPG.generateKeyPair();

    // get Alice's public key and store it to a file
    byte[] mPubKeyEnc = mKP.getPublic().getEncoded();
    FileOutputStream fos = new FileOutputStream("F:\\itso\\ch13\\alice.pub");
    fos.write(mPubKeyEnc);
    fos.close();

    // generate and initialize the KeyAgreement object
    KeyAgreement mKeyAgree = KeyAgreement.getInstance("DH");
    mKeyAgree.init(mKP.getPrivate());
    mKeyAgree.doPhase(mpeerpubkey, true);
    byte[] mSharedSecret = mKeyAgree.generateSecret();
    mKeyAgree.doPhase(mpeerpubkey, true);
    SecretKey mseckey = mKeyAgree.generateSecret("DES");

    // generate and initialize a Cipher object
    Cipher mitsoCipher = Cipher.getInstance("DES/ECB/PKCS5Padding");
    mitsoCipher.init(Cipher.DECRYPT_MODE, mseckey);

    // wait for the file produced by Bob
    boolean read = false;
    while(!read)
        try
        {
            FileInputStream cfistry = new FileInputStream("F:\\itso\\ch13\\bob.cip");
```

Figure 258. (Part 2 of 3). Alice.java

```
                cfistry.close();
                read = true;
            }
            catch(Exception e)
            {
            }

        // get the file produced by Bob
        FileInputStream cfis = new FileInputStream("F:\\itso\\ch13\\bob.cip");
        byte[] cipherdata = new byte[cfis.available()];
        cfis.read(cipherdata);
        cfis.close();

        // decrypt Bob's file and store the decrypted data to a file
        byte[] mydata = mitsoCipher.doFinal(cipherdata);
        FileOutputStream dfos = new FileOutputStream("F:\\itso\\ch13\\alice.dat");
        dfos.write(mydata);
        dfos.close();
        }
        catch(Exception e)
        {
            System.out.println(e);
        }
    }
}
```

Figure 259. (Part 3 of 3). Alice.java

The above program is compiled by entering:

```
javac Alice.java
```

Notice that this program too, like Bob.java, uses F:\itso\ch13 as its working directory, where it looks for the file containing Bob's public key and the file containing the encrypted data, and where it stores the file containing Alice's public key and the file containing the decrypted data.

13.5.2.3 Executing the Programs

Bob's program requires that a string is passed on the command line. Typically this string contains confidential information that Bob encrypts and stores in a file so that only those who hold the secret key can decrypt the message.

This is an example of how Bob could launch his program:

```
java Bob "Credit Card Number 1234 5678 9012"
```

After launching this command, the program runs until Alice stores a file with her public key in the same working directory. For this reason, we open another Command Prompt window and from the same directory, F:\itso\ch13, we issue the following command:

```
java Alice
```

In this case, no particular parameters are required on the command line.

The program can take some minutes to complete, but when it finishes, we can find in the working directory four new files:

1. The file bob.pub containing Bob's public key

2. The file alice.pub containing Alice's public key

3. The file bob.cip containing the information that was passed on the command line of Bob, but in an encrypted form

4. The file alice.dat containing the information of bob.cip after the decryption process has been applied

If the program has been successful, we should see that alice.dat contains the same string that Bob entered on the command prompt when he launched his program.

First of all, we open the encrypted file bob.cip with a text editor, as shown in the following screen:

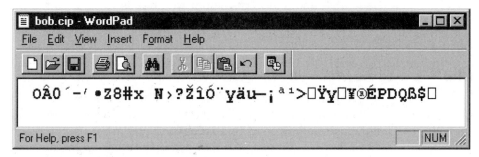

Figure 260. Contents of the Encrypted File bob.cip

Then we open the file alice.dat, which Alice has written after applying the decryption process to the contents of bob.cip, and we find it contains only the following line:

```
Credit Card Number 1234 5678 9012
```

which is exactly the original message entered by Bob. This demonstrates that Bob and Alice have been able to communicate in a secure manner even through a non-secure channel. In fact, using the JCE 1.2 APIs, both Bob and Alice have calculated the same secret key, without the need to exchange it over the network. Then, they have used this secret key to encrypt and decrypt confidential information.

Notice that in a real-life situaltion, Bob and Alice would reside on different machines. In this case, both Bob and Alice should publish their public keys and make them available to third parties.

13.6 Asymmetric Encryption with the Java 2 SDK and JCE 1.2

The output of the GetProviderInfo program, which we showed in 13.3.3, "Algorithms" on page 489, demonstrates that neither the SUN nor the SunJCE provider offer any algorithm available for asymmetric encryption. So private and public keys that can be generated using these two default providers cannot be used to initialize Cipher objects available in JCE. The SUN provider, which comes by default with the installation of Java 2 SDK, Standard Edition, V1.2, supplies cryptography capabilities to generate message digests and digital signatures, but in order to be compliant with the United States export regulations, it does not provide any support for encryption. On the other hand, the SunJCE provider, which is part of the JCE 1.2, only provides a means of symmetric encryption.

However, the provider architecture in Java allows for algorithm and vendor independence, as we saw in 13.3.1, "The Provider Concept in the JCA" on page 484, and a Java developer who needs to write a program implementing asymmetric encryption, can use other providers[9] that supply asymmetric encryption algorithms.

13.6.1 Using Asymmetric Encryption

In 13.4, "Java Cryptography Extension" on page 493 and 13.5, "Java Cryptography in Practice" on page 503 we showed several examples that demonstrate how to write applications that make use of JCE 1.2. We want to show you now an example that demonstrates how the flexibility of the JCE architecture allows asymmetric encryption. We will keep this example general, and we will not use any particular provider that supplies asymmetric encryption algorithms. In other words, we will show you the skeleton of the Java application that performs asymmetric encryption as long as a provider implementing an asymmetric encryption algorithm is installed and configured on the Java 2 SDK platform.

---

[9] Some of these, such as Jsafe, Cryptix and ABA, can be downloaded from the Internet. For further information, see D.1.7, "JCE Providers outside the United States" on page 688.

As we saw in Figure 237 on page 477, applying a digital signature to a message is equivalent to calculating the message digest, and encrypting it with the private key, as long as the algorithms used are the same. In other words:

Signature = Encrypt(MessageDigest)PrivateKey

So, let's see an example that:

1. Creates the digital signature of a file whose name is passed on the command line

2. Creates the message digest of the same file

3. Encrypts the message digest with the same private key used in Step 1 for signing.

On running this program, we expect to see the output produced after signing the file to be the same as that obtained after encrypting the message digest.

First of all, we need to create a KeyPairGenerator object, initialize it, generate the key pair and finally obtain the signature of the file. This part of the program is shown in the following figure:

```
System.out.println("Creating a KeyPairGenerator object...");
KeyPairGenerator KPG = KeyPairGenerator.getInstance("RSA");
System.out.println("Created...");

SecureRandom r = SecureRandom.getInstance("SHA1PRNG");
System.out.println("Random done...");

KPG.initialize(1024, r);
System.out.println("Initialized...");

KeyPair KP = KPG.genKeyPair();
System.out.println("Key pair generated...");
PrivateKey priv = KP.getPrivate();
System.out.println("Algorithm is " + priv.getAlgorithm() + "\n");

System.out.println("Creating a Signature object...");
Signature rsasig = Signature.getInstance("MD2/RSA/PKCS#1");
System.out.println("Created the Signature object...");
rsasig.initSign(priv);

FileInputStream fis = new FileInputStream(args[0]);
```

Figure 261. (Part 1 of 2). AsymmetricEncryption.java – Digital Signature Generation

```
BufferedInputStream bis = new BufferedInputStream(fis);
byte[] buff = new byte[1024];
while (bis.available() != 0)
{
   int len = bis.read(buff);
   rsasig.update(buff, 0, len);
}
bis.close();
fis.close();
byte[] realsignature = rsasig.sign();

System.out.println("Storing the signature in a file...");
FileOutputStream sigfile = new FileOutputStream(args[1]);
sigfile.write(realsignature);
sigfile.close();
```

Figure 262. (Part 2 of 2). AsymmetricEncryption.java – Digital Signature Generation

Next, we create the message digest of the same file. The process of generating a message digest is very similar to that of the digital signature. We create the message digest object by passing the algorithm to be used for digesting to the getInstance() factory method of the MessageDigest class. Next, update the object with the data to be hashed with the update() method and finally calculate the hash using the digest() method.

This is done through the following lines of code:

```
System.out.println("Creating a MD object.....");
MessageDigest classMD = MessageDigest.getInstance("MD2");
System.out.println("Created.....");

FileInputStream cfis = new FileInputStream(args[2]);
BufferedInputStream cbis = new BufferedInputStream(cfis);
byte[] cbuff = new byte[1024];
while (cbis.available() != 0)
{
   int len = cbis.read(cbuff);
   classMD.update(cbuff, 0, len);
}
cbis.close();
cfis.close();
byte[] classdigest = classMD.digest();
```

Figure 263. AsymmetricEncryption.java – Message Digest Generation

After this, we encrypt the message digest using the JCE APIs. To do this, we create a new Cipher object using the getInstance() factory method of the Cipher class, initialize it with the same private key used for signing the file in Figure 261 on page 517 and Figure 262 on page 518 by using the init() method, and finally encrypt the digest with the doFinal() method.

```
System.out.println("Creating a Cipher object...");
Cipher itsoCipher = Cipher.getInstance("RSA/ECB/PKCS1Padding");
System.out.println("Created Cipher object...");
itsoCipher.init(Cipher.ENCRYPT_MODE, priv);
byte[] encMD = itsoCipher.doFinal(classdigest);

System.out.println("Saving the encrypted message digest to a file...");
FileOutputStream encMDfile = new FileOutputStream(args[2]);
encMDfile.write(encMD);
encMDfile.close();
```

Figure 264. AsymmetricEncription.java – Message Digest Asymmetric Encryption

This program produces two signature files that we can compare and verify that they are exactly the same. Notice that the files used in this program are passed on the command line:

1. The file to be signed is passed as the first argument.

2. The file where the digital signature is saved is passed as the second argument.

3. The file where the encrypted message digest is saved is passed as the third argument.

The figure below shows the structure of the program in which you might want to put the blocks described above to generate the signatures:

```
import java.io.*;
import java.security.*;
import javax.crypto.*;

class AsymmetricEncryption
{
    public static void main(String args[])
    {
        if (args.length != 3)
```

Figure 265. (Part 1 of 2). AsymmetricEncryption.java – Structure of the Program

```
            System.out.println("Usage: java AsymmetricEncryption inputFile signFile
                encrDigestFile");
        else
            try
            {
                // Block 1 - Digital Signature Generation
                // Block 2 - Message Digest Generation
                // Block 3 - Message Digest Asymmetric Encryption
            }
            catch (Exception e)
            {
                System.out.println("Caught Exception: " + e);
            }
    }
}
```

Figure 266. (Part 2 of 2). AsymmetricEncryption.java – Structure of the Program

The full program is obtained by inserting in the `try{}` segment the three blocks we have shown in Figure 261 on page 517 through Figure 264 on page 519.

The program can then be compiled with the following command:

```
javac AsymmetricEncryption.java
```

And it can be run by entering a command similar to the following:

```
java AsymmetricEncryption inputFile signFile encrDigestFile
```

The program will run correctly once a provider supporting asymmetric encryption has been installed on the system (see Step 1 on page 299 and Step 2 on page 300). You can either use an existing provider or decide you want to implement your own provider. The way to implement a provider conforming to the JCA framework is explained in the next section.

13.7 How to Implement Your Own Provider

Each provider installed on the JVM supplies implementations of cryptographic services. As we know, the default providers that come with Java 2 SDK, Standard Edition, V1.2 and JCE 1.2 are SUN and SunJCE respectively. Notice that only when JCE 1.2 is installed can the JCE-specific implementations supplied by the provider packages be accessed.

Clients may configure their Java Runtime Environments (JREs) with different providers, and specify a preference order for each of them. The different implementations can vary. They may be software- or hardware-based, and might be platform dependent or independent. If you wish to use your own algorithms you need to create your own provider packages supplying cryptographic service implementations. To implement a provider, you need to do a number of things, as explained in the following sections:

13.7.1 Write the Service Implementation Code

First of all, you need to write the code that will supply algorithm-specific implementations of the cryptographic services you are providing. These can be:

- Ciphers
- Key agreements
- MAC algorithms
- Secret key factories
- Secret key generation services
- Digital signatures
- Message digests
- Key pair generation
- (Pseudo-)Random number generation algorithms
- Key factories
- Certificate factories
- Keystores
- Algorithm parameter management
- Algorithm parameter generation services

For each cryptographic service, you need to create a subclass of the appropriate SPI class. In the subclass, you need to:

1. Supply implementations for the abstract methods, whose names usually begin with `engine`

2. Ensure there is a public constructor without any arguments

   When one of our services is requested, the JVM looks up the subclass implementing that service. The JVM then creates the Class object associated with our subclass, and creates an instance of our subclass by calling the newInstance() method for that Class object. The newInstance() method requires a class to have a public constructor without any parameters. A default constructor without any arguments is automatically generated when a class does not have any constructors. But if a class defines any other constructors, a public constructor without any arguments must be explicitly implemented.

13.7.2 Give the Provider a Name

This short step is important, so that applications can specify this provider by name.

13.7.3 Write a Master Class

The third step is to create a subclass of the java.security.Provider class. The subclass should be a final class, and its constructor should call super(), specifying the provider name (as specified in 13.7.2, "Give the Provider a Name" on page 522), version number, and a string detailing information about the provider and algorithms it supports. For example:

```
super("IBMITSOProvider", 1.0, "IBM ITSO Provider implementing RSA
   encryption and key pair generation, and DES encryption.");
```

So the name is IBMITSOProvider, the version number is 1.0 and the rest is the information about the provider. This information can be retrieved by the applications using the Provider.getInfo() method, as shown in the sample code of Figure 241 on page 489 and Figure 242 on page 490.

For each service implemented by the provider, there must be a property whose name is the type of service, followed by a period and the name of the algorithm, certificate type or keystore type to which the service applies. The type of the service can be:

- Signature
- MessageDigest
- KeyPairGenerator
- SecureRandom
- KeyFactory
- KeyStore
- CertificateFactory
- AlgorithmParameterGenerator
- AlgorithmParameters

The property value must specify the fully qualified name of the class implementing the service. If you are implementing a provider for the JCE 1.2, then the type of service can also be:

- Cipher
- KeyAgreement
- KeyGenerator
- Mac
- SecretFactory

As an example, if our provider implements the Diffie-Hellman key agreement algorithm in a class named DHKeyAgreement, found in the com.ibm.itso.provider package, we will have the following statement:

```
put("KeyAgreement.DH", "com.ibm.itso.provider.DHKeyAgreement")
```

If the cryptographic service is Cipher, the name of the algorithm may actually represent a *transformation* (see 13.4.2, "The Cipher Class" on page 495) and may be composed of an algorithm name, a particular operation mode, and a padding scheme. For example RSA/ECB/PKCS1Padding indicates RSA algorithm, ECB operation mode and PKCS1 padding.

In general, a transformation is of the form *algorithm/mode/padding* or simply *algorithm*. A provider may supply a separate class for each combination of *algorithm/mode/padding*, or may decide to provide more generic classes representing sub-transformations corresponding to *algorithm* or *algorithm/mode* or *algorithm//padding*, in which case the requested mode and/or padding are set automatically by the getInstance() methods of Cipher, which invokes the engineSetMode() and engineSetPadding() methods of the provider's subclass of CipherSpi.

A Cipher property in a provider master class may have one of the following formats:

- Cipher.*algName* for implementing *algName* with pluggable mode and padding
- Cipher.*algName/mode* for implementing *algName* in the specified *mode*, with pluggable padding
- Cipher.*algName//padding* for implementing *algName* with the specified *padding*, with pluggable mode
- Cipher.*algName/mode/padding* implementing *algName* with the specified *mode* and *padding*

Notice that the double backslash (//) means that no mode is specified but only the algorithm and the padding have been specified. If you say *algName/padding*, the provider will take the padding to be a mode.

13.7.4 Compile the Code

Of course the code written needs to be compiled. You can create a ZIP or a JAR file after producing your class files.

13.7.5 Install and Configure the Provider

The provider code you produced must be installed and configured in order for the Java 2 SDK platform to recognize it. This operation can be done by following Step 1 on page 299 and Step 2 on page 300.

13.7.6 Test if the Provider Is Ready

The best way to test if the provider is ready is to write a small program that attempts to find the provider and test if the algorithms are available. For example, you can use the Java program GetProviderInfo, shown in Figure 241 on page 489 and Figure 242 on page 490.

If this is successful, you can test if the services implemented are found. For example:

```
Cipher c = Cipher.getInstance("DES", "IBMITSOprovider");
System.out.println("The Cipher algorithm name is " + c.getAlgorithm());
```

If this succeeds, you can document your provider and use it or make it available for others to use.

13.7.7 Algorithm Aliases

We discuss now another important topic: *algorithm aliases*.

For many cryptographic algorithms, there is a single official *standard name*. For example, *DiffieHellman* is the standard name for the Diffie-Hellman key agreement algorithm defined in PKCS#3. This enables clients to use aliases when referring to algorithms, rather than their standard names. For example, the SunJCE provider's master class, called SunJCE itself, defines the alias DH for the key agreement whose standard name is DiffieHellman. Thus, the following statements are equivalent:

```
KeyAgreement ka = KeyAgreement.getInstance("DiffieHellman", "SunJCE");
KeyAgreement ka = KeyAgreement.getInstance("DH", "SunJCE");
```

Aliases can be defined in the master class. To define an alias, we have to create a property named Alg.Alias.*engineClassName.aliasName,* where *engineClassName* is either Signature, MessageDigest, KeyPairGenerator, KeyFactory, AlgorithmParameterGenerator, or AlgorithmParameters, and *aliasName* is the alias name you define. The value of the property must be the standard algorithm name for the algorithm being aliased.

As an example, the SunJCE provider defines the alias DH for the key agreement algorithm whose standard name is DiffieHellman by setting a property named Alg.Alias.KeyAgreement.DH to have the value DiffieHellman via the following:

```
put("Alg.Alias.KeyAgreement.DH", "DiffieHellman");
```

Similarly, the following line enables users to specify PCKS5 in place of PKCS#5:

```
put("Alg.Alias.PaddingScheme.PKCS5", "PKCS#5");
```

Currently, aliases defined by the SUN and SunJCE provider are available to all clients, no matter which provider clients request. For example, if our provider implements the Diffie-Hellman algorithm, and we do not provide an alias for it, the DH alias defined by SunJCE can still be used to refer to our provider's Diffie-Hellman implementation, as follows:

```
KeyAgreement ka = KeyAgreement.getInstance("DH", "MyPro");
```

Notice that Sun Microsystems states that the aliasing scheme may be changed or eliminated in future releases.

13.7.8 Dependencies on Other Algorithms

Some algorithms require the use of other types of algorithms. For example, a Signature algorithm needs to use a message digest algorithm. To do this we can do one of the following:

- Provide our own implementations for both.

- Let the implementation of one algorithm use an instance of the other type of algorithm provided by a specified provider. Note that using an instance of another type of algorithm is appropriate if the algorithm is provided by the Java 2 SDK or by the same provider. (Otherwise, you must be sure that all clients who will use this provider will also have the other provider installed.)

- Let the implementation of one algorithm use an instance of the other type of algorithm, as supplied by another (unspecified) provider. That is, we can request an algorithm by name, but without specifying any particular provider. This is only appropriate if it is sure that there will be at least one implementation of the requested algorithm installed on each Java 2 SDK platform where our provider will be used.

13.7.9 Default Initializations

In case the client does not explicitly initialize a key pair generator or an algorithm parameter generator, each provider of such a service must supply (and document) a default initialization. For example, the SunJCE provider uses a default modulus key size of 1024 bits for the generation of Diffie-Hellman parameters.

13.7.10 A Sample Master Class

Here is a sample master class for the IBMITSO provider:

```
package com.ibm.itso.provider;

import java.security.AccessController;
import java.security.Provider;

public final class IBMITSOProvider extends Provider
{
   private static String info = "This is a demo provider. It implements DES
algorithms";

   public IBMITSOProvider()
   {
      super("IBMITSOprovider", 1.0, info);
      AccessController.doPrivileged(new java.security.PrivilegedAction()
      {
         public Object run()
         {
            put("Cipher.DES", "com.ibm.itso.provider.DESCipher");
            put("KeyGenerator.DES", "com.ibm.itso.provider.DESKeyGenerator");
            put("AlgorithmParameters.DES", "com.ibm.itso.provider.DESParameters");
            put("SecretKeyFactory.DES", "com.ibm.itso.provider.DESKeyFactory");
            return null;
         }
      });
   }
}
```

Figure 267. IBMITSOProvider.java

Chapter 14. Enterprise Java

The first two parts of this book have described the security issues in running Java programs on a single workstation, usually your PC. But that is only one application area for Java. Java can also be used on a Web server, or any other networked server, in a full-scale client/server approach. In the introduction we stated that security must be *holistic*, as attackers will concentrate on the weakest links. This applies even more forcefully when many computer systems are connected through a network, as there are more possible points to attack.

This chapter describes a number of different architectural approaches, illustrated with real examples that are in use today. We will consider the security implications of these approaches.

Firewalls are often touted as a defense against network attacks. Chapter 15, "Java and Firewalls – In and Out of the Net" on page 583 describes how firewalls work, and what the implications are, to both simple users of Web browsers and to Java application designers.

Cryptography is another valuable tool used to provide integrity, confidentiality and authentication between distributed systems. Chapter 13, "Cryptography in Java 2" on page 475 examines the uses of cryptography to provide security to real-world applications.

14.1 Browser Add-On Applets

Perhaps the simplest use of a Java application is the browser add-on applet to extend the facilities provided by a Web browser. It may be used to enhance the user interface by adding extra interactivity such as context-sensitive help or local search functions. Or it may be used to handle additional data types such as compressed astronomical images or packed database records. These examples depend directly upon the Java security architecture already described, where the security manager and sandbox prevent undesirable access. Because they read data only from the server, if at all, there are no other security issues.

14.2 Networked Architectures

The next level of complexity is seen in network-aware applets, which perform more network operations than simply reading data. Terminal emulators fall into this category. These applets provide the functions of a non-programmable terminal or visual display unit (VDU), connected via a local area network (LAN) to a host system, where the applications are run. An example is IBM Host On-Demand, which emulates a 3270 mainframe display session, communicating with a mainframe over TCP/IP. A graphical representation of IBM Host On-Demand is shown in the next figure:

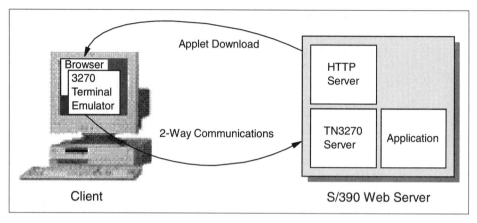

Figure 268. Host On-Demand

When run as applets, such programs are subject to the restrictions on the Java security manager: by default, they may only open a network connection back to the system from which they were downloaded. However, terminal emulation programs usually wish to communicate with many different host systems, not just one. If the host is a large mainframe, crucial to business, its owners may be reluctant to install the TCP/IP software, preferring to remain with systems network architecture (SNA) LANs. On other host systems, it might not be desirable to install, configure, run and maintain a Web server just to download the Java emulator applet, and this approach would still restrict access to that single host.

14.2.1 Applying the Java 2 Access Control Mechanisms

The Java 2 security architecture solves the problem described above. Now, it is still true that downloaded applets are restricted to connect back only to the system from which they are downloaded, but this is only the default configuration. Using the fine-grained access control mechanisms of Java 2, it is now possible to modify this default restriction, and you can specify the details of every socket connection that a particular code source can implement. Notice that this operation is very easy in the Java 2 security model. With the default policy implementation, you simply have to edit the policy file and add the permissions you want. In previous versions of Java, it was necessary to alter the security manager.

14.2.2 Two-Tier Architecture

Another possibility is to run the Java emulator as a stand-alone application, thereby relaxing the restrictions on which hosts the emulator may connect. This is the classic *two-tier* client/server application architecture. The security issues are very similar to running any other executable program, namely that it is wise to use trusted sources of supply only. Java has some safety and security advantages over other binary programs such as EXE files, and digitally signed applets can provide a cryptographic guarantee that the code author is who he says he is.

14.2.3 Three-Tier Architecture

Another solution is to run gateway software on the Web server that holds the Java applet. The applet will communicate over TCP/IP with the gateway software, which can then pass through the messages to the ultimate destination. In the case of 3270 terminal emulation, IBM's Communications Server, which runs on several operating systems, can provide the TCP/IP connection to the Java emulator, and can connect to hosts over both TCP/IP and SNA. This is a *three-tier* client/server application. A graphical representation of this architecture is shown in the following figure:

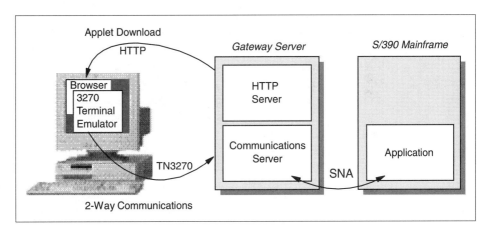

Figure 269. Three-Tier Example

Another approach is to use Web server Common Gateway Interface (CGI) programs[1] to provide the middle tier. The IBM CICS Internet Gateway takes this approach. To the application server, it emulates the functions of a 3270

---

[1] Often termed *CGI-BIN* programs after the directory name where they are conventionally stored.

terminal, but downstream it generates HTML code, which is displayed in the Web browser window. This solution is graphically represented in the following figure:

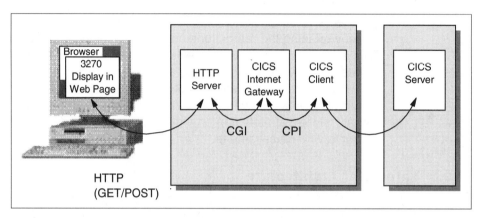

Figure 270. CICS Internet Gateway Example

This avoids using Java altogether in the client. It doesn't provide as much flexibility as the display is restricted to what can be done in HTML, but it may be a simpler solution to the problem.

The gateway server approach can also be used to provide extended facilities to Java applets. The IBM CICS Gateway for Java is a good example of this; it allows a Java applet to access transaction processing capabilities of CICS servers running on a variety of server platforms. This provides a class library package to access CICS functions. The class library itself does not perform the bulk of the functions; instead, it transmits the request to the gateway server, and returns the server's response to the applet. The gateway server is a small program that receives the requests and calls the real CICS client library, which communicates with the CICS system itself. It would be common to run the CICS transaction processing engine on its own system, separate from the Web server, as shown in the following figure:

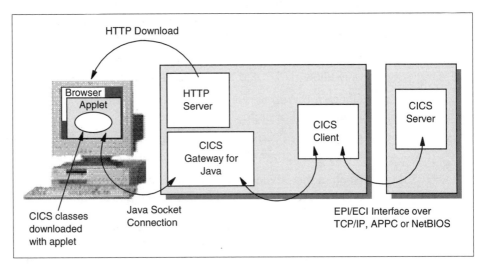

Figure 271. CICS Gateway for Java Example

The security analysis for this type of system is more complex. We wish to ensure the security of the gateway system as well as the systems with which it connects, especially if the server is on the public Internet, where any malicious hacker may attempt to access it. Intranet systems should already have some defenses in place to restrict access to company personnel, but security is still of concern, especially where sensitive data is at risk.

The normal approach is to provide a number of barriers that must be overcome before data access is granted. Often the first barrier is the company firewall system (see Chapter 15, "Java and Firewalls – In and Out of the Net" on page 583 for more on firewalls). Firewalls can check that requests are coming from, and going to, apparently valid addresses; some firewalls will check the data content of selected protocols, but there are limits to what can be checked. There have been several embarrassingly public demonstrations of Web servers whose content has been replaced by derogatory pages, despite firewalls being in place. Often these hackers have succeeded because valid HTTP URL requests to the Web server allowed software to be run on the server which had an accidental *security hole* in it, such as allowing any data file to be read or written, or even executing arbitrary binary code supplied as part of the URL.

Therefore, it is necessary to secure the Web server against as many potential hazards as possible, and also to try to ensure that when (not if) it is compromised, the attacker still does not have access to critical data.

Hardening Web servers against attack has been the subject of several books, such as *Practical UNIX and Internet Security* by Simson Garfinkel and Gene Spafford, so only a brief checklist will be given here:

1. Disable all network services that do not need to be present; if possible only allow HTTP and the gateway protocol.

2. Check the Web server configuration files to allow access only to the required set of pages.

3. Delete any CGI-BIN and other executable programs that are not required; if they are not present, they cannot be run!

4. Restrict the privileges of the Web server program, if possible. UNIX allows it to be run as a normal user, with few access rights.

These guidelines also apply to *any* gateway software being run. Try to ensure it does not provide access to more facilities than needed. In particular, do not depend on the client to validate any requests, but assume that a hacker might have constructed a modified client which can generate *any* possible request. For example, for a 3270 gateway, do not assume that the client will request connection only to a limited set of hosts, but configure the gateway so that those are the only hosts that can be connected to, and that no other host names can be made visible. For database access and transaction processing, make sure the gateway allows no more than the set of permitted requests.

14.2.4 Network Security

The classic three-tier architecture pictures can hide other attack routes. The diagrams shown in Figure 269 on page 529, Figure 270 on page 530 and Figure 271 on page 531 imply that there are separate connections between the client and the Web server/gateway, and the gateway and the end server. However, the real network may not be configured that way. For simplicity or cost, there might be only a single network interface on the Web server, as shown in the following figure:

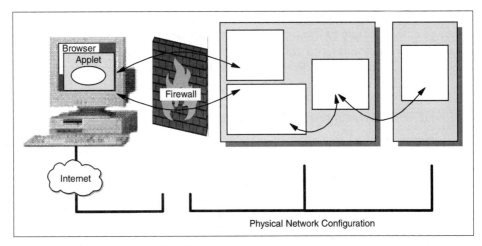

Figure 272. Web Server with One Network Interface

In this case, the third-tier server is on the same network, and can potentially be accessed directly from the firewall. Perhaps the firewall *is* configured correctly, and will prevent direct access to the end server.

But will this be true tomorrow, after additional services have been added? For very little extra cost, the networks can be physically separated by providing two network interfaces in the Web server.[2] This solution is represented in the following diagram:

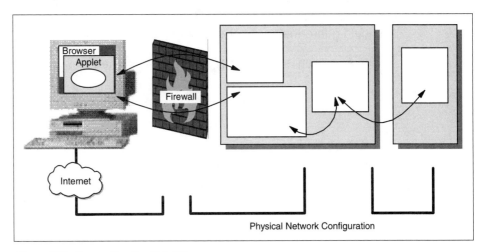

Figure 273. Separating the Third Tier

[2] Make sure the cables are well labeled; there have been cases of firewalls being bypassed when someone tripped over the cables, and plugged them back the wrong way.

Or, a second firewall system can be used. This configuration has the benefit that even if the Web server is compromised, the second firewall still restricts access to the rest of the network. It is more expensive to provide such a *demilitarized zone* (DMZ), but if you already require such a configuration to provide safe Internet connection, there is no extra cost. The cost of a second firewall is likely to be less than the value of the data it protects, so you need to do your own value calculations. A DMZ network environment is graphically represented in the following figure:

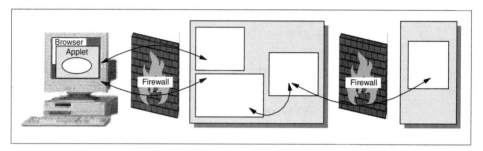

Figure 274. DMZ Network Environment

One additional security barrier to consider using is the type of network itself. You could link the gateway and end server using SNA protocols, or by a small custom-built program communicating over a dedicated serial link. These effectively use the network connection as another firewall; if TCP/IP cannot travel over it, many hacking techniques are simply not possible. Don't forget, though, that if the Web server is totally compromised, the hacker has all your communications software at his disposal, if he can discover it, so you still should guard the third-tier server.

This approach is graphically represented in the following diagram:

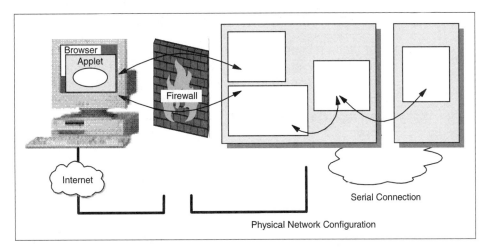

Figure 275. Protection Using Mixed Connection Protocols

14.3 Secure Clients and Network Computers

If you have great concern about what damage an applet may cause on your client, whether by malicious design or by a programming accident, you may wish to consider the network computer (NC) approach. Many types of NCs are now available on the market, with varying feature sets. Some are little different from ordinary personal computers, though they may have sealed cases to prevent expansion. Some may be intended for domestic use, and connect to a television set and a telephone line, for home Web browsing.

The type we are considering here are the diskless clients, such as the IBM Network Station (NS). This is a small book-sized processor unit, without any local disk, which connects to a LAN. It has a display, keyboard and mouse. When switched on, it downloads its kernel software from a server on the LAN, and then downloads applications such as a Web browser and terminal emulator. These allow it to run applications on one or more remote servers. The IBM NS can also download and run Java programs locally, in fact Java is the only published API for running local programs.

In a secure environment, this has some advantages. There is no local disk storage at the NS, so there is little chance of permanent data corruption from malicious or misbehaving software. Although Java programs are not the only things that can run on the NS (it also supports terminal emulation, X-Windows and remote Windows access) there is no capability for integration between the different application types. This means that the Java security restrictions cannot be easily bypassed. All disk storage is held on the servers, allowing a fully managed backup service to be provided. Software updates are performed centrally, reducing administration workload.

For these reasons alone, network computers have a great potential for providing universal access to applications and data, with Java as a key technology. The main impetus behind the network computer is usually the potential for large cost savings. But in the appropriate application areas, the cost savings may be much less important than the other advantages listed above.

14.4 Server-Side Java

We have described the use of Java at the client in these distributed architectures, but what about using Java elsewhere? This can fulfill the goal of *Write Once, Run Anywhere*. It can greatly simplify the work of software developers, especially of distributed architectures. You could argue that the majority of client systems will be PCs running some flavor of Microsoft Windows, so that you can satisfy most people most of the time by only developing a Windows version of your code. This is not true for servers; most of the world's crucial business data is kept on mainframe and UNIX servers. If you develop the server side of your distributed application in Java, it can be run on almost any of these servers, whether they run MVS, VM, OS/390, Windows NT, OS/2, AS/400 or one of the many flavors of UNIX.

Jini Technology

At the other end of the spectrum, the server-side Java might be running in an intelligent peripheral device, such as a printer, modem rack, photocopier or coffee vending machine. These applications are part of the *Jini* connection technology, recently announced by Sun Microsystems. This technology is based on a simple concept: devices should work together. They should simply connect, with no drivers to find, no operating system issues, no cables and connectors.

Jini technology provides simple mechanisms which enable devices to plug together to form a community, put together without any planning, installation, or human intervention. Each device provides services that other devices in the community may use. These devices provide their own interfaces, which ensures reliability and compatibility. Clearly there are immense opportunities to reduce development costs, but there are also clear security implications; imagine the effect of re-programming a rival company's vending machine if you managed to break the access codes!

In many ways, Java is an ideal environment for server applications. The multi-threaded environment is ideally suited for supporting simultaneous requests to a server. Even the standard classes are simplified, as many server programs are unlikely to need the java.awt windowing classes as well as several others, which is where most cross-platform problems have arisen to date.

As an example, the gateway component of the CICS Java gateway could be written in Java, so it could be run on any Web server system without the need for extensive cross-platform porting and testing.

14.4.1 The Cost of Server-Side Java

But what is the cost of this portability? In the case of server-side Java, when Java is used as a program development language, the potential risk is reduced execution performance. This is not always a problem; the next section shows how Java can sometimes *enhance* server performance.

Performance is more important for a server than a client, as the server needs to handle many simultaneous users. Just-in-time (JIT) compilers may help somewhat, but the real solution is to use true Java compilers, at least until processors executing Java bytecode become commonplace. But doesn't this defeat the *Write Once, Run Anywhere* approach? Not entirely, as vendors can still supply system-independent code, which gets compiled once during the installation process.

True compilers can take two different approaches:

1. The first is to treat Java as just another programming language, and compile Java source into native object code for a given machine. This would imply that software would need to be supplied in source form, which would be less attractive to many developers, although it could be passed through an obfuscating program (see 5.4.1, "Beating the Decompilation Threat" on page 134), to remove meaningful identifiers.

2. The second approach, which is likely to be more promising, is to compile Java bytecode, rather than source code, into native object code. This allows the compiler to be run on all the wealth of Java bytecode that is available, not just that supplied by server developers. And since Java bytecode is closely related to source code under normal circumstances, some Java true compilers may provide both options and accept source or bytecode input.

14.5 Servlets

Java is not only used to develop stand-alone programs. In our Web-based world, many of the servers run an HTTP Web server. The traditional approach to add customized function to a Web server has been to write CGI programs.

These CGI programs are stand-alone programs that are called by the HTTP server when it receives requests for specific pages. Rather than return static HTML text, the HTTP server starts the CGI program, and passes to it the user's request, together with many details about the server environment. The CGI program must handle the request, and return HTML text to the HTTP server, which in turn returns it to the user. The following figure offers a graphical representation of this process:

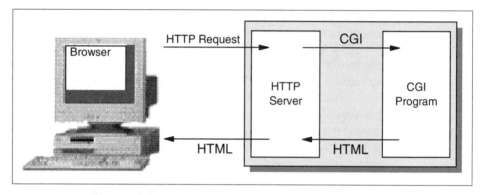

Figure 276. How CGI-BIN Programs Work

Starting the execution of any program, not just a CGI program, can be a lengthy process. Memory needs to be allocated, the program code needs to be read from disk into memory, references to dynamic libraries need to be linked, standard input and output streams need to be created and connected, and finally the program needs to do the processing required.

In a very simple HTTP Web server, multi-threading may not be implemented, which means that no other HTTP requests could be served until the CGI program returns, possibly after many seconds. Most modern HTTP servers support multi-threading (on appropriate operating systems), so this is less of an issue. However, there are still limits to the number of process threads that can be created, and the individual threads still need to wait for the CGI program to complete.

CGI programs are also the target of hackers; many of the successful attacks on Web servers have been through poorly tested CGI programs, which may fail to test the parameters passed to them, or may overflow input buffers when passed data that is too long.

Other alternatives to CGI have been implemented, such as NSAPI from Netscape, MSAPI from Microsoft, or ICAPI from IBM. These permit native software routines to be directly called by the Web server, significantly reducing the startup overhead. However, the add-on routines still need to be compiled for each platform, and the different programming interfaces may not be fully compatible, restricting the choice of Web server to a particular manufacturer (although ICAPI, for example, has been designed to include the NSAPI calls). Program testing is even more important, to prevent badly written software from corrupting the Web server itself.

Java servlets can be employed to overcome these server-side issues. A *servlet* is a platform-independent server-side software component written in Java. Servlets run on a Web server machine inside a Java-enabled server, that is, a server able to start the Java Virtual Machine (JVM) in order to support the use of Java servlets.[3] They dynamically extend the capabilities of the server because they provide services over the Web using the request-response paradigm.

Servlets were introduced to interactively view and modify data and to generate dynamic Web content. From a high-level perspective, the process flow would be:

1. The client sends a request to the server.

2. The server sends the request information to the servlet.

3. The servlet builds a response and passes it to the server. That response is dynamically built and the contents of the response usually depend on the client's request.

4. The server sends the response back to the client.

Servlets look like ordinary Java programs which begin importing some particular Java packages that belong to the Java Servlet API. Since servlets are object bytecodes that can be dynamically loaded off the Internet, we could say that servlets are to the server what applets are to the client. But, since servlets run inside servers, they do not need a graphical user interface (GUI). In this sense servlets are also called faceless objects.

---

[3] Servlets were initially supported in the Java Web Server from JavaSoft. Since then, several other Java-based Web servers have supported the standard Servlet API. A list of Java-enabled Web servers that support the Java Servlet API can be found at http://java.sun.com/products/servlet/runners.html.

14.5.1 Advantages of Servlets

Java servlets offer many advantages:

- A servlet can interact with other resources (files, databases, applets, applications written in Java or in other languages) to construct the response that will be sent back to the client and, if needed, to save information about the request-response interaction.

- With a servlet approach, the server can grant full access to local facilities, such as databases, and trust that the servlet itself will control the amount and precise nature of access that is effectively afforded to external users.

  For example, the Java Servlet API provides all the methods to monitor and verify the origin of all requests. Moreover, the servlet code is not passed to the client, only the results that it produces are. If the code is not passed to the client, it cannot be saved or disassembled, thereby protecting proprietary algorithms built into the servlet.

- Servlets can be client programs of other services, for example, when they are used in distributed application systems.

- It is possible to invoke servlets from a local or remote disk across the network.

- Servlets can be *chained*. This means that one servlet can call another servlet, thus becoming its client. It can also call several servlets in sequence.

- Servlets can be dynamically called from within HTML pages, using the special HTML <SERVLET> tag. This function is also known as *servlet tag technique*.

- The Java Servlet API is protocol-independent. It does not assume anything about the protocol used to transmit it on the Internet. You can write a servlet without having to consider what the transmission protocol will be.

- Like all Java programs, servlets can use all the capabilities of the object-oriented Java language:

  - They can be rapidly developed.

  - Lack of pointers promote robust applications (unlike C).

  - A servlet service routine is only a thread and not an entire operating system process. That is why a servlet can handle connections with multiple clients, accepting requests and downloading responses back to the multiple clients. This is a more efficient mechanism than using CGI-BINs.

- Servlets are portable. They run on a variety of servers without needing to be rewritten.

- Memory access violations are not possible, so faulty servlets will not crash servers.

- Finally, *Java servlets must respect the security rules of the Java platform where they run.*

14.5.2 Servlets and CGI-BINs

From a high-level perspective servlets can perform the same functions as CGI-BINs. However, there are some important differences:

- CGI-BIN applications are difficult to develop since technical knowledge is needed to work with parameter passing, and this is not a common skill. They are not portable: a CGI-BIN application written for a specific platform will only be able to run in that environment. Each CGI-BIN application is part of a specific process that is activated by a client's request and is destroyed after the client has been served. This causes high startup, memory and CPU costs and implies that multiple clients cannot be served by the same process.

- On the other hand, servlets offer all the advantages of Java programs; they are portable and robust applications and they are easy to develop. Servlets also allow you to generate dynamic portions of HTML pages embedded in static HTML pages using the <SERVLET> tag. However, the main advantage of servlets over CGI-BINs is that a servlet is activated by the first client that sends it a request. Then it continues running in the background, waiting for further requests and each request generates a new thread, not an entire process. Multiple clients may be served simultaneously inside the same process and typically the servlet process is destroyed only when the Web server is shut down.

From a security perspective, it must be noted that:

- CGI-BINs programs are typically written in C, C++ or Perl. This means that they are subjected to the security limitations of the operating system only. If further security restrictions need to be applied, these must be coded into the program itself by the CGI-BIN programmer.

- On the contrary, servlets are written in Java and run on a servlet engine JVM. Hence, they are subjected to the security restrictions imposed by the servlet security manager of the platform where they run.

14.5.3 Java Servlet APIs

Servlets use packages found in the Java Servlet API. When you write code for a Java servlet, you must import at least one of the following two packages:

- javax.servlet – for any type of servlet

- javax.servlet.http – for servlets specific to the HTTP protocol

The following table summarizes the structure of the Java Servlet API V2.1[4]:

Table 18. Java Servlet API

	javax.servlet	javax.servlet.http
Interfaces	RequestDispatcher Servlet ServletConfig Servlet Context Servlet Request Servlet Response SingleThreadModel	HttpServletRequest HttpServletResponse HttpSession HttpSessionBindingListener HttpSessionContext
Classes	GenericServlet ServletInputStream ServletOutputStream	HttpServlet HttpUtils HttpSessionBindingEvent Cookie
Exceptions	ServletException UnavailableException	

Servlets are usually created by extending from the HTTPServlet class, which in turn extends GenericServlet, or from the GenericServlet class itself, which implements the Servlet interface. Both the GenericServlet and the HTTPServlet classes contain three methods that they inherit from the Servlet interface: init(), service() and destroy(). These methods, used by the servlet to communicate with the server, are called *life cycle methods*. You will work with these three methods in a slightly different way, depending on whether you are extending the GenericServlet class or the HttpServlet class.

The init() and the destroy() methods have the same properties for the GenericServlet and the HTTPServlet classes, while the service() method must be handled differently when it is based on the GenericServlet class or on the HttpServlet class:

- **The init() method**

  The init() method is run only once when the server loads the servlet and the servlet is started. It is guaranteed to finish before any service() requests are accepted. The servlet can be activated when the server

[4] Information on the latest Java Servlet API can be found at http://java.sun.com/products/servlet/.

starts or when the first client accesses the servlet. The biggest advantage is that the init() method is called only once, regardless of how many clients access the servlet.

The default init() method logs the servlet initialization and it is possible to configure it in order to save other information. The default init() method can usually be accepted as it is, without the need to override it, because it is not abstract. Servlet developers may, if they want, provide their own implementation of this method, overriding it and creating a custom init().

A custom init() is typically used to perform setup of servlet-wide resources only once, rather than once per request. For example, you might want to write a custom init() to load GIF images one time only, where the servlet returns the images multiple times in response to multiple client requests to the servlet. Further examples may be initializing sessions with other network services or getting access to their persistent data (stored in a database or in a file).

- **The destroy() method**

  The destroy() method is run only once when the server stops the servlet and unloads it. Usually, servlets are unloaded when the server is shut down. The default destroy() method also can be accepted as is, without the need to override it, because it is not abstract. Servlet writers may, if they wish, override the destroy() call, providing their own custom destroy() method.

  A custom destroy() method is often used to manage servlet-wide resources. For example, the server might accumulate data when it is running and you might want to save this data to a file when the servlet is stopped.

- **The service() method**

  The service() method is the heart of the servlet. In fact, as we said, the simplest possible servlet defines only the service() method. Unlike the init() and destroy() methods, it is called for each client request, and not only one time in the life cycle of the servlet.

  The service() method must be handled differently when it is based on the GenericServlet class or on the HttpServlet class:

  - If the servlet is based on the GenericServlet class, the service() method is abstract, so you must override it. The service() method obtains information about the client request, prepares the response and returns this response to the client. You should also remember that multiple clients might access the service() method at the same time, so you should consider threads and synchronized code.

- If the servlet is based on the HttpServlet class, the service() method is not abstract. Therefore, you can accept it as it is.

It is through the service() method that the server and servlet can exchange data. In fact, when the server invokes the servlet service() method, it also passes two objects as parameters:

- If the servlet is based on the GenericServlet class, the two objects are instances of:

  - ServletRequest
  - ServletResponse

- If the servlet is based on the HttpServlet class, the two objects are instances of:

  - HttpServletRequest
  - HttpServletResponse

These objects encapsulate the data sent by the client, providing access to parameters and allowing the servlets to report status, including errors if they occurred. The server creates an instance for the request and response objects and passes them to the servlet. Both these objects are used by the server to exchange data with the servlet:

- The servlet invokes methods from the request object in order to discover information about the client environment, the server environment and all the information provided by the client.

- The servlet invokes methods for the response object to send the response that it has already prepared back to the Web server, which then sends it to the client.

14.5.4 Servlet Life Cycle

The servlet life cycle involves a series of interactions among the client, the server and the servlet. This is shown in the following diagram:

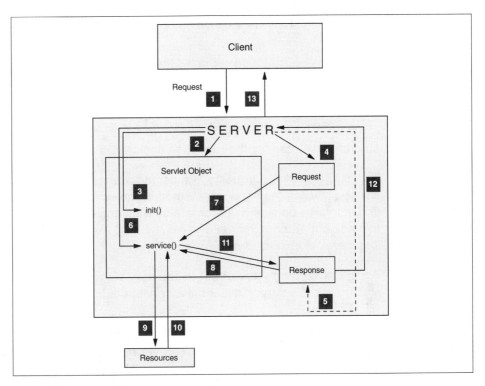

Figure 277. Servlet Life Cycle

The steps are explained below:

1. The servlet is loaded. This operation is typically performed dynamically, that is, when the first client accesses the servlet. In most servers, options are provided to force the loading of the servlet when the server starts up.

2. The server creates an instance of the servlet.

3. The server calls the servlet init() method. This method is called only once during the lifetime of the servlet.

4. A client request arrives at the server and the server creates a request object (ServletRequest or HttpServletRequest).

5. The server creates a response object (ServletResponse or HttpServletResponse).

6. The server invokes the servlet service() method.

7. The service() method takes the request object as one of its two parameters.

8. The service() method takes the response object as the other parameter.

9. The service() method gets information about the request object and processes the request accessing other resources, such as databases, files, etc.

10. The service() method retrieves the necessary information from the resources accessed.

11. The service() method uses methods of the response object.

12. The service() method passes the response back to the server.

13. The server passes the response back to the client.

For additional client requests, the server creates new request and response objects, invokes the service() method of the servlet and passes the request and response objects as parameters. This loop is repeated for every client request, but, without the need to call the init() method every time. The servlet, in general, is initialized only once.

When the server no longer needs the servlets (typically when the server is shut down), the server invokes the servlet destroy() method.

14.5.5 IBM WebSphere Application Server

Before you can run a servlet on a server machine, a Java-enabled Web server must be installed on it. The latest Web servers have settings during their installation to optionally select or deselect the servlet support. If your Web server is not Java enabled, search for the installation of the servlet component on your Web server installation media, and you might be able to selectively install this component alone. If your Web server does not have support for Java, then you should consider installing a Java-enabled Web server.

Alternatively, you might want to install a servlet engine over the Web server. The Web server recognizes the servlet engine as one of its components, and when a request arrives for executing a servlet, the Web server activates the servlet engine, which starts the JVM (if not already started) and runs the servlet.

A very powerful servlet engine comes with IBM WebSphere Application Server[5]. IBM WebSphere Application Server lets you achieve your *Write Once, Run Anywhere* goal for servlet development. The product consists of a Java-based servlet engine that is independent of both your Web server and its underlying operating system.

---

[5] See http://www.software.ibm.com/webservers/appserv/.

WebSphere Application Server offers a choice of server plug-ins that are compatible with the most popular server APIs. The supported Web servers are:

- IBM HTTP Server
- Apache Server
- Domino
- Lotus Domino Go Webserver
- Netscape Enterprise Server
- Netscape FastTrack Server
- Microsoft Internet Information Server

In addition to the servlet engine and plug-ins, WebSphere Application Server provides:

- Implementation of the JavaSoft Java Servlet API, plus extensions of and additions to the API

- Sample applications demonstrating the basic classes and the extensions

- The IBM WebSphere Application Server Manager, a graphical interface making it easy to:

  - Set options for loading local and remote servlets

  - Set initialization parameters

  - Manage servlets

  - Specify servlet aliases

  - Create servlet chains and filters

  - Administer and monitor Enterprise Java Services (EJS) components

  - Enable Lightweight Directory Access Protocol (LDAP) directory support

  - Log servlet messages

  - Enable JVM debugging

  - Monitor resources used by Application Server

  - Monitor loaded servlets, active servlet sessions, and JDBC connections

  - Monitor errors, events, exceptions, and log output

  - Create dumps and data snapshots

  - Dynamically enable and disable tracing

- A connection management feature that caches and reuses connections to your JDBC-compliant databases

When a servlet needs a database connection, it can get one from the pool of available connections, eliminating the overhead required to open a new connection for each request.

- Additional Java classes, coded to the JavaBeans specification, that allow programmers to access JDBC-compliant databases

  These data access beans provide enhanced function while hiding the complexity of using relational databases. They can be used in a visual manner in an integrated development environment.

- Support for dynamic page content called JavaServer Pages (JSP)

  JSP technology lets you produce dynamic Web pages with server-side scripting. The result is to separate your presentation logic (for example, the HTML code that defines your Web site structure and appearance) from your business logic (for example, the Java code that accesses a database for information to display on the Web site). For flexibility, JSP files can include any combination of inline Java, <SERVLET> tags, National Center for Supercomputing Applications (NCSA) tags, and JavaBeans.

- Enterprise Java Services

  This function is provided to run and manage applications coded to Sun's Enterprise JavaBeans (EJB) specification (see 14.7, "Enterprise JavaBeans" on page 580)

- Enablement for LDAP supported directory services

- Modules and a command line interface for integrating Application Server and Apache Server into the Tivoli Management Environment 10 (TME 10) for distributed monitoring and operations

14.5.6 A Sample Servlet

We have seen the structure and the life cycle of a servlet. We are now in a position to write the code for an example servlet, which we call MyRemoteRequest. This servlet is invoked from an HTML page with a form in it. The user enters his or her name and country information. By clicking the **Submit** button of the form, the servlet is invoked. The servlet displays some information about the client and server, reads the contents of a file C:\info.txt residing on the Web server, and displays this information back on the client machine. The block diagram of the client/server interactions is shown in the following figure:

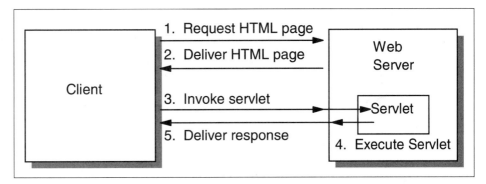

Figure 278. MyRemoteRequest Servlet Block Diagram

The application flow is described in the following list:

1. The user on the client machine requests an HTML page containing a form.

2. The Web server sends the requested HTML page back to the client.

3. The user on the client machine fills out the form and submits it, causing the Web server to invoke the servlet.

4. The servlet processes the client's request and prepares a dynamic response for the client.

5. The servlet sends the dynamic response to the server, which sends it back to the client.

The source code for the servlet MyRemoteRequest is shown in Figure 279 on page 549, Figure 280 on page 550 and Figure 281 on page 551.

```
/*
 * This is an example servlet that echoes to the browser the servlet
 * request information as well as information about the request
 * protocol, requester host name and address, and the receiving
 * server name and port number.
 * The servlet also displays the contents of the file on the Webserver, C:\info.txt
 */

import javax.servlet.*;
import java.io.*;
import java.util.*;

public class MyRemoteRequest extends GenericServlet
```

Figure 279. (Part 1 of 3). MyRemoteRequest.java

```
{
   public void service(ServletRequest req, ServletResponse res) throws IOException
   {
       ServletOutputStream os;
       Enumeration paramNames;
       String paramName, paramValue;

       // set the output content type to HTML
       res.setContentType("text/html");

       // get the  output stream for the response
       os = res.getOutputStream();
       os.println("<CENTER><H2>MyRemoteRequest Servlet</H2></CENTER><HR>");

       // get and print request protocol and scheme information
       os.println("<P>Request protocol is " + req.getProtocol());
       os.println("<BR>Request scheme is " + req.getScheme());

       // get and print requester information
       os.println("<BR>Remote host is " + req.getRemoteHost());
       os.println("<BR>Remote address is " + req.getRemoteAddr());

       // get and print receiver server information
       os.println("<BR>Receiving server is " + req.getServerName() + " on port number "
           + req.getServerPort());

       // put the request parameters into an Enumeration of strings
       paramNames = req.getParameterNames();

       // loop through name Enumeration, get matching value, and print name/value pair
       os.println("<HR><BR><B>Request parameters are:</B>");

       while(paramNames.hasMoreElements())
       {
           // get the next name from the Enumeration of parameters
           paramName = (String)paramNames.nextElement();

           // get the value of the parameter
           paramValue = (String)req.getParameter(paramName);

           // print the name/value pair to the browser */
           os.println("<BR>name = " + paramName + "; value = " + paramValue);
       }
```

Figure 280. (Part 2 of 3). MyRemoteRequest.java

```
      os.println("<HR><BR><B>Contents of file <I>info.txt</I> :</B>");
      try
      {
          String fileName = "C:\\info.txt";
          BufferedReader brIn = new BufferedReader(new FileReader(fileName));
          String lineRead;
          while ((lineRead = brIn.readLine()) != null)
          {
              if (lineRead.length() >0)
                  os.println("<BR>" + lineRead);
              else
                  os.print(lineRead);
          }
      }
      catch (Exception e)
      {
          os.println("<BR>" + e.toString());
          PrintWriter pwOut = new PrintWriter(os);
          e.printStackTrace(pwOut);
          pwOut.flush();
          pwOut.close();
      }

      // close the output stream
      os.close();
  }
}
```

Figure 281. (Part 3 of 3). MyRemoteRequest.java

You can see that the servlet imports the package javax.servlet. There is no main() in a servlet code. The only method that we implement in this servlet is the service() method, which accepts a ServletRequest object req, and a ServletResponse object res. What the servlet does should be clear by reading the comments embedded in the code, but a more detailed explanation follows.

The ServletOutputStream object os is created to write back to the client. The os object is created from the response object, using the res.getOutputStream(). The Enumeration object paramNames is needed to temporarily store the parameter name/value pairs passed from the client to the Web server in the request object, req.

Usually, HTTP data is associated with a specific content type, which can be any of text/data, text/html, image/gif, application/java-archive, etc. The content type tells the browser what kind of data is being supplied to it by the Web server and how to display the data. In our example servlet, we are asking the Web browser to interpret the results of the execution of the MyRemoteRequest servlet as an HTML output. Hence, we set the content type as text/html.

We then obtain the ServletOutputStream os, and print the data to be seen on the browser, all of them embedded in HTML tags. The ServletRequest class has several get methods, such as req.getScheme() and req.getRemoteHost(), which provide information regarding the request object, req, and also the Web client and the server.

The `while` loop prints this information to the output stream. The req.getParameterNames() method obtains the list of the name/value pairs that were sent as part of the client request.

The next `try{}catch(){}` block reads the contents of a text file C:\info.txt and prints it on the client browser. For simplicity, our info.txt file contains only one line:

```
Tigers don't cry!!
```

Any exception that is generated is again printed on the client's browser using the PrintWriter object.

The source code of the servlet we have presented must be compiled. In order for this operation to succeed, the Java compiler `javac` must be able to find the Java Servlet API. The Java Servlet Development Kit (JSDK)[6], which is a basic servlet development environment provided by Sun Microsystems, comes with two JAR files, server.jar and servlet.jar. To compile the above servlet on a Java 2 SDK platform, you should copy these two JAR files to the extensions directory under the Java Runtime Environment (JRE) development directory (see 8.1, "A Note on java.home and the JRE Installation Directory" on page 225), and then issue the command:

```
javac MyRemoteRequest.java
```

Other servlet engines can come with an implementation of the JavaSoft Java Servlet API, plus extensions of and additions to the API. If you are using a different servlet engine, you should follow the directions provided with your servlet engine product to configure the environment correctly before compiling the servlet code and running the servlet.

---

[6] You can download the JSDK from http://java.sun.com/products/servlet/.

The class file produced by the command above must be installed in a special directory that the Web server recognizes as the directory where all the servlets are installed. This is called the *servlet directory*, and its location also depends on the specific servlet engine you are using.

The servlet above is invoked from within the <FORM> of a Web page, whose code is shown in the HTML file in the following figure:

```
<HTML>
   <HEAD>
      <TITLE>myForm servlet</TITLE>
   </HEAD>

   <BODY>
      <CENTER><H2><U>MyRemoteRequest Servlet - Input Form</U></H2></CENTER>
      <P>
      Hi! Fill in your <B>Name</B> and <B>Country</B>, and click on the <B>Submit</B>
         button.
      <P>

      <FORM Action="examples/servlet/MyRemoteRequest" Method="GET">
         Name    : <INPUT Type=input Name="myName" Value="">
         <BR>
         Country : <INPUT Type=input Name="myCountry" Value="">
         <P>
         <INPUT Type="submit" Name="Submit" Value="submit">
      </FORM>
   </BODY>
</HTML>
```

Figure 282. MyRemoteRequest.html

The following figure shows the Web browser window after the user on the client machine has invoked the HTML page and has filled in the form fields:

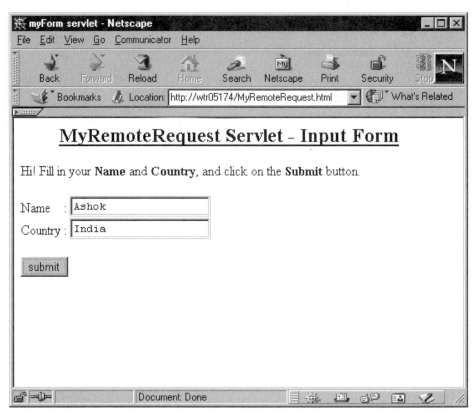

Figure 283. MyRequest.html - Input Form

By clicking on the **Submit** button, the servlet is activated by the Web server. It processes the input from the client and sends a dynamic response back to the client machine. This response is then displayed by the Web browser, as shown in the following figure:

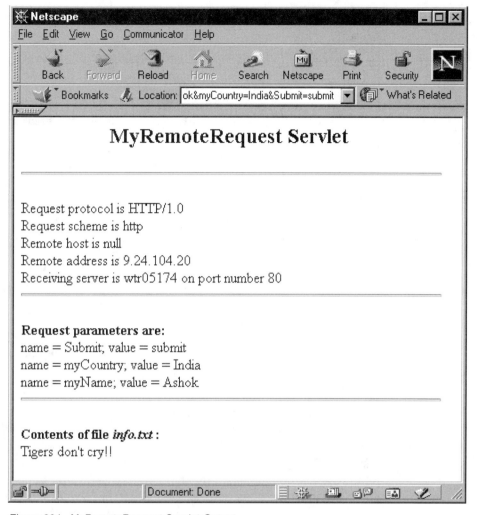

Figure 284. MyRemoteRequest Servlet Output

Notice that the contents of the file info.txt are displayed as well.

We have successfully invoked a servlet on a Web server by sending a request from a client. The same servlet can also be invoked by an HTML page downloaded from a different Web server. This topology is shown in the following diagram:

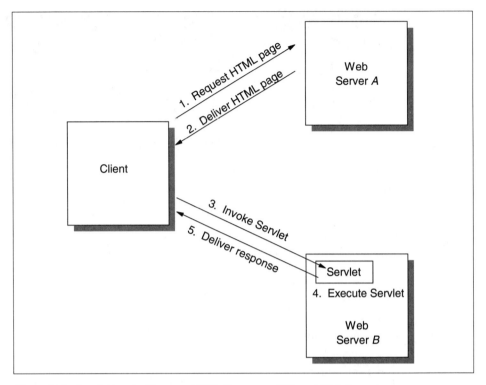

Figure 285. Servlet Invoked from an HTML Page on a Different Web Server

The scenario depicted above is similar to the one we have just described. The only difference is that the HTML page containing the form from which the servlet is invoked resides in Web server *A*, while the servlet resides in Web server *B*. This page is downloaded from Web server *A* to the client machine. When the user on the client machine clicks the **Submit** button, the input from the client machine goes directly to Web server *B*, where the servlet resides. The server processes the information received and sends the dynamic response back to the client. As you can see, Web server *A* just serves the HTML page and is quickly out of the picture.

14.5.7 The Current Servlet Security Model

So far, we have seen two ways in which a servlet can be invoked. Both of these topologies are examples of a servlet that exists on the same system as the Web server. Hence, there are no security restrictions, in terms of the resources the servlet can access. The servlet described in 14.5.6, "A Sample Servlet" on page 548, is allowed to read from the file C:\info.txt without any restriction. Now, we want to examine the scenario where servlet code is

// generate cipher objects for encoding and decoding

```java
Cipher itsocipher1 = Cipher.getInstance ("DES");
Cipher itsocipher2 = Cipher.getInstance ("DES");

// generate a KeyGenerator object
KeyGenerator KG = KeyGenerator.getInstance ("DES");
System.out.println("Using algorithm " + KG.getAlgorithm());

// generate a DES key
Key mykey = KG.generateKey();

// initialize the Cipher objects
System.out.println("Initializing ciphers ...");
itsopcipher1.init(Cipher.ENCRYPT_MODE, mykey);
itsocipher2.init(Cipher.DECRYPT_MODE, mykey);

// creating the encrypting cipher stream
System.out.println("Creating the encrypting cipher stream ...");
FileInputStream fis = new FileInputStream(args[0]);
CipherInputStream cis1 = new CipherInputStream(fis, itsocipher1);

//writing the decrypted data to output file
System.out.println("Writing the decrypted data to output file " + args[1]);
FileOutputStream fos = new FileOutputStream (args[1]);
byte[] b2 =new byte[1024];
int i2 = cis2.read(b2);
while (i2 != -1)
{
    fos.write (b2, 0, i2);
    i2 = cis.read(b2);
}

fos.close();
cis1.close();
cis2.close();
}
catch (Exception e)
{
    System.out.println("caught exception: " +e);
}
```

loaded onto Web server *A* from another remote Web server *B*, and then a client sends a request to Web server *A* to execute the servlet. Note the difference between *invoking a servlet* and *loading a servlet*:

- When we talk about invoking a servlet, we mean that a client requests a Web server to execute a servlet. The servlet is local to the Web server machine, and there is no bytecode transfer across the network. The execution of the servlet is performed in the Web server hosting the servlet, and only the output goes back to the client machine. A scenario showing the invocation of remote servlets is described in 14.5.6, "A Sample Servlet" on page 548. It is important to emphasize that when a servlet is remotely invoked, no code transfer is performed, because only the output of the servlet is transferred across the network, not the servlet itself. For this reason, this operation does not carry any security risks.

- Loading a servlet means that Web server *A* calls and *downloads* the bytecode of a *remote* servlet physically residing on a remote Web server *B*, but this time the execution of the servlet is executed in the Web server *A*. This operation carries security risks because it involves downloading remote code across the network. A remote servlet could represent the same risks as a remote applet: it could steal memory and CPU cycles, introduce a virus, read private information from the local system (such as the file C:\info.txt read by the local servlet in 14.5.6, "A Sample Servlet" on page 548) and then communicate it to another machine in the network, etc.

The remote loading of servlets is graphically represented in the following diagram:

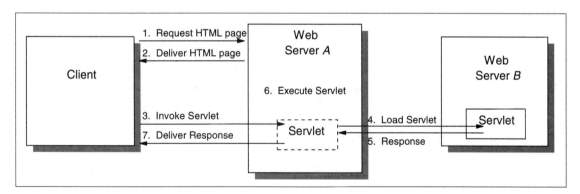

Figure 286. Remote Loading of Servlets

The steps involved are:

1. The client requests a Web page.

2. Web server *A* responds to the client request and delivers the Web page.

3. The client submits a form that sends a specific request to Web server *A*. This request asks the Web server to execute a servlet.

4. Web server *A* does not have the servlet, but loads it remotely from Web server *B*.

5. Web server *B* transfers the bytecode of the servlet to Web server *A*.

6. The remotely loaded servlet runs on Web server *A* and processes a response.

7. The servlet response is sent back to the client.

From the discussion above, it should be clear that Java servlets, like Java applets, must run under a security manager. The servlet security manager controls the resources that servlets can access, much the same way the applet security manager controls the resources that applets can access and the default security manager of the JVM controls the resources accessible by applications.

The current servlet security model is still Java Development Kit (JDK) 1.1-based:

• Local servlets are completely trusted and can access all the system resources (for example, the servlet discussed in 14.5.6, "A Sample Servlet" on page 548 was able to read a file from the local file system).

• Remote servlets can be trusted or untrusted, depending on the digital signature applied to their code:

  • If they are trusted, they can access all the system resources, like local servlets.

  • If they are untrusted, they are constrained by the Java servlet sandbox.

Servlets that are loaded remotely from another server run inside the *servlet sandbox*; this means that they cannot accomplish tasks like network or file access. However, sometimes, it is necessary to trust these remotely loaded servlets and to permit them to access system resources. This can be achieved by signing the JAR file containing the servlet class.

The current servlet security model is represented in the following diagram:

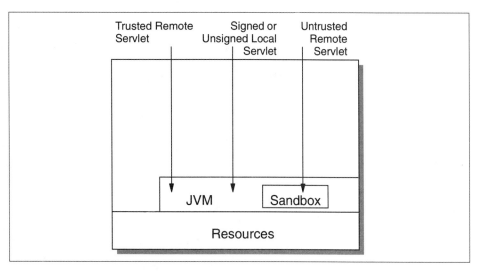

Figure 287. Servlet Security Model

The reason why servlets still run under a JDK 1.1-based servlet security model is only because Java 2 has only recently become available; servlet engines and Java-enabled Web servers have not picked up the new architecture and APIs yet. However, the Java 2 security model is applicable to servlets as well, and as soon as servers are Java 2-enabled, it will be possible to define the exact resources a particular servlet, local or remote, can access, based on the code source of the servlet itself.

14.5.7.1 Enhanced JDK 1.1 Servlet Security Model

Some servlet engines already offer an enhancement of the traditional JDK 1.1 servlet security model, represented in Figure 287 on page 559. For example, IBM WebSphere Application Server allows you to manage users, groups and access control lists (ACLs). To do this it introduces the concept of *security realm*. Realms are security domains, used to organize users, groups and ACLs in a structured way to protect Web resources. Realms are also used to authenticate a client and to decide which remote servlets to trust and what kind of resource access remote servlets can gain.

WebSphere Application Server overwrites the JDK 1.1 servlet security model. For example, a remote unsigned servlet is not necessarily untrusted in WebSphere Application Server, and you can configure the security of the servlet engine so that a remote unsigned servlet is granted specific privileges, as shown in the following diagram:

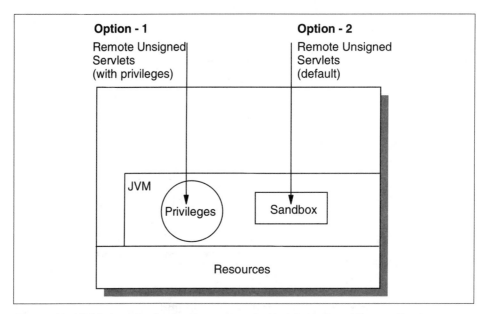

Figure 288. WebSphere Application Server Security Model - Unsigned Remote Servlet

WebSphere Application Server comes with a predefined user who is called unsigned, belonging to a realm called servletMgrRealm. All the permissions granted to unsigned are automatically granted to all the remote unsigned servlets. So, for example, if the servlet MyRemoteRequest discussed in 14.5.6, "A Sample Servlet" on page 548, is remotely loaded and unsigned, it can read the file C:\info.txt only if the user unsigned in the servletMgrRealm has been granted permissions to load servlets and read files:

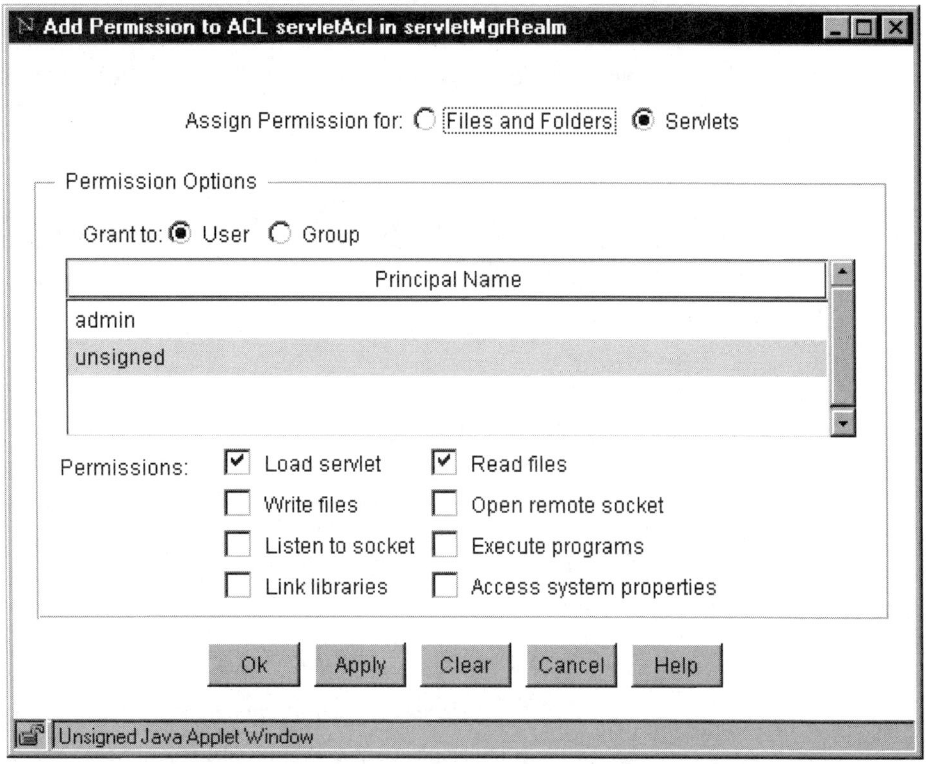

Figure 289. Granting Special Permissions to Unsigned Remote Servlets

In the screen above, if you select only **Load servlet**, an unsigned remote servlet can only be loaded, but then has to run in the default servlet sandbox and cannot have access to any of the system resources. If you select **Read files** as well, then you are granting a remote unsigned servlet the permission to read files – this permission would not be available in the default JDK 1.1 servlet sandbox. Notice that if **Load servlet** is not selected, an unsigned remote servlet cannot even be loaded and so it would not even fall under the default servlet sandbox.

In WebSphere Application Server, a signed remote servlet is not necessarily completely trusted. You can specify the exact permissions that the signer is granted, and all the servlets signed by that user will automatically be granted those permissions.

Servlet signers in WebSphere Application Server are users in the servletMgrRealm. You must first define a user in the servletMgrRealm, and then grant it the necessary permissions. Servlet signers are defined by registering the X.509 certificate of the signer in WebSphere Application Server.

The following figure shows how to grant all the servlets signed by Ashok_Signer the permission to be loaded and read files in the local file system:

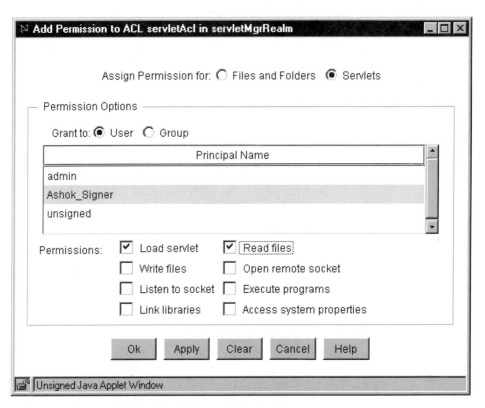

Figure 290. Granting Special Permissions to a Servlet Signer

This way, it is possible to have the servlets signed by signer *A* with a specific set of permissions, servlets signed by signer *B* with another set, servlets signed by signer *C* with yet another set of permissions, etc. There can be also servlets signed by a signer *D* with permissions limited by the servlet sandbox. This scenario is graphically represented in the following diagram:

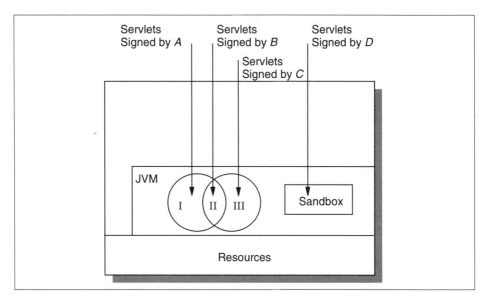

Figure 291. Enhanced Servlet Security Model – Signed Servlet

As you can see, these enhancements permit a better selection of the permissions that can be granted to signed and unsigned remote servlets. However, this security model is still far from the Java 2 security architecture:

- It does not include the concept of code base.
- The number of permissions is limited.
- You cannot specify the target and the actions of any permissions.

These limitations will be solved as soon as servlet engines incorporate the Java 2 security model.

14.6 Distributed Object Architectures – RMI

CGI uses a transaction model: the client issues a transaction request and then waits until the server returns the results. Distributed object architectures are a more elegant approach. Effectively, the *object space* that an applet or application is working with is extended to include objects on different systems. Client-side Java and server-side Java can be combined to create a full distributed architecture, where functions can be split between the client and server to optimize processing and network loads.

Apart from getting object-oriented purists excited, distributed object architectures have a number of advantages over more conventional transactional systems, including security advantages. For example, you can design systems in which mission-critical objects may be kept safe behind a firewall with access allowed only via method calls from clients. This is far safer than shipping data out of the organization to multiple clients who may simultaneously make changes.

To aid the creation of distributed architectures, Java provides a tool kit called Remote Method Invocation (RMI). This extends the Java object model to the network, by allowing objects in one JVM to invoke methods seamlessly on objects in another, remote, JVM. The remote JVM can, in turn, invoke other remote objects.

RMI support in Java 2 SDK, Standard Edition, V1.2 is provided by the java.rmi package and its four subpackages java.rmi.activation, java.rmi.dgc, java.rmi.registry and java.rmi.server.

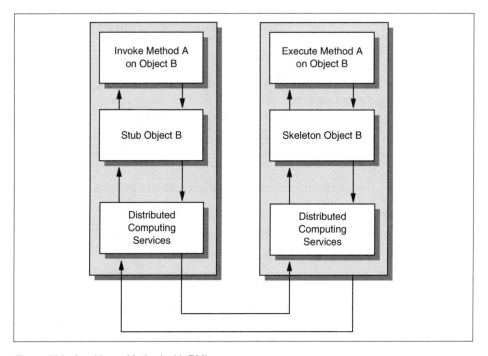

Figure 292. Invoking a Method with RMI

With RMI, an object, B, residing on one machine (the server) may be manipulated by another object, A, on a remote machine (the client). Object B doesn't really exist on the client, rather an alternative object is used as a kind of *stunt double*. This *stub-* or *proxy-object* provides the same interface as the real object B, but under the covers it uses the RMI services to pass method requests over the network to the real object B. Object A therefore doesn't need to know whether object B is local or remote.

If another object, C, needs to be passed between the client and the server – for instance as a parameter for a method – RMI uses a technique called *object serialization* to flatten the object, turning it into a stream of bytes. These are sent to the RMI system on the remote machine, which rebuilds the object C and passes it into the method call. Return values from methods are handled in the same way.

A simple naming service, the RMI Registry, is provided to connect clients and servers together using a URL-style of names, such as *//host:port/name*. A client asks for the remote objects, and the remote server returns the stub object to the client. Developers use the `rmic` compiler to generate the matching stub and skeleton classes for a remote object.

This means it becomes possible to write distributed applications, with little need to be aware of exactly where the software will be executed. A RemoteException may be thrown on error conditions, but apart from that, the program need not be aware that portions are executing remotely.

14.6.1 Stubs and Skeletons

We said that in RMI, an object residing on a server machine may be manipulated by another object residing on a remote client machine. The terms *client* and *server* here apply only for this single call, because in a later transaction the machine that acted as the server can also act as a client and request for a RMI from another machine, which would be the server for this new interaction. When a client object wants to invoke a remote method, it calls a Java method that is encapsulated in a surrogate object called the *stub*. The stub resides on the same machine as the client. The stub then uses the object serialization mechanism of Java to send data in a format suitable for transporting the parameters and the method call to a process on the server. The stub builds an information block that consists of:

- An identifier of the remote object to be used

- An operation number, describing the method to be called

- The marshalled[7] parameters

This information block is sent to the server. A *skeleton* object residing at the server end receives this information block and takes the appropriate actions:

- Unmarshalls the parameters sent by the stub

[7] *Marshalling* is the mechanism of encoding the parameters into a format appropriate to transport objects across the network.

- Calls the appropriate method on the actual object residing on the server

- Captures any exceptions generated due to the call on the server or any return value to be sent back to the stub on the client

- Sends a block in a marshalled form back to the client

Now, the stub receives the response from the skeleton, unmarshalls the return value or the exceptions. The stub is also responsible for passing the return value or the exception to the process that triggered the stub initially.

Stubs and Skeletons in the Java 2 SDK

In Java 2 SDK, Standard Edition, V1.2, an additional stub protocol has been introduced that eliminates the need for skeletons in environments that involve the Java 2 SDK platform only. Instead, generic code is used to carry out the duties performed by skeletons in JDK1.1.

14.6.2 RMI Registry

How does the stub get a handle to the server skeleton object on the server machine? This happens through the RMI registry. The *RMI registry* is a simple server-side name server that allows remote clients to get a reference to a remote object. It is typically used only to locate the first remote object to which an RMI client needs to talk. Then that first object in turn, would provide application-specific support for finding other objects. Once a remote object is registered on the server, callers can look up the object by name, obtain a remote object reference, and then remotely invoke methods on the object.

At the server end, the RMI server source code must bind the server object with a reference to the object and a name (which is a unique string on the RMI registry). This is an example of the code section to register a server object with the RMI registry:

```
// Create a new EmployeeImpl object and register it with the RMI registry
EmployeeImpl emp1 = new EmployeeImpl("Ashok");
Naming.rebind("//wtr05218/ITSO", emp1);
```

The above code registers the EmployeeImpl object emp1 with a registry name ITSO. Notice that wtr05218 in this example is the host name of the server machine.

At the client end, the client code gets a stub to access the server object using the following code:

```
String url = "//wtr05218/";
// Obtain Employee objects by looking up at the RMI registry on the server
Employee c1 = (Employee) Naming.lookup(url + "ITSO");
```

In the above code fragment, you can see that RMI also uses a URL type format (the url String object) to locate the server object entry in the RMI registry, running at the server end.

One Note on Security

For security reasons, an application can bind or unbind only to a registry running on the same host. This prevents a client from removing or overwriting any of the entries in a server's remote registry. A lookup, however, can be done from any host.

Before you execute the server and client Java programs, you must start the RMI registry at the server end. The RMI registry usually runs in background, so the typical command to launch it is:

- On Windows systems:

  ```
  start rmiregistry
  ```

- On UNIX systems:

  ```
  rmiregistry &
  ```

This opens a new window and the RMI registry service is launched. The command above does not produce any output. You can minimize this window.

The RMI registry listens on a default port of 1099. If you wish to run it on a different port, you can start it by specifying the port number on the command line; for example:

```
start rmiregistry 1969
```

If the registry is running on a port other than the default, you must specify the port number in the name handed to the URL-based methods of the java.rmi.Naming class when making calls to the registry. For example, if the registry is running on port 1969, the call required to bind the EmployeeImpl instance emp1 to the name ITSO would be:

```
// Create a new EmployeeImpl object and register it with the RMI registry
EmployeeImpl emp1 = new EmployeeImpl("Ashok");
Naming.rebind("//wtr05311:1969/ITSO", emp1);
```

14.6.3 A Sample RMI Program

In this section, we write an program to illustrate the RMI implementation in Java. This example demonstrates how a downloaded applet on a client browser makes an RMI call to retrieve a message. This message is then displayed on the Web browser where the applet is running.

The following steps are needed:

1. Create the Java and HTML files used in this scenario – Employee.java, EmployeeImpl.java, EmployeeServer.java, EmpApplet.java, Emp.html.
2. Compile the Java files using the Java compiler `javac`.
3. Generate stub and skeleton classes on the server by running the `rmic` command.
4. Start the RMI registry on the server.
5. Run the EmployeeServer program on the server to register objects with the registry.
6. Test the functioning of the RMI setup using the sample DispBindings program.
7. Invoke the applet, that in turn invokes remote methods on the client.

We now explain the details of each step.

14.6.3.1 Creating the Java and HTML Files

In Java, a remote object is an instance of a class that implements a remote interface. Your remote interface declares each of the methods that you would like to call remotely. Hence, we provide the implementation details in an interface, Employee, in the file Employee.java. Normally, the interface class file is present on both the client and the server machine.

This is the source code for the Employee interface:

```
import java.rmi.*;

public interface Employee extends Remote
{
    public String getEmpInfo() throws RemoteException;
}
```

Figure 293. Employee.java

Notice that remote interfaces have the following characteristics:

- The remote interface must be declared public. Otherwise, unless a client is in the same package as the remote interface, the client will get an error when attempting to load a remote object that implements the remote interface.

- The remote interface extends the java.rmi.Remote interface.

- Each method must declare java.rmi.RemoteException (or a superclass of RemoteException) in its throws clause, in addition to any application-specific exceptions.

The method getEmpInfo() declared in the Employee interface is the remote method that the client will be invoking.

Next, we code the EmployeeImpl class that implements the Employee interface. A class that implements a remote interface must do the following:

- Declare that it implements the remote interface.

- Define the constructor for the remote object.

- Provide implementations for the methods that can be invoked remotely.

The source code for the remote object implementation class EmployeeImpl is shown in the following figure:

```
import java.rmi.*;
import java.rmi.server.*;

public class EmployeeImpl extends UnicastRemoteObject implements
Employee
{
    private String empName;

    public EmployeeImpl(String Name) throws RemoteException
    {
        empName = Name;
    }

    public String getEmpInfo()
    {
        return "Hi! I am " + empName;
    }
}
```

Figure 294. EmployeeImpl.java

As a convenience, the implementation class can extend a remote class, which in this example is java.rmi.server.UnicastRemoteObject. By extending UnicastRemoteObject, the EmployeeImpl class can be used to create a remote object that:

- Uses RMI's default sockets-based transport for communication.
- Runs all the time.

Notice that the EmployeeImpl() constructor accepts a java.lang.String object, which is what is returned as part of the message when the getEmpInfo() method is called. The constructor must throw at least a java.rmi.RemoteException.

The getEmpInfo() method is the one invoked remotely by the client.

We are now ready to code the EmployeeServer class. This program, when executed, binds two Employee objects with the RMI registry. These are the requirements for a server class:

- Create and install a security manager.
- Create one or more instances of a remote object.
- Register at least one of the remote objects with the RMI remote object registry.

The code for the EmployeeServer class is shown in the following figure:

```
import java.rmi.*;

public class EmployeeServer
{
    public static void main(String args[])
    {
        // The RMISecurityManager overrides java.lang.SecurityManager -
        // RMIClassLoader will not download any classes from remote locations
        // if no security manager has been set
        System.setSecurityManager(new RMISecurityManager());

        try
        {
            // Create new EmployeeImpl objects and register them with the RMI registry
            EmployeeImpl emp1 = new EmployeeImpl("Ashok");
            EmployeeImpl emp2 = new EmployeeImpl("Ascii");
```

Figure 295. (Part 1 of 2). EmployeeServer.java

```
        // The Naming class provides methods for storing and obtaining
        // references to remote objects in the RMI registry.
        Naming.rebind("//wtr05218/ITSO", emp1);
        Naming.rebind("//wtr05218/Palaya", emp2);
        System.out.println("Naming Rebind was successful");
    }
    catch (Exception e)
    {
        e.printStackTrace();
    }
  }
}
```

Figure 296. (Part 2 of 2). EmployeeServer.java

The EmployeeServer program sets a new RMISecurityManager. A security manager must be running so that the classes that get loaded do not perform operations that they are not allowed to perform. You can use the RMISecurityManager class, provided in the java.rmi package, or another security manager you have implemented. If no security manager is specified, no class loading by RMI clients or servers, is allowed.

In the `try{}catch(){}` block, the EmployeeServer instantiates two EmployeeImpl objects, emp1 and emp2. The EmployeeImpl constructors accept the names Ashok and Ascii respectively and store them. These names, as you remember, are then retrieved by the EmployeeImpl.getEmpInfo() method. The Naming.rebind() method binds the emp1 and the emp2 objects to the RMI registry with the respective names ITSO and Palaya. It is these names that the RMI client refers to (using the Naming.lookup() method), when requesting a reference to the server objects. If the binding is successful, the following message is displayed on the server:

`Naming Rebind was successful`

Notice that wtr05218 is the host name of the server machine.

We have completed the coding for the RMI server modules. We will now start the coding for the client side, which uses the remote service. The client side code includes the applet and the HTML file.

The applet code is shown in the following figure:

```
import java.applet.Applet;
import java.awt.Graphics;
import java.rmi.*;

public class EmpApplet extends Applet
{
    // Data returned from the Remote Method Invocation
    String data = "NULL";

    // empObj refers to the remote object that implements the Employee interface
    Employee empObj = null;

    public void init()
    {
        try
        {
            String param1 = getParameter("emp");
            if (param1 == null)
                param1 = "Palaya";
            empObj = (Employee) Naming.lookup("//" + getCodeBase().getHost() + "/" +
                param1);
            data = empObj.getEmpInfo();
        }
        catch (Exception e)
        {
            System.out.println("EmpApplet exception: " + e.getMessage());
            e.printStackTrace();
        }
    }

    public void paint(Graphics g)
    {
        g.drawString(data, 25, 50);
    }
}
```

Figure 297. EmpApplet.java

The EmpApplet gets the parameter name specified within the <APPLET> tag of
the HTML source. This parameter is stored in the param1 variable and
param1 is used to look up for the server object in the RMI registry. Once the
Employee object is obtained, the getEmpInfo() is called.

Notice that the Naming.lookup() method takes a URL-formatted
java.lang.String object. In this example, the applet constructs the URL string

by using the getCodeBase() method in conjunction with the getHost() method. The constructed URL-string that is passed as a parameter to the Naming.lookup() method must include the server's host name. Otherwise, the applet's lookup attempt will default to the client, and the applet security manager will throw an exception since the applet cannot access the local system, but is instead limited to communicating only with the applet's host.

The HTML file that contains the <APPLET> tag is shown in the following figure:

```
<HTML>
    <HEAD>
        <TITLE>RMI Employee Applet</TITLE>
    </HEAD>

    <BODY>
        <CENTER><H1>RMI Employee Applet</H1></CENTER>
        <H2>Data from <i>EmployeeServer</i></H2>
        <HR><P>
        <APPLET Code="EmpApplet.class" Width=500 Height=120>
            <PARAM Name="emp" Value="Palaya">
        </APPLET>
    </BODY>
</HTML>
```

Figure 298. Emp.html

14.6.3.2 Compiling the Java Source Files
We compile the Java source files using the `javac` command:

```
javac Employee.java
javac EmployeeImpl.java
javac EmployeeServer.java
javac EmpApplet.java
```

The commands above generate a class file for each Java file listed. The Java compiler requires:

- The Employee class file in order to compile EmployeeImpl.java and EmpApplet.java
- The EmployeeImpl class file in order to compile EmployeeServer.java

Therefore, it is important that the Java compiler `javac` finds the classes it needs via the class path. This can be accomplished by running the above commands in the same directory.

We store all the class files generated by the commands above in the public directory D:\WWW\HTML of the Web server machine wtr05218, where Java 2 SDK, Standard Edition, V1.2.1 is installed. The HTML file Emp.html (see Figure 298 on page 573) is stored in the same directory as well. The Web server machine, in this example, is also the RMI server.

14.6.3.3 Generating Stub and Skeleton Classes

The stub and skeleton classes are generated from the EmployeeImpl class by running the rmic command:

```
rmic EmployeeImpl
```

As soon as you run the above command, you will find two new class files in the same directory where EmployeeImpl is: EmployeeImpl_Stub.class and EmployeeImpl_Skel.class.

The rmic command runs with the default -vcompat option, which creates stubs and skeletons compatible with both JDK 1.1 and Java 2 SDK, Standard Edition, V1.2 stub protocol versions. You will need to run the above command if the platform where your RMI program will run is not completely based on Java 2 SDK, Standard Edition, V1.2. For example, if the applet will run on a browser that is not yet Java 2-enabled, and the server runs on Java 2 SDK, Standard Edition, V1.2, your RMI environment is not completely Java 2-based.

In 14.6.1, "Stubs and Skeletons" on page 565, we stated that a client/server environment completely based on Java 2 SDK, Standard Edition, V1.2 no longer requires skeletons. In this case, you should run the rmic command with the -v1.2 option:

```
rmic -v1.2 EmployeeImpl
```

This command creates only the stub class file EmployeeImpl_Stub.class. The skeleton class file is not generated.

14.6.3.4 Starting the RMI Registry

The RMI registry process is started using the command discussed in 14.6.2, "RMI Registry" on page 566. You can minimize the window where the rmiregistry executable is running, and let it run in the background.

14.6.3.5 Running the Server

On the server, it is necessary to register the objects with the RMI registry. To do this, the EmployeeServer program must be launched, and this is done with the command:

```
java EmployeeServer
```

However, even if the command above is launched without invoking a security manager, it throws an AccessControlException and complains that the code does not have the following permission:

```
java.net.SocketPermission wtr05218:1099 connect,resolve
```

In reality, even if not explicitly specified on the command line, a security manager is invoked when the EmployeeServer class is launched. In fact, if you look back at the source code of EmployeeServer (see Figure 295 on page 570 and Figure 296 on page 571), you will see the following line of code:

```
System.setSecurityManager(new RMISecurityManager());
```

It is the EmployeeServer class itself that invokes the RMISecurityManager class.

The RMISecurityManager complains about EmployeeServer's attempt to resolve and connect to the server wtr05218 on the default port 1099; hence, an AccessControlException is thrown. This problem is solved by adding the following grant entry in one of the policy files in effect on the server machine:

```
grant codeBase "file:/D:/WWW/HTML/" {
  permission java.net.SocketPermission "wtr05218:1099", "connect, resolve";
};
```

After granting the permission above, you can launch the EmployeeServer program, which produces the following output:

```
Naming Rebind was successful
```

At this point, a simple test program can verify your RMI setup and see if the RMI server program has registered the server objects correctly. We write a program called DispBindingsList to do this. The source code is shown in the following figure:

```
import java.rmi.*;

public class DispBindingList
{
    public static void main(String args[])
    {
        // Set the RMI security manager
        System.setSecurityManager(new RMISecurityManager());
```

Figure 299. (Part 1 of 2). DispBindingList.java

```
       System.out.println("Getting the Binding List");
       try
       {
           // Get the list of all bound objects using a Naming.list() method call
           String[] bindingList = Naming.list("");
           for (int i=0; i < bindingList.length; i++)
           System.out.println(bindingList[i]);
       }
       catch (Exception e)
       {
           System.out.println("Error: " + e);
           e.printStackTrace();
       }
   }
}
```

Figure 300. (Part 2 of 2). DispBindingList.java

The above program is compiled by entering the command:

```
javac DispBindingList.java
```

We save the class file generated by the command above in the RMI server machine, and we launch it with the command:

```
java DispBindingList
```

Notice that the DispBindingList class also sets the RMISecurityManager as the current security manager, and in order to run correctly it needs the same permissions as EmployeeServer. Therefore, you should grant those permissions to the code source of DispBindingList as well. A quick solution is to save the DispBindingList class file in the same directory where EmployeeServer.class is, and it will be granted the same permissions.

After these security settings are in place, the command above runs correctly and produces the following output:

```
Getting the Binding List
rmi:/Palaya
rmi:/ITSO
```

This output demonstrates that two server objects have been registered correctly: Palaya and ITSO. Any RMI client requesting a remote method invocation on this EmployeeServer can perform either of the following:

```
Naming.lookup("//wtr05218/ITSO")
Naming.lookup("//wtr05218/Palaya")
```

to obtain the corresponding Employee object. The Employee object's getInfo() method would then return `Ashok` if the Naming.lookup() call specifies `ITSO` or `Ascii` if the Naming.lookup() call specifies `Palaya`.

14.6.3.6 Invoking the Applet

If the `rmic` command was launched without any option (see 14.6.3.3, "Generating Stub and Skeleton Classes" on page 574), the applet EmpApplet works from any Web browser or Applet Viewer, as shown in the following figure:

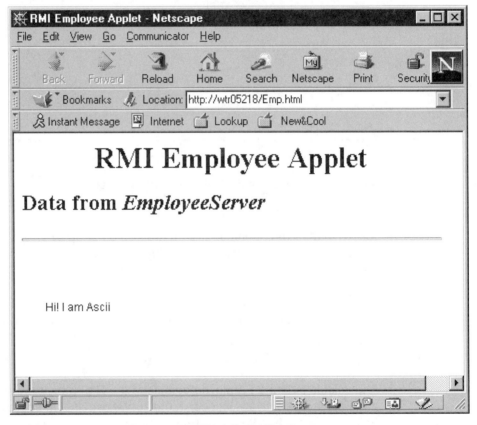

Figure 301. EmpApplet Output on a JDK 1.1-Based Web Browser

On the other hand, if the `rmic` command was launched with the `-v1.2` option, a skeleton object is not generated (see again 14.6.3.3, "Generating Stub and Skeleton Classes" on page 574), and the RMI program works only on an environment that is completely based on Java 2 SDK, Standard Edition, V1.2. In this case, the applet runs correctly in a JDK 1.1-based Web browser only if the Java plug-in is activated and is configured to use a Java 2 JRE (see Chapter 11, "The Java Plug-In" on page 359). Another option is to use the Java 2 SDK, Standard Edition, V1.2 Applet Viewer. This can be launched by entering the following command:

```
appletviewer http://wtr05218/Emp.html
```

The output is shown in the following figure:

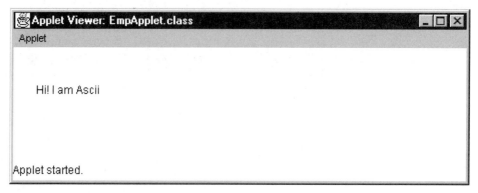

Figure 302. EmpApplet Output on the Java 2 SDK Applet Viewer

As you can see, the applet displays the message:

```
Hi! I am Ascii
```

If now, in the Emp.html file (see Figure 298 on page 573), we change the value of the emp parameter from Palaya to ITSO, the output of the applet will be different:

```
Hi! I am Ashok
```

This conforms to the following two lines of code of the EmployeeServer class:

```
Naming.rebind("ITSO", emp1);
Naming.rebind("Palaya", emp2);
```

These lines bind the Employee objects to the RMI registry with names ITSO and Palaya respectively. Hence, in the applet, we use these names, ITSO and Palaya, to get a handle to the Employee object with the Naming.lookup() method. Once we have the Employee object, we display the string returned by the getInfo() method. The returned string is either Ashok or Ascii, depending on the value of the emp parameter in the Emp.html file.

14.6.4 The Security of RMI

RMI appears to be a straightforward way of creating a distributed application. But there are a number of security issues[8]:

- RMI has a simple approach to creating the connection between the client and server. Objects are serialized and transmitted over the network. They are not encrypted, so anyone on the network could read all the data being transferred.

- There is no authentication; a client just requests an object (stub), and the server supplies it. Subsequent communication is assumed to be from the same client.

- There is no access control to the objects.

- There are no security checks on the registry itself; it assumes any caller is allowed to make requests.

- Objects are not persistent; the references are only valid during the lifetime of the process which created the remote object.

- Stubs are assumed to be matched to skeletons; however, programs could be constructed to simulate the RMI network calls, while allowing any data to be placed in the requests.

- Network and server errors will generate exceptions, so applications must be prepared to handle these.

- There is no version control between stubs and skeletons; thus, it is possible for a client to use a down-level stub to access a more recent skeleton, breaking release-to-release binary compatibility.

A security manager must be set before a remote class can be loaded. For Java applets, the security manager is defined by the Web browser or the Applet Viewer. For Java applications, the security manager can be defined on the command line invocation with the `-Djava.security.manager` option, or it can be defined programmatically within the application itself. There is a java.rmi.RMISecurityManager class available that extends java.lang.SecurityManager and makes extra checks when code tries to access a class package. Specifically, the RMISecurityManager.checkPackageAccess(*pkg*) method consults the package.restrict.access.*pkg* property:

- If the property is set to `false`, the check method returns quietly.

---

[8] At the time of writing this book, the Java RMI Security Extension is a proposed standard extension to add security to Java RMI (see 17.1.4, "Java RMI Security Extension" on page 671). Most of the problems listed here, such as lack of authentication, will be solved by the Java RMI Security Extension.

- If the property is set to `true`, the default SecurityManager's checkPackageAccess() method is called.

If you require a different (more or less restrictive) security policy, you will need to create your own security manager.

If the client and server are connected through one or more firewalls, there are additional issues to be considered. These are covered in 15.7, "Remote Method Invocation" on page 625.

We recommend you only use RMI in pure intranet configurations, or for applications where it cannot usefully be attacked. An inter-company chat system may be a reasonable use of RMI. Closely coupled internal systems might use RMI, if the appropriate access controls are put in place by network and firewall design. But the lack of authentication and access control in the raw RMI must limit its wider use in secure applications.

If you need to create a secure distributed application, you should investigate alternatives to RMI. The Common Object Request Broker Architecture (CORBA) implementations available today provide heavier-weight remote execution methods (see 2.1.3.2, "Some of the Roads to Purity" on page 50), and other suppliers can provide alternatives to RMI.

14.7 Enterprise JavaBeans

As technology evolves, applications are becoming more and more complex. Despite the advancements in both hardware and software, including the emergence of object-oriented technology, it is not getting easier to create applications. An alternative to reducing the logical complexity of applications is to create reusable software components, that is, programs that respect a predefined template and can be easily reused.

Software components must have the ability to be easily assemblable to create applications with much greater efficiency. In other words, a software component should interact with other software components and be able to define useful interfaces that other components can take advantage of.

This brings us to JavaSoft's JavaBeans technology. *JavaBeans* consists of an architecture and platform-independent API for creating and using dynamic Java software components, called Java beans. They can be connected to existing code. The typical phrase associated with Java code is *write once, run anywhere*. With the JavaBeans technology, now we can add: *reuse everywhere*. For this reason, Java beans are useful in many different software and hardware configurations. Also, the same piece of code can be used in different applications.

The JavaBeans API specification defines a Java bean as follows: *a Java bean is a reusable software component that can be visually manipulated in builder tools.*

This definition consists of two totally independent parts:

1. A Java bean is a platform-independent software component
2. A Java bean knows about the tools that will manipulate it and is compatible with those tools

A bean is defined as a software component that can be visually manipulated in builder tools. Java technology is object-oriented and certainly enables you to build reusable objects, but Java itself does not define any mechanism for creating reusable Java objects that can interact with other objects dynamically. JavaBeans, unlike plain Java, provides a framework by which this communication can easily take place.

Besides the JavaBeans technology, JavaSoft has created Enterprise JavaBeans[9], a component architecture for the development and deployment of object-oriented distributed enterprise-level applications. Applications written using the EJB architecture are scalable, transactional, and multi-user secure. These applications may be written once, and then deployed on any server platform that supports the EJB specification. The EJB architecture logically extends the JavaBeans component model to support server components.

Enterprise application systems support high scalability by using a multi-tier, distributed application architecture. A *multi-tier application* is an application that has been partitioned into multiple application components. Multi-tier applications provide a number of significant advantages over traditional client/server architectures, including improvements in scalability, performance, reliability, manageability, reusability, and flexibility.

The essential characteristic of an enterprise Java bean is its extreme flexibility. In particular:

- An enterprise bean's instances are created and managed at run time by a container.
- An enterprise bean can be customized at deployment time by editing its environment properties. This means that you can customize an enterprise

---

[9] See http://www.javasoft.com/products/ejb/.

Java bean to suit the specific requirements of an application through a set of external property values.

- Various *metadata*, such as a transaction mode and security attributes, are separated out from the enterprise bean class. This allows the metadata to be manipulated using the container's tools at design and deployment time.

- Client access is mediated by the container and the EJB server on which the enterprise Java bean is deployed.

This means that the EJB architecture makes it possible to shift most of the burden of implementing security management from the enterprise Java bean to the EJB container and server.

Currently, the EJB 1.0 model utilizes the Java security services supported in JDK 1.1. Java platform security supports authentication and authorization services to restrict access to secure objects and methods. EJB technology automates the use of Java platform security so that enterprise beans do not need to explicitly code Java security routines. The security rules for each enterprise bean are defined declaratively in a set of AccessControlEntry objects within the deployment descriptor object. An AccessControlEntry object associates a method with a list of users that have rights to invoke the method. The EJB container uses the AccessControlEntry to automatically perform all security checking on behalf of the enterprise bean.

Support for security in the EJB architecture includes the existing Java programming language security APIs defined in the core package java.security.

Chapter 15. Java and Firewalls – In and Out of the Net

In this chapter, we consider how Java security can be affected when firewall systems are used on the network.

In particular, we will see how different firewall implementations can affect the proper working of an applet network connection through a firewall.

15.1 What Is a Firewall?

By *firewall*, we mean any computer system, network hardware or combination of them that links two or more networks, and enforces some access control policy between them. Thus one side of the network is protected from any dangers in the other part of the network, analogous to the solid firewalls in buildings, which prevent a fire from spreading from one part of the building to another.

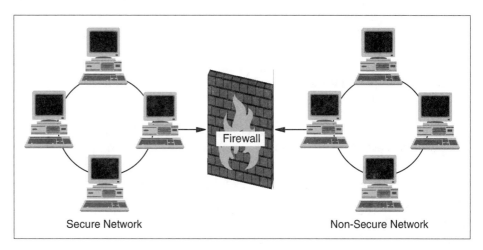

Figure 303. Firewall Representation

Until recent years, very few organizations thought seriously about the need for firewalls, despite the efforts of firewall vendors. Some well-publicized security breaches, when the contents of several public Web sites were vandalized, proved to be an ideal marketing opportunity. Almost any type of access control system was called a *firewall*. The National Computer Security Association (NCSA) has subsequently created tests to enforce minimum standards for a firewall, but that has not stopped some vendors from using the term creatively.

To add to the confusion, sometimes a single hardware system is called a firewall, while other times a complex collection of multiple routers and servers implement the firewall function. But we need to be concerned only with the policies enforced by the firewall, and what the effect is on the data traffic.

15.2 What Does a Firewall Do?

Firewalls can affect any type of network traffic, depending on their configuration. The areas we are especially concerned with are the following:

1. The loading of Java applets from a server to a client

2. Network accesses by Java applets to a server

Firewalls may be present at the client network, the server network, or both. In order to understand the implications, we must understand the basic functions provided by a firewall.

Current literature on firewalls is filled with buzzwords used by specialists to describe the different software techniques that can be used to create firewalls. Techniques include packet filtering, application gateways, proxy servers, dynamic filters, bastion hosts, demilitarized zones, and dual-homed gateways. For the purpose of this book, we can ignore the details of the software technologies, and simply concentrate on what a firewall does with data packets flowing *through* it.

There are several other firewalls functions that have no real effect on Java security; for example, logging, reporting and management functions are available, and these may themselves be written in Java. As an example, the IBM Firewall has a graphical user interface developed in Java.

The basic security functions of any firewall are to examine data packets sent *through* the firewall, and to accept, reject or modify the packets according to the security policy requirements. Most of today's firewalls work with TCP/IP data only, so it is worth seeing what is inside a TCP/IP data packet, in order to understand the firewall's actions.

15.2.1 Inside a TCP/IP Packet

All network traffic exchange is performed by sending blocks of data between two connected systems. The blocks of data are encapsulated within a data packet by adding header fields to control what happens to the data block *en route* and when it reaches its final destination. Network architectures are constructed of layers of function, each built on the services of the layer beneath it. The most thorough layered architecture is the open systems interconnection (OSI) model, whereas other architectures, such as TCP/IP, use broader layer definitions. On the wire, these layers are translated into a series of headers placed before the data being sent, as shown in the following diagram:

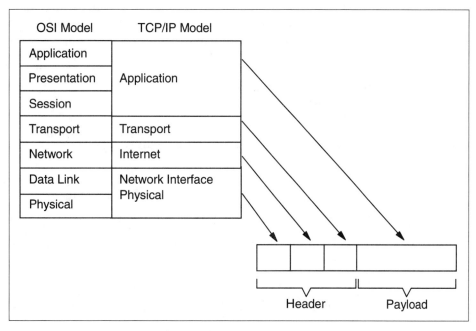

Figure 304. Mapping the Layered Network Model to Packet Headers

The first part of the header, the Data Link/Physical header, is determined by the type of network. Ethernet, token-ring, serial lines, FDDI, and so on, each have their own headers, containing synchronization, start-of-packet identifiers, access control, and physical addresses[1] as required by the network type. There may be fields to distinguish Internet Protocol (IP) packets from other types of packets, such as NetBIOS or SNA. We need to consider only IP packets here.

The next part of the header of IP packets is the standard IP header, which specifies the originator (source) address and the intended recipient (destination) address, together with fields to control how the packet is

[1] Network devices require an adapter to physically attach to the LAN. This adapter must provide both physical and logical capabilities for the device. The adapter contains a unique 48-bit address, assigned to it during the manufacturing process, called *Media Access Control* (MAC). All the MAC addresses are assigned by the IEEE 802 committee. The IEEE provides the vendor building adapters with a range of MAC addresses to use for assigning adapters their unique 48-bit address so that no two adapters should ever have a duplicate address. Ethernet and token-ring require the MAC address for both the origin and the destination adapters when communicating over a LAN. Besides the IP address, the MAC address also must be known when sending data to a LAN-attached device.

forwarded through the Internet. There are two main types of IP headers: the common IP V4 standard, and the new IPv6 standard, which is intended to replace IPv4.

This is followed by the transport layer header, which controls what happens to the packet when it reaches its destination. Almost all the user-level protocols commonly referred to as TCP/IP use either a Transmission Control Protocol (TCP) or a User Datagram Protocol (UDP) header at the transport layer.

Finally, application protocol headers and data are contained in the payload portion of the packet, and are passed from the sending process to the receiving process.

Each of these packet headers contain a number of data fields, which may be examined by a firewall and used to decide whether to accept or reject the data packet.

For current purposes, the most important data fields are:

- **Source IP address** – a 32-bit address (IPv4) or a 128-bit address (IPv6)
- **Destination IP address** – a 32-bit address (IPv4) or a 128-bit address (IPv6)
- **Source port number** – a 16-bit value
- **Destination port number** – a 16-bit value

The source and destination IP addresses identify the machines at each end of the connection, and are used by intermediate machines to route the packet through the network. Strictly speaking, an IP address identifies a physical or logical network interface on the machine, which allows a single machine to have several IP addresses.

The source and destination port numbers are used by the TCP/IP networking software at each end, to send the packets to the appropriate program running on the machines. Standard port numbers are defined for the common network services; for example, by default, an FTP server expects to receive TCP requests addressed to port 21, and an HTTP Web server expects to receive TCP requests to port 80.

However, non-standard ports may be used. It is quite possible to put a Web server on port 21, and access it with a URL of http://*server*:21/. Because of this possibility, some firewall systems will examine the inside details of the protocol data, not just headers, to ensure that only valid data can flow through.

As an elementary security precaution, port numbers less than 1024 are *privileged* ports. On some systems, such as UNIX, programs are prevented from listening to these ports, unless they have the appropriate privileges. On less secure operating systems, a program can listen on any port, although it may require extra code to be written. HTTP Web servers, in particular, are often run on non-standard ports such as 8000 or 8080 to avoid using the privileged standard port 80.

The non-privileged ports of 1024 and above can be used by any program; when a connection is created, a free port number will be allocated to the program. For example, a Web browser opening a connection to a Web server might be allocated port 1044 to communicate with server port 80. But what happens, you may ask, if a Web browser from another client also gets allocated port 1044? The two connections are distinguished by looking at all four values (source IP address, source port, destination IP address, destination port), as this group of values is guaranteed to be unique by the TCP standards.

15.2.2 How Can Programs Communicate through a Firewall?

Simple packet-filtering firewalls use the source and destination IP addresses and ports to determine whether packets may pass through the firewall. Packets going to a Web server on destination port 80, and the replies on source port 80, may be permitted, while packets to other port numbers might be rejected by the firewall. This may be allowed in one direction only and it may be further restricted by only allowing packets to and from a particular group of Web servers, as shown in the following figure:

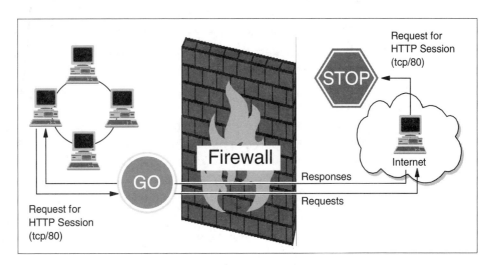

Figure 305. Asymmetric Firewall Behavior

There may be more than one firewall through which data needs to pass. Users in a corporate network will often have a firewall between them and the Internet in order to protect the entire corporate network. And at the other end of the connection, the remote server will often have a firewall to protect it and its networks.

These firewalls may enforce different rules on what types of data are allowed to flow through, which can have consequences for Java (or any other) programs. It is not uncommon to find Java-enabled Web pages that work over a home Internet connection simply fail to run on a corporate network.

There are two problem areas:

1. Can the Java program be downloaded from a remote server?

2. Can the Java program create the network connections that it requires?

The HTTP protocol is normally used for downloading. In order to understand the restrictions that firewalls put on HTTP, especially with regard to proxy servers and SOCKS servers (discussed in 15.4, "Proxy Servers and SOCKS Gateways" on page 596), we will describe this protocol in detail in the next section.

15.3 Detailed Example of TCP/IP Protocol

Let us consider the simple case of a browser requesting a Web page using HTTP. There are two steps to this:

1. First the browser must translate a host name (for example, www.ibm.com) into its IP address (204.146.17.33 in this case). The normal way to do this in the Internet is to use the Domain Name System (DNS).

2. In the second step, the browser sends the HTTP request and receives a page of HTML in response.

15.3.1 DNS Flow (UDP Example)

DNS uses the UDP protocol at the transport layer, sending application data to the DNS (udp/53) port of a name server. The packet header for UDP is shown in the following figure:

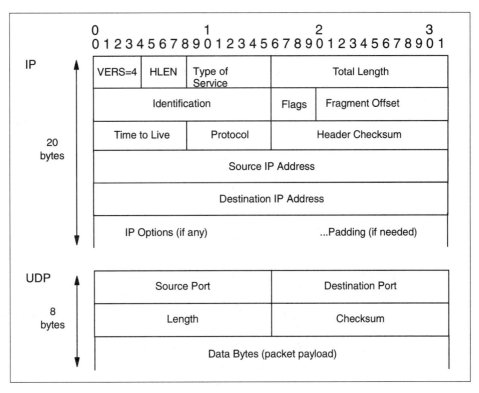

Figure 306. IPv4 and UDP Headers

If the newer IPv6 is used, the header is simpler, but with 128-bit addresses, instead of 32-bit.

The actual DNS request is a simple request and response sequence (see Figure 307 on page 589 and Figure 308 on page 590).

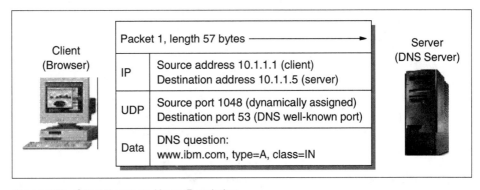

Figure 307. Client Requests Name Resolution

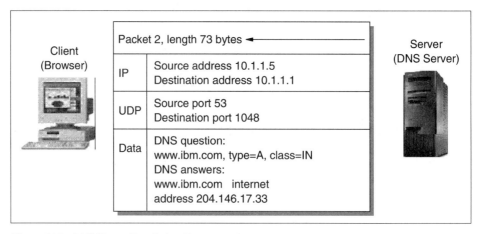

Figure 308. DNS Name Resolution Response

15.3.2 HTTP Flow (TCP Example)

Now the client can request the URL of http://www.ibm.com/example1.html because it knows that the real IP address of www.ibm.com is 204.146.17.33. Requests such as this use TCP at the transport layer to carry the HTTP application data. HTTP is a very simple protocol, where the client requests a particular item of data from the server, and the server returns the item, preceded by a short descriptive header.

TCP headers are similar to UDP but have more control fields to provide a guaranteed[2] delivery service:

---

[2] In this context, guaranteed means that the data will be delivered, or an error will be eventually returned. With UDP, in comparison, data may be discarded without warning.

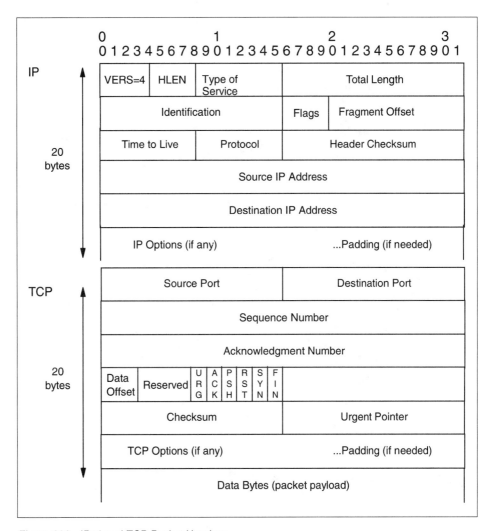

Figure 309. IPv4 and TCP Packet Headers

TCP using IPv6 is similar, with an IPv6 header followed by a TCP header.

The following data packets are sent:

- Packets 1, 2 and 3 establish the TCP connection. The opening connection sequence is sometimes called the *three-way handshake*.

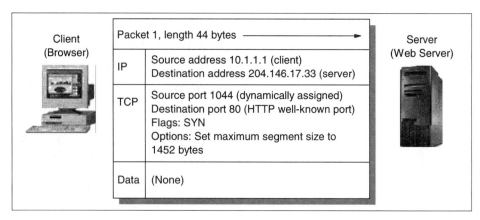

Figure 310. (Part 1 of 3). TCP Handshake

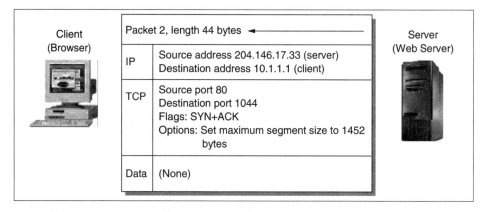

Figure 311. (Part 2 of 3). TCP Handshake

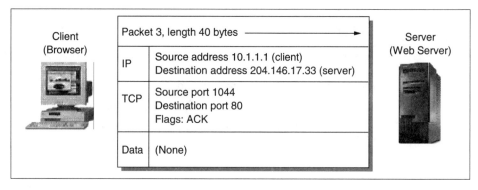

Figure 312. (Part 3 of 3). TCP Handshake

- Packet 4 contains the HTTP request from the browser; you can see the GET request itself, together with other data being passed to the server.

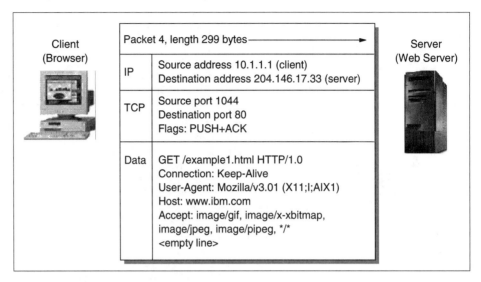

Figure 313. HTTP Request from the Browser

- Packet 5 contains the reply from the server, with the page data preceded by page information. You can see this information by selecting **Page Source** and **Page Info** from the View menu of a Web browser. Larger replies would need to be sent in more than one packet, and the client would periodically send TCP acknowledgment packets back to the server. But only a single item of data is returned, so that the page data, images, applets and other components are returned separately. Using JAR files, several items can now be sent in a single TCP connection, which is more efficient.

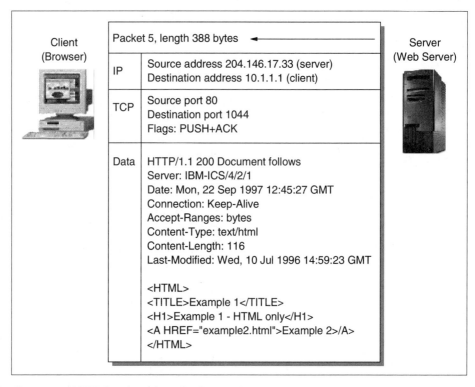

Figure 314. HTTP Response from the Server

- Packets 6 and 7 close the connection from the server end, and packets 8 and 9 close it from the client.

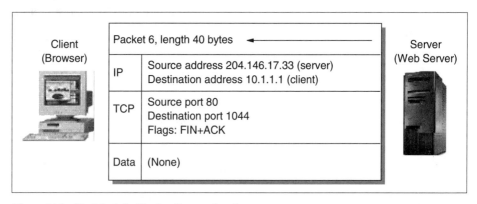

Figure 315. (Part 1 of 4). Closing Connection Sequence

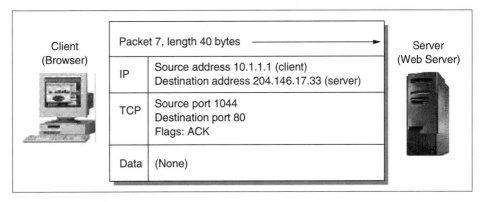

Figure 316. (Part 2 of 4). Closing Connection Sequence

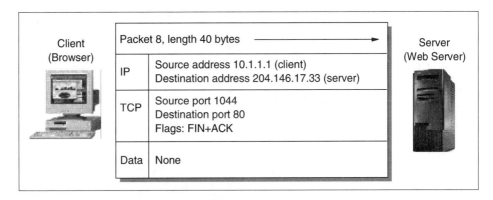

Figure 317. (Part 3 of 4). Closing Connection Sequence

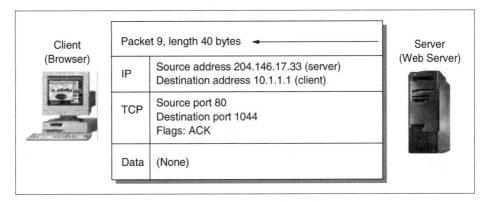

Figure 318. (Part 4 of 4). Closing Connection Sequence

Although at first sight this seems quite complicated, on closer inspection it can be seen as simply sending a request (in readable ASCII text) and receiving a reply, surrounded by packets to open and close the TCP connection.

15.4 Proxy Servers and SOCKS Gateways

Proxy servers and SOCKS gateways are two common approaches used to provide Internet access through corporate firewalls. The primary goal is to allow people within the company network the ability to access the World Wide Web (WWW), but prevent people from outside from accessing the company internal networks.

15.4.1 Proxy Servers

A proxy server's function is to receive a request from a Web browser, to perform that request (possibly after authorization checks), and return the results to the browser.

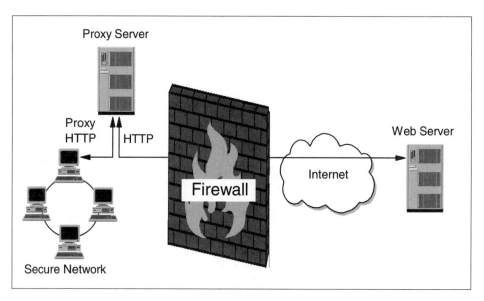

Figure 319. Where a Proxy Server Fits

Instead of sending the following request directly to server www.company.com of:

```
GET /page.html
```

A browser will send a request to proxy.mycompany.com asking:

```
GET http://www.company.com/page.html
```

Then, proxy.mycompany.com will contact www.company.com with the request:

```
GET /page.html
```

There are several advantages to this indirect approach:

- All external Web access can be forced to go through the proxy server, creating a single control point. This is achieved by blocking all HTTP protocol data, except for that from the proxy server itself.

- All pages being transferred can be logged, together with the address of the requesting machine.

- Requests for certain sites can be restricted or banned.

- The IP addresses or names of the internal systems never appear on the Internet, just the address of the proxy server. So attackers cannot use the addresses to gain information about your internal system names and network structure.

- The proxy can be configured as a caching proxy server, and will save local copies of Web pages retrieved. Subsequent requests will return the cached copies, thus providing faster access and reducing the load on the connection to the Internet.

- Web proxy servers usually support several protocols, including HTTP, FTP, Gopher, HTTPS (HTTP with SSL[3]), and WAIS.

- Proxy servers can themselves use the SOCKS protocol to provide additional security. This does not affect the browser configuration.

The disadvantages are that browser configuration is more complex, the added data transfers can add an extra delay to page access, and sometimes proxies impose additional restrictions such as a time-out on the length of a connection, preventing very large downloads.

15.4.2 What Is SOCKS?

The SOCKS protocol is mentioned several times in this section. It is a simple but elegant way of allowing users within a corporate firewall to access almost any TCP or UDP service outside the firewall, but without allowing outsiders to get back inside.

---

[3] For detailed information on the Secure Socket Layer (SSL) protocol, refer to Chapter 16, "Java and SSL" on page 629.

It works through a TCP protocol, SOCKS[4], together with a SOCKS server program running in the firewall system.

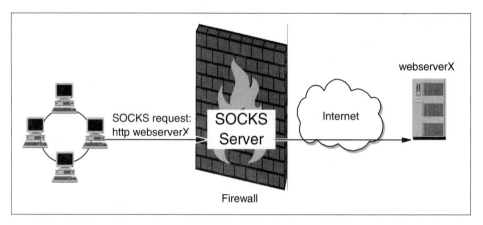

Figure 320. A SOCKS Connection

In basic terms, SOCKS is a means of encapsulating any TCP protocol within the SOCKS protocol. On the client system, within the corporate network, the data packets to be sent to an external system will be put inside a SOCKS packet and sent to a SOCKS server. For example, a request for http://server.company.com/page.html would, if sent directly, be contained in a packet with the following characteristics:

```
Destination address: server.company.com
Destination port: 80 (HTTP)
Data: "GET /page.html"
```

If SOCKS were used, the packet sent would be (effectively):

```
Destination address: socks_server.mycompany.com
Destination port: TCP 1080 (SOCKS)
Data: Destination address = server.company.com,
Destination port = TCP 80 (HTTP),
Data = "GET /page.html"
```

When the SOCKS server receives this, it extracts the required destination address, port and data and sends this packet; naturally, the source IP address will be that of the SOCKS server itself. The firewall will have been configured to allow these packets from the SOCKS server program, so they

---

[4] SOCKS, incidentally, is a shortened version of *socket secure*. Socket is the term used for the data structures that describe a TCP connection.

will not be blocked. Returning packets will be sent to the SOCKS server, which will encapsulate them similarly, and pass on to the original client, which in turn strips off the SOCKS encapsulation, giving the required data to the application.[5]

The advantage of all this is that the firewall can be configured very simply to allow any TCP/IP connection on any port, from the SOCKS server to the non-secure Internet, trusting it to disallow any connections that are initiated from the Internet.

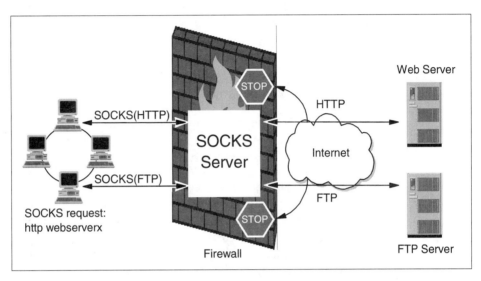

Figure 321. SOCKS Flexibility

The disadvantage is that the client software must be modified to use SOCKS. The original approach was to recompile the network client code with a new SOCKS header file, which translated TCP system calls (connect, getsockname, bind, accept, listen, select) into new names (Rconnect, Rgetsockname, Rbind, Raccept, Rlisten, Rselect). When linked with the libsocks library, these new names will access the SOCKS version, rather than the standard system version. This, therefore, creates a new *SOCKSified* version of the client software.

This approach is still used for clients running on UNIX. However, a new approach has become available for OS/2 and Windows operating systems, where the dynamically linked libraries that implement the TCP calls above are replaced by a SOCKSified version, usually termed a *SOCKSified TCP/IP stack*. This SOCKSified stack can then be used with any client code, without

[5] This description is simplified; in reality, requests between the client and the SOCKS server are in a socket API format, rather than the pure protocol data as shown above.

the need to modify the client. It just requires the SOCKS configuration to be specified, giving the address of the SOCKS server, and information on whether to use SOCKS protocol or to make a direct connection.

The SOCKSified stack comes as standard with OS/2 Warp Version 4 (add-on versions have been produced for OS/2 Warp Version 3), or can be purchased for Windows 95, Windows 98 or Windows NT.

15.4.3 Using Proxy Servers or SOCKS Gateways

We have described three options of providing secure Internet access through corporate firewalls:

1. Using a proxy server
2. Using a SOCKS gateway with a SOCKSified client application
3. Using a SOCKS gateway with a SOCKSified TCP/IP stack

Each of these options has its own advantages and disadvantages for the company network security manager to evaluate for the company's particular environment. But what does the end user need to do to use these options?

Both Netscape Navigator and Microsoft Internet Explorer Web browsers have built-in support for both proxy servers and for the SOCKS protocol. Options are provided to select *either* a proxy server *or* a SOCKS server[6]. But currently, support for SOCKS is limited to specifying the server name; all page requests will be passed to that server, whether or not direct access is possible (as in the case of internal Web servers).

The advantage in using the SOCKSified stack is that it provides better support for deciding whether to use SOCKS or not, rather than sending all requests to the SOCKS server (which may overload it), as well as supporting other clients. This is controlled by a configuration file that specifies which addresses are internal and can be handled directly, and which must go through the SOCKS server. Of course, if you use a SOCKSified stack, you should not enable SOCKS in the browser configuration. Then again, a SOCKSified stack is not available for all platforms, so you may be forced to use the browser's SOCKS configuration.

The SOCKSified stack approach will also work with Java applets run from a Web browser, as the normal java.net classes will use the underlying TCP protocol stack, so this provides a simple way of running Java applets using a SOCKS server through a firewall. But if a SOCKSified stack is not available,

---

[6] Don't select both, or requests will be sent via the SOCKS server to the proxy server, causing unnecessary network traffic.

you will need to SOCKSify the library classes yourself if you have source code, or look for a vendor who supports SOCKS.

15.5 The Effect of Firewalls on Java

Now we will consider the effect of firewalls on Java applets, first from the point of view of loading them, then on the network connections that the applets themselves may create.

15.5.1 Downloading an Applet Using HTTP

Java applets within a Web page are transferred using HTTP when the browser fetches the class files referred to by the <APPLET> tag. So, if a Web page contains the following tag, the browser would transfer the Web page itself first, then the file example.class, then any class files referred to in example.class.

```
<APPLET Code="Example.class" Width=300 Height=300>
   <PARAM NAME=pname VALUE="example1">
</APPLET>
```

Each HTTP transfer would be performed separately (unless HTTP 1.1 is used).

Java Development Kit (JDK) 1.1 and Java 2 SDK, Standard Edition, V1.2, allow a more efficient transfer, where all the classes are combined into a compressed Java Archive (JAR) file. In this case the Web page contains a tag of:

```
<APPLET Archive="example.jar" Code="Example.class" Width=300 Height=300>
</APPLET>
```

If there are problems finding example.jar, or if an older browser is used that still runs a JDK 1.0 Java Virtual Machine (JVM), the archive option is ignored, and the code option is used instead as in the previous example.

15.5.2 Stopping Java Downloads with a Firewall

But what effect do firewalls have on the downloading of Java class files? If the security policy is to allow HTTP traffic to flow through the firewall, then Java applets and JAR files will simply be treated like any other component of a Web page, and transferred. On the other hand, if HTTP is prohibited, then it is going to be very difficult to obtain the applet class files, unless there is another way of getting them, such as using FTP. Quite frequently, Web servers using non-standard TCP ports such as 81, 8000, 8080 may be blocked by the firewall, so if you are running a Web server, stick to the standard port 80 if you want as many people as possible to see your Web pages and applets.

Now since Java is transferred using HTTP, the IP and TCP headers are indistinguishable from any other element of a Web page. Simple packet filtering based on IP addresses and port numbers will therefore not be able to block just Java. If you require more selective filtering, you will need to go one step beyond basic packet filtering and examine the packet payload: the HTTP data itself. This can be done with a suitable Web proxy server or an HTTP gateway that scans the data transferred.

If a Web proxy server is used, a common arrangement is to force all clients to go through the proxy server (inside the firewall), by preventing all HTTP access through the firewall, unless it came from the proxy server itself. If you don't have an arrangement like this, a user can bypass the checking by connecting directly.

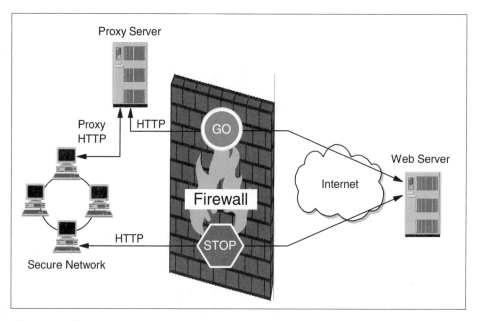

Figure 322. Forcing Connections through a Proxy

So what can we look for, inside the HTTP packet, to identify a Java class file? In an ideal world, there would be a standard Multipurpose Internet Mail

Extensions (MIME) data type for Java classes, so that a Web browser might request:

```
Accept: application/java, application/jar
```

and firewalls could quite easily check for these requests and the Web server Content-Type: replies.

However, in practice servers respond with a variety of MIME types, such as:

```
application/octet-stream[7]
www/unknown
text/plain
multipart/x-zip[8]
application/zip
```

This means it is necessary to examine the actual data being transferred, to see if it might be Java bytecode or JAR files. Bytecode files must start with hexadecimal number 0xCAFEBABE in the first four bytes (see Table 2 on page 125). This string, called the *magic number*, will also be found in JAR files, but as a JAR file may be compressed, a scanner must work harder to find the signature. Commercial products are available that can perform this inspection. They usually work as, or with, an HTTP proxy server, and check all HTTP requests passing through.

Searching for the class file signature in this way is an effective way to stop Java, but it indiscriminately prohibits good code and bad. On the other hand, as we demonstrated in 6.4, "An Incompleteness Theorem for Bytecode Verifiers" on page 183, it is mathematically impossible to build a complete bytecode verifier that determines whether a program is safe or not before it runs. Therefore, rather than stopping all Java programs, a more subtle scanner could extend the principle to other types of *signature*. For example, it would theoretically be possible to filter out any applet that overrode the stop() method (see 7.3.2, "Malicious Applets" on page 195), by analyzing the bytecode in detail.

Of course, in these restrictive environments, you would also want to filter out any other types of executable content that are less secure than Java, such as ActiveX, and maybe JavaScript, executable files, and so on. You would also have to consider other protocols such as FTP, HTTP or FTP encapsulated in SOCKS, and HTTP encapsulated in SSL (which adds the problem of decoding the type of encrypted data).

---

[7] This is valid for class files.
[8] This is valid for JAR files.

We have been focusing on scanning for Java at a single point for the enterprise: the firewall or proxy server. Recent developments by the browser manufacturers and by systems management specialists, such as Tivoli Systems, point to an alternative strategy. They have developed mechanisms for installing and configuring browsers on multiple user systems from a single point. This certainly offers cost savings: a single administrator can be responsible for hundreds of workstations. However, as a security measure it can only work if it is backed up by controls and monitors that prevent individual users from overriding the *official* configuration.

The cleanest solution to the problem of selectively stopping Java is in the use of signed applets. As certificates become used more frequently, it will be possible to permit Java bytecode from sites where you trust the signer (maybe your own company sites), and disallow other sites.

Should You Allow Java through Your Firewall?

Leaving aside the question of how to block Java classes at the firewall, you may be faced with the decision of whether you should allow Java (or any other type of executable content) to travel through the firewall. If your site has public Web servers, then you would expect that Java code is allowed to be sent to the Internet. But you might wish to make restrictions on Java code that can be received.

The most permissive policy is to allow Java to be received, and let users employ their own defenses, or trust in the Java security model. More restrictive policies might allow Java only from trusted Web sites, or not at all. The question that you must ask is: what data is at risk if I allow this? We have shown that, compared with other types of executable content, Java applets are very safe, so if you choose to block applets you should also prevent other downloads. For example, macro viruses contained in word-processor files are a major problem, but few companies would prevent employees from exchanging such files with customers and suppliers.

15.5.3 Java Network Connections through the Firewall

When a Java applet or application wishes to create its own network connections through a firewall, it faces all the difficulties above, and also, for applets, the default security manager restriction of only being able to contact the server from which it was downloaded.

One of the major problems that people have encountered with applets and firewalls is trying to get applets to communicate back to the server through a firewall. There are basically two major approaches that an applet, from behind a firewall, can adopt to retrieve data from a Web server outside the firewall:

1. **URL connection**

   This means using the URL classes from the java.net package to request data from a Web server using HTTP. JDK 1.1 added a new class to this package – HttpURLConnection – as a specialization of the URLConnection class.

2. **Socket connection**

   This involves the use of classes from the java.net package to create socket connections to a dedicated server application.

In 15.6, "Java and Firewall Scenarios" on page 606, we will focus on these two approaches to show you how a Java applet must be written and how the client platform must be configured to allow URL connections and socket connections through different firewall implementations.

The first of the two approaches – URL connection – is the easiest to implement. It is also likely to be the most reliable, because the JVM passes the URL request to the normal browser connection routines to process. This means that, if a proxy is defined, the Java code will automatically use it. However, URL connections suffer from the fact that the server side of the connection has limited capability; it can only be a simple file retrieval, a Common Gateway Interface (CGI) program, a servlet, or similar.

For the second approach – socket connection from the applet to the Web server – the applet will need to choose a port number to connect to, but many will not be allowed through firewall. Some types of applets have no real choice as to port number. For example, IBM Host On-Demand is a Java applet that is a 3270 terminal emulator, hence, needs to use the tn3270 protocol to telnet port 23. It is quite likely that this standard port would be allowed through the firewall; otherwise, encapsulation of tn3270 inside the SOCKS protocol may be the only answer.

Other applets need to make a connection to the server, but don't need any special port. It may be that they can use a non-privileged server port of 1024 or greater, but often these, too, are blocked by simple packet filtering firewalls. A flexible approach is to let the applet be configurable to allow direct connections (if allowed), or to use the SOCKS protocol to pass through the firewall.

Many HTTP proxy servers implement the *connect method*. This allows a client to send an HTTP request to the proxy, which includes a header telling it to connect to a specific port on the real target system. The connect method was originally developed to allow SSL connections to be handled by a proxy server, but it has since been extended to other applications. For example, Lotus Notes servers can use it. The connect method operates in a very similar way to SOCKS and you can implement Java applet connections with it in much the same way as you would with SOCKS.

Another approach is to disguise the packets in another protocol, most likely HTTP, as this will have been permitted through the firewall. This will allow a two-way transfer of data between the applet and server, but will require a special type of Web server. The server will need to act as a normal Web server, to supply the Web pages and applets in the first place, but must be able to communicate with the applets to process their disguised network traffic.

Finally, we want to mention that applets can connect to servers in the network using remote object access mechanisms, such as Remote Method Invocation (RMI) or Common Object Request Broker Architecture (CORBA) (see 2.1.3.2, "Some of the Roads to Purity" on page 50 and 14.6, "Distributed Object Architectures – RMI" on page 563). We will see a practical implementation of these approaches in the next section.

15.6 Java and Firewall Scenarios

In this section we show you how to execute the two approaches discussed in 15.5.3, "Java Network Connections through the Firewall" on page 604 in different firewall environments. The environment setup we use is shown in the following figure:

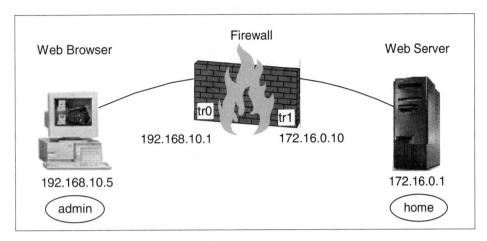

Figure 323. Scenario Environment Configuration

Refer to the table below for the technical details about this test environment:

Table 19. Firewall Client/Server Scenario Environment

Network Object	Host Name	Operating System	Function	IP Address
home	home	Windows NT Server 4.0	Web server	172.16.0.1
non-secure interface	gateway	Windows NT Server 4.0	Firewall non-secure interface	172.16.0.10
secure interface			Firewall secure interface	192.168.10.1
admin	admin	Windows NT Server 4.0	Web browser	192.168.10.5

This test environment is configured with the following products:

- Lotus Domino Go Webserver 4.6.2.5 for Windows NT is installed on the Web server machine

- The firewall machine is installed with IBM eNetwork Firewall 3.2.2 for Windows NT

- On the Windows NT client machine, our tests are based on the most common Java-enabled client platforms:

  - Netscape Navigator V4.5
  - Microsoft Internet Explorer V5
  - Java 2 SDK, Standard Edition, V1.2.1 Applet Viewer

Notice that the version of the JVM shipped with the Netscape Navigator V4.5 and Microsoft Internet Explorer V5 browsers is still 1.1, while the Java 2 SDK, Standard Edition, V1.2.1 Applet Viewer conforms to the Java 2 security model. This will allow us to compare the different permissions that applets can require to implement a connection to their servicing Web server.

In the following section, we describe this process:

1. The client downloads an applet from the Web server.
2. The applet requests for data from the Web server, using a URL connection or a socket connection.
3. The Web server replies back to the client.

We want to see the implications of this communication when the firewall implements one of the following technologies:

- IP filtering
- HTTP proxy server
- SOCKS server

15.6.1 URL Connection

We see now how an applet using the java.net.URLConnection class can connect to its servicing Web server through a firewall. Before we move to a firewall setup, let's understand the working of the applet in a normal client/server environment without any firewall setup. Figure 324 on page 608 and Figure 325 on page 609 show the code of the AppletConnection applet:

```
import java.awt.*;
import java.net.*;

public class AppletConnection extends java.applet.Applet
{
    int javaSize, classSize;

    public void init()
    {
        try
        {
            URL javaURL = new URL(getCodeBase(), getClass().getName() + ".java");
            System.out.println(javaURL);
            URL classURL = new URL(getCodeBase(), getClass().getName() + ".class");
            System.out.println(classURL);
            URLConnection javaURLConnection = javaURL.openConnection();
            URLConnection classURLConnection = classURL.openConnection();
            javaSize = javaURLConnection.getContentLength();
            classSize = classURLConnection.getContentLength();
```

Figure 324. (Part 1 of 2). AppletConnection.java – Used for URL Connection

```
        }
    catch (Exception e)
    {
        e.printStackTrace();
    }
}

public void paint(Graphics g)
{
    Font myFont = new Font("SansSerif", 3, 15);
    g.setFont(myFont);
    g.setColor(Color.black);

    if (javaSize == -1)
        g.drawString("Could not find file : " + getClass().getName() + ".java", 30,
            50);
    else
        g.drawString(getClass().getName() + ".java is " + javaSize + " bytes long", 30,
            50);
    if (classSize == -1)
        g.drawString("Could not find file : " + getClass().getName() + ".class", 30,
            80);
    else
        g.drawString( getClass().getName() + ".class is " + classSize + " bytes long",
            30, 80);
    }
}
```

Figure 325. (Part 2 of 2). AppletConnection.java – Used for URL Connection

We saved this file in the directory C:\itso\ch15 of the Web server machine. In
the same directory, we also save the class file of the applet,
AppletConnection.class, after compiling the source file by entering the
command:

```
javac AppletConnection.java
```

Let us now see what this applet does. After this applet is downloaded onto the
client's Web browser, it establishes a URL connection with the Java file
containing its source code and another URL connection with the class file of
the applet itself. Once these two connections are established, the applet
displays the size of each file on the client's browser.

Now, let us look at the source code to understand how it achieves its purpose.

Java and Firewalls – In and Out of the Net**609**

First of all, the applet imports two packages: java.awt and java.net. These packages are imported so that the applet can use the classes in them:

1. java.awt is necessary for the applet to use the Graphics class in the paint() method.

2. java.net is necessary for the applet to use the URL and URLConnection classes in its init() method and to establish its connections to the Web server that downloaded it.

The URL and URLConnection classes are used twice in the init() method. In fact this applet tries to establish two URL connections with its servicing Web server:

1. The first connection is with the file that stores the Java source code of the applet itself. We create a URL object, named javaURL, that will be initialized to http://*ourWebServer*/itso/ch15/AppletConnection.java.

2. The second connection is with the file that stores the Java class of the applet. For this reason, we created a second URL object, named classURL, that will be initialized to http://*ourWebServer*/itso/ch15/AppletConnection.class.

Note that *ourWebServer* can be either the host name (home) or the IP address (172.16.0.1) of the Web server servicing the applet, depending on whether the client browser invokes the Web server through its host name or through its IP address.

We then create two URLConnection objects, named javaURLConnection and classURLConnection, and we invoke the getContentLength() method on these objects to retrieve the size of each file. The exact number of bytes is then displayed on the client's browser through the paint() method. Notice that the method getContentLength() returns the content length of the resource that this connection's URL references, or returns −1 if the content length is not known. In our applet, the problem of an unknown content length could be generated by the absence of the files in the directory C:\itso\ch15 where the applet looks for the files through the two URL objects created. If the applet does not find the files, the applet will display an error message on the client's browser.

The following figure shows the code for the HTML page through which the applet is invoked:

```
<HTML>
   <HEAD>
      <TITLE>Applet Connection using URL Class</TITLE>
   </HEAD>

   <BODY>
      <CENTER><H2>Applet Connection using URL Class</H2>
      <HR>
      <BR>
      <APPLET Code="AppletConnection.class" Width=500 Height=250>
         <H4>This area contains a Java applet, but your browser is not
Java-enabled.</H4>
      </APPLET>
   </BODY>
</HTML>
```

Figure 326. AppURL.html – Used for URL Connection

We name this HTML file AppURL.html and we store it in the same directory
C:\itso\ch15 where we have also saved AppletConnection.java and
AppletConnection.class.

It is then necessary to add the following line in the Web server configuration
file C:\WINNT\httpd.cnf:

`Pass /itso/* C:\itso\*`

This line is added so that we can load the HTML files under the directory
C:\itso or its subdirectories from a remote client by typing
`http://`*ourWebServer*`/itso/`*directory_name*`/`*file_name*`.html` in the URL
box of the Web browser. The Web server must be restarted after this
modification so that this change is reflected in the Web server's configuration.

Before moving to a firewall environment we see how the applet works in a
normal client/server platform, without any firewall. The HTML page,
AppURL.html, is invoked using the URL
http://172.16.0.1/itso/ch15/AppURL.html from a browser on the Web server
machine, home, only. The applet displayed the length of the
AppletConnection.java and AppletConnection.class file as expected and the
result is shown in the following figure:

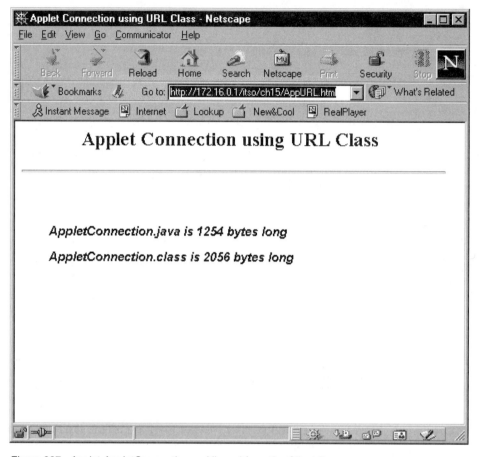

Figure 327. Applet AppletConnection as Viewed from the Client Browser

If you read the source code of the applet AppletConnection, you will see that there are two calls to the System.out.println() method, and the two URL objects javaURL and classURL are passed as parameters. Notice that the println() method automatically converts an Object to a String, using the toString() method. The output of the System.out.println() calls are displayed in the Java Console of the client's Web browser.

So far, everything works as expected. Now, we move to the purpose of this section, which is to test the applet URL connection when the AppletConnection applet is downloaded from the Web server to a client situated in the secure network.

15.6.1.1 IP Filter for HTTP Firewall Configuration

If we configure the firewall to act as an IP filter for HTTP, we get the same results as a normal client/server environment. The reason is that IP filters for HTTP simply permit the HTTP protocol to flow between the client and the server, allowing a TCP/IP connection between a TCP port greater than 1023 on the client and the default HTTP port 80 on the Web server. It is also required that the connection between the client and the server starts from the client side, because for security reasons the firewall will prevent every connection starting from the non-secure network from taking place. The client and the server can speak to each other directly through the filter, since the firewall routes the traffic but does not act on behalf of the client.

The presence of the firewall between the secure and non-secure network does not impact the URL connection established by the applet when the firewall is configured as an IP filter: the URL connection is established correctly on Applet Viewer and on the Netscape Communicator and Microsoft Internet Explorer Web browsers.

15.6.1.2 HTTP Proxy Server Firewall Configuration

What if the firewall acts as an HTTP proxy server? Is the applet still allowed to establish the URL connection to the Web server? The answer is yes, provided that the client machine is configured correctly.

The client must be configured to send its HTTP requests to the HTTP proxy server first. Then it is the proxy that forwards all the client's requests to the Web server, acting on behalf of the client. Web browsers can be configured to do this through a network settings configuration page, where users have to enter the IP address of the secure interface of the HTTP proxy server (192.168.10.1, in our case) and the port used by the proxy to listen for clients' requests (we keep the default port 8080). This needs to be done as all HTTP requests cannot directly reach the Web server, unlike they do when the firewall is simply an IP filter. In fact, clients' requests will now have to be routed through the HTTP proxy server, which by default listens for client HTTP requests on port 8080. The proxy server then forwards each request to the Web server, which by default is listening on port 80 for HTTP requests.

An applet implementing a URL connection executes without any problems in this case also. Problems might occur in a firewalled network when no DNS has been configured to translate host names to IP addresses for hosts located in the non-secure network, or if the firewall has been configured to disable DNS queries. This is a common situation, because DNS is often configured to translate only host names of hosts behind the firewall. What happens is, if you invoke the HTML page using the host name of the Web server, the checkConnect() method in the browser security manager tries to translate the host name to an IP address, to prevent spoofing attacks, but behind the firewall the checkConnect() method fails if the DNS has not been configured. An unexpected SecurityException is thrown and your Web browser displays an error message.

This problem is not present if, when you point your browser to the HTML file, you specify the IP address of the Web server, rather than its host name. In fact, in this case, the getCodeBase() method, which we used in our applet (see Figure 324 on page 608 and Figure 325 on page 609), returns the IP address of the Web server, and no host name translation needs to be done by the security manager. So the URLConnection is still able to access the Java source code file and its corresponding class file.

If you still want to invoke the Web server through its host name and no DNS has been configured to translate host names into IP addresses for hosts located in the non-secure network, you can use the Netscape Navigator browser and enable the following hidden property in the prefs.js configuration file:

```
user_pref("security.lower_java_network_security_by_trusting_proxies", true);
```

With this preference enabled, if the DNS lookup performed by the Netscape implementation of the security manager fails, then the host name of the Web server is relied upon, rather than having a stricter DNS/IP address equivalence. Notice, however, enabling the hidden preference above can impact the security of the system, since it disables the DNS lookup performed by the security manager to prevent spoofing attacks.

We have discussed how a Web browser must be configured to recognize the presence of an HTTP proxy server to which it forwards the requests. What about the Applet Viewer? If we type the following command:

```
appletviewer http://172.16.0.1/itso/ch15/AppURL.html
```

the applet does not execute as expected, because the URL connection fails. This happens because we are trying to access the Web server using a URLConnection object from behind an HTTP proxy server, but since we have not specified that an HTTP proxy server is present in the network, the Applet Viewer, which is unaware of the presence of the HTTP proxy server, still attempts to perform a direct connection and fails. It is therefore necessary to modify the command above. The exact appletviewer command to specify the proxy server host name or IP address, and the port number to which the proxy listens for clients' requests is the following:

```
appletviewer -J-DproxyHost=192.168.10.1 -J-DproxyPort=8080
http://172.16.0.1/itso/ch15/AppURL.html
```

With this command, we get the same successful results as when we run the applet in a Web browser properly configured. Notice that the -J flag of the `appletviewer` command specifies that a `java` command line option follows. In particular, `proxyHost` is used to specify the host name or the IP address of the HTTP proxy server, while `proxyPort` specifies the port at which the HTTP proxy server listens for client connections.

15.6.1.3 SOCKS Server Firewall Configuration

The situation is very similar when the firewall implements a SOCKS server: the applet is able to connect its servicing Web server provided the client platform is correctly configured to recognize the presence of the SOCKS server in the network to which it forwards the requests.

Also in this case, the security manager of the browser performs a DNS lookup, so the considerations about DNS made in 15.6.1.2, "HTTP Proxy Server Firewall Configuration" on page 613 are relevant in this scenario as well.

The situation with the Applet Viewer is slightly different. First of all, to configure the Applet Viewer to contact a Web server in the Internet through a specific SOCKS server, the command to enter must be similar to the following:

```
appletviewer -J-DsocksProxyHost=192.168.10.1 -J-DsocksProxyPort=1080
http://172.16.0.1/itso/fire/AppURL.html
```

In the above command, `socksProxyHost` refers to the SOCKS server's IP address; `socksProxyPort` refers to the port number at which the SOCKS server listens for client connections.

With the command above, the applet works without any restrictions on JDK 1.1. However, this is expected, because the JVM of the browsers that we use is also at a 1.1 level. Interestingly, in the Java 2 SDK platform, the Applet Viewer security manager prevents an applet from connecting to its servicing Web server through a SOCKS server, and the above command works correctly if the following is added to one of the current policy files:

```
grant {
    permission java.net.SocketPermission "192.168.10.1", "resolve";
    permission java.lang.RuntimePermission "readFileDescriptor";
    permission java.lang.RuntimePermission "writeFileDescriptor";
};
```

Figure 328. grant Entry in the Policy File

Notice that 192.168.10.1 is the IP address of the secure interface of the
firewall. This value can be replaced by the host name.

15.6.2 Socket Connection

We see now how an applet using the java.net.SocketConnection class can
connect to its servicing Web server through a firewall. Before we move to a
firewall setup, we want to understand how the applet works in a normal
client/server scenario, without any firewall setup. This is the same thing we
did with the applet implementing the URLConnection in 15.6.1, "URL
Connection" on page 608.

The name of the applet we use here is AppConSock. The figure shows its
source code:

```
import java.awt.*;
import java.net.*;
import java.io.*;

public class AppConSock extends java.applet.Applet
{
    String stringRead;
    StringBuffer displayString = new StringBuffer();

    // The port number the applet connects to for reading the data file
    int portNumber = 80;

    public void init()
    {
        try
        {
            // Open a Socket connection on port portNumber
            Socket s = new Socket(getCodeBase().getHost(),portNumber);
```

Figure 329. (Part 1 of 2). AppConSock.java – Used for Socket Connection

```
            // Assign BufferedReader and DataOutputStream to read and write to the socket
            // on Port 80
            BufferedReader dIn   = new BufferedReader(new
               InputStreamReader(s.getInputStream())));
            DataOutputStream dOut = new DataOutputStream(s.getOutputStream());

            // Write bytes to the socket to get a data file
            dOut.writeBytes("GET /itso/ch15/data.txt \n\n");

            // Read bytes from the Socket
            int count = 0;
            while ((stringRead = dIn.readLine()) != null)
            {
               count += 1;
               if (count > 1)
                  displayString.append(stringRead);
            }

            dIn.close();
            dOut.close();
         }

         catch(Exception e)
         {
            e.printStackTrace();
            displayString.append("Unable to create socket. No data read.");
         }
      }

   public void paint(Graphics g)
   {
      // Set Graphics parameters
      Font myFont = new Font("SansSerif", 3, 15);
      g.setFont(myFont);
      g.setColor(Color.black);

      // Display the string
      g.drawString("Connecting to " + getCodeBase().getHost() + " on Port number " +
         portNumber + " -> ", 30, 80);
      g.drawString(displayString.toString(), 30, 100);
   }
}
```

Figure 330. (Part 2 of 2). AppConSock.java – Used for Socket Connection

The file AppConSock.java is saved in the C:\itso\ch15\ directory of the Web server machine. In the same directory, we also save the class file of the applet, AppConSock.class, after compiling the source file by entering the command:

```
javac AppSockConn.java
```

We have already defined the virtual HTTP mapping for this directory in the httpd.cnf file of the Web server (see 15.6.1, "URL Connection" on page 608).

The AppConSock applet, once downloaded, attempts to retrieve data from a file named C:\itso\ch15\data.txt, this also residing on the Web server. The applet uses a socket connection to read the contents of this file.

The Web server listens for HTTP requests on the default port 80, which must be the port to which Web browsers direct their requests and from which they receive the responses back from the Web server. Similarly, the AppConSock also opens a socket connection on port 80 of the Web Server. It then issues a command:

```
GET /itso/ch15/data.txt
```

on that port, to which the Web server responds by retrieving the C:\itso\ch15\data.txt file and sending it as a response to our AppConSock applet.

URL Mapping

As far as the physical file system on the Web server is concerned, the file data.txt is in the C:\itso\ch15 directory. We have a mapping in our httpd.cnf file for this C:\itso directory. This is the reason why we can access the file data.txt using the URL http://172.16.0.1/itso/ch15/data.txt from a Web browser on a client machine. Our AppConSock applet can also access this file in a way similar to an HTTP request, by creating a socket on port 80 of the Web server and issuing on port 80 the GET command above.

Now, let's look into the source code of the AppConSock applet. The file imports java.awt for graphics, java.net for networking classes and java.io for input and output classes. The input and output classes are needed for reading and writing to the socket, and also reading the data from the file data.txt on the Web server.

We first declare variables to store the string read and the port number (which is 80 for the Web server). The init() method creates a stream socket and connects it to the specified port number on the named host. Note here that, when the HTML page that contains the applet is invoked, if the IP address of the Web server is specified, then it is the IP address of the Web server that is returned by the getCodeBaes().getHost() method of the applet. Otherwise, if the host name is specified in the URL, then getCodeBase().getHost() returns the host name.

If the applet is unable to create a socket on the Web server it throws an exception. This exception can be due to various reasons, such as no route to the Web server host (in this case we will see a NoRouteToHostException) or any other network error. Once the socket is created, the input stream, dIn, and output stream, dOut, are obtained. The applet then requests the data.txt file by issuing a write operation on port 80:

```
GET /itso/fire/data.txt
```

The Web server, on receiving this request on port 80 from the applet, retrieves the /itso/ch15/data.txt file and starts writing to port 80 again. The applet can now start reading from the port using the handle to its socket's input stream dIn. The result of the read operation is then displayed on the client's browser.

If the socket was not created or if there was an exception, then the applet displays the message:

```
Unable to create socket. No data read.
```

The file C:\itso\ch15\data.txt file contains only the following test line:

```
Hi! I am the data file for the Socket Connection Applet.
```

The HTML file, AppSock.html, that we use to invoke the AppConSock applet is shown below:

```
<HTML>
   <HEAD>
      <TITLE>Applet Connection using Socket Class</TITLE>
   </HEAD>

   <BODY>
      <CENTER><H2>Applet Connection using Socket Class</H2></CENTER>
      <HR>
      <APPLET Code="AppConSock.class" Width=500 Height=250>
         <H4>This area contains a Java applet, but your browser is not
            Java-enabled.</H4>
```

Figure 331. (Part 1 of 2). AppSock.html – Used for Socket Connection

```
        </APPLET>
      </BODY>
    </HTML>
```

Figure 332. (Part 2 of 2). AppSock.html – Used for Socket Connection

The AppSock.html file also is saved in the directory C:\itso\ch15.

We show now how the AppSock applet works in a typical client/server environment that does not make use of firewalls. From a client Web browser, we invoke the URL http://172.16.0.1/itso/ch15/AppSock.html, and we can verify that the applet works as expected, as shown in the following window:

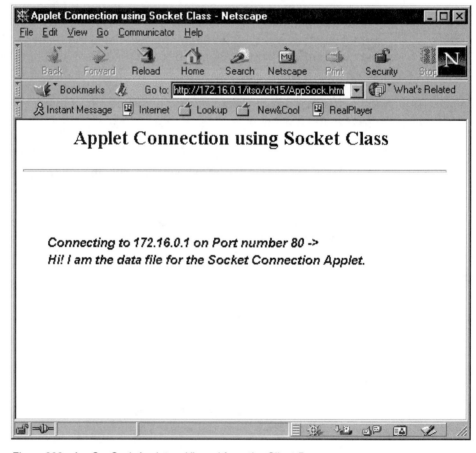

Figure 333. AppConSock Applet as Viewed from the Client Browser

Now, we move to the purpose of this section, which is to verify how the applet socket connection works when the applet, AppConSock, is downloaded from the Web server to a client situated in the secure network.

15.6.2.1 IP Filter for HTTP Firewall Configuration

When a firewall acts as an IP filter for HTTP, the HTTP communication is not broken at the firewall level. The firewall simply forwards packets back and forth between the secure and the non-secure network, verifying that the communication is initiated by a particular client in the secure network on a TCP port greater than 1023, that the destination is the HTTP port (by default, 80) on a specified Web server in the non-secure network, and that the TCP/IP protocol is used. For the rest, client and server can speak directly, and the firewall acts as a router for the communication flow.

For these reasons, an applet that attempts to connect to its originating Web server by using a socket connection executes successfully, and we get the same results as a normal client/server environment that does not use any firewall protection (see Figure 333 on page 620). This would happen by using the most common browsers (Netscape Navigator and Microsoft Internet Explorer) as well as the Java 2 SDK, Standard Edition, V1.2.1 Applet Viewer, which has to be launched with the following command:

```
appletviewer http://172.16.0.1/itso/ch15/AppSock.html
```

Notice that no particular proxy configuration is necessary in the browsers, and also the `appletviewer` command must not be launched with any flag specifying a proxy server or SOCKS gateway. The reason for this is that when a firewall acts as an IP filter, the client in the secure network and the server in the non-secure network can establish a direct connection.

However, if the AppConSock applet tried to open a socket connection on the Web server on any port other than 80, then the connection would be refused with a java.net.NoRouteToHostException being thrown to standard output. This is what the user would see on the client machine:

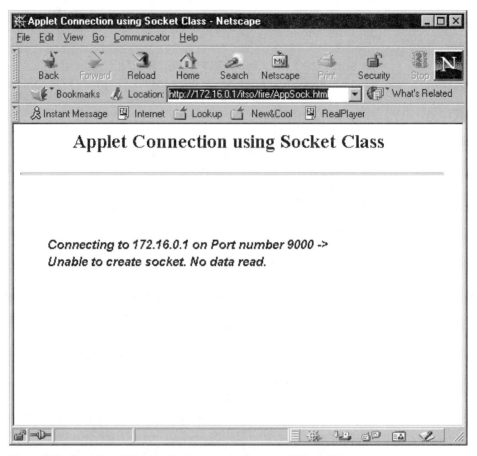

Figure 334. The Firewall Denies the Communication on a Different Port

This would happen because the firewall is configured only to route traffic directed to port 80 on the Web server.

15.6.2.2 HTTP Proxy Server Firewall Configuration

An applet trying to implement a connection to its servicing Web server via the java.net.Socket class is not able to establish a successful connection if the firewall is implementing an HTTP proxy server, and a NoRouteToHostException is thrown to standard output. The problem for HTTP proxy servers is that support for proxy is part of the protocol that you are using over TCP/IP, such as HTTP, FTP, Gopher, etc. (in this case, HTTP). It is therefore not possible to encapsulate the proxy-specific information at the socket layer.

When your browser is configured to submit all its requests to an HTTP proxy server, normal HTTP communication takes place successfully (for example, the HTML page AppSock.html is effectively downloaded in the Web browser). However, an applet trying to implement a socket connection fails for the reasons we have just explained. This would happen also with the Applet Viewer, launched with the same command line options as indicated in 15.6.1.2, "HTTP Proxy Server Firewall Configuration" on page 613.

15.6.2.3 SOCKS Server Firewall Configuration

The situation does not change also when the firewall is configured as a SOCKS server. Even in this case, an applet is prevented from establishing a socket connection with its servicing Web server, and a NoRouteToHostException is thrown to standard output. This happens with a Web browser, correctly configured to forward every request to a SOCKS server, as well as with the AppletViewer, launched with the same command line options as indicated in 15.6.1.3, "SOCKS Server Firewall Configuration" on page 615.

The code for the most common browsers on the market (such as Netscape Communicator and Microsoft Internet Explorer) is SOCKSified, so these browsers do not rely on the underlying operating system to use the SOCKS protocol. This is the reason why, even on a non-SOCKSified operating system, you can configure a browser to use a SOCKS server.

However, the JVM does not use the SOCKS support of the browser, but attempts to use either its own libraries or the underlying operating system resources to route the socket connection requests. Now, with the way SOCKS works, it is possible to put SOCKS support in the java.net.Socket code, resulting in an encapsulating of the SOCKS protocol layer and allowing the enforcement of the security policy without undue negative impact on applications running behind the firewall. This has been done in JDK 1.0.2[9], but unfortunately not in Netscape Navigator. The result is that an applet attempting a socket connection through a SOCKS server will fail on Netscape Navigator V4.5 and will succeed on Microsoft Internet Explorer V5. The only way the applet can work on Netscape Navigator V4.5 is on a SOCKSified operating system, as we will see in 15.6.2.4, "Socket Connections on a SOCKSified Operating System" on page 624.

What happens on the Java 2 SDK Applet Viewer? An applet can perform a socket connection through a SOCKS server, because the java.net.Socket class supports the SOCKS protocol. However, it is necessary that one of the policy files in effect grants the permissions listed in Figure 328 on page 616.

---

[9] In fact, an applet attempting a socket connection through a SOCKS server works correctly on the JDK 1.1. Applet Viewer.

15.6.2.4 Socket Connections on a SOCKSified Operating System

In the OS/2 operating system (at least Warp 4) the basic TCP/IP stack already contains support for SOCKS. In other words, the TCP/IP stack is SOCKSified. Therefore, on this operating system, you will be able to use the class java.net.Socket even if your client machine is running Netscape Navigator and is behind a SOCKS server.

So, if your platform is Netscape Navigator, and your purpose is to run applets that need to implement a socket connection through a SOCKS server, the solution is simple: the operating system of your client machine needs to be SOCKSified. If the operating system of your client platform is not OS/2 Warp 4, but for example, Windows 95, Windows 98 or Windows NT, there are several tools that are able to SOCKSify the TCP stack. One of these is Hummingbird SOCKS Client, which you can download from http://www.hummingbird.com. On a Windows NT system, once you download and uncompress the ZIP file, you have to execute the INSTALL batch file, which will autodetect which version of WinSock is running on your system, and install for that version accordingly. Then you have to edit the SOCKS.CNF file in the C:\WINNT\system32 directory. On our platform (see Table 19 on page 607), the only line that needs to be modified is the following:

```
SOCKD5 @=192.168.10.1 0.0.0.0 0.0.0.0
```

where 192.168.10.1 is the IP address of the secure interface on the firewall machine.

With this configuration in place, you do not have to specify any other proxy or SOCKS server settings in order to use the SOCKS protocol. In other words, a browser does not need to be configured to forward its requests to a SOCKS server, and the Applet Viewer does not require any special command line flag to indicate the presence of a SOCKS server in the network. With a SOCKSified operating system, an applet that implements a socket connection to its servicing Web server will succeed.

15.6.3 Conclusions

The following table summarizes our conclusions with the three types of firewall technologies we have described (IP filter for HTTP, HTTP proxy server and SOCKS server) and the two Java classes we have used to permit the

network connection between the applet and the Web server
(java.net.URLConnection and java.net.Socket):

Table 20. Firewall Technologies and Java Classes for Network Connections

	IP filter for HTTP	Proxy server	SOCKS server	
			Non-SOCKSified client	SOCKSified client
URL connection	Connection permitted	Connection permitted	Connection permitted on Netscape Navigator V4.5 and Microsoft Internet Explorer V5	Connection permitted
			Special permissions must be granted on Java 2 SDK Standard Edition V1.2.1 Applet Viewer	
Socket connection	Connection permitted	Connection denied	Connection denied on Netscape Navigator V4.5	Connection permitted
			Connection permitted on Microsoft Internet Explorer V5	
			Special permissions must be granted on Java 2 SDK Standard Edition V1.2.1 Applet Viewer	

As you can see, the only case where we see a different behavior depending on the Java platform level is when the firewall acts as a SOCKS server on a non-SOCKSified operating system, and the applet implements a URL connection, as discussed in 15.6.1.3, "SOCKS Server Firewall Configuration" on page 615.

15.7 Remote Method Invocation

Java's RMI allows developers to distribute Java objects seamlessly across the Internet. But RMI needs to be able to cross firewalls too.

The normal approach that RMI uses, in the absence of firewalls, is that the client applet will attempt to open a direct network connection to the RMI port (default is port 1099) on the server. The client will send its request to the server, and receive its reply, over this network connection.

The designers of RMI have made provisions for two firewall scenarios, both using RMI calls embedded in HTTP requests, under the reasonable assumption that HTTP will be allowed through the firewall (as the applet was delivered that way). The RMI server itself will accept either type of request, and format its reply accordingly. The client actually sends an HTTP POST request, with the RMI call data sent as the body of the POST request, and the server returns the result in the body of an HTTP response.

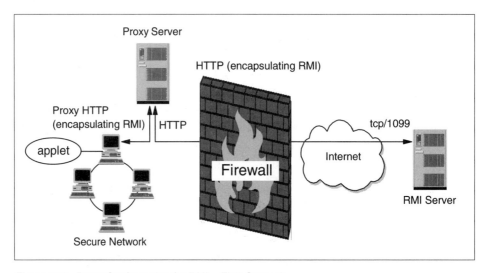

Figure 335. Proxy Configuration for RMI – First Scenario

In the first scenario, we assume that the proxy server is permitted by the firewall to connect directly to the remote server's RMI port (1099). The client applet will make an HTTP POST request to http://*rmi.server*:1099/. This passes across the Internet to the remote server, where it is found to be an encapsulated RMI call. Therefore the reply is sent back as an HTML response. In theory this method could also be used with a SOCKS server, instead of a proxy server, if run by a SOCKS-enabled browser.

As well as assuming that the firewall on the client passes the RMI port, this assumes that the remote firewall also accepts incoming requests directly to the RMI port. But in some organizations, the firewall manager may be reluctant to permit traffic to additional ports such as the RMI port. So an alternative configuration is available, in case RMI data is blocked by either firewall.

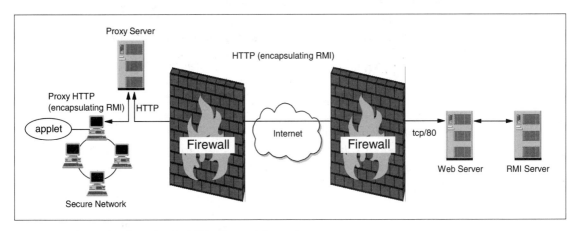

Figure 336. Proxy Configuration for RMI – Second Scenario

In the second scenario, the proxy server cannot use the RMI port directly, so the remote Web server (which supplied the applet) has a CGI-BIN program configured, to forward HTTP on the normal port (80) to the RMI server's port 1099.[10] This CGI-BIN program needs to be installed on the Web server. Once installed, it invokes the Java interpreter on the server, to forward the request to the appropriate RMI server port. It also copies the standard CGI environment variables to Java properties.

So, the client code sends a POST request to http://*rmi.server*/cgi-bin/java-rmi.cgi?forward=1099. The cgi-bin program, java-rmi.cgi, is located in the Web server's cgi-bin directory. The java-rmi.cgi passes the request on to the RMI port specified in the ?forward parameter. The reply will be passed back to the Web server, which adds the HTML header line, and returns the response to the client. In principle, this would allow the RMI server to reside on a different system from the remote Web server, in a three-tier model.

What is Allowed through Your Firewall?

Do you allow your proxy servers access to any TCP/IP port on the Internet? If so, you may allow your internal users to access risky servers; if not, you may prevent them from accessing useful services. You can scan the proxy server log files for non-standard port accesses, to assess the balance of risk.

---

[10] An example CGI-BIN program, java-rmi.cgi, having this purpose, was shipped with the JDK 1.1. This CGI-BIN program is not shipped with the Java 2 SDK, Standard Edition, V1.2.

Fortunately, all the work above is performed automatically in the java.rmi package, so the software developer need not be concerned about the detailed mechanism. It is only necessary to configure the RMI server correctly, and to ensure the client uses the automatic mechanism for encapsulating RMI.

In the current version of RMI, the client stub code checks for the presence (not value) of system properties proxyHost or http.proxyHost, in order to decide whether to try using the HTTP encapsulation. If you are using a Web browser and encapsulated RMI does not seem to work, try explicitly setting these properties, as the browser may be using its own proxy HTTP, without setting proxyHost.

All this automatic encapsulation is not free, of course. Encapsulated RMI calls are at least an order of magnitude slower than direct requests, and proxy servers may add extra delays to the process as they receive and forward requests.

15.8 Summary

We have shown how firewalls provide added security to an organization's network, at the expense of some restrictions on what client users can do. Firewalls use a variety of techniques to provide this security, including packet filtering, proxy servers and SOCKS servers. We have described approaches that can be used with these techniques to allow secure access through the firewalls. We also coded and executed examples of URL connections and socket connections from behind the firewall using proxy and SOCKS, or applying IP filters. These examples showed that the firewalls can impose certain restrictions in a client/server Java communication. A client server application would work perfectly in a normal setup, but the same application might not execute as expected in a firewall environment.

The Java classes that must be used and the type of firewall configurations that must be implemented depend on the factors highlighted in this chapter.

Chapter 16. Java and SSL

In Chapter 8, "Security Configuration Files in the Java 2 SDK" on page 225 and Chapter 13, "Cryptography in Java 2" on page 475, we discussed the capabilities for invoking cryptographic functions from within Java code. We also stepped through a simple transaction, to show the ways that cryptography can be used in an application.

But, as we concluded at the time, most programmers and application designers would prefer ready-built cryptographic protocols, rather than having to create them from the basic elements of encryption and digital signatures. Secure Sockets Layer (SSL) is the most widely used protocol for implementing cryptography in the Web. In this chapter we look at how it can be invoked from within Java.

16.1 What Is SSL?

SSL is a standard protocol proposed by Netscape[1] for implementing cryptography and enabling secure transmission on the Web. The primary goal of the SSL protocol is to provide privacy and reliability between two communicating parties.

As the name suggests, SSL provides a secure alternative to the standard TCP/IP sockets protocol. In fact, SSL is not a drop-in replacement because the application has to specify additional cryptographic information. Nonetheless, it is not a large step for an application that uses regular sockets to be converted to SSL. Although the most common implementation of SSL is for HTTP, several other application protocols have also been adapted.

SSL has two security aims:

1. To authenticate the server and the client using public key signatures and digital certificates.[2]

2. To provide an encrypted connection for the client and server to exchange messages securely.

The SSL connection is private and reliable. Encryption is used after an initial handshake to define a secret key. Message integrity checks are maintained.

Notice that in SSL, symmetric cryptography is used for data encryption, while asymmetric or public key cryptography is used to authenticate the identities of

---

[1] You can find the Internet draft of the SSL V3 specification at http://home.netscape.com/eng/ssl3/draft302.txt.

[2] This is optional. SSL client authentication needs to take place only if a server explicitly requires it. As we will see in Step 3 on page 633, in some cases even the server authentication may be not required.

the communicating parties and encrypt the shared encryption key when an SSL session is established. This way, the shared encryption key can be exchanged in a secure manner, and client and server can be sure that only they know the shared secret key. Also, you have the advantage that client and server can encrypt and decrypt the communication flow with a single encryption key, which is much faster than using asymmetric encryption.

In this way SSL is able to provide:

- **Privacy**

  The connection is made private by encrypting the data to be exchanged between the client and the server. In other words, only they can decrypt it and make sense of the data. This allows for secure transfer of private information such as credit card numbers, passwords, secret contracts, etc.

- **Data integrity**

  The SSL connection is reliable. The message transport includes a message integrity check based on a secure hash function. So there is practically no possibility of data corruption without detection.

- **Authenticity**

  The client can authenticate the server and an authenticated server can authenticate the client (optionally). This means that the information is guaranteed to be exchanged only between the intended parties. The authentication mechanism is based on the exchange of digital certificates.

- **Non-repudiation**

  Digital signatures and certificates together imply non-repudiation. This establishes accountability of information about a particular event or action to its originating entity, and the communications between the parties can be proved later.

For more information about the points discussed above, refer to 13.1, "Security Questions, Cryptographic Answers" on page 475.

SSL is comprised of two protocols: the *record protocol* and the *handshake protocol*. The record protocol defines the way that messages passed between the client and server are encapsulated. At any point in time it has a set of parameters associated with it, known as a *cipher suite*, which defines the cryptographic methods being used.

There are a number of cipher suites defined by the SSL standard, with names that describe their content. For example, the cipher suite named SSL_RSA_EXPORT_WITH_RC4_40_MD5 uses:

- RSA public key encryption for key exchange with an export-strength modulus (see 2.2.3, "United States Export Rules for Encryption" on page 57)
- RC4 cipher for bulk data encryption, using a 40-bit (export strength) key
- MD5 hashing to ensure data integrity

Note that a cipher suite determines:

- The kind of key exchange algorithm used
- The encryption algorithm used
- The digest algorithm used
- Whether the cipher strength is freely exportable outside the United States

The SSL protocol can use different digital signature algorithms for authentication of communication parties. SSL provides various key exchange mechanisms that allow for the sharing of secret keys used to encrypt the data to be communicated. Furthermore, SSL can make use of a variety of algorithms for encryption and hashing. These various cryptographic options defined by SSL, and whether the cipher strength is exportable outside the United States or not, are described by SSL cipher suites.

For example, cipher suite SSL_RSA_WITH_RC4_128_MD5 implies:

- RSA (unlimited) key exchange mechanism
- RC4-128-bit encryption algorithm
- MD5 hash function
- Not exportable

On the other hand, SSL_RSA_EXPORT_WITH_RC4_40_MD5 implies:

- RSA (512-bit) key exchange mechanism
- RC4-40-bit encryption algorithm
- MD5 hash function
- Exportable

When the SSL record protocol session is first established, it has a default cipher suite of SSL_NULL_WITH_NULL_NULL (no encryption at all). This is where the SSL handshake protocol comes in. It defines a series of messages in which the client and server negotiate the type of connection that they can support, perform authentication, and generate a bulk encryption key. At the end of the handshake they exchange ChangeCipherSpec messages, which switches the current cipher suite of the record protocol to the one that they negotiated. This process is graphically represented in the following diagram:

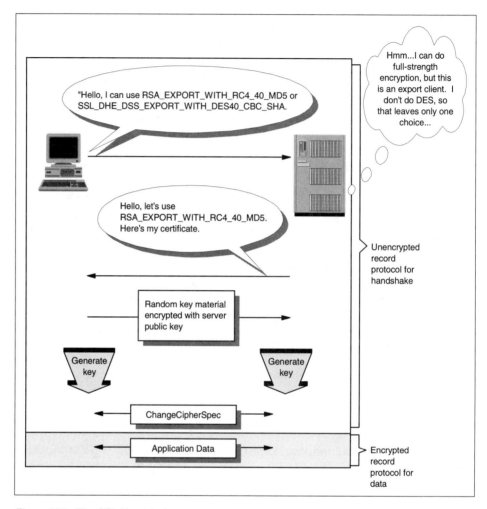

Figure 337. The SSL Handshake

In the case shown in the diagram, only the server is authenticated, so the client does not need to provide a certificate. If client authentication was required, the handshake would be a little longer. In that case the client also sends its certificate or a *no_certificate* message to the server.

Let's now see more details on how an SSL session is activated.

The major elements in an SSL connection are:

1. The cipher suites that are enabled

2. The compression methods that can be used (the compression algorithms are used to compress the SSL data and should be lossless)

3. Digital certificates and private keys, used for authentication and verification

4. Trusted signers (the repository of trusted signer certificates, used to verify the other entities' certificates)

5. Trusted sites (the repository of trusted site certificates)

To speed up connection establishment, the SSL protocol allows reuse of cryptographic parameters of previously established communication sessions between a client and a server. For this reason SSL also maintains a *session cache*.

The steps involved in an SSL transaction before the communication of data begins are described in the following list:

1. The client sends the server a *Client Hello* message. This contains a request for a connection along with the client capabilities, like the version of SSL, the cipher suites and the data compression methods it supports.

2. The server responds with a *Server Hello* message. This includes the cipher suite and the compression method it has chosen for the connection and the session ID for the connection. Normally, the server chooses the strongest common cipher suite. If the server is unable to find a cipher suite that both the client and server support, it sends a *handshake failure* message and closes the connection.

3. The server sends its certificate if it is to be authenticated, and the client verifies it. Optionally the client sends its certificate and the server verifies it.

   When a secure connection requiring SSL server authentication is being established, the server sends a certificate chain[3] to the client to prove its identity. The SSL client will pursue the connection establishment to the server only if it can authenticate the server, or, in other words, verify the signature on the server's certificate. In order to verify that signature, the SSL client needs to trust the server site itself, or at least one of the signers in the certificate chain provided by the server. After verifying the server certificate, the client uses the public key of the server in the next steps of the SSL protocol.

[3] The certification authority (CA) who signed a certificate might not be a known or trusted entity. Hence, for verification purposes, the certificates of the CA, and of the CA that certified this CA, would be required (see 13.1.1.1, "Certificate Hierarchies" on page 479). This is known as a *certificate chain*. You can see a demonstration of this at http://www.thawte.com.

SSL client authentication follows the same procedure: if an SSL server requires client authentication the client sends to the server a certificate chain to prove its identity and the server has to verify it.

We discussed SSL cipher suites earlier in this section. Almost all the SSL cipher suites, with the exception of some anonymous ones, require server authentication and allow client authentication.

4. The client sends the *ClientKeyExchange* message. This is random key material, and it is encrypted with the server's public key. This material is used to create the symmetric key to be used for this session, and the fact that it is encrypted with the server's public key is to allow a secure transmission across the network. The server must verify that the same key is not already in use with any other client. If this is the case, the server asks the client for another random key.

5. When client and server agree on a common symmetric key for encrypting the communication, the client sends a *ChangeCipherSpec* message indicating the confirmation that it is ready to communicate. This message is followed by a *Finished* message.

6. In response, the server sends its own *ChangeCipherSpec* message indicating the confirmation that it is ready to communicate. This message is followed by a *Finished* message.

Now, the client and the server can start communicating in secure mode.

HTTPS URLs

To access SSL Web sites, you need to specify `https` in place of `http` in the URL location, so that the browser is forced to use the HTTPS protocol. This represents one of the most common APIs to SSL on the client side. It layers the HTTP protocol over SSL. The default TCP port at which a Web server listens for HTTP connections is 80 and for HTTPS it is 443.

The java.net.URL class supports, without any modification, the `https://host/object` style URL.

16.2 Using SSL from an Applet

The advantage of a protocol such as SSL is that it removes the need for the application developer to deal with the nuts and bolts of cryptography. There are two ways in which Java can exploit this function: by using the SSL support built into the browser, or by using an SSL class package.

16.2.1 Using SSL URLs with Java

When a webmaster wants users of a site to enter an SSL connection, he or she simply codes a hypertext link with a prefix of `https` in place of `http`. When the user clicks on the link, the browser automatically starts the SSL handshake, connecting to the default SSL port on the server. Any relative URL within an SSL page is also retrieved using SSL. For example, an `<APPLET>` tag could cause the applet bytecode to be encrypted as it passes across the network. More importantly, the user knows that the applet comes from a trustworthy site, because the authentication process in the SSL handshake will have checked the certificate of the server. You will recall that the signature on a JAR file shows only that the creator of the file can be trusted, not the site from which it came (this was discussed in Chapter 12, "Java Gets Out of Its Box" on page 385). By delivering a signed JAR file using SSL, you can add the extra authentication without the Web site having to re-sign the file.

If a Java applet wants to read data from or write data to the server, it can use the URL classes from the java.net package. These allow the Java code to specify the URL of a Web page or CGI program and to receive the output from the URL in an I/O stream. If we change the assignment of the URL to use an `https` prefix, the browser will automatically retrieve the data using SSL.

16.3 Java and SSL with Sun Microsystems

Fetching data using the URL technique is a very simple approach, but it limits the Java program capabilities, because client/server communications can exploit only the capabilities offered by CGI (or another, similar, server interface). Even if this is adequate for the function, it imposes some performance overhead. A direct SSL socket connection between client and server allows more sophisticated and responsive applets to be created. This can be done by using a package that provides SSL function.

Currently, Sun Microsystems provides three packages: javax.net, javax.net.ssl and javax.security.cert. Note that these three packages do not come free with the Java 2 SDK, but are shipped as part of other products, such as Java Server Toolkit (JST) and the HotJava browser. However, these packages are not in their final version yet. Sun Microsystems is planning to make a Java Secure Socket Extension (JSSE) API and reference implementation available in the near future. The JSSE API, which is currently in draft format, will contain the three packages above.

In this section, we evaluate the Sun Microsystems SSL implementation in the JST and we look at the three javax packages one by one.[4] Notice that a strong-cipher version of these packages is available for use in the United States, while a weaker-cipher version is available to be exported outside the United States.

16.3.1 The javax.net Package

This package is not specific to SSL and has two classes in it, namely SocketFactory and ServerSocketFactory, which represent the basic socket and server socket factories respectively:

- **SocketFactory class**

  This class creates sockets. It may be subclassed by other factories, which create particular subclasses of sockets and thus provide a general framework for the addition of public socket-level functionality.

- **ServerSocketFactory class**

  This class creates server sockets. It may be subclassed by other factories, which create particular types of server sockets. This provides a general framework for the addition of public socket-level functionality. It is the server-side analog of a socket factory, and similarly provides a way to capture a variety of policies related to the sockets being constructed. Like socket factories, ServerSocketFactory instances have methods used to create sockets. There is also an environment specific default server socket factory; frameworks will often use their own customized factory.

16.3.2 The javax.net.ssl Package

The javax.net.ssl package is an SSL API, but it does not provide full access to specialized features, sometimes needed by applications, such as the control on what private keys get used.

There are five basic features in this API:

1. SSL sockets and SSL server sockets
2. SSL socket factories
3. SSL-specific session capabilities
4. A handshake completion event facility
5. SSL-specific exceptions

This package has six classes, four interfaces and five exceptions:

---

[4] The API documentation for these packages can be found at http://java.sun.com/security/ssl/packages.html.

- **SSLSocket class**

  SSLSocket is an abstract class extended by sockets that support SSL or IETF Transport Layer Security (TLS) protocols. Such sockets are normal stream sockets (java.net.Socket), but they add a layer of security over the underlying network transport protocol, such as TCP. Those security features include integrity protection, confidentiality, authentication.

- **SSLServerSocket class**

  The server-side implementation of the SSLSocket class is SSLServerSocket. This class is extended by server sockets that return connections protected using the SSL protocol, and that extend the SSLSocket class.

- **SSLSocketFactory class**

  Instances of this kind of socket factory return SSL sockets. An SSL implementation may be established as the default factory.

- **SSLServerSocketFactory class**

  The server-side equivalent of the SSLSocketFactory class is SSLServerSocketFactory. This class creates SSL server sockets.

- **SSLSession interface**

  This interface can be used to describe the current relationship between the server and the client.

- **SSLSessionContext interface**

  An SSLSessionContext is a grouping of SSL sessions associated with a single entity. For example, they could be associated with a server or client who participates in many sessions concurrently. This interface provides methods for retrieving an SSLSession based on its ID, and allows such IDs to be listed.

- **SSLSessionBindingListener interface**

  This interface is implemented by objects that want to know when they are being bound to or unbound from an SSLSession. When either event occurs, it is communicated through an SSLSessionBindingEvent identifying the session into which the object is being bound, or from which the object is being unbound.

- **SSLSessionBindingEvent class**

  This event is communicated to an SSLSessionBindingListener whenever such a listener is bound to or unbound from an SSLSession value. The event's source is the SSLSession to which the listener is being bound, or from which the listener is being unbound.

- **HandshakeCompletedListener interface**

  This interface is implemented by any class that wants to receive notifications about the completion of an SSL protocol handshake on a given SSL connection. When an SSL handshake completes, new security parameters will have been defined. Those parameters always include the security keys used to protect messages. They may also include parameters associated with a new session such as authenticated peer identity and a new SSL cipher suite.

- **HandshakeCompletedEvent class**

  This event indicates that an SSL handshake has completed on a given SSL connection. All of the core information about that handshake's result is captured through an SSLSession object. As a convenience, this event class provides direct access to some important session attributes. The source of this event is the SSLSocket on which handshaking just completed.

- **SSLException class**

  Indicates some kind of error detected by an SSL subsystem.

- **SSLHandshakeException class**

  Indicates that the client and server could not negotiate the desired level of security. The connection is no longer usable.

- **SSLKeyException class**

  Reports a bad SSL key. Normally, this indicates misconfiguration of the server or client SSL certificate and private key.

- **SSLPeerUnverifiedException class**

  Indicates that the peer's identity has not been verified. You may request the identity of the peer. When the peer is not able to identify itself (for example, no certificate, or the particular cipher suite being used does not support authentication, or no peer authentication was established during SSL handshaking) this exception may be thrown.

- **SSLProtocolException class**

  Reports an error in the operation of the SSL protocol. Normally this indicates a flaw in one of the protocol implementations.

16.3.3 The javax.security.cert Package

This package contains two classes and five exceptions, but it can be safely replaced by the more powerful java.security.cert package shipped with the Java 2 SDK.

- **Certificate class**

  This is an abstract class for managing a variety of identity certificates that have different formats but important common uses. For example, different types of certificates, such as X.509, Pretty Good Privacy (PGP) and Simple Distributed Security Infrastructure (SDSI), share general certificate functionality (like encoding and verifying) and some types of information (like a public key).

  X.509, PGP, and SDSI certificates can all be implemented by subclassing the Certificate class, even though they contain different sets of information, and they store and retrieve the information in different ways.

- **X509Certificate class**

  This is an abstract class for X.509 V1 certificates. This provides a standard way to access all the Version 1 attributes of an X.509 certificate. Attributes that are specific to X.509 V2 or V3 are not available through this class, but you can make use of the classes provided by the java.security.cert package of the Java 2 SDK.

- **CertificateEncodingException class**

  A certificate encoding exception is thrown whenever an error occurs while attempting to encode a certificate.

- **CertificateException class**

  This exception indicates one of a variety of certificate problems.

- **CertificateExpiredException class**

  This kind of exception is thrown whenever the current date or the specified date is after the `notAfter` date and time specified in the validity period of the certificate.

- **CertificateNotYetValidException class**

  This kind of exception is thrown whenever the current date or the specified date is before the `notBefore` date and time in the certificate validity period.

- **CertificateParsingException class**

  This exception is thrown whenever an invalid DER encoded certificate is parsed or unsupported DER features are found in the certificate.

16.4 How to Use Java and SSL

In this section we show an example of a client/server communication Java program, implemented in two different fashions:

1. Without SSL, using a typical Java socket connection

2. Using the SSL protocol with the Sun Microsystems API

16.4.1 Skeleton Program without SSL

We write a simple two-way communication program that lets a server and a client talk to each other and terminates the connection once either of them presses Ctrl-Z or Ctrl-C. A Java class called CallReceive.java creates a server when run directly and creates a client when called with an argument. Upon compiling CallReceive.java, three classes are generated: CallReceive.class, Client.class and Server.class. We will show you the single classes that build up this code, and will explain what each class does. At the end, if you want to rebuild the same code, you simply have to concatenate the single pieces of code together.

16.4.1.1 The Main Class of the CallReceive Program

This is the code of the CallReceive class:

```
class CallReceive
{
   public static void main(String args[])
   {
      switch(args.length)
      {
         case 0:
            new Server();
            break;

         case 1:
            try
            {
               new Client(args[0]);
            }
            catch(Exception e)
            {
            }
            break;

         default:
            System.out.println("USAGE: java CallReceive [host]");
      }
   }
}
```

Figure 338. CallReceive.java – CallReceive Class

16.4.1.2 The Server Class

Next, we write the code for the Server class, which listens for clients at a particular port. In this example, we used port 9335. You can pick up any other port number, provided it is not already used by any other applications running on your system.

```
class Server implements Runnable
{
    ServerSocket s;
    Server()
    {
        try
        {
            System.out.println("Server starting...");
            s = new ServerSocket(9335);

            System.out.println("Server started on port 9335");
            System.out.println("Waiting for the client...");

            Socket c = s.accept();
            Thread child = new Thread(this, "IBM");
            child.start();

            System.out.println("Request from Client received...");

            OutputStream out = c.getOutputStream();
            InputStream in = c.getInputStream();

            boolean over = false;
            int b;
            while (!over)
            {
                /* display prompt */
                System.out.print("SERVER:");
                System.out.flush();

                /* Read keyboard input and write to client */
                while ((b = System.in.read()) != -1 && b != '\n' && b != 26)
                {
                    out.write(b);
                }

                if (b == -1 || b == 26) // CLOSE request from server
```

Figure 339. (Part 1 of 3). CallReceive.java – Server Class

```
        {
           over = true;
           System.out.println("<<SERVER closing connection>>");
        }
        else
        {
           out.write('\n');
           System.out.print("CLIENT:\n\t");

           /* Get response from client and display */
           while((b = in.read()) != -1 && b != '\n')
           {
              System.out.print((char) b);
           }

           System.out.print('\n');
           System.out.flush();
           if (b == -1 || b == 26) // CLOSE request from server
           {
              over = true;
              System.out.println("<<SERVER closing connection>>");
           }

           else
           {
              out.write('\n');
              System.out.print("CLIENT:\n\t");

              /* Get response from client and display */
              while ((b = in.read()) != -1 && b != '\n')
              {
                 System.out.print((char) b);
              }

           System.out.print('\n');
           System.out.flush();

           if (b == -1) // Connection closed by client
           {
              over = true;
              System.out.println("<<CLIENT closed connection>>");
           }
        }
}
```

Figure 340. (Part 2 of 3). CallReceive.java – Server Class

```
            out.flush();
        }
        in.close();
        out.close();
        c.close();
        s.close();
    }
    catch(IOException e)
    {
    }
}

public void run()
{
    while (true)
    {
        try
        {
            Socket c = s.accept();
            DataOutputStream out = new DataOutputStream(c.getOutputStream());
            InputStream in = c.getInputStream();

            out.writeBytes("Sorry, busy in a session.");
            out.flush();
            c.close();
        }
        catch(IOException e)
        {
            break;
        }
    }
}
}
```

Figure 341. (Part 3 of 3). CallReceive.java – Server Class

The server waits for a client connection, and as soon as a client connects to it, it starts a session with it. Other clients are not allowed to connect to the same server, and if they try, they get the message

```
Sorry, busy in a session.
```

As you can see, this code makes use of simple I/O statements to allow communication.

16.4.1.3 The Client Class

Finally, we show you the code to create the Client class to connect to the server:

```
class Client
{
    Client(String arg) throws Exception
    {
        int c;

        System.out.println("Requesting connection from " + arg + " on port 9335...");
        Socket s = new Socket(arg, 9335);
        System.out.println("Connected to Server");

        InputStream in = s.getInputStream();
        OutputStream out = s.getOutputStream();

        boolean over = false;
        while (!over)
        {
            /* Get message from server and display */
            System.out.print("SERVER:\n\t");

            while ((c = in.read()) != -1 && c != '\n')
            {
                System.out.print((char) c);
            }

            if (c == -1) // Connection closed by server
            {
                over = true;
                System.out.println("\n<<SERVER has closed connection>>");
            }
            else
            {
                System.out.print("\nCLIENT:");
                System.out.flush();

                /* Read keyboard input and write to server */
                while ((c = System.in.read()) != -1 && c != '\n' && c != 26)
                {
                    out.write(c);
                }
```

Figure 342. (Part 1 of 2). CallReceive.java – Client Class

```
                if (c == -1 || c == 26) // CLOSE request from CLIENT
                {
                   over = true;
                   System.out.println("<<CLIENT closing connection>>");
                }
                else
                {
                   out.write('\n');
                }

                out.flush();
            }
        }
        out.close();
        in.close();
        s.close();
    }
}
```

Figure 343. (Part 2 of 2). CallReceive.java – Client Class

The client requests the server for a connection, and when it connects, the communication can start. Again, the client code uses the same I/O statements to implement the communication as the server code.

16.4.1.4 The import Statements for the CallReceive Program

In order to complete the program, you should not forget the `import` statements that must be added at the beginning of the program:

```
import java.io.*;
import java.net.*;
```

Figure 344. CallReceive.java – import Statements

As you can see, the import statements do not invoke any of the SSL libraries that we have discussed in 16.3, "Java and SSL with Sun Microsystems" on page 635, because this code implements a basic client/server communication without making use of the SSL protocol.

16.4.1.5 Compiling and Installing the CallReceive Program

The entire program can be obtained by concatenating the pieces of code that we have shown here. The sequence should be:

1. `import` statements code (Figure 344 on page 645)

2. Server class code (Figure 339 on page 641, Figure 340 on page 642 and Figure 341 on page 643)

3. Client class code (Figure 342 on page 644 and Figure 343 on page 645)

4. CallReceive class code (Figure 338 on page 640)

The code obtained in this way should be saved as CallReceive.java and compiled through the command:

```
javac CallReceive.java
```

This command will generate three class files in the directory where it is run: CallReceive.class, Server.class and Client.class. These three class files should then be copied to both the client and server machines, or at least they should be saved in a file system shared by both of them.

16.4.1.6 Running the CallReceive Program

The program is launched on both the machines from the directory where you copied the class files. If you enter:

```
java CallReceive
```

the machine where you type this command will automatically act as the server in this scenario. Then, on the other machine, enter:

```
java CallReceive hostname
```

where `hostname` is the host name or IP address of the server. The second machine will automatically act as the client.

Notice that it is possible to run this program on two different command prompts of the same machine, virtually acting as a client and server at the same time.

The following two figures show an example of client/server communication implemented with the CallReceive program. Figure 345 on page 647 is captured on the server, and Figure 346 on page 647 on the client. The three classes are stored in a shared file system, so they are not even physically copied on the local file systems of the two machines.

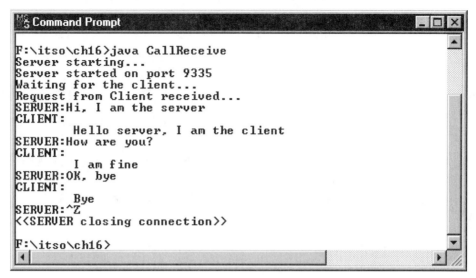

Figure 345. Server Side – without SSL

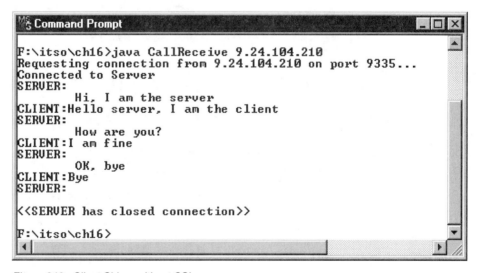

Figure 346. Client Side – without SSL

Notice that in this case the client/server communication is interrupted by the server by pressing Ctrl-Z.

16.4.1.7 Security Implications with CallReceive

We want to demonstrate that this communication is non-secure. To do this, we use Microsoft Systems Management Server (SMS) Network Monitor

Version 4.00.349. This tool can capture and display incoming data being communicated between two machines on the same LAN segment. The following two figures show the TCP/IP frames captured on the server and client machines respectively:

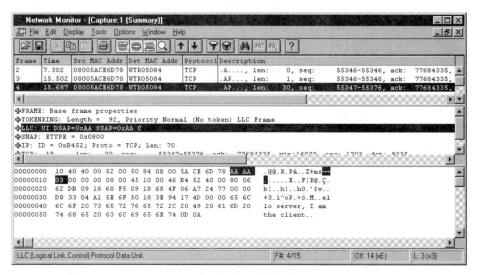

Figure 347. Network Monitor on the Server Side – without SSL

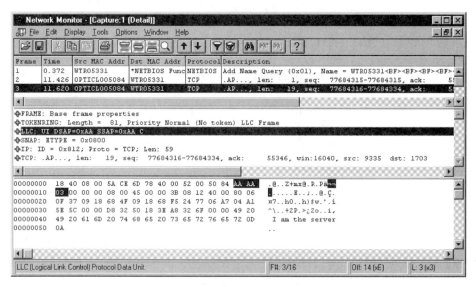

Figure 348. Network Monitor on the Client Side – without SSL

You can clearly see what is being transmitted between the client and the server.

16.4.2 Using SSL with the Sun Microsystems API

Let's see how to modify the program shown in 16.4.1, "Skeleton Program without SSL" on page 640 so that it uses the SSL API provided by Sun Microsystems, thus making the communication secure.

16.4.2.1 The Main Class of the SunSSLCallReceive Program

The code of the main class of the program, SunSSLCallReceive, is shown in the following figure:

```
class SunSSLCallReceive
{
    public static void main(String args[])
    {
        switch(args.length)
        {
            case 0:
                new SunSSLServer();
                break;

            case 1:
                try
                {
                    new SunSSLClient(args[0]);
                }
                catch(Exception e)
                {
                }
                break;

            default:
                System.out.println("USAGE: java SunSSLCallReceive [host]");
        }
    }
}
```

Figure 349. SunSSLCallReceive.java – SunSSLCallReceive Class

As you can see, the SunSSLCallReceive class has substantially the same code as the CallReceive class, shown in Figure 338 on page 640. The only difference being that in this example the client will be represented by a

SunSSLClient class, and the server by a SunSSLServer class, so SunSSLCallReceive must incorporate the new names.

16.4.2.2 The SunSSLServer Class

The server implementation presents some differences. First of all, we create an SSLServerSocket with the following code lines:

```
SSLServerSocketFactory SSLsrvrfact =
    (SSLServerSocketFactory)SSLServerSocketFactory.getDefault();
s = (SSLServerSocket)SSLsrvrfact.createServerSocket(9335);
```

The javax.net package provides the classes ServerSocketFactory and SocketFactory, and these two classes are extended in the javax.net.ssl package by the abstract classes SSLServerSocketFactory and SSLSocketFactory respectively. We create an SSLServerSocket at port 9335 by using the SSLServerSocketFactory class. Again, you can choose any port number, but it should not be one of the standard port numbers used by any other applications on your systems.

In this example, we assume that the server does not require SSL client authentication:

```
s.setNeedClientAuth(false);
```

Also in this example, the server waits for the client to connect. Once the connection is established, you can print the cipher suites supported and enabled using the getEnabledCipherSuites() and getSupportedCipherSuites() methods for the SSLSocket class. For this connection, to keep things simple, we do not provide certificates for the server. For this reason, we enable the supported anonymous cipher suite SSL_DH_anon_EXPORT_WITH_DES40_CBC_SHA. As we said in Step 3 on page 633, in anonymous cipher suites neither the client nor the server is authenticated.

The rest of the code is more or less the same as the Server class code shown in 16.4.1.2, "The Server Class" on page 641, where we did not make use of the SSL protocol:

```
class SunSSLServer implements Runnable
{
    SSLServerSocket s;

    SunSSLServer()
```

Figure 350. (Part 1 of 4). SunSSLCallReceive.java – SunSSLServer Class

```
    {
   try
   {
      System.out.println("Server starting...");
      SSLServerSocketFactory SSLsrvrfact =
         (SSLServerSocketFactory)SSLServerSocketFactory.getDefault();
      s = (SSLServerSocket)SSLsrvrfact.createServerSocket(9335);
      s.setNeedClientAuth(false);

      System.out.println("Server started on port 9335");
      System.out.println("Waiting for the client...");

      SSLSocket c = (SSLSocket)s.accept();
      String[] cipher_suites = c.getEnabledCipherSuites();

      System.out.println("Enabled cipher suites are:");
      for (int i = 0; i < cipher_suites.length; i++)
         System.out.println("   " + cipher_suites[i]);

      String[] encs = new String[cipher_suites.length + 1];

      for (int len = 0; len < cipher_suites.length; len++)
         encs[len] = cipher_suites[len];

      encs[cipher_suites.length]="SSL_DH_anon_EXPORT_WITH_DES40_CBC_SHA";

      c.setEnabledCipherSuites(encs);
      String[] ncipher_suites = c.getEnabledCipherSuites();
      System.out.println("Enabled cipher suites are:");

      for (int i = 0; i < ncipher_suites.length; i++)
         System.out.println("   " + ncipher_suites[i]);

      Thread child = new Thread(this, "IBM");
      child.start();
      System.out.println("Request from Client received...");

      OutputStream out = c.getOutputStream();
      InputStream in = c.getInputStream();
      boolean over = false;
      int b;

      while (!over)
```

Figure 351. (Part 2 of 4). SunSSLCallReceive.java – SunSSLServer Class

```
{
    /* Display prompt */
    System.out.print("SERVER:");
    System.out.flush();

    /* Read keyboard input and write to client */
    while ((b = System.in.read()) != -1 && b != '\n' && b != 26)
    {
        out.write(b);
    }

    if (b == -1 || b == 26) // CLOSE request from server
    {
        over = true;
        System.out.println("<<SERVER closing connection>>");
    }
    else
    {
        out.write('\n');
        System.out.print("CLIENT:\n\t");

        /* Get response from client and display */
        while ((b = in.read()) != -1 && b != '\n')
        {
            System.out.print((char) b);
        }

        System.out.print('\n');
        System.out.flush();

        if (b == -1) // Connection closed by client
        {
            over = true;
            System.out.println("<<CLIENT closed connection>>");
        }
    }

    out.flush();
}

in.close();
out.close();
c.close();
```

Figure 352. (Part 3 of 4). SunSSLCallReceive.java – SunSSLServer Class

```
            s.close();
        }

    catch(IOException e)
    {
    }
}

public void run()
{
    while(true)
    {
        try
        {
            SSLSocket c = (SSLSocket)s.accept();
            DataOutputStream out = new DataOutputStream(c.getOutputStream());
            InputStream in = c.getInputStream();
            out.writeBytes("Sorry, busy in a session.");
            out.flush();
            c.close();
        }
        catch(IOException e)
        {
            break;
        }
    }
}
}
```

Figure 353. (Part 4 of 4). SunSSLCallReceive.java – SunSSLServer Class

16.4.2.3 The SunSSLClient Class

The code of the class implementing the SSL client is similar to the code shown in 16.4.1.3, "The Client Class" on page 644, where we did not make use of the SSL protocol. The modification to incorporate SSL are in the same spirit of what we did in 16.4.2.2, "The SunSSLServer Class" on page 650.

At the client end, by using the SSLSocketFactory class, we create an SSLSocket that tries to connect to the SSLServer. We output the negotiated cipher suite, so that you will notice that the server and the client negotiate on the anonymous cipher suite added.

The code for the SunSSLClient class is shown in the following figure:

```
class SunSSLClient
{
    SunSSLClient(String arg) throws Exception
    {
        int c;
        System.out.println("Requesting connection from " + arg + " on port 9335...");

        SSLSocketFactory SSLfact = (SSLSocketFactory)SSLSocketFactory.getDefault();
        SSLSocket s = (SSLSocket)SSLfact.createSocket(arg,9335);

        String[] cipher_suites = s.getEnabledCipherSuites();
        System.out.println("Enabled cipher suites are:");
        for (int i = 0; i < cipher_suites.length; i++)
            System.out.println("    " + cipher_suites[i]);

        String[] encs = new String[cipher_suites.length+1];
        for (int len = 0; len < cipher_suites.length; len++)
            encs[len] = cipher_suites[len];
        encs[cipher_suites.length]="SSL_DH_anon_EXPORT_WITH_DES40_CBC_SHA";
        s.setEnabledCipherSuites(encs);

        String[] ncipher_suites = s.getEnabledCipherSuites();
        System.out.println("Enabled cipher suites are:");
        for (int i = 0; i < ncipher_suites.length; i++)
            System.out.println("    " + ncipher_suites[i]);

        System.out.println("Connected to Server");
        System.out.println("The one negotiated is " + s.getSession().getCipherSuite());

        InputStream in = s.getInputStream();
        DataOutputStream out = new DataOutputStream(s.getOutputStream());
        out.write('\n');
        out.flush();

        boolean over = false;
        while (!over)
        {
            /* Get message from server and display */
            System.out.print("SERVER:\n\t");

            while ((c = in.read()) != -1 && c != '\n')
            {
                System.out.print((char) c);
```

Figure 354. (Part 1 of 2). SunSSLCallReceive.java – SunSSLClient Class

```
                }

            if (c == -1) // Connection closed by server
            {
                over = true;
                System.out.println("\n<<SERVER has closed connection>>");
            }
            else
            {
                System.out.print("\nCLIENT:");
                System.out.flush();
                /* Read keyboard input and write to server */
                while ((c = System.in.read()) != -1 && c != '\n' && c != 26)
                {
                    out.write(c);
                }

                if (c == -1 || c == 26) //CLOSE request from CLIENT
                {
                    over = true;
                    System.out.println("<<CLIENT closing connection>>");
                }
                else
                {
                    out.write('\n');
                }

                out.flush();
            }
        }

        out.close();
        in.close();
        s.close();
    }
}
```

Figure 355. (Part 2 of 2). SunSSLCallReceive.java – SunSSLClient Class

16.4.2.4 The import Statements for the SunSSLCallReceive Program

In a way similar to what we did in 16.4.1, "Skeleton Program without SSL" on page 640, the pieces of code will have to be concatenated in order to work as a full Java program. The following `import` statements need to be added to the

Java file SunSSLCallReceive.java in order for the program to compile and work correctly:

```
import java.io.*;
import javax.net.ssl.*;
```

Figure 356. SunSSLCallReceive.java – import Statements

As you can see, this time it is necessary to invoke the Sun Microsystems SSL API packages javax.net.ssl instead of the packages java.net, which was used without SSL, as shown in Figure 344 on page 645.

16.4.2.5 Compiling and Installing the SunSSLCallReceive Program
The entire program can be obtained by concatenating the pieces of code that we have shown here. The sequence should be:

1. `import` statements code (Figure 356)

2. SunSSLServer class code (Figure 350 on page 650, Figure 351 on page 651 and Figure 352 on page 652)

3. SunSSLClient class code (Figure 354 on page 654 and Figure 355 on page 655)

4. SunSSLCallReceive class code (Figure 349 on page 649)

The code obtained in this way should be saved as SunSSLCallReceive.java and compiled through the command:

```
javac SunSSLCallReceive.java
```

Notice that the above command will not work if you don't previously copy the JAR file ssl.jar, containing the Sun Microsystems SSL libraries, in the extensions directory of the development environment. For example, on a Windows system, after the default installation of Java 2 SDK, Standard Edition, Version 1.2.*x*, this directory is C:\jdk1.2.*x*\jre\lib\ext.

The command above will generate three class files in the directory where it is run: SunSSLCallReceive.class, SunSSLServer.class and SunSSLClient.class. These three class files should then be copied in both the client and server machines, or at least they should be saved in a file system shared by both of them.

16.4.2.6 Running the SunSSLCallReceive Program
First of all, the JAR file ssl.jar must be copied in the JRE extensions directory of the machines that will act as the SSL client and server in this scenario. The

JRE extensions directory is obtained as the value of the Java Virtual Machine (JVM) internal variable java.ext.dirs, which can be verified using one of the two programs provided in Appendix A, "Getting Internal System Properties" on page 675. After the default installation of the JRE that comes with the Java 2 SDK, the value of this variable is automatically set to C:\Program Files\JavaSoft\JRE\1.2\lib\ext.

The program is launched on both the machines from the directory where you copied the class files. If you enter:

```
java SunSSLCallReceive
```

the machine where you type this command will automatically act as the server in this scenario. Then, on the other machine, enter:

```
java SunSSLCallReceive hostname
```

where *hostname* is the host name or IP address of the server. The second machine will automatically act as the client.

Notice that it is possible to run this program on two different command prompts of the same machine, which will then act as a client and a server at the same time.

The SunSSLCallReceive program is configured to show, immediately after the connection takes place, details about the cipher suites that are enabled and the one that is chosen by the client and the server after negotiating. In this example, the weak-cipher version of the Sun Microsystems SSL API is installed in the system. This version is suitable to be exported outside the United States. This is shown in the following two sessions, captured on the server and client machines respectively:

```
F:\itso\ch16>java SunSSLCallReceive
Server starting...
Server started on port 9335
Waiting for the client...
Enabled cipher suites are:
    SSL_DH_anon_EXPORT_WITH_DES40_CBC_SHA
    SSL_DHE_DSS_EXPORT_WITH_DES40_CBC_SHA
Enabled cipher suites are:
    SSL_DH_anon_EXPORT_WITH_DES40_CBC_SHA
    SSL_DHE_DSS_EXPORT_WITH_DES40_CBC_SHA
    SSL_DH_anon_EXPORT_WITH_DES40_CBC_SHA
```

Figure 357. SunSSLCallReceive Session on the Server

```
F:\itso\ch16>java SunSSLCallReceive 9.24.104.51
Requesting connection from 9.24.104.51 on port 9335...
Enabled cipher suites are:
    SSL_DHE_DSS_EXPORT_WITH_DES40_CBC_SHA
Enabled cipher suites are:
    SSL_DHE_DSS_EXPORT_WITH_DES40_CBC_SHA
    SSL_DH_anon_EXPORT_WITH_DES40_CBC_SHA
Connected to Server
The one negotiated is SSL_DH_anon_EXPORT_WITH_DES40_CBC_SHA
```

Figure 358. SunSSLCallReceive Session on the Client

For the rest, the communication between the two machines is apparently
fairly similar to what you get without SSL (see 16.4.1.6, "Running the
CallReceive Program" on page 646).

16.4.2.7 Security Implications with the SunSSLCallReceive Program

In this section we want to demonstrate that the communication between the
client and the server is secure when using SSL. To do this, we use once again
the Network Monitor tool (see 16.4.1.7, "Security Implications with
CallReceive" on page 647), with which we can verify that, if SSL is used, all
information is encrypted while being transmitted. The following two figures
are captured on the SSL server and client machines respectively:

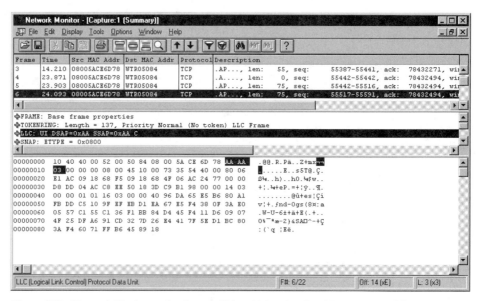

Figure 359. Network Monitor at the Server Side – Using the Sun Microsystems SSL API

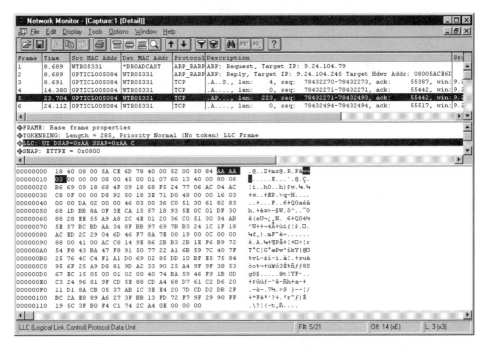

Figure 360. Network Monitor at the Client Side – Using the Sun Microsystems SSL API

All the frames contain similar unintelligible information. This confirms that no sniffing can get to the data if this is sent over a sufficiently strong secured channel using SSL.

16.5 Java and SSL with IBM SSLite

Another way for a Java program to implement a direct SSL socket connection between the client and server is to use the IBM solution *SSLite for Java*, which comes with the package com.ibm.sslite.

SSLite is an SSL V3.0 protocol implementation in Java, targeted especially for applet support. The cryptographic functions used in SSLite are private to the package and cannot be accessed directly by other applications.

IBM SSLite for Java is based on the Java socket API. It provides a set of classes that mirror the java.net socket classes and behave like their java.net equivalents. When creating an SSL socket, an already connected socket can be supplied to be used for the connection. It can also be specified that closing the SSL socket should not close the underlying socket. By these means a number of SSL connections can be created and closed on the same socket.

In the SSLite package the context information for the current SSL connection (in other words, the cipher suite details) is maintained in a Java class named SSLContext. The tricky part is setting up the SSLContext class in the first place. It requires a key ring that is, conventionally, a file containing a database of keys and certificates. An SSL client always needs a key ring, even if client authentication is not in use, because it has to check the validity of the certificate presented by the server. To perform the check, the client needs the certificate for the CA that signed the server's certificate.

The problem with reading a key ring from a file is that normally it is forbidden by the applet security restrictions. One solution to this lies in signed applets, but that can lead to further problems, due to the differences in implementation that we discussed in Chapter 11, "The Java Plug-In" on page 359 and Chapter 12, "Java Gets Out of Its Box" on page 385 (see Table 12 on page 471). The SSLite package provides an innovative alternative, by defining an SSLightKeyRing interface. This means that a key ring can be sent imbedded in the Java class files of the applet, thus avoiding the need for disk I/O. How can the applet know that this key ring (and the CA certificates inside it) can be trusted? The answer is to send the *applet itself* in an SSL URL. The chain of trust from the point of view of the applet is the following:

1. This applet is downloaded from a host that is trusted, because the certificate it sent when downloaded in a URL was signed by an independent, trusted third party (the CA).

2. Therefore, the key ring that the applet includes can also be trusted.

3. Therefore, the CA key in the key ring can be trusted, and the applet can use it to validate the server certificate when the applet starts a connection with SSLite.

This is not a rigorous chain of trust, but even if the applet does not have strong authentication for the server, it can still establish an encrypted session. In other words, privacy of the data is guaranteed, even if authentication of the server is based on doubtful logic.

SSLite also provides a class to manage the SSL session cache. This class provides a method to specify the session cache size which in fact is the maximum number of passive sessions (sessions without connections) that can be maintained at the same time.

Notice that SSLite supports X.509 V3 certificates.

16.5.1 Extensions to the SSL Protocol

IBM SSLite for Java provides two proprietary extensions to the SSL protocol; it defines *compression* methods and *secret-based* cipher suites:

- SSLite provides two proprietary compression techniques based on the java.util.zip package.

- The secret-based cipher suites use secret keys on the client and server sides. There are two key rings, which have to be maintained on the client and server to use these cipher suites: namely *secret* and *peer secret* key rings.

  On the client side, the secret key ring must contain an ID/Secret pair. On the server side, the same ID/Secret pair must be in the peer secret key ring. During the connection establishment, the client sends to the server its ID and uses the corresponding Secret to create the session master secret. Based on the ID received, the server selects the Secret to create its session master secret. The connection establishment succeeds only if the client and server share a common secret. All the rest is according to the SSL protocol.

  The secret-based cipher suites can be used, for instance, to implement password-based server access. In this case the server maintains the ID/Secret pairs of potential users, where the Secret is derived from the user ID and password. On the client side, the user must provide its ID and password to create a connection to the server.

16.5.2 SSLite Key Ring Management Tools

SSLite also provides two tools for SSLite key ring management: the Key Management Tool – a graphical user interface (GUI) utility also known as *keyman* (com.ibm.sslite.tools.keyman) – and the command line tool `keyrng` (com.ibm.sslite.tools.keyrng).

16.5.2.1 The SSLite Key Management Tool keyman

The keyman tool is a GUI utility for management of key ring classes and files. After installing IBM SSLite for Java, the keyman tool can be launched by selecting **Key Management Tool** from the SSLite for Java menu, as shown in the following figure:

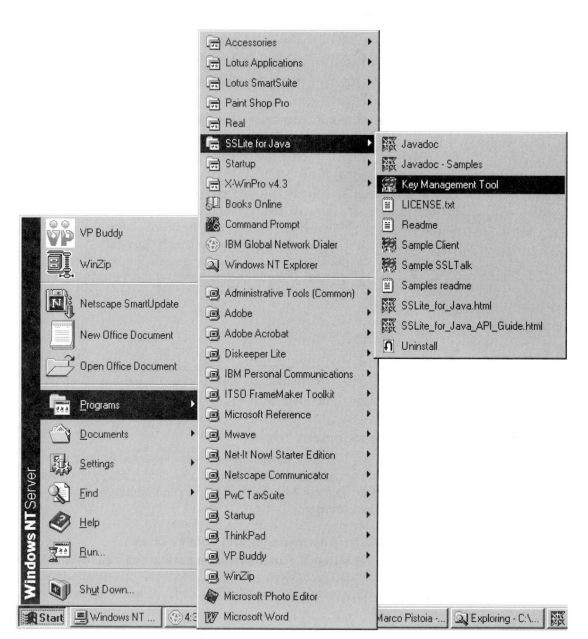

Figure 361. Launching the keyman Tool

The keyman window is brought up:

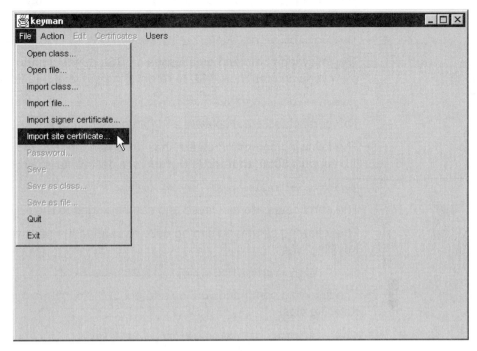

Figure 362. Keyman GUI Tool Available with SSLite

16.5.2.2 The keyrng Command Line Utility

On the contrary, `keyrng` is a command line tool used for management key ring classes, which are Java classes containing a String representation of a key ring repository. This tool can be run from the command prompt. Here are some usage examples that show the various options:

- The following command adds the site certificate stored in the file crt1.cer to KeyRing.class:

```
java com.ibm.sslite.tools.keyrng KeyRing add --site crt1.cer
```

  If KeyRing.class does not exist, it is created by this command. The `keyrng` utility generates a password-protected key ring, unless you do not enter any password.

- The following command adds the CA certificate stored in the file crt2.cer to KeyRing.class:

```
java com.ibm.sslite.tools.keyrng KeyRing add --ca crt2.cer
```

- The following command adds the site certificate stored in the file crt1.cer and the CA certificate stored in the file crt2.cer to KeyRing.class:

```
java com.ibm.sslite.tools.keyrng KeyRing add --site crt1.cer --ca crt2.cer
```

- The following command adds the contents of the key ring class AdditionalKeyRing.class to KeyRing.class:

  ```
  java com.ibm.sslite.tools.keyrng KeyRing add --class AdditionalKeyRing
  ```

- The following command establishes an SSL connection to the server www.verisign.com, port 443, to retrieve the server's certificate chain:

  ```
  java com.ibm.sslite.tools.keyrng KeyRing connect www.verisign.com
  ```

  The certificates are displayed and can be added to the KeyRing.class.

- The following command establishes an SSL connection to the server litzner, port 8050, to retrieve the server's certificate chain:

  ```
  java com.ibm.sslite.tools.keyrng KeyRing connect litzner:8050
  ```

  The certificates are displayed and can be added to the KeyRing.class.

- The following command can be used to change the password of the KeyRing.class:

  ```
  java com.ibm.sslite.tools.keyrng KeyRing password
  ```

- The following command verifies and prints the contents of the KeyRing.class:

  ```
  java com.ibm.sslite.tools.keyrng KeyRing verify
  ```

  This command prompts the user whether to delete the certificates it is unable to verify.

- The following command option is used to selectively delete key ring items of the KeyRing.class:

  ```
  java com.ibm.sslite.tools.keyrng KeyRing delete
  ```

IBM SSLite for Java ships a sample KeyRing class, com.ibm.sslite.keyring.KeyRing. The session screen shown in the following figure demonstrates how to use the verify option of the keyrng tool to see the contents of the sample KeyRing class:

```
F:\itso\ch16>java com.ibm.sslite.tools.keyrng
com.ibm.sslite.keyring.KeyRing verify
Password for com.ibm.sslite.keyring.KeyRing.class: sslite
------------------------- Key ring entry: 1 -------------------------


  Entry type: Private Certificate Chain

  Certificate: Yours
```

Figure 363. (Part 1 of 2). keyrng Session Screen

```
          Key : RSA/512 bits
      Subject: Java Security, NCSD, IBM, US
       Issuer: Java Security, NCSD, IBM, US
   Valid from: Tue Mar 23 21:35:16 EST 1999
     Valid to: Wed Mar 22 21:35:16 EST 2000
Finger print: 83:4C:37:DD:76:5B:C7:E4:AD:AF:19:23:DD:F7:81:D2


F:\itso\ch16>
```

Figure 364. (Part 2 of 2). keyrng Session Screen

16.5.3 SSL Server Authentication with IBM SSLite for Java

SSL server authentication is more sophisticated with IBM SSLite for Java
than with the Sun Microsystems APIs. In fact, as soon as an attempt is made
to establish an SSL connection that requires server authentication, the
following Java Security warning message pops up on the SSL client machine:

Figure 365. SSL Server Authentication with IBM SSLite for Java

This warning message is displayed when the server certificate cannot be
verified based on the information contained in the client's public key ring. We
opt to use the C:\WINNT\Profiles\Administrator\SiteCer.db certificate
repository to identify the server certificate and we click on **Continue**. The
following message is displayed:

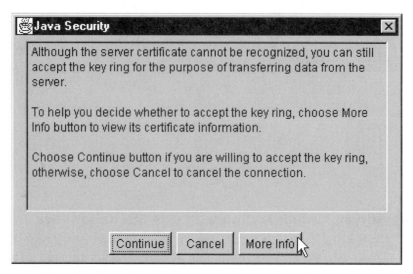

Figure 366. Java Security Warning Message

We want to know more details about the server certificate before deciding to accept it. For this reason, we click **More Info**. In this scenario, we are using the KeyRing sample class shipped with IBM SSLite for Java. Therefore, the details on the server certificate are the same as we got with the keyrng command line utility (see Figure 363 on page 664 and Figure 364 on page 665), as follows:

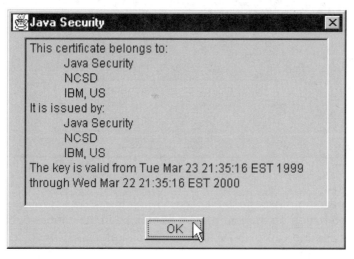

Figure 367. Server Certificate Details

We click **OK** and then, in the Java Security window shown in Figure 366 on page 666, we click **Continue**.

At this point, the user on the client system has the option to select whether to accept the key ring for only this connection or forever. If the user selects to trust it forever, a further warning message is displayed, as shown in the following figure:

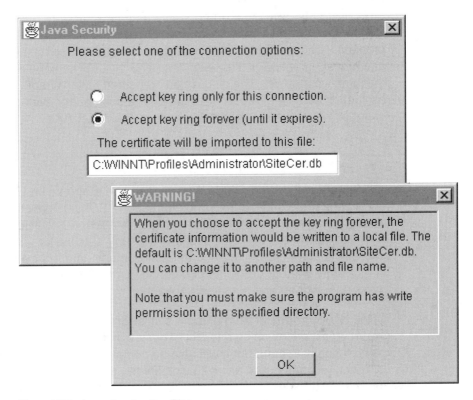

Figure 368. Accepting the Key Ring

16.6 Conclusions

The Sun Microsystems SSL API provides abstract classes to implement SSL. IBM SSLite is more sophisticated. However, with IBM SSLite we have to set up an SSLContext before we start communication at both ends even though we do not want to use client authentication (or server authentication for anonymous cipher suites).

SSLite has been targeted especially toward applet support. Concerns such as the size of the package were central to SSLite development. SSLite also provides two key management tools. On the contrary, with the javax SSL APIs found in the JST, there are currently three major problems:

1. Dependencies on the java.security package
2. No standard public key ring format
3. No management APIs

Dependencies on the java.security package create problems when working on browser platforms that do not implement java.security, such as Netscape Communicator and Microsoft Internet Explorer. Moreover, compatibility problems are generated by the absence of a standard public key ring format and management APIs. However, the javax SSL APIs in the JST are not in their final version yet. The discussion presented in this chapter is based on an evaluation version of those APIs, which are still under development. Some changes will appear in the final version of the JSSE APIs.

16.7 Summary

The history of the World Wide Web is based on pragmatism. For example, no one would argue that sending uncompressed ASCII text data on sessions that are set up and torn down for every single transaction is efficient in any way. However, this is what HTTP does, and it is very successful. The reason for its success is that it is simple enough to allow many different systems to interoperate without problems of differing syntax. The cost of simplicity is in network overhead and a limited transaction model.

Using cryptography in Java offers a similar dilemma. It is possible to write secure applications using a toolkit of basic functions. Such an application can be very sophisticated, but it will also be complex. Alternatively, using SSL URL connections offers a way to simplify the application, but at the cost of application function. SSL Java packages, such as SSLite, provide a middle way, retaining simplicity but allowing more flexible application design.

Chapter 17. Epilogue

This book has shown you how the Java security model has evolved from the basic sandbox of JDK 1.0 to the fine-grained access control model of Java 2 SDK, Standard Edition, V1.2, passing through the binary security model of JDK 1.1.

In this chapter, which represents the epilogue of this long adventure through Java security, we describe the future security developments of this fashionable and complex programming language, and summarize the reasons why today Java can really help application developers, network administrators, managers and common Internet users improve the security of their platform.

17.1 Future Directions of Java

How is the Java security model going to change in the future? What is the direction of its evolution?

In this section, we will answer these questions according to the information that is publicly available on the JavaSoft Web site http://www.javasoft.com.

17.1.1 Java 2 SDK – The Path Ahead

We have seen how the integrity and trustworthiness of downloaded applets can be determined, but can you be sure that the Java 2 SDK downloaded is the correct software? At present, the answer to this question is *no* because there is no provision for signed core classes, extension classes and native DLLs, by which a user could verify the authenticity of the software received. At some point, Java will have a solution to this problem of correctness of software and insurance that it has not been tampered with, which is the primary security requirement. In addition, signing the system classes would give them a protection domain.

Also, it would be desirable that the policy files had some kind of protection, such as encryption, and the Policy Tool were compatible with this new type of protected storage. This would be an additional level of security, though not a fool-proof measure, to protect against tampering with these files.

Another problem is that currently, the digital signature algorithm supported on the Java 2 platform is DSA/SHA1 (see Chapter 11, "The Java Plug-In" on page 359 and 12.7, "Future Developments" on page 470). The most popular certification authorities (CAs) do not seem to be accepting this format because the *de facto* standard is RSA/MD5. Moreover, the Java Plug-in is currently unable to verify applets that were signed using RSA. Therefore, to use the cryptography capabilities of Java 2 in a real-life situation, you would need to install the software of a provider that enables you to use the RSA algorithm for public key encryption. These problems will be solved once the Java 2 SDK and the Java Plug-in provide RSA signature support.

17.1.2 Resource Consumption Management

Java should develop mechanisms to guard against the *denial of service* type of attack, where the attacker tries to consume as much of the CPU cycle time as possible (by keeping the CPU busy in some silly activity), so that all other requests to the CPU remain unattended. An example denial of service attack is shown in 7.3.2.1, "Cycle Stealing" on page 195.

Resource consumption management is relatively easy to implement in some cases, such as limiting the number of windows any application can pop up at any one time. On the contrary, it can be quite hard to implement efficiently in other cases, such as limiting memory, CPU or file system usage. The JavaSoft security developers plan to coherently address such issues in the future.

17.1.3 Java Authentication and Authorization Service

The Java 2 SDK provides a means to enforce access controls based on *where code came from* and *who signed it*. The need for such access controls derives from the distributed nature of the Java platform, where, for instance, a remote applet may be downloaded over a public network and then run locally.

The Java 2 SDK, however, still lacks the means to enforce similar access controls based on *who runs the code*. To provide this type of access control, the security architecture of the Java 2 SDK requires additional support for authentication (determining who's actually running the code), and requires extensions to the existing authorization components to enforce new access controls based on who was authenticated.

The Java Authentication and Authorization Service (JAAS)[1] extends the security architecture, providing mechanisms to authenticate subjects, execute code on behalf of subjects, and grant permissions to subjects. The result is that access control policies can be based on both what code is being executed and who is executing that code.

---

[1] See http://java.sun.com/security/jaas/.

17.1.4 Java RMI Security Extension

The Java Remote Method Invocation (RMI) Security Extension[2] further extends the Java 2 security architecture to distributed systems, providing mechanisms to mutually authenticate client and server subjects during a remote call, protect the communication from third parties, and execute code in the server on behalf of the client's subject.

The API for this extension is intentionally at a very high level; cryptographic mechanisms and protocols are not exposed, so that code written to the API is more portable. An underlying service provider interface (SPI) allows specific mechanisms and protocols to be configured into the framework.

17.1.5 Arbitrary Grouping of Permissions

Sometimes it is convenient to group a number of permissions together and use a shorthand name to refer to them. For example, if we would like to have a permission called SuperPermission to include (and imply) both the following:

```
FilePermission("-", read,write)
SocketPermission("*", "connect,accept")
```

technically we can use the class Permissions or a similar class to implement this super permission. And such grouping can be arbitrarily complicated.

The more difficult issues are the following:

1. To understand what actual permissions one is granting when giving out such a super permission, either a fixed and named permission class is created to denote a statically specified group of permissions, or the member permissions need to be spelled out in the policy file.

2. Processing the policy file (or, more in general, the policy) can become more complicated, because the grouped permissions may need to be expanded. Moreover, nesting of grouped permission increases complexity even more.

17.1.6 Object-Level Protection

Given the object-oriented nature of the Java programming language, it is conceivable that developers will benefit from a set of appropriate object-level protection mechanisms that:

- Goes beyond the natural protection provided by the Java programming language

- Supplements the thread-based access control mechanism

[2] See http://java.sun.com/products/jdk/rmi/.

One such mechanism is SignedObject (see 10.1.9, "The SignedObject Class" on page 316). Parallel to this primitive, JavaSoft provides SealedObject, which uses encryption to hide the content of an object. Due to current United States export control regulations on the use of encryption, the SealedObject class is provided separately from the Java 2 SDK (see 13.4.7, "The SealedObject Class" on page 501).

GuardedObject is a general way to enforce access control at a per class/object per method level (see 10.1.2, "Guard Interface and GuardedObject Class" on page 298). This method, however, should be used only selectively, partly because this type of control can be difficult to administer at a high level.

17.1.7 Subdividing Protection Domains

A potentially useful concept not currently implemented is that of *subdomains*. A subdomain is one that is enclosed in another. A subdomain would not have more permissions or privileges than the domain of which it is a subpart. A subdomain could be created, for example, to selectively further limit what a program can do.

Often a domain is thought of as supporting inheritance: a subdomain would automatically inherit the parent domain's security attributes, except in certain cases where the parent further restricts the subdomain explicitly. Relaxing a subdomain by right amplification is a possibility with the notion of trusted code.

For convenience, we can think of the system domain as a single, big collection of all system code. For better protection, though, system code should be run in multiple system domains, where each domain protects a particular type of resource and is given a special set of rights. For example, if file system code and network system code run in separate domains, where the former has no rights to the networking resources and the latter has no rights to the file system resources, the risks and consequence of an error or security flaw in one system domain is more likely to be confined within its boundary.

17.1.8 Running Applets with Signed Content

The JAR and manifest specifications on code signing allow a very flexible format. Classes within the same archive can be signed with different keys, and a class can be unsigned, signed with one key, or signed with multiple keys. Other resources within the archive, such as audio clips and graphic images, can also be signed or unsigned, just like classes.

This flexibility brings about the issue of interpretation. The following questions need to be answered, especially when keys are treated differently:

1. Should images and audios be required to be signed with the same key if any class in the archive is signed?

2. If images and audios are signed with different keys, can they be placed in the same Applet Viewer or Web browser page, or should they be sent to different viewers for processing?

These questions are not easy to answer, and to be the most effective, require consistency across platforms and products. The JavaSoft intermediate approach is to provide a simple answer – all images and audio clips are forwarded to be processed within the same applet class loader, whether they are signed or not. This temporary solution will be improved once a consensus is reached.

Moreover, if a digital signature cannot be verified because the bytecode content of a class file does not match the signed hash value in the JAR, a security exception is thrown, as the original intention of the JAR author is clearly altered. Previously, there was a suggestion to run such code as untrusted. This idea is undesirable because the applet class loader allows the loading of code signed by multiple parties. This means that accepting a partially modified JAR file would allow an untrusted piece of code to run together with and access other code through the same classloader.

17.1.9 Java 2 Platform, Enterprise Edition

The Java 2 Platform, Enterprise Edition (J2EE) is the newest addition to the Java platform family. The Java 2 Platform, Enterprise Edition, is a platform for building *n*-tier Java-technology-based applications across the enterprise.

The J2EE, is a complete infrastructure for Enterprise JavaBeans (EJB) technology (see 14.7, "Enterprise JavaBeans" on page 580). It is designed to ensure that the *write once, run anywhere* principle applies to the server side of enterprise computing just as the Java 2 Platform, Standard Edition (J2SE) works on the client side. By providing a complete set of standard services available to every enterprise bean, the J2EE provides a way for organizations to develop and deploy applications as modular components that can be easily reused, and that scale to the range of enterprise servers.

17.2 Conclusion

The authors believe that Java provides a powerful tool with which to create secure computer systems. This security does not depend on the underlying operating system; indeed, insecure PC operating systems will benefit, while secure operating systems like MVS and UNIX will have their security enhanced, using the same portable software as that on the PC. Java is sufficiently secure to allow other software to be run safely, even if it came from a dubious source.

This security depends on vigilance by the users, in ensuring that the software that they must trust does not contain any loopholes, and is correctly configured. Undoubtedly, Java implementation flaws will continue to emerge and so continuing vigilance is needed.

The most publicized (and hence quickly fixed) flaws have appeared in the Java Virtual Machine (JVM). We believe that the next generation of flaws will appear in situations where Java is working together with other types of client executable content. For example, it is now very common to find Web pages that use a bewildering mixture of technologies – Java, JavaScript, ActiveX, Macromedia Shockwave and other plug-ins, dynamic HTML, and so on. Each of these works within its own zone of protection, which may overlap but are not identical. The wily cracker can take advantage of this fact to bypass the restrictions of one technology by exploiting another. Fixes for this type of exploit will probably not appear so quickly, because each component may be working correctly on its own terms.

Signed content (all types of content, not just Java) offers one solution to these problems, by guaranteeing the integrity of its source. But there are dangers here also. Cryptography is not a simple subject and it is important to mask complexity from the end user. At the time of writing, the variety of different approaches to signed content reflects the difficulty of doing this. We hope that a consistent approach will soon emerge. One area that merits attention is the question of how to warn the user that some component of a Web page wants to perform some potentially dangerous function. The problem is that the user becomes *click-happy*. When confronted by an endless sequence of dialog boxes warning of one thing or another, it is too easy to just keep clicking **OK**. We need a method that makes it clear that, for example, a request by a Java applet to read environmental information is potentially an order of magnitude less dangerous than allowing an ActiveX control to run.

Java 2, because of its unique design, offers many safety and security advantages over alternative approaches. In this book we have illustrated this fact and, we hope, given you some insight into how to create secure Java applications, how to protect Java assets, and how to use Java securely.

Appendix A. Getting Internal System Properties

In this appendix, we show two simple programs that can be used to get system properties.

A.1 Program GetAllProperties

The GetAllProperties program saves the values of all internal Java Virtual Machine (JVM) properties to a text file named properties.lst in the current directory. The following figure shows the code of this program:

```java
/**
 * GetAllProperties.java
 */
import java.lang.*;
import java.util.*;
import java.io.*;
import java.security.*;

class GetAllProperties
{

    public static void main(String[] args)
    {
        Properties p;
        FileOutputStream f;

        try
        {
            p = System.getProperties();
            f = new FileOutputStream("properties.lst");
            p.store(f, "Java 2 properties");
            System.out.println("All done - Results are in file properties.lst");
        }
        catch(Exception e)
        {
            System.err.println("Caught exception " + e.toString());
        }
    }
}
```

Figure 369. GetAllProperties.java

Compile this program by entering:

```
javac GetAllProperties.java
```

and run it with this command:

```
java GetAllProperties
```

It will produce the following output:

```
All done - Results are in file properties.lst
```

On opening the properties.lst text file with a text editor, you will be able to see all the JVM internal properties. Example values are shown in the following figure:

```
#Java 2 properties
#Wed Apr 14 13:09:02 EDT 1999
java.specification.name=Java\ Platform\ API\ Specification
awt.toolkit=sun.awt.windows.WToolkit
java.version=1.2.1
java.awt.graphicsenv=sun.awt.Win32GraphicsEnvironment
user.timezone=America/New_York
java.specification.version=1.2
java.vm.vendor=Sun\ Microsystems\ Inc.
java.vm.specification.version=1.0
user.home=C\:\\WINNT\\Profiles\\pistoia.000
os.arch=x86
java.awt.fonts=
java.vendor.url=http\://java.sun.com/
file.encoding.pkg=sun.io
user.region=US
java.home=D\:\\Program\ Files\\JavaSoft\\JRE\\1.2
java.class.path=.
line.separator=\r\n
java.ext.dirs=D\:\\Program\ Files\\JavaSoft\\JRE\\1.2\\lib\\ext
java.io.tmpdir=C\:\\TEMP\\
os.name=Windows\ NT
java.vendor=Sun\ Microsystems\ Inc.
java.awt.printerjob=sun.awt.windows.WPrinterJob
java.library.path=C\:\\WINNT\\SYSTEM32;.;C\:\\WINNT\\System32;C\:\\WINNT;
    C\:\\WINNT\\SYSTEM32;C\:\\WINNT;C\:\\MWW32\\BIN;C\:\\MWW32\\MODEM;
    D\:\\Program\ Files\\Personal\ Communications;
    D\:\\jdk1.2.1\\bin;d\:\\notes\\
java.vm.specification.vendor=Sun\ Microsystems\ Inc.
sun.io.unicode.encoding=UnicodeLittle
file.encoding=Cp1252
```

Figure 370. (Part 1 of 2). JVM Internal Properties in the Text File properties.lst

```
java.specification.vendor=Sun\ Microsystems\ Inc.
user.name=pistoia
user.language=en
java.vendor.url.bug=http\://java.sun.com/cgi-bin/bugreport.cgi
java.vm.name=Classic\ VM
java.vm.specification.name=Java\ Virtual\ Machine\ Specification
java.class.version=46.0
sun.boot.library.path=D\:\\Program\ Files\\JavaSoft\\JRE\\1.2\\bin
os.version=4.0
java.vm.info=build\ JDK-1.2.1-A,\ native\ threads,\ symcjit
java.vm.version=1.2.1
java.compiler=symcjit
path.separator=;
user.dir=F\:\\SG24-2109-01\\itso\\ax01
file.separator=\\
sun.boot.class.path=D\:\\Program\ Files\\JavaSoft\\JRE\\1.2\\lib\\rt.jar;
  D\:\\Program\ Files\\JavaSoft\\JRE\\1.2\\lib\\i18n.jar;
  D\:\\Program\ Files\\JavaSoft\\JRE\\1.2\\classes
```

Figure 371. (Part 2 of 2). JVM Internal Properties in the Text File properties.lst

It is important to emphasize that the GetAllProperties application should be run without the `java` flag `-Djava.security.manager`, or the following AccessControlException will be thrown:

```
Caught exception java.security.AccessControlException: access denied
(java.util.PropertyPermission * read,write)
```

This exception is thrown because the default security manager denies access to the system properties unless permission is explicitly granted in one of the current policy files. Assuming that the GetAllProperties class resides in the F:\itso\ax01 directory, the following lines added to the user's policy file will enable the program to read the system properties and write the results to the properties.lst file in the same directory:

```
grant codeBase "file:/F:/itso/ax01/" {
  permission java.util.PropertyPermission "*", "read, write";
  permission java.io.FilePermission "properties.lst", "write";
};
```

As you can see, GetAllProperties must be granted read and write access to the Java system properties. This is because java.lang.System.getProperties() calls the default SecurityManager.getPropertyAccess() method with no arguments. This in turn calls the checkPermission() method, passing in the following permission argument:

```
java.util.PropertyPermission("*", "read,write")
```

When the default security manager is invoked, GetAllProperties also requires write access to the file properties.lst.

A.2 Program GetProperty

If you need to know the value of a single system property, the program GetProperty works well for you. The code for this program is shown in the following figure:

```java
/**
 * GetProperty.java
 */
import java.lang.*;
import java.security.*;

class GetProperty
{
    public static void main(String[] args)
    {
        String s;
        try
        {
            if (args.length > 0)
            {
                s = System.getProperty(args[0], "name " + args[0] + " not specified");
                System.out.println(args[0] + " property value is: " + s);
            }
            else
            {
                System.out.println("Property name required");
            }
        }
        catch(Exception e)
        {
            System.err.println("Caught exception " + e.toString());
        }
    }
}
```

Figure 372. GetProperty.java

GetProperty prints out the value of the JVM internal property represented by the String argument passed to it on the command line. Compile it with the following command:

```
javac GetProperty.java
```

It takes as a command line argument the name of the property whose value you want to know. For example:

```
java GetProperty java.home
```

produces an output similar to the following:

```
java.home property value is: D:\Program Files\JavaSoft\JRE\1.2
```

Notice that in this case also the GetProperty program works correctly if no security manager is invoked. If the default security manager is invoked with the -Djava.security.manager flag, then the command above throws the following exception:

```
Caught exception java.security.AccessControlException: access denied
(java.util.PropertyPermission java.home read)
```

In order to prevent the system from throwing this exception, and assuming that the GetProperty class resides in the F:\itso\ax01 directory, the following lines should be added to one of the current policy files:

```
grant codeBase "file:/F:/itso/ax01/" {
  permission java.util.PropertyPermission "java.home", "read";
};
```

Or, more generically, you can replace java.home with the wildcard (*) so that the permission above applies to all the system properties:

```
grant codeBase "file:/F:/itso/ax01/" {
  permission java.util.PropertyPermission "*", "read";
};
```

You can notice that GetProperty needs only the following permission:

```
java.util.PropertyPermission "*", "read"
```

The reason this program requires only read permission is that java.lang.System.getProperty() calls the default SecurityManager.getPropertyAccess() method with a String argument representing the system property that must be read. This in turn calls the checkPermission() method, passing in the following permission argument:

```
java.util.PropertyPermission("*", "read")
```

Note that this differs from the permission argument passed to the checkPermission() method in the GetAllProperties example (see A.1, "Program GetAllProperties" on page 675).

Appendix B. Signature Formats

Both fields and methods have *signatures* within the Java class file. They are a shorthand to describe the *type* (of a field) and the *return type* and *parameters* (of a method). Signatures are constructed using characters or strings to represent the various data types.

The following table indicates how data types are represented by characters or strings:

Table 21. *Data Type Representations in Method Signatures*

Type	Character or string used in signature
long	J
byte	B
character	C
double	D
float	F
integer	I
object reference	L*classname*[a]
short	S
boolean	Z
array	[*datatype*

a. The class name here is the full name of the class with slashes (/) in place of dots (.)

The *signature of a field* is simply the character or string representing its data type.

The *signature of a method* consists of a pair of parentheses enclosing a list of the characters or strings representing the data types of the parameters, separated by semicolons. The parentheses are followed by the data type of the return type of the method. The character v indicates that the method returns no value (its return type is void). Otherwise, the descriptor indicates the type of the return value.

The following table shows some examples:

Table 22. Examples of Signatures

Type	Signature	Description
char[]	[C	An array of character
String	Ljava/lang/String	A Java string
Object[][]	[[java/lang/Object	A two dimensional array of objects
void methodName()	()V	A method taking no parameters and returning no value
int methodName(String, int)	([Ljava/lang/String;I)I	A method taking a String and an integer value and returning an integer

Notice that a class cannot declare two methods with the same signature, or a compile-time error occurs.

Appendix C. X.509 Certificates

X.509 is one of the most common formats for signed certificates. It is largely used by JavaSoft, VeriSign, IBM and many other companies for signing e-mail messages, authenticating program code and certifying many other types of data. In its simplest form, an X.509 certificate contains the following data:

1. Version of the certificate format[1]

2. Certificate serial number

3. Identifier of the signature algorithm[2]:

   - Algorithm ID
   - Parameters passed to the algorithm

4. Name of the signer of the certificate[3]

5. Period of validity[4]:

   - Begin date
   - End date

6. Name of the certified entity[5]

7. Public key of the certified identity[6]:

   - Algorithm ID
   - Parameters passed to the algorithm
   - Public key value

8. Signature[7]

All the data in a certificate is encoded using two related standards called Abstract Syntax Notation (ASN.1) and Distinguished Encoding Rules (DER).

---

[1] This identifies which version of the X.509 standard (V1, V2 or V3) applies to this certificate (see C.1, "X.509 Certificate Versions" on page 684).

[2] This identifies the algorithm used by the *certification authority* (CA) to sign the certificate.

[3] The X.500 name of the entity that signed the certificate. This is normally a CA. Using this certificate implies trusting the entity that signed this certificate. Note that in some cases, such as root or top-level CA certificates, the issuer signs its own certificate.

[4] Each certificate is valid only for a limited amount of time. This period is described by a start date and time and an end date and time, and can be as short as a few seconds or almost as long as a century.

[5] The X.500 name of the entity whose public key the certificate identifies. This field conforms to the X.500 standard, so it is intended to be unique across the Internet. This is the *distinguished name* (DN) of the entity, for example: CN=Milind Nagnur, OU=OSRM, O=Price Waterhouse C=IN. These refer to the subject's *common name* (CN), *organizational unit* (OU), *organization* (O), and *country* (C).

[6] This is the public key of the entity being named, together with an algorithm identifier that specifies which public key cryptosystem this key belongs to and any associated key parameters.

[7] Hash code of all the preceding fields, encoded with the signer's private key. Thus the signer guarantees that a given entity has a particular public key.

C.1 X.509 Certificate Versions

Several modifications have been made to the features and information content of an X.509 certificate in each subsequent version:

1. X.509 V1 has been available since 1988, is widely deployed, and is the most generic.

2. X.509 V2 introduced the concept of subject and issuer unique identifiers to handle the possibility of reuse of subject and/or issuer names over time.

3. X.509 V3 is the most recent (1996) and supports the notion of extensions, whereby anyone can define an extension and include it in the certificate. Some common extensions in use today are:

   - KeyUsage, which limits the use of the keys to particular purposes such as signing-only. The associated private key should only be used for signing certificates and not for Secure Sockets Layer (SSL).

   - AlternativeNames, which allows other identities to also be associated with this public key, for example DNS names, e-mail addresses, or IP addresses.

Appendix D. Sources of Information about Java Security

This appendix contains information about Internet resources and interesting Java security sites. It is in two parts: the first covers companies involved in Java development, and the second contains sites that are maintained at educational establishments or by individual experts within those establishments.

This appendix lists some of our information sources and gives you the opportunity to consult them for different views of Java security. These sources can also help you stay abreast of new Java developments via the Web.

D.1 Companies

There are many companies that maintain Java security sites; it would be an impossible task to list them all. For this reason we have decided to concentrate on the few companies that are at the cutting edge of the Java phenomenon.

D.1.1 JavaSoft

- The main JavaSoft URL is:

  http://www.javasoft.com

  This is an excellent Web page and one to keep a regular check on, because it has many links to various topics related to Java. Many of these are not directly related to security, but have a bearing on it; for example, new versions of the development kit and standardization activity.

- There is also a page dedicated to security:

  http://www.javasoft.com/security

  This page contains links to downloads and documentation for the latest JavaSoft Java security packages.

  These documents are very well constructed and easy to follow; however, they assume a high level of knowledge from the user. As an example of this, there are manual pages for UNIX commands that are not easy to understand if you are not a UNIX user.

  This page also contains links to other pages which, in general, describe various parts of Java specifications such as the Java cryptographic architecture.

  The JavaSoft security page also contains links to frequently asked questions (FAQs), white papers, presentations and other articles. In particular, you may wish to refer to the JavaSoft archives. These archives date back to November 1996 and contain a massive amount of information about problems encountered in the development of the various Java tools.

- One especially interesting link is the Java 2 security tutorial:

http://java.sun.com/docs/books/tutorial/security1.1/index.html

Reading this tutorial, you will learn the definitions of various cryptography terms, and see an overview of the Java security API and its core classes. You will then learn how to produce digital signatures for data, and how to verify the authenticity of such signatures. The author of the tutorial is Mary Dageforde.

- Another link of particular interest is the following:

http://java.sun.com/products/jdk/1.2/docs/guide/security/index.html

This page is full of links to other pages, where you can learn about the Java 2 security architecture, APIs and tools.

- The Java Cryptography Extension (JCE) home page is:

http://java.sun.com/products/jce/

Here you will find information and a link to download the JCE. Note that downloading cryptographic products is limited by the United States export rules for encryption.

D.1.2 Sun

- The Sun home page URL is:

http://www.sun.com

As the originator and primary force behind Java, you would expect it to feature in many parts of the Sun site. So, for example, the Sun news highlights include many Java-related developments.

- The URL for the main page for specifically Java-related issues is:

http://www.sun.com/java

This page has links to many Java-related topics and it also leads you back to the JavaSoft Web site.

D.1.3 IBM

- The IBM home page URL is:

http://www.ibm.com

There are many Java-related links from this page.

- The URL of the main page for Java information is:

  http://www.ibm.com/java

  This page also has a number of links to various pages.

- The easiest way to approach the Java IBM Web page is to link to the site index page:

  http://www.ibm.com/Java/siteindex.html

  This page lists all of the Java-related topics on this site in alphabetical order.

- The IBM alphaWorks Web page is very interesting:

  http://www.alphaworks.ibm.com/

  alphaWorks' mission is to provide early adopter developers direct access to IBM's emerging alpha-code technologies. Many of these technologies are developed in Java.

- The IBM WebSphere Web page is:

  http://www.software.ibm.com/webservers/

  From this Web page, you can download trial copies of WebSphere Application Server and WebSphere Studio. These two products allow you to develop and run powerful server-side Java applications.

- The IBM SecureWay Web page is:

  http://www.ibm.com/secureway

  This page contains a lot of security-related links.

D.1.4 Microsoft

- The Microsoft home page URL is:

  http://www.microsoft.com

  Although late to join the Java fold, Microsoft now offers a range of products for developing and running applications written in Java.

- The URL of the main page for Java-related issues is:

  http://www.microsoft.com/java

  This page has links to many Java-related topics such as news, issues and trends, technical information and the Microsoft SDK for Java. There are also related topics, which change frequently, such as information about bugs found in beta versions of products that can be downloaded from the Microsoft site.

- The URL for the main page about Java security is:

http://www.microsoft.com/java/security

This page at first appears to be for a user who knows very little or nothing at all about Java security, but there are some very good links to more technical information. We found that a more effective way to get the required information from the Microsoft site was to use the internal search function. Searching for Java security produced more than 50 hits, although a number of them were for material that is available only to members of the Microsoft Developers Network.

D.1.5 Reliable Software Technologies

RST performs research and consults in all aspects of the security, safety, and testability of computer systems. They work closely with academics, in particular the Princeton Safe Internet Programming team (see D.2.1, "Princeton" on page 689). The RTS home page has the following URL:

http://www.rstcorp.com

D.1.6 JavaWorld

- The JavaWorld home page URL is:

http://www.javaworld.com

This page also has a number of links to various pages.

- An interesting link from the home page goes to the JavaWorld Book Catalog Web page:

http://www.javaworld.com/javaworld/books/jw-books-security.html

Here you can find a link to the most recent Java security books and publications.

D.1.7 JCE Providers outside the United States

The United States government has placed restrictions on the export of cryptographic technology. The following are Web sites of JCE providers outside the United States:

- The Australian Business Access (ABA) JCE Web site is:

http://www.aba.net.au/solutions/crypto/jce.html

The ABA JCE is an implementation of the JCE API as defined by Sun Microsystems, plus a provider of underlying cryptographic algorithms.

- The Forge Cryptographic Provider Web site is:

http://www.forge.com.au/

The Forge Cryptographic Provider is a full-featured JCE 1.2-compliant cryptographic provider. This product offers RSA key generation, an RSA key factory and digital signatures using the RSA and MD5 algorithm. The Forge Cryptographic Provider 1.1 also includes a digital signature for use with SSL/TLS. The provider comes with complete source code and is available as a free download.

- The DSTC Java and Cryptography and Security Web site is:

http://security.dstc.edu.au/projects/java/release.html

The JCSI product is released by DTSC. It incorporates a JCE implementation, an associated security provider, and a public key infrastructure (PKI) library and tools. This software is free for non-commercial use and can be downloaded in source form.

D.2 Universities

There are many universities that maintain Java sites and Java security sites; it would be an impossible task to list them all. For this reason, we have decided to concentrate on the universities whose pages we found most useful and informative. There is also a brief list at the end of this section that contains some other Java sites that you may find interesting.

D.2.1 Princeton

Princeton University is the leading center for Java security research. The main Java security page is:

http://www.cs.princeton.edu/sip

This page contains information and links about Java security.

The purpose of this site is to study the security of widely used Internet software, especially mobile code systems like Java, ActiveX, and JavaScript. They try to understand how security breaks down, and to develop technology to address the underlying causes of security problems.

This Web site has links to many publications about Java security.

D.2.2 Yale

- A Java security site worth visiting at Yale is:

http://pantheon.yale.edu/~dff/java.html

This site is mainly a collection of links to other Java security sites.

- Another interesting Yale site is the following:

  http://daffy.cs.yale.edu/java/java_sec/java_sec.html

  This site gives a good breakdown of Java security and some good guidelines for security measures to take.

D.2.3 Others

The following pages are from other university sites that have some worthwhile information and links:

- A page of information put together by Patricia Evans (a graduate student at the University of Victoria) is:

  http://gulf.uvic.ca/~pevans/java.html

- A list of Java security resources provided by Steven H. Samorodin of the UC Davis Security lab can be found at the following URL:

  http://seclab.cs.ucdavis.edu/~samorodi/java/javasec.html

- An entry for Java security in the Gene Spafford of Purdue University's security hot list is found at the following Web site:

  http://www.cs.purdue.edu/coast/hotlist/network/java.html

- A page at the University of Utah, devoted to Java security is:

  http://www.cs.utah.edu/~gback/javasec

  It includes pointers to talk slides, and a few pointers to related Web sites.

- A page on security flaws in Java implementations, maintained by a research group at the University of Washington, is the following:

  http://kimera.cs.washington.edu

  They implement a new Java security architecture based on factored components for security, performance, and scalability.

- The University of Arizona has a Web page devoted to the Sumatra Project. Here you can find an interesting link to Java Hall of Shame:

  http://www.cs.arizona.edu/sumatra/hallofshame/

- JAWS (Java Applets With Safety) is an Australian National University project using theorem-proving technology to analyze safety and security properties of Java Applets. The home page for JAWS is:

  http://cs.anu.edu.au/people/Tony.Dekker/JAWS.HTML

Appendix E. What's on the Diskette?

The diskette that accompanies this book contains the following:

- **The sample code**

  All of the samples contained in the book are on the diskette, both as source Java and as compiled class files. Because of government restrictions on encryption, the Java programs in Chapter 13 and 16 that use encryption are not included on the diskette.

- **Some useful links**

  There is a table of HTML links to Java and security Web sites that we found useful while creating the book.

E.1 How to Access the Diskette

To access the contents of the diskette, simply point your Web browser at file index.html in the diskette root directory and follow the links you find there.

Appendix F. Special Notices

This publication is intended to help Java users to exploit the strengths of Java and make it more secure. The information in this publication is not intended as the specification of any programming interfaces that are provided by Java 2 SDK, Standard Edition, V1.2. See the PUBLICATIONS section of the IBM Programming Announcements for more information about what publications are considered to be product documentation.

References in this publication to IBM products, programs or services do not imply that IBM intends to make these available in all countries in which IBM operates. Any reference to an IBM product, program, or service is not intended to state or imply that only IBM's product, program, or service may be used. Any functionally equivalent program that does not infringe any of IBM's intellectual property rights may be used instead of the IBM product, program or service.

Information in this book was developed in conjunction with use of the equipment specified, and is limited in application to those specific hardware and software products and levels.

IBM may have patents or pending patent applications covering subject matter in this document. The furnishing of this document does not give you any license to these patents. You can send license inquiries, in writing, to the IBM Director of Licensing, IBM Corporation, North Castle Drive, Armonk, NY 10504-1785.

Licensees of this program who wish to have information about it for the purpose of enabling: (i) the exchange of information between independently created programs and other programs (including this one) and (ii) the mutual use of the information which has been exchanged, should contact IBM Corporation, Dept. 600A, Mail Drop 1329, Somers, NY 10589 USA.

Such information may be available, subject to appropriate terms and conditions, including in some cases, payment of a fee.

The information contained in this document has not been submitted to any formal IBM test and is distributed AS IS. The information about non-IBM ("vendor") products in this manual has been supplied by the vendor and IBM assumes no responsibility for its accuracy or completeness. The use of this information or the implementation of any of these techniques is a customer responsibility and depends on the customer's ability to evaluate and integrate them into the customer's operational environment. While each item may have been reviewed by IBM for accuracy in a specific situation, there is no guarantee that the same or similar results will be obtained elsewhere. Customers attempting to adapt these techniques to their own environments do so at their own risk.

Any pointers in this publication to external Web sites are provided for convenience only and do not in any manner serve as an endorsement of these Web sites.

Any performance data contained in this document was determined in a controlled environment, and therefore, the results that may be obtained in other operating environments may vary significantly. Users of this document should verify the applicable data for their specific environment.

The following document contains examples of data and reports used in daily business operations. To illustrate them as completely as possible, the examples contain the names of individuals, companies, brands, and products. All of these names are fictitious and any similarity to the names and addresses used by an actual business enterprise is entirely coincidental.

Reference to PTF numbers that have not been released through the normal distribution process does not imply general availability. The purpose of including these reference numbers is to alert IBM customers to specific information relative to the implementation of the PTF when it becomes available to each customer according to the normal IBM PTF distribution process.

The following terms are trademarks of the International Business Machines Corporation in the United States and/or other countries:

IBM ®

AIX	AS/400
VisualAge	CICS
WebSphere	eNetwork
SP	IBM Registry
System/390	MQ
Network Station	OS/2
OS/390	S/390

The following terms are trademarks of other companies:

C-bus is a trademark of Corollary, Inc. in the United States and/or other countries.

Sun, Sun Microsystems, the Sun Logo, SunWorld, SunPlaza, Sun SITE, and all Sun-based trademarks and logos, Java, Java 2, HotJava, JavaScript, the Java Coffee Cup Logo, JavaWorld, and all Java-based trademarks and logos, the Duke Logo, Jini and the Jini Logo, Solaris, Netra, Ultra, NFS, and The Network Is The Computer are trademarks or registered trademarks of Sun Microsystems, Inc. in the United States and other countries.

Microsoft, Windows, Windows NT, and the Windows logo are trademarks of Microsoft Corporation in the United States and/or other countries.

PC Direct is a trademark of Ziff Communications Company in the United States and/or other countries and is used by IBM Corporation under license.

ActionMedia, LANDesk, MMX, Pentium and ProShare are trademarks of Intel Corporation in the United States and/or other countries. (For a complete list of Intel trademarks see www.intel.com/tradmarx.htm)

UNIX is a registered trademark in the United States and/or other countries licensed exclusively through X/Open Company Limited.

SET and the SET logo are trademarks owned by SET Secure Electronic Transaction LLC.

Other company, product, and service names may be trademarks or service marks of others.

Appendix G. Related Publications

The publications listed in this section are considered particularly suitable for a more detailed discussion of the topics covered in this redbook.

G.1 International Technical Support Organization Publications

For information on ordering these ITSO publications see "How to Get ITSO Redbooks" on page 699.

- *Internet Security in the Network Computing Framework*, SG24-5220
- *Network Computing Framework Component Guide*, SG24-2119

G.2 Redbooks on CD-ROMs

Redbooks are also available on the following CD-ROMs. Click the CD-ROMs button at `http://www.redbooks.ibm.com/` for information about all the CD-ROMs offered, updates and formats.

CD-ROM Title	Collection Kit Number
System/390 Redbooks Collection	SK2T-2177
Networking and Systems Management Redbooks Collection	SK2T-6022
Transaction Processing and Data Management Redbooks Collection	SK2T-8038
Lotus Redbooks Collection	SK2T-8039
Tivoli Redbooks Collection	SK2T-8044
AS/400 Redbooks Collection	SK2T-2849
Netfinity Hardware and Software Redbooks Collection	SK2T-8046
RS/6000 Redbooks Collection (BkMgr)	SK2T-8040
RS/6000 Redbooks Collection (PDF Format)	SK2T-8043
Application Development Redbooks Collection	SK2T-8037

G.3 Other Publications

These publications are also relevant as further information sources:

- Li Gong, *Inside Java 2 Platform Security*, Addison-Wesley
- Mike Morgan, *Using Java 1.2*, Que
- Scott Oaks, *Java Security*, O'Reilly
- Jonathan Knudsen, *Java Cryptography*, O'Reilly
- McGraw, Felten, *Java Security*, Wiley Computer Publishing

- Elliotte Rusty Harold, *Java Network Programming*, O'Reilly
- Kim Topley, *Core Java Foundation Classes*, Prentice Hall
- Douglas R. Stinson, *Cryptography Theory and Practice*, CRC Press
- Rita C. Summers, *Secure Computing*, McGraw-Hill
- Gamma, Helm, Johnson, Vlissides, *Design Patterns*, Addison-Wesley

How to Get ITSO Redbooks

This section explains how both customers and IBM employees can find out about ITSO redbooks, redpieces, and CD-ROMs. A form for ordering books and CD-ROMs by fax or e-mail is also provided.

- **Redbooks Web Site** `http://www.redbooks.ibm.com/`

  Search for, view, download or order hardcopy/CD-ROM redbooks from the redbooks web site. Also read redpieces and download additional materials (code samples or diskette/CD-ROM images) from this redbooks site.

  Redpieces are redbooks in progress; not all redbooks become redpieces and sometimes just a few chapters will be published this way. The intent is to get the information out much quicker than the formal publishing process allows.

- **E-mail Orders**

  Send orders via e-mail including information from the redbooks fax order form to:

	e-mail address
In United States	usib6fpl@ibmmail.com
Outside North America	Contact information is in the "How to Order" section at this site: `http://www.elink.ibmlink.ibm.com/pbl/pbl/`

- **Telephone Orders**

United States (toll free)	1-800-879-2755
Canada (toll free)	1-800-IBM-4YOU
Outside North America	Country coordinator phone number is in the "How to Order" section at this site: `http://www.elink.ibmlink.ibm.com/pbl/pbl/`

- **Fax Orders**

United States (toll free)	1-800-445-9269
Canada	1-403-267-4455
Outside North America	Fax phone number is in the "How to Order" section at this site: `http://www.elink.ibmlink.ibm.com/pbl/pbl/`

This information was current at the time of publication, but is continually subject to change. The latest information may be found at the Redbooks Web site.

IBM Intranet for Employees

IBM employees may register for information on workshops, residencies, and redbooks by accessing the IBM Intranet Web site at `http://w3.itso.ibm.com/` and clicking the ITSO Mailing List button. Look in the Materials repository for workshops, presentations, papers, and Web pages developed and written by the ITSO technical professionals; click the Additional Materials button. Employees may also access MyNews at `http://w3.ibm.com` for redbook, residency, and workshop announcements.

IBM Redbook Fax Order Form

Please send me the following:

Title	Order Number	Quantity

First name _____ Last name _____

Company _____

Address _____

City _____ Postal code _____ Country _____

Telephone number _____ Telefax number _____ VAT number _____

☐ Invoice to customer number _____

☐ Credit card number _____

Credit card expiration date _____ Card issued to _____ Signature _____

We accept American Express, Diners, Eurocard, Master Card, and Visa. Payment by credit card not available in all countries. Signature mandatory for credit card payment.

Glossary

3270   Usually any of a family of block-mode VDUs, including the IBM Model 3270

AWT   Abstract Windows Toolkit, the Java package for creating GUIs

CGI   Common Gateway Interface, an interface that allows server-side executable code to be invoked as a URL

CICS   customer information control system

CERT   Computer Emergency Response Team, an organization that acts as a clearing house of information about security problems

CORBA The Common Object Request Broker Architecture, a standard for implementing a distributed object architecture

DES   Data Encryption Standard, a bulk (symmetric key) encryption algorithm

DMZ   Demilitarized zone, used here to indicate the portion of a network surrounded by firewalls

DNS   Domain Name System

FTP   File Transfer Protocol

GET   An HTTP command which requests the server to send data to the client

Gopher An information service providing linked pages

HOD   Host On-Demand, an IBM 3270 terminal emulator

HTML   Hypertext markup language

HTTP   HyperText Transfer Protocol

HTTPS   HTTP encapsulated in SSL protocol

ICMP   Internet Control Message Protocol

IIOP   Internet Inter ORB Protocol, a specification for the way that ORBs communicate

IP   Internet Protocol

IPv4   Version 4 of Internet Protocol

IPv6   Version 6 of Internet Protocol

JCA   Java Cryptography Architecture

JCE   Java Cryptography Extension (the parts of JCA that cannot be exported from the United States)

JVM   Java Virtual Machine

key pair A matching pair of public and private keys, used for digital signatures and public key encryption

LAN   local area network, with typical bandwidth greater than 4 Mbps

MD5   A message digest (secure hash) algorithm from RSA Corp

MIME   Multipurpose Internet Mail Extensions

NetBIOS LAN protocol generally used by PCs

ORB   Object Request Broker, a program that provides services to enable the use of distributed objects

PC   Personal Computer

POST   An HTTP command that sends client data to the server

RC4   A bulk (symmetric key) encryption algorithm that allows variable key sizes

RMI   Remote Method Invocation, a technique to allow Java on one system to access objects on another

RSA   Rivest, Shamir and Adleman formed the RSA corporation to market cryptographic software and algorithms, in particular the public key encryption mechanism that also bears their initials

SHA   Secure Hash Algorithm

SNA   Systems Network Architecture

SOCKS A protocol used to encapsulate other TCP protocols

SSL   Secure Sockets Layer

TCP/IP Often used as a generic term for the suite of TCP, IP and related protocols

TCP Transmission Control Protocol

UDP User Datagram Protocol

URL Uniform Resource Locator

VDU visual display unit

WAIS Wide Area Information Service

WAN wide area network, with typical bandwidth less than 4 Mbps

WWW World Wide Web, usually refers to systems using HTTP

Index

Symbols
${/} 96, 247, 256
${file.separator} 247
${java.home} 85, 87, 255, 256
${user.home} 247, 256

Numerics
0xCAFEBABE 126, 177, 603
100% Pure Java 50, 404

A
Abstract Syntax Notation (ASN.1) 683
ACC_FINAL 126
ACC_PUBLIC 126
access control 54, 59, 476, 528
   access control and permission APIs 482
   access control APIs 304
   access control list (ACL) 324
      Acl interface 324
      AclEntry interface 324
   access controller 98
   AccessControlContext class 305
   AccessControlException 304
   AccessController class 304, 344
   checkConnect() method 614
   checkCreateClassLoader() method 194
   checked exception 353
   checkPackageAccess() method 240
   checkPackageDefinition() method 241
   checkPermission() method 190, 211, 344
   checkRead() method 218
   checkWrite() method 206, 218
   doPrivileged() method 92, 305, 350, 357
   lexical scoping of privilege modification 76, 78, 216, 304, 350
      privileged blocks usage 354, 358
      privileged code 350
      PrivilegedAction interface 305
      PrivilegedActionException 353
      PrivilegedExceptionAction interface 305, 353
access flag 126
ActiveX 603
   ActiveX control 363, 438
Ada 120

algorithm 306, 483, 489
   algorithm aliases 524
   AlgorithmParameterGenerator class 322
   AlgorithmParameterGeneratorSpi class 322
   AlgorithmParameters class 322
   AlgorithmParameterSpec interface 323
   NoSuchAlgorithmException 485
AllPermission class 317, 340
anonymous cipher suites 634, 650
API object 489
applet security 14
Applet Viewer 16, 21, 99, 188, 623
   appletviewer command 147, 615, 621
      -J-DproxyHost flag 615
      -J-DproxyPort flag 615
      -J-DsocksProxyHost flag 615
      -J-DsocksProxyPort flag 615
applets with signed content 672
application 5
   application class path 45, 89
   application domain 82
   application security 26
architectures 36, 50
Archive attribute 274
asymmetric encryption 55, 477, 516
   Java 2 asymmetric encryption support 516
attack applets 9
attack types 59, 66, 193
attributes table 126
authentication 6, 475, 478
authenticity 630
AWTPermission class 342

B
Base 64 format 262, 264, 266
BASIC 120
BasicPermission class 317, 341, 345
binary trust model 59
Blowfish 492
boot class path 84, 110
   -bootclasspath flag 85, 86
   -Xbootclasspath flag 85
bulk encryption 54, 477
bytecode 4, 7, 36, 117, 136, 537
   bytecode compilers 120
   bytecode hosing 134
   bytecode instructions 175

bytecode integrity check   178
bytecode verifier   178, 180, 183, 603

C

C   3, 67, 118, 127, 541
C++   5, 7, 118, 124, 541
CA keystore   401
cacerts keystore file   233
   cacerts default password   234
casting operations   176
CERT Coordination Center   11
cert7.db certificate database file   419
certificate
   Certificate class   318, 323
   certificate expiration date   478
   certificate hierarchies   479
   certificate revocation list (CRL)   78, 323, 491
      CRL class   323
      generateCRL() method   324
      X509CRL class   323
      X509CRLEntry class   323
   certificate signing request (CSR)   78
   certificate validity   268
   CertificateFactory class   324
   CertificateFactorySpi class   324
   generateCertificate() method   324
   public key certificate   9, 59, 478, 479
   self-signed certificate   18, 480
   server certificate   402
certification authority (CA)   360, 683
   CA key database   393
   CA private key   403
CGI-BIN programs   62, 529, 532, 541, 605, 627
Chinese Remainder Theorem (CRT)   324
CICS
   CICS client   530
   CICS server   530
   IBM CICS Gateway for Java   530
   IBM CICS Internet Gateway   529
cipher
   Cipher Block Chaining (CBC)   492
   Cipher class   495, 507
   Cipher Feedback (CFB)   492
   cipher strength   58
   cipher suites   630
      anonymous cipher suites   634, 650
      SSL secret-based cipher suites   661
   CipherInputStream class   496

CipherOutputStream class   496
   ciphertext   476
class area   112
class file format   124
class file verifier   9, 45, 47, 70, 110, 112, 168, 192
   class integrity check   177
   file integrity check   177
   JVM security elements interdependence   192
class loader   8, 45, 46, 70, 110, 145, 192
   class loading process   150
   ClassLoader   47, 90, 111, 470
   default class loader   146
   delegation model   152, 163
   ExtClassLoader   148
   extension framework   86
   extensions class loader   148
   internal class loader   146
   Java 2 class loading mechanism   89
   JVM security elements interdependence   192
   native method loader   113
   null class loader   146
   primordial class loader   146, 149, 153
   RMIClassLoader   156
   SecureClassLoader   90, 111, 147, 149, 322
   URLClassLoader   147, 149
class path   45, 84
   application class path   45, 89
   boot class path   84, 110
     -bootclasspath flag   85, 86
   class search path   83
   CLASSPATH   46, 84, 87, 110, 146, 147, 193
   -classpath flag   83, 147, 151
   -cp flag   83, 147, 151
   -extdirs flag   87
   extension class path   45
   java.class.path   88, 149
   java.ext.dirs   105, 153
   JVM class path   45, 84
   sun.boot.class.path   84, 153
   system class path   45, 84
   user class path   89
   -Xbootclasspath flag   85
classes   42, 119
classes.zip file   84
client key database   399
client store   452
COBOL   118, 120, 124
code base   94, 318
   code base URL directory   252

ITSO Redbook Evaluation

Java 2 Network Security
SG24-2109-01

Your feedback is very important to help us maintain the quality of ITSO redbooks. **Please complete this questionnaire and return it using one of the following methods:**

- Use the online evaluation form found at http://www.redbooks.ibm.com/
- Fax this form to: USA International Access Code + 1 914 432 8264
- Send your comments in an Internet note to redbook@us.ibm.com

Which of the following best describes you?
_ **Customer**   _ **Business Partner**   _ **Solution Developer**   _ **IBM employee**
_ **None of the above**

Please rate your overall satisfaction with this book using the scale:
(1 = very good, 2 = good, 3 = average, 4 = poor, 5 = very poor)

Overall Satisfaction   _____

Please answer the following questions:

Was this redbook published in time for your needs?   Yes___ No___

If no, please explain:

_____

_____

_____

_____

What other redbooks would you like to see published?

_____

_____

_____

Comments/Suggestions: **(THANK YOU FOR YOUR FEEDBACK!)**

_____

_____

_____

_____

LICENSE AGREEMENT AND LIMITED WARRANTY

READ THE FOLLOWING TERMS AND CONDITIONS CAREFULLY BEFORE OPENING THIS SOFTWARE MEDIA PACKAGE. THIS LEGAL DOCUMENT IS AN AGREEMENT BETWEEN YOU AND PRENTICE-HALL, INC. (THE "COMPANY"). BY OPENING THIS SEALED SOFTWARE MEDIA PACKAGE, YOU ARE AGREEING TO BE BOUND BY THESE TERMS AND CONDITIONS. IF YOU DO NOT AGREE WITH THESE TERMS AND CONDITIONS, DO NOT OPEN THE SOFTWARE MEDIA PACKAGE. PROMPTLY RETURN THE UNOPENED SOFTWARE MEDIA PACKAGE AND ALL ACCOMPANYING ITEMS TO THE PLACE YOU OBTAINED THEM FOR A FULL REFUND OF ANY SUMS YOU HAVE PAID.

1. **GRANT OF LICENSE:** In consideration of your payment of the license fee, which is part of the price you paid for this product, and your agreement to abide by the terms and conditions of this Agreement, the Company grants to you a nonexclusive right to use and display the copy of the enclosed software program (hereinafter the "SOFTWARE") on a single computer (i.e., with a single CPU) at a single location so long as you comply with the terms of this Agreement. The Company reserves all rights not expressly granted to you under this Agreement.

2. **OWNERSHIP OF SOFTWARE:** You own only the magnetic or physical media (the enclosed software media) on which the SOFTWARE is recorded or fixed, but the Company retains all the rights, title, and ownership to the SOFTWARE recorded on the original software media copy(ies) and all subsequent copies of the SOFTWARE, regardless of the form or media on which the original or other copies may exist. This license is not a sale of the original SOFTWARE or any copy to you.

3. **COPY RESTRICTIONS:** This SOFTWARE and the accompanying printed materials and user manual (the "Documentation") are the subject of copyright. You may not copy the Documentation or the SOFTWARE, except that you may make a single copy of the SOFTWARE for backup or archival purposes only. You may be held legally responsible for any copying or copyright infringement which is caused or encouraged by your failure to abide by the terms of this restriction.

4. **USE RESTRICTIONS:** You may not network the SOFTWARE or otherwise use it on more than one computer or computer terminal at the same time. You may physically transfer the SOFTWARE from one computer to another provided that the SOFTWARE is used on only one computer at a time. You may not distribute copies of the SOFTWARE or Documentation to others. You may not reverse engineer, disassemble, decompile, modify, adapt, translate, or create derivative works based on the SOFTWARE or the Documentation without the prior written consent of the Company.

5. **TRANSFER RESTRICTIONS:** The enclosed SOFTWARE is licensed only to you and may not be transferred to any one else without the prior written consent of the Company. Any unauthorized transfer of the SOFTWARE shall result in the immediate termination of this Agreement.

6. **TERMINATION:** This license is effective until terminated. This license will terminate automatically without notice from the Company and become null and void if you fail to comply with any provisions or limitations of this license. Upon termination, you shall destroy the Documentation and all copies of the SOFTWARE. All provisions of this Agreement as to warranties, limitation of liability, remedies or damages, and our ownership rights shall survive termination.

7. **MISCELLANEOUS:** This Agreement shall be construed in accordance with the laws of the United States of America and the State of New York and shall benefit the Company, its affiliates, and assignees.

8. **LIMITED WARRANTY AND DISCLAIMER OF WARRANTY:** The Company warrants that the SOFTWARE, when properly used in accordance with the Documentation, will operate in substantial conformity with the description of the SOFTWARE set forth in the Documentation. The Company does not warrant that the SOFTWARE will meet your requirements or that the operation of the SOFTWARE will be uninterrupted or error-free. The Company warrants that the media on which the SOFTWARE is delivered shall be free from defects in materials and workmanship under normal use for a period of thirty (30) days from the date of your purchase. Your only remedy and the Company's only obligation under these limited warranties is, at the Company's option, return of the warranted item for a refund of any amounts paid by you or replacement of the item. Any replacement of SOFTWARE or media under the warranties shall not extend the original warranty period. The limited warranty set forth above shall not apply to any SOFTWARE which the Company determines in good faith has been subject to misuse, neglect, improper installation, repair, alteration, or dam-

age by you. EXCEPT FOR THE EXPRESSED WARRANTIES SET FORTH ABOVE, THE COMPANY DISCLAIMS ALL WARRANTIES, EXPRESS OR IMPLIED, INCLUDING WITHOUT LIMITATION, THE IMPLIED WARRANTIES OF MERCHANTABILITY AND FITNESS FOR A PARTICULAR PURPOSE. EXCEPT FOR THE EXPRESS WARRANTY SET FORTH ABOVE, THE COMPANY DOES NOT WARRANT, GUARANTEE, OR MAKE ANY REPRESENTATION REGARDING THE USE OR THE RESULTS OF THE USE OF THE SOFTWARE IN TERMS OF ITS CORRECTNESS, ACCURACY, RELIABILITY, CURRENTNESS, OR OTHERWISE.

IN NO EVENT, SHALL THE COMPANY OR ITS EMPLOYEES, AGENTS, SUPPLIERS, OR CONTRACTORS BE LIABLE FOR ANY INCIDENTAL, INDIRECT, SPECIAL, OR CONSEQUENTIAL DAMAGES ARISING OUT OF OR IN CONNECTION WITH THE LICENSE GRANTED UNDER THIS AGREEMENT, OR FOR LOSS OF USE, LOSS OF DATA, LOSS OF INCOME OR PROFIT, OR OTHER LOSSES, SUSTAINED AS A RESULT OF INJURY TO ANY PERSON, OR LOSS OF OR DAMAGE TO PROPERTY, OR CLAIMS OF THIRD PARTIES, EVEN IF THE COMPANY OR AN AUTHORIZED REPRESENTATIVE OF THE COMPANY HAS BEEN ADVISED OF THE POSSIBILITY OF SUCH DAMAGES. IN NO EVENT SHALL LIABILITY OF THE COMPANY FOR DAMAGES WITH RESPECT TO THE SOFTWARE EXCEED THE AMOUNTS ACTUALLY PAID BY YOU, IF ANY, FOR THE SOFTWARE.

SOME JURISDICTIONS DO NOT ALLOW THE LIMITATION OF IMPLIED WARRANTIES OR LIABILITY FOR INCIDENTAL, INDIRECT, SPECIAL, OR CONSEQUENTIAL DAMAGES, SO THE ABOVE LIMITATIONS MAY NOT ALWAYS APPLY. THE WARRANTIES IN THIS AGREEMENT GIVE YOU SPECIFIC LEGAL RIGHTS AND YOU MAY ALSO HAVE OTHER RIGHTS WHICH VARY IN ACCORDANCE WITH LOCAL LAW.

ACKNOWLEDGMENT

YOU ACKNOWLEDGE THAT YOU HAVE READ THIS AGREEMENT, UNDERSTAND IT, AND AGREE TO BE BOUND BY ITS TERMS AND CONDITIONS. YOU ALSO AGREE THAT THIS AGREEMENT IS THE COMPLETE AND EXCLUSIVE STATEMENT OF THE AGREEMENT BETWEEN YOU AND THE COMPANY AND SUPERSEDES ALL PROPOSALS OR PRIOR AGREEMENTS, ORAL, OR WRITTEN, AND ANY OTHER COMMUNICATIONS BETWEEN YOU AND THE COMPANY OR ANY REPRESENTATIVE OF THE COMPANY RELATING TO THE SUBJECT MATTER OF THIS AGREEMENT.

Should you have any questions concerning this Agreement or if you wish to contact the Company for any reason, please contact in writing at the address below.

Robin Short
Prentice Hall PTR
One Lake Street
Upper Saddle River, New Jersey 07458

About this diskette

The diskette that accompanies this book contains the following:

The sample code

All of the samples contained in the book are on the diskette, both as source Java and as compiled class files. Because of government restrictions on encryption, the Java programs in Chapter 13 and 16 that use encryption are not included on the diskette.

Some useful links

There is a table of HTML links to Java and security Web sites that we found useful while creating the book.

How to Access the Diskette

To access the contents of the diskette, simply point your Web browser at file index.html in the diskette root directory and follow the links you find there.

How to Get the Same Software Material from the Web

The same software material is available on the Internet from the IBM redbooks Web server. Point your Web browser to ftp:// www.redbooks.ibm.com/redbooks/SG242109.

Alternatively, you can go to http://www.redbooks.ibm.com and select **Additional Redbook Material** (or follow the current instructions provided, since the Web pages change frequently).

Technical Support

Prentice Hall does not offer technical support for this software. However, if there is a problem with the media, you may obtain a replacement copy by e-mailing us with your problem at:

disc_exchange@phptr.com